Dedication

To Joan Paterson, *my true companion*

About the Author

Jack B. Rochester is an instructor and professional writer specializing in computers and information technology. His first encounter with computers was in the U.S. Air Force, batch processing with an IBM 701 and punch cards. The author of seven books, including the popular *The Naked Computer* (William Morrow, 1983), he has been writing about computers since 1980. His articles have appeared in such publications as *Computerworld, The Boston Globe, Harvard Business Review, InfoCom Review, Omni, USA Today, U.S. News & World Report*, and others. He has provided editorial consulting services to such firms as Coopers & Lybrand Global L.L.P. Telecommunications Group, New York; International Data Corporation, Framingham, Massachusetts; A.T. Kearney, Inc., Chicago, Illinois; and The Massachusetts Computer Software Council, Boston, Massachusetts.

Jack holds a master's degree from California State College at Sonoma. He has written several computer textbooks and has taught computer courses for ten years at Babson College, Stonehill College, Plymouth (N.H.) State College, and elsewhere. He currently teaches the Introduction to Computers course at Colby-Sawyer College in New London, New Hampshire. In 1987, he was named one of "323 People Who Made the Boston Computer Society." He is a member of the advisory council of the International School of Information Management and is listed in the *International Businessmen's Who's Who* and *Contemporary Authors*.

Preface

Using Computers and Information: Tools for Knowledge Workers is a textbook that takes its title seriously. Its premise is that people, whom we refer to as *knowledge workers*, use computers and information to perform knowledge work. Without people, the work that computers perform would be meaningless. Together, computers and information contribute to the creation of knowledge work—work that has *added value*, thanks to the computer system.

My objective in writing this text is to explain the importance of computer technology in a meaningful and interesting context for people with little or no computer background. I don't feel that it's enough to tell you what bits and bytes are without explaining how a person working with a computer uses them in the process of creating useful information. It is not necessarily valuable to know the clock speed of a microprocessor without understanding it as part of the *better, faster, cheaper* paradigm that drives the computer industry. There is little point in explaining application software unless you understand it in relation to the data processing operations. In short, there is no point in *describing* technology without *showing* how it actually works and explaining how to become skillful and productive in using computer tools to obtain and work with information.

Using Computers and Information is the work of an instructor who has devoted over 15 years of his life to computer journalism and writing about information technology. This book represents what I have learned from spending ten years in the classroom teaching the Introduction to Computers course to people just like you. The book is also the product of a collaborative workgroup, one that reaches back to 1987 and the author's first text, *Computers for People,* and culminates with the knowledge workers who made this book a reality in the fall of 1995. This workgroup is composed of intelligent, insightful, dedicated, and hard-working teachers across the country who were willing to read this manuscript and critique it candidly.

The publishing professionals at Que Education and Training, through their diligence and creativity, demonstrated this book's thesis: that knowledge workers, using computers and a variety of software applications, can be extraordinarily productive. These knowledge workers created this beautiful book—from its cover to the interior design, drawings and illustrations, and page layout—using the technology that this book explains. The organization of the text and content is as much a product of their vision as it is mine, although I assume total responsibility for its content, accuracy, and timeliness.

Organization

This text is organized into four parts:

- An Introduction to the Computer System
- Computer Hardware
- Computer Software
- How Knowledge Workers Use Computer Systems

Each part begins with "The Knowledge Worker Interview," a question-and-answer interview conducted over the Internet with people using computers in their professions. These interviews are intended to convey the challenge and excitement of contemporary knowledge work.

Each chapter begins with an introduction to the topic, followed by modules with course content. Chapters conclude with approximately 30 review and discussion questions, followed by two features: "Ethics" and "The Learning Enterprise."

"Ethics" discusses an ethical issue related to chapter content. These ethical issues have been drawn from a variety of well-qualified books, magazine articles, and Internet resources. The "Ethics" sections are highly focused and provocative, and are accompanied by review questions to promote critical thinking and discussion. These sections can also be used for essay assignments.

"The Learning Enterprise" is an interactive business simulation that can be managed as a class project or as individual assignments. "The Learning Enterprise" enables students to create a new enterprise—a business, non-profit organization, or government agency—and determine its mission. The class breaks into functional workgroups that make decisions, set goals and objectives, and literally run an enterprise, all while using computer systems and information to do so. Individual knowledge workers and workgroups are assigned activities that progress toward a functioning organization by the end of the book. In addition, each chapter has specific World Wide Web sites on the Internet where students can go for more information about "The Learning Enterprise".

Each chapter is divided into several modules. A module is designed to be studied as a separate, distinct *stand-alone* body of information. Each module covers a single topic comprehensively and is designed as one contact hour's assignment.

The pages of *Using Computers and Information* are not cluttered with numerous sidebars, callouts, boxed features, and decorative photographs. Instead, each module has just a few simple features carefully chosen to enhance understanding of the subject:

- *"Home Page"* is a feature found within each module. The term is borrowed from the Internet's World Wide Web, an increasingly valuable source of information. Like its on-line counterpart, the "Home Page" is a montage of text and graphics that focuses on describing and illustrating an interesting and relevant topic. Three or more Review Questions accompany each "Home Page" feature.
- *"Issues and Ideas"* explores a concern or aspect related to the module's topic. This feature is designed to inspire critical thinking and encourage discussion—in writing, in class, or in groups. Many of these sections, written by real people, were drawn verbatim from primary sources, including the Internet, and are identified as such. Three or more Critical Thinking questions accompany each "Issues and Ideas" section.

Many modules feature two-page spreads that delve deeply into the technical aspects of the topic. These features have been drawn from a variety of books, such as *How Microprocessors Work* and *How The Internet Works*, published by Ziff-Davis and Que. These highly visual illustrations make the topics come alive.

Using Computers and Information: Tools for Knowledge Workers has been written with the sincere belief that the study of computers is eminently worthwhile, both as an intellectual pursuit and as a means of acquiring invaluable skills. Understanding the universal presence and extraordinary influence of computers in society is a responsibility. Knowing how computers work and how to use them makes us eminently employable in this, the Information Age.

Acknowledgments

Many people helped make this a book.

My deepest appreciation to Chris Katsaropoulos, whose vision has powered this book from the first discussions. His team-building skills were what made it possible to bring this book to print in less than a year.

Betsy Brown proved to be a project coordinator, art researcher, permissions manager, and teammate par excellence. Thanks for all your hard work and patience, Betsy.

Jeannine Freudenberger, the senior production editor who created this book, page by page, from electronically transmitted binary files, has proven tireless and good-spirited in spite of delays, problems, and complexities beyond imagine. I am proud to be the author of this, Jeannine's last Que book before her well-deserved retirement.

Joan Paterson of East-West Editorial worked tirelessly beside me on this book, from inception to conclusion. She managed many aspects of this project, including manuscript development, the review process, developmental editing, copy editing, coordination with Que production, and so many hundreds of major and minor details that I could not possibly list them all. She is not only my companion but also my publishing partner.

I would also like to thank Sheila Cunningham, Managing Editor; Anne Jones for her elegant book design; Kathy Ruggles for her cover art; Ryan Oldfather for his wonderful illustrations; Garrett Pease for his technical editing; and Jodi Jensen, Ginny Noble, and Sally Yuska for their copy and production editing.

Special thanks to Anthony N. Quinn, Chairman of the Business Department at Colby-Sawyer College. After a 25-year career at IBM, Tony knows knowledge work and computers, and I greatly appreciate his patience and support and that of all my friends, colleagues, and students at Colby-Sawyer. Thanks also to my son Joshua, whose experience as a student and a knowledge worker have been the source of inspiration, council, and advice for many years. Mike Antonucci, my oldest and best friend and constant supporter of my college textbook writing. Dr. James Martin, unquestionably the most erudite and knowledgeable expert in the computer industry, whose prolific writing and incisive and provocative thoughts on business and information technology have been an inspiration to me throughout my computer journalism career.

Charles P. Lecht, (1933-1992), my mentor and my friend who taught me a deeper wisdom about computers and their influence in our lives. I still miss you, Charley. Special appreciation to Webb Castor, a wise and witty man; Elisa Klosterman at Cunningham Communications for her professionalism in helping me with Motorola; Garth Chouteau of Stormfront Studios for our long, long-distance work together; John and Rosalie Babiarz, for their expert counsel in real-world computing; to our four featured knowledge workers, Tonya Antonucci, Bruce Gee, Jolin Marie Salazar-Kish, and Rich Tennant— brave cyberpilgrims on the Information Superhighway; to the many professional marketing, media relations, and publicity people with whom I had the pleasure of working; and to John Woods for his initial encouragement to write this book for Que.

The following colleagues were members of the book's academic advisory board and reviewers, and I am grateful for all the hard work they put into reading and commenting on this manuscript. It would not be as good a book were it not for their tireless scrutiny:

Virginia Anderson, University of North Dakota; Michael Atherton, Mankato State University; Bruce Black, Polk Community College; Fred Bounds, Dekalb College; Barbara Comfort, J. Sargeant Reynolds; John LaPonte, Southern Connecticut State University; Darlene De Vida, Lower Columbia College; Philip East, University of Northern Iowa; Elaine Haight, Foothill Community College; James LaSalle, University of Arizona; Pete Maggiacomo, Sinclair Community College; Nat Martin, University of Rochester; Elizabeth Oddy, SUNY-Oswego; Pat Ormond, Utah Valley State College; Domenick Pinto, Sacred Heart University; Herbert Rebhun, University of Houston-Downtown; Bruce Reinig, University of Arizona; Judy Scheeren, Westmoreland Co. Community College.

Jack B. Rochester
Cherry Hill Farm
Grafton, New Hampshire
December, 1995

A Guide to the Supplements

Annotated Instructor's Edition (1-57576-060-6). The *AIE*, written by the author, contains Lecture Notes and Discussion Points to enhance the class discussion.

Student Study Guide (1-57576-329-X). The *Student Study Guide* is exceptionally well integrated with the text. Appealing to students with diverse learning styles, it requires students to think critically in analyzing the concepts they have learned and in applying them to a variety of challenging questions.

Instructor's Resource Manual (1-57576-328-1). The *Instructor's Resource Manual* provides expert guidance for teaching even the most challenging topics. This manual includes unique instructional activities for effective lectures as well as course outlines for instructors who use alternative syllabi. A *MultiMedia Curriculum Guide*, which correlates the PowerPoint Electronic Transparencies and *Interacting with Your Computer* CD-ROM, is also included.

Computerized Test Bank (incorporating On-Line Testing) (1-57576-330-3 for DOS, 1-57576-332-X for Macintosh, and 1-57576-331-1 for Windows 3.1/Windows 95). This test bank takes testing beyond assessment to provide another opportunity to teach your students the computer concepts they'll need for the future. Three levels of questions—factual, conceptual, and applications-based—are designed to actively promote critical thinking and problem-solving skills.

PowerPoint Electronic Transparencies (1-57576-327-3). Over one hundred bullet-point presentation slides that correspond to the text outline are available as convenient, easy-to-use PowerPoint electronic transparencies.

Interacting with Your Computer CD-ROM (0-7897-0340-8 for Windows 3.1, 0-7897-0344-0 for Macintosh). This interactive CD-ROM combines crystal-clear images, animated sequences, and audio for the Windows and MAC platforms.

The Quest Custom Publishing Program. This program is brought to you courtesy of our parent corporation. Macmillan Computer Publishing, the publisher of the most complete library of computer information in the world, proudly presents the most comprehensive custom publishing program in the world! Quest gives you a comprehensive menu of selections from your computer application specialists at Que Education & Training *and* all the imprints of Macmillan Computer Publishing—Hayden, New Riders Press, Que, Sams, Sams.net, and Ziff-Davis. Only Que Education & Training understands that every computer course is different—from course objectives and teaching styles to course length and class demographics. Provide us with a menu, and we'll create the book!

Essentials. These hands-on tutorials for short courses of 8 to 12 contact hours are designed to be used separately or as computer lab application modules to accompany *Using Computers and Information: Tools for Knowledge Workers*. The primarily four-color modules, presented in a project-driven chapter format, cover the essential elements of leading applications for Windows 3.1 and Windows 95 platforms. The tutorials are designed for a broad spectrum of majors, although the business examples and the case problems contained in the end-of-chapter material also make them suitable for use in Schools of Business. Each *Essentials* volume is sized at 8 1/2 × 11 inches for maximum screen-shot visibility. Many of the attractive, yet affordably priced, books in this series range in length from 100 to 200 pages, although integrated suite manuals range in length from 400 to 500 pages. Manuals can be custom-built to your specifications through the Quest program.

SmartStarts. This series, suitable for use in courses of 12 to 24 contact hours, offers extended practice for major software applications in DOS, Windows 3.1, and Windows 95 platforms. Each two-color *SmartStart* volume is approximately 300 to 350 pages in length. This series is also part of the Quest program.

For more information about the *Using Computers and Information* ancillary package or our on-line access program, please visit our Web site (http://www.mcp.com); contact your local Que Education & Training representative; or contact Susan Dollman at Macmillan Computer Publishing, 201 W. 103rd Street, Indianapolis, IN 46290. Ms. Dollman may also be reached at CompuServe 75462,3444, Internet: sdollman@que_edtr.mcp.com, or AOL: sdollman@aol.com. Videotapes of broadcast quality are also available to adopters. Please contact your local representative for details.

Table of Contents

Preface

USING COMPUTERS

AND
INFORMATION

TOOLS FOR KNOWLEDGE WORKERS

Jack B. Rochester
Colby-Sawyer College

Using Computers and Information

Library of Congress Catalog No.: 95-70950

ISBN: 1-57576-059-2

99 98 97 96   4 3 2 1

Interpretation of the printing code: the rightmost double-digit number is the year of the book's printing; the rightmost single-digit number, the number of the book's printing. For example, a printing code of 96-1 shows that the first printing of the book occurred in 1996.

Screens reproduced in this book were created using Collage Plus from Inner Media, Inc., Hollis, NH.

Trademark Acknowledgments

President and Publisher
David P. Ewing

Associate Publisher
Chris Katsaropoulos

Product Marketing Manager
Susan J. Dollman

Managing Editor
Sheila B. Cunningham

Senior Editor
Jeannine Freudenberger

Production Editors
Jodi Jensen, Virginia Noble, Sally A. Yuska

Acquisitions & Art Coordinator
Elizabeth D. Brown

Cover Design
Kathy Ruggles

Book Design
Anne Jones

Illustrator
Ryan Oldfather

Publisher's Assistant
Angie Denny

Formatter
Alison Scott

Production Team
Mary Ann Abramson, Charlotte Clapp, Jeanne Clark, Terrie Deemer, Cheryl Dietsch, Mike Dietsch, Tim Griffin, Mike Henry, Louisa Klucznik, Brian-Kent Proffitt, Laura Smith, SA Springer

PART I

AN INTRODUCTION TO THE COMPUTER SYSTEM

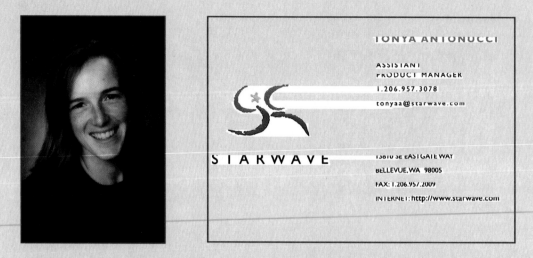

TONYA ANTONUCCI

ASSISTANT
PRODUCT MANAGER
1.206.957.3078

tonyaa@starwave.com

STARWAVE

13810 SE EASTGATE WAY
BELLEVUE, WA 98005

FAX: 1.206.957.2009

INTERNET: http://www.starwave.com

Knowledge Worker Interview with Tonya Antonucci

Tonya was born on March 30, 1968, in Biloxi, Mississippi, and now lives in Kirkland, Washington. She graduated from Stanford University in 1990 with a B.A. in political science and a minor in economics.

Author: Where do you work?

Tonya: I'm a product manager in the Online Group at Starwave Corporation. I'm responsible for *Outside On-line* on the Internet's World Wide Web. It's an on-line publication for outdoor enthusiasts, offering current news on adventure sports and environmental issues, forum discussions with outdoor experts, advice on traveling and buying gear, and the ability to read and search issues of *Outside* magazine.

Author: What's your job like?

Tonya: Marketing on-line publications is unlike traditional marketing in a few key ways. First, the on-line publication isn't a finished product that ships to target markets. It evolves and changes daily. So I meet with the editorial staff of *Outside Online* almost every day to discuss and plan upcoming content, contests, and on-line surveys, to name a few. I write press releases and prepare informative documents explaining our publication. I'm on-line a lot, generating awareness about *Outside Online* on the Internet and with various communities of users on commercial services, such as America Online. Other activities on any given day include buying advertising, securing new content, forming partnerships for promotional activities, working on long-range marketing plans, and attending trade or consumer shows.

Author: What do you like about your employer and your work?

Tonya: Starwave is a start-up technology company, founded in 1993. We're young people, we work long hours, and we're dedicated to delivering products we believe in. What's uniquely attractive is our market position. We've established ourselves as early leaders in on-line publishing, and there's a certain pride or "top dog" mentality that motivates everyone to keep improving and stay ahead of the curve.

Author: How do you view the future of knowledge work?

Tonya: Business today is conducted at light-speed, and computers are largely responsible for that, no question. In the corporate world, most communication is conducted via computer networks.

An Introduction to the Computer System

Sting Live!

Got something you'd like to say to Sting? Ask the rock superstar about his CD-ROM, *All This Time*, and other scintillating topics in the *Mr. Showbiz* Celebrity Lounge, Tuesday, November 7, at 7 p.m. EST

(4 p.m. PST)

about   faq

For example, I'll send e-mail to a guy ten feet away, just because it's faster and more efficient than a face-to-face exchange. The future of knowledge work in society is more nebulous to me. Certainly, the sheer volume of people on-line is staggering; however, most surveys also show that both hardware and on-line access are still clearly divided between the "haves" and the "have-nots." So until technology is accessible and affordable for more of society, it's difficult to assess the societal impact.

Author: Where do you think future opportunities lie?

Tonya: Given the explosive growth of publishing on the Internet and on-line services, there are opportunities in all facets of my industry. Demands will be high for programmers, writers, editors, and business majors savvy in advertising, marketing, customer support, and operations.

Author: What advice would you give today's college student?

Tonya: If you hope to graduate and move directly into the field of electronic publishing, you face some competition from old-school print publishers and other media professionals who are crossing over to the new medium. Some will be your parents' age, with loads of editing, marketing, and general business experience. College students have access to cutting-edge technology and resources that bring you quickly up to speed. Take advantage of that and get some experience, too. At the same time, be sure you're sharpening your basic communication skills. Although the electronic medium is different, being able to speak and write intelligently and cogently is still an asset.

Author: Tell us about your computer system.

Tonya: I use a Hewlett-Packard xm2 (486DX2-66 MHz) with 32MB of RAM, running Windows 95. I use Micrsoft Excel and Word a lot, but I'm always connected to the Internet via a T-1 line and have 14.4bis external modem connection to America Online, Prodigy, and the Microsoft Network (MSN).

Author: What are your favorite non-work uses for the computer?

Tonya: Games are a hit with me. I enjoy *Myst*—of course, who doesn't? I have an instructional rock-climbing CD, and I have to admit I'm partial to the new Sting CD we've produced here at Starwave.

Author: What do you do for fun?

Tonya: Soccer is my part-time obsession. I've played soccer ever since I was 8 years old. I was assistant coach for the Stanford Women's Soccer team the first year they went to the NCAA final four tournament. I'm still extremely competitive, and that continues to motivate me on the soccer field. I play in a women's league with other former college players, and I'd like nothing more than for our team, the Saints, to win a national championship.

WHAT IS A KNOWLEDGE WORKER?

CHAPTER 1

What the lever was to the arm, the computer is to the brain.

Charles P. Lecht, computer futurist

In the Industrial Age, work skills were often defined by physical strength or the ability to operate specific types of machinery. Intelligence and knowledge weren't primary considerations for the jobs for the average worker. Today it's pretty much the other way around: intelligence and knowledge are prerequisites for good jobs. And the Information Age is rapidly creating new occupations that require computer skills.

The term *knowledge worker* was first coined in 1966 by Peter F. Drucker, one of the twentieth century's foremost thinkers in the field of business management. Drucker taught business and management for many years at Claremont Graduate School in California. (The college's Drucker Management Center is named for him.) He has also written dozens of books on business.

In his book *Managing for the Future: The 1990s and Beyond*, Drucker writes, "For 30 years, from the end of World War II to the mid-1970s, high-paying jobs in all developed countries were concentrated in unskilled blue-collar work. Now a majority of the new high-paying jobs are in knowledge work: technicians, professionals, specialists of all kinds, managers. The qualification for the high-paying jobs of 20 years ago was a union card. Now it is formal schooling."[1]

Knowledge work is not new. It used to be called white-collar or clerical work, but most knowledge work today involves computers. By refining and organizing the data it processes, the computer *adds value* to clerical work, producing information that can be used in many ways. The people who perform knowledge work are called *knowledge workers*. The computer adds value to knowledge work and enhances the knowledge workers' *personal productivity* by helping them complete tasks more quickly and obtain valuable information.

---

1. Peter F. Drucker. *Managing for the Future: The 1990s and Beyond* (New York: Truman Talley Books/Plume, 1993), 131.

Module A

Types of Knowledge Workers

Why It's Important to Know

Almost every educated member of the Information Age is or will become a knowledge worker. Understanding the scope of knowledge work and the purpose behind knowledge work—increased productivity—will give you insight into the evolving opportunities in the business workplace.

What is a knowledge worker? A **knowledge worker** is someone who routinely uses information in his or her work. Using a computer to work with information enhances a knowledge worker's productivity. A knowledge worker is the single most critical component in a computer system. Knowledge workers are people from many walks of life; those who routinely use computers have the following characteristics:

- They are skilled in the use of computers.

- They know how to work with computer-based information.

- They understand how the computer benefits their work and the enterprise.

- They regard the computer as a productivity tool.

Knowledge workers may be employed in an *enterprise*, or organization, of any size, large or small, for a wide range of tasks. The enterprise may be a business, a governmental agency, or a not-for-profit organization. Knowledge workers also may be self-employed, working in their own offices as doctors, attorneys, certified public accountants, or any one of thousands of other occupations, or working from home as marketing representatives, freelance writers or editors, consultants, and so on. Sales representatives or managers are knowledge workers, too.

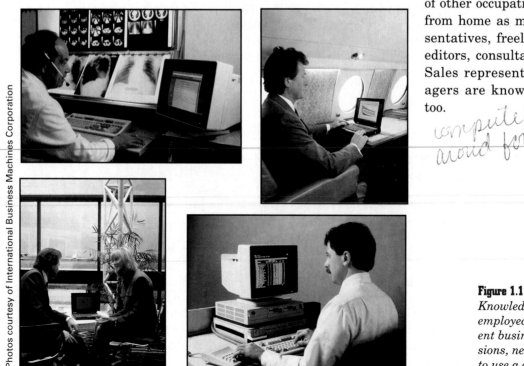

Photos courtesy of International Business Machines Corporation

Figure 1.1
Knowledge workers, employed in many different businesses and professions, need to know how to use a computer.

Today's knowledge worker needs to understand how to use a personal computer, how to work with computer-based information, and how computer systems benefit business. For example, Diane is a video designer who owns her own small business. Kevin is the TV advertisement manager for a large Boston advertising agency; he is in charge of producing animated video clips, such as morphs, for TV ads. Diane and Kevin work together as a team: one is a contract knowledge worker, the other a staff knowledge worker. They both hire various freelance artists and designers, most of whom work from home or "cottage industry" studios to help prepare video clips for use in commercials produced for the ad agency's clients.

Figure 1.2

Lately, Diane and Kevin have been asked to produce some videos and special graphics for clients who have a home page on the Internet. The Internet is the on-line computer network, often called the Information Superhighway, that is attracting millions of new subscribers. A home page is a combination of written text, graphic design, photos or pictures, sometimes moving video, and *hypertext links*, which enable you to find related information. So now Diane and Kevin are working

Courtesy of International Business Machines Corporation

with other knowledge workers who have skills in desktop publishing, on-line computer communications, and the creation of home pages and other information services on the Internet. Kevin and Diane never dreamed that they would be creating ad material for a computer network, but they're pretty excited about exploring this new opportunity.

You too are a knowledge worker. You may be preparing for a career in knowledge work in office automation, science, research, public relations, account supervision, social work, sports management, travel, education, children's literature, or a number of other occupations. More than likely, no matter what you do, you'll be using a computer for at least part of your knowledge work.

Knowledge Worker Productivity: An Example

Knowledge workers use computers and information in many, many ways; often the process is highly personal. Here is an example. Follow figures 1.3 through 1.7 as you watch this knowledge worker, Kathleen, an editor at a publishing company, prepare for a 3 o'clock meeting to confer about the new book she is interested in publishing (see figure 1.3).

At the weekly meeting, any editors who want to offer a contract to an author must present a report called a publishing proposal. Our editor Kathleen arrives at work that morning and powers up her personal computer. She starts the word processing and spreadsheet applications. Her publishing proposal is nearly written; it needs only some final touches. Kathleen uses some word processing procedures to make her report more interesting to read; she adds different typefaces and boldfacing and centers the beginning list, as shown in figure 1.4.

Figure 1.3
Kathleen uses her computer to prepare her presentations.

Courtesy of International Business Machines Corporation

Figure 1.4
Kathleen uses word processing's formatting features to create an attractive document that invites the reader to read it.

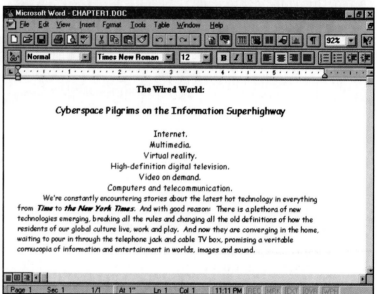

When the proposal is completed, Kathleen gets the book production figures from the publishing company's corporate mainframe computer and enters them into her spreadsheet. Using specific procedures (known as spreadsheet formulas) for processing the data, Kathleen begins preparing sales figures, printing costs, marketing costs, and so forth, which she then copies into her document (see figure 1.5).

The numbers show that her book could do extremely well. Using the graphing feature in her spreadsheet, she turns the spreadsheet numbers into a bar chart. Then she copies the chart into her publication report, as shown in figure 1.6.

Next she reads, edits, and formats her document carefully. Once it's perfect, she prints six copies of the proposal on a color printer and puts them in binders (see figure 1.7).

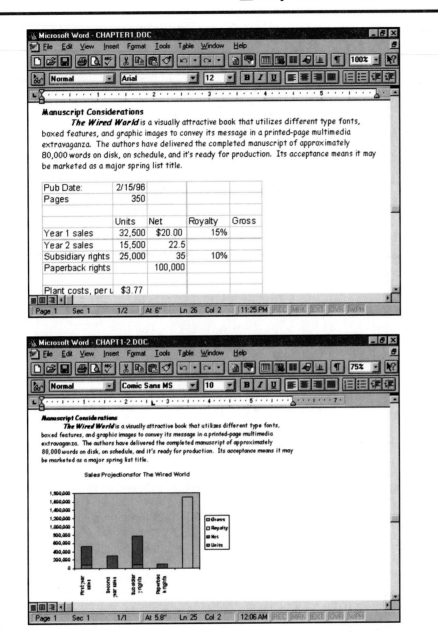

Figure 1.5
Kathleen works with the spreadsheet data and brings it into her document.

Figure 1.6
Kathleen uses the cut-and-paste feature of her software to combine text and graphics.

Kathleen smiles; she's prepared a document that presents the book proposal information clearly. As she walks down the hall to the meeting, she thinks, "I'm going to get the green light to publish this book, and it's going to be my first best-seller!"

As this example demonstrates, from an employer's standpoint, one goal of knowledge work is to increase knowledge worker productivity so that the employee is, in a sense, profitable. Another goal is to make the organization as a whole less costly to operate; one way to accomplish the second goal is to hire and retain good people. It costs four times as much to lose and retrain a knowledge worker as it does to keep that worker.

Figure 1.7
The final printout shows a professional-looking document.

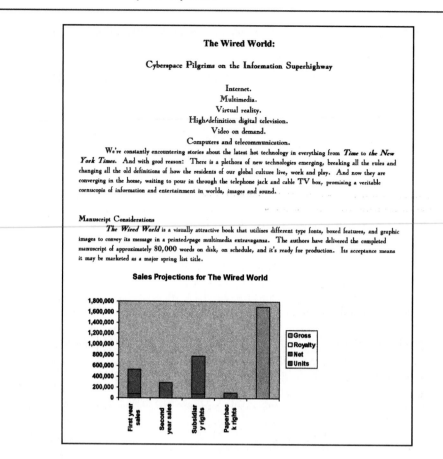

The Wired World:

Cyberspace Pilgrims on the Information Superhighway

Internet.
Multimedia.
Virtual reality.
High-definition digital television.
Video on demand.
Computers and telecommunication.

We're constantly encountering stories about the latest hot technology in everything from *Time* to *the New York Times*. And with good reason: There is a plethora of new technologies emerging, breaking all the rules and changing all the old definitions of how the residents of our global culture live, work and play. And now they are converging in the home, waiting to pour in through the telephone jack and cable TV box, promising a veritable cornucopia of information and entertainment in worlds, images and sound.

Manuscript Considerations

The Wired World is a visually attractive book that utilizes different type fonts, boxed features, and graphic images to convey its message in a printed-page multimedia extravaganza. The authors have delivered the completed manuscript of approximately 80,000 words on disk, on schedule, and it's ready for production. Its acceptance means it may be marketed as a major spring list title.

Sales Projections for The Wired World

[Bar chart with y-axis from 0 to 1,800,000 in increments of 200,000; x-axis categories: First year sales, Second year sales, Subsidiary rights, Paperback rights; legend: Gross, Royalty, Net, Units]

Knowledge Work Today and Tomorrow

Courtesy of The Bettmann Archive

Courtesy of International Business Machines Corporation

Figure 1.8
The old compartmentalized office is disappearing.

Becoming a highly skilled, valuable knowledge worker does not necessarily mean "rising to the top" in the traditional sense. In the information-based enterprise, knowledge is not power as we have come to understand it, because most people have access to information. Thus, managers don't necessarily know more than their subordinates in all phases of the job. Everyone has a high degree of *information literacy*, meaning all workers know what information they need in order to do their work and where to find this information. In the social organization of tomorrow's enterprise, information literacy and knowledge work tend to make everyone peers.

To quote Peter Drucker, with whom this chapter opened:

To be information literate, you begin with learning what it is you need to know. Too much talk focuses on technology, even worse on the speed of the gadget, always faster, faster. This kind of "techie" fixation causes us to lose track of the fundamental nature of information in today's

HOME PAGE

WORKING AWAY FROM "WORK"

The following is an excerpt from a book by Danny Goodman entitled *Living at Light Speed: Your Survival Guide to Life on the Information Superhighway*:

> Telecommuting—the ability to work at a location other than the central office—is already a common practice for millions of knowledge workers in the United States. Obviously some jobs—such as service jobs dealing with customers who venture out into the real world for shopping and entertainment—don't lend themselves to telecommuting. But . . . employers whose primary tasks are computer and/or telephone-based can perform that work virtually anywhere phone lines run.
>
> Working out of the office takes on many forms. It could mean working from home, from a small satellite office closer to home than the main office, or from a self-contained office in your car or briefcase if you work "in the field." Typical tools for telecommuters are the telephone and personal computer (equipped with a telephone modem, which allows the computer to communicate with electronic mail and other main office services via standard telephone lines).

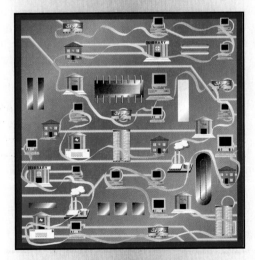

The Information Superhighway.

> Depending on your communication needs, a fax machine and pager may also be part of the arsenal (although personal computers can handle fax tasks these days without much difficulty).
>
> The Los Angeles earthquake of 1994 hit many knowledge workers and their employers very hard. In that megalopolis, commutes of one or more hours each way in normal circumstances had been common. But when the earth shook enough to close major highways for months, each one-hour trip took two to three hours. To help employees whose jobs were already suited to telecommuting, a number of companies allowed them to work from home or satellite offices for part of each week.[2]

HOME PAGE REVIEW QUESTIONS

1. At one time, work involved going to a specific place of business. What factors have changed this definition?
2. What electronic devices, or *knowledge worker tools*, have made telecommuting work possible?
3. The definition of work in question 1 implies that all your work is conducted at the place of business. What are the implications of having your telecommuting

---

2. Danny Goodman. *Living at Light Speed: Your Survival Guide to Life on the Information Superhighway* (New York: Random House, 1994), 110–111.

organization. To organize the way work is done you have to begin with the specific job, then the information input, and finally the human relationships needed to get the job done.[3]

Knowledge work is steadily assuming larger proportions. According to several worldwide studies, urban centers in Canada, the United States, Europe, and other developed countries are increasingly using computer technology and thus evolving *knowledge-based* cities. These knowledge-based cities are characterized by (1) a concentration of scientists and engineers; (2) business, university, and governmental research activities; (3) a high degree of interaction between individuals and the various institutions; and (4) a positive image that attracts college graduates to knowledge work. Clearly, the decade of the 1990s and the new millennium that follows are an exciting time for knowledge work.

Knowledge Workers: The Most Important Element

People are the most important component in any computer system. Knowledge workers are found in many different occupations in modern business, adding value to data and turning it into useful information. By and large, they enjoy their work, but it wasn't always that way.

A hundred years ago, office workers were treated in much the same way as factory workers, performing rote tasks under strict supervision. Today's knowledge workers and the work they perform have redefined office work. In many instances, knowledge work has significantly altered the established organizational hierarchy, turning managers into their own secretaries and administrative assistants into decision makers.

There are two types of knowledge workers, characterized by the way they work: collaborators and power users.

Courtesy of The Bettmann Archive

Figure 1.9
The office of the nineteenth century.

Collaborators

Knowledge workers used to be defined by the department they worked for or their function in the enterprise. Today, people are selected to work together for their knowledge and skills to accomplish a task or project. Once a project is completed, the group may be given a new project, or the workers may be reassigned as a group to work on the next project. This method is termed **collaboration**, and it simply means working together. The knowledge workers working together are often referred to as a **work group**. In the book *Workplace 2000*, these work groups are called teams and are

---

3. T. George Harris. "The Post-Capitalist Executive: An Interview with Peter F. Drucker," from *The Evolving Global Economy* (Kenichi Ohmae, ed., Boston: Harvard Business School Press, 1995), 230–233.

described this way: "Both physically and emotionally the team will be like a small business unto itself; teams will be analogous to small shops or boutiques in a shopping mall—each shop is a part of a larger whole, but separate and distinct."[4]

Figure 1.10
Collaboration breaks down the artificial departmental groups of the past and creates relationships based on the need to work together with information.

Power Users

Certain knowledge workers are able to assimilate and learn to use computer technology more quickly than others. A **power user** is a knowledge worker who can learn to use new applications quickly, has mastered most of an application's advanced features, and may know some application programming techniques.

He or she understands the business and work group objectives, as well as the computer systems in use (often personal computers), and is able to help formulate strategies for getting the most productivity from computers for the work group. For example, Sarah, the graphic designer who uses a PowerPC Macintosh in the advertising department, is a power user. So is Mike, the sales representative who has developed a sophisticated customer database on his notebook computer for maximum productivity.

InfoWorld magazine described a power user this way: "Some end-users learn enough . . . to qualify as power users: those people whose computing skills are beyond the scope of the occasional user's but not at the level of the system administrator. These people like to fiddle with their environments."[5] Almost any knowledge worker can become a power user willing to share computer skills and knowledge with other knowledge workers to help them solve business problems and become more productive.

---

4. Joseph H. Boyett and Henry P. Conn. *Workplace 2000: The Revolution Reshaping American Business* (NY: Dutton, 1991), 255.

5. Robert A. DelRossi. "Democratic Data Tools," *InfoWorld*, October 23, 1995, 84.

Figure 1.11
This power user works at the Help Desk in this large company, helping knowledge workers learn new techniques and solve problems in using their computers.

The Future of Knowledge Work

One thing can be said about knowledge work with certainty—there will be more of it. W.W. Castor, an information age futurist and consultant, cites the heavy investment made by American industry in knowledge work: back in 1990, it was 75 percent of the industrial workforce; today, it is more like 90 percent. Even with this investment, most of the information—about 90 percent—is still in paper form, and the amount of paper is growing from 4 trillion pages per year to an estimated 8 trillion pages per year by the end of the decade.[6]

At the same time, it's interesting to note that a recent U.S. government study concluded that by the year 2000, three out of five jobs for which people will need to be trained and educated *do not exist today*. Moreover, these jobs will almost certainly involve the use of a computer and working with information. Clearly, it is in your best interest to become a highly competent knowledge worker.

Knowledge Check

1. What is the most important element in a computer system?
2. What is the main reason a knowledge worker uses a computer?
3. List some specific productivity problems confronting today's knowledge worker.
4. Where do knowledge workers get data?
5. Knowledge workers turn data into what?

Key Terms

collaboration   knowledge worker   power user   work group

---

6. W.W. Castor. "The Information Age and the New Productivity," unpublished report, 20–21.

ISSUES AND IDEAS

How (Not?) to Resolve Conflict

Consider the issues in the following story submitted to the Internet RISKS Forum by David Miller; then answer the questions at the end.

STUDENTS SUE COLLEGE OVER COMPUTER COURSE
(originally appeared in the *Wall Street Journal*, May 9, 1995, page A1)

Two students won the lawsuit they brought against New York's Pace University when an instructor for a beginner's course in computing gave a homework assignment the students thought was too hard: calculating the price of an atom of aluminum on Friday given such information as the price of aluminum on Wednesday, the rate change between the prices of the metal on Wednesday and Friday, the atomic mass of aluminum, the value of Avogadro's number (6.02×10 to the 23rd power), etc., etc. The students handled their own case against the university, and asked the teacher to answer such questions as: "Do you think this was a good choice for a beginning class?" The judge decided: "Students are consumers. There is nothing holy or sacred about educational institutions."

The judge seemed to mistake the product of educational institutions as being the work that is given out (rather than the learning that results from doing the work).[7]

CRITICAL THINKING

1. List the facts in this story.

2. Present an argument in favor of the example the instructor used, and then present an argument against the example.

3. Given what we are told, do you think that the judge's decision was based on (a) consumer protection issues, (b) the idea that computers are inherently difficult, or (c) any other reason you can think of?

4. Given what we know, was this the best way for the students to resolve the issue with their instructor?

5. Research this story by locating the original *Wall Street Journal* article and several other sources, and write a brief paper about the subject.

---

7. Adapted from RISKS Forum 17.12.

Module B

Computer Literacy and Productivity

Why It's Important to Know

> **Developing computer literacy is similar to joining a sports team. Computer literacy gives you a sense of confidence and accomplishment as well as the basic skills with which to become more creative and productive with your PC.**

Computer literacy is (1) being knowledgeable or educated in how to use a computer and (2) having an understanding of the computer's impact on our daily lives. In addition, computer literacy means using computers properly and ethically.

Most people in our culture would agree that it is useful to know how to turn on a computer and perform a simple task like word processing (which is the most frequently used application). Computer literacy includes a number of intermediate stages: mastering the operating system and operating environment, identifying software and hardware problems, correcting software and hardware problems. The most skillful and computer-literate knowledge worker may be a power user.

It is likely that you'll be using computers frequently in your work. Computer literacy is an essential skill for people in the 1990s, but we gain this skill incrementally. We do not need to know everything about computers or understand how to use every aspect of an application all at once; it's far better to learn new things as we discover a need for them. This text takes that approach: First, you'll learn a little; then, as you progress, you'll learn a little more.

Productivity

The basic idea behind automating tasks and processes with computers is to make people more productive—to increase productivity. The term **productivity** refers to the measurement of an enterprise's efficiency, often defined by labor, or worker productivity. At first, the computer was put to work performing long, complex mathematical equations. The computer has been used for many years to improve white-collar, or knowledge worker, productivity. And even though worker productivity in the United States is among the highest in the world, productivity gains from computers have not come as quickly or as plentifully as expected, as the Home Page feature explains.

HOME PAGE

THE PRODUCTIVITY PARADOX

Dr. Peter G.W. Keen is a highly respected information technology consultant and university professor. Here are his views on the "productivity paradox."

Economist Stephen Roach coined this term, productivity paradox, to describe the negligible payoff from more than $100 billion spent on information technology by financial services companies in the 1970s and 1980s. The paradox is, that after this massive investment, which more than doubled the IT (information technology, or computer for short) capital deployed per worker, productivity increased only 0.7 percent a year, whereas that of U.S. manufacturing during the same period increased 3.5 percent a year.

Courtesy of The Bettmann Archive

"The way of paradoxes is the way of truth. To test Reality we must see it on the tight-rope. When the Verities become acrobats we can judge them."
— *Oscar Wilde*

Roach attributes the lack of improvement in productivity to misallocation of priorities and overinvestment in administrative systems. He now sees a major shift that targets marketing, customer service, and value-added applications. He, along with many other observers, argues that U.S. productivity in banking is not the highest in the world.

The productivity paradox reflects an ongoing concern of business executives that their own firms have poured money into IT with little if any return and an ongoing concern of researchers and consultants about how to measure the value of IT. There are many problems (including in Roach's analysis) in assessing the true costs of IT, especially regarding support, education, and maintenance; choosing a fair time frame in which to determine payoffs from long-term capital investments; and defining and measuring productivity.[8]

HOME PAGE REVIEW QUESTIONS

1. What is the productivity paradox?
2. Do you think that similar productivity problems have occurred in industries other than financial services?
3. Is it possible that companies failed to take into account the learning curve when they invested in computers and immediately expected productivity improvements?

---

8. Peter G.W. Keen. *Every Manager's Guide to Information Technology*, Second Edition (Boston: Harvard Business School Press, 1995), 228–9.

How Productivity Views Have Changed

From the late 1800s, when the typewriter was introduced, to the late 1900s, the way work was accomplished in business offices changed very little. Manual typewriters became electric typewriters, but typists still worked in "typing pools" (see figure 1.12). Paper documents accumulated everywhere and were stored in filing cabinets. Perhaps most important, the *procedures* that office workers used to work with information and with each other changed very little.

Courtesy of The Bettmann Archive

Figure 1.12

A typing pool, circa 1900.

Computer technology in the 1980s dramatically changed the office environment. The personal computer began replacing typewriters. Secretarial jobs began to disappear as more knowledge workers used PCs to create, edit, and print their own documents. Most still worked with printed paper documents, but the *speed* with which knowledge workers processed transactions was picking up. First, it was overnight delivery services, like Federal Express; then the desktop facsimile machine changed forever the meaning of "You want it when?" Procedures *were* changing.

But all was not rosy. A hard lesson business had to learn was that computers alone do not improve productivity. In fact, early less sophisticated computer hardware and software sometimes *retarded* productivity. The equipment was often difficult to use, although learning about hardware was nothing compared to learning to use the software. Some applications took as much as 50 hours of practice for the basics. Companies began sending knowledge workers to one-, two-, even three-day seminars to learn how to use a spreadsheet application. Many more hours were spent back in the office trying to master the procedures; the result was lost productive hours when the knowledge workers should have been performing their regular work. Some companies gave their key people PCs to work on at home so that they could spend more time practicing and learning.

Courtesy of International Business Machines Corporation

Figure 1.13

Many companies soon realized that it was cost-effective to have knowledge workers get specific training in PC hardware and software procedures rather than to have them waste productive time trying to learn on their own.

Over time, hardware and software were designed to resemble more closely actual work processes—the way people do their work. With these design changes, real productivity improvements began to occur.

In the past, for example, a single knowledge worker might have been responsible for collecting, organizing, analyzing, and formatting a printed monthly report of his or her department's activities. Now, several people—the supervisor, the analyst, the sales manager—contribute information based on their individual areas of expertise. They use data stored on a disk or captured via data communications. They may use several different applications to work with the data. Significant tables or charts are electronically turned into overhead transparencies or color slides. Indeed, the report may be distributed electronically rather than on paper. The subsequent meeting to discuss the report's contents may occur on-line through electronic mail without all parties present in the same conference room. In fact, the sales manager, who is on the road with her salespeople, could participate from a remote site using a notebook computer.

All these components—knowledge workers, better hardware, and easy-to-use software—enhance productivity to some extent. However, reaching the goal of higher productivity depends on improved procedures. The computer can only emulate the way people and business work. If the processes and procedures are still back in the typewriter era, increasing productivity will be hard. Today, companies have to look at the entire business—not just at buying more computers—if they want real productivity gains.

Courtesy of Silicon Graphics, Inc.

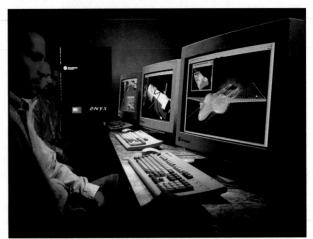

Figure 1.14
Computers and communications have redefined the way people work together.

Knowledge Check

1. What is computer literacy?
2. Why is productivity such an important business goal?
3. How do procedures affect productivity?
4. Why can't computers improve productivity on their own?
5. How can knowledge workers help improve productivity?

Key Terms

computer literacy   productivity

ISSUES AND IDEAS

After Work, What?

Jeremy Rifkin is considered one of the country's foremost thinkers and is the author of more than a dozen books on economic trends and issues relating to science, technology, and culture. In his book *The End of Work,* he writes:

> The Information Age has arrived. In the years ahead, new, more sophisticated software technologies are going to bring civilization ever closer to a near-workless world. In the agriculture, manufacturing, and service sectors, machines are quickly replacing human labor and promise an economy of near automated production by the mid-decades of the twenty-first century. The wholesale substitution of machines for workers is going to force every nation to rethink the role of human beings and the social process. Redefining opportunities and responsibilities for millions of people in a society absent of mass formal employment is

Courtesy of International Business Machines
Corporation

likely to be the single most pressing social issue of the coming century.

While the public continues to hear talk of better economic times ahead, working people everywhere remain perplexed over what appears to be a "jobless recovery." Every day, transnational corporations announce that they are becoming more globally competitive. We are told that profits are steadily rising. Yet, at the same time, companies are announcing massive layoffs. In the single month of January 1994, America's largest employers laid off more than 108,000 workers. Most of the cutbacks came in service industries, where corporate restructuring and the introduction of new laborsaving technologies are resulting in greater productivity, larger profits, and fewer jobs.

Rifkin believes technology has accomplished many wonderful things, but at the expense of the economic well-being of most working people. Technology was supposed to free workers from hard labor and give us more leisure, yet he says, that dream "seems further away now, at the dawn of the Information Age, than at any time in the past half century."9

CRITICAL THINKING

1. Has your assumption been that the Information Age would produce more jobs? Or more specifically, more *knowledge worker* jobs?

2. Is a shrinking labor force a natural evolution of industrialization? Is it a bad thing? Should we be doing more thinking about the way work and leisure are changing—such as how a large nonworking society will be supported?

3. John Lennon of The Beatles once said, "Work is life, you know, and without it, there's nothing but fear and insecurity." What happens if we have a society where most of the people no longer work? Will people be happy, satisfied, and secure?

---

9. Jeremy Rifkin. *The End of Work: The Decline of the Global Laborforce and the Dawn of the Post-Market Era* (New York: Tarcher/G.P. Putnam's Sons, 1995), 3–4, 13–14.

ETHICS

Are You Productive?

Although it's fair and reasonable to place some blame for low productivity on the learning curve and the length of time needed to master an application, knowledge workers should check their work habits as well. Many hours a day are lost to nonproductive activities, such as fine-tuning the computer system, playing games, sending nonbusiness mail messages, and so forth. Although no one expects the knowledge worker to spend eight hours a day being 100 percent productive, frivolous activities need to be taken into account.

What amount of time in nonproductive activities is reasonable? Consider breaks: most employees are given two breaks a day, about 20 minutes each. That may be a good ratio for business versus pleasure computing. But being honest with yourself and adhering to sensible ethical standards should tell you that any activities that do not contribute to the overall good of the company should be left to personal time. Taking paper, pens, and other office supplies home for personal use is considered pilfering or theft. Using the telephone for personal calls is generally frowned on as well, and the same can be said for taking computer time and resources for personal use.

Critical Thinking

1. What constitutes proper ethical behavior at work? Is it based on your ethics or regulations the company sets?

2. Do some research: call the human resources directors at several local companies and ask for the company's ethical standards or code of conduct. Ask whether each company has guidelines for computer use.

3. If a company expects you to do some of your work at home, do you think it's fair to use some of the company's time for nonproductive activities?

THE LEARNING ENTERPRISE

The Learning Enterprise

The Learning Enterprise is a modern company for which you and your class work. It is an employee-owned enterprise that you create from scratch, and you choose by consensus its name; type of enterprise (business, not-for-profit, or governmental agency); and mission. This project is ongoing, and you'll continue it during your studies in this course.

The Learning Enterprise is comprised of *knowledge workers*, organized into *work groups* that function together in different synergies to accomplish the stated mission. Your enterprise gathers, interprets, and assimilates *information* that is used (a) to create value-added services or products for customers, whether they are buyers, volunteers, members, or a constituency, and (b) to enhance learning opportunities for employees of The Learning Enterprise. Excellence, added value, and "customer satisfaction" are the company's goals.

Your first task is to determine the type of enterprise, describe its mission, and develop a set of guidelines for its knowledge workers. These guidelines describe the most important characteristics of the work and the well-being of the knowledge workers. Because the enterprise is employee-owned, the mission is determined by consensus among its knowledge workers. Therefore, each person in the class must submit a mission statement and set of guidelines by answering the following questions, using the examples provided. Then, you will collaborate to decide on the final choices for your enterprise. Each subsequent chapter gives the next step in creating your new organization.

Examples

Type of Enterprise	Name	Mission Statement
Business	Mountain Goat Bikes	To develop a space-age mountain bike.
Not-for-Profit	Save the Forests	To develop a program to save the South American rain forests.
Governmental Agency	Information Literacy for All	To create an information literacy program for the general public.

Knowledge Worker Guidelines

1. The knowledge workers form work groups to accomplish tasks.
2. The Learning Enterprise uses the latest computer technology to provide high-quality information.
3. All knowledge workers are peers and have equal decision-making votes.

Chapter Review

Fill in the Blank

1. The term *knowledge worker* was first coined by _____.
2. Knowledge workers routinely work with _____ in their work.
3. Most knowledge work requires the use of a(n) _____.
4. The computer adds _____ to knowledge work and enhances the knowledge worker's _____.
5. Characterized by the way they work, there are two types of knowledge workers: _____ and _____.
6. The capability to work at a location other than the central office is called _____.
7. Knowledge workers working together are often called a(n) _____ or _____.
8. Knowledge work used to be called _____ or _____ work.
9. Reaching the goal of higher productivity lies in improved _____.
10. In the _____, computer literacy is a prerequisite for a good job.

True/False

1. Computer literacy is not an essential skill for knowledge workers in the 1990s.
2. The basic idea behind automating tasks and processes with computers was to make people more productive.
3. Providing specific training in PC hardware and software procedures for employees is not cost-effective for a company.
4. One way employers can make an organization less costly to operate is to hire and retain good people.

Review Questions

1. What is a knowledge worker?
2. List four characteristics of knowledge workers.
3. Name some of the places knowledge workers can be found.
4. List four characteristics of knowledge-based cities.
5. How are information literacy and flat organizations changing the nature of working in organizations?

Discussion Questions

1. Discuss some of the benefits of telecommuting both for yourself and for your employer.

2. A knowledge worker might be a collaborator or a power user. Discuss these two ways of working.

3. Describe some of your personal knowledge worker characteristics—for example, how you work with information, computers, and other people.

4. Discuss the effects of computers on our daily lives. Use specific examples.

INTERNET DISCOVERY

To meet some knowledge workers, log on to Netizens, a group of "net citizens" at the following address:

http://www.gnn.netizens/index.html

To learn more about collaboration and workgroups, use this site:

http://www.collaborate.com

To research business subjects, use the following address:

http://www-elc.gnn.com/gnn/bus/index.html

WHAT IS INFORMATION?

*Raw data can be, but isn't necessarily, information, and,
unless it can be made to inform, it has no inherent value. . . .
Information anxiety . . . is the black hole between data and
knowledge, and it happens when information doesn't tell us
what we want or need to know.*

Richard Saul Wurman, *Information Anxiety*[1]

Data in its raw form is what the computer works with.
Information is what people want as a result of data processing. Information is an organized collection of facts or data.
Studying a significant accumulation of high-quality information can lead to knowledge. Knowledgeable people are called
knowledge workers.

Finding reliable information can be a problem. How can you
tell when you're getting accurate, up-to-date, high-quality
information? How can you tell when it's biased? How about
plain old wrong?

Another problem is that people continue to find new ways to
package and deliver information. Remember when we thought
there were too many magazines? Forget that. Who has the
time or energy to get through the few we subscribe to, much
less browse at the newsstand?

But forget newspapers, magazines, books. Do you get too
many phone calls? What do you do when your answering
machine or voice mail box is full? And by the way, did you
read all your electronic mail today?

And do you know what? Right now, somebody is probably trying to figure out yet another way to deliver information.

Data. That's what we have. Information. That's what we want.
We use the computer to help us organize the data and present
it in a form we can use. That form is information.

---

1. (New York: Doubleday, 1989), 34, 38.

CHAPTER 2

Module A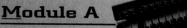

Working with Information

Why It's Important to Know

> **Information is the result of data processing operations. It is what knowledge workers work with on computers. Information models show us how the way we use information can help us perform more valuable work.**

In 1956, Harvard sociologist Daniel Bell identified most of Western civilization as entering the "post-industrial society," or what we now call the Information Age. Simply put, the **Information Age** describes a society in which information takes on the following three characteristics:

- It is a *commodity*, just as steel, plastic, cars, stereos, and other manufactured products are commodities.

- It has *value*; companies carefully guard the formulas for their products and all kinds of market data.

- It is *bought and sold*, whether in the form of a magazine, an on-line data file, or a computerized list of customer names.

Figure 2.1

Characteristics of information in the Information Age.

Although information has not replaced manufacturing, nor is it yet considered part of the Gross National Product, information is an essential aspect of many human activities. Hardly a week goes by without our hearing a news story that contains useful information. It is not uncommon to see machinists working on the factory floor with a computer monitor close by, referring to it for specifications and part numbers as they work (see figure 2.2). In fact, it's nearly impossible to imagine any human undertaking where retrieving, evaluating, or disseminating information isn't integral.

Courtesy of International Business Machines Corporation

Figure 2.2
This PC on a manufacturing shop floor is connected to a powerful mainframe.

Data to Information: An Example

Understanding the purpose and value of information is essential for anyone entering the business world of the 1990s. Many experts believe that the term *information* has become ambiguous and that much of what we assume to be information is simply data. To become information, data must have form and must be applied to a specific situation. Information then leads to knowledge, which enhances understanding.

Information is intangible. In fact, what one person thinks of as information may be data to another. For example, say that Ted, director of product marketing, writes a report for Louisa, his manager. Figure 2.3 shows that report.

Figure 2.3
Ted's memo is light on data and even lighter on information.

July 12, 1996

TO: Louisa

FR: Ted

RE: Fall Marketing Campaign

We've got all four product launches together now. We'll roll out new marketing for each one about every six weeks.

    Cindy: sweaters

    Tina: backpacks

    Otto: boots and socks

    Dave: jackets and anoraks

Thanks, Ted

Louisa hands the memo back to him and says, "Ted, you told me who is assigned to what, but you haven't given me the status of these projects. I need to know when you plan to begin each of these marketing campaigns. I need launch dates, a description of the brochures and TV ads, freebies, and expected market response." Ted gave Louisa some data, but he didn't transform it into real information.

The computer is capable of processing data and organizing it. Sometimes we expect the computer to provide information. Even when it does, a human is needed for understanding and interpretation. That's why the people aspect of the computer system is the most important.

Two Information Models

Two information models can help you learn how to think about information: a model for how people work with information and a model for how computers work with information.

The Human Model

The human model has nothing to do with using computers. Here is how Richard Saul Wurman describes this visual model for understanding the various types of information that people deal with in daily life. The model is comprised of concentric rings (see figure 2.4).

Figure 2.4

The information rings widen and expand from the individual to society.

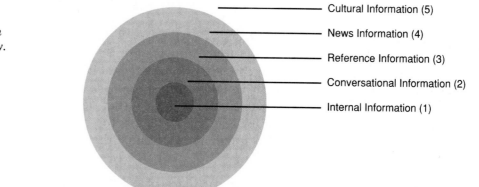

Cultural Information (5)

News Information (4)

Reference Information (3)

Conversational Information (2)

Internal Information (1)

1. Internal information about our physical and mental selves
2. Conversational information about informal and interpersonal interactions
3. Reference information, such as a telephone directory or dictionary
4. News information, such as current industry or world events
5. Cultural information, including history, philosophy, the arts, and so on

One of the primary skills in working with information is recognizing what kind of information you're using and knowing how to put it into proper context. For example, if you have a headache (circle 1 in figure 2.4), you don't want to assume that there is a mass outbreak of headaches in North America (circle 4). But if your hands or rear gets numb while riding your bike (circle 1), you could turn to another source of information to see whether anyone else has the problem (level 3). So you see, once understood in context, information becomes far more valuable.

HOME PAGE

WHAT IS A FINDOLOGIST?

Since the advent of the personal computer, a number of new careers have emerged. One is information broker, a person who works at home (or in an office) with a PC, telephone line, and databases to obtain computer-based information for clients. Ellen Lizer, an information broker in Beverly Hills, California, calls herself a findologist.

Many people who have turned to information brokering as a career were laid off during the corporate downsizings of the late 1980s and early 1990s. They are computer-literate people (many of whom work at home) who understand the value of information to professional people and companies. Derek Pugsley is a findologist in Toronto, Ontario, Canada. He created a thriving one-person business within a year; he now has between 40 and 50 clients for whom he regularly obtains information.

Courtesy of International Business Machines Corporation

Findologists need several essential skills. They must have computer abilities—know the hardware and software. They must have researching skills—especially the ability to find data in large computer databases quickly and efficiently. Then the findologist must organize the data into useful information and present it clearly and concisely in a written (word processing) and a data-oriented (database management system) report. Finally, the findologist needs good business skills in order to work with people, to manage projects successfully, and to operate the business so that it is successful and profitable.

Findologists are often retained by a company so that they're available to do custom research whenever needed. A marketing manager may require a competitive market analysis, or company managers may want an up-to-date profit and loss analysis of competitors. Knowledge of where to find the information quickly and the ability to organize and present it in a useful way make findologists valuable. Findologists work with information, as do all people using computers. What's different is that findologists are actively engaged in buying and selling information.

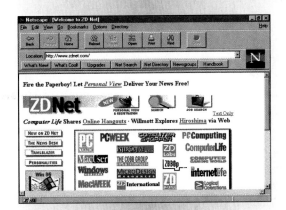

HOME PAGE REVIEW QUESTIONS

1. Where does an information broker, or findologist, obtain information?

2. What skills does a findologist need to be successful?

3. What kinds of diverse purposes might a findologist collect information for?

The Information Tree

The second information model, the information tree, demonstrates information within a computer context. Dr. Robert Lucky, executive director of research at Bell Labs, a respected technology think tank, wrote an interesting book entitled *Silicon Dreams*. He writes:

> Perhaps information itself is best described in terms of organization, implying that organization per se is the intellectual effort that manufactures information out of such raw material as observation. The more the organization, the higher the level of information. In contrast, where there is total disorder there is no information. The level of organization can be described in terms of a hierarchy, where we have borrowed the words sometimes used as synonymous with information to indicate the levels of organization—data, information, knowledge, and wisdom.[2]

Lucky goes on to say that data is the raw material from which information is extracted. Information is the data after it has been organized, as in a newspaper. "When we take in information ourselves, for example by reading, and consciously or not store it in our minds with the rest of our remembered information, we create something personal, and at a higher level of organization. Now we call it knowledge." Lucky concludes by saying that **wisdom** is organized, distilled, and integrated **knowledge**. An integrated base of knowledge makes it possible to create new knowledge. You can visualize this concept by referring to the information tree in figure 2.5.

Figure 2.5

A tree receives food from the ground; the computer accepts data as input. The tree trunk represents the processing; the branches and leaves represent the output. As the leaves store the food, the computer stores data, which becomes information.

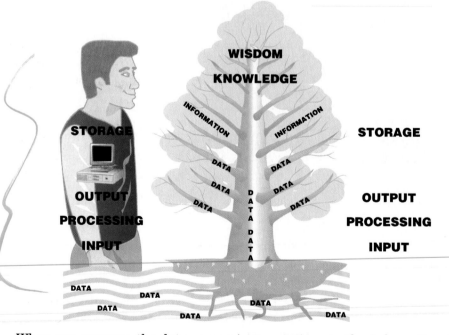

When you compare the data processing operations to the information tree, remember that you're comparing the computing machine to the human mind. We do not have computers that are capable of producing knowledge or wisdom (even though we may in the future). For now, producing knowledge and wisdom is left to humans. However, it's nice to know that computers can be a big help with the first three levels.

---

2. Robert W. Lucky. *Silicon Dreams* (New York: St. Martin's Press, 1989), 20.

Knowledge Check

1. What are the three characteristics of information in the Information Age?
2. List some business and personal activities in which you are regularly involved, and write down the type of information you use in each.
3. What are the five aspects of the information tree?
4. How does the information tree compare to the steps in data processing?
5. Where does the human mind take over on the information tree?

Key Terms

information   Information Age   knowledge   wisdom

ISSUES AND IDEAS

Does Knowledge Confer Power?

It has been said that control of information is an important aspect of power, and that true power comes from knowledge. Here are some quotations that refer to power. Comment on each individually; the four "Critical Thinking" questions correspond to the four quotations.[3]

1. "Knowledge is the most democratic source of power."

> **Alvin Toffler (b. 1928), U.S. author.** *Powershift: Knowledge, Wealth, and Violence at the Edge of the 21st Century*, Part 1, Chapter 2, "The Democratic Difference" (1990).

2. "Can the knowledge deriving from reason even begin to compare with knowledge perceptible by sense? No doubt the number of people crass enough to rely exclusively on the former and scorn the latter are sufficient in themselves to explain the disfavor into which everything deriving from the senses has gradually fallen. But when the most scholarly of men have taught me that light is a vibration, or offered me any other fruits of their labors of reasoning, they will not have rendered me an account of what is important to me about light, of what my eyes have begun to teach me about it, of what makes me different from a blind man—things which are the stuff of miracles, not subject matter for reasoning."

> **Louis Aragon (1897–1982), French poet.** *Paris Peasant*, "Preface to a Modern Mythology" (first published 1926; repr. 1971).

---

3. Quotations in this "Issues and Ideas" were taken from the CD-ROM, Microsoft Bookshelf, available from Microsoft Press.

3. "There are three principal means of acquiring knowledge available to us: observation of nature, reflection, and experimentation. Observation collects facts; reflection combines them; experimentation verifies the result of that combination. Our observation of nature must be diligent, our reflection profound, and our experiments exact. We rarely see these three means combined; and for this reason, creative geniuses are not common."

Denis Diderot (1713–84), French philosopher. "On the Interpretation of Nature,"
no. 15 (1753; repr. in *Selected Writings*, ed. by Lester G. Crocker, 1966).

4. "Knowledge is and will be produced in order to be sold, it is and will be consumed in order to be valorized in a new production: in both cases, the goal is exchange. Knowledge ceases to be an end in itself, it loses its use-value."

Jean François Lyotard (b. 1924), French philosopher. *The Postmodern
Condition: A Report on Knowledge, Introduction* (1979).

CRITICAL THINKING

1. What are the democratic aspects of knowledge? How is knowledge regarded in totalitarian or communist societies?

2. Is it plausible to say that knowledge derived from reason *complements* knowledge derived from nature? Or are the two mutually exclusive?

3. How do observation of nature, reflection, and experimentation apply to acquiring knowledge with a computer system?

4. Information is a commodity. Is knowledge also a commodity? Where is it bought and sold? What kind of knowledge would you be willing to pay for or exchange something for? What does Lyotard mean by the last sentence?

Module B

The File

Why It's Important to Know

Understanding the file is a prerequisite to performing any work with the computer. Knowing how to recognize different kinds of files, how to create them, and how they are stored and organized is key to using software productively and managing data effectively.

One element all programs have in common is the file. You'll be working with files for a long time, so you need to know what they're all about.

The **file** is a group of related records, or a collection of related data, identified and stored with a unique name. The file is the primary unit of data storage in DOS-based computers (and most others). A file may contain program instructions; or it may contain data in the form of text, numbers, images, and so forth. There are several kinds of files:

- Files that are unique to the *operating system*, such as COMMAND.COM in DOS

- Files that both the operating system (and operating environment) and applications use, such as printer drivers, which print files

- Files with data only—not programs—created by people working with a program or application, such as a word processing document or database report

DOS File Names

Each file in DOS has a unique **file name**, which can be up to eight characters long. The file name may be followed by a period (often called a *dot*) and then an optional three-character **file name extension**. For example, figure 2.6 diagrams the file name PRINT.COM, a DOS file.

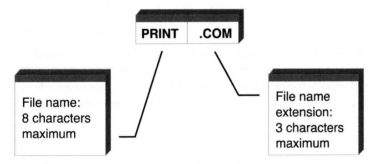

Figure 2.6
The elements of a DOS file name.

DOS requires special file name extensions for certain types of DOS and program files. The applications you use often insert their own file name extensions to make it easy to see what program created the files. But in most cases, you can give files you create any extension you want—or no extension.

If you're using a Macintosh or Windows 95, you won't need to be concerned about file name extensions or the limitations of an eight-character file name. Both programs allow you to create long, English-like file names. For example, the old DOS file name for this chapter was CH2INFO.DOC, but the new long name is Chapter 2, What Is Information.

Even so, knowing which files do what is helpful. To help you identify them, figure 2.7 shows examples of the different types of files and their file name extensions.

Figure 2.7
*Different kinds of files
have different file name
extensions.*

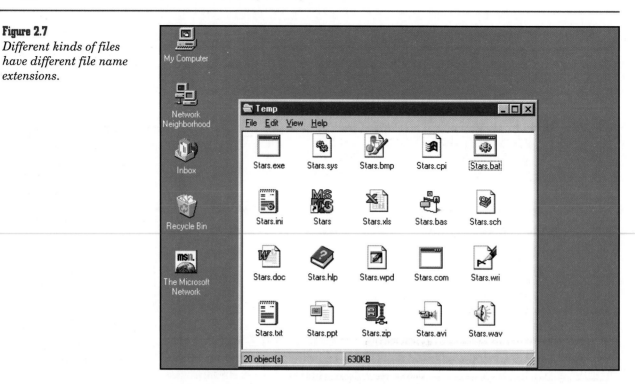

The Directory and the Folder

DOS stores files on a disk in directories. A **directory** is a list of the files stored on a disk or a portion of a disk. The primary directory is called the **root directory**, and every disk has one. DOS also allows you to create additional **subdirectories** under the root directory. Subdirectories help keep your programs and data well organized and easy to find.

Each application program is stored in its own subdirectory and can have a number of subdirectories of its own that store ancillary programs as well as your data files. Working with directories has become easier in Windows 95 because of the Macintosh-like folders. The folder takes the place of a directory, and folders are organized in the same way DOS organizes directories. Files, stored within folders, are called documents.

HOME PAGE

THE POST-INFORMATION AGE

"Computing is not about computers anymore. It is about living," says Nicholas Negroponte, professor of Media Technology and the founding director of the Media Lab, a high-tech think tank on the MIT campus in Cambridge, Massachusetts. In his book *Being Digital*, a collection of essays that were first published in *Wired* magazine, Negroponte writes about what he calls the post-information age:

> The transition from an industrial age to a post-industrial or information age has been discussed so much and for so long that we may not have noticed that we are passing into a post-information age. The industrial age, very much an age of atoms, gave us the concept of mass production, with the economics that come from manufacturing with uniform and repetitious methods in any one given space and time. The information age, the age of computers, showed us the same economies of scale, but with less regard for space and time. The manufacturing of bits could happen anywhere, at any time, and, for example, move among the stock markets of new York, London, and Tokyo as if they were three adjacent machine tools.

In the post-information age, we often have an audience the size of one. Everything is made to order, and information is extremely personalized. A widely held assumption is that individualization is the extrapolation of narrowcasting—you go from a large to a small to a smaller group, ultimately to the individual. By the time you have my address, my marital status, my age, my income, my car brand, my purchases, my drinking habits, and my taxes, you have me—a demographic unit of one. . . .

True personalization is now upon us. It's not just a matter of selecting relish over mustard once. The post-information age is about acquaintance over time: machines understanding individuals with the same degree of subtlety (or more than) we can expect from other human beings, including idiosyncrasies (like always wearing a blue-striped shirt) and totally random events, good and bad, in the unfolding narrative of our lives.[4]

HOME PAGE REVIEW QUESTIONS

1. What exactly is the Information Age? Do some library research, and find some articles that explain it.

2. How does Negroponte compare the Information Age to the Post-Information Age?

3. Is the Information Age, as Negroponte characterizes it, more concerned with data or with information?

Nicholas Negroponte, Director of the MIT Media Laboratory

Courtesy of MIT Media Lab

4. Nicholas Negroponte. *Being Digital* (New York: Alfred A. Knopf, 1995), 163–65.

Figure 2.8 shows a simplified root directory and subdirectory structure beside a folder structure from the Explorer program in Windows 95. As with DOS files, directory names are eight characters in length, but both directory names and file names can be 256 characters long in Windows 95. However, an eight-character file name and a file name extension are assigned, just in case the file is used by an older system.

A DOS directory   An Explorer directory

Figure 2.8

A file manager like the Explorer in Windows 95 makes working with files and directories much easier.

File Formats

Every application creates files in a unique format. A **file format** is a series of patterns, standards, and codes that identify the unique data stored in the file by the application that created it. The format of a spreadsheet file is very different from that of a database file; even two different word processing programs format files differently. More advanced applications have a **file conversion utility** that translates files from other formats—for example, Microsoft Word for Windows can convert files created in WordPerfect—so that the program you're using can read and edit the files. Most applications offer several options for opening and saving files, as figure 2.9 shows.

Figure 2.9

Always pay close attention to the Save as type box in the Save As or Open dialog box.

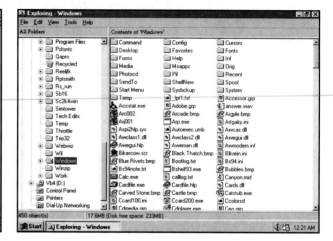

The one universal file format is **ASCII**, an acronym for the American Standard Code for Information Interchange. The ASCII character set is basically what you see on your keyboard, plus a few additional characters. This character set consists of 96 upper- and lowercase letters and 32 non-printing control characters. Almost all computers can understand ASCII characters, so it is commonly used in communications. Word processing programs can save files in ASCII format (also called text format) so that they can be transmitted to another computer and then easily read by word processing programs.

Knowledge Check

1. What is the computer's primary unit of storage?
2. For what are file name extensions useful?
3. What type of directory must every disk have?
4. What is the other type of directory called?
5. The distinctive way an application prepares its files is called what?
6. What is the universal file format?

Key Terms

ASCII	directory	file	file conversion utility
file format	file name	file name extension	root directory
subdirectory			

ISSUES AND IDEAS

A Human Approach to Files

Alan Cooper, author of the book *About Face*, writes: "The term 'computer literate' is really a euphemism. It means that the person so labeled has been trained in the irrational and counterintuitive way that file systems work. And once you have been properly subverted into thinking like a computer nerd, the ridiculousness of the file system no longer seems so obvious."[5]

The way files are created, named, stored, and retrieved was set up long ago to make it easy for the computer to do its work. That was back in the days when there were many limitations and restrictions in the hardware and software. For example, the hardware was slow, and the storage space was limited, so economy was needed in all things.

Today we don't really have these problems. We have fast computers and lots of space, so storing long file names isn't a problem. But in many respects, we still work with files in the same way we did ten, even twenty, years ago.

---

5. Alan Cooper. "Fighting Files with Files," *InfoWorld*, Sept. 4, 1995, 53-56. Excerpt from *About Face* (Indianapolis: IDG Books).

Why? Primarily it's one of those "if it isn't broke, don't fix it" issues. Equally, everybody knows pretty much how to do things the way they are designed now. Unfortunately, such a viewpoint doesn't take into consideration that there are many thousands, even millions, of new knowledge workers every year.

Cooper believes that names should have an easily identifiable relationship with the applications used to create them. He says an invoicing program should call its files "Invoice," instead of "File" as it appears in the File menu. Some Microsoft applications have partially implemented this approach: Word calls its files "documents," and Excel calls its files "sheets," but not, however, in the File menu.

"Changing the name and contents of the File menu violates an established, though unofficial, standard," Cooper writes. "I have tremendous respect for standards, unless they are wrong. This one is wrong, and its existence makes computing difficult for every user—particularly newcomers."[6]

CRITICAL THINKING

1. Do you think that the current file methodology for Windows is, as Cooper suggests, "irrational and counterintuitive"?

2. Describe your "mental model" for how files should be organized on the computer.

3. Have you found it difficult to learn the way files are named and organized on the PC compatible? How about the Macintosh? Is there any significant difference between the two?

4. Find Cooper's article or book and read further. What do you think of his new method?

Module C

The Document

Why It's Important to Know

> **The computer works with files. Knowledge workers create documents. Creating a document is more interesting and requires different skills than simply working with a file. Knowing how to work with documents helps make you more productive and the knowledge work you perform more valuable.**

At this point, it's fair to say that the modern computer can actually produce a rudimentary type of information. Once output has been generated—even if it's simply on the monitor screen—if the output is in an understandable form, it could be considered information. But how do we use that information, and how do we share it with others? Increasingly sophisticated application software has given us tools that enable us to add value to information by creating something known as the *document*.

---

6. Ibid.

A **document** is a self-contained work, created by a knowledge worker using a computer and an application; this document can be saved as and later retrieved as a file. Another way of stating this distinction is that a file contains data, but a document is a file in which the data has had *value added*. In other words, the raw data in the file is transformed into information that a person can understand and use. *Value-added* is a business term meaning that something with its own intrinsic value has been made even more useful or meaningful through specific enhancements. In the case of creating a value-added document from a file, consider this example:

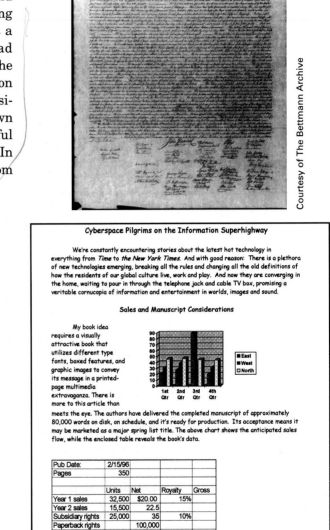

Courtesy of The Bettmann Archive

Cyberspace Pilgrims on the Information Superhighway

We're constantly encountering stories about the latest hot technology in everything from *Time* to *the New York Times*. And with good reason: There is a plethora of new technologies emerging, breaking all the rules and changing all the old definitions of how the residents of our global culture live, work and play. And now they are converging in the home, waiting to pour in through the telephone jack and cable TV box, promising a veritable cornucopia of information and entertainment in worlds, images and sound.

Sales and Manuscript Considerations

The Wired World is a visually attractive book that utilizes different type fonts, boxed features, and graphic images to convey its message in a printed-page multimedia extravaganza. The authors have delivered the completed manuscript of approximately 80,000 words on disk, on schedule, and it's ready for production. Its acceptance means it may be marketed as a major spring list title.

Pub Date:	2/15/96			
Pages	350			
	Units	Net	Royalty	Gross
Year 1 sales	32,500	$20.00	15%	
Year 2 sales	15,500	22.5		
Subsidiary rights	25,000	35	10%	
Paperback rights		100,000		
Plant costs, per u	$3.77			

Figure 2.10

There's a good reason the Founding Fathers referred to the Declaration of Independence as a document. Like the document on the right, it has far more value than the piece of paper with words written on it on the left.

Cyberspace Pilgrims on the Information Superhighway

We're constantly encountering stories about the latest hot technology in everything from *Time* to *the New York Times*. And with good reason: There is a plethora of new technologies emerging, breaking all the rules and changing all the old definitions of how the residents of our global culture live, work and play. And now they are converging in the home, waiting to pour in through the telephone jack and cable TV box, promising a veritable cornucopia of information and entertainment in worlds, images and sound.

Sales and Manuscript Considerations

My book idea requires a visually attractive book that utilizes different type fonts, boxed features, and graphic images to convey its message in a printed-page multimedia extravaganza. There is more to this article than

meets the eye. The authors have delivered the completed manuscript of approximately 80,000 words on disk, on schedule, and it's ready for production. Its acceptance means it may be marketed as a major spring list title. The above chart shows the anticipated sales flow, while the enclosed table reveals the book's data.

Pub Date:	2/15/96			
Pages	350			
	Units	Net	Royalty	Gross
Year 1 sales	32,500	$20.00	15%	
Year 2 sales	15,500	22.5		
Subsidiary rights	25,000	35	10%	
Paperback rights		100,000		
Plant costs, per u	$3.77			

A document usually contains data in the form of text and graphic characters, but a document is also something more. It is the record of an exchange of information between two parties. The most common types of business documents are the following:

- Business letter (formatted text)
- Sales report (text and spreadsheet data)
- Sales territory (text and customer database)
- Management report (text and spreadsheet data)
- Product fact sheet (graphics with text)
- Product or service brochure with database of authorized sales and service locations

- Company or customer newsletter with graphics

- Consumer owner's manual (text and graphics)

- Technical product documentation (text and graphics)

Most of the work you'll be doing with the computer will involve creating documents. Refer to figure 2.11, which shows how a word processing program keeps track of your work with a document. The following paragraphs summarize some of the most important characteristics of a document.

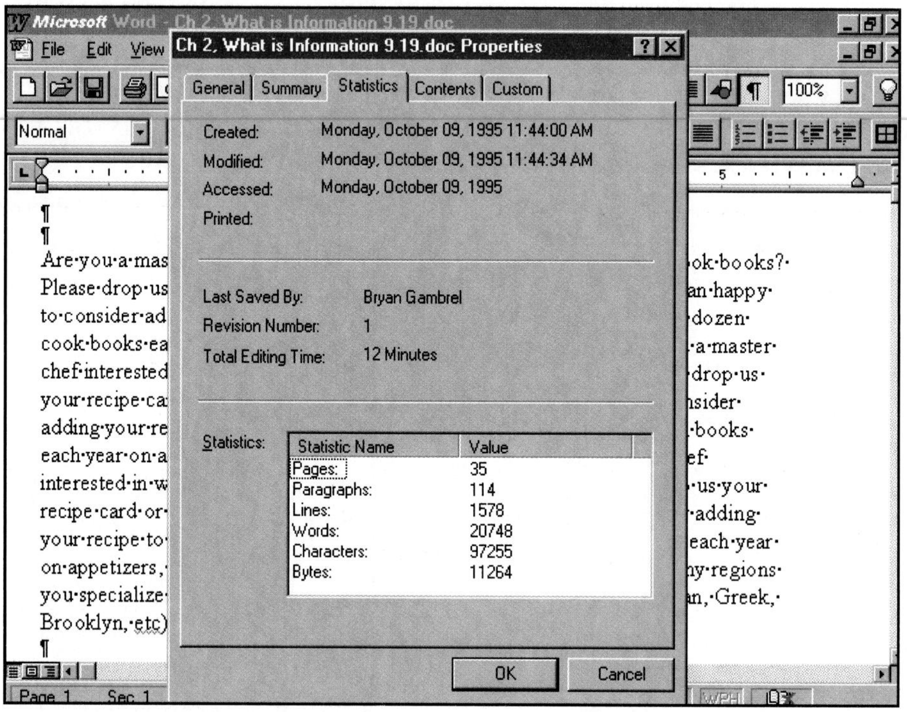

Figure 2.11
In Microsoft Word for Windows 95, you can click Properties in the File menu and get a quick update of your document work.

A document has an author. Clearly, a human being has created the document and added value to the data. In some businesses, more than one author may have worked on a document. For example, the news story in a newspaper is a document used by many people, many times a day. The reporter writes the story, the story editor edits it, the news editor gives it a title, an artist prepares a graphic or photo to accompany it, and the production editor lays it out. Authorship gives a document unique qualities; in a sense, the difference between a file and a document is like the difference between data and information.

A document has a life cycle that extends over time and in space. Over *time* the document's content has immediate and possibly long-range value. In *space*, the document has a distinct style. If on paper, the document must conform to business or company requirements for quality and presentation—for example, as a management report or an advertising brochure. A poorly written or carelessly prepared document is perceived as having low value and thus usually has a shorter life cycle.

A document can take many forms. The most common form is paper, but a document can remain a file on a disk, used solely on computers. An example is the Help feature built into most applications. Help is a document in electronic form that is primarily used on the screen, although it can be printed.

A document can also be electronically transmitted from computer to computer using various communications programs. For example, an Internet home page is a sophisticated electronic document.

A document contains information. Data is static. Information in a document is dynamic. Data is a spreadsheet worksheet without any explanation. Information is a spreadsheet worksheet that shows how changing figures represent a trend or predicts the possibility of some future event.

A document is dynamic. Data, such as manufacturing production schedules, becomes information when it includes equipment status, vacation schedules, adjustments of production runs to advance sales orders, and so on. This type of document could have a never-ending life span as it constantly circulates between managers and departments, as it is constantly revised and updated, and as people continue to derive useful information from it.

A document is more than just text and graphics. A picture or graphic image conveys information and adds value to text, but it is not the only way to create a document. Today's complex electronic documents often use presentation graphics or photos, but they can also contain

- Moving video, such as a clip from a videotape or television program

- Editing comments, either as text or recorded audio messages

- Alarms that signal deadlines or due dates

- Key words, special symbols, or other indicators that perform other tasks or provide links to other documents and information

These complex documents rival the printed magazine page with its text and graphics complexity (see figure 2.12).

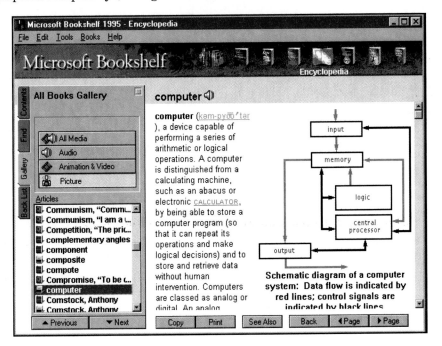

Figure 2.12
A document containing text and complex graphics.

HOME PAGE

THE DIGITAL LIBRARY

Access to documents in libraries can become a real time and space problem: you must have the time to go to the space where they're stored. But many libraries are going digital, which means that we will be able to use their resources at our home computers. This change solves the time and space problem: using a computer, we can quickly travel through electronic space to the library!

One of the first digital libraries was at Cornell University. Over one-third of the books in the world's libraries are deteriorating, due to the "brittle book" problem. As a result of manufacturing process changes made about 1850, book life is no longer measured in centuries but in decades.

Cornell University has two libraries that contain more than 5 million books, including world-renowned collections of the poets William Wordsworth and Petrarch. Xerox is working with Cornell, supplying technology and expertise for its Commission on Preservation and Access project development team. Over the project's life span, about a thousand books will be scanned into a digital format.

Cornell has a large collection of valuable older books on mathematics that are turning brittle. One such volume is the *Traite D'Analyse* by H. Laurent, a French work on calculus published in 1885. It was preserved in digital form using the Xerox DocuTech Production Publisher.

The DocuTech machine is designed to accept both text and images from either paper or electronic sources; to digitize them; and then organize, design, format, and print them in another new form. Large pages can be reduced, and small pages enlarged. Photographs can be scanned and then prepared for printing. Text and images can be moved, resized, or reformatted in a variety of ways.

Cornell has identified a number of benefits to digital preservation. There is no loss of information; the book appears in its original format. For example, the *Traite D'Analyse* is reproduced with its complex and varied mathematical symbols, its boldfaced and italicized type, and even a blob of printing ink that stuck to the type.

More recently, the Library 2000 group at the MIT Lab for Computer Science was formed as part of a five-university project working on digital libraries. One of the group's highest priorities is replication, which will make the contents of library after library available to just about anyone with access to a computer and the electronic networks.

Courtesy of Xerox Corporation

The DocuTech machine: a high-tech cross between a copier and a printing press.

HOME PAGE REVIEW QUESTIONS

1. What advantages do digital libraries offer?

2. How do digital libraries disseminate information?

3. Does your college library or one near you offer digital information? What form does it take? Find out how you can gain access to it.

Working with Documents

Figure 2.13 shows a typical document *life cycle,* a business term used to refer to the stages in a document's creation and use. The document is the company's manufacturing process manual. A manager has read and reviewed it and determined that it is out of date. The manager has written an accompanying document—a memo—to all the key managers and initiated a review for revising and updating the manual. Follow through the document processing life cycle in figure 2.13.

1. *Input.* The manager asks the managers for their ideas, suggestions for revision, and other thoughts regarding document content.

2. *Processing.* The other managers have *appended* the memo with typed comments, voice-recorded comments, and annotated graphics.

3. A new memo document is created.

4. *Output.* The manager has coordinated all the editing and revision suggestions into a new memo document, and the printout is circulated for review and approval.

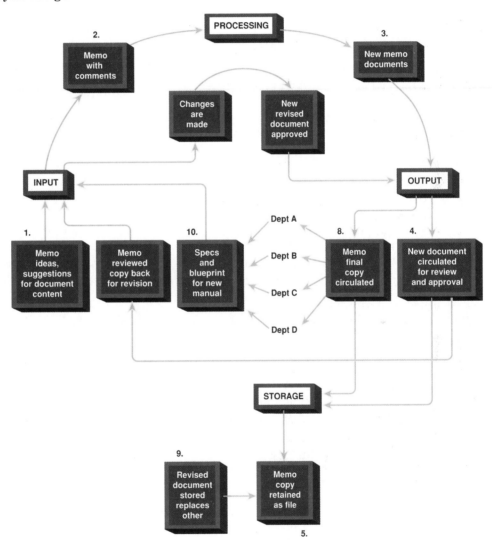

5. *Storage.* A copy of the memo document is retained in permanent storage.

6. *Input.* Managers' revisions are made.

7. *Processing.* The other managers review, revise, and approve the changes to the document.

8. *Output.* The manager prints and circulates the final document.

9. *Storage.* The revised document is stored and re-used as the guidelines and instructions for revising the manufacturing process manual document.

Figure 2.13
The document processing life cycle is like the computer system's data processing cycle. As the data is refined into information, certain steps are repeated.

10. *Information.* The memo becomes the specifications and blueprint for the new manufacturing process manual. It re-enters the document processing life cycle and eventually is printed and/or electronically distributed to the people who will do that work.

As you can see, the document life cycle is the same as the data processing process except that some of the steps are repeated. The document and the information it contains are refined and improved through continual or repeated processing. This refining process is one of the major advantages in using a computer: the computer encourages constant improvement because the processing step makes revising and refining work so easy.

Document-based information is the next great frontier for white-collar work. Data created by a number of applications—including word processing, spreadsheets, database management systems, drawing and drafting programs, and many others—most frequently appears in a document of some kind. New computer systems for working with and managing the document have emerged—and continue to emerge. These systems include desktop publishing, electronic publishing, multimedia systems, text retrieval systems, the Xerox DocuTech machine, and others.

Researchers at the Xerox Palo Alto Research Center, in Palo Alto, California, have been studying the document concept for a number of years. They are constantly trying to determine how knowledge workers can use the computer system most effectively to achieve high-productivity work. One thing they have learned is that what knowledge workers need "is not so much information retrieval itself" but better, more useful, and more powerful information-based work processes.

These researchers have also drawn the following conclusions:

> From a user's point of view, document retrieval and other forms of information retrieval are almost always part of some larger process of information use. Examples are *sensemaking* (building an interpretation of understanding of information, *design* (building an artifact), *decision making* (building a decision and its rationale), and *response tasks* (finding information to respond to a query).

> In each of these cases:

> • Information is used to produce information, or to act directly

> • The new information is usually at a higher level of organization relative to some purpose.[7]

Knowledge Check

1. In what ways does creating a document add value to data?
2. What is the significance of a document's having an identifiable author?
3. What different elements, besides text and presentation graphics, might you expect to see in a document?

---

7. George G. Robertson, Stuart K. Card, and Jock D. Mackinlay. "Information Visualization Using 3D Interactive Animation," *Communications of the ACM* (April 1993), 58–59.

4. Name some of the more common business documents.

5. What steps in the document process are often repeated?

6. Explain how repeated processing produces superior information.

Key Terms

copyright   document

ISSUES AND IDEAS

Who Owns Information?

When information is authored or digitally stored, we often encounter the **copyright** problem. Who owns information? This question becomes pervasive as we enter the full-blown Information Age. Indeed, one of the responsibilities we have as computer-literate people is to recognize information ownership and areas involving copyright.

There are three primary areas of information ownership and copyright: personal, business, and external sources.

- *Personal.* You have the copyright and intellectual ownership to any thing you write or create, without having to register such ownership legally or formally.

- *Business.* Generally, your employer owns any forms of information you create while on the job.

- *External.* You are responsible for acknowledging and obtaining permission to use any information you obtain that was created and/or published by others, whether printed, copied, or stored in any information retrieval system (such as a computer).

Violation of someone else's copyright can be a serious matter. The U.S. Copyright Law of 1978 protects your original work for your lifetime plus 50 years when you put *Copyright* © followed by your name. (It is recommended, however, that you register your work with the U.S. Copyright Office for protection in case of a lawsuit.) The Copyright Law also provides for stiff penalties for copyright violation and plagiarism. But above all, remember that copyright applies to your unique and individual expression in writing. Neither facts nor ideas can be copyrighted. Put another way, data cannot be copyrighted, but information, which is the product of the human mind can be copyrighted.

CRITICAL THINKING

1. Can information be copyrighted?

2. What are some of the new developments that make access to copyrighted information easier and thus more vulnerable?

3. What is required for you to have copyright to information you have created?

ETHICS

Respecting Information Ownership

Working with information that belongs to others requires a moral and ethical commitment on your part to maintain confidentiality when asked to do so. During the world wars, to ensure that confidences and secrets were kept, people used the phrase, "Loose lips sink ships." The same statement is true in business today; company secrets that leak out could cost millions. Employees are often asked to sign a confidentiality agreement when they begin work with a new employer; these agreements often specify that no company secrets be divulged for a period of time after the person has left the company as well.

In a number of industries, including the software industry, outsiders often must be included on projects the company is developing. In this case, the company asks the consultant, journalist, or other nonemployee to sign a *nondisclosure agreement* that legally ensures the person's silence. One software company sent to people testing a prerelease version of the program a memo that read in part:

> Please remember that use of ___ and the Beta (software) is governed by the terms of the Non-Disclosure or Beta Agreement that you have signed. The ___ Program and Documentation constitute protected intellectual property of XYZ and its suppliers. You have agreed not to distribute or copy the (software) for any other party without XYZ's written permission.

Sometimes people abuse this trust. A consultant gives a tip to a friend at lunch, who buys the company stock. This, essentially, is insider trading. A journalist, preening his or her ego, decides to break the story a week before the official announcement. What is gained in the short term is lost in the long term. If we have loose lips, or if we have been careless with the confidences entrusted to us, this reputation precedes us. Trust, once it is broken, is difficult to reestablish.

Critical Thinking

1. What does it mean to give your word that you'll maintain a confidence?

2. Imagine a scenario in which you violate a confidence in your work or another relationship in your life. Now imagine the consequences. What ethical boundaries have you crossed? Would it be worth it?

3. Is it any more important to maintain high ethical standards in your work relationships than it is in your personal relationships?

THE LEARNING ENTERPRISE

The Learning Enterprise

At this point, your class has determined the type of enterprise and its mission. You've also established a set of guidelines for the knowledge workers' environment. Now it's time to create the departments and functions in which the knowledge workers will work. Make your selections from the following list, depending on the type of enterprise you've created. The letters in parentheses indicate which are most appropriate for what: B stands for business, N for not-for-profit, and G for governmental agency. For example, a governmental agency won't need Sales and Marketing, and a business won't need Program Development. Add or modify any departments or functions you choose.

Accounting and Financial Management (B, N, G)

Community Relations (N, G)

Creative Resources (B, N, G)

Decision Support and Management (B, N, G)

Human Resources (B, N, G)

Insurance (B, N, G)

Legal (B, N, G)

Long-Range Planning (B, N, G)

Management Information Systems (B, N)

Manufacturing (B)

Program Development (N, G)

Research and Design (B)

Sales and Marketing (B)

When you have described your organization, determine how information will be used. Use the two information models to do so.

1. Create the circular human model, and show how the departments and functions interact and how information flows between them.

2. Create the information tree, and show how the information will be used to develop and improve your information flows.

Next, make a list of the types of documents each part of the organization will be creating and where the documents will flow: inside—between departments and functions—and outside—to customers or supporters, to the press, and so on.

Finally, write down possible ethical issues of information ownership that might arise in your new organization, and discuss how you can deal with them.

Chapter Review

Fill in the Blank

1. _____ is the end result of data processing operations.
2. A(n) _____ translates a file created in another application so that the application you are using can read and edit it.
3. The universal file format, _____, stands for _____.
4. An organized collection of facts is called _____.
5. Two useful information models are (a) _____ and (b) _____.
6. A group of related records is called a(n) _____.
7. A list of the files stored on a disk is called a(n) _____.
8. The primary directory that is always present is called the _____.
9. A DOS file name can be up to _____ characters long and is followed by a(n) _____ and a three-character _____.
10. A self-contained work created by a knowledge worker using a computer is called a(n) _____.

Circle the Correct Answer

1. The computer's primary unit of storage is a (document, file).
2. Computers work with (files, documents) and people work with (files, documents).
3. (Data, Information) is an organized collection of facts.
4. Computers help us organize (data, information) and present it in an organized form called (data, information).
5. (Wisdom, Knowledge) is organized, distilled, and integrated (wisdom, knowledge).

Review Questions

1. Define file, and describe three kinds of files.
2. Explain the difference between root directory and subdirectory.
3. Define document, and list some common types of business documents.
4. Describe at least three characteristics of documents.
5. Describe the document life cycle, and compare it to the data processing cycle.
6. How does the human model of information apply to the way you work with information?
7. Give an example of the information tree in your work with information.
8. What materials can be copyrighted and what cannot?

Discussion Questions

1. What are the democratic aspects of knowledge? How is knowledge regarded in totalitarian or communistic societies?
2. What does Negroponte mean by "being digital"?
3. How do you feel about computers storing personal information about yourself?
4. How do information models help us deal with all the various types of information that surround us?
5. What would be the most valuable use for digital libraries for you?

INTERNET DISCOVERY

Here are some Web site examples of the three kinds of enterprises mentioned.

Business (specialized bicycles):

http://www.specialized.com

Not-for-profit (The Rand Organization):

http://www.rand.org

Government (The Small Business Administration):

http://www/sbaonline.sba.gov/

You can search for other not-for-profits using the keyword **nonprofit** in Yahoo.

WHAT IS SOFTWARE?

Another way to think of software is this: It's the thoughts computers have.

John Gantz, veteran computer industry analyst, International Data Corporation

Software. The word is so new that it didn't appear in the 1971 edition of the *Oxford English Dictionary*. Yet software has created an entirely new industry and is changing the way we think. For example, did you know that compact discs and tapes for stereos are now referred to as software? And a recent *New Yorker* cartoon shows two adults saying to their child, "We're neither hardware nor software. We're your parents."

Software. It's that seemingly intangible component that makes computers so versatile. Without software, computers would be of little value, like an auto engine without a transmission and drive train. Software helps us perform the tasks that control the machine. More importantly, software performs many tasks that people used only to *think* about.

Software. In a way, it's like magnetic magic.

Computer software, quite simply, is defined as the programs and instructions that tell the computer what to do. This chapter covers the three basic types of software:

- *System software*, which controls the computer's primary operations

- *Operating environment software*, which is used with both system software and application software

- *Application software*, which knowledge workers use for specific tasks

CHAPTER 3

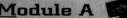

Module A

System Software

Why It's Important to Know

> **System software manages the entire computer system. You can't use the computer or your application software properly unless the system software is running properly. All programs require system software in order to operate. Understanding system software makes knowledge workers more skillful.**

Just flipping on the personal computer's power switch is not enough for you to begin using it. The computer must have instructions for the tasks it is to perform. These instructions come in the form of software.

Every computer must perform primary tasks, functions, and self-checks on itself each time the power is switched on in order to ensure that all the hardware is in proper working order. These tasks and checks come from the instructions in the system software. **System software** consists of all the programs used to operate and maintain a computer system. You won't be able to use your computer and the application software properly unless everything checks out at the system level.

Figure 3.1
System software is an intermediary between the hardware and the application program.

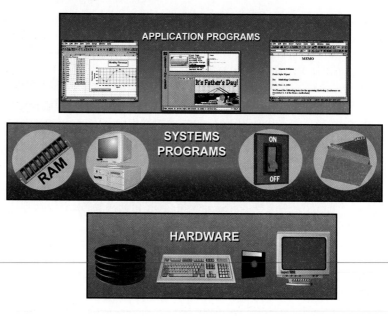

The following list describes the three types of DOS system software:

1. **BIOS**, the **basic input/output system**, is made up of programs permanently stored in the computer. The BIOS programs load the operating system and also check and coordinate the peripherals, such as the keyboard, monitor, and disk drives. BIOS is often casually referred to as system software.

2. **DOS**, the **disk operating system**, is the collection of programs that *manage* the computer's internal functions and *control* the computer's operations.

3. System-level **utility programs** provide additional capabilities and sometimes ease of use. Some are included with the operating system and others (often called *add-ons*) are purchased separately.

Now you are ready to take a closer look at each of these types of system software.

BIOS: Basic Input/Output Software

The basic input/output software is comprised of specific system software instructions, embedded in the computer's memory chips, called **read-only memory,** or **ROM**, so named because the instructions it holds cannot be changed. BIOS instructions form a *permanent* part of the computer's circuitry.

When you turn on the computer, an automatic software routine begins in BIOS to load the operating system software from a computer disk and prepare the computer system for use. This process, called a **boot**, or *booting the system*, loads the initial software instructions from ROM into the other type of computer memory called **random-access memory,** or **RAM**, a form of temporary storage where instructions and data are kept while being used. The system loads these instructions without assistance. The term *boot* comes from the old saying, "pulling oneself up by one's own bootstraps," referring to someone who is able to achieve a goal without assistance. Starting a program in the early days of computers was called *bootstrapping*, later shortened to just boot.

The computer also runs initial routine BIOS checks to make sure, for example, that the keyboard is connected and the disk drives are working. Most of the BIOS instructions occur without your being aware of them. However, one you can often watch on the monitor when you first turn on the power is the computer checking its RAM. You'll see the words "RAM Test" or "Memory Test," and you may even see numbers, similar to a digital watch display, spinning away. Once booting is complete, you can begin issuing commands to the computer system.

Programs and instructions you're currently using, as well as the data you're working with, are *temporarily* stored in RAM.

DOS: Disk Operating System

System software also includes the operating system software, called DOS on PC compatibles, which controls the execution of computer programs. DOS is a set of programs and instructions that are *temporarily* loaded into the computer's random-access memory (RAM) from a computer disk—hence the term *disk* operating system. DOS is stored temporarily in two senses of the word. One, DOS must be loaded from the disk into random-access memory each time the PC is booted. Two, DOS is a program that has been changed and improved many times over the years, which means that a newer version can be loaded and run in place of an older one.

Together, the BIOS and DOS awaken your PC hardware and enable you to control your personal computer (see figure 3.2). DOS is responsible for managing all the input and output tasks, such as ensuring that when you type a character on the keyboard, that exact character appears on the screen and is stored in memory.

How the BIOS Works with Software

Figure 3.2
How the BIOS works with DOS.

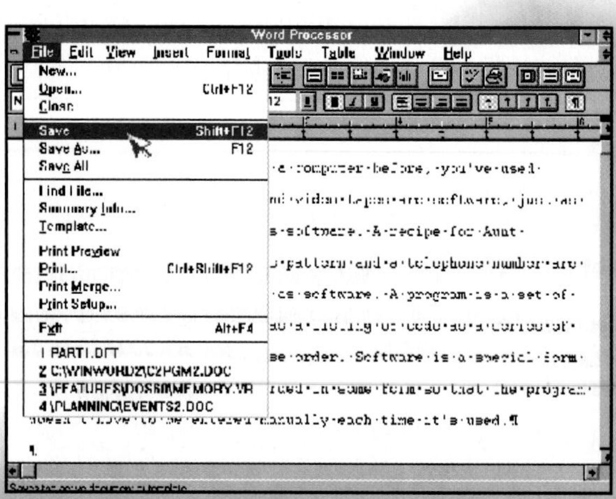

❶ When you choose the commands for saving a file in your word processor, the word processor sends the command and the data to be saved to the operating system. (In a Windows enviroment, Windows acts as an extension of the operating system to help handle command operations.)

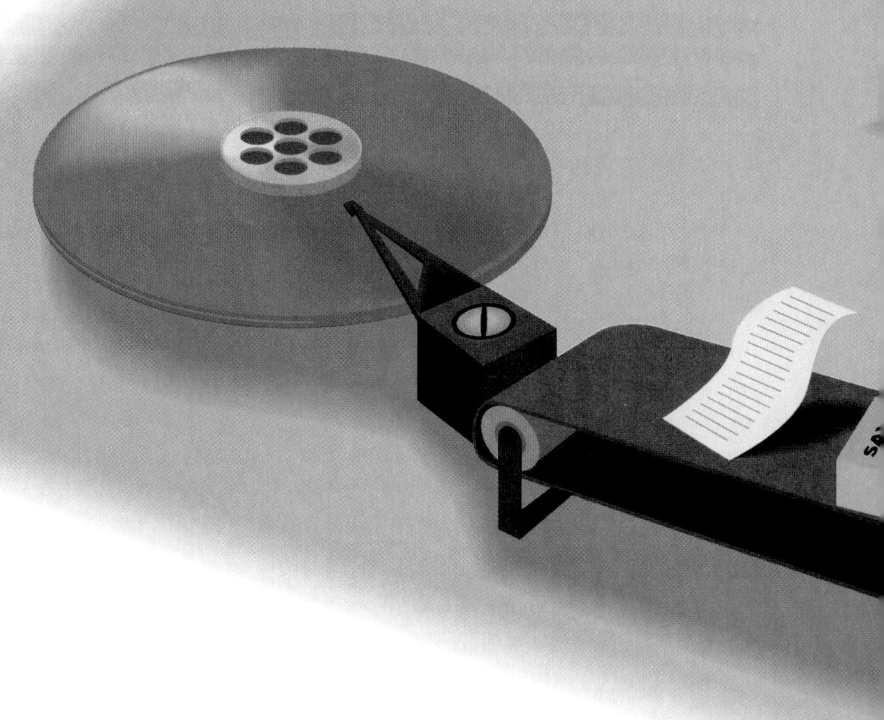

❹ The BIOS instructions are translated into the electrical signs needed to move the drive's read/write heads to the proper locations on the disk and to create the magnetic signals that record the data on the disk's surface.

Courtesy Ziff-Davis Press

2 The operating environment checks to make sure that the command to save data has no problems. For example, the operating environment makes sure that the file name is a legal one and that you're not trying to save over a file that's marked read-only. If everything is OK, the operating environment turns the job of writing the data to disk over to the BIOS.

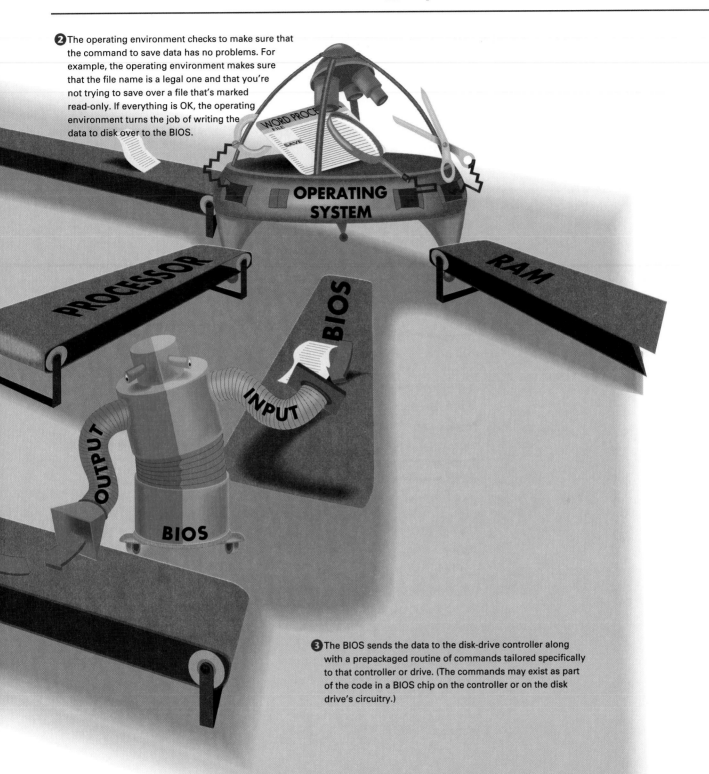

3 The BIOS sends the data to the disk-drive controller along with a prepackaged routine of commands tailored specifically to that controller or drive. (The commands may exist as part of the code in a BIOS chip on the controller or on the disk drive's circuitry.)

On older machines, DOS acts as a kind of supervisor between you and the application program you're using. On newer machines, you rarely use DOS; instead, you use the operating environment software to issue DOS commands. But DOS is still there, controlling and managing the basic computer operations.

Referring again to figure 3.2, notice that DOS performs four important operations essential to the hardware:

1. *Input and output control.* Note the input traveling along the conveyor belt. DOS manages both the data and the peripheral hardware, such as the keyboard and monitor. If your keyboard cord accidentally is unplugged, the operating system displays a keyboard error message on your monitor.

2. *Processor task scheduling.* See the operating system studying its instructions? The processing hardware can manage only one task or instruction at a time, and organizing and prioritizing the processing is DOS's responsibility.

3. *Data management and storage.* DOS has special "conveyor belts," one to send data to RAM and another to send data to disk storage. DOS ensures that data is organized and stored accurately in both temporary and permanent storage; DOS also lets you assign names and locations to the files in which you store the data.

4. *Commands.* Notice the instructions between input and the BIOS? You use a command language to issue instructions in DOS. The **command language** is a collection of terms, often called *keywords*, and special *expressions* that the operating system understands and executes. You use many commands for working with the data you've created and stored in files. Some frequently used commands are COPY, DELETE, MOVE, PRINT, RENAME. You'll learn how these command language keywords and expressions are commonly used when you read the next module.

You direct and control some of these DOS operations when you work with application software, but other operations are performed through the operating environment software without your intervention. Yet all four types of operations are necessary for smooth computer performance. A basic knowledge of these four operations helps you understand what happens when you're using the more complex and sophisticated operating environment software, as well as individual software applications. For example, when you issue the command to print in word processing, you're actually issuing the command to DOS.

The Macintosh System

The Macintosh needs system software to run, just as a PC compatible does. The Mac also has its own unique operating environment software. Today, the two computers are very much alike. Microsoft saw the advantages in the Macintosh operating system's ease of use and recognized that people using DOS-based computers wanted this ease of use with their PCs.

But the two computers have some important differences, too. For instance, you never see the system checks and BIOS routines on the Mac screen; you see only the happy clock face that indicates "something is happening, so please wait until you see the pointer." Once you do see the pointer, you can begin using the Mac's software. The Macintosh system software consists of the following elements:

- The *Macintosh operating system*, MacOS, a small portion of the system software. Similar to DOS, it is a collection of programs, some of which are stored in ROM and some on disk.

- The *Macintosh Toolbox*, which gives the Mac its distinctive screen appearance and provides a collection of procedures and functions that are used by the applications and make it possible for them to run. The Toolbox is also responsible for the way the operating environment works and for ensuring that all applications look and work in similar ways. The Toolbox functions between the system software and the Finder.

- The *Finder*, the operating environment software that displays the various folders, disk drives, and trash can icons, and from which applications are started. The Finder is the only system software that you actually see and use.

The Macintosh has had an easy-to-use operating environment since its introduction in 1984. Apple takes great pride in how intuitively easy using the Mac is. You work with folders and documents rather than directories and files. You can give documents long names, a feature of Windows 95 not found in previous versions of Windows or DOS. The Mac and its operating system were designed almost from scratch instead of being based on existing system software, as was the case with DOS. You can see how the Mac operating system is organized in the Home Page feature.

Like DOS, the Mac operating environment has gone through a number of revisions and improvements over the years, culminating in the new 1996 version, named Copland after the contemporary composer Aaron Copland. While still in development, Copland promises to improve the Mac in these ways:

- Make computers easier to learn and use by letting people customize the way the operating environment looks and works and by providing active assistance when the user needs help.

- Make designing, presenting, and communicating information easier with two-dimensional and three-dimensional graphics as well as video and sound.

- Make obtaining and using information simple through the concept of the mailbox and by offering new ways to search for and manage files and information.

- Make the operating environment powerful enough to support people working in teams with documents and through videoconferencing.

Even though the Macintosh is an excellent machine, its one lingering problem has been its small market share—only about 9 percent. PC compatibles dominate the market, due in part, no doubt, to the PC's lower price tag—about one-third less than an equivalent Macintosh. As is often the case, superior technology does not achieve market dominance. Reasons for this include the following:

- Lower price

- First in the market

- Popular, widely used application

- Compatibility with other computers

Apple continues to strive for technological superiority, but in many respects, it is difficult to distinguish the PC from the Mac.

Utility Software

Computers have always had utility software, or utility programs. They accompany operating system software to perform such tasks as printing what's on the screen, formatting a disk, or setting the date and time. We often take these built-in utilities for granted because an operating system just wouldn't be complete without them. Yet sometimes a built-in DOS utility is less than satisfactory. Perhaps it's hard to use. Maybe it doesn't have all the functions we need. That's why software developers have created separate systems-level utility programs.

There are three basic types of utility software, as seen in figure 3.3.

Figure 3.3
Utility software is used at all three major levels of software: operating system, operating environment, and application.

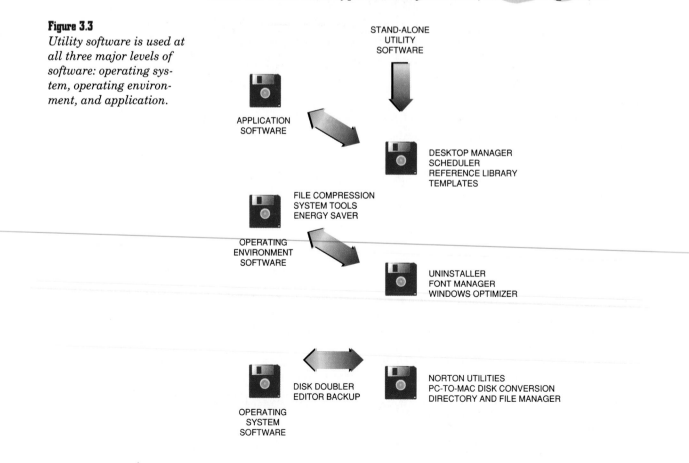

HOME PAGE

THE MAC ROM

2 The application document doesn't have to know exactly where in ROM the procedures are located: The application calls a table, which then directs it to the ROM routines. This way, the ROM on each new model of Macintosh can be different with out affecting software compatibility.

3 A series of Toolbox sets of routines called managers are enacted. This drawing depicts some of the main managers, but the Toolbox contains many others. The Menu Manager handles how a menu works. The Window Manager keeps track of multiple windows open on the desktop. The Resource Manager enables the application to read and write system resources, such as the fonts, which reside on the start-up disk.

4 QuickDraw, the Mac's graphics controller, displays the cursor and draws the menu on the screen while erasing the part of the screen behind every menu. QuickDraw also draws the text, graphics, windows, and everything else on the screen.

5 Toolbox routines make the calls to the operating system, telling it to interact with the Mac hardware. In this example, the Toolbox tells the operating system to save a copy of the file to the hard disk.

6 The File Manager allows the application to access the system on the hard disk where the file is being stored. The Save command replaces an older version of a file with the newer version.

1 When the user issues a command in an application, such as pulling down a menu and selecting the Save command, the application makes calls to the Macintosh Toolbox in ROM, which in turn triggers a chain of procedures.

9 When you quit an application after you save your file, the Process Manager terminates the application, removing it from RAM, The Process Manager launches an application when a user double-clicks its icon. It is the job of this manager to share the Mac's CPU among multiple open applications, providing the multitasking environment of System 7 and of MultiFinder in System 6.

7 In this case, the Device Manager sends data to the hard disk through the SCSI port. It also handles the sending or receiving of data to the Mac's other input/output ports, such as the modem, printer, and ADB ports.

8 The Memory Manager allocates and manages the portion of memory used by an application. When an open file is saved, the Memory Manager lets the other managers know where in RAM the file can be found. The memory allocation is constantly changing, depending on what the user is doing within an application.

MAC FACT

Mac ROM often contains extra space, which Apple sometimes fills with nonessential data that can be accessed by programmers in the know. Sometimes this material is fun stuff, and other times it is experimental data that Apple is considering for future models. The ROM of the first Mac Classics contained an entire System folder that could be used to start the Mac without the use of a hard or floppy disk. The key combination that invoked this hidden System folder at start-up, ⌘-Option-X-O, was disabled after a few months of production.

HOME PAGE REVIEW QUESTIONS

1. Why do you think that Mac system software and DOS system software are similar?
2. Compare several features of the Macintosh operating system software with those of DOS, Windows, and Windows 95.
3. Why do you suppose that average technology prevails over superior technology?

These types of utility software are as follows:

1. *System-level utility programs* work with the operating system. Some (a simple text editor, for instance) come with the operating system. Others are required for using a peripheral; a mouse or printer requires special software, called a *driver*, to operate correctly. Some add-on programs, such as Norton Utilities, provide additional functions. These utilities have become so useful that many have been incorporated into the operating system or operating environment software.

Figure 3.4
Norton Utilities, an operating system-level utility.

2. *Operating environment-level utility programs* perform operating system functions and enhance the human-computer interface operations. The After Dark screen saver program is one popular environment-level utility (see figure 3.5).

Figure 3.5
After Dark, an operating environment-level utility.

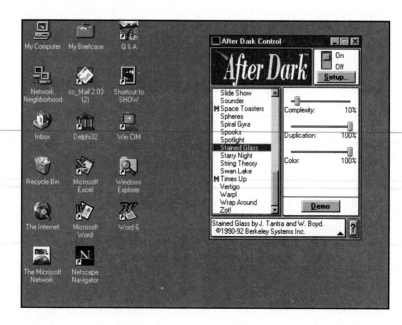

3. *Application utility programs* augment and extend the usefulness of application programs. Some utility programs, such as spelling checkers, are now integrated with word processing software. Others, like Design Portfolio, provide design templates for a variety of business forms, from letters to reports to faxes, as well as an address book (see figure 3.6).

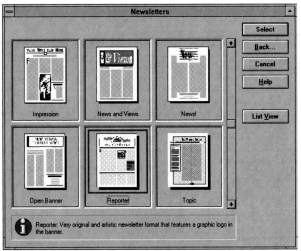

Screenshots Courtesy of Streetwise Software

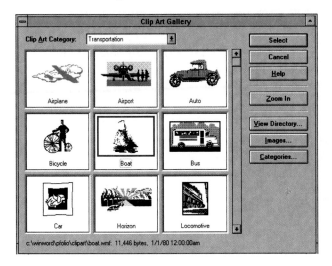

Figure 3.6
Design Portfolio, an application-level utility.

Now that you understand system software and DOS, you can see that you won't actually interact much with them—at least not without the excellent assistance of operating environment software and something called the graphical user interface. With the release of Microsoft Windows 95, there is less need for a separate operating system. For DOS, Windows 95 is the beginning of the end. The DOS operating system was integrated with Windows to create Windows 95 in order to make PC compatibles easier to use. But just in case you ever need to use DOS, it's still there, available for your use just like any other application.

Knowledge Check

1. Name three types of software that comprise system software.
2. Where are BIOS instructions stored?
3. What does DOS stand for?
4. What is the command language used for?
5. Why do we need utility programs?

Key Terms

basic input/output system (BIOS)

bug

disk operating system (DOS)

read-only memory (ROM)

utility program

boot

command language

random-access memory (RAM)

system software

ISSUES AND IDEAS

The Story of the Bug

The term **bug** has been around for quite a while, but it has a unique significance in the history of computing. In the early 1940s, a programming team was working with one of the earliest computers, the Mark I at Harvard, when the machine suddenly stopped. According to the late Grace Murray Hopper, a leading figure in computing for most of her life, the computer stopped because a bug—in this case a moth—had flown into a relay, causing it to malfunction. The moth was taped into the log book, which reads:

> 1545 [hours] Relay # 70 Panel F (moth) in relay. First actual case of bug being found.

But today, according to the article "Attack of the Swarming Bugs" by Carole Patton, bugs are an everyday fact of life:

> The text of the December 1994 issue of Bruce Brown's *BugNet* newsletter reads like an encyclopedia of software snafus.
>
> . . .The infinite combinations of hardware and software mean software developers can't test the product on every machine using all configurations. And the tendency to rush new, not-completely-tested software out the door because of deadlines, shorter product-creation cycles, and computer-press expectations seems to be standard operating procedure. "The developers are under tremendous pressure to bring out new products," says Brown, "if only because the richest part of their income cycle is at the outset, when the product is fresh and competitors haven't caught up with the new features yet, and the poorest part of the cycle is at the end of a version's run, when an upgrade is expected momentarily."
>
> The increasing sophistication of many software packages along with the piling on of features, makes for more buggy software, adds Brown, joking about database products that add word processors to "let you spell-check your spreadsheets. Developers keep reaching a little farther, and the more terrain the features cover, the greater the chance something will not work right. In a static world of features, bugs wouldn't be a problem. But they keep making programs bigger and faster, so it's a moving target."[1]

CRITICAL THINKING

1. Unfortunately, a great many software bugs are discovered by purchasers after a new program is on the market. Why do we have to

---

1. CIS Online News, June 24, 1995.

suffer software failures and, in effect, debug software for its maker? What do you think might improve this situation in the future?

2. After reading this article, do you think that software publishers honestly try to get rid of all the bugs before they release the software?

3. Should programs with serious bugs that destroy data, cause damage, or result in losses for the business purchaser be subject to consumer protection laws?

Module B

The Operating Environment

Why It's Important to Know

The graphical user interface, found in operating environment software and application software, provides the easiest way to issue commands and instructions to the computer system. Knowing how to use the interface properly and well makes your computer work simpler, easier, and more fun.

The operating system determines how certain things look on the monitor. The operating system also is the means of executing commands for the application software. To say that the on-screen view and the actual procedures for using the operating system are enhanced means that the human-computer interface has been improved.

The Human-Computer Interface

As you know, a computer system requires a person, software, and hardware (in addition to data and procedures). When you sit down in front of a computer, you form part of the **human-computer interface**, or the way the computer and its software are presented to the human who is using them. The operating environment software was developed to improve the human-computer interface. The human-computer interface consists of five levels, as shown in figure 3.7.

Perhaps the most distinguishing characteristic of the human-computer interface is the way knowledge workers issue commands to the computer system. Three basic types of human-computer interfaces are available for personal computers today: the command line interface; the menu-driven interface; and the graphical user interface, or GUI.

Figure 3.7
*In order to make comput-
ers easier to use, it is necessary to add another
layer of software between
the system software and
the application software.*

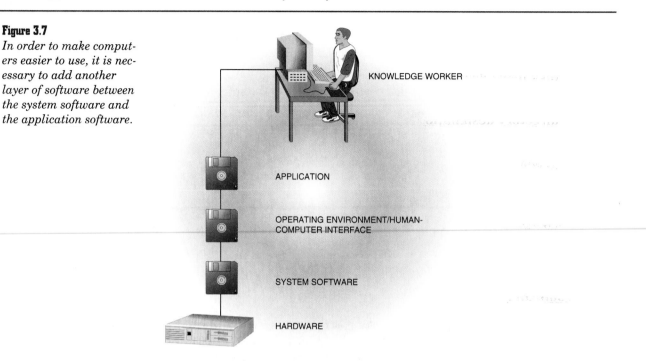

KNOWLEDGE WORKER

APPLICATION

OPERATING ENVIRONMENT/HUMAN-
COMPUTER INTERFACE

SYSTEM SOFTWARE

HARDWARE

The Command Line Interface

DOS is used to issue commands and instructions to the computer. When you
start the computer and it has finished its system checks, you may see a
screen that looks like the one in figure 3.8. This screen represents the first
and simplest type of interface. It's called the **command line interface**
because you are required to type the exact command on the line you see.
When you're looking at the command line interface you're interacting with
DOS itself, so it is not considered a separate operating environment. Once a
command is typed, you must press the Enter or Return key to actually issue
that command.

Figure 3.8
*The DOS command line
interface.*

Viewing from left to right, the command line interface has these distinguishing features:

- The **disk drive designation**, a letter telling you which drive is "logged," or in use.

- The **directory designation**, indicating which directory you are presently using. If no directory is indicated, you are in the root directory.

- The **prompt**, a character or message that tells you that the computer system is ready to accept a command or input. The DOS prompt is a right-pointing arrow that looks like this: >

- The **cursor,** usually a blinking rectangle or a blinking underline that tells you where the next keyboard character typed will appear on the screen. The cursor (which is not visible in the figure) appears just to the right of the prompt or last character typed.

- A **command**, the instruction you give to the computer. For example, *DIR* is the command to list all the files and directories on the logged disk. The command is typed on the **command line**, which is the blank space to the right of the cursor.

The Menu-Driven Interface

As more people with little experience began using computers, these users wanted a human-computer interface to help them remember commands or select the next task. One of the first friendly interfaces was called a menu because it presented a list of the commands, tasks, or projects the user most often worked with. The **menu-driven interface** was developed to make the command line interface easier to use. The simplest menu interfaces were *batch files*, which some knowledge workers created for themselves, and only launched applications. Commercial offerings were called *shells*, or utility programs, and could issue DOS commands as well. Figure 3.9 shows a menu-driven interface program. The menu has been redesigned and continues to be used in the graphical user interface, which you learn about next.

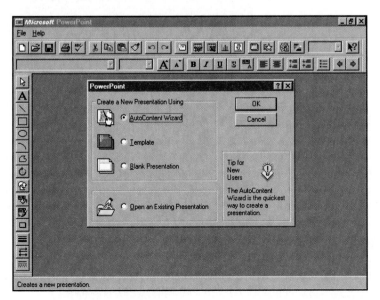

Figure 3.9
A menu interface helps users get started.

The Graphical User Interface (GUI)

The graphical user interface is the most sophisticated human-computer interface in use today. A **graphical user interface**, or **GUI** (pronounced "gooey"), is a software design that enables knowledge workers to use *color and graphics*, *icons*, *pull-down menus*, and a *pointing device* to issue commands and instructions. Most software being designed today incorporates these features.

GUI software is often referred to simply as the operating environment. The **operating environment** is a type of software between the operating system and the application software, that makes the computer system easier to use. Strictly speaking, the simple menu-driven interface is an operating environment, although it lacks the range of features in today's GUI. Generally speaking, an operating environment is graphical and has many features that make it useful and desirable. It's a complete and self-contained program, which we can use to issue commands and perform tasks that otherwise would have required using the operating system or systems utilities.

The two most popular operating environments in use today are Windows for PC compatibles and the Finder for the Macintosh, both shown in figure 3.10. Now take a closer look at the GUI's main characteristics.

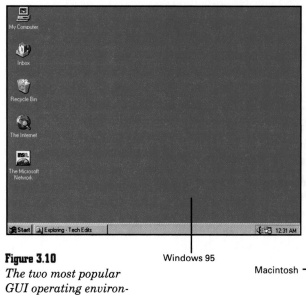

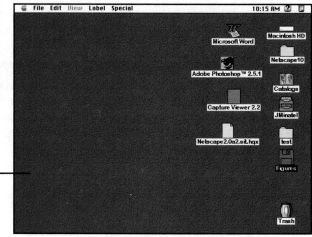

Windows 95

Macintosh

Figure 3.10
The two most popular GUI operating environments.

Color and Graphics

The GUI makes extensive use of *color*, which makes the screen more attractive and helps make programs easier to use. We can recognize a color or a shape more easily than a line of text, so finding things is easier. When the human-computer interface was monochrome, or one color (often green), and programs were capable of displaying only text, the interface was harder to use. For example, underlining a word meant typing a hidden command by pressing the Control key and a letter, like this: ^Iwedge^I. In many programs, the control characters weren't even visible, so there was no visual way to recognize where you had underlined a word—you simply had to wait until you printed the document. Color made it possible to mark text in color, and graphics made it possible to see the actual underlining.

Icons

An **icon** is another type of graphics, an on-screen symbol that represents a program, a data file, or some other entity or function.

 Clicking the Word icon starts the program.

Documents are kept in folders.

Completed works are documents or files created by an application.

The Print function (an operating system function) is often found as a button on the taskbar.

Pull-Down Menus

A **pull-down menu** is a menu of commands or selections. You choose the pull-down menu from a **menu bar**. As you can see in figure 3.11, the menu concept has been improved. Related or associated commands are grouped under each selection on the menu bar. For example, the pull-down menu under File displays several selections for working externally with files. The Edit pull-down menu lists commands to work within files. This feature makes it convenient for you to issue commands because you don't have to worry about typing them correctly at the command line interface. The GUI operating environment does it for you.

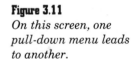

Figure 3.11
On this screen, one pull-down menu leads to another.

Pointing Device

Both icons and pull-down menus rely on the use of a pointing device. The **pointing device**—usually a mouse—controls the **pointer**—usually an arrow—on the screen. The pointing device takes the place of the keyboard arrow keys for moving around the screen. Choosing icons, such as the one showing a printer, takes the place of typing the command and pressing the Enter key.

As you move the pointing device, the arrow moves on the screen. When you're issuing commands, clicking icons, and opening pull-down menus, the pointer is normally an arrow. It changes to different shapes, however, according to the work you're doing, as you'll see when you work with different applications. If you want to start an application, you move the pointer to the application's icon and click it. If you want to use commands or functions in a pull-down menu, you move to the menu bar and click the name of the menu you want; then you move to the command you want and click again.

Look and Feel

Each operating environment has a kind of personality of its own, often referred to as its *look and feel*. The designer's goal is to make the interface look and feel as *intuitive* as possible. Using the interface should be a matter of natural common sense. Ideally, you should be able to figure out what the icons stand for, how to issue commands, and where to find functions, with little or no help.

The interface design is integral to the operating system software and affects both the operating environment and the application software. The design must accurately represent all the operating system commands and functions, because many of them are used by the operating environment as well as the application software. The interface design must also create a visual and organizational GUI model for other programs so that the look and feel of the application software closely resemble the look and feel of the operating environment. Figure 3.12 shows the screens of a number of the most popular and widely used GUI operating environments. Based on what you have just learned, look closely to see both the similarities and differences among them.

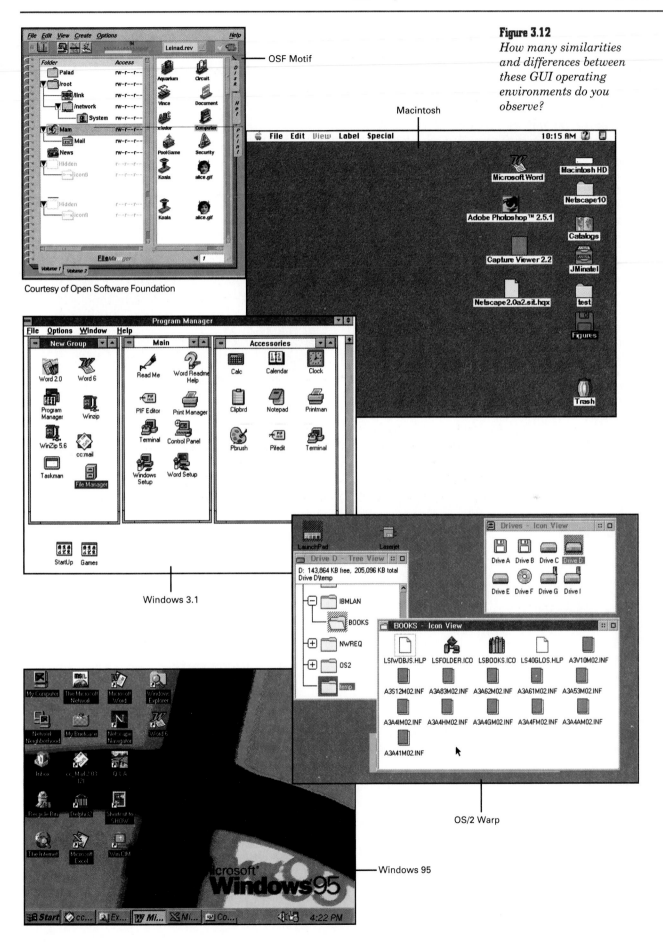

Figure 3.12
How many similarities and differences between these GUI operating environments do you observe?

HOME PAGE

THE FUTURE OF THE HUMAN-COMPUTER INTERFACE

One of the greatest technology think tanks in the world is Xerox Corporation's Palo Alto Research Center (PARC), which celebrated its 25th anniversary in 1995. PARC pioneered many computer innovations that we take for granted today, including the human-computer interface. Steven Jobs, Apple Computer's cofounder, visited PARC in the early 1980s and saw the Xerox Star workstation, with its mouse, graphic screen, and icons. He vowed to develop a similar computer that anyone could learn to use, and the result was the Macintosh.

Stuart Card is a cognitive psychologist and computer scientist who has been developing user interfaces at PARC since its beginning. He knows how much research has gone into inventing and refining user interfaces, which at PARC date back to the early 1970s. The Macintosh, he writes, was "widely cited as the first commercially successful use of a graphical user interface. The first Apple introduction of this technology on the LISA failed, as did the second, the LISA 2, as did the third, the Macintosh 128. Only on the fourth try, the Macintosh 512, was there commercial success. But this machine had no user interface invention, it just used the design settled earlier in the series. Most of the real invention in this design, in turn, actually occurred in the designs of the Xerox SmallTalk and the Xerox Star systems and related design at PARC. . . . Some ideas in these systems can be traced back even further."[2]

A more recent innovation from PARC is the *Information Visualizer,* or *IV.* An IV is a three-dimensional, animated tool that turns the computer screen into a passageway which leads to various types of information. Card says that the old ways of retrieving information are based on *content,* such as words or dates. The new way is to present information in the same manner in which the brain thinks about it: in structure and context as well as content.

The PARC workstation screen presents an *overview* room with twelve information visualiz-

ers, or screens. Eleven are 3-D rooms; the knowledge worker moves from one to another via connecting "doors." One IV room displays the Xerox organizational chart. Previously, it was an 80-page document, like one created in word processing. In the IV, it is a rotating drum with revolving names. When a person is chosen, the name is moved to the front of the screen, like a label, but the relationship to others in the organization is graphically presented.

Courtesy of Xerox Corporation

By clicking the mouse, the knowledge worker can *navigate* closer to the individual. All screen objects, such as name labels, are *interactive,* which means that they can be changed or moved into various relationships, as in a work group. The view can be narrowed on the person, displaying a color photograph, biography, papers the person has written, and other public information. The view can also be widened to show the person's office, the floor plan for the work group, and biographies and other information about fellow knowledge workers. In fact, the interactive nature of the screen objects even permits showing parallels or differences between the various individuals' work.

Stuart Card believes that the ultimate goal of interface design is to make the interface vanish. Today, too much manipulation of the computer system is required. An ideal interface takes the focus off the machinery and puts it on the work.

Scientists and engineers at PARC will be the first knowledge workers who get to take advantage of IVs. But Card and his team are working to develop IVs that help visualize information for business applications.

2. Stuart K. Card. "Pioneers and Settlers: Methods Used in Successful User Interface Designs," a Xerox PARC monograph, Dec. 12, 1994, 6–7.

HOME PAGE REVIEW QUESTIONS

1. What computer's GUI was designed after the Xerox Star computer?
2. Discuss the idea of replacing text documents with visual rooms and people. Is it a good idea?
3. Is Card's goal of making the interface vanish entirely a good idea? Why?

Advantages of the GUI Operating Environment

The advantages of the GUI operating environment over its predecessors are easy to see. Humans are visual creatures. Eighty percent of what we learn is received from images, so a graphical user interface is indeed more intuitive than the command line interface. The GUI is also much easier to learn and use. In addition to its graphical aspects, today's GUI operating environment offers several other advantages:

- *Multitasking.* The capability to start and use more than one program at a time on a single computer system. Once the programs are open, you can switch among word processing, the spreadsheet, and any of a number of other application programs. **Multitasking** also lets you print one file while you're working with another. In this case, the application you're working with is said to be in the *foreground*, and the other is said to be in the *background*; thus, you may hear the term *background printing*.

- *Consistent application design and function.* All the applications have the same or a similar look and feel. When DOS reigned and there was no common operating environment, every application functioned differently. If you didn't use an application frequently, you could easily forget the commands. Pioneered by the Macintosh, the graphical operating environment standard demands consistency in screen layouts, use of icons, and contents of pull-down menus. One application should look and work as much like the next as possible, regardless of the type of application software or the company that created it.

- *File compatibility.* Modern operating environments also ensure a high degree of file compatibility. Applications designed to work under the Mac or Windows operating environment have almost 100 percent compatibility, which makes it possible for knowledge workers to share information more easily. For example, a freelance writer preparing a story for a magazine using Microsoft Word, a Windows-based word processing program, can be assured that the editor at the magazine will be able to edit the file using Windows and Microsoft Word.

- *Cut and paste.* An operating environment permits moving portions of files between applications. This procedure is called **cut and paste**: you can *cut* a portion of your spreadsheet and *paste* it into the report you're writing in word processing. You can also *copy* a portion of text and paste it elsewhere.

- *Accessories.* Operating environments usually come with a number of small programs that act like desktop accessories. Some of these small, simple programs are often referred to as **applets**, which are small applications that work only within the operating environment. Others are utility programs, which perform specific tasks. All are electronic replacements for the items normally found on a knowledge worker's desk, and they make working with the computer easier and more interesting. Accessories include a clock, a calendar, an appointment book, an alarm clock, an address book (and telephone dialer), a scratch pad for notes, and a calculator. Because you have multitasking, these accessories are always readily available even while you're using other applications.

Most of us derive pleasure and enhanced productivity from working with GUI operating environments. However, if you ever need to use DOS, the understanding you've gained in these pages will help you. The operating environment most of us will use is called Windows or Windows 95. The second most popular one is the Macintosh.

But these environments may not be the only ones: Now there is a new-generation operating environment called the social interface. The *social interface* is designed primarily for home users. It uses familiar scenes, like a small town or a home, and friendly characters or animals to perform tasks. Yet the social interface should appeal to business as well, says *InformationWeek* magazine.[3] Figure 3.13 shows some of the leading social interfaces.

Figure 3.13
Out with the old, in with the new: the social interface is redefining ease of use.

Packard Bell Navigator —

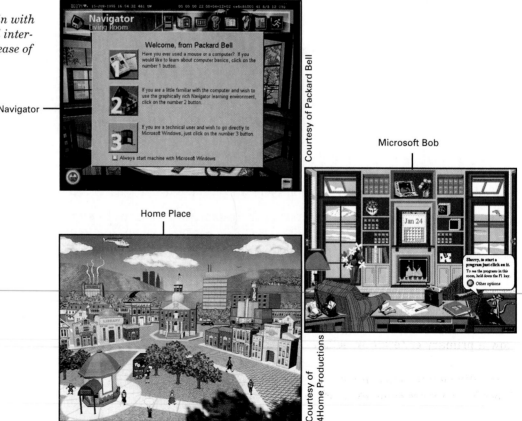

Home Place

Microsoft Bob

---
3. Joseph C. Panettieri. "PCs Gain Social Skills," *InformationWeek*, July 3, 1995, 32–42.

Knowledge Check

1. Name the five levels of the human-computer interface.
2. What is an advantage of the command line interface? A disadvantage?
3. Why is it important that the operating environment and application software look similar?
4. Describe multitasking and tell why it's useful.
5. Identify the following on the screen shown:
   a. pointer
   b. menu bar
   c. icon
   d. File menu
   e. disk drive designation

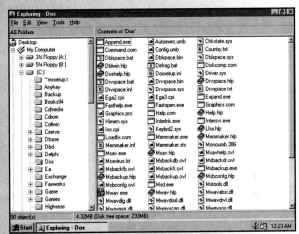

Key Terms

applet	command	command line
command line interface	cursor	cut and paste
directory designation	disk drive designation	graphical user interface (GUI)
human-computer interface	icon	menu bar
menu-driven interface	multitasking	operating environment
pointer	pointing device	prompt
pull-down menu		

ISSUES AND IDEAS

What Is Ease of Use?

Ease of use is the primary goal of computer hardware and software makers. For example, creating and printing a chart in Lotus 1-2-3 for Windows is much simpler than it was in the previous DOS version because ease of use is now a primary criterion in software design. Yet with every new innovation, it seems that both hardware and software become more complex. *Ease of use* is the flip side to *better, faster,* and *cheaper:* we want our PC to do more, but it becomes a more complex machine as its capabilities increase.

John Sedgwick, in an article entitled "The Complexity Problem," writes:

> One leading manufacturer (of watches) was distressed to discover that a line of its particularly advanced digitals was being returned as defective by thousands, although the watches actually worked perfectly well. Further investigations revealed that they were coming back soon after purchase and thereafter in two large batches—in the spring and the fall, when the time changed.
>
> Charles Mauro, a consultant in New York City, is a prominent member of a branch of engineering generally known as ergonomics, or human-factors research—the only field specifically addressing the question of product usability. Mauro, who has won many awards for industrial design and human-factors research, was brought in to provide some help to the watch manufacturer, which was experiencing what Mauro calls "the complexity problem." With "complexity" defined as "a fundamental mismatch between the demands of a technology and the capabilities of its user," the term nicely captures the essence of our current technological predicament. . . . About the digital-watch manufacturer Mauro asks, "Can you believe the company actually expected you to carry around a thirty-page manual in your wallet?"[4]

CRITICAL THINKING

1. Research the term *ease of use* to see what others have said or written about it. Then read several articles about computer training and education. Is ease of use the real factor, or is it proper training and education?

2. What are your responsibilities in terms of self-education? Was it reasonable for the watch manufacturer to expect owners to read the instruction manual? How much time do you think you should be expected to devote to studying software instruction manuals or using the computer's built-in Help features?

3. Look around your world. How many other technological devices do you operate? What is their ease of use rating on a scale of 1 to 10? Which are the most intuitive?

4. Keep a journal of your work with the computer, recording your problems with ease of use, occasions when you needed help and how you got it, and a list of the tasks you learned to perform intuitively.

---

4. *The Atlantic Monthly*, March 1993, 96.

Application Software

Why It's Important to Know

> **Application software is what knowledge workers use most frequently. Six or more applications are commonly used in business and enterprise today. Once you are familiar with them, you'll know how to pick the right application for the right task.**

Application software is the third type of computer software. It's also the software you'll use most. An **application** is a specific purpose for which the computer is used. ENIAC, the first computer, was built for a single application: calculating missile trajectories for the Allies during World War II. Today, an application may be used for writing a term paper or short story, creating a health and fitness program, preparing a budget or paying bills, or designing and publishing a newsletter.

Application software refers to programs designed to perform tasks with the computer. As you know, application software requires system software in order to operate. Operating environment software enhances the ways we use application software.

Today we have many thousands of applications to choose from. And when working in an operating environment, we can use more than one at the same time. For convenience, this book refers to application software simply as an application. The most popular applications for personal productivity are the following:

- **Word processing** enables you to create, write, edit, proofread, and format documents for printing.

- **Spreadsheets** perform *number processing* and electronically simulate an accountant's worksheet, enabling you to add and revise numerical data and formulas for a wide variety of financial work.

- **Database management systems**, or **DBMS**, perform *fact processing* and are used to enter, organize, format, and retrieve data in a variety of different formats and then print that data in a report.

- **Communications software** turns the computer into a terminal for transmitting and receiving data to and from other computers, commonly over phone lines. A popular use for communications software is to connect to the Internet.

- **Presentation graphics** performs image processing, combining simple line drawings and art from slides or overhead transparencies with text and paper reports for use in business presentations.

- **Desktop publishing**, or **DTP**, combines text (from word processing), graphics, and data from other applications and formats them on pages suitable for professional publishing—books, magazines, pamphlets, newsletters, and so on.

Figure 3.14
Macmillan is the largest publisher of computer books in the world. These books attest to the popularity of these software applications.

From reading these brief descriptions, you can see that each of these applications is quite different from the others, yet all perform their work in an essentially similar pattern of steps and functions. When you sit down to use the computer, you begin a *work session*. In this module's work session, you learn about this common functionality in applications.

A Work Session

Any work session begins with switching on the power and booting the computer. First, ROM instructions run their system checks. Next, DOS is loaded. After that, Windows is loaded. When it's finished, you see a screen that looks similar to the screen shown in figure 3.15.

Figure 3.15
The opening screen in Windows 95: this view shows one of several Desktop Themes from which you can choose.

HOME PAGE

TIPS FOR BUYING PERSONAL COMPUTER SOFTWARE

People usually buy their application software in a retail store, such as Egghead Software, or from a mail-order software company. Both retail stores and mail-order houses offer discounts and guarantee software—you can bring it back if you don't like it—but how do you know what's the best choice for you? There is a bestseller list, but it doesn't tell you whether the software fits your expertise level or needs. Most buyers need more help. You may find this checklist useful in making your selection:

1. List the tasks you would like the application to perform.

2. Determine whether the features of a particular application match your task list.

3. Make sure that the application runs on the hardware and operating system you use. Some applications are designed exclusively for certain brands of personal computers and operating systems.

4. Find out how much memory the application requires and make sure that your personal computer has enough memory to support the application. Also find out whether any other software is required, such as a specific version of an operating system or operating environment.

5. Use it! Determine whether the application is easy to use. Many retail software stores permit you to return or exchange software (but be sure to ask about this before you buy).

6. See whether the application includes good documentation. If it doesn't, software- and hardware-specific books, written by knowledgeable people, are available in bookstores and com-puter retail stores.

7. Check the on-line Help built into the application, and try it out for ease of use.

8. Some applications offer a technical support number you can call when you have problems. Is there an additional charge for this support? Is there a toll-free 800 telephone number? What is the average waiting time on the phone before a support person picks up your call?

9. Is the application copy-protected? Most are not these days. If it is, does the copy-protection make the program hard to install on your personal computer or awkward to use? Does the publisher provide backup disks? Is there a charge for them?

10. Read reviews and advertisements in trade publications. Is the application highly regarded by users or testing labs?

11. How long has the application been on the market? Check the version number or the copyright dates listed on the package. Applications are updated every few years; make sure that you're not paying new-version price for an older version. Mail-order companies often sell previous versions at greatly reduced prices. Again, check the reviews; sometimes an earlier version is better than the latest one! (After you buy, mail in your warranty card so that you will be notified when a new version is available; often you'll get a reduced "upgrade" price.)

12. If you haven't yet purchased your personal computer, conventional wisdom suggests that you choose the application(s) you like and then buy the appropriate computer system. In many cases, you must make compromises between software and hardware; try to make as few as possible. If you're like most people, the commitment means that you'll probably have to live with your system for quite a while.

Courtesy of Egghead Software

This software retailer provides a selection guide for purchasing software.

Now you can select an application from the Windows 95 Start bar. After you point to Start, the application menu appears. You see a number of icons and accompanying titles, each representing an application. Move the pointer to the one you want, and click the pointing device. You have sent a message from the operating environment to *execute* a command—in this case, loading a program by starting a file with a file name extension that is either EXE or COM. Now you see the monitor screen change as the application is loaded; an hourglass may appear to indicate "Wait, I'm performing the task you asked, but it's taking a little time." Once opened, most applications display a blank screen, indicating that a new file is open and ready for you to begin data processing.

The Work Session Process

Each time you work with the computer, you are using one of the data processing operations: input, processing, output, storage. These same four operations occur whenever you use an application. We call these operations the *work session process*, a term that is simply a guide to understanding how to work effectively with any application. Regardless of the type of application, these steps typically occur during a work session:

- *Input*: You begin typing characters (letters, numbers) to create your work.

- *Processing*: The computer captures your work and allows you to issue commands to move, rearrange, modify, format, delete, and the like. Your work is held in RAM (memory) for processing.

- *Output*: Your work is displayed on the monitor as it is processed and/or printed.

- *Storage*: Your work being held in RAM is saved as a file or document on a disk.

Once the data process-ing is completed and your work is printed on paper (or other med-ium), you have *information* in a form suitable for people to understand and use.

Any time you're work-ing with an application, you are involved in one of these four work ses-sion steps. If you experi-ence a problem or lose your place, so to speak, ask yourself which one of the steps you were last doing. This knowl-edge will make getting back on track easier.

A good tip to remember is this: *Never begin an operation or function unless you know how to end it.* For example, if you're going to cut and paste something, be sure that you know where you are going to *cut from* and where you are going to *paste to* before you begin. Always be able to backtrack so that you can at least get back where you started.

Figure 3.16
A knowledge worker performing the four oper-ations in a work session.

Working with the Application

The idea behind both the operating environment and compatible application software is to create a standardized look and feel. First, you learn how the pointer changes; then you become familiar with the screen.

The Pointer

When you're working solely in the operating environment, the pointer is just that: a pointer or arrow. It is used to issue commands.

When you're working with an application, the pointer issues commands but also assumes a second task. When you move it into the work area—where you actually enter data—the pointer changes into an **I-beam pointer**. You can position the I-beam pointer where you want to work next. Clicking the mouse button creates a vertical bar called an insertion point.

Like the DOS cursor, the **insertion point** identifies where the next charac-ter you type will appear. Once you have set the insertion point, you can move the I-beam pointer anywhere you like. You can move it to a place where you want to insert a character or word, you can move it to the top of the screen to issue a command, or you can move it to the side of the screen where it's not in the way.

The Screen

A number of features are common to the human-computer interface of both the Windows operating environment and applications designed for it. Starting at the top of the Windows 95 screen shown in figure 3.17, here are those used most often:

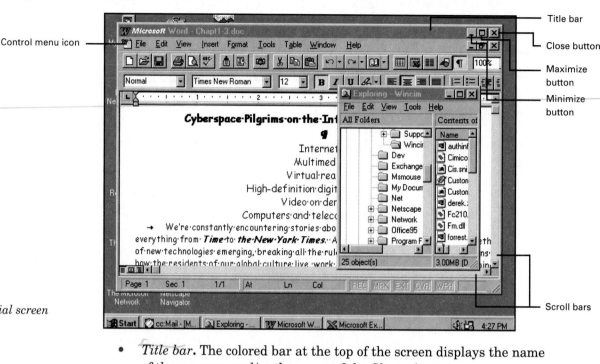

Figure 3.17
Some special screen features.

- *Title bar.* The colored bar at the top of the screen displays the name of the program and/or the name of the file you're using.

- *Control-menu icon.* At the left end of the title bar—clicking this icon displays commands for managing the window or screen you're using.

The following three buttons are at the right end of the title bar:

- *Minimize button.* Shrinks the application window while keeping it active and operational; watch the window reduce its size into its button on the Start bar (and make a sound as it does so). Often used to "park" an application temporarily until you need it again.

- *Maximize / Restore button.* Used to change the screen size of the application. If it's showing a double window, the application is full-size. If it's showing a single larger window, you can see other open windows behind it. Useful when *cascading* (showing overlapping windows) or alternating between applications, or when you want to compare data or files in different applications.

- *Close button.* Click the X and the file closes, just as if you had selected Close from the control-menu icon.

- *Scroll bars.* Along the right side and across the bottom of the screen (just above the status bar) are the vertical and horizontal scroll bars.

Scrolling is the action of moving the contents of a file through the window you view, either vertically (up and down) or horizontally (left and right). If you touch the pointer to an arrow at either end of a scroll bar and hold down the pointing device button, you move through the screen or file contents in that direction. Move the pointer to the square button, and hold down the pointing device button; move the box to scan through the document. The box also shows you where you are relative to the full length of the document. Note, however, that activating the scroll bars to move somewhere else in the file does *not* move the cursor. It stays where you left it until you click the pointing device button in the work area again.

You also see the menu bar and the toolbar, both of which you learned about in the preceding module. The menu bar is fairly standard among applications. The buttons on the toolbar differ, however, because applications perform different tasks. For example, you may want to change line spacing in word processing, but you don't have as much need for using formulas and percentages as you do in a spreadsheet.

When ending a work session, you must save your files and exit the application. To save your file, go to the File menu and select Save; type a name in the text box, and click the OK button. Once the operation is completed, go to the control-menu icon or back to the File menu and select Exit. This procedure enables you to quit the application and ensures that everything has been properly saved.

Now you'll find yourself in Windows, which you must also shut down before switching off the computer. Move to the Start button, select Shut Down, and make the appropriate selection, normally "Shut down the computer?" and wait until you see the message, "It is now safe to turn off your computer."

Exiting applications and following shutdown procedures, regardless of whether you're using a Macintosh or a PC compatible, are extremely important. Failure to do so can result in losing work and changing the software settings. You can easily forget that you have several applications open or several files in one application open. Some applications need to verify certain menu settings or the time and date.

Simply turning off the power without following proper closing, exiting, and shutdown procedures could result in serious problems. Play it safe: take the time to finish what you started in the prescribed manner.

Software Ambiguity

All software—regardless of its purpose, the company that published it, or any other factor—has a certain degree of ambiguity in its operations. The *American Heritage Dictionary* defines *ambiguous* as "Open to more than one interpretation." **Software ambiguity** means that there is more than one way to perform a given task or execute a command. In the case of exiting Windows applications, there is more than one way to quit:

1. Select Close from the control-menu icon on the title bar.
2. Hold down the Alt key and simultaneously press the F4 key.
3. Double-click your pointing device on the control-menu icon.
4. Select Exit from the File menu.

In many cases, you'll find commands and functions on the menu bar repeated on the toolbar. Print is a good example.

Figure 3.18
Software ambiguity often means that there is more than one good way to issue a command or instruction.

Why this ambiguity? Part of the answer lies in the design. Many of the current Windows programs began as DOS programs and used simple key combinations to issue commands. Then the menu concept was implemented and replicated the key commands, such as Alt+W and F4. The menu bar was then improved on by the toolbar.

All these options continue to be available in most applications, and that's good. The ambiguity gives us a choice in how we want to use the application; after all, no two people perform a task in exactly the same way. Ambiguity enables each of us to find the most comfortable and convenient ways for ourselves (see figure 3.18). Explore the options, and find the way you like best to control your software.

Types of Application Software

Most application programs for personal computers—word processing, the spreadsheet, the DBMS—are commonly known as **stand-alone** applications. This name simply means that the application works alone, by itself. In the past, stand-alone applications weren't capable of easily exchanging data. In the Windows environment, you can use a variety of stand-alone programs and easily cut and paste data between them.

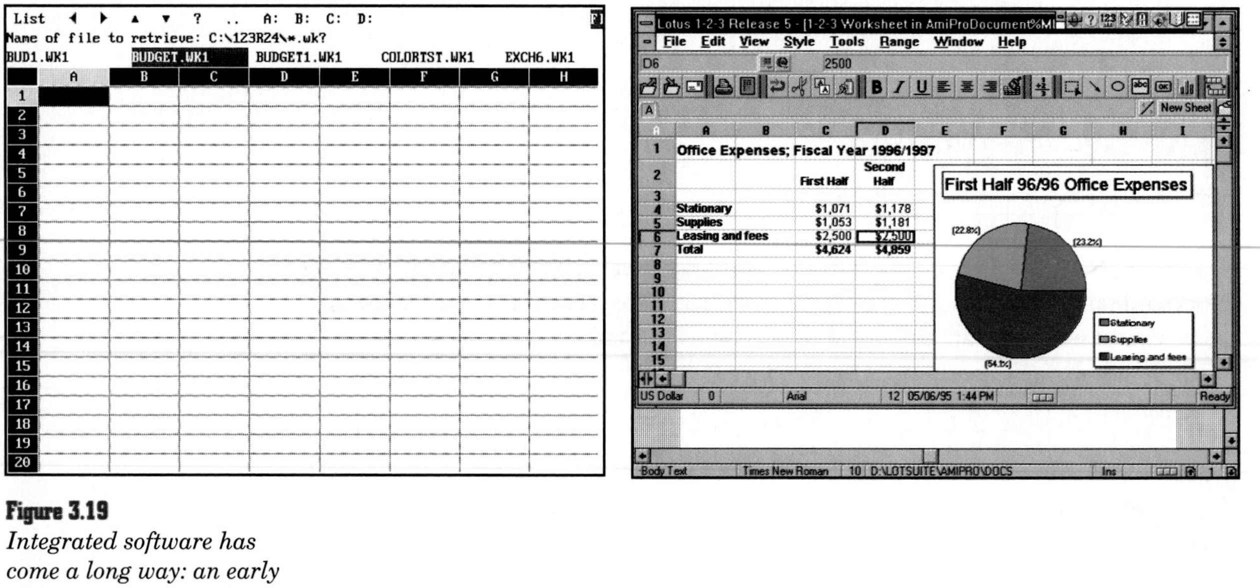

Figure 3.19
Integrated software has come a long way: an early version of Lotus 1-2-3 and the latest Lotus SmartSuite in 1995.

However, there is still a look-and-feel issue to stand-alone applications. The major distinction has led three major software companies—Microsoft, Novell, and Lotus (now part of IBM)—to introduce integrated software packages with word processing, spreadsheet, DBMS, and often several other applications. Microsoft offers Microsoft Office and Microsoft Works, Novell has Perfect Office, and Lotus has SmartSuite.

Integrated software combines into a single program or suite of programs several stand-alone applications that are capable of freely exchanging data with each other. Integrated software has several advantages:

- You can switch from one application to another just by clicking an icon.

- The applications all work similarly so that the degree of ambiguity is lessened. For example, Microsoft's integrated applications all use a Wizard to create new document formats. If you know how to use the word processing Wizard, learning how to use the Wizard in companion applications is relatively simple.

- Because the applications work similarly, you are familiar with terminology and technology. For example, a table in one application won't be called a chart in another, and the icons on the toolbar for cutting and pasting will always be the same.

- Files transferred from one application to another retain all their original formatting. For example, data from the columns in a spreadsheet worksheet will be perfectly aligned when pasted into a word processing document.

- Integrated packages are usually less expensive than the same applications purchased separately.

Integrated software is not new. The first integrated package for PCs was Lotus 1-2-3, which was three applications in one: spreadsheet, DBMS, and graphics. Over time, it was thought that the operating environment would reduce the need for integrated software because most of the advantages just described were built in. However, software publishers have always designed and executed their applications just a little differently, each thinking these features would ensure competitive advantage. The end result was that switching—say from the WordPerfect word processing program to the Lotus spreadsheet—still required a mental shift.

For that reason and many others, the market has drifted back to integrated software. And although each integrated package has all the primary applications and works pretty much the same way, each does have its own distinctive look and feel. Customers have expressed their preferences by what they purchase and, for the most part, have chosen a camp to stick with: Lotus/IBM, Novell/WordPerfect, or Microsoft. Yet each company continues to sell its individual applications separately as well.

Knowledge Check

1. When you begin a work session, which programs are loaded, and in what order?
2. To what is the work session process identical?
3. What actions in the work session process correspond to the processing step (refer to figure 3.18)?
4. What should you know before you start a command or action?
5. What steps should you follow before you switch off the computer's power?
6. What is an example of software ambiguity?
7. Why might you prefer to use integrated software?

Key Terms

application	application software	communications software
compound document	database management system (DBMS)	desktop publishing (DTP)
I-beam pointer	insertion point	integrated software
presentation graphics	scrolling	software ambiguity
spreadsheet	stand-alone	word processing

ISSUES AND IDEAS

What Is a "Killer Application?"

The search for the next big "killer application" has been going on ever since Dan Bricklin and Bob Frankston created the first spreadsheet program, VisiCalc, for the Apple II in 1979. A *killer app* is a program that's an instant hit, one whose usefulness is immediately apparent. Lotus Notes, a multipurpose application designed to be used by many people working together, is generally considered a killer app since it was largely the reason IBM bought Lotus. Paul Keegan, writing in *The New York Times Magazine*, puts it this way: "Just as the Lotus spreadsheet gave companies a reason to buy IBM personal computers in the 80's, the company (IBM) is now gambling that Notes will be the leader in the next big wave of business computers. . . ."[5]

Software developers are always on the lookout for the next great killer app—perhaps because they hope to make a killing on it. Some of the software technologies that have the capability to create the future killer app include artificial intelligence, neural networks, speech recognition, international language translation, pen-based computing, and videoconferencing. As yet, none of them has reached killer status.

5. Paul Keegan. "The Office That Ozzie Built," *The New York Times Magazine*, October 22, 1995, 50.

Perhaps the next contender is a type of software that is used to create something called the compound document. This software can almost be considered another layer of software between the operating environment and the applications. Simply defined, a **compound document** is a single file that has been created by two or more applications. For example, a document that has text from word processing and a worksheet from a spreadsheet *and can be opened and used by either application* is a compound document.

Both Apple and Microsoft are hotly competing in the compound document arena, creating software that works with their operating environments and applications to make the new software easy to use and versatile. Apple's software, jointly developed with IBM, is called OpenDoc. Microsoft's version is called OLE, for Object Linking and Embedding. If the compound document works, and works well, it could change the way we work with computers. In an IBM technical white paper, the software is described in this manner:

> OpenDoc is a compound document component architecture. Designed initially by Apple Computer to provide an object-oriented end-user environment, the concept of a compound document has evolved far beyond the original word processing focus. A compound document in this new environment has become analogous to a structured container that allows a variety of functions or data (that is, objects) developed for different purposes to appear as a united application.

The *objects* referred to are portions of the document: text, graphics, a portion of a spreadsheet, a list of names. When you click text in OpenDoc, the menu for, say, word processing tasks appears so that you can perform its specialized tasks. Likewise, if you click the graphic image, the graphics application's menu appears, and so forth. The idea is that no matter what application created the objects, they can be harmoniously integrated into the compound document.

The compound document's future is promising, for it represents a step away from working with data and one toward working with information. Instead of starting a specific application to work with a document, we open documents that are served by the applications. What might be next? Is it possible that we could reach a point where applications don't actually make an appearance on-screen—don't require us to use menus or click icons—but instead work in the background? Beyond that point, is it possible that we could begin working with an idea and then let the software find the best application, or applications, with which to express that idea? Now that just might be a killer application.

CRITICAL THINKING

1. What are the incentives behind creating a killer application?

2. How might a software company determine and define a killer app?

3. How would you use compound document technology?

4. Give some thought or discussion to what you and your colleagues might like to have in a "killer" software application.

ETHICS:

Who Owns Software?

If you walk into a retail store or call a mail-order company to buy software, you pay for it—but you don't own it. Instead, you've purchased a license to use that software, as set forth in the license agreement that comes with it. By virtue of the fact that you've purchased the software license and broken the shrink wrap, you accept the terms of the license. You ought to read it and see what you've agreed to.

There are, however, several kinds of software, not sold in normal commercial channels, that reflect what might be called a "people's ethos." The way these kinds of software are sold or distributed places the ethical responsibility for their continued presence in the market and even their improvement squarely on the user's shoulders.

Shareware is software that has been developed primarily by small companies or self-employed programmer-entrepreneurs. Like commercial software, it is copyrighted, but it is made available on a trial basis. If you like it, mail your check; if you don't like it, don't use it. Shareware is usually inexpensive.

Public domain software is *not* copyrighted and can be freely distributed without obtaining permission or paying a fee to the author.

Freeware is copyrighted software that can be used without paying a fee; it cannot be resold for profit.

The man who has campaigned longest and hardest to keep software free is Richard M. Stallman, who was on the faculty at MIT for many years. Stallman created an editing program called EMACS, which was infinitely customizable by anyone who used it. Stallman sought to keep it that way, with the only caveat being that whoever used EMACS and modified it would return the improved version for others to use. "I called this arrangement the EMACS commune," Stallman wrote. "As I shared, it was their duty to share; to work with each other rather than against."[6] Stallman rebelled against the commercialization of software, and for many years has waged a campaign to make all software free.

6. Steph Levy. *Hackers* (New York: Dell, 1984), 416.

Critical Thinking

1. What statement are programmers who create noncommercial software making about commercial software?

2. Why might you have doubts about the quality and integrity of noncommercial software? Would it affect your decision to purchase or use it?

3. Is someone who uses a shareware program and doesn't pay for it any less a software pirate than a someone making illegal copies of a copyrighted program?

4. Do you agree or disagree with Richard Stallman's desire to keep software free? Defend your position.

THE LEARNING ENTERPRISE

The Learning Enterprise

Your enterprise now has a mission and an organizational structure, and you have finished a rough blueprint of your information resources. In this chapter, the objective is to give each knowledge worker a work assignment and to determine the workers' software needs and requirements.

The first task is for each person in your department or function is to choose a job. The group must make these decisions together so that all agree on the department needs and individual assignments and you can make sure that there is no duplication. Each person writes down his or her job title and a description of the duties, using the form given in this problem. Bear in mind that you'll be working together and sharing information.

The next decision is to select applications from the list of six provided in the chapter. This consideration affects the choice of the operating environment. Your enterprise is a fairly typical one, so about 90 percent of your organization will be using PC compatibles with Windows 95, and about 10 percent will be using Macintosh personal computers.

If your departments have approximately five knowledge workers, and if the application is well suited to a departmental task, let one person choose a Macintosh.

Uses for PC compatibles and Macintoshes usually break out this way:

PC

   Word processing

   Spreadsheet

   Database management system (DBMS)

   Communications

   Presentation graphics

   Desktop publishing

Macintosh

   Word processing

   Spreadsheet

   Presentation graphics

   Desktop publishing

1. Write down the applications you think you'll be using, and make a list of the documents you might create with each application. Use the list of documents you developed in Chapter 2 to create this list.
2. Create a model for a compound document. Draw or describe it, and explain how it would be useful in your own personal tasks. Show how you might use it to share information with your fellow knowledge workers.

SAMPLE FORM

Name:

Job Title:

Job Description:

Information Responsible For:

Duties in the Work Group:

Type of Computer and Operating System:

Applications Used:

Compound Document:

Chapter Review

Fill in the Blank

1. To perform specific tasks, a computer needs _____, which come in the form of _____.
2. The programs that operate and maintain a computer system are called _____.
3. There are three types of PC system software: (a) _____, (b) _____, (c) _____.
4. The automatic software routine that starts a computer system is called a(n) _____.
5. There are three types of utility software: (a) _____, (b) _____, (c) _____.
6. The way the computer and its software are presented to people is called the _____.
7. There are three basic types of human-computer interfaces for PCs: (a) _____, (b) _____, (c) _____.
8. The _____ is a vertical bar that tells you where the next character typed will appear on the screen.
9. A(n) _____ is an on-screen symbol that represents a program, a data file, or function.
10. GUI stands for _____.

Circle the Correct Answer

1. A (prompt, disk drive designation) is the character or message that tells you that a computer system is ready to accept a command or input.

2. The (menu, BIOS) has been re-created as a pull-down feature in the graphical user interface.

3. (Multitasking, Typing commands) is a major advantage of the GUI.

4. Knowledge workers use the (operating environment, applications) most frequently.

5. The (pointer, I-beam) is used to issue commands in the GUI.

6. The (toolbar, status bar) contains icons for the most frequently used commands.

7. The (scroll bar, menu bar) is used to move through a document.

8. The (PC compatible, Macintosh) was the first PC to have ease of use built into its operating environment.

Review Questions

1. What is software ambiguity, and why do we need to be aware of it?

2. Describe the steps in a work session.

3. Explain the advantages of the GUI operating environment over DOS.

4. What is the purpose of using an integrated software package?

5. Do all computers require system software?

6. Identify the following aspects of the application screen.

Title bar

Menu bar

Toolbar

Scroll bar (vertical)

Scroll bar (horizontal)

Status bar

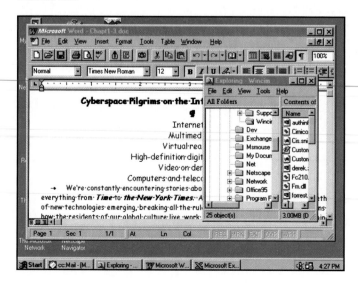

Discussion Questions

1. Describe the evolution of the human-computer interface from the simple command line to the multifunctional graphical user interface.

2. Why do the four steps in a work session correspond to the four data processing steps?

3. Why do Windows and the Macintosh Finder appeal to knowledge workers?

4. Discuss examples of software ambiguity in respect to (a) intentional features designed to offer optional ways to perform a task or command and (b) difficult or complex features in which procedures are unclear or difficult to perform.

5. Discuss the advantages and disadvantages of stand-alone applications versus integrated software packages.

6. As discussed in the Home Page, what are the most important criteria for buying application software?

INTERNET DISCOVERY

Here are some Web sites to help you explore the different types of software. You can select all these sites from Yahoo menus. First, using your Web browser software, type **Yahoo.com** or select it. Then move down the alphabetical listing to **Computers and Internet** and select it. Look for the following:

Operating systems: DOS, Macintosh OS, and Microsoft Windows

The topic **User interface** has information of interest.

For application software, use this URL:

http://www.bgnett.no/linker/pc.eng.html

Here you'll find thousands of programs described. Select five that interest you.

WHAT IS A COMPUTER?

There is no reason for any individual to have a computer in the home.

Kenneth W. Olsen, founder and retired president of Digital Equipment Corporation, the second-largest computer maker in the world, in a 1977 speech

A computer is a device that accepts *data*, performs arithmetic or logical operations that manipulate or change the data, and produces new results from that data. *Information* is derived from data. A human being is involved in many of the operations the computer performs, especially in working with the results the computer produces. Computers are capable of manipulating and changing data, which may take many different forms: text characters, numbers, graphic images, representational symbols such as © for copyright, the Greek letter sigma (Σ), and even musical notation, for example, the treble clef.

After reading this definition, you might think that many machines or devices qualify as computers—and you'd be right. Computers come in many shapes and sizes. There are computers seen and unseen—from large, extraordinarily powerful computers used in weather forecasting to computers so small that they can be inserted into a human vein. Our studies focus on computers we can see and use, primarily in the world of work and business.

This book's primary focus is the personal computer, which you study in Module A. In Module B, you learn about the other types of computers. Module C explains how the computer works and how it processes data to turn it into useful information.

CHAPTER 4

Module A

The Personal Computer

Why It's Important to Know

The personal computer is the most widely used computer today. Once you understand the PC's hardware components, you'll know how all computers work, regardless of size.

The quest for computer literacy begins with the personal computer for most of us. The **personal computer** is a self-sufficient computing machine equipped with everything necessary for a person to perform data processing tasks. The personal computer has the following characteristics:

Figure 4.1
An example of a modern personal computer.

- It is a *stand-alone* computing machine; it contains all the necessary software and hardware required to do its work.

- It is designed for use by a single individual.

  - It is usually small enough to fit on a desktop or to stand beside a desk.

    - The average person can afford it.

There are many brands of personal computers, also known as **PC**s. IBM was the first formally to use the name—the IBM Personal Computer. Today, thousands of companies make PCs based on the original IBM design. These machines are known as *PC compatibles,* or *clones*. Companies such as Acer, Compaq, Dell, Hewlett-Packard, IBM, Tandy, and Zeos make PC compatibles.

The other popular PC is the Macintosh, made by Apple Computer, Inc. In 1995, three companies began making *Mac compatibles*, or clones. The first, Power Computing Corporation's PowerWave, is intended for sophisticated graphics designers, multimedia applications, and scientific uses. Radius Inc. and DayStar Digital also make Mac compatibles. Some other notable PCs are discussed in the Home Page feature.

The PC is sometimes called a *microcomputer*, a name reflecting two of the PC's primary characteristics. One, it uses a single integrated circuit chip called a *microprocessor* to perform data processing. Two, the PC is smaller than a mainframe or a minicomputer. *PC* and *personal computer* and *microcomputer* all mean the same thing.

The Modern Desktop PC

A personal computer represents a complete computer system. We character-ize the **computer system** as being composed of *people* using *data* and *pro-cedures* to work with *hardware* and *software* to create the end result, useful *information*. Without people, there can be no computer system, for comput-ers are operated *by* people and produce information *for* people. The five aspects of the computer system are *people, data, procedures, hardware*, and *software*.

In addition to the standard desktop model, personal computers come in many sizes: There are portables, laptops, notebooks, and palmtops. The most powerful models are called workstations.

The most common personal computer, however, is the desktop PC. Its main advantages are low cost, convenience, and expandability. It is *inexpensive* because of mass production and *convenient* because most people can easily learn to operate it, and it can be *expanded* or modified with add-on parts and components.

The personal computer system is made up of several types of hardware com-ponents. The following sections give you a closer look.

Hardware

Figure 4.2 shows a state-of-the-art personal computer. The physical com-puter itself is referred to as hardware. **Hardware** refers to any and all the components or physical devices—things we can touch and feel. Hardware includes the external cabinet and any electrical, electronic, or mechanical components either inside the cabinet or connected to it. Here are the most common personal computer hardware components:

- Processing hardware
- System unit
- Read-only memory (ROM)
- Random-access memory (RAM) — *wasn't really imp. till windows - multiple applications at once.*
- Secondary storage (floppy disk drive)
- Secondary storage (hard disk drive)
- Secondary storage (CD-ROM)
- Keyboard
- Pointing device
- Monitor
- Printer
- Routing components
- Control components

K - kilobytes Kilobytes - (1000 bytes)

m - mega bytes - (1,000,000 bytes)
G - giga bytes - (Billion !!)
T - tera bytes - trillion !!

Figure 4.2
The modern PC has all these hardware components.

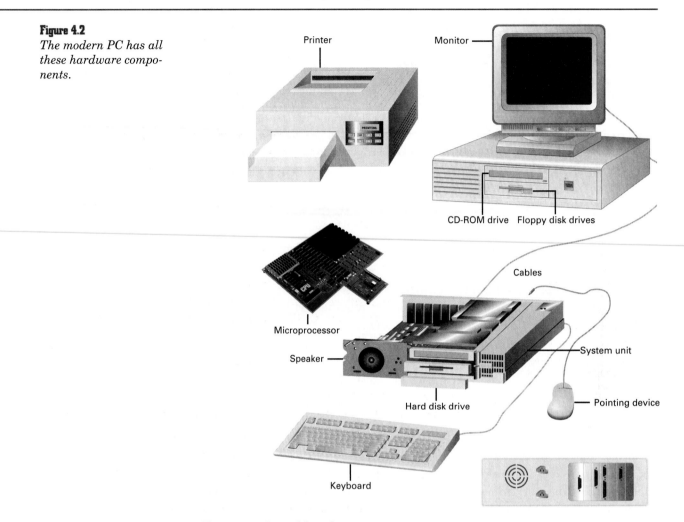

Processing Hardware

The most important kind of hardware is called **processing hardware**. This category includes all the components and physical devices necessary for the actual computing, or processing of data. The most important processing component is the microprocessor. The processing hardware is stored on a large printed circuit board, called the main circuit board, inside a cabinet called the **system unit**. The system unit is, essentially, the computer itself. It is where all computer processing activities take place.

Memory

Inside the system unit on the main circuit board, are two types of **memory**, which make up the computer's primary storage for instructions and data. Read-only memory, or ROM, is so named because the instructions it holds cannot be changed. Random-access memory, or RAM, is a form of temporary storage where instructions and data are kept while being used. RAM is sometimes called *main memory* or *primary storage*.

Now, refer to figure 4.2 to see how these hardware components are connected to make up a PC. They can be organized into the following groups: processing, memory, secondary storage, peripherals, and routing and control components.

HOME PAGE

PC GENESIS

The year 1995 marked the twentieth anniversary of the personal computer—at least as we know it today. Several prior claims to the title of "First Personal Computer" were made, all after the fact. For example, the Honeywell H316 "Kitchen Computer" was introduced in 1969 for the price of $10,600, and the IBM 5100 "desktop computer" required a pretty big desk and wallet, too—it sold for $20,000. Early personal computers were like the old Volkswagen beetle: they came with only the bare essentials, and most of the work was do-it-yourself. Their owners had to know a great deal more about computers than today's personal computer users. Here are some of history's notable PCs.

• The *Altair 8800*, introduced as a kit in the April 1975 issue of *Popular Electronics*, is generally considered the first modern personal computer. It had no monitor and no keyboard, just toggle switches and blinking lights.

The Altair 8800, 1975.

• The Apple I was built in a garage. In 1976, Steve Jobs and Steve Wozniak, two friends who grew up in Silicon Valley in northern California, combined their talents, sold a VW microbus to raise money, and launched an industry. Two hundred Apple I's were sold; the new, improved version was called the Apple II. In 1984, Apple introduced the Macintosh, which its inventor, Steve Jobs, dubbed "insanely great."

• Tandy/Radio Shack introduced the *TRS-80* hot on the heels of the Apple II in 1977. Because Radio Shack's management wasn't sure of much interest in personal computers when the TRS-80 Model I came off the assembly line, the company made

only enough for each retail store to have one. The doubts were unfounded: the TRS-80 sold very well, and today Tandy is sold in Radio Shack stores everywhere.

The Apple I, 1976.

The TRS-80, 1977.

• On August 12, 1981, IBM introduced the *IBM Personal Computer*. The press release included a photo of two children using the computer to play games. Businesses bought 100,000 machines the first year, and it dawned on IBM—and the industry—that the PC was not a toy.

The IBM Personal Computer, 1981.

- Adam Osborne was a technical writer and visionary, who introduced the world's first portable personal computer in 1981. Dubbed the *Osborne-1*, it weighed 28 pounds, fit under an airline seat, and came with all the necessary software programs. Although short-lived, the Osborne-1 launched the quest for smaller and portable personal computers—which have evolved to the *notebook computers* of today.

The Osborne-1, 1981.

- In 1982, Xerox developed the *Star* computer, a prototype with many advanced features that made it very easy to learn and use. Today, the Star is best known as the computer that inspired Steve Jobs to create the Lisa, which became the Macintosh, the first commercial PC to employ many of the Star's innovations.

The Star, 1982.

- The Personal Digital Assistant, or *PDA*, is the smallest personal computer currently available. Unlike its counterparts, the PDA usually employs a special stylus for writing on the screen. The first PDA was Apple's *Newton*, introduced in 1993. Although you may not want to write a novel using a PDA, it's handy for taking notes and keeping track of appointments. Most PDAs can also send and receive phone calls, faxes, and electronic mail messages.[1]

The Apple Newton PDA.

HOME PAGE REVIEW QUESTIONS

1. From what year do we commonly date the first personal computer?

2. What company is a major player among PC compatibles?

3. What company has been a leading innovator in PCs?

4. Who invented the first portable computer?

---

1. Rochester and Gantz. *The Naked Computer*, and additional author research.

Secondary Storage

Mounted in the system unit are several types of secondary storage devices: the floppy disk drive, the hard disk drive, and the CD-ROM drive. **Secondary storage** refers to the hardware components that enable you to store programs and data permanently, or indefinitely, so that they may be used again. **Storage devices** are usually housed in the system unit.

RAm - primary storage
everything else - secondary storage

Peripheral Hardware

The second kind of hardware is **peripheral hardware**. A **peripheral** is a hardware component that is physically separate from but connected to the processing hardware. The connections for peripherals are mounted in or on the system unit cabinet. Some peripherals are essential for doing work. You use the **keyboard** to enter data and instructions. A **pointing device** is another input peripheral that works with the keyboard; the most common pointing device is the **mouse**. You use the **monitor**, or video display screen, to view your work. The **printer** provides a finished paper printout of the results of your work.

Routing and Control Components

Other hardware components direct the instructions and/or data from one component to the next, making sure that each does its task properly. Some of these components are complex electronic circuits and may reside within the system unit. Others are cables and other connecting devices between the system unit and the peripherals.

These hardware components are common to all computers, large or small. A personal computer has a single system unit, or cabinet; one model is the *desktop,* and the other is the *tower,* which stands on the floor (see figure 4.3). A larger computer's processing hardware may fill many refrigerator-size cabinets. Because a PC is used by one individual at a time, it has only one of each primary kind of peripheral. In contrast, a larger computer usually has hundreds of keyboards and monitors enabling many people to use the computer at the same time.

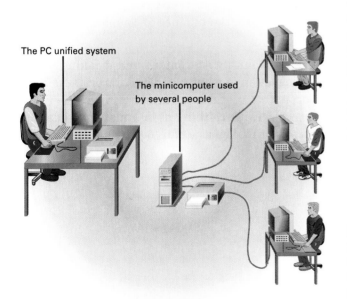

The PC unified system

The minicomputer used by several people

Figure 4.3
The PC is a unified system for one user. The minicomputer or mainframe is used by many people at the same time.

Software

The term **software** refers to the programs and instructions that tell the computer what to do. In general, when you or I use a computer, we are trying to accomplish a task or solve a problem. We use the computer to work more efficiently. Software, in the form of *programs*, or *instructions*, tells the computer what to do. For example, a software program may perform simple calculations, dial a phone number, print a document, or alphabetize a list of customer names. Software is one of the five components in the *computer system*.

Figure 4.4
People called programmers create programs for knowledge workers to use.

Programs or instructions must be created in a specific language that the computer can understand. A **programmer** is a person who understands the problem or task and can turn it into instructions the computer understands. This process is called **programming**. Programmers create software, which is stored on computer disks for the computer to use, as illustrated in figure 4.4.

The specific tasks we ask the computer to perform are often referred to as *procedures*; a procedure is a set of clearly defined steps. For example, you might ask the computer to prepare the season statistics for a favorite athlete or team. The mathematical formulas you enter are the *procedures*, and when they are properly organized, you have a program capable of working with the *data*, which in this case is the player's or team's record. The computer, using the program it has been given, processes the data, and the result is *information:* a batting average, the number of completed passes, or the win/loss record, for instance.

Information is processed data. It is data with content and meaning, which give the data added value. Information is what a person interprets from the data, interpretations that people find useful in a variety of ways (see figure 4.5). One knowledge worker says, "I like to think of information as 'data in formation,' or ordered in a way that makes it useful to you—so that you can use it for some purpose."

Figure 4.5

Data in formation: These young fans can discuss their favorite player's performance much more easily when the data is well-organized. Each of these baseball cards is like a database of player statistics.

Knowledge Check

1. Name some of the primary characteristics of a personal computer.
2. What is a PC compatible?
3. Name the two types of hardware.
4. What type of hardware is kept in the system unit?
5. Name one or two examples of a peripheral.
6. Where is data held temporarily? Permanently?
7. What must the computer have in order to accomplish a task or solve a problem?

Key Terms

computer system	hardware	keyboard
memory	monitor	peripheral
peripheral hardware	personal computer (PC)	pointing device
printer	processing hardware	programmer
programming	secondary storage	software
storage device	system unit	

ISSUES AND IDEAS

What Is a Microcomputer?

Ted Nelson, widely considered one of the true visionaries of computers, has argued vigorously—and humorously—against the term *microcomputer:*

> So-called *microcomputers* are no different, were never any different from regular computers.
>
> *Micro-* is properly a prefix for things that deal with smallness, not for things that embody it. A microSCOPE looks at small things, a microTOME slices thinly. . . . There is no difference between the "micro-computer" of the seventies and the "minicomputer" of the sixties. It's on a desk? There were minicomputers on desks. It's for one individual to use? That started in 1960.
>
> My point is that the so-called microcomputer is NO DIFFERENT FROM WHAT CAME BEFORE, EITHER IN FUNCTION OR SIZE. No, "micro-computer" is a marketing term, cleverly concocted to suggest inferiority without actual difference. Like certain racial terms. . . . There are no words as foolish as "microcomputer" in other fields, because in any other field a comparable word would be too silly.[2]

CRITICAL THINKING

1. Get a second opinion from someone who feels that *microcomputer* is a perfectly valid term.
2. Why do you think that Nelson is so adamant about this terminology?
3. Is this argument basically philosophical—a computer is a computer is a computer—or is it, as Nelson suggests, an attempt to belittle the micro-computer?

M̲odule B

Other Types of Computers

Why It's Important to Know

The computer has evolved over time, growing smaller, more powerful, more useful, and less expensive. Knowledge workers may spend most of their time using PCs, but they are likely to come in contact with many other types of computers as well.

The computer has evolved over the past fifty years. Leaving behind the notion that the world would need only a few very large computers, we have seen computers proliferate while at the same time they grew smaller and smaller. Three words characterize the evolution of computers: *better, faster, cheaper* (see figure 4.6).

2. Ted Nelson. *Computer Lib* (Redmond, WA: Tempus Books/Microsoft Press, 1987), 45.

- Computers have become much *better* at their tasks; they are less prone to breakdowns and are capable of doing far more than their predecessors of even five years ago. Computers have evolved from being capable of performing only one task at a time, such as calculating a complex mathematical equation, to performing simultaneously a multitude of tasks, such as accounting, order processing, inventory control, and financial analysis.

- Computer speeds have increased; today's personal computer is *faster* in every respect than yesterday's mainframe computer. (But today's mainframe has also grown correspondingly faster.)

- Computers continue getting *cheaper* as their performance improves. The first commercial PCs appeared in the mid- to late 1970s and cost at least $10,000 each; five years later, in 1981, the first IBM PC cost $5,000. Today, you can own a PC twenty times faster than the first IBM PC for one-third the price.

Analog display

Digital display

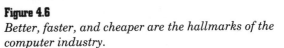

Photos courtesy of Ford Motor Company

Figure 4.6

Better, faster, and cheaper are the hallmarks of the computer industry.

At one time, people thought that personal computers were not capable of performing sophisticated tasks. This idea has proved false. On the other hand, not long ago people thought that the large computers used in business would soon be obsolete. Today, we realize that we need both large and small computers to handle all the various needs of complex organizations. This module describes some of the other types of computers you're likely to encounter.

The Modern General-Purpose Computer

The earliest computing devices, dating back hundreds of years, were mechanical. All the types of computers you will study in this module are electronic, digital computing machines that date back to the 1940s. The term **electronic** refers to a machine that uses such components as vacuum tubes, transistors, or silicon chips. All electronic devices, whether a vacuum tube-powered stereo amplifier or a transistor radio, require electricity. **Digital** means a computer that uses the binary arithmetic system as the basis for its operation. *Binary arithmetic* uses only two digits: the 0 and the 1, and is compatible with the way electronic switching circuits work in computers—on/off, on/off, on/off.

Most modern computers used in government and business are **general-purpose computers**. *General-purpose* means that the computer can be adapted to a variety of tasks without modifying or changing its basic design when a task changes. This characteristic is very important. It distinguishes the computer from nearly every other type of machine or device. For example, you cannot use a toaster to make orange juice or a saw to bore holes in wood; yet a computer can handle tasks from word processing to accounting at the touch of a key. A PC is a general-purpose computer. The photo essay in figure 4.7 shows a variety of computers and their uses.

Figure 4.7
Different types of computers.

Courtesy of International Business Machines Corporation

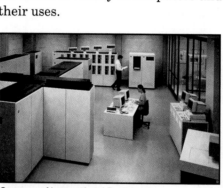

Courtesy of International Business Machines Corporation

Courtesy of Apple Computer, Inc.

Courtesy of Hewlett-Packard

Courtesy of Apple Computer, Inc.

Courtesy of Cray Research, Inc.

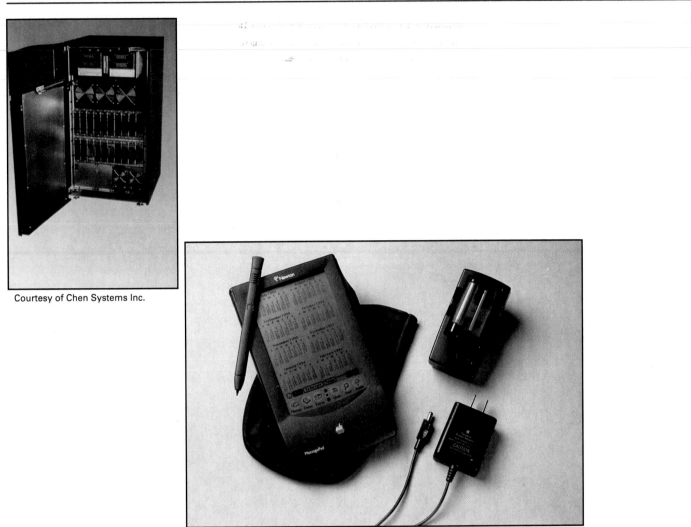

Courtesy of Chen Systems Inc.

Courtesy of International Business Machines Corporation

The Special-Purpose Computer

In contrast to the general-purpose machine is the **special-purpose computer**. As its name implies, it is used for a single, unique purpose or application. The earliest computers were used in research labs for a single purpose—conducting lab experiments or calculating such things as prime numbers. Over time, a variety of interesting uses for special-purpose computers have emerged—from oil prospecting to supporting the astronauts on space missions. These computers have proven equally as useful as their general-purpose counterparts. A popular example of a special-purpose computer is a video game, such as Sega or Nintendo. These special-purpose computers use microprocessors that are as powerful as those of personal computers. The number of special-purpose computers is growing; today's automobile has as many as 50 special-purpose computers, for everything from anti-lock braking to curtailing emissions.

Types of Modern Computers

Even though personal computers are on the cutting edge of technology, big computers haven't gone away. Business, government, research labs, non-profit organizations, and many other social institutions need computers of all sizes to accomplish the tasks necessary to remain viable, competitive, and productive. Here are the other types of computers in use today:

- The *workstation:* a more powerful desktop computer than a PC

- The *minicomputer,* or midrange computer: small but expandable

- The *mainframe* computer: a large system

- The *parallel processing computer:* a mainframe-power supercomputer that uses more than one processor

- The *supercomputer:* the world's fastest computer

The Workstation

Figure 4.8
A typical workstation.

Courtesy of Silcon Graphics, Inc.

A **workstation**, like its personal computer counterpart, is a computer that fits on a desk and is usually used by a single individual (see figure 4.8). A workstation may be a more powerful than average PC, or it may be a specialty computer made by a computer company such as Sun Microsystems, or it may be a PC that has more than one type of processor. A workstation may use a special operating system that lets it be shared by several users. The workstation combines the ease of use and convenience of a personal computer with some of the power and functions of larger computers. It is often used for special applications, such as drafting or designing. Workstations usually cost more than most individuals can afford for personal use.

Workstations were first used by engineers to design everything from airplanes to computers. Today, workstations are widely used in a great variety of organizations and industries. An example is the desktop publishing workstation system. It is often used in companies where publishing is the primary or secondary business, such as a publisher of newsletters or a software company that writes and produces the documentation manuals for its software. Desktop publishing workstations are designed to work with large or complex documents and enable writers, editors, graphic artists, and page layout specialists to perform their specialized tasks on a document while sharing a single system.

The Minicomputer

The **minicomputer** is a versatile, medium-sized computer designed so that many people can use it at the same time (see figure 4.9). The mini was introduced as a smaller, less expensive alternative to the mainframe. Early minis were designed for use in a variety of special-purpose tasks, such as manufacturing, engineering, science, and process control. Minis have been used to

- Provide instructions for manufacturing equipment, such as presses or robots
- Operate guidance systems for aircraft
- Measure seismographic fluctuations in dangerous mines
- Regulate such things as temperature in cooking vats of soup, spaghetti sauce, or chocolate

Figure 4.9
A minicomputer.

Courtesy of International Business Machines Corporation

Yet over time, the mini became a viable general-purpose computer for business, serving the needs of a small to medium-sized company or a department of division of a larger company. You may see minis in use at your college, often managing the electronic card catalog in the library. Many of the sharp distinctions between mainframes and minis, between minis and workstations, and between workstations and powerful personal computers have been blurred by technological advances and the changes to better, faster, and cheaper. Today, most general-purpose minis can perform tasks that once required a mainframe. Minis are often called *midrange* computers. Minis are frequently connected to other minis and are often used to provide connections between mainframe computers and personal computers.

For example, Kentucky Fried Chicken built an information system designed to support its home-delivery service. The company installed Hewlett-Packard and IBM midrange computers in its central offices and PCs in the local stores. When orders are received at the central locations, a midrange computer determines the nearest retail outlet and electronically forwards the order. The system is so advanced that it provides the delivery person with a street map. This system enables KFC to capture valuable customer information just once—at the first contact. KFC hopes to link its computer system to interactive television technology so that in the future, customers can place orders directly through their TVs.[3]

Mainframe Computers

The first computer used in business was the mainframe computer. A **mainframe** is a large, general-purpose computer capable of performing many tasks simultaneously while hundreds, even thousands, of people use it at the same time. A mainframe is made up of many cabinets filled with electronic gear connected to the main computer cabinet, which led to its being called a mainframe (see figure 4.10).

Figure 4.10
A mainframe computer.

Courtesy of International Business Machines Corporation

Mainframes have dominated the corporate and governmental computing market for many years and may do so for many years to come. Yet, like any computer, the equipment must be upgraded and replaced from time to time. The Federal government is known to use computer systems far past their prime, an unwise practice when a mission is critical. *The New York Times* reported in a front-page story that the Federal Aviation Administration (FAA) is using mainframe computers that are more than 25 years old "and long past due for replacement, but updated technology has been delayed because contractors have not been able to write the software for new equipment." The IBM 9020e Display Channel Complex mainframe computers, which have been in use at major U.S. airports since the early 1970s, are becoming unreliable. "Cables are brittle, vacuum tubes do not stand too much handling, circuit boards can break when flexed, and transistors can fail under the strain of testing," the *Times* reports.[4] So far, the expertise of human air traffic controllers and the ability to repair the computers quickly has warded off accidents.

3. Mary Hayes. "KFC's Delivery Challenge," *Information Week*, July 18, 1994, 58–9.

4. Matthew L. Wald. "Aging Control System Brings Chaos to Air Travel," *The New York Times*, August 20, 1995, 1, 32–33.

In the 1980s, people found many uses for the personal computer in business, and it was soon obvious that the mainframe needn't be used for all computing tasks. In fact, many companies have shifted various tasks off the mainframe and on to minis and personal computers. The mainframe is still a viable computer. It is commonly used as a storehouse for vast amounts of data—such as financial management, accounting, personnel, and inventory—that organizations need to operate properly.

Parallel Processing Computer

Most computers have a single processor; the **parallel processing** computer has many processors, all running simultaneously—in parallel. A bank's automated teller machine (ATM) is a good example. Suppose that the bank has one ATM in the lobby, and ten customers walk in to use the ATM. One customer wants to make a deposit, another a withdrawal, another a payment on her car loan, and another just wants to check account balances. Customers have to wait in line to perform their transactions. But if the lobby has ten ATMs, no one has to wait, and the computer can perform all the different transactions in parallel.

Parallel processing computers now come in many different sizes and designs. One of the latest parallel processing computers is the Chen Systems CS-1000, installed at the Oak Ridge National Laboratory in Tennessee (see figure 4.11). This computer is used to manage the lab's Financial Automated Management Environment, in order to make the financial information stored there available to other organizations within the Lockheed Martin Energy Systems Corporation. The CS-1000 has eight processors, each the same as a very powerful PC's microprocessor, but it is possible to upgrade the computer to a total of 256 processors.

Courtesy of Chen System Inc.

Figure 4.11
Steve Chen with a Chen Systems parallel processing computer.

The Supercomputer

The **supercomputer** is the most outstanding example of a special-purpose computer. Supercomputers are the most powerful computers on earth. They usually perform a single very complex task at a time—a task that requires massive processing power (see figure 4.12). For example, a supercomputer may be given the task of analyzing the way a chemical carcinogen attaches itself to a DNA molecule; this task might take hours, days, or even weeks to compute. Once that task is completed, the supercomputer can be used for another task. It can even be put to work as a general-purpose computer.

Figure 4.12

A supercomputer: Thinking Machines' Connection Machine.

Courtesy of Thinking Machines Corporation

Supercomputers are most often used in experimental governmental and scientific research facilities, such as the Lawrence Livermore Labs in California, the Los Alamos National Laboratory in New Mexico, and the National Center for Supercomputing Applications at the University of Illinois at Champaign-Urbana. But supercomputers are also used in business and government. For example, Electricité de France, the national electric utility company of France, has two Cray supercomputers in use for scientific purposes. One application, called neutron scattering, performs over 200 tasks to help determine that a nuclear reactor is safe when workers are changing or reloading the uranium rods in the core. The other application is a study and training simulator for post-accident operations at a nuclear power plant.[5]

Many businesses found uses for supercomputers, and a variety of new machines were introduced to meet the market needs. Today, computers that perform parallel processing and supercomputing tasks are known as *high-performance computing systems*, defined in *I/S Analyzer* as "the most powerful machines in their class, whether they be mainframe, minicomputer or workstation. In other words, a supercomputer is a high-performance mainframe; a parallel or massively parallel computer is a high-performance minicomputer. . . ."[6] Large manufacturing companies often make a supercomputer available to engineers and specialists in research and design. Financial firms and brokerages have used supercomputers to analyze market trends, and credit card companies have found supercomputers useful for making highly accurate predictions of credit card fraud. However, the demand for supercomputers is shrinking as less expensive alternatives become available.

5. Jack B. Rochester. "High-Performance Computing," *I/S Analyzer*, May 1991, 7–8.

6. Ibid., p. 4.

HOME PAGE

ENIAC: THE FIRST ELECTRONIC DIGITAL COMPUTER

In 1937, the League of Nations commissioned a group of the world's best minds to forecast future technologies. When these experts submitted their report, it contained no mention of a computer. Yet even as the group convened, John Atanasoff, a physics professor at Iowa State University, was at work on the first electronic computer.

Many of his ideas found their way into ENIAC, the Electronic Numerical Integrator and Calculator. ENIAC was a project commissioned by the U.S. Army's Ordnance Department, which was looking for a better way to plot ballistics trajectories. John Mauchly and J. Presper Eckert headed the project, which began in 1943 at the University of Pennsylvania. Some of the best academics in the country worked on ENIAC.

Courtesy of Charles Babbage Institute, University

Some of the ENIAC engineers.

When ENIAC was completed in 1946 at a cost of $3 million, it stood two stories high, weighed 30 tons, and covered an area the size of two football fields. Its electronic circuitry was comprised of 18,000 vacuum tubes, 70,000 resistors, 10,000 capacitors, and 6,000 switches that made up 100,000 circuits. When ENIAC was turned on, it was said, the lights of Philadelphia dimmed. Yet ENIAC was not much more complicated than a modern handheld calculator or digital wristwatch and could perform a mathematical computation about as fast.

World War II ended in 1945, before ENIAC could fulfill its original purpose. However, ENIAC was put to work on calculations for atomic bomb research at the Los Alamos, New Mexico, government research laboratories. Today, some portions of ENIAC are on display in the Smithsonian Institution in Washington, D.C.

ENIAC was a special-purpose computer. Mauchly and Eckert designed its descendant, UNIVAC (for Universal Automatic Computer), as a general-purpose machine. They formed their own computer company to build UNIVAC, but they were not good businessmen and eventually had to sell their interests to Remington Rand.

Courtesy of International Business Machines Corporation

Eckert stands proudly near the ENIAC computer.

The UNIVAC I was introduced in 1951, and the U.S. Bureau of the Census received the first one to tabulate census statistics. The government also bought two more. Shortly thereafter, a computer made its first television appearance. UNIVAC was used to predict the 1952 Presidential election—and it did a good job. UNIVAC predicted that Dwight Eisenhower would win 438 electoral votes to Adlai Stevenson's 93. The actual count was 442 to 89.

The next year, General Electric became the first private business to buy a computer. Then other businesses began clamoring for UNIVACs, which were sold in rapid succession to Metropolitan Life Insurance, U.S. Steel, DuPont, and Franklin Life Insurance Company.

HOME PAGE REVIEW QUESTIONS

1. What modern device is comparable in speed to the original ENIAC?
2. Where can you see ENIAC today?
3. What was the first commercial version of the ENIAC called?
4. Where was the first one installed?

The *better, faster, cheaper* progress in computing machines has led to an exciting new paradigm for determining how computers are used, as shown in figure 4.13.

Figure 4.13
MIT's Athena is one of the country's most advanced computing systems.

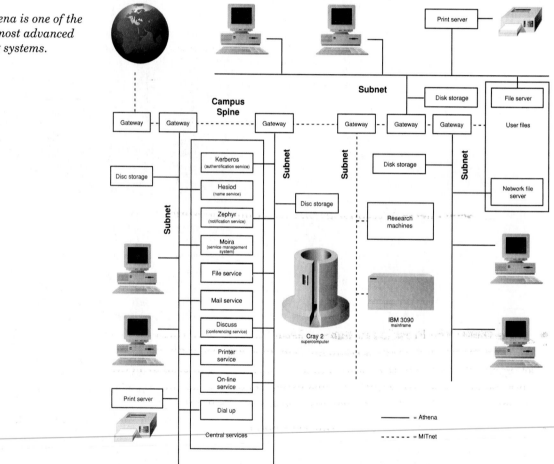

In the past, computers of all sizes were viewed as separate machines, unable to connect with others. Today, we more commonly think of the computer *system* as an electronic infrastructure for a business, not unlike the human nervous system. As the diagram shows, today we think far less about the type or size of the computer we're using and far more about the computing *resources* and the *information* we need to do our work.

Knowledge Check

1. What three words describe the growth and progress of the computer industry?
2. What are the two prime characteristics of the modern general-purpose computer?
3. Why is using binary arithmetic important for computers?
4. What distinguishes the general-purpose computer from other machines?
5. What is the difference between a mainframe computer and a minicomputer?
6. How is the role of the mainframe changing?
7. How has the minicomputer business changed?
8. What are the primary uses for workstations?
9. What is the trend with special-purpose supercomputers?

Key Terms

digital	electronic	general-purpose computer
mainframe	minicomputer	parallel processing
special-purpose computer	supercomputer	workstation

ISSUES AND IDEAS

How Does Technology Affect Society?

What are the social effects of technology on society and the world? Consider these events:

- Around the year 1000 A.D., a Spaniard named Magnus invented a brass counting machine that looked like a human head. It had figures instead of teeth and looked so diabolical that priests destroyed it with clubs.

- In the 1600s, the Frenchman Blaise Pascal built a calculating machine for his father to use in his accounting. The machine could do the work of six people and so outraged the citizens that, fearing unemployment, they rioted in the streets. Pascal, disgusted, renounced all interests in science and mathematics and devoted the rest of his life to God.

- In 1799, an Englishman named Edward Ludd organized disgruntled factory workers, who followed him from factory to factory destroying machines. Ludd left his imprint in the term *Luddite,* which describes someone who resists new technology.

- In the 1800s, Dutch factory workers, driven to work ever faster, kicked their wooden shoes into factory machines to slow or shut them down. Their shoes were called *sabots,* and their act became known as *sabotage.*

In his book *Rebels Against the Future,* Kirkpatrick Sale writes that "Industrialism is always a cataclysmic process, destroying the past, roiling the present, and making the future uncertain. It is the nature of the industrial ethos to value growth and production, speed and novelty, power and manipulation, all of which are bound to cause continuing, rapid, and disruptive changes at all levels of society."

Sale also assails technology's effects on nature: "Since technology is, by its very essence, artificial—that is to say, not natural, a human construct not otherwise found in nature, where there is no technology—it tends to distance humans from their environment and set them in opposition to it, and the larger and more powerful it becomes the greater is that distance and more effective that opposition. . . . At a certain point, one that we have reached in the 20th century, technology can completely overwhelm so many other elements of that world as to threaten its continued existence...."[7]

CRITICAL THINKING

1. What lessons about technology and society do the examples portray?
2. Do you, like author Sale, see technology as an unnatural power or a force bent on the destruction of nature or society?
3. What are the ethical aspects of the "technosphere"? Of the "biosphere"?

The Millennium Bug

When programmers began creating software in the 1950s and 1960s, they didn't design programs to read dates beyond December 31, 1999. The millennium bug means that once the date changes to January 1, 2000, software will stop working. In addition, the millennium bug is likely to produce a vast array of accounting errors, such as adding a hundred years of interest instead of interest for one year.

Data Dimensions, a computer consulting firm, says the software conversion project to update the U.S. Government's computers could cost as much as $75 billion in equipment and labor. A typical federal agency will have to convert as many as 100 applications, which will take up to 60,000 people-days (people-days is a way to measure programming work).

The millennium bug has been a subject of discussion on the RISKS Forum on the Internet for years. Dr. Stan Niles reported that "The Social Security Administration (SSA) is the only agency to begin the task of millennium conversion, which is expected to take the SSA seven years."

Jim Huggins of the University of Michigan wrote that the *Detroit News* (12/2/95) reported that the average Fortune 500 company will spend $100 million to convert its own systems. He also writes

> Bill Schoen, a computer programmer from Ford who the article states was the first to write about the 2000 problem in 1983, says he contacted every Fortune 500 company about the problem at that time, but few were

---

7. Kirkpatrick Sale. *Rebels Against the Future: The Luddites and Their War on the Industrial Revolution; Lessons for the Computer Age* (Reading, Massachusetts: Addison-Wesley, 1995), 264–267.

interested. "The people that were in positions of power then were going to be retired long before this problem kicked in. They didn't care about a mess they weren't going to be around to clean up."

For more online information about the millennium bug and a Frequently Asked Questions (FAQ) file, use this URL:

http://www.year2000.com/

CRITICAL THINKING

1. Why do you suppose that the original programmers—and the governmental agencies—were so short-sighted about this problem?

2. Will it *always* take seven years to correct the dates? Do some research on your own to find out what agencies other than the SSA are doing about the problem.

3. Will the millennium bug affect your personal computer? Do some research and find out.

Module C

Computer Operations and the Data Processing Process

Why It's Important to Know

Once you understand the four data processing steps, you'll have a basic understanding of what the computer is doing as you use it. You'll know what each hardware component does, and you'll be able to learn application software more quickly and easily.

In the earlier definition of a computer, you learned that the computer accepts data. The term **data** is defined as facts, numbers, and other symbolic representations, suitable for communication or interpretation, that can be processed by a computer (see figure 4.14). At the simplest level, this definition means that when you type the letter *a* on the keyboard, the computer processes the symbol as the letter *a* and then displays it on the monitor.

---

8. RISKS Forum 17.09, filename time2000.rch

Figure 4.14
Data consists of letters, numbers, symbols—anything that is suitable for communication.

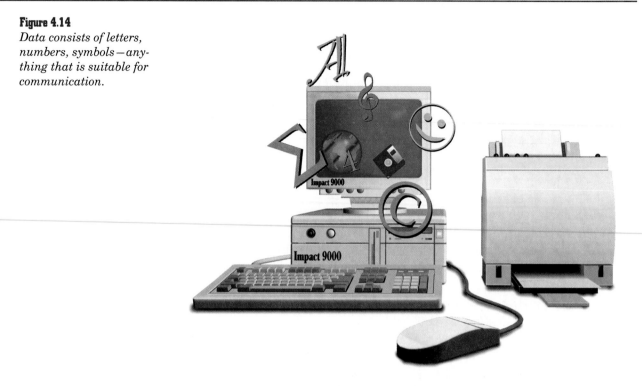

Note: Strictly speaking, a single unit of data is called a *datum*; data is the plural term. Using the word *data* to refer to both singular and plural forms is commonly accepted.

When people or a computer do something with data, we call the procedure *processing*. **Data processing** is the activity of the computer system. This term describes the specific procedures required to prepare, manipulate, and store data. Once data processing has occurred, the product can be made into useful information for people. Data is the raw material of information. *People,* using their mental capabilities, turn the *data* from computers into useful *information* through understanding, integrating, and applying it in the world.

How Computers Perform Data Processing

We commonly turn to computers to help us solve a problem or to perform a task that would take too long or be too difficult to do ourselves. The problem or task must be presented in a specific and precise manner. If it is not, the computer can't perform properly. As you learned in Module A, computers need instructions, in the form of programs, to solve problems and perform tasks.

An **instruction** is typically a group of characters organized in an action statement, which the computer understands and can execute. For example, an action statement might be to add 2 plus 3. An organized set of instructions is called a program. A **program** is a complete sequence or set of instructions directed to a specific purpose, written in a language the computer understands and executes (see figure 4.15).

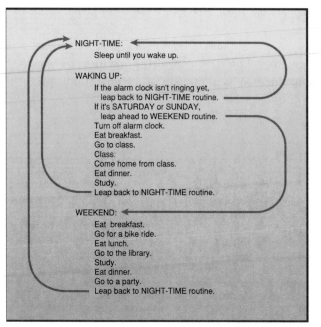

Figure 4.15
An instruction is a line of code; a program is a group of instructions.

Programs can be simple or sophisticated—the more sophisticated, the more complex the results. Sophisticated programs are often a collection of simple programs that have been designed to work together. Here are a few examples:

Simple	Sophisticated
Calculator	Spreadsheet
Clock	Appointment Scheduler
Notepad	Word Processing
Cardfile	Database Management System
Line Printer	Type Font Manager
Phone Dialer	Communications Management Program

Computer Operations

The computer performs two types of operations on data: arithmetic and logical. The **arithmetic operations** a computer performs are simple addition and subtraction. For example, adding the numbers 2 plus 3 equals 5. To subtract 2 from 3 the computer also adds, but it does so by creating a negative number so that –2 plus 3 equals 1.

The **logical operations** a computer performs compare values in order to perform logical tests and make decisions. For example, is the number 2 *greater than* (expressed with the $>$ sign) or *less than* (expressed with the $<$ sign) the number 6? As you can see, the fundamental way computers operate is simple. In fact, data processing involves only four steps.

The Four Data Processing Steps

You can now put everything you have just learned into a practical context so that you can better understand how the computer performs its tasks. Processing data with a computer involves four specific steps: input, processing, output, and storage (see figure 4.16).

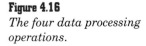

Figure 4.16
The four data processing operations.

1 INPUT
When you type characters into the word processor, they are stored as ASCII codes, shown here as numbers, in a section of memory set aside for them. As you type text or scroll through a document, the word processor reads more text and formatting codes from RAM and processes them through a display driver.

2 PROCESSING
If the word processor is DOS-based, the driver uses the PC's BIOS to translate ASCII codes to text. The BIOS matches a table of ASCII numbers to their corresponding bitmapped patterns of screen pixels, which are then lighted to form characters. A formatting code activates an alternative pattern built into the BIOS, causing the text to be displayed as bold or underline.

3 OUTPUT
When the word processor sends text to be printed, a printer driver performs a similar function to translate text and formatting into the patterns of dots created by all printers, whether dot-matrix, bubble-jet, or laser.

4 STORAGE
Output may also be directed to RAM or to a disk drive for permanent storage.

When we give the computer instructions or data, this step is called **input**. An instruction is either an arithmetic operation, such as addition, or a logical operation. The data consists of the numbers, for example, 2 and 3. When the computer performs the addition of 2 plus 3, it is **processing**, as you have already learned. The product of the processing, or the answer, is **output**—in this case, the number 5. Needless to say, you don't often use the computer to perform tasks that a simple calculator can do. The example of adding 2 plus 3, however, demonstrates the simplicity of the computing process. The computer is no more complicated than this; its primary virtues are its speed and versatility. It is able to count and compare very, very rapidly.

Once the data is processed and output has been produced, there is an additional step. It is **storage**, or holding the data in computer memory. This storage may be for a short, indefinite period, or permanent, depending on the type of storage you choose.

You can summarize these four important steps in data processing as follows:

1. *Input*. Either instructions or data
2. *Processing*. The computer carrying out its instructions, either an arithmetic or logical operation, on the data
3. *Output*. The data produced after processing
4. *Storage*. The option of retaining the data temporarily or permanently

Data processing has one final aspect. As said before, a person forms part of the computer system, for without people, the computer's work has little purpose. The computer can accept input, process data, produce output, and store data all day long, but unless a human uses this data for something, it is still just plain old computer data. The purpose behind data processing is to give the person, or knowledge worker, something useful. Once the raw data has been processed, it has had value added to it. The result, in most cases, is *information*—data presented in a meaningful form that people can use. That information can be simple, like a list of names and addresses, or it can be complex, such as a list of every female customer who bought a Ford Explorer with the Eddie Bauer options package in August of 1991. Typically, the information resulting from the four data processing steps is what we see displayed on the monitor or printed on the printer.

HOME PAGE

UNDERSTANDING COMPUTER HARDWARE AND DATA PROCESSING

Learning to use a personal computer is really no more difficult than learning to program a VCR. In fact, given the number of VCRs that constantly blink 12:00, some might think it's easier! Contrary to popular opinion, it's difficult to damage a personal computer in normal usage; at the very worst, you might lose something you typed. Here are the three most important things to remember:

1. *Take your time.* You don't need to rush. Look at the screen, make sure that you know where you are and what you're going to do *before* you do it.

Screen A.

2. *Do everything carefully.* Press keys carefully, and be sure to look and see whether everything is as it should be on the monitor. If it's not, be sure that you know what to do to reverse the last step you took or to get out of the situation.

3. *Never start something you don't know how to end.* Before you start the computer and its programs, be sure that you know how to exit the programs properly before you switch off the power. Before you start an action within a program, such as moving text or copying formulas, be sure that you know how to conclude that action with the desired outcome or results. Think about each step you must perform before you begin.

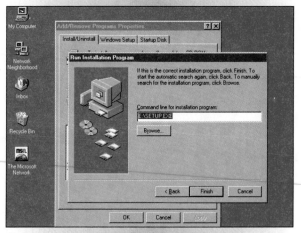

Screen B.

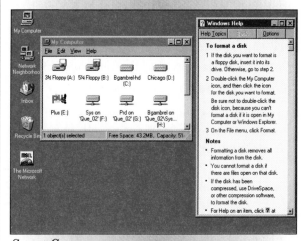

Screen C.

If you follow these three simple guidelines, you'll have very few problems working with your personal computer.

HOME PAGE REVIEW QUESTIONS

1. How can you tell what is active in Screen A?

2. How can you tell which button is active (the one to click) in Screen B?

3. What's a good thing to do when you're not certain about a procedure (Screen C)?

Knowledge Check

1. What is data?
2. What is data processing?
3. Of what is a program comprised?
4. What kind of computer operation adds two numbers?
5. What kind of computer operation compares two numbers?
6. What are the four data processing steps?

Key Terms

arithmetic operation	data	data processing	input
instruction	logical operation	output	processing
program	storage		

ISSUES AND IDEAS:

Lottery Computer Runs Amok

Date: Tue, 16 May 1995 07:50:47 -0700

From: Bruce Findlay

Subject: "Double your fun" (CA lottery woes)

Excerpted from the local paper of record, the *San Jose Mercury News* [probably on 15 May 1995, which is when a similar item appeared in the *San Francisco Chronicle*. PGN]:

> Lottery computer gets ahead of itself
>
> California Lottery officials scrambled Sunday to make amends for a computer glitch that unexpectedly halted sales three hours early for the weekend's $3 million jackpot. By mistake, the computer began issuing tickets for Wednesday's upcoming drawing instead—causing anger and confusion for lottery players and retailers around the state. . . . Lottery officials decided Sunday that players affected by the mix-up will have their tickets honored in both contests. . . . Lottery spokesman said an employee of Sacramento's GTECH, which runs the lottery computer, was conducting routine maintenance when he mistakenly entered a command that closed the draw pool for Saturday's drawing. . . . it wasn't clear how many tickets were sold during the three hours but GTECH has promised to make up any losses to the state.

RISKS? Where do I start? Why was an employee able to disturb what is supposed to be an unriggable game? If GTECH does not know how many tickets were sold, how will the loss be made right. And since when does basic operator error mean the same thing as "computer glitch?"[9]

---

9. Source: RISKS Forum 17.13, filename lottery.rch

CRITICAL THINKING

1. Many computer experts have often expressed the view that computers should not be allowed in such activities as elections or games of chance like lotteries. What problems do you see in this situation?

2. Is it possible that the computer is being improperly blamed for the error?

3. What might be a possible *long-term* solution to this problem?

ETHICS

Respect and Privacy in the Workplace

Human beings tend to be competitive and want to get ahead in life. It's no secret that certain people will do unethical—even illegal—things to make money or advance their careers. This fact becomes an issue of particular concern in the office, where unethical people can easily gain access to your computer and the data stored in it.

Knowledge workers must work together to achieve common goals. There should be respect for the rights and privacy of others and their data in the workplace. In the real world, however, unethical people most likely will violate other people's rights and read private or personal files. In fact, some have been known to sabotage a colleague's work in an attempt to make him or her look bad. To some extent, security systems should take care of this problem, but as the old saying goes, locks keep only honest people honest. What can you do about this problem? Don't create temptations.

- Always keep your computer secure. Remember, the computer and its data are your employer's property. Don't leave it accessible to others when you're away from your desk. Conceal your password, and follow the company's security precautions.

- Be sure that all your important work is backed up and stored in more than one physical location—on more than one computer system or on a disk you keep with you.

- Keep your personal data on a separate floppy disk. Lock it in your desk or take it home with you at night.

- Finally—and this is the hardest part—realize that you are part of the problem as well as part of the solution. Encourage your fellow employees, through polite conversation and personal example, to behave ethically. Find mutually shared values and beliefs, and don't be afraid to discuss them; people who are basically moral and honest find it difficult to do wrong to those they know personally. And when you see illegal or unethical things occurring, discuss them with your manager or supervisor. To do otherwise makes you an accomplice to wrongdoing, and it also makes it easier to look the other way the next time something happens.

Critical Thinking

1. How would you react if when discussing computer security and ethics you heard a fellow employee say, "Well, everyone's doing it, so why should I care?"

2. Plan a computer security and ethics workshop for your class or the place you work. Make a list of the topics you want on the program.

3. Discuss how you would deal with an employee who violated company policy.

THE LEARNING ENTERPRISE

Most enterprises the size of yours need many different types of computers. Although most knowledge workers use PCs in their daily work, they may need programs that are running or data that is stored on other computers. For example, the marketing manager may need to review the personnel files of an employee up for review. The manufacturing manager may want to check last year's production figures. The purchasing agent may want to solicit prices for raw materials from several different vendors.

All these and many more tasks require the use of all kinds and sizes of computers. In many cases, the PCs are connected in some way to the other organizational computers. Your organization should evaluate its computing needs and determine what, if any, other computers it needs to have, or needs to be connected to in order to share programs and data.

Your assignment is to

1. Prepare a report stating what computers you need.

2. Describe the tasks and purposes the computers will be used for.

3. Determine where the computers should be located.

Here are some guidelines to follow in choosing the computing machines:

- Workstations are used by engineers, designers, desktop publishers, or power users.

- Minicomputers are used as departmental or organizational computers to serve a group of knowledge workers, or in special-purpose tasks described in Module B.

- Mainframes are used primarily at the enterprise level for general-purpose tasks described in Module B.

- Supercomputers are used by engineers and scientists.

Here are two additional assignments:

1. Review the Ethics section at the end of the chapter. All knowledge workers must prepare security statements stating how they will secure their computer and data, and what measures they believe should be taken to ensure respect and privacy for all.

2. Appoint one knowledge worker to collect and assemble all the responses, prepare a summary, and distribute it to (a) everyone in the department and (b) each of the other departments or functions.

Chapter Review

Fill in the Blank

1. The personal computer, or PC, is sometimes called a(n)
   _____.

2. The smallest personal computer currently available is the PDA, or
   _____.

3. The most powerful desktop computer is called a(n) _____.

4. The most important kind of hardware is called _____ hardware.

5. A second kind of hardware, _____ hardware, is physically separate from, but connected to, the hardware described in question 4.

6. The PC has a single system unit, or cabinet. One model is the desktop and the other, which stands on the floor, is called a(n) _____.

7. A(n) _____ computer uses the binary arithmetic system as the basis for its operation.

8. Binary arithmetic uses only two digits: the _____ and the _____.

9. The processor performs two types of operations: _____ and _____.

10. A(n) _____ is a sequence or set of instructions.

Circle the Correct Answer

1. The first personal computer was a kit introduced in a magazine in (1975, 1985) by (IBM, Altair).

2. A complex set of instructions is called a (procedure, program).

3. In order to perform (programs, procedures), computers use (programs, procedures).

4. Computer instructions that cannot be changed are stored in (RAM, ROM).

5. Computer instructions and data that are being used are stored temporarily in (RAM, ROM).

Review Questions

1. Describe several characteristics of personal computers.
2. List the five aspects of a computer system.
3. List a primary hardware component from each of the following groups: (a) processing, (b) memory, (c) secondary storage, (d) peripherals, (e) routing and control components.
4. Name the two kinds of computer memory.
5. Describe the following peripheral devices: (a) keyboard, (b) pointing device, (c) mouse, (d) monitor, (e) printer.
6. Besides the PC, what are some other kinds of computers in use today?
7. What are the four steps in data processing?
8. In a few words, describe each of the following types of computer: (a) workstation, (b) minicomputer, (c) mainframe, (d) parallel processing computer, (e) supercomputer.

Discussion Questions

1. Using an example from your personal experience(s), explain how the four data processing operations are used.
2. Research a specific technology, such as the cotton gin, automobile, or computers, and find an example of how society reacted to its introduction. Look for a popular book, song, movie, work of art, or other media of the time.
3. Create a list of ten Do's and Don'ts for computer ethics and security.
4. Discuss the different purposes for each of the types of computers. In what ways are all computers alike?

INTERNET DISCOVERY

Explore these Web sites to learn more about various types of computer hardware and computer companies:

yahoo.com/Business_and_Economy/Companies/Computer

Then select from the listing:

mainframes

supercomputers

workstations

Or use these URLs:

http://www.ibm.com (IBM)

http://www.pc.ibm.com/ (IBM personal computers)

http://www.digital.com (Digital Equipment Corp.)

PART II

COMPUTER HARDWARE

Chapter 5   **The System Unit**

Chapter 6   **Peripherals**

KNOWLEDGE WORKER INTERVIEW WITH RICH TENNANT

E-mail address: the5wave@tiac.net

Rich was born in Chicago on May 15, 1947. He attended the College of DuPage, the Chicago Academy of Fine Arts, and the Berklee College of Music in Boston. Rich's interests have taken him in many directions: from selling vacuum cleaners, to acting, to gourmet catering, to working as a paralegal, to playing jazz piano, to painting houses.

Rich never considered a career in computers, but one day found himself working as a typesetter at *Computerworld,* a weekly newsmagazine. In the throes of boredom, he began doodling. Unfortunately, he was caught. Fortunately, it was by the art director. Rich soon found that there was a huge market for good cartoons about the computer industry. That was in 1981, and the phone hasn't stopped ringing since. Today, he runs his business from his home/studios in Rockport, Massachusetts, producing and licensing The 5th Wave cartoons to companies and publications in the US and abroad.

Author: What's your day like?

Rich: By the time I arise on Monday mornings, my staff has the office humming. She hands me a fax from *Federal Computer Week* with a few stories from the forthcoming issue that give me ideas for the editorial cartoon. I pick one I think has the best potential for a dramatic visual statement; then I make notes and begin some sketches.

By Tuesday, I'm really starting to warm up. I talk to the editor of *Computerworld* about my weekly cartoon. My staff calls Federal Express—that's the signal to increase my productivity, and by the end of the day I ship the finished cartoons to both publications. I spend the rest of the week producing 5th Wave cartoons for books, direct market and advertising campaigns, and other ongoing clients.

Author: For example?

Rich: Take *PC Magazine.* Please! I peruse the latest issues, primarily the ads, to keep abreast of current trends—then I relate them to what feels like odd or quirky elements of our culture. These are four-color cartoons for the "Abort, Retry, Fail?" humor page.

I've also produced cartoons for a European print media campaign for Micro Focus, a software company. I did an original cartoon for a calendar cover for Acer personal computers. I've also done lots of illustrating for several computer books. And you can always see

COMPUTER HARDWARE

my collected work in my books, *The 5th Wave: BYTE-ing Humor*, and *Version 2.0*, proudly published by Andrews & McMeel.

Author: What does "The 5th Wave" refer to?

Rich: Alvin Toffler, in his book *Future Shock*, calls the Information Age the third wave. The 5th Wave is simply the silly side of the third wave.

Author: What kind of computer do you use in your work?

Rich: I have a Power Macintosh with a 17-inch NEC color monitor, a Power 28.8 data/fax modem, and a laser printer. The computer is for office work; I do my illustrating by hand. But I have a custom font that emulates my cartoon lettering. Now my staff can type and print captions on the computer and strip them into the drawings. We scan my cartoons into an image database where they are stored digitally, so that they can be faxed or e-mailed as files to clients.

Author: How do you view the future of knowledge work?

Rich: Well, I hope computers will become more transparent!— meaning we'll use them without having to see them or twiddle with them all the time. I also think there'll be lots more dumb "little"computers dedicated to doing one or two things, like hooking up to the Internet, instead of one big smart desktop mainframe that does things we never wanted to do in the first place.

Author: Where do you think future opportunities lie?

Rich: In what? The computer industry? How do I know, I'm a cartoonist!. . . Opportunities also lie in creating easier links between technology and humans. The person who makes a fortune won't be the one that builds a bigger, faster, better VCR, but the one who makes it easier to set the digital clock.

Author: What advice would you give today's college student?

Rich: Most fifth-graders can give more advice about learning to use a computer than I can. Nevertheless, don't worry too much about how the computer does what it does or your head will explode (this has actually happened to several people). Instead, try to recognize the *patterns* in how the computer does what it does. Each function, isolated, is more difficult to retain. Look at the *interrelatedness* of several functions.

Author: What are your favorite nonwork uses for the computer?

Rich: Solitaire, collecting and organizing stories, letters, anecdotes, and scanned images of my family.

Author: What do you do for fun?

Rich: I still play jazz piano, I love to cook, and I collect science-fiction and horror movies from the 1950s.

THE SYSTEM UNIT

To see a world in a grain of sand
And a heaven in a wild flower,
Hold infinity in the palm of your hand
And eternity in an hour.

William Blake (1757–1827), "Auguries of Innocence" in *Poems from*
the Pickering Manuscript

Blake wrote these words more than 200 years ago, but they could almost describe today's silicon chip, an *integrated circuit,* or IC for short, created from silicon that has been refined from ordinary beach sand.

Complex computer circuitry that once filled entire rooms now rests in a sliver of silicon you can hold on the tip of your finger. ENIAC, two stories high and covering 15,000 square feet, was composed of 18,000 glass vacuum tubes that made up 100,000 circuits. A 1/4-inch-square integrated circuit contains more than a million circuits. Is it any wonder we call it a miracle?

Integrated circuits fill the system unit, carrying out various instructions. In this chapter , you take a closer look at computer hardware. First, you lift the cover off the system unit and look inside, where millions of electronic circuits are busily performing tasks that turn data into information and everyday office workers into knowledge workers. Then you take a close look at the chip that does the computer processing and examine the types of data processing that computers perform.

Module A

The Main Circuit Board

Why It's Important to Know

The main circuit board is the central nervous system of the computer. All the most important components are either mounted on it or connected to it.

The **main circuit board** is where the computer's primary electronic circuitry resides. The main circuit board, which used to be called the motherboard, contains a number of electronic components that are essential in the processing and storage operations in some of the routing and control operations. Think of the main circuit board as a silicon city, where all the necessary functions and services can be found without having to travel elsewhere.

Figure 5.1 shows an actual main circuit board, which is commonly found in the bottom of the system unit. Although main circuit boards, like cities, are often laid out differently, they all have certain components and circuitry.

Figure 5.1
The main circuit board is an electronic computer city.

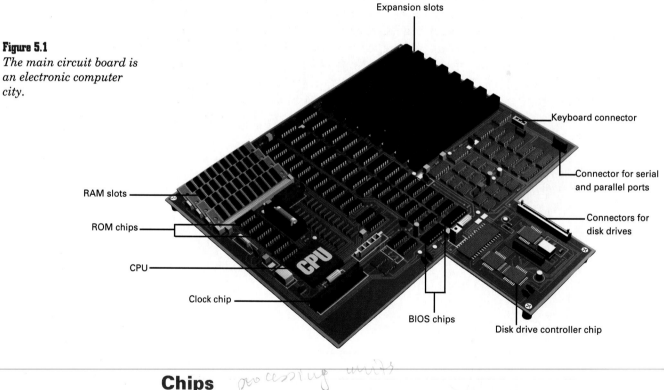

Chips

Integrated circuit chips are used in several different ways in a computer:

1. CPU (microprocessor chip). You'll quickly recognize the microprocessor: It's the largest single chip. In some older PCs, you'll find a numeric coprocessor chip.

2. ROM chips

3. RAM (SIMMs). Note that the SIMMs are actually sets of ICs (integrated circuits) used for random-access memory (RAM), mounted on a small connector card similar in appearance to the expansion cards mounted in the expansion slots at the rear of the board.

4. Video display controller chip

5. Disk drive controller chips. Note that the video display controller chip and disk drive display controller are normally found on expansion cards, a topic explained in a later section.

6. Coprocessor chip. In some PCs, the **coprocessor** is a microprocessor support chip that takes over when additional or special processing is needed. The most common uses for the coprocessor are math-intensive and graphic applications. With the advent of the Intel 80486 series microprocessor (and higher) and the Motorola 68040 series microprocessor (and higher), the coprocessing functions were combined in a single microprocessor chip.

Ports

A **port** is a connection from the main circuit board to a peripheral device. The peripheral is connected to the port by a special cable. Another term for port is *interface*, a word that is used to describe any situation in computing where two different aspects of the computer system meet to pass data back and forth. There can be various interfaces between hardware, software, and people. In the case of a port, however, the interface is hardware to hardware. Ports are arranged along the rear of the main circuit board and provide connections through the back of the system unit. Ports commonly connect the main circuit board to the following:

- Keyboard
- Monitor
- Printer
- Mouse (or other pointing device)
- External modem (used for communications)
- Joystick (used for games and simulation)

Figure 5.2
The ports connect the computer's main circuit board to the peripherals and thus to the knowledge worker.

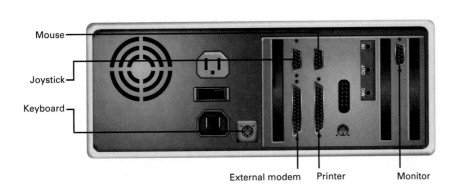

Mouse

Joystick

Keyboard

External modem   Printer   Monitor

Expansion Slots

Note the long plug-in strips at the left rear of the main circuit board. These strips, or receptacles, are called **expansion slots**, and expansion cards are inserted into them. An **expansion card** is a printed circuit card with circuitry that gives the computer additional capabilities. You may hear an expansion card referred to as an adapter card, or simply a *card*. Figure 5.3 shows an expansion card. Some cards are essential—for example, the video driver card; it has a port into which the monitor is plugged.

Figure 5.3

Expansion cards slip into slots facing the rear of the computer. If any have ports, they are accessible from the back.

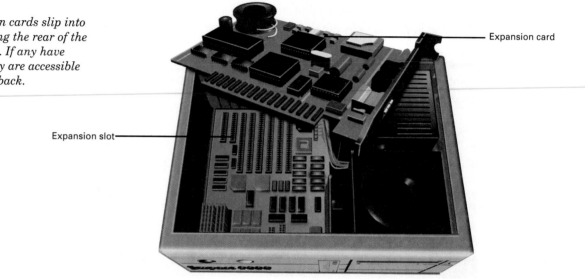

Expansion card

Expansion slot

Expansion cards are used to connect the following devices to the main circuit board:

- Video monitor
- Disk drive
- Scanner
- External CD-ROM
- Internal modem
- Audio
- TV tuner
- Networking

And one other device is connected to the main circuit board. It's the computer's built-in speaker that beeps at you occasionally.

The Bus

This microscopic city that we call the main circuit board has one more important aspect—the bus. Like a bus that takes you from place to place in the city, the bus whisks the electronic bits—those 1s and 0s discussed earlier—from place to place on specific, predefined routes. A main circuit board's **bus** is an electronic pathway between various computer components.

HOME PAGE

COMPUTER SYSTEMS ARE LIKE HOME THEATER SYSTEMS

You can think of the computer as a home theater system. At the heart of the home theater is the audio-video receiver, which is like the personal computer system unit. Both systems have a number of peripherals connected; some are input, others output. Compare the two as shown in the illustration.

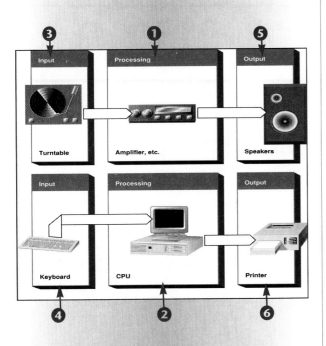

Computers are like stereos.

1. The amplifier receives input, in the form of electrical signals, from a tuner, turntable, or CD player.

2. The computer's processor receives input from the keyboard.

3. The tuner or turntable sends electrical signals to the amplifier.

4. The keyboard sends commands and instructions to the processor.

5. The amplifier processes the specific signals from an input device, amplifies the signal, and then sends sound output to listening devices, such as speakers or headphones.

6. The computer processes the data (input) and sends output to the monitor or printer.

The portable, or notebook, computer is like a stereo boom box. All the components—usually excluding the printer, which is analogous to the speakers—are contained within the system unit. Take a look around a personal computer and explore its peripherals, which are capable of doing a great deal more than a stereo's.

Both computer systems and home theater systems have forms of storage media that can be recorded on, or *written to*, such as computer disks and audio or video tapes. *Write* means the same thing as *record*.

The two most common types of storage devices for personal computers are floppy disks and hard disks. The home theater system's storage devices are a cassette tape deck or a VCR.

Both systems also use devices that can only play, or *read*, media. *Read* means the same thing as *play back*. For example, compact disc players play back prerecorded CDs but cannot record on them—at least not yet!

HOME PAGE REVIEW QUESTIONS

1. Create a chart that compares the components of the computer and home theater system.

2. How does this comparison help you understand the computer's four data processing operations? Why do you suppose they're so similar to the home theater system?

3. What does *write* mean the same thing as? What does *read* mean the same thing as?

4. What is the home theater's main read/write device?

5. What output component do both systems have in common?

Differences in Buses

Figure 5.4
A bus is a thoroughfare for travel in the electronic city.

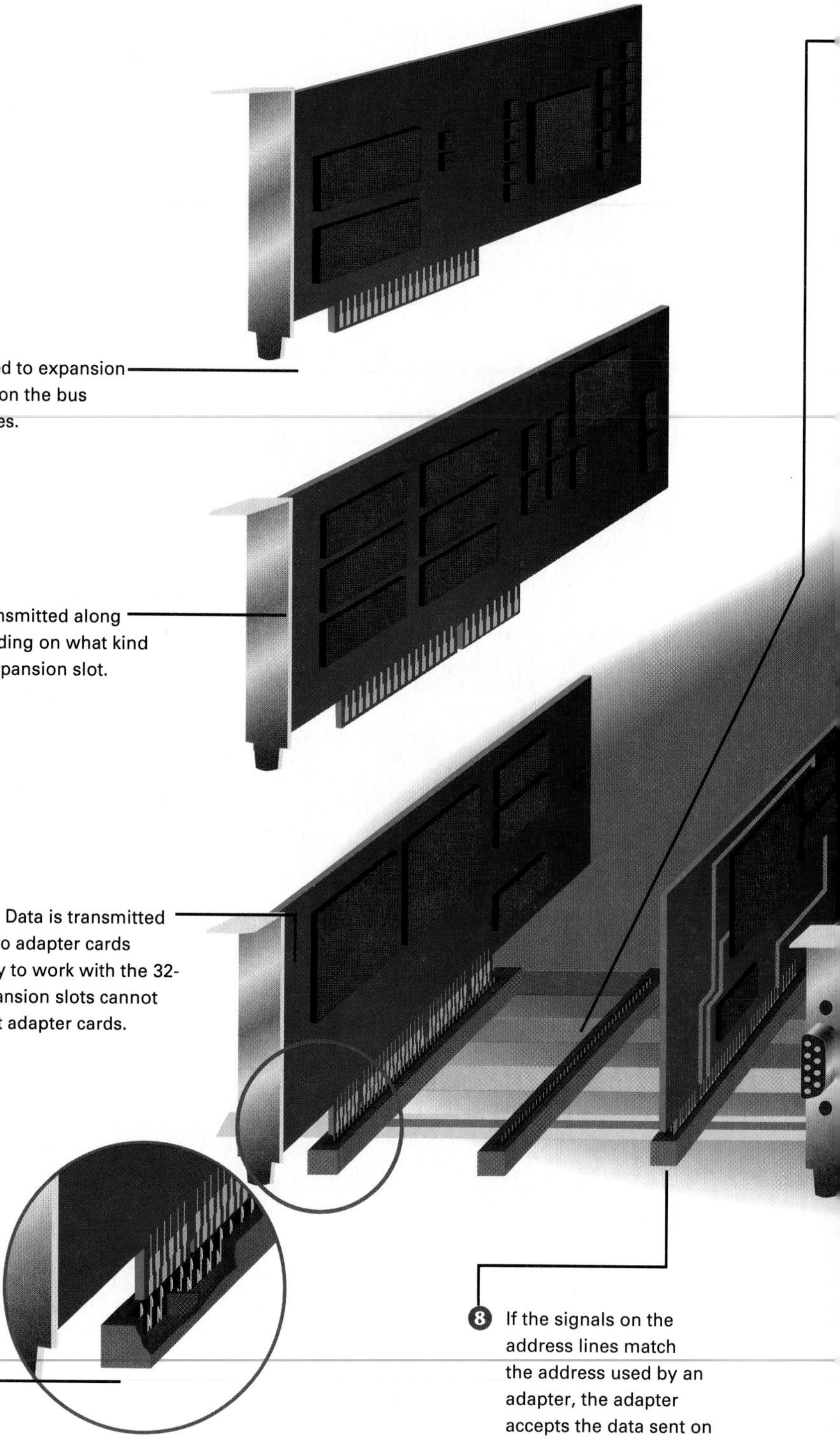

8-bit bus. Data is transmitted to expansion slots and other components on the bus along only 8 parallel data lines.

16-bit or ISA bus. Data is transmitted along either 8 or 16 data lines, depending on what kind of adapter card is used in an expansion slot.

EISA or MCA bus. Data is transmitted along 32 data lines to adapter cards designed specifically to work with the 32-bit buses. MCA expansion slots cannot accept 8-bit or 16-bit adapter cards.

EISA adaptability. The design of EISA expansion slots allows 8-bit or 16-bit boards to enter only far enough to make contact with a row of 16 connectors that handle data based on the ISA bus. But boards designed specifically for the EISA slot can enter farther and align their connectors with 32 special slot connections that handle data based on EISA specifications.

8 If the signals on the address lines match the address used by an adapter, the adapter accepts the data sent on the address lines and uses that data to complete the write command.

Courtesy of Ziff-Davis Press

Data Traveling along the Bus

1 Signals from the processor or other components travel along several parallel circuit lines. The number of lines depends on the type of architecture used for the bus. The simplest of them—the 8-bit bus used in the original IBM PC—uses 62 lines to connect to adapter cards. Any signal sent to an adapter card is received by all adapter cards.

2 Eight lines transmit electrical power to the adapter cards. Different lines carry different voltages.

3 Eight to thirty-two lines are used to transmit all data, regardless of whether the data is destined for memory chips, a display adapter, or a disk controller.

4 Twenty lines carry information to specify the address for which the data is intended. Each expansion card uses a specific, unique address—from among those available in the first megabyte of memory— that can be addressed by the operating system.

5 The remaining lines are used to pass control signals for common specific commands, such as read and write commands for memory and for each input/ output device.

6 Each adapter card along the bus constantly looks for appropriate signals along the command lines. When a signal appears on the write command line, for example, all the I/O devices recognize the command, and the memory circuits do not.

7 The I/O adapters alerted by the write command turn their attention to the address lines. If the address specified on those lines is not the address used by an adapter, the adapter ignores the signals sent on the data lines.

Note: Recently, the *local bus* for communicating with peripherals has gained in popularity. The design overcomes the speed limitation imposed on all other bus designs. The original bus was designed to run at 8MHz, which was roughly twice as fast as the original IBM PC's 8088 processor. As processor speeds increased to 10MHz, 25MHz, 50MHz, and faster, the bus speed stayed at 8MHz. The local bus is designed to transmit 32 bits of data at the local speed of a PC's processor. Usually, a PC with a local bus limits that architecture to one or two slots, used for display adapters or disk controllers, where speed is most crucial. Slower conventional expansion slots are used to communicate with the serial and parallel ports and with the keyboard, where speed is not crucial.

Personal computers have four bus pathways:

- The *data bus*, which sends bits of your data back and forth between the microprocessor and random-access memory during processing and temporary storage

- The *address bus*, which facilitates the assignments of processed data to specific memory locations in RAM

- The *control bus*, which carries the microprocessor's control unit signals from the currently running program to the proper peripherals

- The *expansion bus*, which connects the expansion slots to the computer, making the expansion cards an integrated electronic part of the computer

A fifth bus, the *local bus*, is often used instead of the expansion bus for operations that require a high-speed data transfer. For example, a local bus often links the microprocessor directly to the video card expansion slot.

Data (or bits) is transferred down the computer's busways in sets. Think of our city streets and the number of lanes; a two-lane street is like a two-bit wide bus. The wider the bus, the faster the computer can transfer data from one component to another. Not all buses are the same size; for example, the Pentium microprocessor has a 32-bit address bus, but a 64-bit data bus, making its processing very fast indeed.

Knowledge Check

1. Where does the computer's primary electronic circuitry reside?
2. What is the most important chip on the main circuit board?
3. What is the purpose of a port?
4. What are expansion slots used for?
5. Name an essential expansion card.
6. How is a local bus different from other buses?
7. Why is a 32-bit bus preferable to a 16-bit bus?

Key Terms

bus	coprocessor	expansion card
expansion slot	main circuit board	port

ISSUES AND IDEAS:

Computers—The Fine Line between New and Used

When is a new computer not new? Apparently when it's built with used and returned parts. There are legal distinctions between new and used products. Yet some computer makers remove from returned computers parts that are in good condition and reinstall these parts on other computers. How best to inform the public? A *Business Week* article states:

> Compaq Computer Corp. tried everything. There were lots of advertising, lawsuits, pleas to state attorneys general. Then Compaq sued Packard Bell in Federal District Court in Wilmington, Delaware, charging the company with false advertising. The suit came after Packard Bell PCs had outsold Compaq's for three straight quarters. Compaq's gripe: Packard Bell wasn't telling consumers that some of its computers were made with used parts.

> The distinction between new and used can be a fine one. Clothing and other goods are commonly returned to mail order houses and department stores, where they are put back on the shelves to be resold as new. A computer processor that has been used for several thousand calculations is indistinguishable from one just off the shelf. Indeed, manufacturers routinely "burn in" their products by running them for several hours to test them.

In this instance, the issue of used parts was not raised by a consumer protection agency but rather by a PC maker that uses only new parts. The company found itself in head-to-head competition with a competitor that routinely installed "serviceable used parts." But in its advertising, Compaq accused Packard Bell of selling "used computers."

The article further states that "Packard Bell recertifies good components from computers returned by customers and uses them to build new computers. Other PC makers do the same. Compaq uses only new components, selling returned machines as used in its factory store in Houston."[1]

CRITICAL THINKING

1. How would you define a new computer with "serviceable used parts"? Is it a new computer?

2. Does the fact that "other PC makers do the same" make the practice right?

3. What would be a satisfactory disclaimer for a PC containing used parts? How would the disclaimer apply to the burn-in period?

4. Has Compaq performed a public service by bringing this matter to the attention of the public? Would Compaq's efforts affect your decision to purchase a computer from Compaq? From Packard Bell?

---

1. Larry Armstrong and Gary McWilliams. "A PC War That's Not Exactly PC," *Business Week,* July 10, 1995, 42.

5. When purchasing a new computer, knowing what you know, would you ask about new versus used parts?

6. Research the lawsuit and find out what disposition has been made of the charges.

Module B

The Central Processing Unit

Why It's Important to Know

Processing is the most important activity of the computer. Without a processor, the computer wouldn't be a computer. To understand how the central processing unit does its work is to understand the nature and purpose of the computer.

The **central processing unit**, or **CPU**, is the computer's processing, control, and internal storage circuitry. The CPU is an integrated circuit chip containing the electronic circuitry that controls the interpretation and execution of instructions that are issued by an input device. But what exactly is an integrated circuit, and why do we use it?

The Integrated Circuit

Early computers were plagued by problems associated with the *vacuum tube*, a large, fragile electronic device that generated excessive heat and was relatively unreliable.

Courtesy of International Business Machines Corporation

The *transistor* replaced the vacuum tube. The transistor was small and simple and put out very little heat. Scientists and engineers were soon at work seeking ways to reduce the already small transistor and to improve its performance. Their work led to the silicon wizardry called an integrated circuit, or IC. An **integrated circuit** is a small chunk of silicon semiconductor material that contains hundreds of thousands to millions of electronic circuits. Each integrated circuit replaces one or more vacuum tubes, and an IC generates very little heat. An IC is often called a *chip* (see figure 5.6).

Figure 5.5
Smaller, faster, cooler: the vacuum tube was replaced by silicon circuits.

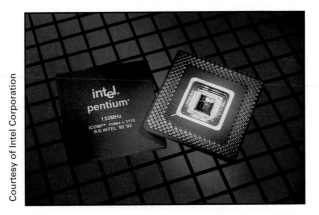

Courtesy of Intel Corporation

Figure 5.6
The Pentium is an example of an integrated circuit chip mounted inside a special case with electrical connectors that plug into a printed circuit board.

Types of Integrated Circuits

Integrated circuits perform many tasks today, depending on how they are designed and programmed. They are found in wristwatches, cameras, phones, cars, musical instruments—the list is endless. In computers, ICs may be any of the following:

- A central processing unit, or microprocessor
- A ROM (read-only memory) chip
- A RAM (random-access memory) chip
- A cache chip, which is a special type of memory
- A controller chip, used for routing electrical signals from one place to another—for example, between input and output devices

As you might expect, the most demanding task for an IC is as the computer's engine. That IC is called the microprocessor.

The Microprocessor

In large computer systems, a number of ICs may work together to perform the tasks of the CPU. A personal computer has only one engine—a very powerful one. The **microprocessor** is the personal computer's CPU on a single integrated circuit. It is an integrated circuit chip that combines the processing functions that required multiple—sometimes hundreds of—components or circuits in older, larger computers. The microprocessor is absolute proof that the computer industry's anthem is "better, faster, cheaper." In the case of microprocessors, cheaper means that each successive generation delivers more computing power for the same or lower cost.

Clock Speed

Regarding the *faster* aspect, a personal computer microprocessor measures CPU speed based on an internal timer, or clock. Thus, the measure is called **clock speed**. The clock speed is the pace at which processing takes place—the faster, of course, the better. Clock speed is measured in **Hertz**, which is a unit of measurement of electrical vibrations. One Hertz equals one cycle per second. The basic unit of CPU speed calculation is one million Hertz (Hz)—one megahertz, abbreviated MHz. The early personal computer performed significantly more slowly than minis and mainframes, but during the past few years, PCs have shown a more than tenfold increase in microprocessor speed. In fewer than ten years, clock speeds went from 4.77 MHz to 50 MHz, then to 66 MHz, to today's 100 MHz or more. The Home Page of this module tells the evolution of microprocessors and their speeds in MHz.

Microprocessors are found in cash registers, video games, toys, automobiles, stereos, and appliances, to name just a few uses. Now that you know a little about how ICs are used in computers, you are ready to explore their history.

The Evolution of the Integrated Circuit

The IC was created by Jack St. Clair Kilby, who was an engineer at Texas Instruments in Dallas. This electronics firm was working on what the engineers called "Micro Modules," miniaturized circuits for the military. Jack realized that because all "the components could be made of a single material (silicon), they could also be . . . interconnected to form a complete circuit." This discovery meant that all three main components in a circuit—the transistor, the resistor, and capacitor—could be placed, or *integrated*, on a single slice of silicon. Kilby created the first integrated circuit in 1958. Because electricity didn't have to travel as far, the circuits were faster.

In 1968, a microelectronics firm named Intel started up near Palo Alto, California, an area that has come to be known as Silicon Valley. Marcian E. "Ted" Hoff, a Stanford University graduate and an engineer at Intel, was asked to design a set of 12 chips for electronic calculators; each chip would perform certain functions. Ted considered this design inefficient, so he redesigned the twelve chips into four chips sharing a single processor that could be programmed to perform many tasks. This technique was exactly what mainframe computers did using far more circuits. Ted's creation was named the Intel 4004, and the company often referred to it as "a computer on a chip," or what we call a microprocessor today. The Intel 4004 was the first in a family of Intel microprocessor chips that led to the IBM PC.

Intel is the leading manufacturer of microprocessors for PCs. The other primary microprocessor manufacturer is Motorola, whose microprocessor is commonly used in Macintosh computers. Intel and Motorola have kept technologically neck-and-neck in introducing newer, more powerful, and more sophisticated microprocessors. Table 5.1 shows this evolution.

Table 5.1
The Evolution of Microprocessors

CPU Mfr	Date of Intro	Clock Speed (Mhz)	Word size (bits)	Used in/Comments
Intel				CISC Microprocessors
8086	1978	4.77	16	PS/2 Model 25
8088	1978	4.77	8	IBM PC
			10	PC XT
80286	1984	10-20	16	IBM PC AT
80386DX	1986	16-33	32	Compaq Deskpro 386
80386SL	1987	16-33	32	Power Saver - laptops
80386SX	1988	16-33	16	compatible with 286

CPU Mfr	Date of Intro	Clock Speed (Mhz)	Word size (bits)	Used in/Comments
80486DX	1989	25-33	32	1 million transistors; pipeline processing; first built-in numeric coprocessor
80486DX2	1992	50-66	32	OverDrive upgrade chip
80486DX4	1993	75-100	32	triples DX speed
80486SL	1990	25-33	32	Power Saver - laptops
80486SX	1990	25-33	32	no numeric coprocessor
Pentium (80586)	1993	66-133	32	3 million transistors; 2 pipelines; "CRISC" chip; cache memory
Pentium Pro (80586)	1996	133-200+	32	5.5 million transistors; CRISC; "superpipeline" for 2 instructions per cycle
P7	1998			RISC
Motorola				CISC microprocessors
68000	1979?	8-16	16/32	for workstations
68020	1984	25	32	4× faster than 68000
68030	1987	20-50	32	virtual memory mgmt, numeric coprocessor
68040	1989	25	32	"RISC-like;" analogous to Intel 486DX; numeric coprocessor
68040V	1993	25-33	32	Power Saver version for PowerBook laptops
68060	1994	50-66	32	RISC-like hybrid; 3 instructions per cycle
Apple/IBM/Motorola/PowerPC				RISC microprocessors
PowerPC601	1994	66-80	32	3 instructions per cycle; Apple PowerMacintosh
PowerPC 602	1994	80	32	games, multimedia, graphics; 1 instruction per cycle
PowerPC 603	1994	66-80	32	3 instructions per cycle; for portables
PowerPC 604	1994	100-133	32	4 instructions per cycle; work stations, parallel processing
PowerPC 620	1995	133-410	64	technical and scientific work stations, servers

The Anatomy of the CPU

Figure 5.7 illustrates a typical microprocessor. It contains a number of components: the most critical are the control unit (CU) and the arithmetic/logic unit (ALU). Strictly speaking, the *processor* includes the CPU and main memory. The CPU integrated circuit chip (the control unit and the arithmetic/logic unit) is physically separate from the main memory integrated circuit chips— ROM and RAM. Working together, the three components—the CU, ALU, and main memory—perform the computer's processing functions.

HOME PAGE

AND THE WINNER IS . . . CISC OR RISC?

Today, we have personal computers that are based on many different microprocessors and operating systems. All microprocessors process instructions; it's the way they do it that makes them different. As the song goes, it isn't what you do, it's the way you do it.

Recently, IBM and Motorola teamed up to create the next-generation personal computer microprocessor. It is a RISC chip, different in design from the existing generation of CISC chips. Briefly, the difference between them is the following:

- **CISC** stands for **Complex Instruction Set Computing**. A CISC microprocessor, or CPU architecture, and its operating system design enable the microprocessor to recognize 100 or more instructions; engineers thought this number sufficient to carry out most computations. The instructions are very powerful, but the required complexity means that an instruction takes many clock cycles to execute. In a CISC chip, instructions are represented by additional instructions that are stored in ROM and referred to as *microcode*. CISC architecture has been used since the beginning of computers and is the prevailing architecture for most PCs in use today. The Intel Pentium microprocessor is a CISC chip.

The integrated circuit is, in its way, as beautiful as Blake's poetry.

Courtesy of Digital Equipment Corporation

The Alpha chip: Although the CISC and RISC chips look alike, they work very differently.

- **RISC** stands for **Reduced Instruction Set Computing**. A RISC microprocessor, or CPU architecture, uses a condensed set of instructions for its operating system. RISC microprocessors have the advantage of simplicity and elegance over CISC microprocessors. A RISC instruction is executed directly, without microcode, and is usually executed within a single clock cycle. This direct execution makes RISC chips extremely fast. The Digital Equipment Corporation Alpha RISC chip is twice as fast as the Pentium chip.

The most popular CISC microprocessor chip today is the Intel Pentium, followed closely by the 486. The Intel Pentium is available in speeds from 60 MHz to 150 MHz. It's not uncommon to see an advertisement with the graphic "Intel Inside" displayed, although Intel has plenty of competition from other chipmakers, such as Cyrix and AMD.

The Motorola microprocessors used in Macintosh computers are CISC chips, too. But as mentioned earlier, Motorola and IBM now offer PCs that use the PowerPC RISC microprocessor.

However exciting a new technology is, older technologies are kept alive by the huge investments individuals and companies have already made. The entire computer industry, as well as big business, has invested heavily in CISC—what if the RISC computers are incompatible? Another factor in the competition between RISC and CISC is the abundance

Courtesy of Intel Corporation

of existing software for CISC machines, which means continuing support of that technology. These and many questions concerning the RISC versus CISC question are difficult to answer.

Courtesy of International Business Machines Corporation

The PowerPC's chip: PowerPCs are the first personal computers to result from the joint IBM-Apple venture with RISC microprocessors.

The debate over reduced-instruction-set computing versus complex-instruction-set computing typically focuses on which architecture is better, rather than which architecture best handles a specific set of problems. RISC is fast, but simple applications like word processing do not require greater speed. CISC computers offer a wide diversity of applications, but these applications are often constrained by fundamental limitations in the CPU (or microprocessor) design. RISC is well suited for applications requiring

great power, complexity, and diversity, such as computer-aided design (CAD) or any application serving many knowledge workers.

Converging forces may make choosing one or the other unnecessary. The newest CISC microprocessors, such as the Intel Pentium, are capable of RISC speeds, and the distinctions are beginning to blur. And RISC workstations are now capable of utilizing several different operating systems, such as Windows, Macintosh, and UNIX—often simultaneously—so the workstations can run a wide variety of application software. Perhaps at some point in the not-so-distant future, it won't really matter whether you're CISC or RISC.

HOME PAGE REVIEW QUESTIONS

1. What does CISC stand for?

2. What does RISC stand for?

3. What is currently the most popular Intel microprocessor, and what is its speed range?

4. What companies are collaborating on the latest RISC microprocessor, and what is it called?

Microprocessor

Figure 5.7
The brain in the machine: the microprocessor. Note the presence of the control unit and the arithmetic / logic unit. Main memory is on separate ICs.

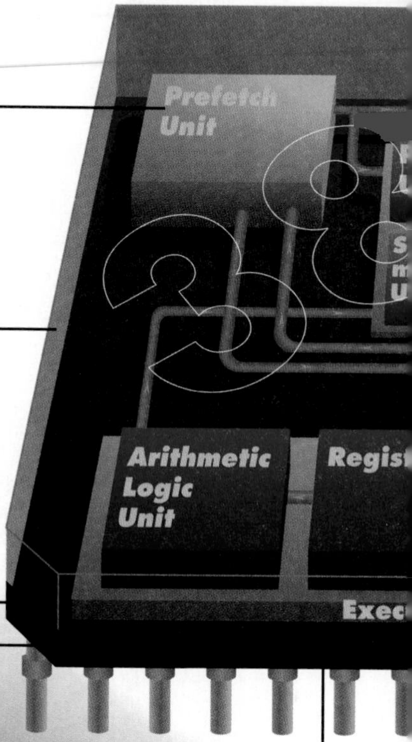

2 At the same time, the segment and paging units convert the location of that instruction from a virtual address, which software understands, to a physical address (an actual location in memory), which the bus interface unit understands.

1 The prefetch unit, which queues instructions for processing, asks the bus interface unit to retrieve from memory the next instruction—in this example, a command to add two numbers. The goal of the prefetch unit is to make sure that the instruction decode unit won't have idle time while it waits for its next instructions.

9 The control unit tells the bus interface unit to store the sum in RAM. The segment and paging units translate the virtual address specified by the control unit for that sum into a physical address, completing the instruction.

8 The arithmetic logic unit, which is the microprocessor's calculator, produces the sum of the number that was just retrieved from RAM and the first number that had been stored in the internal registers.

7 The bus interface unit locates and retrieves the number stored at that address. The number travels back through the protection test unit to the execution unit, where it is stored in one of the chip's internal registers. The registers function as a combination scratch pad and working memory for the execution unit. A similar operation results in the second number also being fetched to the execution unit.

Prefetch Unit

Arithmetic Logic Unit

Regis

Exec

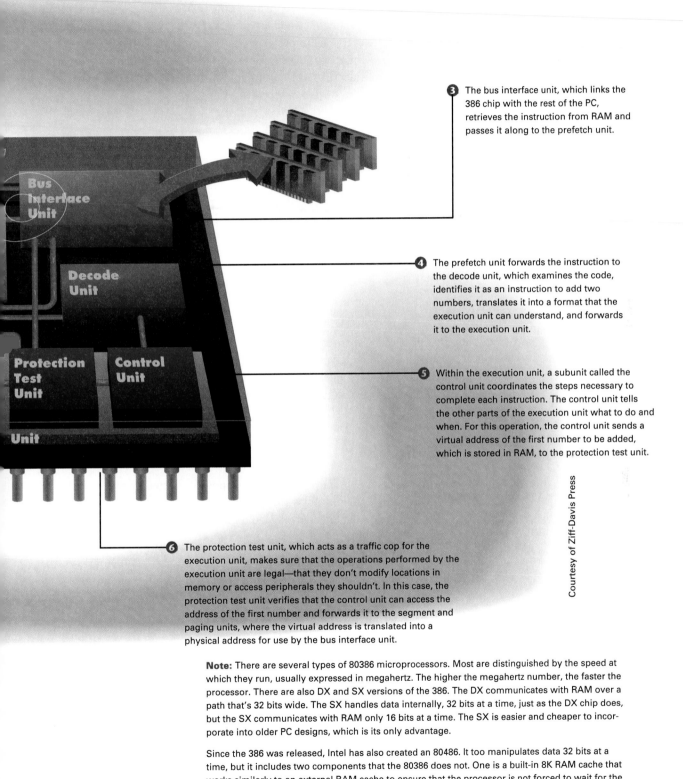

3 The bus interface unit, which links the 386 chip with the rest of the PC, retrieves the instruction from RAM and passes it along to the prefetch unit.

4 The prefetch unit forwards the instruction to the decode unit, which examines the code, identifies it as an instruction to add two numbers, translates it into a format that the execution unit can understand, and forwards it to the execution unit.

5 Within the execution unit, a subunit called the control unit coordinates the steps necessary to complete each instruction. The control unit tells the other parts of the execution unit what to do and when. For this operation, the control unit sends a virtual address of the first number to be added, which is stored in RAM, to the protection test unit.

Bus Interface Unit

Decode Unit

Protection Test Unit

Control Unit

Unit

Courtesy of Ziff-Davis Press

6 The protection test unit, which acts as a traffic cop for the execution unit, makes sure that the operations performed by the execution unit are legal—that they don't modify locations in memory or access peripherals they shouldn't. In this case, the protection test unit verifies that the control unit can access the address of the first number and forwards it to the segment and paging units, where the virtual address is translated into a physical address for use by the bus interface unit.

Note: There are several types of 80386 microprocessors. Most are distinguished by the speed at which they run, usually expressed in megahertz. The higher the megahertz number, the faster the processor. There are also DX and SX versions of the 386. The DX communicates with RAM over a path that's 32 bits wide. The SX handles data internally, 32 bits at a time, just as the DX chip does, but the SX communicates with RAM only 16 bits at a time. The SX is easier and cheaper to incorporate into older PC designs, which is its only advantage.

Since the 386 was released, Intel has also created an 80486. It too manipulates data 32 bits at a time, but it includes two components that the 80386 does not. One is a built-in 8K RAM cache that works similarly to an external RAM cache to ensure that the processor is not forced to wait for the data it needs. The other component is a built-in math coprocessor. The *coprocessor* is a set of instructions streamlined for handling complex math.

The Control Unit

The **control unit**, or **CU**, is the part of the CPU that directs the step-by-step operation of the computer. Like a traffic policeman directing cars, the CU is in charge of obtaining and processing instructions. The control unit directs electrical impulses between itself, the ALU, and main memory. In more recent machines, the CU gets help from input and output control circuits that control operations between the CPU and the peripheral devices. These electrical impulses consist of the data, the instructions being processed, and the input and output control signals.

The Arithmetic/Logic Unit

The **arithmetic/logic unit,** or **ALU**, performs two types of operations: arithmetic and logical. The ALU is responsible for making comparisons for the control unit in order to determine whether processing operations are mathematical or logical. The **arithmetic operations** are addition, subtraction, multiplication, and division. The **logical operations** compare two pieces of data to determine whether one is greater than, less than, or equal to the other.

Arithmetic Operations

Even though addition, subtraction, multiplication, and division are listed, the ALU is actually capable of performing only addition—but very fast addition. If the ALU is asked to perform subtraction, it adds negative numbers. The multiplication and division also are accomplished by complex addition operations.

Logical Operations

Logical operations specify to the CPU the relationship between two quantities or states. These operations play many important roles in computing by comparing data and values. There are three logical operations:

- *Greater than (>) condition.* The new data or value is larger than the existing one. For example, the bank's computer checks to see whether the amount you want to withdraw from the ATM is *greater than* the prescribed $350 daily limit—or greater than the balance in your account.

- *Less than (<) condition.* The new data or value is smaller than the existing one. For example, an inventory management program alerts the purchasing manager that the stock of size 9 ski boots has fallen below six pairs, which is *less than* the required stock level.

- Equal to (=) condition. The new data or value is supposed to be the same as the existing one. For example, the spelling checker in word processing compares a word you type with the word in its dictionary, looking for a 100 percent equal to match.

Knowledge Check

1. From what common material are integrated circuits made?
2. What does the term *integrated* mean?
3. What four tasks do ICs perform in computers?
4. What tasks does the CPU perform?
5. What two components make up the CPU?
6. What three components make up the processor?
7. What is an arithmetic operation?
8. What are the three types of logical operations?

Key Terms

arithmetic operation	arithmetic/logic unit (ALU)
central processing unit (CPU)	clock speed
complex instruction set computing (CISC)	control unit (CU)
Hertz	integrated circuit
logical operation	microprocessor
reduced instruction set computing (RISC)	

ISSUES AND IDEAS

Birth of the RISC Microprocessor

International Business Machines Corporation was once considered the premier computer company and a "blue chip," or consistently high-value, stock. But in their book *Computer Wars*, author Charles H. Ferguson and Charles R. Morris state that IBM lost its hegemony during the 1980s and has never regained it. Consider the story of how IBM forfeited "one of the most important technologies in the recent history of computing, known as RISC, which IBM once had all to itself."

RISC was invented by John Cocke, a senior scientist at IBM's Yorktown Heights Research Center.

. . . Cocke's work at IBM was kept secret for more than a decade, but by the end of the 1970s, similar ideas were bubbling up in the academic computer science community, particularly at Berkeley, through the work of David Patterson, and at Stanford under John Hennessy. (Both had students who had worked at IBM Yorktown as summer interns.) Patterson spent a sabbatical at DEC (Digital Equipment Corporation) in 1979 and . . . in 1980, with the help of a Defense Department grant, he and a graduate student designed a new microprocessor called RISC I— the first use of the name *RISC*. IBM disclosed its own work on RISC only in 1982, and then very guardedly, at a conference at which all the main academic players were present. Patterson's work led directly to Sun Microsystems' highly successful SPARC RISC microprocessor, while Hennessy left academia to found MIPS. MIPS and Sun processors dominated the RISC market during the last half of the 1980s.

Cocke, on the other hand, worked on RISC for almost fifteen years before IBM introduced a product—the 1986 RT PC workstation, an abject failure. The story of how IBM squandered a decade's head start in RISC holds important clues about what was going wrong at the company.[2]

CRITICAL THINKING

1. The authors state that Cocke's research was "kept secret for more than a decade." How did it leak out?

2. IBM lost the battle for dominating the personal computer (CISC) market, then lost the RISC market as well. Research IBM and determine why a great company that has dominated the mainframe market since the late 1960s might have made these business blunders.

3. Using the Internet's World Wide Web, research the three companies the authors mention as leaders in RISC technology to determine the "state of the art" for each:

   MIPS: MIPS: http://www.mips.com

   Silicon Graphics: http://www.sgi.com

   Sun Microsystems: http://www.sun.com

2. Charles H. Ferguson and Charles R. Morris. *Computer Wars: How the West Can Win in a Post-IBM World* (New York: Times Books, 1993), 39–40.

CPU Operation

Why It's Important to Know

> **When the CPU performs the four data processing operations on data or instructions, the procedure is called the machine cycle. Data must be properly represented for processing to occur. The faster data and instructions are processed, the better.**

The CPU, by itself, can do nothing; it is like an engine without fuel. The CPU must receive instructions and data through main memory in order to do processing. Knowledge workers provide the input and use the output. The typical processing sequence is represented in figure 5.8.

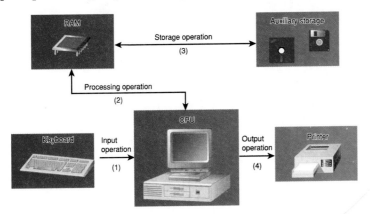

Figure 5.8
The CPU in action: input, processing, output, and storage are the four data processing operations that occur with every single instruction.

As you know, when it comes to computing, there's no such thing as too fast. Computers use several techniques to increase their operating speed. Main memory and secondary storage play a significant role in enhancing the computer's processing speed—in more ways than one.

The Registers

The CPU can perform its processing faster when instructions and data are nearby. That's why both the control unit and ALU have **registers**, high-speed temporary storage areas, to hold both instructions and data during processing. Because registers are built into the CPU integrated circuit chip, they are electrically very close to the control unit and ALU; hence, they enhance processing speed. There are several types of registers:

- The **instruction register** holds an instruction—for example, to add, to multiply, or to perform a logical comparison.

- The **storage register** temporarily holds data retrieved from RAM, prior to processing.

- The **accumulator** temporarily stores the results of continuing arithmetic and logical operations.

Remember, registers are short-term memory storage areas; they hold instructions or data only during a processing sequence; then they pass the data or instruction back to RAM. Main memory (RAM) and secondary storage (disk storage) can be organized into the memory hierarchy pyramid shown in figure 5.9.

Figure 5.9

The memory hierarchy pyramid.

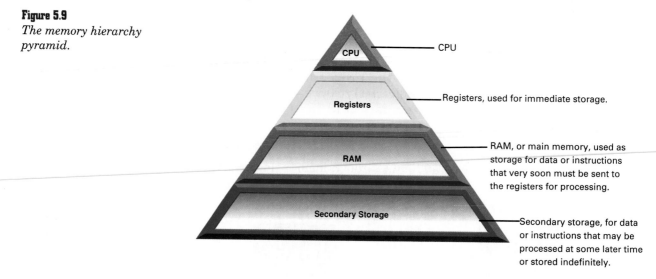

CPU

Registers, used for immediate storage.

RAM, or main memory, used as storage for data or instructions that very soon must be sent to the registers for processing.

Secondary storage, for data or instructions that may be processed at some later time or stored indefinitely.

As you can see, the closer the type of memory (or storage) to the CPU, the more immediate and critical the need for speed. This subject is covered later in this module, but first, you need to take a closer look at the instructions and data being processed.

Data Representation

What, you might ask, do these instructions and data that are being held temporarily in registers look like to the computer? Our everyday language symbols—the characters on the keyboard—must be translated into the binary language the computer understands. This means of translation is called **data representation**. The computer understands only the binary language of 1s and 0s. When 1s and 0s are linked in a unique string, they create a representation the computer understands. Each 1 or 0 is a *bit*, and the representation they form—a letter or number, for example—is called a *byte*. But bytes have to be properly represented before they can be processed.

Bytes are organized into words for presentation to the processor. In computing, a **word** is a logical unit of information, made up of bits and bytes, that can be stored in a single memory location. *Word length* is the term used to describe a word's size, counted in number of bits. To a computer, a word is not the same as a word in our language. Most bytes represent just one letter, digit, or symbol. Several bytes are needed to represent most human language words.

Once the instructions and data are in a language the computer understands, the CPU can perform its processing. The sequence of steps by which an instruction is processed is called the *machine cycle*.

The Machine Cycle

The length of time the CPU takes to process one machine instruction, or word, is called a **cycle**. The cycle is a useful measure of CPU performance, in the same way that *horsepower* is used as a measure for internal combustion engines.

Information systems professionals often use cycles as a way to monitor computer resources consumption. For example, more cycles for automated teller machines' (ATM) transactions are needed late in the afternoon, when people who have left work are making withdrawals for purchases at the grocery store.

Machine cycle is the term used to describe the steps involved in processing a single instruction. Figure 5.10 shows the CPU machine cycle. Actually, it is comprised of two cycles: the instruction cycle and the execution cycle.

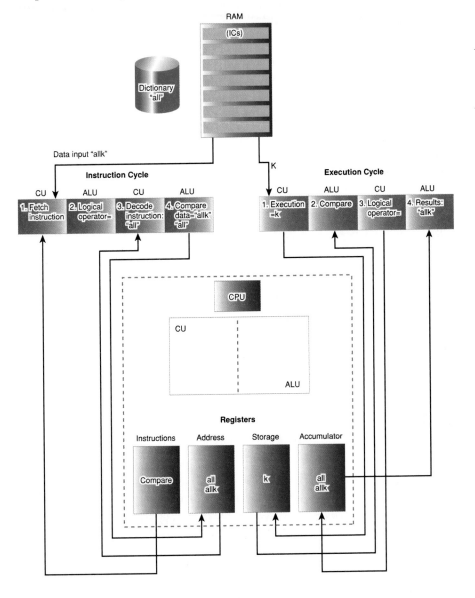

Figure 5.10
The machine cycle processes a single instruction. A typical personal computer's CPU processes millions of instructions per second.

Take the example of spell-checking a word—not to be confused with the logical-unit-of-information word just discussed, but a real English-language word—to see how the machine cycle works. The word is *all*, but you have mistakenly typed a fourth character so that it reads *allk*. The ALU has performed its equals condition operation on the first three letters and is beginning on the fourth. As you work through the following paragraphs, refer to figure 5.10.

The Instruction Cycle

In the **instruction cycle**, sometimes called the *I-cycle*, the control unit of the CPU retrieves an instruction from RAM and gets ready to perform processing. Note in figure 5.10 the four steps in the instruction cycle:

1. The control unit retrieves from primary memory the next instruction for execution—in this case, an instruction that compares two values to see whether they are equal.

2. The control unit decodes the instruction, to issue the logical operation comparing the fourth letter of the word. (The word, previously considered *all*, is now determined to be *allk*.)

3. The control unit puts the part of the instruction for the equals condition into the instruction register; it's now waiting for the ALU to compare the fourth letter.

4. The control unit now puts into the address register the portion of the instruction that indicates where the needed data—the *k*— is located.

To summarize, the computer now has the equals (=) instruction ready and waiting in the instruction register, and the data (the *k*) ready and waiting in the address register.

The Execution Cycle

The next phase is the **execution cycle**, or *E-cycle*, in which the data is located and the instruction is executed. Again, there are four steps. You can follow them in figure 5.10:

1. Using the equals condition instruction, the control unit retrieves the *k* from RAM and places it in a storage register.

2. The command to compare is issued.

3. The ALU performs its equals (=) condition logical operation on the values it has found in the storage register and the accumulator (which is holding the results of performing the equals condition on the first three letters of the word).

4. The result of the operation is placed in the accumulator, replacing the values previously stored there. The word has now been completely— and incorrectly—spelled as *allk*. The spelling checker, not having found such a word, will ask you to verify its spelling.

The computer machine cycle is very fast—a mere fraction of a second. It's an important measure of computer performance. Computer professionals often refer to *cycle time* when discussing computer performance. Cycle time can be important to you when you're standing in front of an automated teller machine waiting for your cash withdrawal. Now take a look at just how fast CPUs really operate.

Speed

The measure of CPU performance is in **million instructions per second**, or **MIPS**. The VAX line of Digital minicomputers range from 1 to 12 MIPS. The IBM 3090 mainframe line ranges from 30 to 60 MIPS. The Intel microprocessor has experienced a dramatic increase in performance, as shown in figure 5.11.

With the 80486, Intel introduced *pipelining*, a new method of retrieving and decoding instructions during the machine cycle. The 80386 microprocessor took two or more clock cycles to process a single instruction. The new pipeline hardware design made it possible for the 80486 to process one instruction in one cycle, or tick of the clock.

The fastest computers are supercomputers, where the measure is in **floating operations per second**, or **FLOPS**, a distinctly mathematical term. Supercomputers perform FLOPS by the millions—called megaflops, or MFLOPS—and even by the billions—gigaflops. The next generation of supercomputers will perform in the teraflops range, or trillions of floating-point operations per second.

The machine-cycle distinction between different classes of computers is blurring; however, PCs are not equal in power to minis, mainframes, or supercomputers. Some other considerations are the amount of RAM, the use of multiple processors, and the number of users and applications that are simultaneously on the system.

Figure 5.11
*Microprocessor performance
put to use.*

Courtesy of Ziff-Davis Press

❶ The first PC's were very simple compared with today's versions. The original PC communicated using cryptic words, the language of DOS, which sometimes resembled English. The logic and reasoning behind the C:\>DOS prompt escaped many would-be users. Graphics and even color were beyond the capability of the 8088 microprocessor powering these first PCs. Although revolutionary, the PC was used as little more than an advanced adding machine or typewriter that could store documents and files.

Calculation   Word Processing

"MIPS"
Millions of instructions per second

4004 processor
0.06 MIPS

8088
0.75

1971

Year Introduced

6 This power is also being put to good use in software applications that link computers in the work place. Electronic mail and large databases accessed by multiple users across wide area networks (WANS) are now possible with the horsepower available on the desk top PC.

7 Video conferencing capabilities are now available on the PC. The performance of the newest generation of microprocessors enables the PC to process the enormous quantity of digital information required to display video in real time and to move it over communication lines.

5 PC hardware is also benefiting from the microprocessor's increase in performance. Color monitors have become a standard PC feature. The microprocessor can now process the high-resolution color data required for popular video standards, such as VGA and Super VGA. Today the amount of video information processed by the microprocessor is more than ten times greater than that of the original PC.

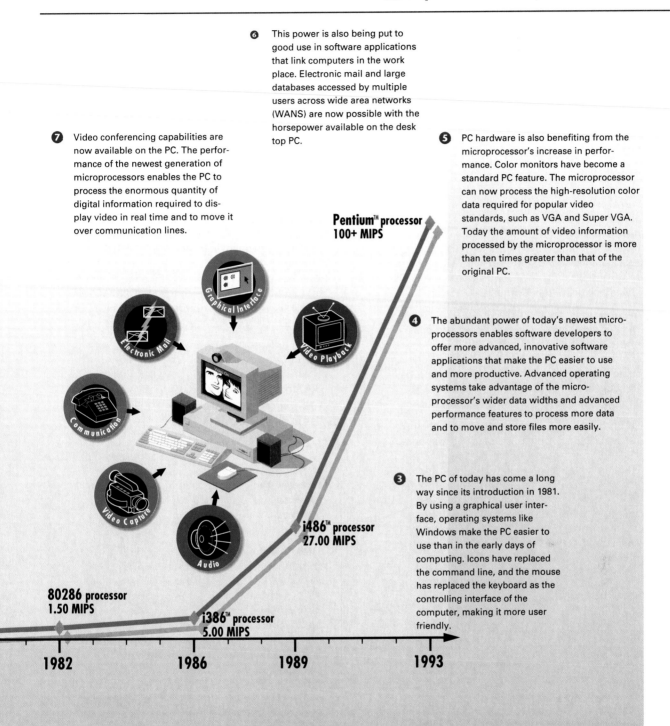

Pentium™ processor 100+ MIPS

i486™ processor 27.00 MIPS

80286 processor 1.50 MIPS

i386™ processor 5.00 MIPS

1982   1986   1989   1993

4 The abundant power of today's newest microprocessors enables software developers to offer more advanced, innovative software applications that make the PC easier to use and more productive. Advanced operating systems take advantage of the microprocessor's wider data widths and advanced performance features to process more data and to move and store files more easily.

3 The PC of today has come a long way since its introduction in 1981. By using a graphical user interface, operating systems like Windows make the PC easier to use than in the early days of computing. Icons have replaced the command line, and the mouse has replaced the keyboard as the controlling interface of the computer, making it more user friendly.

2 The performance level of the microprocessor has increased dramatically over a short period of time. This graph shows a rapid rise as measured by MIPS. The increased performance allowed the PC to evolve from a simple business machine to a vital interactive communications tool, capable of electronically linking to remote sources of data and making vast amounts of information available at the home or office.

HOME PAGE

THE HEART AND SOUL BEHIND THE MACHINE

The following excerpt from the book *The Soul of a New Machine* by Tracy Kidder describes the work of Steve Wallach, the computer science architect who designed the CPU for the Data General MV/8000, the "Eagle," a brand-new superminicomputer that upstaged rival Digital Equipment Corporation's machines. The computer was introduced on April 29, 1980, and was a great success. Tracy Kidder won the Pulitzer Prize for the book. This excerpt is from the chapter "Wallach's Golden Moment."

In computers, an architecture describes what a machine will look like to the people who are going to write software for it. It tells not how the machine will be built, but what it will do, in detail. Drawing up such a blueprint would be the crucial first technical act in the making of this 32-bit, fully Eclipse-compatible computer. . . .

[Steve] Wallach had now spent more than a decade working on computing equipment. He'd had a hand in the design of five computers—all good designs, in his opinion. He had put himself into those creatures of metal and silicon. And he had seen only one of them come to functional life, and in that case the customer had decided not to buy the machine.

. . . The soles of Wallach's cowboy boots faced his office door. He was stretched out in his chair, his feet up on his desk. . . . Conceiving architectures was his job, and Eagle was the only project around that needed an architect.
. . . Wallach returned to West's office, and now, at long last and sniffing, he said, "Okay, Tom, one more time."

. . . Wallach went to his office and closed the door. Some months later, a careful examination of Wallach's quarters revealed many scuff marks etched in shoe polish low down along his walls, and there was a dent higher up on one wall. These were bruises, left over from Wallach's labor on the machine.

When he sat down, alone, in his office, Wallach reasoned that since the whole purpose of this ridiculous undertaking was 32-bit-hood—the enlargement of the Eclipse's logical-address space from 65,000 to 4.3 billion storage compartments—he might as well begin by figuring out how the compartments would be organized ("managed") and the information in them protected. He further decided—he called this "the methodical engineering approach"—to worry about memory management first. Clearing a place on his desk, he placed a yellow legal pad in front of him and drew a picture of the standard 32-bit address—a box containing 32-bits. . . . He began to divide up the space inside this box.

If you imagine the computer's storage—its memory—to be a large collection of telephones, then what Wallach was doing might be described as designing a logical system by which phones and groups of phones could be easily identified—a system of area codes, for instance.

. . . The first three bits of the address would contain the segment number of a memory compartment—in the telephone analogy, a given compartment's area code. The other bits would define the rest of the address . . . the "instruction set."

These are the basic operations that the computer's builders equip it to perform. Typically, instructions bear such names as ADD, which means the computer should perform addition, and Skip On Equal, which tells the machine to compare two values and if they are equal to skip the next step in a program. Today, there are a couple hundred instructions or so in most minicomputers' sets. A large part of the art of designing a computer's architecture lies in selecting just the right set of instructions and in making each instruction as versatile as possible.[3]

---

3. Tracy Kidder. *The Soul of a New Machine* (Boston: Atlantic-Little, Brown, 1981), 67–85.

1. Does this short excerpt bring the human element of computer design and CPU operation to life for you? Explain.

2. How did this piece help you understand the importance of memory management?

3. Relating it to the telephone number analogy, why is a longer (32-bit) instruction better?

4. William Strunk, Jr., used to advise writers to "omit needless words." Does it seem like the same advice applies to selecting the instructions for a computer?

Knowledge Check

1. What is the purpose of the registers?
2. What are the three types of registers?
3. Why does the CPU need data representation?
4. What is processed during one machine cycle?
5. What are the two types of machine cycles?
6. What term describes the length of time necessary to process an instruction?
7. What is the measure of the speed of microprocessor CPUs?

Key Terms

accumulator	cycle	data representation
execution cycle	floating operations per second (FLOPS)	instruction cycle
instruction register	machine cycle	million instructions per second (MIPS)
registers	storage register	word

ISSUES AND IDEAS:

Corporate Responsibility and Damage Control

Read the following electronic mail item, and assess the problem as it is explained.

From: [several anonymous sources]

Subject: My Perspective on Pentium—AGS

Date: 27 Nov 1994 19:31:21 GMT

Andy Grove has asked me to post the following for him. Since it is the weekend and we are out of the office, I am posting from my home system.

Richard Wirt

Director SW Technology

Intel Corp

This is Andy Grove, president of Intel. I'd like to comment a bit on the conversations that have been taking place here. First of all, I am truly sorry for the anxiety created among you by our floating point issue. I read thru some of the postings and it's clear that many of you have done a lot of work around it and that some of you are very angry at us.

Let me give you my perspective on what has happened here.

The Pentium processor was introduced into the market in May of '93 after the most extensive testing program we at Intel have ever embarked on. Because this chip is three times as complex as the 486, and because it includes a number of improved floating-point algorithms, we geared up to do an array of tests, validation, and verification that far exceeded anything we had ever done. So did many of our OEM customers. We held the introduction of the chip several months in order to give them more time to check out the chip and their systems. We worked extensively with many software companies to this end as well.

We were very pleased with the result. We ramped the processor faster than any other in our history and encountered no significant problems in the user community. Not that the chip was perfect; no chip ever is. From time to time, we gathered up what problems we found and put into production a new "stepping"—a new set of masks that incorporated whatever we corrected. Stepping N was better than stepping N minus 1, which was better than stepping N minus 2. After almost 25 years in the microprocessor business, I have come to the conclusion that no microprocessor is ever perfect; they just come closer to perfection with each stepping. In the life of a typical microprocessor, we go thru half a dozen or more such steppings.

Then, in the summer of '94, in the process of further testing (which continued thru all this time and continues today), we came upon the floating point error. We were puzzled as to why neither we nor anyone else had encountered this earlier. We started a separate project, including mathematicians and scientists who work for us in areas other than the Pentium processor group, to examine the nature of the problem and its impact.

This group concluded after months of work that (1) an error is only likely to occur at a frequency of the order of once in nine billion random floating point divides, and that (2) this many divides in all the programs they evaluated (which included many scientific programs) would require elapsed times of use that would be longer than the mean time to failure of the physical computer subsystems. In other words, the error rate a user might see due to the floating point problem would be swamped by other known computer failure mechanisms. This explained why nobody—not us, not our OEM customers, not the software vendors we worked with, and not the many individual users—had run into it.

As some of you may recall, we had encountered thornier problems with early versions of the 386 and 486, so we breathed a sigh of relief that with the Pentium processor we had found what turned out to be a problem of far lesser magnitude. We then incorporated the fix into the next stepping of both the 60 and 66 and the 75/90/100 MHz Pentium processor along with whatever else we were correcting in that next stepping.

Then, last month Professor Nicely posted his observations about this problem and the hubbub started. Interestingly, I understand from press reports that Prof. Nicely was attempting to show that Pentium-based computers can do the jobs of big time supercomputers in numbers analyses. Many of you who posted comments are evidently also involved in pretty heavy duty mathematical work.

That gets us to the present time and what we do about all this.

We would like to find all users of the Pentium processor who are engaged in work involving heavy duty scientific/floating point calculations and resolve their problem in the most appropriate fashion including, if necessary, by replacing their chips with new ones. We don't know how to set precise rules on this so we decided to do it thru individual discussions between each of you and a technically trained Intel person. We set up 800# lines for that purpose. It is going to take us time to work thru the calls we are getting, but we will work thru them. I would like to ask for your patience here.

Meanwhile, please don't be concerned that the passing of time will deprive you of the opportunity to get your problem resolved—we will stand behind these chips for the life of your computer.

Sorry to be so long-winded—and again please accept my apologies for the situation. We appreciate your interest in the Pentium processor, and we remain dedicated to bringing it as close to perfection as possible.

I will monitor your communications in the future—forgive me if I can't answer each of you individually.

Andy Grove

CRITICAL THINKING

1. This memo from the president of Intel Corporation is a response to a problem with the Pentium microprocessor. In essence, it's an apology and a voluntary recall. Is this a good response to an admittedly minor problem?

2. Do you feel that Intel should have caught this bug before the manufacturing began?

3. Why, as illustrated in this example, are bugs so difficult to find?

4. What role and what position should consumers take in instances like this?

Module D

Computer Memory

Why It's Important to Know

> **Memory works hand in hand with the CPU. There are two types of memory, ROM and RAM, and they have an impact on every aspect of the work we do with the computer.**

Memory is the general term used to describe *where* the computer holds data and instructions before and after processing. Memory's job is *temporarily* storing the instructions and data in the computer. Memory is divided into two major categories:

- *Read-only memory*, where permanent instructions are stored

- *Random-access memory*, where data and instructions are temporarily stored

In this module, you learn about these two types of memory and a third kind—cache memory.

Think of computer memory this way: You're going to learn to play racquetball. *Read-only memory* is the rule book that explains the game—the rules that are the same every time you play. *Random-access memory* is a play-by-play description of the game you're playing right now, at this very moment. In this text, RAM is also called primary storage. *Auxiliary storage* is permanent storage—the videotape of today's game—which you can replay later to improve your moves.

Read-Only Memory

You know that ROM is called *Read-Only Memory* because it holds instructions that can only be read by the computer but not changed or written to. These permanent instructions—the racquetball rules and regulations—are used to start the computer. ROM instructions direct many of the computer's operations that never vary in their execution. ROM instructions are generally stored in integrated circuit chips.

ROM holds the start-up instructions, sometimes called the bootstrap routine, that begin when the computer power is turned on. This process is what we mean when referring to *booting* the computer. Each computer's start-up program is a little different, but in general its tasks are to

- Check the amount of RAM

- Establish connections with the video controller and monitor

- Ensure that external connections, such as the keyboard or printer, are operational

- Identify auxiliary storage devices
- Load the operating system
- Execute any other instructions it finds on a disk

ROM is a form of **nonvolatile memory**, which means it is specifically designed to store data even when the computer is powered down.

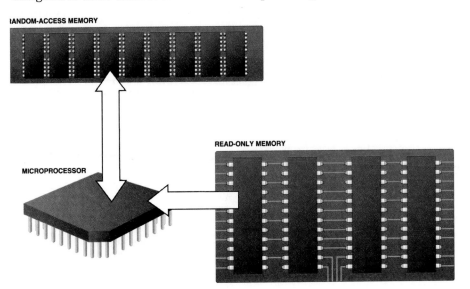

Figure 5.12
ROM holds permanent instructions that can only be read by the computer but not changed or written to.

Random-Access Memory

Random-access memory, or RAM, is the primary storage area. RAM is working memory and is directly controlled by the computer's processor. Together with the control unit and arithmetic/logic unit, random-access memory is the third component of the processor.

Random-access memory assists the CU and the ALU by temporarily holding the programs being executed and the data being processed. Random-access memory commonly takes the form of a number of ICs, electrically connected to and close to the CPU chip. These connections and the closeness are important, for they make it possible for the processor to obtain data and instructions directly from RAM and to perform processing with great speed.

Another aspect of RAM affects processing speed: its size. Think of RAM as a container: the larger it is, the more programs and data it can hold. The more it can hold, the faster the CPU can access it. The RAM in large computer systems is immense, and in recent years, the PC's RAM capacity has grown as well. Fifteen years ago, the first PCs were limited to 64 kilobytes (K). Five years ago, most PCs had 2 megabytes (M) of RAM; today, the average PC has 8M. That number will soon be 16M, then 32M, and most probably 64M—*one hundred thousand times more* than the early PCs.

Random-access memory is often called memory, main memory, main storage, internal storage, or primary storage. All these names refer to the fact that RAM is a working partner with the CPU. Unlike ROM, RAM is read/write memory. It not only assists in processing tasks, but it also directs its contents to output devices, such as the monitor and printer, or to auxiliary storage. RAM works with the CPU to **read**, or get, data and instructions from a source, such as the keyboard. RAM and the CPU also work together to **write**, or transfer, data to other devices like auxiliary storage. As you will see, auxiliary storage is also read/write memory.

Also unlike ROM, random-access memory is short-term, volatile memory. **Volatile memory** means that the instructions and data held in RAM are replaced by new instructions and data; RAM contents are lost when electrical power to the computer is cut off. For that reason, saving your important work in auxiliary storage is essential—in the same way that it's fine to remember your plays in that racquetball game you just played, but it's even better to get instant replays whenever you like.

Figure 5.13

RAM, ROM, and cache memory all work together to increase the speed of processing.

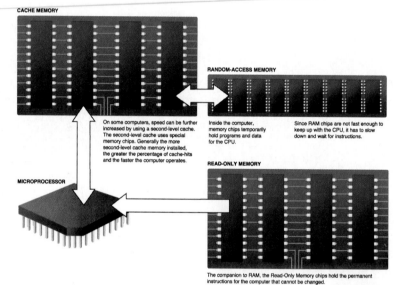

CACHE MEMORY

RANDOM-ACCESS MEMORY

On some computers, speed can be further increased by using a second-level cache. The second-level cache uses special memory chips. Generally the more second-level cache memory installed, the greater the percentage of cache-hits and the faster the computer operates.

Inside the computer, memory chips temporarily hold programs and data for the CPU.

Since RAM chips are not fast enough to keep up with the CPU, it has to slow down and wait for instructions.

MICROPROCESSOR

READ-ONLY MEMORY

The companion to RAM, the Read-Only Memory chips hold the permanent instructions for the computer that cannot be changed.

Cache Memory

The most recent development in memory is the cache memory. A *cache* is a place to keep something safe. **Cache memory** is a special set of very fast random-access memory chips used to store data that the CPU most frequently accesses from RAM. These chips are called static random-access memory, or SRAM, chips, and they are directly connected to the CPU. Because of this direct connection, cache memory can deliver data to the CPU at the speed of processing. And as we know, when it comes to speed, every little bit helps.

HOME PAGE

BITS AND BYTES

The key to understanding how memory and storage work is understanding the basic units of storage. You know that a gallon is 128 ounces, and a foot is 12 inches. We use many forms of capacity and measurement for different objects and systems. This fact is also true of computers.

The most basic unit of capacity in a computer system is the bit. The term **bit** stands for *bi*nary dig*it*. A bit is the basic unit of data recognized by a computer.

Computers like to keep things simple, so there are only two types of bits. That's because at their most basic level, computers understand only the language of electricity: positive and negative, or on and off. What we get is this: one bit stands for *on* and is represented by the number *1*. The other bit stands for *off* and is represented by the number *0*. This designation is an example of the **binary number system**—a mathematical system based on just two numbers or digits.

Computer designers realized that they could make computers work faster by grouping bits together for presentation to the CPU. This grouping is like our language—it's easier for us to speak in words than to spell out each letter as we talk to one another. The term we use for a group of bits is a byte. A **byte** is a group of bits on which the computer can operate as a unit. Most modern computers have eight bits to a byte. The relationship between bits and bytes is shown in the accompanying figure.

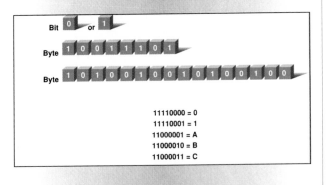

A byte can be operated on as a unit. What does that mean? Well, computer designers looked for the most common characters we use when working with information and identified 128 letters, numbers, and symbols—pretty much the characters you see on typewriter keys. These characters were identified as the *standard ASCII character set*. Later, a number of foreign language, technical, and block graphics characters were added, doubling the number to 256 characters; this set is called the *extended character set*. Each of these characters is represented as a byte, made up of eight bits in a distinct and unique order.

What does this information have to do with RAM and data storage? First, note that the binary number system is called a *base 2* number system, because it has only two numbers, or values. By contrast, we use the *base 10* number system in our everyday lives. Using base 10, we count by powers of 10—10, 100, 1000, and so on. Using the base 2 system, we count by powers of 2.

A very important measure of the computer's capacity is the number of bytes of memory storage it has. We are always interested to know how much storage capacity we have in RAM, as well as in auxiliary storage. Running out of memory or storage space can cause programs to misbehave or result in losing valuable data. This capacity is commonly counted in the thousands of bytes available, called **kilobytes** (**K**), but using the base 2 number system. Therefore, 1 kilobyte, or 1K, is 2^{10} bytes, or 1,024 bytes (roughly a thousand bytes).

When memory and storage go into the millions, they are measured in **megabytes** (**M**): 1M is 2^{20}, or 1,048,576 bytes (roughly 1 million bytes). For example, most modern personal computers have at least 8M of RAM. But there's more.

A **gigabyte** (**G**) is 2^{30}, or 1,073,741,824 bytes (approximately 1 billion bytes). It's becoming increasingly common to see PCs equipped with 1G of auxiliary storage.

A **terabyte** (**T**) is 2^{40}, 1,099,511,627,776 bytes, or approximately 1 trillion bytes or 1 million megabytes.

TERM	WHAT IT MEANS
Byte	One character
Kilo	Metric for "one thousand"
Mega	Metric for "one million"
Giga	Metric for "one billion"
Kilobyte (K)	One thousand characters
Megabyte (M)	One million characters
Gigabyte (G)	One billion characters

And just to put things into a little perspective, there are approximately 100 billion cells—100 gigacells—in the human brain.

HOME PAGE REVIEW QUESTIONS

1. What is a bit?

2. How many bits are in a byte?

3. What is an example of the kind of character represented by a byte?

4. Why is it important to know how much memory and storage capacity the computer has?

Hardware Memory Management

Memory management has been a critical hardware technology concern for most of the PC's fifteen-year life span. Early memory IC chips held approximately 16,384 kilobits, or 16K bits. Four such chips provided the computer with 64K bytes of RAM. Software placed increasing demands on memory management and soon there were memory ICs with 64K bits capacity, then 256K bits capacity. Eight 256K-bit ICs gave the computer 2M bytes of RAM.

However, as memory requirements grew, so did the number of chips that needed to be installed. One-quarter to one-third of the main circuit board might be taken up with memory ICs. Upgrades required special tools and great care in removing and installing the ICs.

Both problems were solved by a more advanced type of IC called a **single in-line memory module**, or **SIMM**. Figure 5.14 shows a SIMM, which you can see looks like a small circuit board. SIMMs snap into sockets mounted on the main circuit board. The most commonly used SIMMs are 4M bytes capacity; a pair make 8M of RAM, and four make 16M of RAM.

Figure 5.14
SIMMs have made upgrading memory much easier.

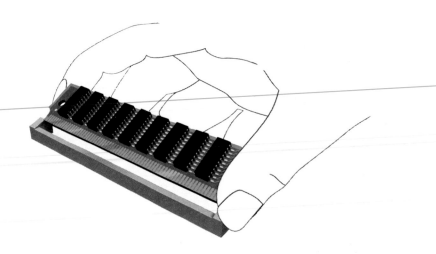

SIMMs take up less space on the main circuit board, are easy to install, and are designed to permit further RAM expansion—always an important consideration. As one veteran knowledge worker says, "The amount of RAM you need is usually one and a half times more than you currently have."

All these hardware advances were wonderful, but operating system software had not kept up. DOS imposed a maximum memory limitation of 640K. Because it was theoretically possible to access many *megabytes* of memory, the 640K barrier had to be broken. This need ushered in more sophisticated memory management techniques, called *extended* or *expanded* memory manager programs. These memory managers held programs or data in *upper memory*—that above 640K—until they were needed and then swapped them in and out of base memory.

Memory management schemes work well, but they add complexity to the way hardware and software interact and limit the performance and efficiency inherent in today's fast, sophisticated PC. Newer operating systems, such as Windows 95, have made memory limitations a thing of the past.

Knowledge Check

1. What are some of the tasks that ROM's permanent instructions perform?
2. What is another common name for random-access memory?
3. What is the difference between RAM and ROM?
4. What is the difference between volatile and nonvolatile memory?
5. Why has memory management been an important issue?
6. Why is it easier to upgrade SIMMs than it is to replace RAM chips?

Key Terms

binary number system	bit	byte
cache memory	gigabyte (G)	kilobyte (K)
megabyte (M)	nonvolatile memory	read
single in-line memory module (SIMM)	terabyte (T)	volatile memory
write		

ISSUES AND IDEAS

Computer Error: Who's Really to Blame?

Study this story from the RISKS Forum and evaluate the author's premise, stated in the Subject line.

Date: Mon, 20 Mar 1995 20:21:24 -0400 (EDT)

From: Cynthia P. Klumpp

Subject: Reevaluating Our Trust in Computers

With the increasing involvement of computers in our daily lives, the number of errors occurring is also increasing. Errors seen many times in the past are still occurring while new errors are cropping up with the use of new technology. The dependent relationships between the software, hardware, data input (whether it is by a person or computer generated), procedures, and the communication links [RISKS-9.61], create a very complex environment.

The blind trust we have in computers and the people who operate or program them may need to be reevaluated. In other words, can and should we always trust a computer operator or a computer with the ever increasing processing of data which affects our lives and then look to blame when failure occurs?

Or should we decrease or adjust the trust we place on data input and computers?

While I was doing a search for articles at the library on the periodical database and happened to be short of time one night, the computer froze suddenly for no apparent reason. I had already spent 30 of my precious 90 minutes reading abstracts and marking (to print) the ones I thought were relevant. I had not yet printed the abstracts when the computer stopped responding to keystrokes. I asked the reference librarian if there was anything that could be done. He said "Not usually, but try [Ctrl] Z or [Ctrl] [Enter]." I did—but nothing happened. He shrugged. I shrugged and laughed, then moved over to another machine to start my work all over again. . . . how fitting. I would not have enough time to make copies of the articles I searched for and would have to return another day.

I probably should not have trusted the computer to get me smoothly through my work that night; I left no time for computer error expecting the computer to be 100% reliable.

Critical Thinking

1. Consider the writer's closing comment. Was it realistic of her to expect the computer to be 100 percent reliable?

2. What might the writer have done to ensure the safety of her work?

3. How does the writer feel about taking personal responsibility versus blaming the computer for errors? What similar instances of each have you encountered?

4. Is the primary issue trusting the computer or being a computer-literate knowledge worker?

5. What did the writer learn about leaving enough time to deal with problems?

Methods of Data Processing

Why It's Important to Know

Different computer systems process data in different ways, depending on the importance of the data and the most efficient way to do the processing.

All computers perform the four data processing operations: input, processing, output, and storage. However, not all computers perform these four operations in the same manner. Various methods of data processing have come about during the computer's 50-some years of existence. By and large, these methods are evolutionary in nature: They evolved from simple batch processing, which occurred at set intervals, to more sophisticated real-time and interactive processing, which take place almost instantaneously. Processing has improved as hardware and software have improved.

Batch Processing

In the early years of business data processing—the 1950s and 1960s—computer processing was done in batches. **Batch processing** means that the data is collected in a batch over a period of time, then usually input, processed, and output in one session. One big factor in batch processing was the way instructions and data were stored: on punched cards, also called IBM cards, shown in figure 5.15.

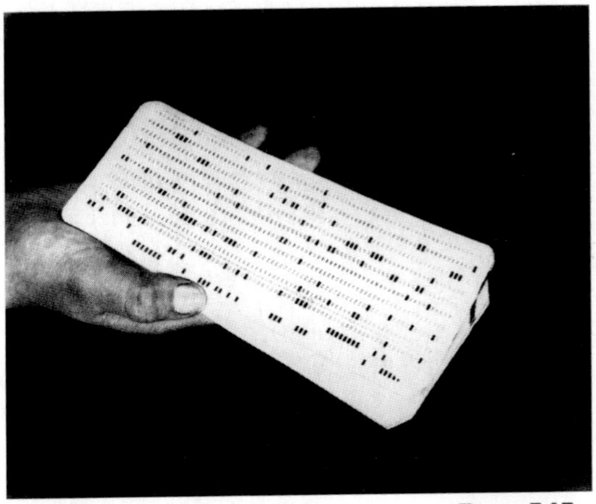

Batch processing helps people use the computer more efficiently; the computer can be used for important tasks during the day and perform the more repetitive and less important tasks overnight. Batch processing is best suited to tasks where there are many transactions to perform or tasks that are not particularly time-sensitive, such your monthly checking account statement from the bank.

Courtesy of International Business Machines Corporation

Figure 5.15

For example, say that a steel company makes concrete reinforcement bars only once a week, on Thursday. The company accumulates hundreds of orders Monday through Wednesday; the computer batch processes them Wednesday night. The computer tallies the orders, determines how much steel to make on Thursday, and prepares the invoices and shipping forms so that the orders can be shipped to customers on Friday.

Transaction Processing

Transaction processing means that data is processed as soon as it is input. The term *transaction* refers to an exchange between two parties, such as placing an order, shipping merchandise, or purchasing or renting something. Transaction processing is more frequently used as people and organizations require more speed and efficiency in handling transactions. You may hear it referred to as *on-line transaction processing*, or OLTP. The term *on-line* means that the computer or terminal you are using is directly connected to another computer that is doing the processing.

Figure 5.16

An on-line transaction processing screen.

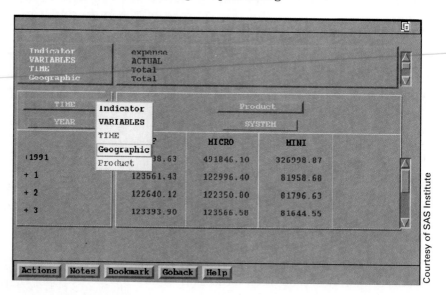

Courtesy of SAS Institute

For example, an order entry system at a mail-order sporting goods company allows the operator to enter the transaction immediately, producing an invoice and sending the paperwork to the warehouse for packing and shipping. Another example is a retail clothing store. When the salesperson scans the bar code on the product tag, the item is removed from the inven-tory count, the price is recorded on the cash register, its purchase is recorded in the customer's database file, and, if desired, a replacement item is ordered.

Real-Time Processing

If batch processing is the computer saying "I'll do it later" and transaction processing is "I'll take care of that promptly," then real-time processing is the computer saying "We've got to do it right now!"

Real-time processing is processing data immediately, as soon as it is input, and producing output just as immediately. The first computer to operate in real-time mode was the IBM AN/FSQ-7, better known as the Semi-Automatic Ground Environment (SAGE) system (see figure 5.17). SAGE, which went into operation in 1958, was the U.S. Air Force's means of early warning in case of an enemy air attack. The Air Force used 53 SAGE computers; the last one ceased operation in 1983.

Real-time computing is still associated with aircraft: computers used for air traffic control use real-time computing to warn of a possible mid-air collision. A smaller and more recent example of a real-time processing computer is the one that operates antilock disc brakes in automobiles. If the application is critical, a real-time computer can make a difference.

Interactive Processing

The types of processing discussed so far concern large computer systems. A term not often heard is **interactive processing**, which refers to a computer that can display the output so that changes may be made or errors corrected before the processing operation is completed. The way PCs process could be called interactive because all four data processing operations are, in effect, coordinated interactively by the knowledge worker.

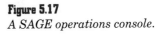

Figure 5.17
A SAGE operations console.

For example, data in a spreadsheet appears in columns with all the numbers totaled. Yet the knowledge worker can change the numbers or the mathematical equations at any time—repeating the input, processing, and output operations over and over until she gets the results she wants to store. Because the four operations are so closely coupled in PC hardware, everything happens quickly and interactively.

Compare this example with the transaction processing system in the retail store. Suppose that you purchase five items of clothing. The salesperson scans the five tags, and the purchases are processed. If you suddenly decide that you don't want one item, the clerk has to process another separate transaction to remove the item. If this system were an interactive one, the clerk could cancel the transaction by simply highlighting and deleting it on the monitor screen.

Parallel Processing

All the types of data processing described so far use *serial processing*, which means that only one instruction can be processed, by a single processor, at a time. Serial processing was the first type of processing invented, and it is still the dominant computer architecture. But the future holds great promise for parallel processing.

A **parallel processing** computer has more than one CPU, so that it can process instructions and data through multiple CPUs simultaneously. In serial processing, each instruction or transaction must wait in a queue to be processed. It's like going to a bank where there is only one teller. With parallel processing, there are many tellers; instructions or transactions are routed to the next one available and promptly processed. Each CPU has its own memory but often acts in concert with the others, each taking part of a processing job and performing the entire task far more quickly than a single-CPU computer could perform it. Parallel processing requires special software programs.

Sequent Computer Systems was the first company to make parallel processing machines that use an array of off-the-shelf microprocessors. Sequent considers the microprocessors as "building blocks for large-scale systems," ranging from a simple configuration of four to a maximum configuration of 250 or more. The parallel processing computer is ideally suited to high-volume processing, such as a World Wide Web site that must serve millions of visitors each day.

Courtesy of Computer Systems, Inc.

Figure 5.18

A Sequent parallel processing computer.

Another example is Millipore, an environmental testing company. Millipore changed from old, slow batch processing to parallel processing. On the old system, a request might not be filled for several days. On the new system, requests were filled with what was termed "stunning" performance. The old system ran at 27 MIPS; the new Sequent system ran at 350 MIPS. Millipore began creating a parallel processing environment in order to have on-line transaction processing that computerized its operations from beginning to end.[4]

A parallel processing computer typically has from 4 to 128 CPUs. When those numbers rise to the hundreds or even thousands of processors, the processing is called **massively parallel processing**, or **MPP**. A massively parallel processor can reach and exceed supercomputer speeds. For example, Prudential Securities ran benchmark tests on a set of financial analysis tasks. For the same tasks, a powerful minicomputer took 16,000 minutes, and a Cray supercomputer took 100 minutes. An Intel Hypercube performed the task in a few minutes.[5]

4. Jack B. Rochester. *I/S Analyzer*, "High-Performance Computing," May 1991, 8–11.

5. *Ibid*., pp. 3–4.

HOME PAGE

JOHN VON NEUMANN AND THE STORED PROGRAM CONCEPT

He was born in Budapest, Hungary, on December 23, 1903. John von Neumann earned his PhD in physics at the age of 22 and in 1927 became a scholar at the University of Berlin. Four years later, he joined the faculty at the Institute for Advanced Study at Princeton University in Princeton, New Jersey.

Von Neumann's head was filled with so many ideas, and he was so busy, that he allowed himself only five hours of sleep at night. During World War II, Johnny, as his friends called him, consulted in weather forecasting and ballistics and on the Manhattan Project—the atomic bomb. His work led to an interest in computers, and he became a technical advisor at the Moore School of Engineering at the University of Pennsylvania, where ENIAC was being built.

Courtesy of Richard Goldstein, RAND Corporation

In 1945, as a result of conversations regarding computer design, von Neumann wrote a paper entitled "First Draft of a Report on Edvac." Edvac was ENIAC's predecessor. This now-famous paper set forth for computer operation the precepts that have dominated the way computers are built ever since.

6. Rochester and Gantz. *The Naked Computer*, 70–71.

To the computer, instructions and data are indistinguishable; without knowing which was which, the computer would manipulate either. The paper explains how the computer instructions would be stored and how to handle the data separately from the instructions. This idea became known as the *stored-program concept*, and it is still the prevailing theory for serial-processing computers today.

John von Neumann died at the age of 53, a victim to bone cancer he most likely contracted from exposure to radiation. "I've met Einstein and Oppenheimer and Teller and a whole bunch of other guys," Professor Leon Hartman of Case-Western Reserve once said, "and von Neumann was the only genius I ever met. The others were supersmart . . . but von Neumann's mind was all-encompassing."[6]

HOME PAGE REVIEW QUESTIONS

1. What was the concept about which von Neumann wrote?

2. What is the computer incapable of doing unless otherwise directed?

3. What type of computer still uses the concepts developed for Edvac?

Knowledge Check

1. What was the earliest type of processing?
2. What makes transaction processing superior to batch processing?
3. What are the advantages of interactive processing?
4. When is real-time processing an advantage?
5. Why is parallel processing an advantage?

Key Terms

batch processing

parallel processing

interactive processing

real-time processing

massively parallel processing (MPP)

transaction processing

ISSUES AND IDEAS:

Buy Now or Later?

When is the best time to buy a PC? Many people have the impression that they should wait because prices are going to fall. However, the truth is that prices have been falling since 1982, and they will continue to fall. The price of a PC today will be less in the future, that's for certain; and tomorrow's computers will be more powerful and will have more features, too. But that was as true in 1982 as it is today.

There is the true story of a man who bought an Apple II, investing over $6,000 in hardware and software. After the IBM PC was introduced, the man soon realized that it had many features and a variety of software he desired. Yet he could not bring himself to sell his old Apple system because he could not get his money back out of it. He had mistakenly thought of the computer as an investment rather than as a consumable.

The best time to buy a computer is right now, because you can begin using it as soon as you have it. If you wait, you lose out by not having the use of the computer for all that time. You also lose the ability to gain proficiency and skills, which will make the learning curve much steeper when you finally do purchase a computer. The best decision is to buy the computer when you need it and keep it for as long as it is useful. You don't need to buy a new computer every time a new model is introduced—not even every year. Buy a new one when the features and benefits are such that it is hurting your productivity not to have the new model. You'll find a good way to dispose of your old computer, have no fear. Some of them find their way into dorm rooms at college campuses!

CRITICAL THINKING

1. From a financial standpoint, what is the best way to view a computer purchase?

2. What are the constraints that keep you or people you know from buying a computer?

3. If price were no object, what would be your reasons today for buying a new computer?

ETHICS

Professional Conduct and a Code of Ethics

Civilized, respectful conduct and behavior based on a code of ethics apply to all citizens. This statement is also true for people who create computer systems and those who use them. The Association of Computing Machinery, or ACM, approved an updated Code of Ethics in 1992. It states that "Commitment to ethical professional conduct is expected of every voting, associate, and student member of the ACM."[7] Classified as "1. General Moral Imperatives," the Code states that ACM members will do the following:

1. Contribute to society and human well-being.
2. Avoid harm to others.
3. Be honest and trustworthy.
4. Be fair and take action not to discriminate.
5. Honor property rights including copyrights and patents.
6. Give proper credit for intellectual property.
7. Respect the privacy of others.
8. Honor confidentiality.

Critical Thinking

1. Discuss each of these moral imperatives and create an example from
    a. Society
    b. Your social group
    c. Your work or profession (such as student)
    d. Your personal life
2. What imperatives seem most difficult to sustain?
3. What examples of good ethical behavior can you cite? Bad ethical behavior? Which list is longer, and why do you suppose that is?

---

7. "ACM Code of Ethics and Professional Conduct," from *Computers, Ethics and Social Values*, Deborah G. Johnson and Helen Nissenbaum, eds. (Englewood Cliffs: Prentice-Hall, 1995), 598–601.

THE LEARNING ENTERPRISE

Now that you have determined all the hardware needs for your enterprise—and before you go on to the software requirements—it is time to consider some of your human resources. Your objective is to determine what skills, training, and support the knowledge workers in each department or function will need to maximize their productivity. This determination, of course, also involves the application of computer technology.

In order to reach this objective, you must think of the enterprise's goal as a business process. Dr. Peter G.W. Keen describes it this way: "Existing business processes are built around a division of labor that has created 'stovepipe' functional departments that make simple work complex. By taking a fresh look at the processes that most affect customer satisfaction and service, firms can . . . fundamentally transform the organization and mobilize the company's culture and information technology."[8]

What is a business process? James Cortada and John Woods define it this way: "Any activity or a collection of activities that takes inputs and transforms and adds value to them, and then delivers an output to an internal or external customer. A process has distinct start and end points and includes actions that are definable, repeatable, predictable, and measurable. A process always has a specific purpose that has value to some customer."[9]

For example, accounting and financial management will certainly need a larger, more powerful computer system as the enterprise grows more profitable, and that acquisition means people to operate and program the computer system. Other knowledge workers will need training in order to use it. Computer systems in other departments may need to be reconfigured to exchange data with the new accounting system; that may mean a need for power users with special skills.

But before these things can be determined, accounting needs to understand the overall enterprise process: what decision support's and management's objectives are, and how the work process flows from R&D to manufacturing to sales and marketing. The company certainly doesn't need to go to all the trouble and expense unless there is a need and unless the new system will contribute to the goals of the enterprise.

---

8. Peter G. W. Keen. *Every Manager's Guide to Information Technology*, Second Edition (Boston; Harvard Business School Press, 1995), 80.

9. James Cortada and John Woods. *McGraw-Hill Encyclopedia of Quality Terms and Concepts* (New York: McGraw-Hill, 1995), 264.

Your first task is to define the process that flows throughout your enterprise and gives it purpose. Make sure that yours is not a "stovepipe" organization that doesn't communicate with other departments and functions. Then, each department or function must coordinate its objectives and requirements with Human Resources and Management Information Systems to determine its needs. As you work on this project, it's a good idea to appoint an emissary who coordinates with other groups. Fill in the tasks each group must address:

Accounting and Financial Management:

Community Relations:

Creative Resources:

Decision Support and Management:

Human Resources:

Insurance:

Legal:

Long-Range Planning:

Management Information Systems:

Manufacturing:

Program Development:

Research and Design:

Sales and Marketing:

Chapter Review

Fill in the Blank

1. The _____ contains the computer's primary circuitry.
2. A hardware-to-hardware interface, or _____, connects the main circuit board to the peripheral devices.
3. The _____ is a microprocessor support chip used when additional or special processing is needed.
4. A small chunk of silicon semiconductor material that contains hundreds of thousands to millions of electronic circuits is called a(n) _____.
5. An electronic pathway on the main circuit board is called a(n) _____.
6. The computer's processing, control, and internal storage circuitry is called the _____, or _____.
7. The _____, or chip, replaced the vacuum tube in computers.
8. The integrated circuit that drives the computer's central processing unit is called the _____.
9. The machine cycle processes _____ instructions.
10. The two types of operations the CPU performs are _____ and _____.

Circle the Correct Answer

1. CPU clock speed is measured in (Hertz, Baud).
2. The most common CPU architecture today is (CISC, RISC).
3. The CPU architecture that has the minimum number of instructions is (CISC, RISC).
4. (Registers, Secondary storage) are closest to the CPU for fastest processing.
5. The measurement of processing performance is (CISC, MIPS).
6. The memory that cannot be changed is called (RAM, ROM).
7. The memory that holds instructions and data is called (RAM, ROM).
8. The most efficient way to install random-access memory on the main circuit board is with (SIMMs, RISC).

Review Questions

1. Where does the computer's primary electronic circuitry reside?

2. How are external peripherals, such as the monitor, connected to the computer?

3. Expansion cards give additional capabilities to computers. Name several of these capabilities.

4. What is the connection used by the printer called?

5. Describe the different kinds of memory and tell how each is used: cache, registers, ROM, and RAM.

6. What is the purpose of data representation, and how does it affect processing speed?

7. Describe the measures of memory and storage.

Discussion Questions

1. Refer to the Home Page discussion in Module B. Find chips that are capable of processing more than one instruction per machine cycle. Look up processor speeds for earlier microprocessors, and compare them to today's faster chips. Discuss these speed increases in relation to any other technology and its implications. What if another technology had realized this kind of improvement in the same relative length of time?

2. Discuss the machine cycle, and explain why it's important to have instructions and data stored ever closer to the CPU, such as with cache memory. What is the purpose of closer storage?

3. Discuss the different types of processing explained in Module E, their history, and what each is best suited for.

4. Discuss the emerging technologies of parallel processing and RISC technology in comparison to von Neumann's stored program concept and the single-instruction processing technology prevalent today. What are the advantages?

INTERNET DISCOVERY

Learn more about commerce and the functions of your enterprise on the Galaxy Web site. You'll find many categories to explore: Business Administration, General Resources, and a number of sites with function-specific information. Each knowledge worker should find at least one useful document. Log on to the following site:

http://galaxy.einet.net/galaxy/Business-and-Commerce.html

PERIPHERALS

We can write off the peripherals, as they're called (the input, output and storage devices), as plain ordinary machines, doing what they do out of electromechanical necessity. A coded electrical pulse comes down the line, the juice flows in, and they do what they're wired to do. No choice. . . . Peripherals just follow orders.

Phil Bertoni, Strangers in Computerland[1]

Peripherals, or peripheral hardware, accomplish the data processing steps of input, output, and storage. Peripherals work with the processor—the computer itself—and deliver results to the knowledge worker. Peripherals are the CPU's senses. Without peripherals, we could not issue instructions to the computer, nor could the computer process data or the knowledge worker obtain the information. Peripherals are connected to the main circuit board, either by an expansion slot or with a cable plugged into a port. Peripheral devices fall into four categories: input, output, storage, and communication devices. The first two work hand in hand; that's why we often refer to them as *I/O*, or *input/output*, devices.

1. (New York: Vintage Books, 1983), 17, 71.

CHAPTER 6

Module A

The Computer Interface

Why It's Important to Know

> **The computer interface is the way peripheral devices are connected to the computer's main circuit board. The computer interface has three aspects: physical, logical, and human.**

Interface is probably one of the most misused words in the English language. People often mistakenly use the word as a verb to describe communications or interactions between people. Yet **interface** is more appropriately used as a noun that names the point where a peripheral device or a human meets the computer.

Interfaces are categorized in three types:

- *The physical interface.* The ports and connecting cables between the main circuit board and peripheral devices.

- *The logical interface.* The software that enhances communication and operations between the computer and the peripheral.

- *The human-computer interface.* The point at which the knowledge worker comes in physical contact with the computer system. The ergonomic design aspects of peripherals can benefit the human-computer interface, making the computer easier to use and enhancing productivity.

Now you are ready to look more closely at each type of interface.

The Physical Interface

Whether you can use a particular peripheral device with a certain processor depends on the availability of the correct physical interface. The **physical interface** is a connection between two hardware devices. The most common physical interfaces connect the system unit and peripheral devices. Another type of physical interface is the expansion slot, which connects an expansion card to the main circuit board.

Either the system unit or the external peripheral device—sometimes both—has a physical interface connection called a port. The port is a connection designed to manage the flow of data between the two devices. A cable or wire is often needed as a connection between the peripheral and the system unit. Figure 6.1 shows the ports on the back of a PC.

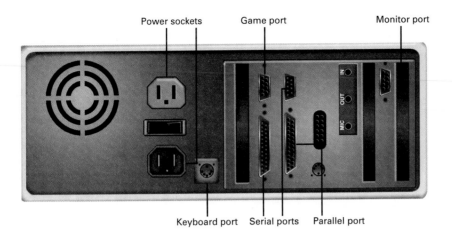

Power sockets   Game port   Monitor port

Keyboard port   Serial ports   Parallel port

Figure 6.1
*Ports are plug-in recepta-
cles on the back of the
computer.*

Some peripherals—such as the pointing device, the keyboard, and the monitor—have their own cables, which connect directly to the main circuit board
or to an expansion card. A joystick has its own port, called a **game port**.
Other peripherals use a standardized physical interface called a serial or
parallel port.

The **serial interface** is used to connect a variety of devices, usually a
mouse or modem. **Serial** means that the data passes through the interface
sequentially, one bit at a time. Serial ports are named COM1, COM2, and so
on. The serial interface is explained in figure 6.2.

The **parallel interface** is commonly used to connect the printer. **Parallel**
means that several bits of data pass through the interface simultaneously;
for example, eight bits of data are transmitted through eight separate wires
in the cable, side by side, at the same time. Parallel ports are named LPT1,
LPT2, and so on. The parallel interface is explained in figure 6.3.

Two other physical interfaces warrant mention. The **Integrated Drive
Electronics**, or **IDE**, interface is used with hard disk drives in PC compatibles. Its older counterpart, the ESDI (Enhanced System Device Interface),
required a controller card plugged into an expansion slot in order to provide
an interface to the hard disk drive. IDE redesigned the interface so
that most of the controller electronics are mounted directly on the hard disk
drive itself; no controller card or expansion slot is required. Some large
disk drives (1G and over) and CD-ROM drives use the high-speed *Enhanced
IDE*, or *EIDE*, interface.

The other physical interface is the **Small Computer System Interface**, or
SCSI (pronounced "scuzzy"). Using a SCSI is like having a separate parallel
interface, external to the main circuit board, into which you can connect
hard disk drives, CD-ROM drives, printers, modems, scanners, and so on. As
many as seven devices can be connected to a single SCSI port (six with a
Macintosh), although only one device can be in use at a given time.

Serial Port

Figure 6.2

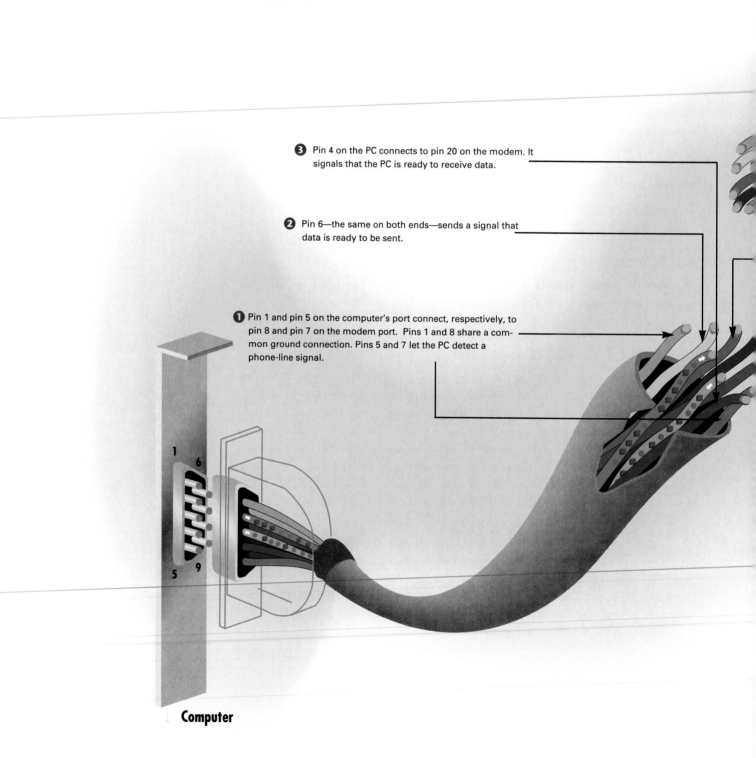

3 Pin 4 on the PC connects to pin 20 on the modem. It signals that the PC is ready to receive data.

2 Pin 6—the same on both ends—sends a signal that data is ready to be sent.

1 Pin 1 and pin 5 on the computer's port connect, respectively, to pin 8 and pin 7 on the modem port. Pins 1 and 8 share a common ground connection. Pins 5 and 7 let the PC detect a phone-line signal.

Computer

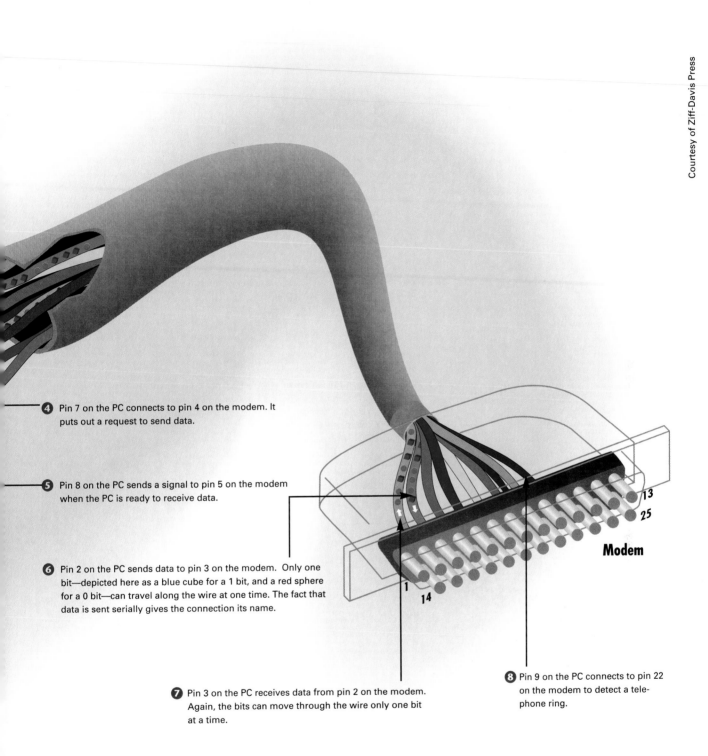

4 Pin 7 on the PC connects to pin 4 on the modem. It puts out a request to send data.

5 Pin 8 on the PC sends a signal to pin 5 on the modem when the PC is ready to receive data.

6 Pin 2 on the PC sends data to pin 3 on the modem. Only one bit—depicted here as a blue cube for a 1 bit, and a red sphere for a 0 bit—can travel along the wire at one time. The fact that data is sent serially gives the connection its name.

13

25

Modem

1

14

8 Pin 9 on the PC connects to pin 22 on the modem to detect a telephone ring.

7 Pin 3 on the PC receives data from pin 2 on the modem. Again, the bits can move through the wire only one bit at a time.

Parallel Port

Figure 6.3

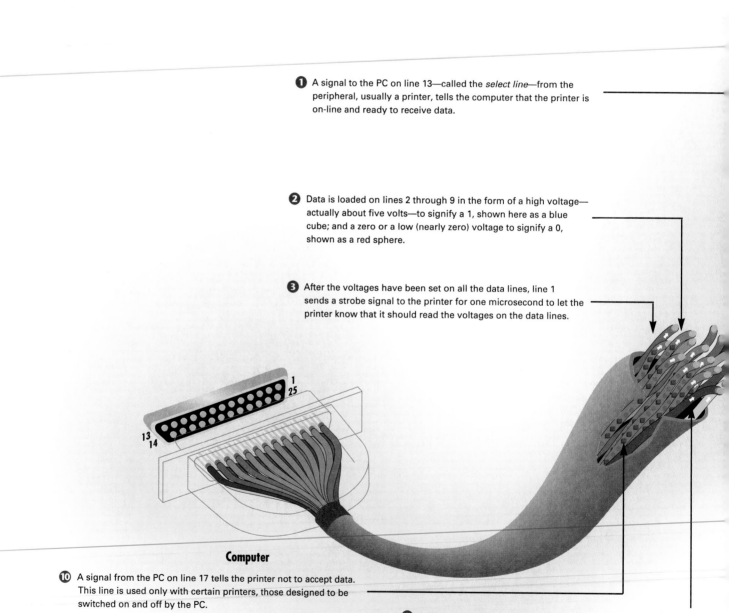

❶ A signal to the PC on line 13—called the *select line*—from the peripheral, usually a printer, tells the computer that the printer is on-line and ready to receive data.

❷ Data is loaded on lines 2 through 9 in the form of a high voltage—actually about five volts—to signify a 1, shown here as a blue cube; and a zero or a low (nearly zero) voltage to signify a 0, shown as a red sphere.

❸ After the voltages have been set on all the data lines, line 1 sends a strobe signal to the printer for one microsecond to let the printer know that it should read the voltages on the data lines.

Computer

❿ A signal from the PC on line 17 tells the printer not to accept data. This line is used only with certain printers, those designed to be switched on and off by the PC.

❾ A low-voltage or zero-voltage signal from the PC on line 14 tells the printer to advance the paper one line when it receives a carriage-return code. A high-voltage signal tells the printer to advance the paper one line only when it receives a line-advance code from the printer.

Courtesy of Ziff-Davis Press

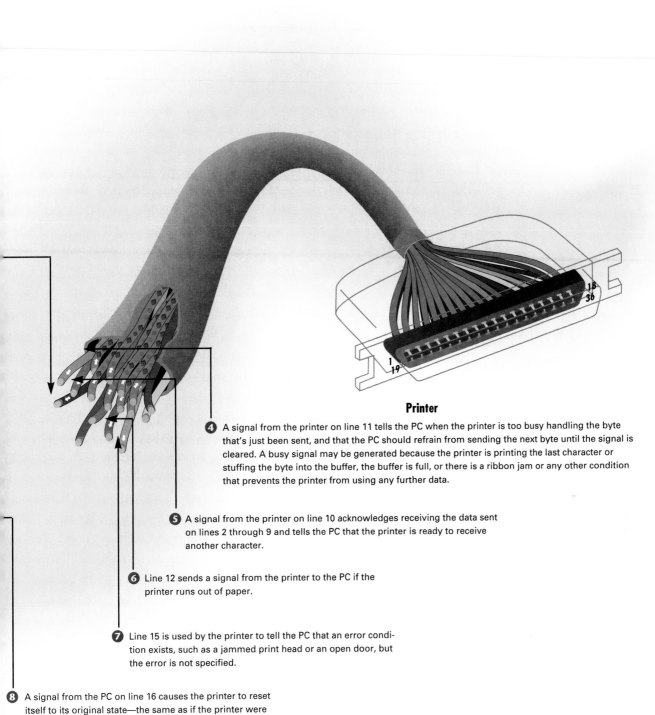

Printer

4 A signal from the printer on line 11 tells the PC when the printer is too busy handling the byte that's just been sent, and that the PC should refrain from sending the next byte until the signal is cleared. A busy signal may be generated because the printer is printing the last character or stuffing the byte into the buffer, the buffer is full, or there is a ribbon jam or any other condition that prevents the printer from using any further data.

5 A signal from the printer on line 10 acknowledges receiving the data sent on lines 2 through 9 and tells the PC that the printer is ready to receive another character.

6 Line 12 sends a signal from the printer to the PC if the printer runs out of paper.

7 Line 15 is used by the printer to tell the PC that an error condition exists, such as a jammed print head or an open door, but the error is not specified.

8 A signal from the PC on line 16 causes the printer to reset itself to its original state—the same as if the printer were turned off and on.

Note: Lines 18 through 25 are simply ground lines.

An advantage of using the SCSI is the capability to connect many peripherals to a single port. Another advantage is that each peripheral is an "intelligent" device, meaning that it can communicate with other devices independently of the computer. Thus, the data on one SCSI storage device could be backed up to another SCSI storage device while the computer is busy with other tasks. Connecting several devices at once is called *daisy-chaining*.

The Logical Interface

In the early days of computing, changing from one peripheral to another meant reprogramming the computer—often necessitating flipping switches and recalibrating electronic circuits. This task could take hours to complete.

Today, most peripherals with special functions come with their own software so that they'll work properly with the rest of the system. This software is the **logical interface**, which sets up a form of communication between hardware devices so that they "talk" to one another.

A common logical interface is printer driver software, often referred to as a *device driver*, but usually just called a **driver**. Printers have become sophisticated devices with their own internal languages for creating type fonts and graphics. The driver sets up a logical interface with the commands issued from the operating system and ensures that the data sent from the processor is correctly translated to the printed copy.

As peripheral devices grow more sophisticated and do more, the logical interface—the drivers—becomes more feature-laden. The Microsoft mouse and Microsoft Natural Keyboard come with driver software called IntelliType Manager, which enables you to customize these input devices to suit your needs and preferences (see figure 6.4).

Figure 6.4
With IntelliType Manager, you can customize the way your keyboard and mouse perform.

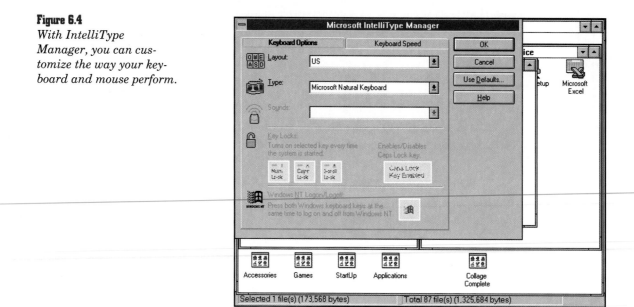

The Human-Computer Interface

The point at which people use input and output devices is referred to as the human-computer interface. One goal for many designers is to provide the most humanlike interface possible—with aspects that are easy for people to understand intuitively. In other words, we should be able to communicate with the computer as simply as we do with another person.

In the simplest terms, designing for a good human-computer interface means that the keyboard—the most commonly used input device—responds well to the touch. Engineers study the *human factors*, concerns such as the key's length of travel, the kind of clicking sound it should make and at what point during the keystroke, spacing of the keys, and much more. The study of **ergonomics** explores the human factors surrounding the design of computers, office environments, furniture, and other aspects of the work area in order to make them more healthy and easy for people to use.

A good human-computer interface also means a video monitor that is clear, adjustable, and easy on the eyes. The trend in monitors is toward flat screens; a very-fine-grain display; low radiation emission; and the capability to adjust the color, contrast, brightness, and image according to personal preferences.

The human-computer interface is primarily concerned with peripherals, but as you will see, it also extends to software design, such as the graphic user interface.

Courtesy of Nanoa Corporation

Figure 6.5
This monitor has its own programmable microprocessor that enables the knowledge worker to set his or her own preferences.

Peripheral Devices and the Human-Computer Interface

A *peripheral device* performs input, output, or storage functions and is connected to the CPU through the main circuit board. Without peripheral devices, the CPU is of no use to people. Figure 6.6 shows a variety of peripherals that connect to a personal computer. Some are externally connected, and others are plugged into the main circuit board's expansion slots inside the system unit.

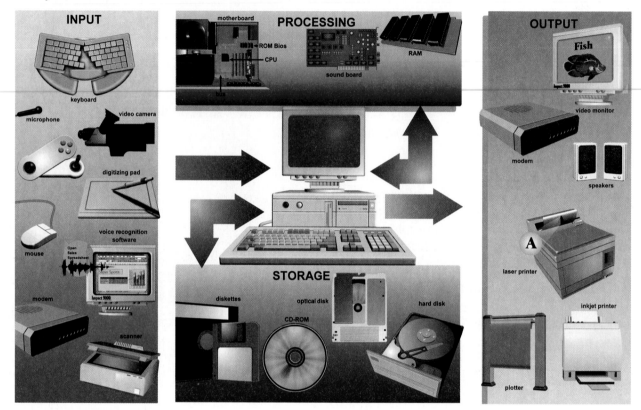

Figure 6.6
Peripheral devices have been designed for many different tasks and the individual needs of many different knowledge workers. All the peripherals, external and internal, connect to the main circuit board

HERMAN HOLLERITH AND THE FIRST I/O DEVICE

Herman Hollerith had a problem to solve: how to count the 1890 census data in less than the seven years it had taken to do the 1880 census. Hollerith applied punched card technology, invented by the Frenchman Joseph-Marie Jacquard for knitting machines, to mechanical tabulating machines. This card, called the Hollerith card, was the size of a dollar bill. By 1884, Hollerith had developed an electro-mechanical tabulating machine. It used some of the same technology as an electric telegraph and had the same mechanical counters as an adding machine.

Herman Hollerith.

The *punched card* had a pattern of holes punched in it to code the program instructions. To read the cards, the machine made electrical contact by means of pins passing through the holes in the card and touching a bath of mercury below. The machine could read from 50 to 80 cards a minute. Counting the census involved tabulating data on 62,622,250 citizens. That amounted to 2 billion holes in punched cards. Hollerith's machine did the job in just over two years. An article in a magazine of the time said, "This apparatus works as unerringly as the mills of the gods, and beats them hollow as to speed."

Hollerith leased his equipment to the U.S. government and to other countries. In 1896, he formed the Tabulating Machine Company. That company became International Business Machines, and the punched card became the IBM card. Over the years, billions and billions of punched cards have been used for storing programs and data. But now, other more efficient forms of input and output have replaced the punched card. The last IBM punched card plant closed its doors in 1986. Today, the Bureau of the Census uses the most modern VAX computers from Digital Equipment Corp. Yet it took as long to process the census in 1990 as it did in 1890, primarily because the population has grown so much.

Punched cards as input. The computer must read each card to process instructions.

HOME PAGE REVIEW QUESTIONS

1. What did the company that Hollerith started become known as?
2. Why do you think that punched cards are less efficient than newer I/O devices?
3. What type of processing do you think the punched cards best support—batch or transaction?

Knowledge Check

1. What three functions do peripherals perform?
2. Name the two ways peripherals are connected with computers.
3. Name two common I/O devices.
4. What is a peripheral-to-computer connection called?
5. What is a human-to-peripheral connection called?

Key Terms

driver	ergonomics	game port	Integrated Drive Electronics (IDE)
interface	logical interface	parallel	parallel interface
physical interface	serial	serial interface	Small Computer System Interface (SCSI)

ISSUES AND IDEAS

Is There Sexism in Computing?

Feminism and political correctness have removed many sexist and racially sensitive terms from our language. Yet some terminology in the field of computing lingers, giving people reason for concern.

One sexist term crops up when you are using the operating system to work with a disk. If the operating system is unable to perform the desired task, a message that reads "Abort, Retry, Fail?" appears.

Another term that has caused great offense is *motherboard*, which is used in place of main circuit board. Ports are referred to as "female connectors" and plugs as "male connectors." One educator describes these terms as "archaic and obscene."

CRITICAL THINKING

1. Why do you think that sexist terms came to be used in the first place? Did people realize they were "sexist"?
2. Do you find any of these terms offensive? State your reasons.
3. Why is it usually better to have terms that accurately describe an object—such as the main circuit board—than to use a less accurate, analogous term?
4. Think of some other terms, like *abort*, from your experience. Can you suggest alternatives?

Input Devices

Why It's Important to Know

> **Input devices are used to issue instructions and enter data. Specific input devices have been designed for specific tasks or to work with specific types of software. Designing input devices that are easy to use is a high priority.**

Input devices perform the two most basic computing tasks: issuing commands and entering data. The simple input activity is **data entry**: the process of entering data into computer memory and issuing commands that tell the processor how to work with the data. For example, if you place a mail order, the customer service representative fills out an order form on the screen and then issues the instruction to save the order in a file. This data processing activity occurs concurrently with the actual order processing.

The CPU cannot produce any meaningful output until data is input for the CPU to process. Once data is available, someone must give the CPU instructions for what to do with the data. There are many different types of input devices with which to enter data and issue instructions. Most input devices depend on knowledge workers' using their fingers and their eyes to perform data entry—although, as you shall see, that too is changing.

The Keyboard

When Christopher Sholes invented the typewriter, he significantly advanced written communications. However, he had to do so with available technology. The keys were attached to long bars with the type characters on the end; they traveled forward and struck the paper through an inked ribbon to make an impression. Typing too fast caused the bars to get tangled, so Sholes designed the typewriter keyboard to slow the typing process. We call this the QWERTY keyboard, and it is the one most people use for typewriters and computers alike.

The Standard Computer Keyboard

The first computer keyboards were nearly identical to a typewriter's keyboard, with one or two additional keys for issuing computer-related commands. The character keyboard contains all the *alphanumeric* characters (letters and numbers) that are used in daily English. Both Macintosh and PC-compatible computers have a *101-key enhanced keyboard*. A PC version is shown in figure 6.7. The 101-key keyboard adds to the standard typewriter keyboard the arrays of keys identified in the figure.

Function keys, F1 to F12, usually across the top of the keyboard

System keys for use by the operating system, the operating environment, or applications

A *numeric keypad* that resembles an electronic calculator's keypad

Figure 6.7
The IBM enhanced keyboard.

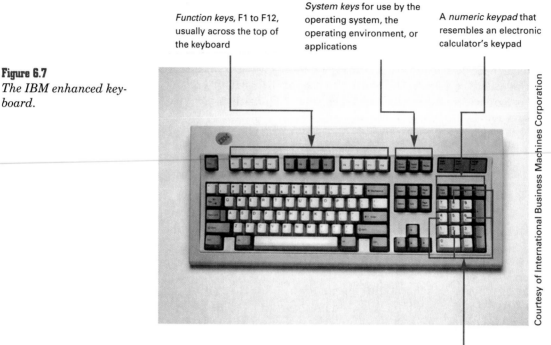

Courtesy of International Business Machines Corporation

Four *cursor-movement* keys

Some keyboards have additional keys that can be programmed to perform specific tasks. For example, the Macintosh has an "Apple key" for issuing commands. Holding it down and pressing a second key initiates a command. For example, +O opens a file. Some PC-compatible keyboards now have a "Windows key" that displays the Windows 95 "Start" main menu when pressed. In most cases, you can issue any command initiated by the pointing device by using keyboard keys in various combinations.

Figure 6.8
Follow the color coding as you read the discussion of the personal computer keyboard features.

Toggle keys   Numeric keypad

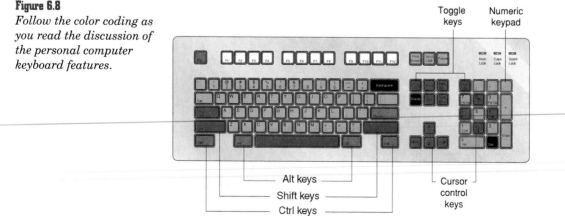

Alt keys
Shift keys
Ctrl keys

Cursor control keys

To the left of the alphanumeric keys are the **Caps Lock** and **Shift** keys, used to type capital letters. Caps Lock is a *toggle* key; it alternates between two related tasks, or turns a task on or off, each time it's pressed. When you press Caps Lock, you will probably see on your keyboard a light indicating that Caps Lock is toggled on. Now you type all capital letters. When you press Caps Lock again, it toggles off for normal typing. The Shift key types a capital letter only as long as you hold Shift down.

To the right is a second Shift key, and above it the **Return** key, often displaying **Enter** and referred to as the Enter key. The Enter key takes the place of the typewriter's Return key, which was used at the end of a line of typing to move down one line. You press Enter to complete and issue a command or instruction to the computer software—either the operating system or an application. In this respect, pressing Enter takes the place of clicking the mouse's primary button. In word processing, the Enter key inserts a *hard return* when you want to end a line or a paragraph. Above the Enter key is the **Backspace** key, which deletes the last character typed. Holding Backspace down deletes every character to the left until you release the key.

In the center of the keyboard and below the alphanumeric keys is the **space bar**, used to insert blank spaces between characters or words. To either side, note the **Control (Ctrl)** and **Alternate (Alt)** keys; they are used with standard keyboard keys to issue commands or instructions to the application software.

Above the alphanumeric keypad is another row of keys. At the far left is the **Escape (Esc)** key. This key was once used either to stop a task in progress or to exit from an application program altogether, but over the years its uses have changed. In the Windows operating environment, Escape is used with the Alt key to switch between programs. In such programs as Microsoft Excel, the Esc key is used to cancel an operation.

Directly to the right of the Esc key are the **function** keys, which perform commands or instructions for the specific application program you're using. For example, pressing F5 in Microsoft Word issues the Go To command: *go to* a specific page number, section, footnote, and so on. The function keys often duplicate commands that are available by using the Shift, Alt, or Control key in combination with other keys; for example, holding down the Ctrl key and pressing G is another way to use Go To. Another way to use Go To is to use the Edit pull-down menu.

Just to the right of the function keys are three system keys. These keys are used primarily for system software functions and not often needed by knowledge workers. However, you may use the first key, **Print Screen**, to capture and print the screen exactly as you're viewing it.

The middle set of keys to the right of the alphanumeric keys are used in most programs. The first is the **Insert** key which, like Caps Lock, is a toggle key. In Insert mode, every character you type is inserted at the position of the insertion point (the vertical bar), pushing ahead all the text following it. Nothing is deleted; every new character you type is inserted into the existing text. If you press the Insert key, it toggles to Typeover mode, where every character you type replaces any character that was there previously. Typeover mode, sometimes called Overstrike mode, deletes each old character as you type a new character. There is no keyboard indicator light for the Insert/Typeover key, but you can check its status in the application's status line if it has one.

You can use the **Home**, **End**, **Page Up**, and **Page Down** keys with the cursor keys, depending on the way the programmers designed the application software. For example, in most spreadsheets, the Home key takes you to the first cell on the left or to cell A1. In most word processing programs, Page Up and Page Down take you backward or forward a screen at a time.

In addition to the Backspace key, there is a **Delete** key. It removes the character on which the insertion point rests, and continues to remove every character it rests on as long as you press Delete. The Backspace key deletes to the left; the Delete key deletes to the right.

The lower keys to the right of the alphanumeric keys are the **cursor-control** keys. These four arrow keys move the insertion point around on-screen as you work—from cell to cell in the spreadsheet and through the lines of written text in word processing.

At the far right side of the keyboard is the numeric keypad, so called because it is laid out like the keys on an electronic calculator. On most computers, the numeric keypad is toggled on automatically, and the keypad is ready for working with numbers. This keypad is especially handy if you're using the calculator or the spreadsheet program. You can see that the surrounding keys are used to add, subtract, multiply, and divide—the four primary mathematical functions. The second Enter key is conveniently placed beside the numeric keypad.

When you press the **Num Lock** key—the third toggle key discussed here—the numeric keypad becomes a second cursor-movement keypad. When Num Lock is toggled off, the **2**, **4**, **6**, and **8** keys become cursor-control keys identical to the arrow keys. In this mode, the **0** (zero) key becomes a second Insert key, and the decimal point becomes a second **Delete** key, identical to the other Delete key.

Other Keyboard Designs

We take the QWERTY keyboard for granted, but in 1936, August Dvorak designed a far more efficient keyboard (see figure 6.9). The Dvorak keyboard places the most frequently used keys under the strongest fingers, reducing wasted finger motions and awkward strokes. The Dvorak also permits faster typing speeds with more comfort and fewer typing errors.

Figure 6.9

The Dvorak keyboard is an illustration of how the most efficient and superior technology is not necessarily the one in widespread use.

The axiom about building a better mousetrap and the world rushing to your door doesn't seem to hold true for keyboards. People seem to be overly cautious when it comes to changing something as basic as the keyboard. Why don't more people use the clearly superior Dvorak keyboard? The simple answer is that they learned to type on the QWERTY, and it is hard for most people to change and learn another method.

Yet there are some QWERTY keyboard innovations that don't require us to change the fundamental way we input. Here are a few examples.

The *Microsoft Natural Keyboard* is designed with special keys and shortcuts to make Microsoft Windows 95 easier to use (see figure 6.10). The overall shape of this keyboard and the way it is split and angled make it an innovative and ergonomic advance in keyboard design. It also

Courtesy of Microsoft Corporation

Figure 6.10

has three additional keys: a "Windows key" on either side, between the Ctrl and Alt keys, that calls up the Start menu; and a third programmable key beside the Windows key on the right. A Microsoft advertisement says that "you are connected, fitted, ergonomically and intuitively one with the machine."[2]

The *Alps GlidePoint Keyboard and TouchPad* combines an ergonomic keyboard and a unique pointing device that looks like a small screen. You move the pointer by moving your fingertip on the screen, and you issue commands by tapping (see figure 6.11). The model designed for use with PC compatibles has features that take particular advantage of Windows 95. A Macintosh version is also available.

The *Wireless Keyboard and Mouse touchpad* replace cables with a wireless transmitter and receiver, which makes it possible to compute up to 30 feet from the computer. It's a standard keyboard layout but with a touchpad pointing device. The idea of a wireless keyboard isn't new, however; IBM tried it 15 years ago with its PC Junior, one of the biggest flops in the personal computing industry.

2. *PC Week*, July 1995, 72–3.

Figure 6.11
*Alps GlidePoint Keyboard
and TouchPad.*

Courtesy of ALPS

Pointing Devices

Several types of pointing devices are used to move the cursor; these devices usually work with a keyboard. Pointing devices commonly have two or three buttons that are used to issue commands to the computer.

Regardless of the type of pointing device you use, you will perform certain common actions. To **point** is the act of moving the pointing device to an object on-screen. The next step is to make a selection, commonly called a **click**. *Point and click* is the way you issue commands to modern computers. For example, you *point* the arrow at the printer icon and then *click* to issue the command to print.

The pointing device can also be used for a variety of tasks within a specific application. For example, you use the pointing device to highlight a block of text that you want to move or delete in a pair of actions called *click and drag*. **Drag** refers to holding down the pointing-device button while you move the pointer through data. You place the pointer or cursor at the beginning of the text and press and hold the mouse button; then you drag the cursor to the end of the selected section. As the cursor moves through the text, it is highlighted. **Highlighting** means that the selection's appearance has been changed, either by reversing the characters or changing the display color. When the button is released, the highlighting ends, and the pointing device is ready to issue another command. Then the highlighted block of data can be deleted, moved, or copied. Figure 6.12 shows a block of highlighted text in word processing.

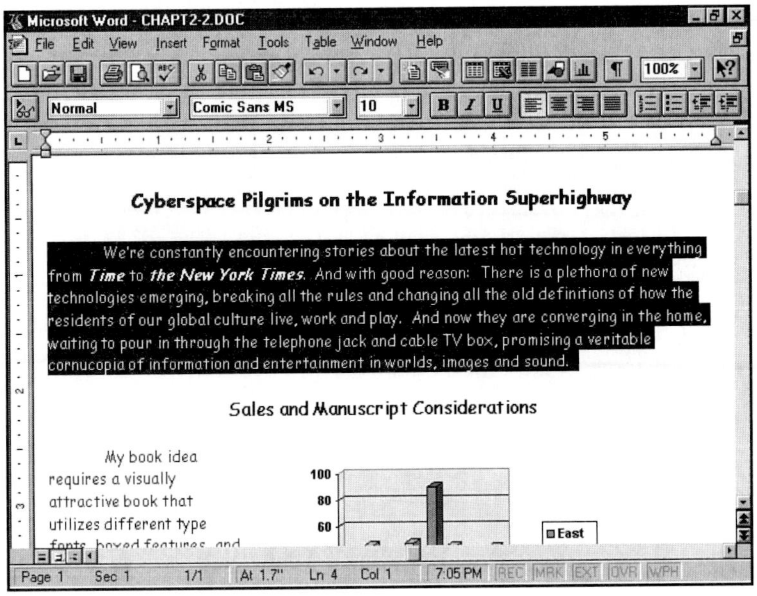

Figure 6.12
Once text is highlighted, it can be cut and moved, deleted, or copied.

The Mouse

The most common pointing device is the *mouse*, so named because it has a wire, or "tail," attached to the computer. Douglas Englebart pioneered the mouse. His first model, built in 1963, was made of wood and used two wheels for movement (see figure 6.13). At the time, he and his colleagues at Xerox's highly respected Palo Alto Research Center (PARC) were also exploring such futuristic concepts as the workstation, graphic user interfaces, and networking, to name a few.

Courtesy of Doug Englebart

Figure 6.13
Doug Englebart's first mouse prototype.

Other Pointing Devices

Another commonly used pointing device is the **trackball**, which performs like a stationary, upside-down mouse. Figure 6.14 shows two types. Many people prefer the trackball over the mouse because the trackball does not require as much hand-eye coordination, nor does it require the extra desk space necessary to move the mouse. Most portable laptop computers use a built-in or clip-on trackball. The touchpad, mentioned earlier with keyboards (refer to figure 6.11), is also available separately.

Figure 6.14

Courtesy of International Business Machines Corporation

Courtesy of International Business Machines Corporation

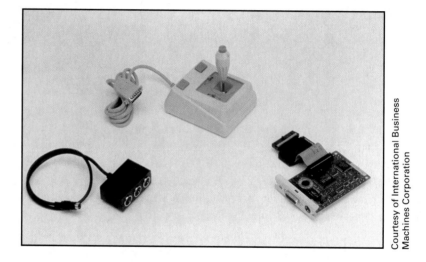

Courtesy of International Business Machines Corporation

The **joystick** is another pointing device, one usually associated with playing computer games. Joysticks used to produce jerky movement and can be awkward to hold; however, newer models, such as the one shown in figure 6.14, use advanced technology for smooth movement and are ergonomically designed to fit the hand.

Writing and Drawing Input Devices

There are several ways to use a device similar to a pen for entering data. One is the **light pen**, used to draw, write, or issue commands when it touches the specially designed video monitor screen (see figure 6.15). For example, a circuit designer can draw the interconnecting wires in electronic circuits with a light pen. The light pen was originally developed for computer-aided drafting at MIT in 1964 and is now used in some types of hand-held personal computers.

Even simpler than the light pen is your finger, which you can use as an input device on a video monitor with a **touch-sensitive screen** (see figure 6.15). You may have used a touch-sensitive screen to get information at a fast-food restaurant, an airport, or a grocery store.

A drawing tablet, or **digitizer**, is similar to the touch-sensitive screen and makes a good input device (see figure 6.15). Some digitizers have a form overlay that the data entry clerk fills out with a light pen or stylus. Others have more sophisticated stylus or pointing devices that are useful for designers, architects, artists, desktop publishers, or map makers, to name a few. The cartoonist Skip Morrow uses a digitizing tablet to produce work such as *The Official I Hate Cats Book*.

Courtesy of Ford Motor Company

Figure 6.15
The light pen, the touch screen, and the digitizer provide means of data input.

Video Input

With a video digitizer peripheral, you can use images from video cameras, camcorders, VCRs, and optical disc players for input to computers, either as static "snapshots" or digitized moving video. You can then use these images in many different ways. A series of snapshots can describe a process, such as the assembling of a machine or an athlete's movements. The most recent video input device is the **digital camera**, which takes still photographs and transfers them directly into the computer through the serial port. A digital camera is shown in figure 6.16.

Text Input

One of the most tedious data entry tasks is to retype text. It is also a task that is apt to produce many errors. The use of an input device to scan text from the printed page into the computer began as an attempt to reduce errors in data entry while speeding up the process as well.

Courtesy of Logitech

Figure 6.16

HOME PAGE

ERGONOMICS

Ergonomics is the science that studies how to best create a comfortable and safe working environment in which people can be productive without pain. For example, there are certain ways a person should sit in a chair if he wants to be comfortable and reduce pain and pressure to the lower back (especially if he will be sitting for long periods of time). Most computer furniture and peripheral manufacturers are now taking ergonomic considerations into account when designing their merchandise because workers' pain and discomfort not only lowers productivity, it also increases medical costs.

Ergonomics has become a real concern recently, mainly because the number of workers who regularly use computers has increased in the last decade. The problem arose when companies incorporated technological advancements (such as using word processing programs on a PC instead of using a typewriter) without adjusting work environments. People who were used to springy typewriter keys and manual carriage returns started to experience wrist and hand pain when using their computers.

The cause of the pain eventually became apparent: the workers were holding their wrists at unnatural angles for extended periods of time with no breaks. The actual pain is caused by pressure on the median nerve, a nerve that runs through the carpal tunnel of the wrist. (The carpal tunnel is a circle of eight bones in the wrist through which nerves and tendons run to the hand.) When the nerve is pinched or compressed, it causes numbness,

tingling, and pain in the fingers. The condition is called Carpal Tunnel Syndrome (CTS), and it is becoming increasingly common in workers who spend long hours typing on keyboards. The syndrome used to be considered an excuse for lazy workers to stop working, but as more cases were reported, it was soon evident that the most diligent workers were affected because they were more likely to type longer without breaks.

Carpal Tunnel Syndrome has recently been compared to other repetitive stress injuries (RSIs), which until now have mainly been associated with factory workers and people whose jobs require them to perform the same action repeatedly. RSI is not a new phenomenon; it already costs about $7 billion a year from lost worker productivity combined with medical costs. With more and more workers developing Carpal Tunnel Syndrome, that number will probably skyrocket—unless employers can improve their workers' environments.

Carpel tunnel

Median nerve

An ergonomic keyboard by Apple computers

Courtesy of Apple Computer, Inc.

Simple equipment improvements that can be made to a computing area include

- **Wrist rests** A small foam-covered, shelf-like unit placed in front of a keyboard on which the typist can rest his wrists. A wrist rest helps to ensure that the wrists are flat (parallel to the floor), which reduces the risk of CTS.

- **Adjustable keyboards** Many keyboard manufacturers have developed more ergonomically correct keyboards. Some of these keyboards are separated into adjustable sections so the worker can position the keys at a more comfortable level. Other "keyboards" have eliminated keys altogether: they rely on finger pressure instead of hand movement. One new keyboard is split into two sections that are more vertical than horizontal, which means the user's palms face each other while he is typing. This position is desirable because wrists are more comfortable in a vertical

position than they are in a horizontal position (as most traditional keyboards force them to be).

- **Adjustable keyboard drawers** A tabletop is very rarely the ideal position for a keyboard. The keyboard should be on a special shelf or drawer that can be adjusted for each individual user. The keyboard should then be positioned so that the user does not have to bend her wrists to type on it when the elbow is bent at a 45-degree angle. The wrists should be flat at all times in order to avoid CTS. In addition, the knees should not bump the keyboard drawer.

- **Monitor stands and glare guards.** To avoid unnecessary eye strain, the monitor should be at eye level or slightly lower. If it is lower than eye level, it should be tilted upward a bit. The monitor should be roughly two feet away from the eyes. If glare is a problem, there are several glare guards on the market that help reduce eyestrain. Glare guards are basically screens that prevent reflections on the monitor from the many light sources in a room.

- **Adjustable chairs** A good chair allows a person to adjust not only the height, but also the backrest and armrests. The seat of the chair should be positioned so the user can sit in it with his feet flat on the floor; the backrest should give support to the person's

Courtesy of Alpha Books

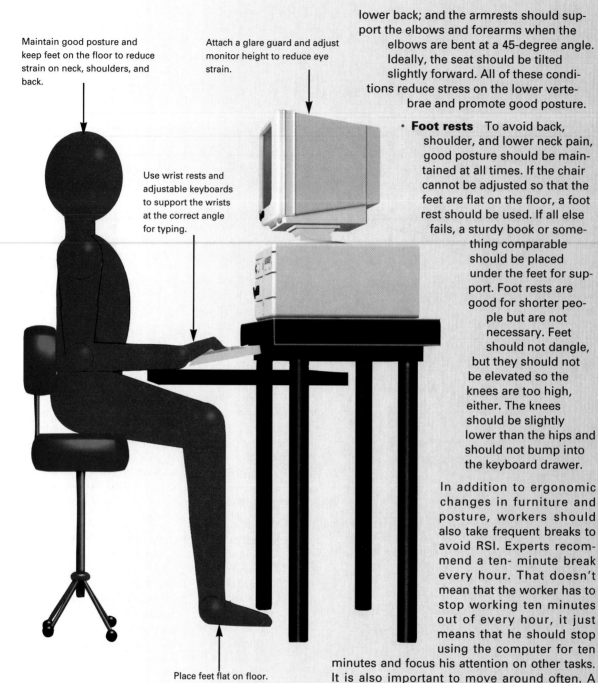

Maintain good posture and keep feet on the floor to reduce strain on neck, shoulders, and back.

Attach a glare guard and adjust monitor height to reduce eye strain.

Use wrist rests and adjustable keyboards to support the wrists at the correct angle for typing.

Place feet flat on floor.

lower back; and the armrests should support the elbows and forearms when the elbows are bent at a 45-degree angle. Ideally, the seat should be tilted slightly forward. All of these conditions reduce stress on the lower vertebrae and promote good posture.

- **Foot rests**   To avoid back, shoulder, and lower neck pain, good posture should be maintained at all times. If the chair cannot be adjusted so that the feet are flat on the floor, a foot rest should be used. If all else fails, a sturdy book or something comparable should be placed under the feet for support. Foot rests are good for shorter people but are not necessary. Feet should not dangle, but they should not be elevated so the knees are too high, either. The knees should be slightly lower than the hips and should not bump into the keyboard drawer.

In addition to ergonomic changes in furniture and posture, workers should also take frequent breaks to avoid RSI. Experts recommend a ten- minute break every hour. That doesn't mean that the worker has to stop working ten minutes out of every hour, it just means that he should stop using the computer for ten minutes and focus his attention on other tasks. It is also important to move around often. A worker should not sit in the same position for a long time.

Since using the computer can often cause eye-strain, it is important to exercise the eyes every once in a while. Try this simple trick: focus on something far away (look out a window, or look up at the ceiling), and then focus on something close (like your hand). Repeat this ten times. This exercise uses all the muscles in the eye, and allows them to refocus easily on the computer screen once a person begins working again. There are also software and shareware programs on the market that will help exercise the eyes to reduce eye strain.

Another concern about frequent computer use that has recently come to light is that computer monitors (except the LED screens used in portable computers) emit extremely low frequency magnetic fields (ELFs). Exposure to such fields over time has not yet been proven to cause harm, but scientists are warning users to be careful. These fields are the most powerful along the sides of the monitor, so users should be careful when sitting too near other computers. Be sure to remain at arm's length from the front of the monitor as well; the electron beams that light up the display flow out of the front of the monitor and may also cause harm. (This is similar to the warning about sitting too close to a television set.)

CARPAL TUNNEL SYNDROME

A painful condition of the wrist and hand resulting in tingling and numbness of the fingers. Carpal Tunnel Syndrome is caused when the median nerve is pinched or compressed, usually resulting from long periods of time spent typing at a keyboard with the wrists held at unnatural angles.

RSIs

Stands for repetitive stress injuries. RSIs are caused by jobs requiring repetitive actions, such as those found in factories. RSIs are common among today's computer users who type at the computer for long periods of time without the proper equipment or setup. Carpal Tunnel Syndrome is a repetitive stress injury.

ELFs

ELFs are extremely low-frequency fields emitted by computer monitors that are suspect in causing harm if the user is sitting too close to the monitor. Although there is no scientific data proving such suspicions, users are warned not to sit too close to the sides of the monitor where the ELFs are the strongest.

HOME PAGE REVIEW QUESTIONS

1. Is your dorm room, campus lab, or office workspace ergonomically correct? Cite the aspects that are not.

2. What do you think is the greatest detrimental ergonomic factor for you personally?

3. List the reasons why you believe ergonomics is important, both to knowledge workers and to the organizations where they work.

A **scanner** uses a light-sensitive device to enter text or graphics, depending on the software. Early scanners used a process called **optical character recognition**, or **OCR**. Early optical character reading equipment could recognize only text printed in OCR type, as shown in figure 6.17. Today, scanners can read just about any type font (including OCR). Their reading capability and the degree of accuracy in text input is largely dependent on the text, or character, recognition software used. Scanners can also scan in graphic images. The *flatbed scanner* allows you to feed in sheets continuously. The *hand-held scanner* can capture images from source material such as a soft drink can label that can't be conveniently fed through a flatbed scanner (see figure 6.18).

Figure 6.17

00197 OCR-A 12 **187** H 2.58 mm F 0.968

ABCDEFGHIJKLMNOPQRSTUV
WXYZ
1234567890 .￢:¡&?
HAMBURGEFONSTIV. SINCE 1886 LINOTYPE HAS BEEN A
LEADER IN THE FIELD OF TYPEFACE DEVELOPMENT AND

00198 OCR-B 12 **187** H 2.46 mm F 1.016

abcdefghijklmnopqrstuvwxyz
ABCDEFGHIJKLMNOPQRSTUVWXYZ
1234567890 .,:;"'ß&!?
Hämbûrgefönstiv. Since 1886 Linotype has been a
leader in the field of typeface development and

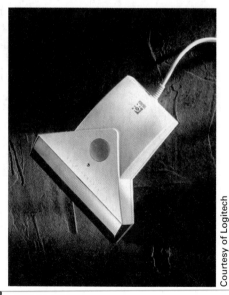

Courtesy of Logitech

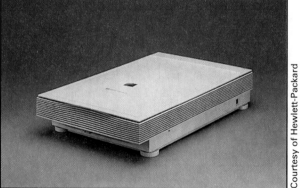

Courtesy of Hewlett-Packard

Figure 6.18

Voice Input

Perhaps the easiest way to enter data into a computer is by speaking; this is called voice input or **voice recognition** (see figure 6.19). Because of different pronunciations and regional accents, however, the knowledge worker must teach the computer to understand his or her voice. Raymond Kurzweil leads voice recognition research with his Voicesystem, which can understand over 5,000 words. Doctors, notorious for bad handwriting, have successfully used the Voicesystem when evaluating patients and diagnosing illnesses.

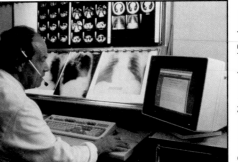

Courtesy of International Business Machines Corporation

Figure 6.19

Source Data Automation

Source data automation refers to data fed from a machine or device directly into the computer without human intervention. Three types of media are commonly used, and each requires a special reader:

- **Magnetic ink character recognition** (**MICR**) enables the computer to recognize characters printed with magnetic ink. MICR is used by banks for processing checks.

- **Magnetic strip**, used on the backs of credit cards and bank debit cards, enables readers, such as an automated teller machine (ATM), to read account information.

- **Data collection device**, commonly used by sales and inventory people, checks and orders stock in retail stores or supermarkets. You may see these people standing in the shopping aisle, scanning *Universal Product Code (UPC)* symbols, often called *bar codes*, on bags of potato chips; they are counting what's in stock. They may use a light pen attached to a laptop or palmtop computer, or the hand-held computing device may have a bar code reading tip built in. During restocking, the number of bags sold will automatically be replenished when the hand-held data collection device is linked to its host computer.

The **point-of-sale terminal** (**POS**), used by grocery stores and businesses, is usually part of the checkout register. The POS terminal scans the bar codes of the UPC to register the price, which is programmed into the host computer, as well as to deduct the item from inventory. Figure 6.20 shows methods of source data input.

Figure 6.20

Input Devices for the Disabled

Some small computer companies have made interesting advances in input devices developed to aid the disabled. Voice recognition is one of these techniques, although not the only one. Stephen Hawking is the brilliant physicist who is almost completely immobilized from a rare type of sclerosis. Unable to use either his arms or his voice, Hawking wrote his best-selling book, *A Brief History of Time*, by using a mouthstick to press the computer's keys. Special keyboards have been developed for people with cerebral palsy and muscular dystrophy. For the eyesight-impaired, there is a special Braille keyboard that translates phrases into conventional letters and words. Scanners referred to as *readers* are also used as input devices for both text and Braille.

People who can't move their limbs but have some head movement can use special pointing devices that attach to their heads. One such device is a small projector-like device that projects a beam of light at a simulated keyboard. By holding the beam of light briefly on the selected key, the user sends the character as input to the computer. The IBM National Support Center for Persons with Disabilities is researching the creation of a brain-wave scanner. By reading electrical brain waves, the scanner would sense when the person thought about an object, such as a baseball, causing the word to appear on-screen. Figure 6.21 shows an input system for the physically challenged.

Figure 6.21

Courtesy of International Business Machines Corporation

Knowledge Check

1. What is the most common input device?
2. Name two tasks a pointing device performs.
3. What type of software depends on the use of a pointing device?
4. What is a scanner commonly used for?
5. What advantages does voice recognition offer?
6. Name three different input devices.
7. Describe two kinds of source data input.

Key Terms

click	data collection device
data entry	digital camera
digitizer	drag
highlighting	joystick
light pen	magnetic ink character recognition (MICR)
magnetic strip	optical character recognition (OCR)
point	point-of-sale terminal (POS)
scanner	source data automation
touch-sensitive screen	trackball
voice recognition	

ISSUES AND IDEAS:

More on Ergonomics

The Joyce Institute is an ergonomics training and consulting firm head-quartered in Seattle, Washington. Founded by Marilyn Joyce in 1981, the company has helped over 750 organizations in the U.S., Canada, the United Kingdom, Mexico, Europe, and Asia. Among its notable accomplishments are the designs of the Microsoft mouse and the Microsoft Natural

Keyboard. Both were created by Edie Adams, who graduated from the University of Calgary with a master's degree in Industrial Design and Ergonomics.

The Joyce Institute has a program called "Practical Office Ergonomics," which helps organizations learn how to maximize their human investment through enhancing the well-being of knowledge workers who work in an office environment and use computer equipment. The course deals with issues such as these (adapted from the "Practical Office Ergonomics" brochure, The Joyce Institute):

Problems	Causes	Solutions Modifications/Major Changes
Visual		
Eyestrain	Glare/light	Lighting/glare control
Blurred vision	Display quality	Workstation arrangement
Headache	Workstation layout	Screen design
	Time in VDT	Eye care policy
	(monitor) use	Ergonomics training
Musculoskeletal		
Back pain	Awkward positions	Work surfaces
Neck/shoulder pain	Static posture	Seating
Arm/hand disorders	Repetitive motions	Accessories/storage
Carpal tunnel syndrome	Emotional stress	Ergonomics training
Environmental		
Low productivity	Crowded space	Space design/colors
Worker unrest	Excessive noise	Acoustics
Turnover	Fear of radiation	Radiation studies
		Ergonomics training
Organizational		
Stress	Poor communications	Job design
Morale	Unrealistic expectations	Communication
Quality concerns	Poor job design	Policies
Poor customer service	Monitoring	Ergonomics training

CRITICAL THINKING

1. Have you experienced any of the ergonomic problems described? Explain what they were and what, if anything, was done to correct them.

2. Why would an organization pay a consulting firm to help the organization improve ergonomics?

3. Present your own view of why an ergonomically correct work environment is good for morale, productivity, and communications.

Output Devices

Why It's Important to Know

Output devices make it possible to work with the results of computer processing. A variety of innovative technologies produce output tailored to specific needs—both human and organizational.

As the acronym I/O implies, you don't have much use for input without output. Output refers to displaying or printing the processed data. Output is delivered in a form that knowledge workers can understand, and turns into *results* or a form that can be read by another machine. (Refer to figure 6.6 in Module A for examples of different output devices.)

As input, or data entry, methods have improved, the forms of output have kept pace. Today, most output is visual, commonly produced by two devices: a monitor or a printer.

Types of Computer Output

Most computer output comes in one of the following forms:

- *Text output* is simply the alphanumeric characters that make up our language. Text output appearance ranges from typewritten to typeset quality.

- *Graphic output* includes line drawings, maps, presentation business graphics, computer-aided design, computer painting, and photographic reproduction.

- *Sound output* ranges from the message beeps produced by the computer system to the human voice to music.

- *Video output* is photographs or moving images such as television and videotaped material.

It is becoming more common to see text and graphics output combined in a printed document. But the PC is also capable of displaying complex screen documents that combine not just text and graphics, but sound and moving images as well (see figure 6.22). Now take a look at the devices that provide us with the output we need.

Figure 6.22

This screen, from Multimedia Beethoven, displays output in the form of Beethoven's musical score, text, and sound—the actual music from the score. The program also displays drawings and illustrations of Beethoven.

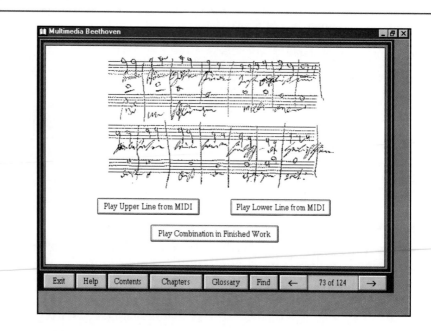

Types of Output Devices

Text and graphic output devices fall into two categories: hard copy and soft copy. **Hard copy** is output you can hold in your hands, such as a printed sheet of paper. Once the output is printed in hard copy, the computer cannot change it. The most common hard-copy output device is the printer. **Soft copy** refers to output we cannot touch, such as video or audio. The most common soft-copy output device is the video monitor. This module discusses each in detail, as well as several other forms of output.

The Printer

A printer provides hard copy output on paper. There is a printer for every need and every pocketbook. The basic criteria for evaluating printers include the following:

- *Quality* of the printed output

- *Speed* at which printed pages are produced

- *Sound level* during printing

- *Cost* of printing media, such as ribbons, ink cartridges, and toner cartridges

- *Conservation* of paper

Printers fall into two primary categories, impact and nonimpact:

- **Impact printers** print characters by striking the paper. This category includes dot-matrix and letter-quality printers.

- **Nonimpact printers** form a character by other means. This category includes laser and inkjet printers.

Examples of output from three types of printers is shown in figure 6.23 so that you can compare their quality.

```
''I don't 'think them up,' to use your phrase.  They come from some
other place, really, it's hard to tell you where it is, but I can
feel it right there and it makes me think of Montana, Big Sky
Country.  When I'm a cowboy on that range, nothing can stop me.''
```

Dot-matrix

```
"I don't `think them up,' to use your phrase.  They come
from some other place, really, it's hard to tell you where
it is, but I can feel it right there and it makes me think
of Montana, Big Sky Country.  When I'm a cowboy on that
range, nothing can stop me."
```

Laser

```
from some other place, really, it's hard to tell you where
it is, but I can feel it right there and it makes me think
of Montana, Big Sky Country.  When I'm a cowboy on that
range, nothing can stop me."
```

Inkjet

Figure 6.23
Output from dot-matrix, laser, and inkjet printers.

Impact Printers

An impact printer produces a character by using a mechanism that presses against an inked ribbon on paper. Impact printing was the first printing technology. In the early days of computing, typewriters were adapted to printing. They were followed by dot-matrix printers. As nonimpact printing becomes better and less expensive, both of these older printing technologies are being used less.

Letter-Quality Printing

Letter-quality printers are most like typewriters and produce the same high-quality output. The two most common letter-quality technologies are the daisy wheel and the thimble. The *daisy wheel* resembles a daisy; a print hammer strikes each "petal" against a ribbon to form the impression. The *thimble* resembles the IBM Selectric "golf ball" but, like the daisy wheel, uses a print hammer. Letter-quality printers can print on form-feed or individual sheets of paper and can print carbon copies. They offer a wide selection of interchangeable type fonts; however, you cannot change fonts in the middle of a print job because the change necessitates changing the daisy wheel or thimble. Nor can letter-quality printers print graphics. The impact printer's other major disadvantages are cost, noise, and slow speed.

Dot-Matrix Printing

Dot-matrix output is produced by printers that use wires in the print head. These wires extend out in different patterns, pressing against the ribbon to print the characters on the paper. For this reason, dot-matrix printers can produce both text and graphics (see figure 6.24). Although fast, dot-matrix printers are noisy. Some have single-sheet feeders, but they are wasteful when they use form-feed paper. The wires in the print head wear out ribbons very quickly. **Dot-matrix printers** are the least expensive.

Figure 6.24

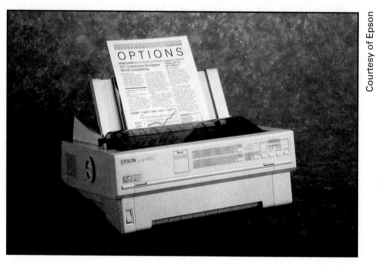

Courtesy of Epson

The first dot-matrix printer for a personal computer was created by the Japanese company, Epson, which in Japanese means literally "son of EP." The EP stands for electronic printer, which was part of an extremely accurate timing device that Seiko, Epson's parent company, built for the 1964 Summer Olympics in Tokyo. It was used to clock various events and print the winning times. The timing device became the quartz watch, and the electronic printer became the dot-matrix printer.

Early dot-matrix printers had nine wires in the print head and were very fast, but the print quality was often unacceptable for professional or business documents. To improve quality, printer makers created 24-pin print heads, which produce **near-letter-quality (NLQ) output**. The primary disadvantages of dot-matrix printers are that they are noisy and their print quality is often below business standards. Dot-matrix printers usually print on continuous-feed (tractor-feed) paper, which wastes a sheet of paper with every printing. Printouts must be separated along perforations, which is tedious and annoying.

Nonimpact Printing

Nonimpact printing is the dominant technology and will likely be so for some time to come. Early nonimpact printers used thermal paper; if you buy something to eat at a snack bar in Chicago's O'Hare airport, your receipt will probably be a thermal printout on a special silvery paper—a technology that dates back to the 1970s. The early color inkjets, used to print architectural drawings and engineering schematics, led the way to today's inkjet printers for PCs.

Laser Printing

The **laser printer** provides high-quality nonimpact printing. Output is created by directing a laser beam onto a drum to create an electrical charge that forms a pattern of letters or images. As the drum rotates, it picks up black toner on the images and transfers them to paper. The laser printer, like the one shown in figure 6.25, is probably the most popular printer in use.

Laser printers have the advantages of speed and a wide selection of type fonts, as well as high-quality graphics. A variety of fonts permit many type sizes, as well as italic and boldface text. Laser printers for personal computers can print as many as eight pages per minute; commercial laser printers, such as those that produce bank statements, can print 400 to 500 pages per minute. Another name you may hear is *page printer*, a printer that prints an entire page of paper at once. By contrast, dot-matrix and letter-quality printers print one line at a time.

Courtesy of Hewlett-Packard

Figure 6.25

Laser printing offers the highest quality text and graphics printing for the desktop. A laser printer does a fine job, printing up to 300 dpi, or dots per inch. Newer laser printers designed specifically for high-quality desktop publishing output can print at twice the resolution—600 dpi. Linotype printers double that number to 1200 dpi and are used for commercial printing, such as magazines and brochures.

Color laser printers promise to be the next great advance. Although laser printer prices have fallen dramatically over the past few years, the primary disadvantages are expensive maintenance and the high cost of toner cartridges. Laser printers often have hardware peripherals of their own, such as add-on memory boards that help speed printing, and a special kind of adapter card that allows them to be shared by more than one computer.

Inkjet Printing

The first inkjet printers were used for high-volume, high-speed printing, such as direct mail brochures. An **inkjet printer** transfers characters and images to paper by spraying a fine jet of ink. Like laser printers, inkjet printers can print many different typestyles and graphics. In recent years, inkjet printing has come to the personal computer, offering nearly the quality—if not quite the speed—of a laser printer but at a more affordable price. Color inkjet printers produce excellent quality and are a low-cost alternative to color laser printing. Some inkjet printers, like the one shown in figure 6.26, have removable inkjet cartridges so that they can print in black and white or in color.

Figure 6.26

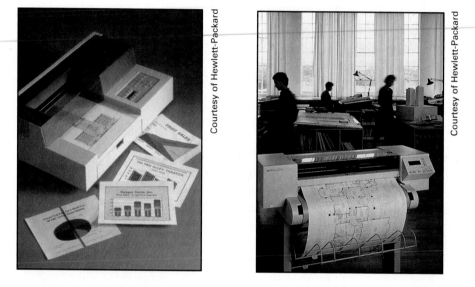

Courtesy of Hewlett-Packard

Courtesy of Hewlett-Packard

Plotters

The **plotter** uses moving ink pens or electrostatic charges to create large or complex scientific and engineering drawings, as well as other graphics, often in color (refer to figure 6.26). Color plotters use ink pens that switch on and off according to instructions from the computer and software. Plotters can create very large documents; for example, a chip designer created a schematic drawing of an integrated circuit 7 by 9 feet.

Thermal Printing

As the name implies, a **thermal printer** uses heat to form a nonimpact image on chemically treated paper. Thermal printing combines high speed with a low-maintenance printing technology; however, the paper is expensive and not as desirable as plain bond paper. Thermal printing is mostly used for low-cost calculators or high-quality color printing, although the new thermal printers can print on plain paper.

Table 6.1 presents an evaluation of different printing technologies, evaluated in terms of their output quality, printing speed, sound level, and cost factors.

Table 6.1
Comparing Popular Printing Technologies

Type	Speed	Print Quality	Font Selection	Graphics/ Quality	Color/ Quality	Noise	Cost
Dot-matrix 9-pin	250 cps	Fair	Good	Yes/low	Yes/fair	High	Low
Dot-matrix 24-pin	80 cps	Good	Good	Yes/high	Yes/fair	High	Medium
Letter-quality	50-80 cps	Excellent	No	No	No	High	High
Laser	8+ ppm	Excellent	Excellent	Yes/high	Yes/high	Medium	High
Inkjet	12+ ppm	Excellent	Excellent	Yes/high	Yes/high	Low	Medium

The Video Monitor

The video monitor, or display, provides soft copy output. The most common video monitors, such as those used with personal computers, are similar to a television screen; both use a cathode ray tube (CRT) to project an image. Video monitors come in either monochrome or color. A *monochrome* display is a single color displayed against a different colored background, such as green on green, amber on black, or white on black. A color display can show a variety of colors.

Types of Video Displays

Resolution is the term used to describe the degree of detail in a video display. The higher the resolution, the sharper and crisper the characters or images. For example, a conventional television display is **low resolution**—you can see lines, jagged edges, and graininess in the image. The newer, high-definition displays (HDTV) are **high-resolution** sets that display a picture as sharp and crisp as a film image in a Hollywood movie. The same is true with high-resolution computer monitors; they have crisp text letters and smooth edges to graphics. Computer monitor resolution is measured according to *dot pitch*, which determines the smallest dot a monitor is capable of displaying. *InfoWorld* newsmagazine rates monitors with a dot pitch of 0.28 or 0.27 as sufficient for most business applications[3]; the best ones have a dot pitch of 0.24 or even less.

The Macintosh was the first to offer a *bit-mapped display*, which had extremely high-resolution although it was monochrome, or black and white. **Bit map** means that each dot on the screen, called a **pixel** (for picture element), is represented by one bit (a 1 or 0) by the computer.

3. Jill Welch, Ana Orubeondo, Jeff Senna, and Michelle Murdock, "Big Screen Test, Take 10," *InfoWorld*, November 20, 1995, 74–86.

A bit-mapped display

A monochrome display

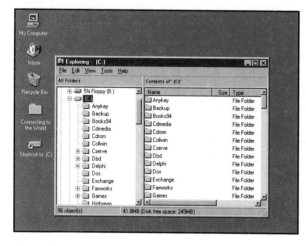

A color display

A high-resolution display

Figure 6.27

Notice the difference in clarity in the different kinds of screens.

Bit-mapped graphic is the color version of a bit map display. In a color bit map, each pixel identifies a number—for example 1 to 256 on a 256-color palette—indicating what color that pixel should be. Bit-mapped graphic displays are very good for graphics and also easy on the eyes. The text counterpart is the *bit-mapped font*, where each alphanumeric character is composed of a pattern of dots. The finer the dot pattern, the higher the resolution—meaning the longer we can look at it without eye fatigue. Figure 6.27 compares different kinds of screens.

Early monitors had *character-mapped* displays, which are not as high in resolution as a bit-mapped display. To overcome the grainy display, successive generations of personal computers have used improved video display technologies. The first color display, called CGA or *color graphics adapter*, could display up to 16 colors. The EGA or *enhanced graphics adapter* had better resolution and a palette of 64 colors.

EGA was followed by VGA, or *video graphics array*, which is even sharper than high-definition television (HDTV) and has a palette of 256 colors. VGA monitors use bit-mapped technology and are compatible with previous video standards, so older computers can be upgraded to the newer monitors.

The standard today is called SVGA, or *Super VGA*; it was approved in 1992 by the Video Electronics Standards Association. SVGA allows for easier installation and configuration of high-level video boards that work with the older video graphics array (VGA) technology. Super VGA offers the highest resolution, which means that more can be displayed on the screen. For example, a CGA or EGA monitor could display only 24 lines of text on the screen in word processing. Super VGA not only displays many more lines but also enables the knowledge worker to customize the display in a variety of ways. With an SVGA display, you can show one, two, or even four complete pages at a time.

Special Characteristics of Monitors

Most computer systems come equipped with a 14-inch or 15-inch monitor, but bigger is often better. Monitors also come in 17-inch, 19-inch, and even 21-inch sizes, measured diagonally like TV sets. Newer monitor screens are flatter and thus can display more image from edge to edge than older monitors displayed. Better monitors use glare-free glass and incorporate automatic degaussing to cut down on static electricity, which often coats the screen with dust. In order to provide a colorful, high-resolution graphic image, monitors demand a better video expansion card, often referred to as a *graphics adapter* (see figure 6.28).

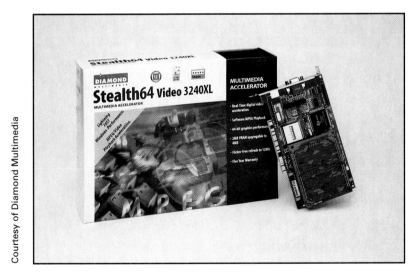

Courtesy of Diamond Multimedia

Figure 6.28
The Diamond Stealth is a popular graphics adapter card.

Modern monitors also come with a logical interface, or driver software, that allows choices among display characteristics and energy-saving options. The user can change the type of color scheme as well as the size of the screen display—for example, from a larger display of 480 by 640 pixels to a smaller, finer-detailed display of 1024 by 1280, which allows more of the graphic to be displayed. Many newer monitors incorporate an Energy Star feature (see figure 6.29). Monitors consume more electricity than any other computer component. If you have not used an input device after a certain length of time, an Energy Star-compliant monitor first goes into low-power standby mode and then shuts off its power completely. For example, you might go to standby mode after 10 minutes and power down after 20 minutes. Touching the mouse or a key usually reawakens the monitor.

Figure 6.29

A menu for using an Energy Star-compliant monitor.

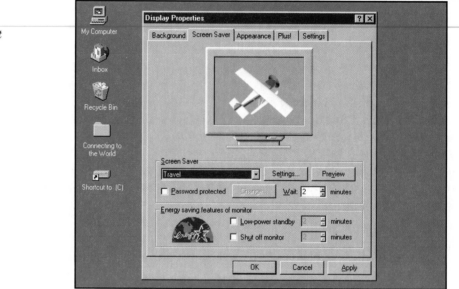

Special Video Displays

Some computers require special display technology, because of power requirements or the needs of special application software. Here are a few examples. The **gas plasma** display is easy to recognize because it is a deep monochrome orange. It is a flat-panel display composed of three sheets of glass with plasma, an illuminant gas, between them. When electricity is connected, the screen glows.

The gas plasma display has several distinct advantages:

- It is very thin, so a screen can be hung on a wall.

- It has no limit to its size; one could be as large as a movie screen.

- It is extremely easy on the eyes.

Some laptop computers use a gas plasma display, making it possible to view the screen from any angle and in any light.

The **liquid crystal display** (**LCD**) is also a flat-screen display commonly used with laptops. To make LCD screens easier to read in dim or bright light, they are *backlit,* or lighted from behind the screen. Better laptops are equipped with a color LCD display. Figure 6.30 shows an LCD display.

Courtesy of Toshiba

Figure 6.30
A crystal-clear laptop color LCD display.

LCD displays come in two types: active matrix and passive matrix. An active matrix display is a full-color display with excellent resolution and contrast, used in better laptops. The older passive matrix display is less expensive and has lower resolution and contrast.

The Terminal

All types of computers, not just personal computers, have computer video monitors. When a monitor is combined with a keyboard and connected to a computer that is somewhere else, the monitor-keyboard combination is called a **terminal**. A terminal has no system unit of its own but instead shares one with other terminals. Mainframes, minicomputers, and workstation systems use multiple terminals, each of which consists of a video monitor for output and a keyboard for input. A PC can also be used as a terminal. These terminals can be used for anything from data entry to computer-aided design (CAD). There are two basic types of terminals:

- The **dumb terminal** performs the simplest input and output operations but no processing. A bank ATM is a dumb terminal.

- The **smart terminal** may have its own CPU or processing capabilities, as well as a built-in disk drive for storage. A point-of-sale (POS) cash register and a personal computer are examples of a smart terminal. You may hear the term **intelligent terminal**, which is essentially the same thing.

Computer-to-Machine Output

Computer output can also be sent to another machine, a device, or another computer. For example, computers are used for process control in factories, buildings, and even the home. With **computer-to-machine output**, the I/O process controls machine operations, maintains heating and cooling, and turns lights on and off at prescribed times. At a Panasonic factory in Japan, computer-controlled robots make vacuum cleaners without any human help (unless something breaks).

It's possible to produce high-quality color slides directly using computer-to-machine output. By means of a camera-like device connected to the computer interface, the image on the screen, whether text, graphics, or both, is output to 35mm film, which is exposed just as it would be in a camera. The film is then developed normally, and the slides are often used for presentations.

Another interesting computer-to-machine output task involves computer-output microfilm. **Computer-output microfilm** (**COM**) uses miniature photography to condense, store, and retrieve data on a film-like media called *microform*. The two most common types of microform are *microfiche*, 4-by-6-inch sheets of film, and *microfilm,* which comes in rolls. Both are used with special readers that magnify the information and display it on a screen. Microforms hold up well under sustained usage. You'll probably find them used in your college library.

Computer output, such as newspaper copy, canceled checks, or invoices, is sent to a special COM machine that reduces it in size and then records it 10 to 20 times faster than printing. The film is developed and copied for distribution. For example, book distributors prepare weekly microfiches listing books by title, author, price, and number in stock. A single sheet of microfiche holds almost 1,000 sheets of standard paper.

Voice Output

Speech synthesis, or **voice output**, is the machine's capability to "speak" like a human. Some computer programs already talk to us, as shown in figure 6.31. The soft drink machine thanks us for our purchase. Autos tell us to buckle our seat belts. Directory information gives us a telephone number. Speech synthesis programs are built into some software programs, such as an encyclopedia, to pronounce the selected word through a speaker.

But when will computers be able to converse with us like the HAL 9000 in the movie *2001: A Space Odyssey*?

Dave Bowman: Hal, switch to manual hibernation control.

HAL: I can tell from your voice harmonics, Dave, that you're badly upset. Why don't you take a stress pill and get some rest?

Dave: Hal, *I* am in command of this ship. I order you to release manual hibernation control.

HAL: I'm sorry, Dave, but in accordance with special subroutine C1435-dash-4, quote, "When the crew are dead or incapacitated, the onboard computer must assume control," unquote. I must, therefore, overrule your authority, since you are not in any condition to exercise it intelligently.

Dave: Hal, I am not incapacitated. Unless you obey my instructions, I shall be forced to disconnect you.

HAL: I know you have had that on your mind for some time now, Dave, but that would be a terrible mistake. I am so much more capable than you are of supervising the ship, and I have such enthusiasms for the mission and confidence in its success.[4]

Figure 6.31
The Talking Clock has an announcer who tells you the time and reminds you of appointments you've made.

Raymond Kurzweil, the man who created the Voicesystem mentioned earlier, thinks that we will have natural-sounding speech synthesis by the first decade of the next century. He describes a practical use for speech synthesis: a language translation telephone system. It uses three technologies: automatic speech recognition for voice input, language translation performed as real-time processing, and speech synthesis for voice output. Then two people, regardless of their native language, can speak to each other over the telephone or understand one another during meetings of the United Nations, as if they were both speaking the same language.

---

4. Arthur C. Clarke, *2001: A Space Odyssey* (New York: New American Library, 1968), 145.

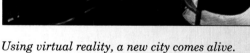

VIRTUAL REALITY: THE ULTIMATE I/O?

Virtual reality is an artificial, three-dimensional reality created by a computer. Virtual reality (VR) involves as many human senses as possible, creating an information-rich environment almost as complex as natural experience. Through the use of special gloves and stereoscopic eyewear, a user feels almost a part of the virtual world. Cyberspace, a term coined by William Gibson in the novel *Neuromancer* refers to this artificially created world.

Using virtual reality, a new city comes alive.

Using virtual reality, a pilot, a surgeon, or an air-traffic controller can practice his craft without endangering himself or others. Designers can study the forces of nature (water and air flow) on their aircraft and building designs. City planners can foresee future needs for water, electricity, and traffic control before new buildings are constructed. And chemists, geneticists, and molecular engineers can manipulate models to investigate new theories.

Virtual reality dates back to early flight simulators used in WWII to train young pilots. Hollywood got into the act some time later with Cinerama, VistaVision, Sensorama, 3-D glasses, Sensurround, Dolby, and THX stereo, which were all designed to enhance the reality of the movie-going experience. Recently, for the movie *Jurassic Park*, the sound was placed on a laser disk (and not encoded on the film) to improve its quality when replayed. This created the effect that the dinosaurs in the movie were right there in the theater.

In the '60s, Ivan Sutherland designed the first head-mounted graphics display and the first interactive computer screen, called the Sketchpad. In the '70s, artist Myron Krueger created Video Place, a user-responsive computerized environment. When a person walked into Video Place, he was surrounded by video images that changed according to his movements. SuperCockpit, a flight simulator developed in 1981, used head-mounted displays to create an artificial world through which a pilot could fly. NASA improved this system with its Virtual Interface Environment Workstation, composed of 3-D stereo sound, head-mounted displays, computer-generated graphics, and a DataGlove. The DataGlove was designed by Jaron Lanier and Tom Zimmerman in order to create a virtual guitar playing experience. Lanier and

A realistic virtual reality experience involves viewpoint, navigation, manipulation, and immersion.

Zimmerman later founded VPL Research, the first of many VR suppliers.

To be effective, virtual reality involves several techniques: viewpoint, navigation, manipulation, and immersion. *Viewpoint* is created by simulating the position of the user's eyes within a virtual (computer-created) world. *Navigation* is the process of moving the user's viewpoint from one position to another within the VR environment. Navigation is normally controlled through special eyepieces that track the movement of a user's eyes, calculating the approximate change in view. Through *manipulation*, the user's hands join his eyes in the virtual world. Wearing special gloves fitted with electrical connections leading to the computer, the user can reach out and pluck an object off a table. *Immersion* is the extent to which the user is drawn into the VR world—the measure of how realistic the simulation is. However, virtual reality has not yet reached the point where total immersion is possible. The main problem is that the sense of touch is so very hard to simulate with machinery.

Although there are no programs available today that attempt a true virtual reality experience, there are many programs available for fun and entertainment. Among these are flight simulators (such as Falcon 3.0), action-adventure games (such as Shadowcaster), 3-D animation programs (such as Animator and 3-D Studio), and a relatively inexpensive VR creator (called VR Studio). In addition, with popular games such as SimAnt and SimEarth, a user can create his own world and test how that world functions. Various VR simulators are also available as shareware on popular BBSs and information services such as CompuServe.

How Does It Work?

To create realistic visuals, a headset is used that places a small viewing screen in front of each eye. When the user moves his head, the headset transmits the movement data to the computer, which makes the appropriate changes to the on-screen image.

Creating realistic sound in a VR world is a bit more complicated. Stereo creates the effect of moving sounds by making the sound a little louder in one earpiece than in the other, but the sound always stays "inside" the user's head. Truly realistic sound must come from somewhere in the three-dimensional space of the virtual world. The Convolvotron headset utilizes a complicated set of mathematical formulas to make small adjustments to a digitized sound wave, making it appear as if the sound is coming from various directions.

The most difficult sense to duplicate is the sense of touch. Using a glove-like device, it is possible to duplicate a small range of senses. One such glove employs small air bladders that inflate and deflate, applying differing amounts of pressure to various parts of the hand. Another type of glove uses an arrangement of pistons to apply pressures to the fingers. Still another contains special wires that, when heated, simulate the feel of different textures.

Garage Virtual Reality

Also known as desktop virtual reality, this is the most common type of virtual reality program available. Mostly made up of games that allow the user to experience a scaled down version of a virtual world, garage virtual reality uses the PC's monitor as the window into the virtual world.

HOME PAGE REVIEW QUESTIONS

1. What input devices does VR use?
2. What output devices does VR use?
3. Name the four techniques involved in VR.
4. What are the two most popular uses for VR?

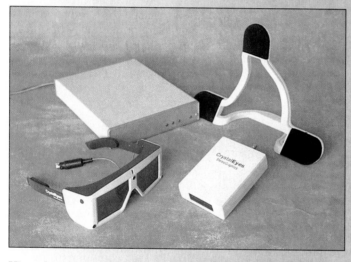

Virtual reality equipment.

Courtesy of Alpha Books

Knowledge Check

1. What are the two types of output called?
2. Give examples of low-resolution and high-resolution monitors.
3. What are the two types of terminals?
4. What are the two categories of printers?
5. List the different types of printers, and characterize the quality of their output.
6. What is a main advantage of computer-output microfilm?

Key Terms

bit map	bit-mapped graphic
computer-output microfilm (COM)	computer-to-machine output
dot matrix	dot-matrix printer
driver	dumb terminal
gas plasma	hard copy
high resolution	impact printer
inkjet printer	intelligent terminal
laser printer	letter-quality printer
liquid crystal display (LCD)	low resolution
near-letter-quality (NLQ) output	nonimpact printer
pixel	plotter
smart terminal	soft copy
terminal	thermal printer
virtual reality	voice output

ISSUES AND IDEAS

Virtual Reality: "Seasick in Cyberspace"

A *Business Week* article reported that several years ago, Sega had dropped plans for a virtual-reality game system because "some users who donned Sega's prototype head-mounted display (HMD) suffered jarring symptoms, from nausea to sore eyes—a suite of complaints the VR community calls 'cybersickness'. " The article reports:

These side effects were no sudden revelation. After 30 years of experience with VR for flight and weapons training, the U.S. military today often grounds pilots who experience queasiness during simulations—a condition it calls "simulator sickness."

Now, as a wave of VR products approaches the consumer market, manufacturers of HMDs, gloves, and PC add-on boards fear that eye injuries or LSD-style "flashbacks"—and ensuing litigation—could hobble the budding VR market.[5]

---

5. Neil Gross, with Dori Jones Yang and Julia Flynn, "Seasick in Cyberspace," *Business Week*, July 10, 1995, 110–113.

The article goes on to cite the following problems:

- *Eyestrain.* Squinting at low-resolution images in a cheap head-mounted display (HMD) can strain your eyes. So can poorly crafted spatial illusions. Some doctors suggest limiting exposure to one hour.

- *Simulator sickness.* Nausea and confusion occur when head position and visual signals are out of synch. Effects vary with individuals but appear most likely with low-end systems that display fewer than 60 frames per second.

- *Flashbacks.* Virtual reality creates audio and visual illusions of motion but lacks other physical cues. To resolve the conflict, the brain forges new neural pathways, which can cause flashbacks hours later.

But Sega has developed a new HMD. "Paired with the powerful, 32-bit Saturn machine Sega just released in the U.S.," the article says, "it will deliver a 'knock-your-socks-off experience,'" says Steven Payne, Sega's vice president of product development. He says that the company plans "a battery of new [health] tests" before the new product is released.

CRITICAL THINKING

1. Get a copy of the *Business Week* article and any others on the subject. Assess the risk involved. Is it an acceptable or unacceptable risk?

2. The government has so far not stepped in to regulate VR gear. Do you think that they should? Should *caveat emptor* be the rule?

3. Are the risks any more serious than, say, carpal tunnel syndrome?

4. Is the virtual reality experience worth all the attention it receives?

The Perfect Peripheral

What is the perfect peripheral? Create a "pro and con" list for each of the most important input and output devices you learned about in this chapter, listing their strengths and weaknesses. Use this analysis to speculate about and discuss the ideal input peripheral and output peripheral.

CRITICAL THINKING

1. What senses would the peripherals require?

2. How would the peripherals improve the way we use computers? Would they make computer better, faster, less expensive, easier?

3. Would the peripherals be difficult to learn to use, or intuitive?

Secondary Storage Devices

Why It's Important to Know

> **Knowing how to store your work safely is one of the most important things you can learn about using a personal computer. Understanding the way memory and storage work together with your data is a basic skill in using applications.**

You've finished your knowledge work on the computer, and you want to go home. Where are you going to keep your work? Can't put it in your backpack. Can't put it in your pocket. Can't even put it in your three-ring binder. Before you power off the PC, you have to store your work. That's what you use the secondary storage device for.

Secondary storage is permanent storage that supplements primary storage, or RAM. You may also hear it called *auxiliary storage*. Secondary storage is nonvolatile storage, which means that it is more permanent. Programs and data are safely saved even after the computer is turned off. Figure 6.6 in Module A shows the various types of secondary storage devices in their relationship to the computer.

Secondary storage is RAM's partner. In fact, RAM is sometimes called the "working memory" of the computer because RAM holds the data and instructions during data processing. When the proper instructions are given, the data being held temporarily in RAM is sent to secondary storage for safekeeping. Table 6.2 summarizes the characteristics of each type of storage.

Table 6.2
Comparing the Characteristics of Memory and Storage

Name	Primary Storage	Secondary Storage
Alternate name	Main memory	Auxiliary storage
Storage medium	RAM (IC chips)	Disk
Storage medium is	Volatile	Nonvolatile
Type of storage	Temporary	Permanent
Location	Main circuit board	Peripheral (storage) device

Using Memory and Storage: An Example

Suppose that you use word processing to write a short memo so that you can see how primary storage, or RAM, and secondary storage, such as a floppy disk, work together. Follow along in figure 6.32 to see what happens at each stage.

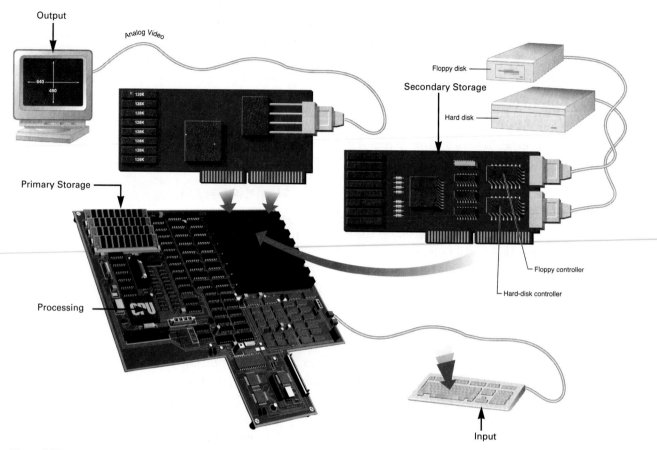

Figure 6.32

How memory and storage work during data processing.

1. *Input*. You type a short memo that reads, "Department meeting at 3:00 p.m. today."

2. *Processing*. The CPU executes the instructions to turn the keystrokes into characters.

3. *Output*. The characters are displayed on the monitor.

4. *Primary storage*. The memo is stored temporarily in RAM.

5. *Secondary storage*. At this point, you could also send the memo from RAM's working memory to a secondary storage device, where you could save it permanently on disk.

The Difference between Memory and Storage

Computers differentiate between main storage and secondary storage in terms of speed and efficiency. RAM storage is very fast because it's usually a chip on the main circuit board, physically close to the CPU. The shorter the distance the electrical signals have to travel, the faster the processing. Secondary storage is usually slower, not solely because of the electrical distance but also because secondary storage involves some type of mechanical operation. For instance, disk drives must spin the disk to store and retrieve data. Consider the speed and efficiency of RAM versus secondary storage:

Random-access memory. It takes the computer 80 nanoseconds (ns) to access RAM.

Secondary storage. It takes the computer 30 milliseconds (ms) to access a disk.

A secondary storage device is a hardware component that has the capability to read and write data and instructions, just as RAM does. One big difference between the two is that secondary storage is at least long-term, if not permanent. Another difference is that the secondary storage device uses a form of media to read to and write from.

Media refers to the physical material on which secondary storage devices store data and instructions. The most common type of media used with computers is *magnetic media*, usually a magnetically coated disk or a form of magnetic tape.

Secondary storage is the critical link between input and output. Secondary storage is permanent storage. Once data is safe in secondary storage, it can be recalled again and again. Application programs can be stored and reused. A report can be revised and printed in fresh copies; new figures can be inserted into a budget spreadsheet and recalculated; an address book database can be updated when a friend moves.

Types of Secondary Storage

There are two methods for storing and accessing instructions or data in secondary storage: direct access and sequential access. **Direct access**, sometimes called *random access*, means that the data is stored in a specific location so that any data can be found quickly. This technique is similar to selecting a song on a compact disc; it doesn't take the CD player any longer to find and play selection 8 than selection 3. Direct access is the most widely used secondary storage method. The most common direct-access storage medium is the disk.

Sequential access means that the data is stored and accessed in a set order, perhaps alphabetically or by date and time. The most common sequential storage medium is magnetic tape on reels or cassettes. Just as you must search sequentially for a particular song on a cassette, so the computer must sequentially search for data. Today, sequential-access storage is used mostly to make protective, or backup, copies of data stored on direct-access devices.

The term **backup** describes the process of making copies of program files or data files for safekeeping. Backups are the best insurance in case of computer or hard disk failure (sometimes called a crash). The simplest backup process on a personal computer is copying data to a floppy disk. It is essential that you back up all your data often—and certainly every time you make any changes.

When you purchase an application software package, the publisher recommends that you make backups, or working copies, of your original disks. A working copy is an exact copy of the original program disks. Keep the original disks in a safe place.

Secondary storage technology has improved dramatically over the years. In many cases, what was once a widely used secondary storage medium is today's backup medium. Next, you'll examine the types of secondary storage peripheral devices most commonly used today. Continue referring to figure 6.6 in Module A to identify the various peripheral devices.

Direct-Access Storage Devices

Direct-access storage devices, or **DASD**, are magnetic disk drives used for secondary storage. They may be either floppy disks or hard disks. We have Alan Shugart of IBM to thank for inventing magnetic disk storage. He built the first hard disk drive for the RAMAC computer in 1957 and invented the floppy disk in 1961.

DASD drives use a moving **read/write head** that scans the magnetic surface of the disk. We say that the head is *reading the disk* when it retrieves data or instructions and that it is *writing to disk* when it stores data or instructions.

How RAM and DASD Work Together

Where do the data or instructions go to when read from disk? Where do they come from before being written to disk? The answer is to and from RAM. Instructions and data are held in memory during processing; then they are sent to secondary storage. The data you're currently working with is held in RAM and then *copied* to secondary storage media and saved as a file. Once data is copied, it exists in identical form in RAM and on disk. If you begin working again with the data—for example, the memo you wrote earlier— the version in RAM is changed, but the version on disk remains unchanged *until you save the file again.* Always keep this fact in mind when you're working with the computer.

The DASD read/write head floats above the spinning disk surface on a cushion of air. As you can see from figure 6.33, this cushion is very thin. Think of a Boeing 747 flying an inch above the ground at 3,000 miles per hour, and you get an idea of the close tolerances. You can also see why it's so important to keep disks clean. When the head encounters a particle of foreign matter that causes it to fail in either reading or writing to the disk, you have a head crash.

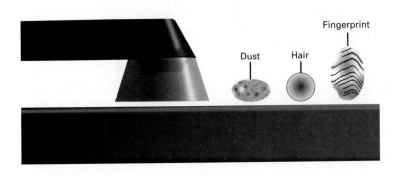

Figure 6.33
Read/write head clearance on a hard disk.

Figure 6.34 shows how a disk is magnetically laid out into tracks and sectors. **Tracks** are concentric circles on which data is recorded. **Sectors** are pie-shaped wedges that compartmentalize the data into the addresses for the head to locate. In addition, multiple hard disk drives organize tracks into **cylinders**, a vertical stack of tracks which, again, make it easier to locate data. Let's take a closer look at the various DASDs.

What Happens When You Format a Disk?

A disk starts out very unstructured—just a lot of little bits of magnetic stuff without any organization, rhyme, or reason. Before the system can start writing files to it, the disk must have a structure—a gridwork into which the information can be placed.

Formatting a disk is the process of putting the gridwork on the disk and building the organizational structure so that files can be found. Once a disk is formatted, it's ready for the system to write data to it.

Figure 6.34

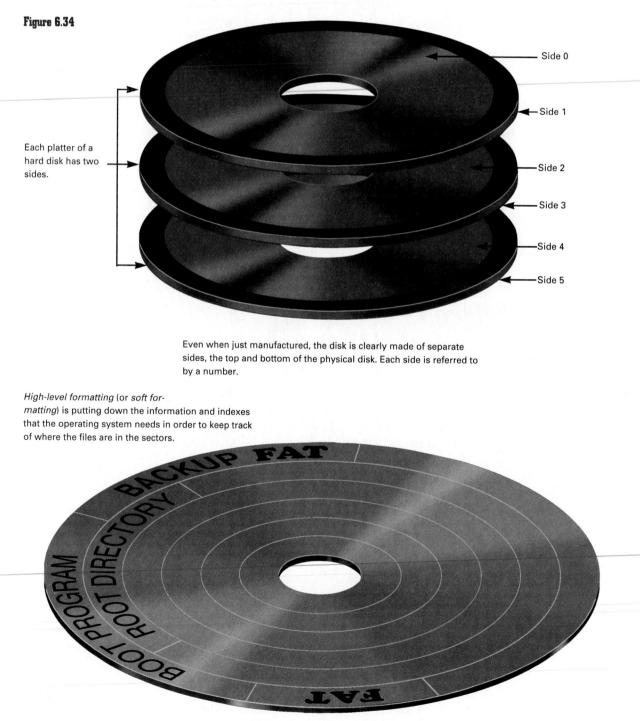

Side 0

Side 1

Each platter of a hard disk has two sides.

Side 2

Side 3

Side 4

Side 5

Even when just manufactured, the disk is clearly made of separate sides, the top and bottom of the physical disk. Each side is referred to by a number.

High-level formatting (or *soft formatting*) is putting down the information and indexes that the operating system needs in order to keep track of where the files are in the sectors.

BACKUP FAT

BOOT ROOT DIRECTORY

BOOT PROGRAM

FAT

Formatting organizes disks into numbered rings, called *cylinders*. A cylinder on a single side is referred to as a *track*.

Each track is broken up into numbered pie slices, called *sectors*. Each sector stores 512 bytes of information.

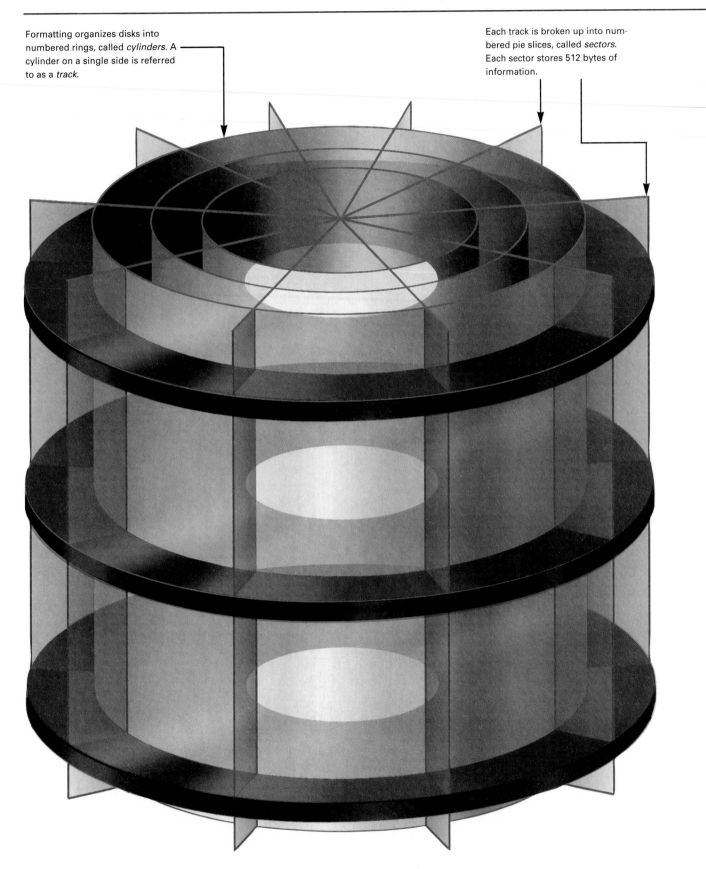

The process of magnetically raking out the separate tracks and marking where each sector starts is called *low-level formatting*. It is the same regardless of operating system.

The Floppy Disk

The **floppy disk** is an inexpensive, removable storage medium for storing instructions and data. Floppy disks come in two popular sizes: 5.25-inch *minifloppy* and 3.5-inch *microfloppy* for most computer systems. The first floppy disks were 8 inches in diameter; over the years, floppy disks have become smaller while increasing in data capacity—and becoming far less floppy in the bargain.

One technique was to develop **double-sided** disks that could be written to on both sides; then **double-density** was added, doubling capacity again. The 3.5-inch disks are identified as "DSDD" and hold 720K. Another innovation was **high-density** disks, which doubled and quadrupled the number of tracks and sectors. Today, a 5.25-inch disk can hold as much as 1.2M, although this size is falling into disuse. A 3.5-inch disk commonly holds 1.44M or even 2M and is often identified as "MF-2HD," for "microfloppy, double-sided, high-density." An *extra-high density* 3.5-inch disk can hold as much as 2.88M to 4M. Figure 6.35 shows various disks and their capacities.

Figure 6.35
Not only is disk storage space increasing, but storage techniques are becoming more innovative as well.

Today's microfloppy can store from 720K to 2.88M.

The portable Zip Drive uses a special 3.5-inch disk that holds 100M.

The floppy disk drive begins to spin when it begins a read or write operation, timing the speed of rotation very precisely. Figure 6.36 shows a floppy disk with the metal shutter moved aside to reveal the disk within. Once the shutter is moved, the head moves back and forth across the disk. First, the head moves out to the edge of the disk, a process called **indexing**, which means finding the index of file locations on the disk. After the disk is indexed, the head scans the spinning disk to locate sectors where data or program instructions are stored.

The floppy disk is one way that a personal computer software program is distributed by the publisher to the consumer. With hard disk drives as standard equipment on personal computers these days, programs are often copied to the hard disk and then used. The original program disks are stored for safekeeping. Conversely, hard disk drives—depending on their size—may be backed up on floppy disks. Therefore, floppy disks are both direct-access storage devices and backup storage devices—but they are being replaced by newer technologies for both uses.

The Hard Disk Drive

A **hard disk drive** is a secondary storage medium that uses from two to eight disks, or *platters*, permanently sealed in a case. Each has its own read/write head, but all move together to read and write to the disk. Figure 6.37 shows a typical multiple-disk platter.

Hard disk drives operate similarly to floppy disk drives. A floppy disk is made of coated mylar plastic, but a hard disk is made of aluminum and coated with the same magnetic material. Hard disks are hermetically sealed in a metal case to prevent smoke, dirt, and other contaminants from entering. Today's personal computer uses either 3.5-inch or 2.5-inch hard disk drives, which have also helped make laptops smaller and lighter. Computers of all types and sizes, including mainframes, minis, and workstations, use disk drives.

For many years, the hard disk was referred to as a fixed disk because it was fixed in place. That fact, however, is no longer always true. Today, we have the convenience of *removable hard disk drives* for personal computers. Removable drives offer several advantages. One, your data is secure because you can take it home with you. Two, removable drives make it easy to copy data from one computer to another. Three, storage capacity is expanded because you can remove a drive that is full and replace it with a fresh one.

Besides its higher storage capacity, the hard disk drive provides much faster access to data or instructions than a floppy disk drive. One reason for this speed is that the disk spins much faster. This speed is extremely important in large businesses, where there may be scores, even hundreds, of disk drives, each holding anywhere from many billion to several trillion bytes of data.

CD-ROM

Compact disc read-only memory (**CD-ROM**) is an optical disc that holds approximately 650M, the equivalent of four hundred fifty-two 1.44M floppy disks. A CD-ROM, just like its musical counterpart the compact disc, is written to only once. Thus, a CD-ROM containing information, or the CD containing music, is manufactured, or "published," as a way to distribute its contents, much the same way that book publishers distribute information in printed and bound books.

Using 3.5-Inch Floppy Disks

The little 3.5-inch floppy disk may look like the 5.25-inch disk's kid brother, but if so, he's not only younger and smaller, but tougher and smarter as well.

The well-protected disk stores anywhere from 720K for the double-density disks (which define the low end), through the 1.44-megabyte high-density disks that most new machines can read and write, up to the extended-density 2.88-megabyte disks that are starting to be supported in advanced machines.

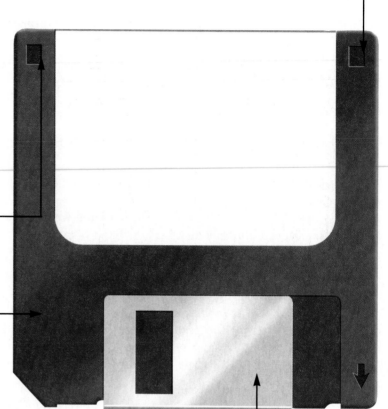

This hole indicates a high-density disk. Double-density disks don't have the hole.

The case is made of a rigid plastic. This disk isn't made to survive bending; it's made to avoid bending. Just because it's in a hard case, don't confuse it with a hard disk!

. . . it presses against an armature that swings back and pushes downward, pulling the disk into the drive . . .

When you push a 3.5-inch floppy disk into its drive . . .

. . . while it slides open the shutter, exposing the disk.

Meanwhile, a simple lever system cocks springs on either side of the disk and pushes a button out. At a press of that button, those springs will shoot the disk out of the drive.

Figure 6.36

This plastic *write-protect switch* on the back of the disk can be used to cover or reveal the hole in the disk.

Information can be written to the disk only when the hole is covered.

The metal hub helps protect the disk's rigidity better than the hollow center of the larger disk.

This spring-loaded metal shutter protects the magnetic disk from dirt and scratches, and then slides away when the disk is inserted into the machine.

A light emitting diode (LED) shines on the upper-right corner of the disk. If the photoreceptor on the other side detects the light passing through, it knows this disk is write-protected, and the drive can then only read the disk and not write on it. Some drives detect the hole using a physical switch instead of an LED.

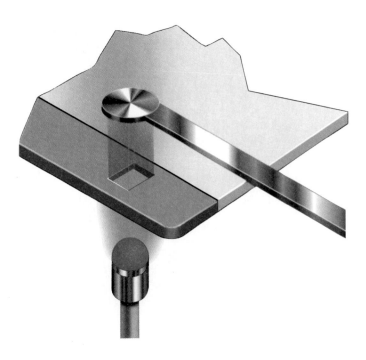

Using Hard Drives

The hard drive is the powerhouse of long-term data storage. It's fast and powerful. When hard drives were originally launched, their 5- to 10-megabyte storage capacity seemed vast. Now you would be hard-pressed to find a new hard drive smaller than 40 megabytes. Most people buy hard drives that store hundreds of megabytes, and some store gigabytes (a *gigabyte* is 1,024 megabytes).

Figure 6.37

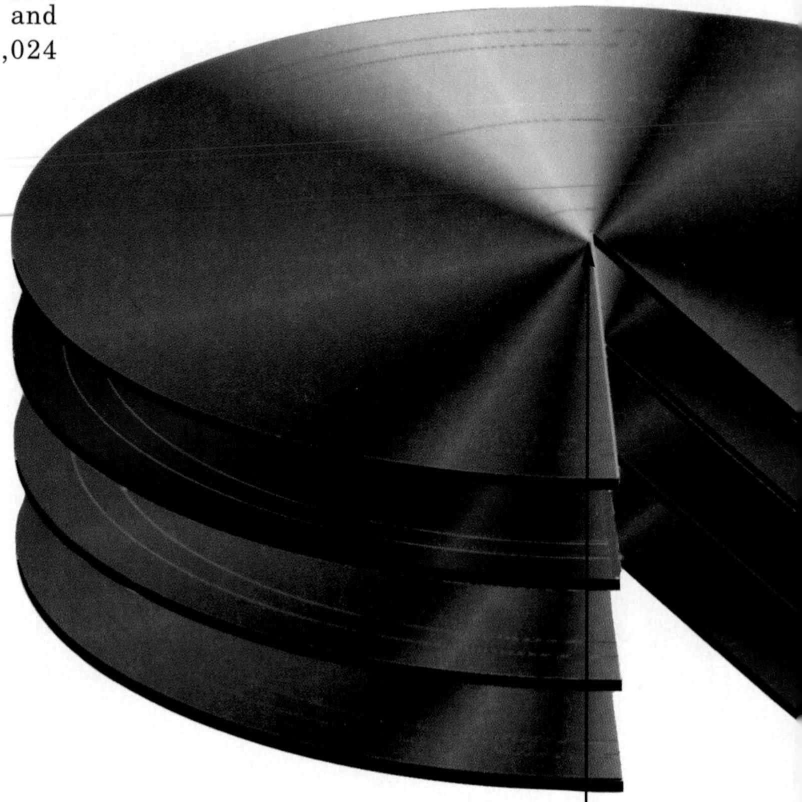

The hard disk drive has multiple *platters*. The exact number of platters varies from drive to drive, but both sides of all the platters are always used. Each is made of an aluminum alloy or a ceramic material, which is what makes the hard disk hard. The platter is coated with magnetic material far more sensitive than that on a floppy disk.

The disks spin on a single spindle at speeds of around 60 to 100 times per second.

The hard disk can spin faster than the floppy because the head never actually touches the disk; instead, it flies over (or under) the disk at a low height, able to detect and alter the magnetic status on the disk without actually touching it.

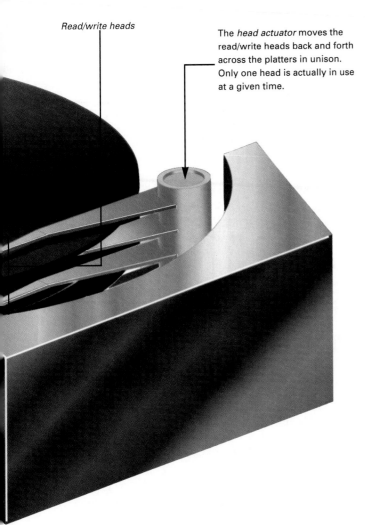

Read/write heads

The *head actuator* moves the read/write heads back and forth across the platters in unison. Only one head is actually in use at a given time.

Because they are so delicate, the platters and head mechanism are sealed in an airtight chamber.

Facts

Access time is how long a drive takes to move the disk heads into position to read a requested piece of information. This time is measured in *milliseconds* to thousandths of a second. The smaller the access time is, the faster the hard disk operates. Most disks sold these days run between 10 and 20 milliseconds.

Because hard disks are so delicate, they should be protected from vibration or sudden impact, particularly while the computer is on and the disk is running.

Hard drives are sometimes called *fixed disks* because the platters are fixed in place and not designed to be taken out of the drive. Some manufacturers now make removable hard disks; they generally involve sealed cartridges containing not only the platters but also the read/write heads and other parts of the mechanism.

HOME PAGE

THE AMAZING GROWTH OF HARD DISK DRIVES

An anomaly of hard disk drives is that as they have grown in capacity, they have also shrunk in size. Over the years, mainframe and minicomputer disk storage capacity grew, but the disks were always rather large. The smaller personal computer required a smaller drive. The first hard disk drives for PCs were the same size as their floppy disk drives: 8 inches, then 5.25 inches.

In 1983, a speaker at the monthly Boston Computer Society meeting was asked when the price of hard disk drives was coming down. He replied that if anyone saw a 10M hard disk drive for under $1,000, they should snap it up. A hundred dollars per megabyte was considered a very good price.

Today's hard disk drives sell for about *30 cents* a megabyte—or less. Five years ago, most PCs came with an 80M drive. Three years ago, it was 120M. Today, it's at least 350M, probably 540M, and possibly 850M. You can buy a 1.2G hard disk drive for less than $300.

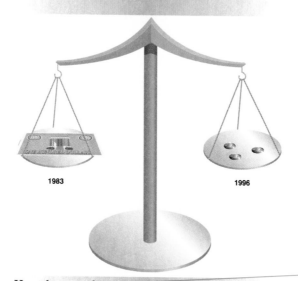

1983   **1996**

How the cost of one megabyte of disk storage has declined.

As storage capacity has increased, so has reliability. Ten years ago, a hard disk drive might last two, perhaps three, years at best. Today's drives have a life expectancy—and often a warranty—for five years. Few things were more unpleasant than powering up your computer to find that the hard disk drive had crashed.

Although that's still an ever-present danger, good utility programs now help you monitor your hard drive's health.

Hardware and software exist in synergy. Large-capacity drives make it possible to have larger, more complex, and thus more useful, programs. Larger programs create the need for a larger hard disk drive. Thus, the two industries ensure each other's future. Expect to be buying larger and larger capacity hard disk drives for a long time to come.

Compression is another approach to disk storage. Utility software that effectively doubles the storage capacity of a disk is available. For example, a program called DriveSpace, which comes with Windows 95, compresses an entire hard disk drive, which then is treated as if it were a compressed file on another disk drive.

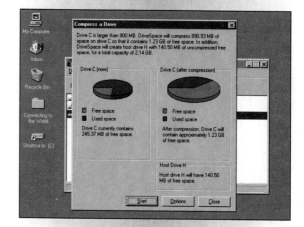

How DriveSpace works.

HOME PAGE REVIEW QUESTIONS

1. Chart how the hard disk drive's price per megabyte has dropped over the years.

2. Along with lower prices and more storage, what else are we getting in the bargain?

3. Why do we need so much more storage?

CD-ROMs are made of aluminum and coated with a tough plastic surface, as shown in figure 6.38. Data is stored in *pits*, or indentations, and *lands*, or bumps, that are etched into the reflective surface with a laser beam. Thus, the data is permanently etched on the CD-ROM and cannot be changed. For that reason, we call CD-ROM technology *read-only storage*, in the same way that ROM is read-only memory. A laser beam in the CD-ROM drive reads the data in a spiral track from the outer edge into the center, much like the old phonograph records the music CD replaced. On a CD-ROM, however, this single track is divided into sectors of equal length. Files are stored in consecutive sectors.

Because of its huge data capacity, the CD-ROM is frequently used for storing more than just text. It can hold large quantities of music, audio, graphics, and video as well. These capabilities make it useful as a way to deliver programs with entertainment and instructional content, such as computer games or encyclopedias.

In addition, the CD-R0M is a convenient way to distribute software and is rapidly replacing the floppy disk. For example, the full version of Windows 95 comes either on 16 floppy disks or on one CD-ROM. Another reason for its popularity is the ease and economy of manufacture. A factory that makes music CDs can make CD-ROMs just as easily and inexpensively.

In 1995, more than 10,000 CD-ROM titles were available. They've become so popular that each week on the television program "c|net Central," computer industry journalist John Dvorak reviews new CD-ROM titles.

For a long time, CD-ROM drives were very slow in accessing the programs and data stored on them. In recent years, drives have doubled (2×) and quadrupled (4×) in speed; the latest boost is to 6×, so that you don't have to sit and wait. For the present, CD-ROM is a read-only technology. Better CD-ROM drives conform to the Microsoft Personal Computer (MPC) standard and come equipped with a headphone jack on the front so that you can listen to music CDs while you work. Although CD-ROM is, by definition, a read-only technology, expect that to change in the future.

Optical Disk Storage

The term **optical disk** is generally used to refer to other types of laser disks besides the CD-ROM. Optical disks come in several sizes and formats:

- The 12-inch *laser videodisk* is also used in home videodisk players and holds a billion bytes, or one gigabyte.

- The *magneto-optical disk*, either 3.5-inch or the same size as a CD-ROM, can be written to and read from. A 3.5-inch holds up to 230M, and a CD-ROM up to 680M. Unlike regular CD-ROMs or laser disks, magneto-optical disks can be rewritten to.

- The *write once, read many* (WORM) is an optical CD-ROM disk that can be written to by the user but cannot be erased. A WORM disk can hold up to one terabyte; however, the advent of fully readable and writable optical disks has made WORMs less desirable.

Figure 6.39 shows how optical disks work.

CD-ROM

The CD in CD-ROM stands for *compact disc;* they are exactly like audio CDs, and many computer CD-ROM drives can be used to play audio CDs. The ROM stands for *read-only memory,* because your computer can only read information from the CD-ROM; it cannot save information on a CD-ROM.

CD-ROMs are used to distribute large programs and vast amounts of information. A CD-ROM disk holds more than 600 megabytes, making applications possible that were previously impractical. Entire encyclopedias are available on a single CD-ROM, as are large libraries of programs and of art.

Information is coded on a series of pits and bumps (or *lands*) that spiral out from the center of the disc. These pits are so small and narrow that the spiral goes around tens of thousands of times.

Plastic coating

Aluminum

The data on the disc is read from the bottom. The labeling information is on the top, where it will not block the light from reflecting off the data.

Figure 6.38
A CD-ROM primer.

A miniature laser . . .

. . . shoots a tight thin beam of light . . .

. . . which travels through a series of lenses and optical devices to aim and focus it on the disk above.

The light passes through the disc's plastic and reflects off the pit or land in the aluminum plate. Pits reflect light badly, while lands reflect it well.

The reflected beam is bounced to a photoreceptor, which can tell whether is was a pit or a land by how much light is reflected.

The data is passed as a series of electrical blips to the electronics of the CD-ROM drive, which interprets it and sends back the information to the controller.

Facts

CD-ROMs are very reliable. The data is physically fixed in place, so it can't get messed up the way magnetic media can. As long as you keep the bottom surface of a CD from getting scratched, it should keep the data safe for decades.

CD-ROMs spin at variable rates. The motor spins the disc at more revolutions per second when reading data near the center than reading data at the edge. This method lets it read the pits at the same rate no matter what part of the disc is being read.

Although there is rarely a need to play music faster, there is always a need to try to read data faster, so CD-ROM manufacturers have come up with double-, triple-, and even quad-spin CD-ROMs, which can read the CD two, three, and even four times as fast.

Spin rate is not the only speed factor. Access time, the amount of time it takes to find where a given file starts on the disk, makes a major difference in how long you have to wait for your information. Even the fastest CD-ROM drives today take more than 20 times as long to find the start of a string of data as a fast hard drive does.

Multisession CD-ROM drives can read CDs of a special format that can be updated.

Optical Disks

CD-ROMs show that lasers can be used to read information very precisely, making storage of large amounts of information possible. Unfortunately, CD-ROM drives can only read information; they cannot store it.

Drive manufacturers have created a number of types of disk drives that use a laser both to read and to write information, which are all referred to as *optical drives*. These drives can hold large amount of information on removable disks, but they all have significant limitations as well. However, they may be the direction for the future of mass storage.

Figure 6.39
A primer on optical disks.

One type of optical disks uses the laser to actually burn pits into the disk, which are then read in the same way that CD-ROMs are read. Once a pit is burned into a disk, there is no way to unburn it, so you can never erase or write over information. It's there forever, and all you can do is read it. Because of this, these disks have the odd name of *WORM disks*. (WORM stands for write once, read many.)

Magneto-optical (M-O) drives take advantage of the scientific relationship between heat, magnetism, and light to store a lot of information, using both laser and magnetic heads. Information is stored magnetically, but using a metal substance that holds on to its polarity tightly. Heat will encourage any magnetic substance to change its polarity. When writing to a disk, the M-O drive has to let the disk spin by the heads twice. On the first spin, the laser puts out a strong beam of light. This heats up all the magnetic bits, allowing the magnetic head to set them to zero.

Facts

The biggest drawback of all these systems is expense. Floptical drives are the cheapest of the three, available in the $500 range. They also hold the least; the typical floptical system stores about 20 megabytes on a $20 floptical disk. Magneto-optical and WORM drives that will store up to a gigabyte of information are available, but the drives cost around $3,000, and the disks themselves are expensive, generally in the $50 to $250 range.

There aren't standards for some types of optical disks, so you can't just take an optical disk out of one drive and put it into another. A disk might work only with drives from the manufacturer who designed it. (Magneto-optical disks are the exception; a standard for single-sided M-O disks that store 128M has taken hold, and a double-sided 256M standard is emerging.)

Because of these limitations, optical disks are nowhere near as prevalent as their magnetic cousins.

A *floptical drive* is like a floppy disk drive, reading and writing data magnetically. More data is fit on the disk by making the tracks of data much thinner. The laser acts like a car headlight, finding the specially etched lines that separate the tracks of the data, and checking to make sure the head stays in the right track, which allows data to be used more precisely and enables more data to be fit on the disk.

On the second spin, the laser heats up just the bits that are to be set to one, and the magnetic head changes only those bits.

Light is made up of vibrations, and magnets have the capability to change the direction in which the wave is vibrating. To read the disk, the laser bounces a weak beam of light off the stored bit. If the reflected light is vibrating one way, the system knows that it's a 1, and another way, that it's a 0.

Courtesy of Ziff-Davis Press

Sequential-Access Storage Devices

Today, **sequential-access storage devices** are most commonly used for backup purposes. No one wants to wait for data that is stored sequentially on tape these days!

Reel-to-Reel Tape

Reel-to-reel magnetic tape was once a primary means of storage for mainframes. After disk storage was introduced, reel-to-reel tape became a backup storage medium. It probably won't be used at all for much longer. One reason is that tape cartridges are inexpensive and much easier to work with. Another reason is that loading and unloading reel-to-reel tapes require a person, often called a "tape hanger," and personnel who want to do the job are scarce. The same thing happened in home recording: reel-to-reel tape was replaced by the compact cassette.

Figure 6.40

Courtesy of International Business Machines Corporation

In an interesting reversal, CD-ROM is being used to back up reel-to-reel tape at the Harvard-Smithsonian Astrophysics Laboratory. Satellites collected celestial images and data for many years, transmitting the information back to earth, where it was stored on reels of magnetic tape. Now that the tape is growing old and subject to deterioration, data could be lost. So the tapes are being copied on to CD-ROMs and sent to scientists at observatories all around the world. What once could be used only by an institution with a large computer system and software capable of handling the tape reels is now available to many more researchers.

Tape Cartridges

Early tape cartridges were nothing more than the Philips compact cassette most people use to listen to music. In time, a better-quality tape was used, but slow speed was still a problem. This factor led to specially designed tape cassettes for backup, called **quarter-inch cartridges** (**QIC**), and special **streaming tape drives** that are quite similar to QICs. Figure 6.42 shows several of these tape cartridges.

QICs offer several other distinct advantages. They have greater capacity than reel-to-reel tape, are easier to handle and are considerably more compact. Cartridges come in a library system, as shown in figure 6.41, with a robot arm that loads and unloads them. The robot has an eye that searches for a cartridge by reading the bar-code serial number on the tape cartridge. The robot can find and load a cartridge in 10 seconds. No more tape hangers.

Courtesy of TRW Information Services

Figure 6.41
A tape cartridge library.

Tape Drives

Magnetic tape cartridges for PCs fill a very important niche—they store a lot of information in a removable form. Hundreds, sometimes thousands, of megabytes can be stored on a single tape.

Because files are spread all across a long tape, there is no way of getting to any individual piece of information. As such, while tape drives can store a lot of information cheaply, they aren't very good for day-to-day storage use.

They are, however, excellent for making backup copies of information stored elsewhere in case something goes wrong (if, for example, a disk gets damaged or a file is accidentally and irretrievably deleted). The entire contents of a hard drive can fit on a single cartridge.

The basics of a cartridge tape are simple, much like an audio tape. The tape (iron oxide on a ribbon of mylar plastic) goes between two reels inside the cartridge. A tape head reads and writes the information magnetically.

Figure 6.42
QICs now dominate the market for PC backup and are getting smaller and more convenient all the time.

There are a number of different types of tape systems available, using different types of cartridges and different sizes of tapes.

Some tape systems store the information in a single line on a tape, and then, when they hit the end of the tape, switch direction and move to another line. This way, dozens of tracks can be recorded on a single tape.

Facts

The earliest IBM PCs sometimes used a cassette tape drive as their primary storage medium. Floppy disk drives were an option costing hundreds of dollars, and it was a long time before a hard drive was an assumed part of a basic PC setup. These early cassette drives used standard audio cassettes, which were far slower and less precise than the high-speed, high-precision specialty cassettes used to back up hard drives these days.

The spinning read/write head automatically checks each bit immediately after writing it.

Other tape systems store information in diagonal lines across the tape. This allows information to be stored more quickly, because the tape doesn't have to move as much when the bits are grouped across the width of the tape.

Tape cartridges make backing up a hard disk drive much easier, even though it takes some time. The disk is faster than a DASD, although the tape is slow and sequential. Tape drives and cartridges are often expensive as well. Purchasing a second identical hard disk drive and using it for backup isn't a bad idea. Whichever you use, please develop a regular backup procedure—every week, for example. It's a little extra effort, but as one knowledge worker says, "The computer can make an extra copy of your work unattended, and you'll probably never need to use this backup copy. But if you ever do have to use the backup, you won't mind the time it took to make it."

Knowledge Check

1. Name the two types of storage.
2. What is the difference between direct access and sequential access?
3. Name several types of direct-access storage devices (DASD).
4. What is meant by the term *media*?
5. What does it mean to make a backup?
6. Why have CD-ROMs become so widely used for computers?
7. What has been a major disadvantage of optical storage?
8. What is a major advantage of tape cartridges?

Key Terms

backup	compact disc read-only memory (CD-ROM)
cylinders	direct access
direct access storage device (DASD)	double-density
double-sided	floppy disk
hard disk drive	high-density
indexing	media
optical disk	quarter-inch cartridge (QIC)
read/write head	sectors
sequential access	sequential-access storage device
streaming tape drive	tracks

ISSUES AND IDEAS

The Digital Disk

How would you like to have a single compact disc (CD) format that plays music, contains computer data, holds an entire movie (maybe two!), and your favorite video games as well? How would you like to have a single CD player that plays any or all of these different types of discs? No more separate music CDs and computer CD-ROMs, no more 12-inch laserdisc movies, no videotapes, no game cartridges.

Enter the digital disk. Lawrence B. Johnson, writes in *The New York Times*:

> The proposed video disk is a high-density version of the familiar 4.7-inch music compact disk. Both fall into the category of CD-ROM: they are playback devices only. Where the music CD has a storage capacity of about 680 million bytes (megabytes), all the digital video disk formats [three have been proposed] offer storage in the billions (gigabytes).
>
> What all these approaches share is a highly sophisticated digital compression technology called MPEG-2 (pronounced EM-peg, for the Motion Picture Experts Group). . . . Demonstrations of the MPEG-2 compression suggest that the digital video disk could deliver a better picture than that obtained from laser disks. [MPEG-2 is now in use with digital satellite (DSS) transmission of television and music broadcasts.]
>
> Nearly lost in the movie orientation of these auspicious developments are the new disk's staggering implications for music recording. . . .
>
> Certainly, the little disks should be handy enough . . . and it's only realistic to expect a new generation of machines that will play any sort of CD-ROM you might care to pop in: movies, music, games. The lone compromise to convenience may be the play-only nature of the disks, though the coming years well may bring an affordable system for in-home recording of both movies and music on disks. . . .
>
> Perhaps the commonality of the little disk, its slickness and even its charm will carry the day for the new high-density video medium.[6]

CRITICAL THINKING

1. What single characteristic makes the new disk, in Johnson's words, a CD-ROM?

2. Make a list of the similarities mentioned between the digital disk and computer storage media, as well as the terminology both share.

3. Would you make the investment in a new CD player that played all types of digital disks? How much would you spend?

4. If they were both priced competitively, would you purchase a digital CD movie over a VHS videotape movie? Would you rent a digital CD movie over a VHS videotape movie, even if it cost, say, a dollar more?

5. What would be the impact of the digital CD on the computer industry? The music industry? The movie industry? Make a list of its pros and cons.

---

6. Lawrence B. Johnson, "The Digital Disk is (Almost) Here," *The New York Times*, September 10, 1995, 45–46.

Module E

Communications Devices

Why It's Important to Know

Being a knowledge worker in the Information Society means sharing data and information. This sharing is often done over communications networks. Communications devices are the hardware used to facilitate this sharing.

Let's be honest. Just about anything could be considered a communications device if it helps two people understand one another. But now let's be realistic. Some communications devices are more efficient than others. Computers are pretty efficient, and they're becoming more versatile at communicating all the time.

What kind of communications are we talking about? James Martin, a noted industry expert, defines **telecommunications** this way in The James Martin World Seminar:

Any process that permits the passage from a sender to one or more receivers of information of any nature, delivered in any usable form (printed copy, fixed or moving pictures, visible or audible signals, etc.) by means of any electromagnetic system (electrical transmission by wire, radio, optical transmission, guided waves, etc.). [Telecommunications] includes telegraphy, telephony, video-telephony, data transmission, etc.]

Today, it is common to hear the term *communications* used in place of telecommunications or data communications. So, if you're going to use your computer for communications, what do you have to do? First, you must make a connection with another computer. Most people use the phone lines and the telephone networks to make this connection. We refer to this physical means of communication as a *communications channel*. But computers and people speak different languages, and you need to understand the difference.

Analog and Digital Communications

Telephone systems were designed to carry analog signals. An **analog signal** is continuous and changes in tone, pitch, and volume, like our voices. A **digital signal** is a single discrete signal, a steady stream of pulses that do not change in tone, pitch, or volume. Digital signals are the only language that computers understand. The same is true of fax machines. Figure 6.43 offers a visual example of the differences between digital and analog signals.

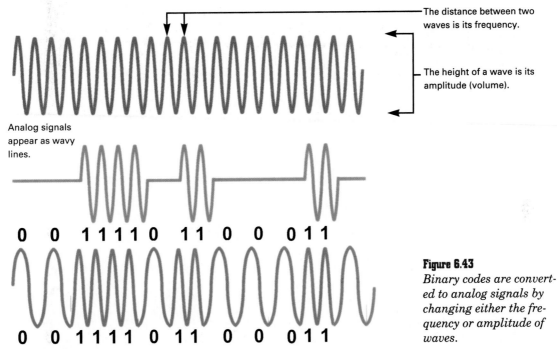

The distance between two waves is its frequency.

The height of a wave is its amplitude (volume).

Analog signals appear as wavy lines.

0   0   1 1 1 1 0   1 1   0   0   0 1 1

0   0   1 1 1 1 0   1 1   0   0   0 1 1

Figure 6.43
Binary codes are converted to analog signals by changing either the frequency or amplitude of waves.

A series of digital signals makes up a data transmission, like a series of letters makes up a word. When a modem (or fax) connection is made, you hear a high-pitched squeal. This sound is a **carrier**, or carrier signal, a tone which indicates that the computer is available. After connection, the carrier signal is modulated to convey the binary information of the computer over the telephone line.

Fiber optic cable, which is wire made from glass, is being installed at an incredible pace in order to wire the Information Superhighway. Fiber optic cable is capable of carrying vast amounts of data, whether analog or digital. The amount of data that can flow through a communications channel is referred to as **bandwidth**. Fiber optic cable has far greater bandwidth than the copper wire used in homes and businesses. Other high-bandwidth communications channels include wireless and satellite-based networks.

Next, we need a communications device. The most common communications device is a modem. It's used extensively with personal computers and can communicate with various other communications devices connected to large systems. Various communications devices are shown in figure 6.44.

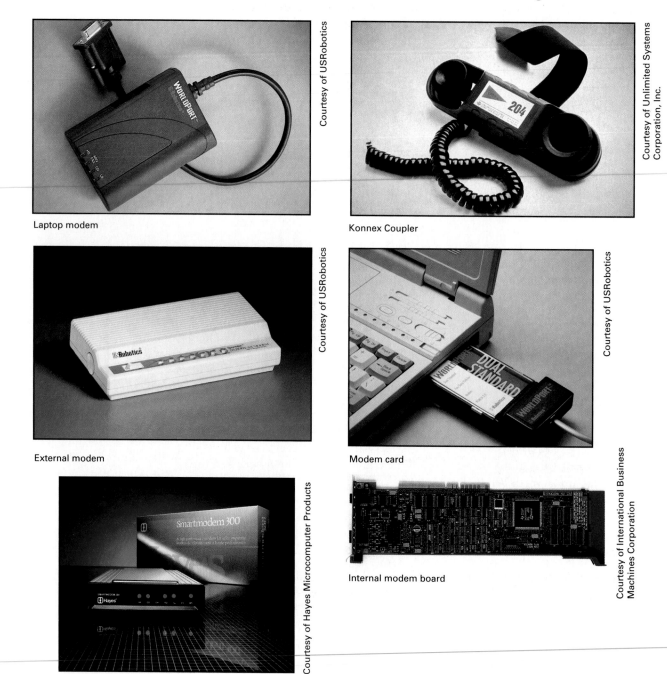

Laptop modem

Courtesy of USRobotics

Konnex Coupler

Courtesy of Unlimited Systems Corporation, Inc.

External modem

Courtesy of USRobotics

Modem card

Courtesy of USRobotics

Hayes Smartmodem

Courtesy of Hayes Microcomputer Products

Internal modem board

Courtesy of International Business Machines Corporation

Figure 6.44

The Modem

A **modem** is a hardware device that enables computers to communicate through telephone lines. The word *modem* is a combination of the terms *mo*dulator and *dem*odulator. You connect a terminal or personal computer to a modem, and the modem to the telephone line, as illustrated in figure 6.45. At the sending end, the modem **modulates**, or converts, the computer's digital signals so that they can be transmitted over the analog phone line. At the receiving end, the modem **demodulates**, or reconverts, the analog telephone signals back into digital signals the computer understands. When the all-digital Information Superhighway is complete, we won't need to use modems any longer.

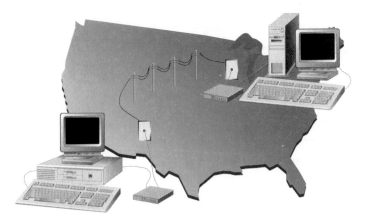

Figure 6.45
Signals leaving the modem are analog until they reach the modem at the other end.

Types of Modems

Modems come in many shapes and designs, as figure 6.44 shows. Briefly review the different types in use today. Identify each modem as you read these descriptions.

The Acoustic Coupler Modem

The earliest modem was called an **acoustic coupler**; it has two cups into which the telephone receiver fits. The acoustic coupler enables you to use almost any phone with a handset to transmit data from a computer. The acoustic coupler has had a resurgence of interest in recent years. One reason is the advent of very small notebook computers, which are convenient to use in a phone booth or even from a cellular phone in an auto.

The External Modem

The acoustic coupler modem was followed by the **external modem**. It is enclosed in a case and has LED lights that signal its activities, so you know when it's working and what it's doing. The external modem connects to the computer with a cable and has a receptacle for a modular phone plug (see figure 6.46). This modem can be easily moved or shared between computers.

Figure 6.46
External modems hook up to the serial port of the computer.

The Smart Modem

The **smart modem** contains advanced circuitry that was created by Hayes Microcomputer Products, the modem company that coined the term. Most modems are considered smart modems these days. The smart modem performs many functions for the knowledge worker. It can do the following:

- Issue its own commands to get a dial tone (called the AT command set)

- Automatically dial a number or answer the phone

- Redial a busy number over and over

- Adjust to the characteristics of the modem to which it is connecting

- Provide a visual signal showing what the modem is doing (such as the data transmission speed, connection made, sending or receiving data, and so on)

- Provide audible monitoring through a speaker

The smart modem is a great advance. By contrast, the first modems of the 1960s had to be taken apart and rewired simply to dial a different telephone number. Figure 6.47 shows the modem's circuit board and components.

Figure 6.47
The circuit board for an external modem is similar to an internal modem, which has electrical connections for the expansion slot.

The Internal Modem

The **internal modem** is on an adapter card that slips into an expansion slot inside your computer (see figure 6.48). This modem is on if the computer is on, although it has no LED indicator lights. Because the internal requires no housing or lights, it is often less expensive than an external modem.

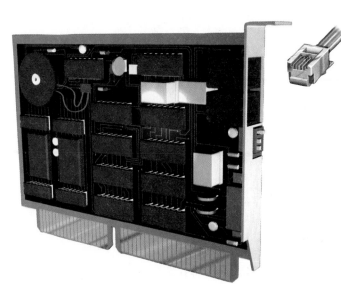

Figure 6.48
Internal modems go into a slot on the computer.

The Modem-on-a-Chip

Space is at a premium in portable and laptops, so modems must be very small. The modem-on-a-chip is a complete modem, with all its functions on a single integrated circuit chip (see figure 6.49). All it needs is its connection to the phone line.

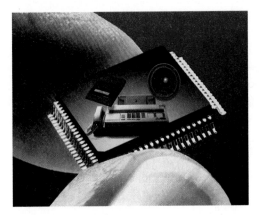

Figure 6.49
How small can you get? This is the entire modem for a notebook computer.

HOME PAGE

AN INVENTION IN SEARCH OF A USE

Across the nation, thousands of people sign on to bulletin board systems every day to perform a wide range of tasks, from downloading important business information to ordering groceries. The inventors of the first BBS didn't have such commercial uses in mind on a snowy Chicago day in 1978. Ward Christensen and Randy Suess were simply two snowbound computer hobbyists who needed an easier way to

transfer data to one another than sending cassette tapes in the mail.

The preceding summer, Dennis Hayes shipped the first hobbyist modem, the 300-baud internal modem. Hayes built the first Smartmodems on his kitchen table in small production runs of five. The Smartmodem was the missing component needed to make the connection between computers and telephone lines. In the setup manual, Hayes wrote that modems could be used for a number of applications, including establishing a bulletin board.

Christensen and Hayes knew each other from industry meetings. So when Christensen called Hayes on the snowy Saturday, Hayes agreed to donate a modem for use in their history-making project.

While Suess worked on the hardware side, Christensen wrote the bulletin board program patterned after corkboard bulletin boards used to post information for a computer club. With that program finished, all the components—computer, phone line, modem, and software—came together to produce the first BBS . . . in the world.[7]

The first Hayes Smartmodem.

HOME PAGE REVIEW QUESTIONS

1. Who built the first modems for personal computers?

2. What was the first use for a PC modem?

3. What was the speed of the first PC modem?

7."The First BBS" in *Official Hayes Modem Communications Companion* (San Mateo, CA: IDG Books, 1994), 26.

Modem Speed

Modems are also classified by data transmission speed, measured as **baud rate**. The **baud** is a unit for measuring signal speed and is roughly equivalent to one **bit per second** (**bps**). Although bps is more accurate, baud rate is the more commonly used term for assessing modem speed.

Early personal computer modems could transmit at only 300 bps, but 2400-bps and 9600-bps modems soon became common. As more people wanted to use various communications services, the demand for faster access grew, and new standards with them. Today, the two most popular modems are these:

- V.32bis, or 14,400 bits per second (referred to as 14.4Kbps).

- V.34, or 28,800 bits per second (referred to as 28.8Kbps); also called V.FAST, it is the fastest possible standard that will operate on conventional phone lines.

Fax Modems

Facsimile, or *fax* for short, refers to the transmission and reception of digitized images over telephone lines. Facsimile turns text, characters, graphics, and other types of images into patterns of tiny dots. Stand-alone fax machines have been in use for many years, but they should not be confused with the computer, which transmits digital bits, not dots. Most stand-alone faxes transmit at 9600 baud.

For a short while, a fax expansion card for PCs was on the market. It was called a *fax board*, and accompanying software enabled you to read the incoming fax. Some of these cards could send only, while others were able to send and receive. The fax board was usually sold with a separate scanner for fax input. The entire setup was awkward, and a prerequisite was calling the party to whom you wanted to fax to make sure that the software and hardware were prepared to receive a transmission.

Recently, however, we have seen a marriage of modems and fax, and the result is the **fax modem**, which can send and receive faxes as well as data. Like other modems, a fax modem may be either internal or external. The speeds of the data modem aspect are generally faster than the fax modem aspect. The fastest fax standard is 14.4, but 9600 is more common.

A great advantage is to use the fax modem to fax a document as a computer file. You don't need to print the file and then feed the pages into a fax machine. The fax modem is highly suited to faxing a document created by the computer and application software, directly from the computer. But the fax modem lacks the capability to scan noncomputer documents, such as a magazine article or photograph. For this task, using a stand-alone fax machine is still easier.

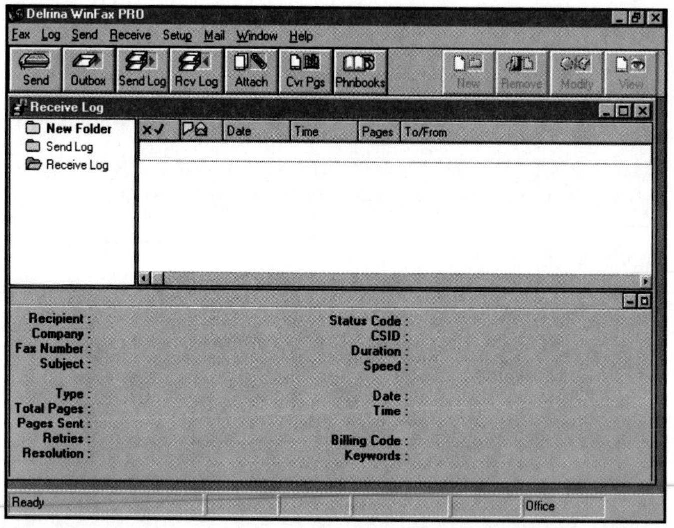

Figure 6.50
Fax software makes setting up for faxing quick and easy.

A scanner peripheral can, of course, be added to the computer, but it is less expensive simply to use the stand-alone fax machine as a scanner—as long as you don't need to save the scanned data as a computer file. Remember, it is dots, not digital. Fax modems can fax to a stand-alone fax machine, and vice versa.

Using the computer as a full-time, send-and-receive fax machine is a decision you need to consider carefully. The single greatest disadvantage is that your computer must be on and the fax modem software loaded at all times. By comparison, the stand-alone fax machine consumes far less power than a computer.

Computers and facsimile have been combined to deliver information. Fax-back systems like Special Request are designed to enable callers to dial a voice phone number and listen to a recording that lists such things as ski reports, sports information, product descriptions and prices, investment tips, and interest rates. Then the prospective customers can request specific documents by pressing numbers on the phone keypad, followed by the fax number. The documents are faxed almost immediately.

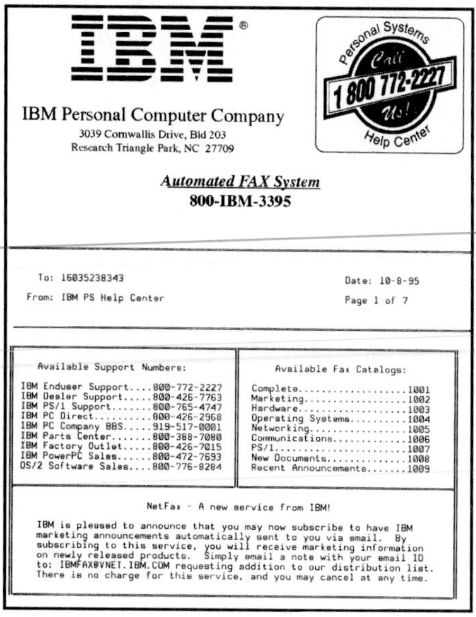
IBM®

IBM Personal Computer Company
3039 Cornwallis Drive, Bld 203
Research Triangle Park, NC 27709

Personal Systems Call 1 800 772-2227 Us! Help Center

Automated FAX System
800-IBM-3395

To: 16035238343
From: IBM PS Help Center
Date: 10-8-95
Page 1 of 7

Available Support Numbers:

IBM Enduser Support....800-772-2227
IBM Dealer Support.....800-426-7763
IBM PS/1 Support.......800-765-4747
IBM PC Direct..........800-426-2968
IBM PC Company BBS.....919-517-0001
IBM Parts Center.......800-388-7080
IBM Factory Outlet.....800-426-7015
IBM PowerPC Sales......800-472-7693
OS/2 Software Sales....800-776-8284

Available Fax Catalogs:

Complete....................1001
Marketing...................1002
Hardware....................1003
Operating Systems...........1004
Networking..................1005
Communications..............1006
PS/1........................1007
New Documents...............1008
Recent Announcements........1009

NetFax - A new service from IBM!

IBM is pleased to announce that you may now subscribe to have IBM marketing announcements automatically sent to you via email. By subscribing to this service, you will receive marketing information on newly released products. Simply email a note with your email ID to: IBMFAX@VNET.IBM.COM requesting addition to our distribution list. There is no charge for this service, and you may cancel at any time.

Figure 6.51
This document was sent by a fax information service.

Network Adapters

The trend in communications is to connect personal computers in networks. A **network** is a computer-based communications and data exchange system that connects two or more computers, using hardware and software. Networking enables many knowledge workers to share programs and data, and to communicate with each other using e-mail. In fact, networking is changing the way people work together.

A <u>**network adapter**</u> is an expansion card that physically connects the computer to the network. It has processing and memory capabilities, and it is designed to work with specific types of networks. Some of these types of networks are known as Ethernet, token ring, and ARCnet. Networking software runs on all computers connected in the network.

Most network adapters are a conventional expansion card plugged into an expansion slot on the main circuit board. The card is connected to the network and the other computers through cabling. The cable may be a phone cord, coaxial cable, or fiber optic cable.

The pocket network adapter is often used with portable or notebook PCs. This adapter plugs into the parallel port, making it possible to connect quickly to the network, join the group, and get productive.

Knowledge Check

1. How do we commonly use the word *telecommunications*?
2. What is the most common communications peripheral for a PC?
3. What are the fastest communications speeds available today?
4. What is the *more accurate* measurement of communications speed?
5. What is a fax modem unable to do?
6. What is the usual speed of a fax modem?
7. What is the purpose of a network adapter?

Key Terms

acoustic coupler	analog signal	bandwidth	baud
baud rate	bits per second (bps)	carrier	demodulate
digital signal	external modem	facsimile	fax modem
internal modem	modem	modulate	network
network adapter	smart modem	telecommunications	

ISSUES AND IDEAS

Faxes—From Dots to Bits

The major issue remaining in the integration of fax documents and documents created by a software application is this: faxes are made up of dots, and document files are made up of bits and bytes. An attempt to bring the two together is called *binary file transfer*, or BFT. Here is an explanation:

> BFT is a file transfer protocol, but it is specifically for fax modems and the software that works with fax modems. It enables you to send a binary file at the same time you send a fax message.
>
> For example, you can send a cover page explaining a detailed spreadsheet and send the large spreadsheet file at the same time. This means you don't have to send the [spreadsheet's worksheet] as a fax. . . . The difference is that with BFT . . . instead of converting the attachment into a fax image and sending it as a fax [it is sent as a binary file].
>
> . . . Receiving BFT transmissions is even easier than sending them. You receive the transmission as you would receive a normal fax. . . . After receiving a BFT transmission, you treat it as any other fax transmission, with one exception. [The fax message is an attachment that is opened as a file.][8]

BFT works very well with documents created by computer applications. Yet it does not address the document that was originated outside the computer—the magazine article, the photograph, and so on. These documents, scanned in and translated into dots, cannot be stored as files unless optical character recognition (OCR) software is used—and then OCR does not work with 100 percent accuracy. A key to successful BFT is that both computers must be using a software program that can work with binary file transfers. Most major fax software programs now support BFT, and some operating environments now support it.

CRITICAL THINKING

1. What major problem does BFT solve?
2. What kind of document can be sent via BFT? What kind of document cannot?
3. What are the technical requirements for sending and receiving BFT?
4. Do you think this solves the problem of "dots to bits"? Defend your position.

---

8. *Using WinFax PRO 4* (Indianapolis: Que, 1994), 369–374.

ETHICS

Altering Facts and Reality with Computers

What promises to provide us with the most dramatic steps forward in making computers more useful also holds an inherent danger: altering facts and reality. A scanner could be used to enter the letterhead of the President of the United States, and someone could add text that declares war on China. Anything from a business card to a birth certificate could conceivably be falsified. A person's signature can be scanned from one document and inserted in one that he or she did not author—say, an order or a promise of some sort—and faxed to another party as authentic.

Similarly, a photograph can be input and then doctored by computer processing to remove or insert images. We have seen this process at computer trade shows, performed by people demonstrating the powers and features of their products. In one instance, a photograph showed a building and an American flag. The image was scanned into the computer, and using a graphics program, the demonstrator literally erased the flag from the photo. What would happen if a photograph were doctored to show an innocent person as the perpetrator of a crime?

Over the past few years, a debate has grown up over fact versus fiction on television news and documentaries. Reenactments of actual events have been filmed with actors, often with hypothetical scenarios of what really happened. Many people feel that it is neither ethical nor proper to present re-creations as actual events; however, television executives seem to feel that this technique is a valid method of depicting events as close to the way they actually occurred as possible.

Computers can be used—and misused—in the same way. A computer simulation could show a warplane attacking an American ship. A journalist's video image could be altered so that she appeared to be reporting on a fictitious event. If these and similar events occur, where—and how—can we draw the line between appearance and reality?

There is nothing particularly new about falsifying documents, but the computer makes it easier—it doesn't take expensive, specialized equipment. What's more, the computer makes it seem like fun or entertainment. The demonstrator at the trade show did not exhibit feelings of guilt or remorse over falsifying or altering the photograph; on the contrary, she seemed to feel that it was a technological achievement.

It is this attitude that the average computer user must recognize and avoid. There is a sense of accomplishment associated with performing computer tasks. That is all the more reason we must be careful constantly to ask ourselves whether we are acting prudently, ethically, and legally with our computers.

Critical Thinking

1. How do you feel about the fact that technological advances in peripheral devices have made it easier to falsify images with a computer?

2. What social measures should be taken to correct the situation? For example, should the demonstrator at the trade show be warned, fined, or punished?

3. Is there an ethical line that can be drawn between private, personal use of altered images and those used in public or for consumption by others?

4. In the latter instance, should there be a disclaimer, as on cigarettes?

THE LEARNING ENTERPRISE

In the preceding chapter, you made many of the determinations regarding the people, the computer systems, and the business process. In this assignment, you have an opportunity to take what you've learned about refining goals and pinpointing how computer systems are to be used, and then apply that knowledge in a very practical way: to optimize your personal computer system.

You've already determined what kind of personal computer you're going to use, and primarily what kind of application software. As you know from studying this chapter, there are many different kinds of peripherals. Most are designed to enhance productivity; some are designed for special purposes as well. Now you can pick and choose the ones best suited to your work.

First describe the type of interfaces, or special characteristics of interfaces, that you need:

Physical:

Logical:

Human-computer:

Ergonomics:

Now place a check mark in the box beside each peripheral you choose. Then write a brief description of *how* you plan to use it to improve your personal productivity.

☐ Keyboard

☐ Pointing device

☐ Writing or drawing device

☐ Video input

☐ Text input

☐ Source data automation

☐ Input devices for the disabled

☐ Printer (type)

☐ Video monitor (type)

☐ Terminals

☐ Computer-to-machine output

☐ Voice output

☐ RAM (amount)

☐ Floppy disk drive(s)

☐ Hard disk drive(s)

☐ CD-ROM drive

☐ Optical disk storage

☐ Sequential access storage devices

☐ Modem (type, speed)

☐ Fax modem

Chapter Review

Fill in the Blank

1. The connection between two hardware devices is called a(n) _____ interface.

2. A(n) _____ interface connects a variety of devices, such as a mouse or a modem.

3. A(n) _____ interface is used to connect the computer to the printer.

4. The study of _____ explores the human factors surrounding the design of computers, office environments, furniture, and other aspects of the work area in order to make them more healthy and easy for people to use.

5. An electronic pathway on the main circuit board is called a(n) _____.

6. The _____, or chip, replaced the vacuum tube in computers.

7. The integrated circuit that conducts the computer's processing is called the _____.

8. The process of entering data into computer memory and issuing commands that tell the processor how to work with the data is called _____.

9. A light-sensitive input device used to enter text or graphics is called a(n) _____.

10. Data transmission speed is measured as _____ rate.

Circle the Correct Answer

1. (Analog, Digital) signals are continuous and change in tone, pitch, and volume.

2. (Analog, Digital) signals do not change in tone, pitch, or volume and are a single discrete signal or steady stream of pulses.

3. The term used to describe the degree of detail in a video display is (resolution, gas plasma).

4. (Impact, Nonimpact) printers print characters by striking the paper.

5. Laser and inkjet printers are (impact, nonimpact) printers.

6. The main advantage of the CD-ROM is (speed, storage capacity).

7. The floppy disk and the hard disk store data (magnetically, sequentially).

8. Microprocessors are used in (mainframes, personal computers).

Review Questions

1. Name three types of interfaces.

2. What are the advantages of using a small computer system interface (SCSI)?

3. Software that sets up a form of communication between hardware devices so that they "talk" to one another is called what kind of interface?

4. Briefly describe the purpose of the following pointing devices: (a) Mouse, (b) Trackball, (c) Touchpad, and (d) Joystick.

5. Briefly describe the purpose of the following writing or drawing input devices: (a) Light Pen, (b) Touch Screen, and (c) Digitizer.

6. Describe different specific uses for the following kinds of computer output: (a) Text, (b) Graphic, (c) Sound, and (d) Video.

7. What is the difference between hard copy output and soft copy output?

8. What is a secondary use for hard copy?

9. Explain the difference between a modem and a facsimile machine.

10. When do you need a sequential access storage device?

Discussion Questions

1. Discuss the advantages of voice recognition over other kinds of computer input such as keyboards or touch screens.

2. Working with a classmate, consult the ergonomics Home Page diagram. Measure each other to meet all the criteria, and then record your impressions of how it feels to work in an ergonomic position.

3. Discuss your ideas about what would make an ideal human-computer interface.

INTERNET DISCOVERY

Each knowledge worker should bring to class a document or reference to one peripheral that is innovative, useful, or new. Print the home page or send for a brochure. You can research peripherals at the following site:

http://www.yahoo.com/Computers_and_Internet /Hardware/Peripherals/

PART III
COMPUTER SOFTWARE

Chapter 7   Operating Systems and Operating Environments

Module A   Common Operating Systems
Module B   Common Operating Environments
Module C   Working with the Graphical User Interface and Multitasking

Chapter 8   The Word Processor

Module A   The Word Processing Process
Module B   Word Processing Basic Tools and Advanced Features

Chapter 9   The Spreadsheet

Module A   The Spreadsheet Process
Module B   Spreadsheet Basic Tools and Advanced Features

Chapter 10   Database Management Systems

Module A   The Database Management System Process
Module B   DBMS Tools and Advanced Features
Module C   The Personal Information Manager

Chapter 11   PC Communications

Module A   The PC Communications Process
Module B   PC Communications and the Internet
Module C   The World Wide Web and Browser Software

Chapter 12   Presentation Graphics and Desktop Publishing Software

Module A   Presentation Graphics
Module B   Desktop Publishing

Bruce Gee
Product Manager
Entry Macintosh Products

Apple Computer, Inc.
1 Infinite Loop, MS: 306-4ES
Cupertino, California 95014
408 974-3457
Fax: 408 862-5059
AppleLink: GEE

初級マッキントッシュ製品
製品課長
ブルース・ジー

アップルコンピュータ株式会社
米国カリフォルニア州クパティーノ 市
インフィニット　ループ1番地
Tel : (408) 974-3457
Fax : (408) 862-5059
AppleLink: GEE

Knowledge Worker Interview with Bruce Gee

E-mail address: GEE@APPLELINK.APPLE.COM

Bruce was born in Sacramento, California, on April 10, 1962. He holds an undergraduate degree in economics from Stanford University and an MBA from the Sloan School of Management at the Massachusetts Institute of Technology in Cambridge. He currently lives in Palo Alto, California, with his wife and son.

Author: Where do you work?

Bruce: At Apple Computer, Inc., in Cupertino, California. I'm part of the team responsible for designing, building, and marketing the Performa line of Macintosh computers sold to homes and schools. My job is a mix between marketing, engineering, and manufacturing. To the engineering and manufacturing teams, I'm their marketing person. To the marketing folks, I'm their engineering and manufacturing contact. It's fun to work with these different functional teams within Apple.

Each day, I spend about half my time in meetings. In addition to meeting with the project team, I spend a fair amount of time listening to what customers want and need in our future products, talking with independent software developers who create programs for the Mac, and making product presentations to our salespeople. The rest of my day is filled with reading and writing e-mail (about 50 to 100 messages a day), talking on the phone, and preparing for meetings.

Author: You must use computers quite a bit.

Bruce: Yes. I use a Power Macintosh 8500 at work, a Performa 5200 at home, and a PowerBook 540C notebook for travel. I'm constantly using AppleLink, Apple's private network, for e-mail, Excel, Word, and Persuasion, which I use for making presentations to educators. And I like to play lots of games.

Author: What do you like about your employer and your work?

COMPUTER SOFTWARE

Bruce: Apple Computer is a great place to work, full of fun, smart, and energetic people. It's an environment that encourages creativity and fosters teamwork. At Apple, we create really cool products.

Sometimes I think I have the best job in the world. I get to work on products that millions of people will use every day for work, education, and play. People don't just use their Macs; they love them. It really makes the work enjoyable when you realize that someone benefits from your hard labor.

Author: How do you view the future of knowledge work?

Bruce: Today, we spend a lot of our time looking for things—data. Unfortunately this is too difficult, slow, or expensive—or, for most of us, the data is inaccessible. In the future, computers will make it easy to find the information we need. As these barriers disappear, we can spend more time analyzing, or just plain enjoying, what we have already found.

Author: Where do you think future opportunities lie?

Bruce: While computers have become a natural and obvious way many people write letters, work with numbers, and do other tasks, we still have to consciously think about using them. The challenge is not just to make computers easier to use, but to make them transparent—so we forget (or don't even realize) that we are using one.

Author: What advice would you give today's college student?

Bruce: Here are two things to remember. First, technology continues to advance at a rate that sometimes boggles the mind. Computers will be faster, cheaper, and easier to use next year—and the next year—and the year after that. Second, computers aren't the answer to everything. They are just tools for people to use to make our lives easier, more productive, and more fun.

Author: What are your favorite nonwork uses for the computer?

Bruce: Besides the standard address book and home finance tracking, I use my Mac and Adobe Premiere to create fun cards and newsletters to send to friends and family. My next goal is to use Avid VideoShop to edit home movies with titles and fancy special effects. I also enjoy woodworking, gardening, a few sports, and being a dad.

OPERATING SYSTEMS AND OPERATING ENVIRONMENTS

It is pretty cool that the products we work on empower individuals and make their jobs more interesting. It helps a lot in inventing new software ideas that I will be one of the users of the software so I can model what's important.[1]

Bill Gates, chairman and cofounder, Microsoft Corporation

System software includes the operating system (or OS), which controls the execution of computer programs, and the operating environment software that runs on top of the OS. System software runs the computer system, performing a variety of fundamental operations. These operations include

- Starting the computer and making sure that its hardware components are operational

- Controlling and managing peripherals

- Retrieving, loading, executing, and storing application programs

- Storing and retrieving data and files

- Performing system utility functions

- Controlling programming tools

- Acting as an intermediary between the user or application program and the computer hardware to control and manage the operation of the computer

The system software is the resident authority in your computer, regardless of which application and computer you are using. System software must be utterly reliable. Consider the responsibilities of MVS, the operating system for IBM's mainframe computers. It is made up of 520 million 8-bit characters, coded into 13 million instructions. One MIS department has seven interconnected CPUs, with about 15,000 terminals in more than 450 locations, running under the MVS operating system. Between 500 and 700 knowledge workers may have access to the CPU at a time, concurrently using between 300 and 400 different applications.

1. Peter Kent. *The Complete Idiot's Guide to the Internet,* Second Edition (Indianapolis: Que, 1994), 73–90.

Module A

Common Operating Systems

Why It's Important to Know

> **The operating system is essential software, coordinating all activities between hardware and software components.** Although you may use only one operating system, sometimes you need to be familiar with others.

This module is an introduction to the various operating systems you may encounter as a knowledge worker. Without the operating system, no computer processing can take place. Having as little interaction with the operating system as possible is preferable; productivity depends on using application programs.

Personal Computer Operating Systems

Two types of personal computer operating systems are in use today: stand-alone and network. *Stand-alone* means dedicated to a single computer system, working all by itself. Network operating systems are designed for two or more knowledge workers who share various resources.

Stand-Alone PC Operating Systems

In the beginning, all PC operating systems were stand-alone because PCs were designed for individual use. The idea was to provide a single, integrated computer system, dedicated to the needs of an individual knowledge worker. A *stand-alone PC operating system* is designed to support just one computer system—the processing, software applications, and individual knowledge worker. Here are the most popular stand-alone PC operating systems:

- *MS-DOS,* usually referred to as simply *DOS,* is the most common personal computer operating system. It was developed by Microsoft Corporation of Redmond, Washington. MS-DOS stands for Microsoft Disk Operating System. The current version, MS-DOS 7.0, is integrated into Windows 95; Microsoft does not plan to release another separate version of DOS.

- *PC DOS* is similar to MS-DOS but was developed specifically for the IBM PC. Both MS-DOS and PC DOS have been greatly improved with the addition of color, graphical screens, and extra utilities. IBM believes that there are still many DOS users for its current version, PC DOS 7, which the company continues to sell separately (see figure 7.1).

```
                        PC DOS Shell
File  Options  View  Tree  Help
C:\DOS
 ⊟A    ⊟B    ■C    ⊟D
            Directory Tree                    C:\DOS\*.*
 ⊟ C:\                          ↑  ⊞ 4201     .CPI      6,404  04-09-91  ↑
    ⊟ DATA                         ⊞ 4208     .CPI        720  04-09-91
    ⊟ DOS                          ⊞ 5202     .CPI        395  04-09-91
       ⊟ DATA                      ⊞ 7201     .CPI     17,089  05-27-88
       ⊟ PCM                       ⊞ 7202     .CPI        459  05-27-88
       ⊟ SYSTEM                    ⊞ 865      .CPI      9,920  11-17-94
       ⊟ UTILS                     ⊞ 912      .CPI      9,920  11-17-94
    ⊟ MOUSE                        ⊞ 915      .CPI      9,920  11-17-94
    ⊟ MSOFFICE                     ⊟ ACALC    .EXE     22,851  11-17-94
    ⊟ OLD_DOS.1                    ⊞ ADMIN    .PRF        715  11-17-94
    ⊟ PCDOS                        ⊞ ANSI     .SYS      8,906  11-17-94
    ⊟ SETUP                        ⊟ APPEND   .EXE      7,735  11-17-94
    ⊟ STACKER                      ⊞ APPNOTES .TXT      9,701  04-09-91
    ⊟ STEPUP                    ↓  ⊟ ASSIGN   .COM      5,102  11-17-94  ↓
                                  Main
 ⊟ Command Prompt                                                       ↑
 ⊟ Editor
 ⊟ MS-DOS QBasic
 ▦ Disk Utilities



                                   ↳


                                                                        ↓
 F10=Actions   Shift+F9=Command Prompt                          3:34p
```

Figure 7.1
*PC DOS was developed
specifically for the
IBM PC.*

- *OS/2,* or Operating System/2, was jointly developed by Microsoft and IBM for the latter's PS/2 line of personal computers. OS/2 was so named because it was the second generation of DOS. OS/2 offers features not found in DOS: more RAM capacity, which enables it to run more complicated applications; multitasking capabilities; and a graphical user interface (GUI). The OS/2 GUI, called Presentation Manager, enables you to run several applications in *windows*, or individual boxes displayed on the monitor screen.

  IBM has taken over all OS/2 development and has released a new version called *OS/2 Warp*. It is a direct competitor of Microsoft Windows.

- *Windows* began life as a shell utility program for DOS. But as the popularity of the Macintosh grew, Microsoft began developing Windows in earnest. Knowledge workers could choose to run their PCs with DOS alone or to use both Windows and DOS. Today, in Windows 95, DOS and Windows act as one.

- *MacOS,* the Macintosh operating system, uses icons and graphics instead of the command line common to DOS and OS/2. Apple has improved MacOS many times, from its introduction to the most recent System 7, which has both multitasking and built-in networking capabilities. MacOS System 8 (code-named Copland), scheduled for release in 1996, is faster, incorporates OpenDoc, and has improved graphics and multimedia capabilities.

Network PC Operating Systems

A **network operating system**, or NOS, operates separately but in addition to a stand-alone OS. The NOS coordinates activities among various computers and peripherals—ranging from disk drives to printers—connected in a network. One computer may be designated as the file server and may also be where the NOS resides, issuing its commands to the other PCs and devices.

The main purpose for a NOS is to enable people to share applications, files, and printers. A network version of an application can be licensed and installed on the server, then loaded as needed on to individual PCs in the network. Files can be copied, shared, and exchanged. All knowledge workers can share one printer. Following are a few of the popular network operating systems; most share similar features:

- *AppleShare* is the NOS for Macintosh PCs. All the devices are connected in the AppleTalk network, and one Macintosh is designated as the file server.

- *NetWare* was created by Novell, a networking company that also owns WordPerfect. There are two versions of NetWare, one for PC compatibles and one for the Macintosh.

- *OS/2 Warp Connect* is IBM's version of OS/2 Warp for networked PCs.

- *Windows for Workgroups* is Microsoft's version of Windows for networked PCs. It is ideal for small networks. The newer Windows 95 can also be used in a network.

- *Windows NT* is Microsoft's full network version of Windows, the first in the line to do away with DOS and act as a fully integrated operating system for networking (see figure 7.3). Windows NT is designed for high-performance environments where PCs and workstations are used.

Figure 7.2
The Novell Corsair GUI is used in many business offices.

Courtesy of Novell, Inc.

Figure 7.3
Windows NT is Microsoft's full network version of Windows.

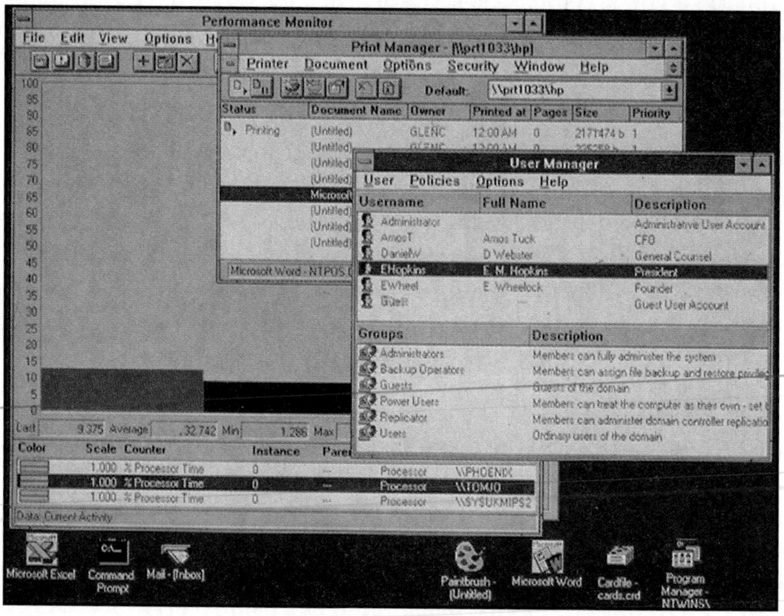

Minicomputer Operating Systems

Minicomputer operating systems are more complex than systems for personal computers. Most are multiuser, multiprogramming systems that control an extensive array of peripheral devices. Minicomputer operating systems are fast, handle large volumes of data, and perform many I/O operations.

UNIX is an operating system developed at AT&T Bell Laboratories in New Jersey. Although it began as a minicomputer operating system, today UNIX also runs on PCs and workstations. UNIX was designed to offer a powerful and convenient programming environment for experienced users. UNIX commands are abbreviated—steps required by many simpler operating systems are eliminated to make UNIX faster. Novice users often find UNIX unfriendly and unforgiving. A small mistake using DOS can be a big one with UNIX!

People who want to do many things concurrently or who want to do one thing while the computer is working on another find UNIX especially valuable. UNIX enables you to run several subprocesses or user sessions simultaneously. Each subprocess can perform several tasks at once.

UNIX use is widespread, especially in the college community. Its popularity is due in part to its being a portable operating system. **Portable** means that UNIX can be used on many different computers, regardless of their manufacturer. For example, NASA uses 200 workstations and 30 servers from nine computer manufacturers, each with a different version of UNIX, but all can communicate with one another.

VMS is the operating system Digital Equipment Corporation developed for its family of VAX (Virtual Address Extension) computers. *VMS* stands for *Virtual Memory System.* It is a proprietary operating system.

VMS uses a technique called the Swapper to make the virtual memory seem larger than it actually is. It "swaps" user sessions into and out of the CPU and its RAM very quickly, so each user feels that he or she has exclusive access to processing. VMS is one of the most popular operating systems for minicomputers. It is an ideal operating system for networking, where its versatility and high level of security facilitates support for many different computer platforms. Table 7.1 shows some of the most important VMX commands. Note that they maintain an ease-of-use factor.

Mainframe Operating Systems

One of the main advantages of using mainframes is that they permit the largest number of knowledge workers to use the computer system and its application software concurrently (at the same time). In addition, many different kinds of peripherals and auxiliary storage devices can be connected to the mainframe. In fact, a mainframe can send different types of output to a number of different printers or other output devices all at the same time. Another advantage of mainframes is their capability to work with large amounts of data. These advantages, and many others, are possible because of the sophisticated operating systems mainframes employ. Mainframe operating systems are *multiuser* (many simultaneous workers), *multiprogramming* (many concurrent tasks) systems that can perform at greater processing speeds than either personal computer or minicomputer operating systems.

Table 7.1
Digital Minicomputer VMS Commands

Command	Function
AUTHORIZE	Allocates system resources to users
COPY	Copies a file from one disk or directory to another
DELETE	Deletes a file
DIFFERENCE	Shows the difference between two files
DIRECTORY	Lists contents of the default directory
EDIT	Edits a file
HELP	Displays help on commands
LOGIN/LOGOUT	Begins/ends a user session
MAIL	Sends/reads mail messages
PURGE	Deletes prior versions of the files
RECOVER	Restores a file lost by system failure
RENAME	Changes file names
SET DEFAULT	Sets default disk and directory
SET PASSWORD	Sets a new user password
SHOW PROCESS	Shows use of system resources
SHOW PROTECT	Shows users allowed access to a file
SHOW QUEUE	Lists printer and batch jobs being executed or waiting to be executed
SHOW USERS	Lists current users of computer
SPAWN	Begins a user session within an active user session

MVS, developed by IBM, is a well-known operating system in the mainframe world. MVS specializes in batch processing, which involves collecting large numbers of user requests or programs for processing at a later time. Batch processing is used primarily for large, periodic jobs such as corporate billing or payroll.

MVS also has extensive multiuser capabilities—thousands of people can share the computer and the applications running on it. MVS was created using principles established during Project MAC (Multiple-Access Computer) at the Massachusetts Institute of Technology in the 1960s. Project MAC's goal was to create a **time-sharing** computer, a computer that can be used by many people simultaneously for different purposes or applications.

Mainframe computers have tried to remain viable in a world that continues to move toward desktop computers connected in networks. IBM has introduced a new suite of MVS system software programs to make its mainframes more compatible with the new computing environment. This new software forms the core of a new operating system IBM is tentatively calling OS/390, named for its top-of-the-line mainframe computers.

HOME PAGE

HERE'S LOOKING AT UNIX, KID

Dennis Ritchie and Ken Thompson created the UNIX operating system in 1969 out of frustration with the inefficient and inflexible alternatives available to them. Little did they know that their creation would one day run on hundreds of thousands of computers around the world.

UNIX is the operating system running on most of the computers connected to and serving the Internet. So, from time to time, you'll have to know UNIX commands to gain access to the programs or data stored on a remote computer. Here are some things you'll need to know about UNIX, excerpted from *The Complete Idiot's Guide to the Internet*:

Even if you have a menu, you'll eventually want to go to the [UNIX] shell to do something, because . . . you might need to . . . transfer files back to your computer or to view files stored in your home directory on the hard disk. . . . How do you get to the shell? It may be there immediately when you log in; if not, you can choose it from the menu that appears instead.

Shell takes [you] to the UNIX operating system. . . . To use the shell, you need a basic understanding of UNIX commands. . . . Unlike DOS, which uses the backslash (\) character to separate directories in a path, UNIX uses the front slash character (/) to separate them.[2]

One place where you'll see a UNIX command line is in the World Wide Web's Universal Resource Locator, or URL. The command line is a way to address a request to a specific computer on the Web and a specific file of information stored in its directories. Here is how you could address one WWW document:

http://www/usnews.com/repub/gingrich.html

Other UNIX commands that you need to know follow.[3] Note that UNIX is case sensitive, which means that it distinguishes between uppercase and lowercase letters. All commands are typed in lowercase.

logon	The process of typing a logon name and password each time you begin a work session with a UNIX computer
passwd	Enables you to change your password
ls list	Displays the file names in a directory
ls	Displays all files
ls-a -l	Displays all contents and file information
cd	Changes the directory, combined with a new directory name: cd text
mkdir	Makes a new directory: mk text
rmdir	Removes a directory: rm text
rm	Removes (deletes) a file: rm software.doc
cat	Reads a text file (complete): cat software.doc
more	Displays the contents of a text file one page at a time: more software.doc
mv	Moves a file from one directory to another: mv software.doc
man	Reads the on-line UNIX manual of commands; requires some knowledge of what you're looking for, such as man whois
Ctrl-d	Cancels any operation, returning to the previous starting point
logout	Ends the work session with the UNIX computer, but not all UNIX systems use the same commands. Follow logout with exit, then logoff; or try bye or off. Some may use Ctrl-d.

HOME PAGE REVIEW QUESTIONS

1. Where are you likely to encounter computers running UNIX?
2. When typing UNIX commands, which (diagonal) slash do you use?
3. What must you do when you start and end a work session with a UNIX computer?
4. What is important to remember when typing UNIX commands?

---

2. Peter Kent. *The Complete Idiot's Guide to the Internet*, Second Edition (Indianapolis: Que, 1994), 73–90.

3. Compiled from *ibid.* and *Internet Starter Kit* by Adam C. Engst, Corwin S. Low, and Michael A. Simon (Indianapolis: Hayden Books, 1994).

Figure 7.4
MVS code is widely used on mainframes.

```
//*          ---------------------------------------------------------------------------  00000010
//*          FORTCLG-FORTRAN COMPILE, LINK, AND EXECUTE.                                   00000020
//*          ---------------------------------------------------------------------------  00000030
//           PROC DECK=NODECK, SOURCE=,MAP=NOMAP,LOAD=LOAD, LIST=NOLIST                    00000040
//FORT       EXEC PGM=IEYFORT,REGION=100K,                                                00000050
//                PARM='&DECK,&SOURCE,&MAP,&LOAD,&LIST'                                    00000060
//SYSPRINT    DD SYSOUT=A                                                                  00000070
//SYSPUNCH    DD SYSOUT=B                                                                  00000080
//SYSLIN      DD UNIT=SYSDA,SPACE=(CYL,(1,1)),DISP=(,PASS)                                 00000090
//LKED        EXEC PGM=IEWLF440, COND=(4,LT,FORT),REGION=96K                               00000100
//                PARAM=(XRAM,LIST,LET)                                                    00000110
//SYSLIB      DD DSN=&&FORTLIB1,DISP=(SHR,PASS)                                            00000120
//           DD DSN=&&FORTLIB2,DISP=(SHR,PASS)                                             00000130
//SYSLMOD     DD DSN=&&GOSET(GO),DISP=(,PASS),UNIT=SYSDA,                                  00000140
//           SPACE=CYCLE,(1,1,1))                                                          00000150
//SYSPRINT    DD SYSOUT=A                                                                  00000160
//SYSUT1      DD DSN=&&SYSUT1,UNIT=SYSSQ,SPACE=(1024,(100,50),,,ROUND)                     00000170
//SYSLIN      DD DSN=*.FORT.SYSLIN,DISP=(OLD,DELETE)                                       00000180
//           DD DDNAME=SYSIN                                                               00000190
//GO          EXEC PGM=*.LKED.SYSLMOD,COND=((4,LT,FORT),(4,LT,LKD))                        00000200
//FT05F001    DD DDNSMR=SYSIN                                                              00000210
//FT06F001    DD SYSOUT=A                                                                  00000220
//FT07F001    DD SYSOUT=B                                                                  00000230
//*          ---------------------------------------------------------------------------  00000240
```

Trends in Operating Systems

Personal computer operating systems, such as the new MacOS System 8 for the Macintosh, are becoming increasingly sophisticated. Not only do they handle the traditional chores of managing memory and controlling peripherals, they now include such features as user-friendly interfaces, different fonts, and networking capabilities. In addition, multiuser, multiprogramming, and multitasking capabilities, previously found only in mainframe and minicomputer operating systems, are now available with personal computer operating systems.

In the past, computer manufacturers chose to keep the operating systems they developed for their computers **proprietary**, which means that the exact workings of these operating systems were private, protected information. If you wanted to use a particular manufacturer's hardware, you had to use the operating system designed for it and no other. For many years, the Macintosh operating system was proprietary.

The opposite of a proprietary product is an **open system**, which means it is not the exclusive property or design of one software or hardware vendor. UNIX is an example of an open system; it can be modified and adapted for use with any manufacturer's hardware. Because the inner workings of UNIX are available to the public, anyone can develop applications to work on this operating system.

UNIX is the first *nonproprietary* operating system that works with personal computers, workstations, minis, and mainframes.

As mentioned, the trend in operating systems is toward open systems. DOS and Windows are essentially open systems. Apple, in a desire to increase its acceptance and become more "open," has licensed its MacOS to other hardware companies to build Macintosh PC compatibles. IBM and Apple have announced plans to make the latest version of the MacOS run compatibly on PowerPC computers.

The operating system is undeniably an essential link in the computer system. It links the CPU, peripherals, software, data, and knowledge worker, much in the same way the human nervous system links the brain to the spinal cord, limbs, and sensory organs for smooth functioning. And although the operating system performs many of its functions autonomously, there are still times when we need to direct its tasks.

Knowledge Check

1. What kind of software is the operating system?
2. Identify the main functions of an operating system.
3. What is the most common personal computer operating system?
4. What is a multiuser system?
5. Define the term *multitasking*.
6. What is a portable operating system?
7. What is the difference between a proprietary system and an open system?

Key Terms

network operating system   open system   portable   proprietary
time-sharing

ISSUES AND IDEAS

Is Microsoft a Great Competitor or a Monopoly?

Consider the issues in following story by James Gleick in *The New York Times Magazine*; then answer the questions at the end.

The Government's lawyers are engaged in the third major phase of an investigation that may prove to be the most important, and the most difficult, in the century-old history of antitrust law. Its target is a scrappy, young, fast-moving company with a mere 18,000 employees—a fraction of the size of IBM and AT&T, the last great subjects of antitrust action. Microsoft does not control a manufacturing industry. . . . Microsoft's strategic monopolies—for it does possess and covet monopolies, despite vehement denials from its lawyers—are in a peculiarly subtle and abstract commodity: the standards and architectures that control the design of modern software.

. . . The vast majority of the world's personal computers—estimates range from 80 percent to more than 90 percent—run on Microsoft software from the instant they are turned on. . . . By making connections among all . . .levels of modern computing, and by exerting control over the architectures that govern these connections, Microsoft is in the process of transforming the very structure of the world's computer business.

The essence of antitrust is an American view that the public has interest in preventing excessive concentration of economic power. . . .Monopolies become their own worst enemies—particularly in businesses that live or die by technological innovation. They get soft. They make poor research choices. They bleed both profit and invention.

. . . a comment by Senator Bob Dole . . : "Let us understand what is going on here. A company develops a new product, a product consumers want. But now the Government steps in and is in effect attempting to dictate the terms on which that product can be marketed and sold. Pinch me, but I thought we were still in America."

Gleick says that a few years ago several operating systems were available for PCs, but today the Microsoft architecture is firmly established and has become the standard, in the same way the 60-Hz electrical current is the standard in the U.S. Gleick does not believe that the U.S. Government should break Microsoft apart, as is often the case in antitrust actions. Instead, he argues that the government should require Microsoft to "make its operating system, and the web of standards surrounding it, truly and permanently open."[4]

CRITICAL THINKING

1. Discuss both sides of the monopoly issue, and make a list of the pros and cons.

2. Research other antitrust actions by the U.S. Government and their eventual outcomes.

3. Debate some what-if situations for Microsoft. How might the government break up the company, and what would happen if it did? What would happen if it didn't?

4. In general, do you believe that the government should intervene in free enterprise?

---

4. James Gleick. "The Microsoft Monopoly," *The New York Times Magazine,* November 5, 1995, 49–65.

Common Operating Environments

Why It's Important to Know

> **The use of an operating environment and its accompanying graphical user interface is becoming more widely accepted as the standard for most computer systems. Operating environments make it easier to work with both the operating system and applications.**

Most computer systems have an operating environment with a graphical user interface. The reason is simple: this type of operating environment is easy to use. Most knowledge workers don't want to become computer experts. They have tasks they want to accomplish, and the computer makes their work faster, easier, and sometimes more fun.

As John Pivovarnick says in *The Complete Idiot's Guide to the Mac*, "In computerese, the environment is much like the environment of the world at large, or your work environment. It's the atmosphere, surroundings, and even the decor of your computer."[5]

The command to save a file may vary from one operating system to another and may be difficult to remember. However, the purpose of a universally used button with a disk icon is easily recognized. This module explores the characteristics of the most widely used operating environments.

The Macintosh Operating Environment

The operating environment the Macintosh was modeled on was originally developed at the Xerox Palo Alto Research Center (PARC), where the mouse also was invented. Xerox PARC created a workstation called the Xerox Star in 1980, with a graphical screen and icons. It became the model for the Macintosh.

The Mac's operating environment is called the **Finder**, and its opening screen, shown in figure 7.5, is the desktop.

The opening desktop screen is simple and uncluttered. System information—including drives in use, the printer icon, and the trash can—is displayed vertically on the right side of the desktop as icons.

The menu bar displays the basic commands needed for navigating the system. From left to right, these menus are as follow:

- The Apple icon is the pull-down menu for desk accessories.

- The File menu works with folders and windows.

---

5. John Pivovarnick. *The Complete Idiot's Guide to the Mac,* Second Edition (Indianapolis: Alpha Books, 1994), 49.

- The Edit menu works with files and data.

- The View menu changes the way files are displayed in folders or on the desktop.

- The Label menu color-codes folders, files, and icons.

- The Special menu performs utilities, such as emptying the trash or ejecting a disk.

- The Apple Guide icon provides help.

- The Application icon enables you to use the multitasking feature to switch between the Finder and open applications.

Figure 7.5
The Macintosh Finder displays this desktop opening screen.

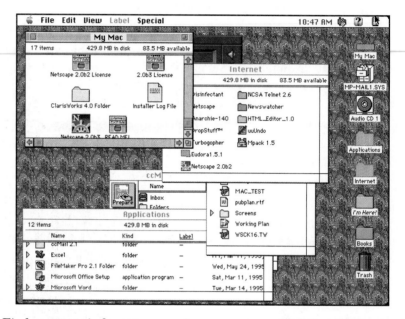

The Finder uses windows to organize programs and data, which are stored in folders. A program folder usually has an identifying icon, such as an X for Microsoft Excel. Folders holding data resemble a conventional manila file folder. Files are stored in both program and data folders. The file icon for files you create with applications looks like a sheet of paper with a corner turned down.

Folders and files have been attractively redesigned in System 8. A click of the mouse button selects an item, which then darkens. Files may be moved between folders by clicking the icon and dragging it to its new location.

The Finder is loaded when you power up the Macintosh. When you have finished your work session, click the Special menu, and select Shut Down. This step ensures that all applications will be closed and all files will be stored safely. Then you are ready to switch off the power. If a floppy disk is in the drive, it will eject automatically.

Microsoft Windows 3.1

Windows 1.01 was introduced in November 1985. It was awkward and slow, and few applications were available for it. (Although DOS applications will perform under Windows, applications must be specifically created or rewritten to take advantage of Windows and its GUI.) Windows didn't gain wide acceptance until the release of Windows 3.0 in 1990.

Windows 3.1, released in 1992, became a mature product; many bugs had been corrected and it included many more features that knowledge workers had requested (see figure 7.6). Windows for Workgroups 3.11, which is used in networks, looks just like Windows 3.1.

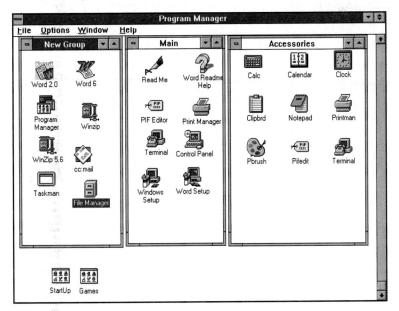

Figure 7.6
Windows 3.1 became the standard for desktop computing.

Here are the primary software modules that comprise Windows 3.1. Refer to figure 7.6 as you study these modules.

The **Program Manager** is the first screen you see in Windows. It is in charge of the operating environment and all applications and performs the same essential tasks as the Finder on the Macintosh. Note how applications, displayed as icons, are grouped into functional categories in group windows. The active window is in the center of the screen; inactive windows appear as small, square icons at the bottom of the screen.

The Program Manager is a window itself. Its design is a model for how all Windows 3.1 windows and applications appear on the screen. The *title bar* tells you the name of the program. The button on the left is the *Control menu*, with various options for managing the active window you're using. Buttons at the right end open, close, and resize the window. The *menu bar* displays pull-down menus of Windows commands:

- The File menu contains commands for working with programs and program groups.

- The Options menu presents alternatives for the way windows are displayed.

- The Window menu presents alternatives for the way program icons are displayed and provides a menu for switching among various windows.

- The Help menu provides guidance and instruction.

Windows also enables you to create a Startup group of programs that are launched with Windows. You can see the icons for those programs in the Startup group window. Then, when you boot the computer or start Windows, all these applications are launched automatically.

The **File Manager** enables knowledge workers to work with drives, directories, and files, either graphically as icons or in a conventional tree directory structure. File Manager graphically depicts each of the computer's disk drives; you change drives by pointing to the one you want and clicking. Using the mouse, you click files, drag them to the new directory, and then drop them in place. This technique eliminates typing long, tedious move and copy commands, although you do have that option in File Manager.

The other major feature of Windows is the *Control Panel*, a window with the various computer hardware and environment settings. Typically, the Control Panel enables the knowledge worker to change the following:

- The colors Windows uses

- Typefaces, or fonts

- The printer or printers

- The sound (turning it on or off)

- The date and time

Windows is started from DOS. At the end of a Windows work session, you must use the Control menu or File pull-down menu to exit Windows. This step saves your work and automatically exits any open programs (the one exception is DOS programs, which must be manually closed and exited) before returning you to the DOS prompt. Figure 7.7 summarizes the way Windows runs applications.

Windows 95

The introduction of Windows 95 on August 24, 1995, in contrast to the release of Windows 1.01 a decade earlier, was probably the greatest media event of the year. Windows 95 has integrated DOS so that the operating system and operating environment act as one. Yet DOS is still available, as if it were any other application.

My Computer takes the place of the previous Program Manager. You do not have to perform DOS functions from, for example, the File Manager. Instead, you use a program called Explorer, which works with Windows 95 folders and files. The overall Windows 95 environment is more Mac-like. As industry commentator John C. Dvorak says, "They've taken a lot of ideas from the Mac. There is no difference. It is a Mac. They've done everything they can to make it like a Mac."[6]

---

6. John C. Dvorak, quoted on *C-Net Central*, week of July 31, 1995.

HOME PAGE

WINDOWS 95 TIPS

1. Use the Desktop Themes that come with Microsoft Plus! to customize your desktop. Each one has its own color schemes, images, and sounds. Use the Appearance option to change colors. And be sure to learn about Windows 95's many multimedia features.

2. If more than one person uses your computer, create shortcuts using program folders for each different worker. That way, each can have his or her own unique desktop.

3. Learn the various features of Cut and Copy and Paste or Paste Special. You'll be able to do better on-line file transfers, and this knowledge will help you learn how to create compound documents with OLE.

4. If you want to capture a screen and print it, press the PrintScrn button; then open the WordPad accessory, and click the Paste icon. Now you can print the screen and save it as a Word file.

5. Install your most frequently used programs on the Start menu. The menu choice is called Startup and can be modified using the Taskbar command in the Settings submenu. Locate the executable file, click it, and drag it to the Start Menu folder.

6. Create shortcuts to the programs or functions you use most frequently.

7. Subscribe to an on-line forum to learn more about Windows 95 and other software you use. You'll find other people who share your interests and who may be able to help you solve problems. Two forums are the Macmillan Computer Publishing Forum on CompuServe (go macmillan) and the Internet's World Wide Web (http://www.mcp.com).

8. Take advantage of Windows 95's communications capabilities. Not only can you connect to on-line services, send and receive e-mail, and log on to the Internet, you can also send faxes and use Win95 to dial phone calls.

9. Take advantage of Win95's capability to upload and download files between a desktop computer and a notebook computer.

10. Choose some good books that will help you explore Windows 95's many features and capabilities. Some come with disks or CD-ROMs that have additional programs, games, and useful tools.

How Windows Runs Windows Applications

Figure 7.7

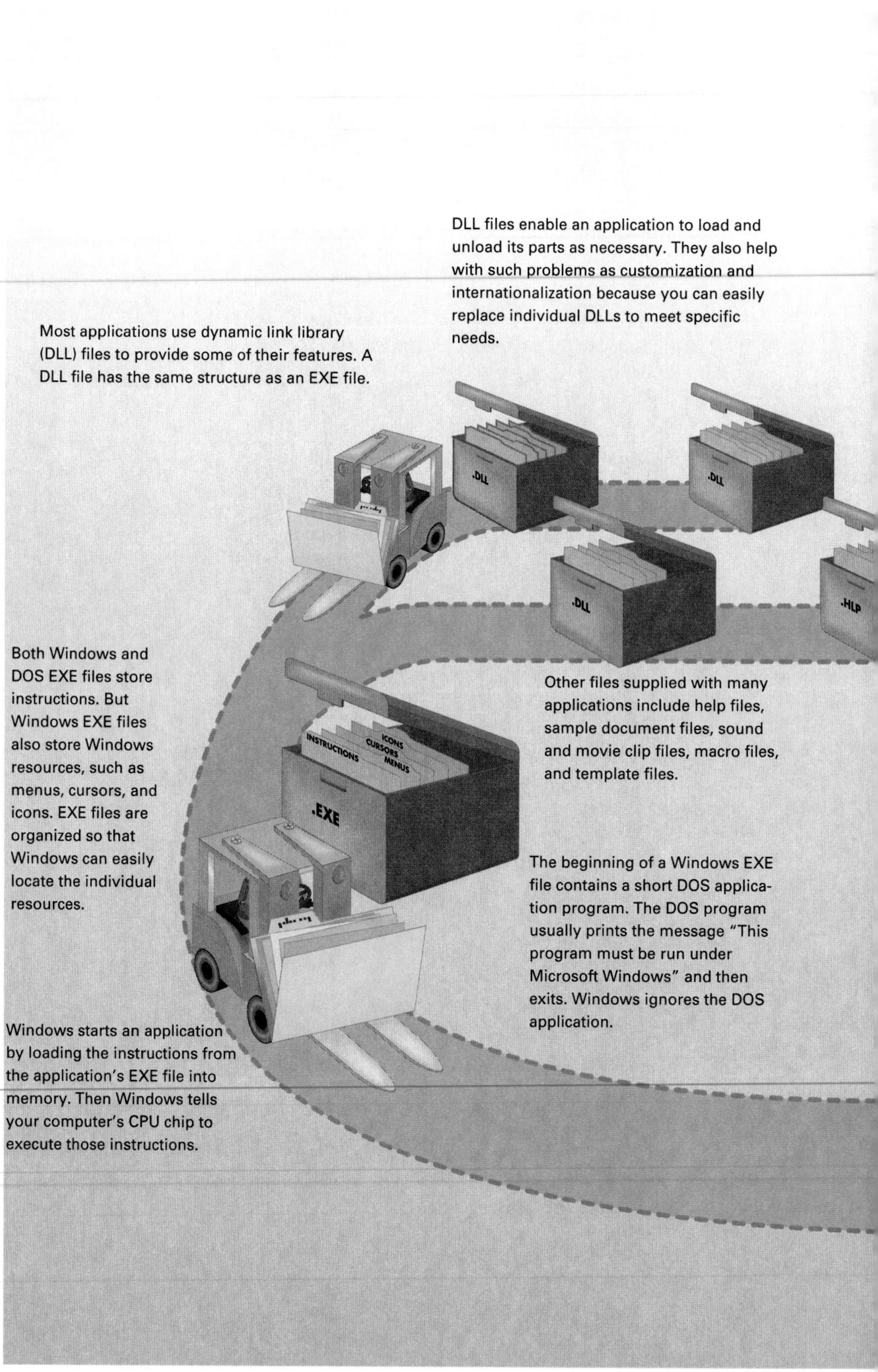
Windows starts an application by loading the instructions from the application's EXE file into memory. Then Windows tells your computer's CPU chip to execute those instructions.
Both Windows and DOS EXE files store instructions. But Windows EXE files also store Windows resources, such as menus, cursors, and icons. EXE files are organized so that Windows can easily locate the individual resources.
Most applications use dynamic link library (DLL) files to provide some of their features. A DLL file has the same structure as an EXE file.
DLL files enable an application to load and unload its parts as necessary. They also help with such problems as customization and internationalization because you can easily replace individual DLLs to meet specific needs.
Other files supplied with many applications include help files, sample document files, sound and movie clip files, macro files, and template files.
The beginning of a Windows EXE file contains a short DOS application program. The DOS program usually prints the message "This program must be run under Microsoft Windows" and then exits. Windows ignores the DOS application.
.EXE
INSTRUCTIONS
ICONS
CURSORS
MENUS
.DLL
.DLL
.DLL
.HLP

Once an application has finished initializing, it enters a more reactive state, in which it waits for messages to arrive. Each time a message arrives, the application processes the message and then waits for another message to arrive. Waiting for messages is important because other Windows applications then have a chance to execute so that Windows runs several applications at once.

When an application starts to execute, it works with Windows to create its main windows, to load menus and other resources, and to perform other initialization chores. During this phase of operations, which typically lasts only a few seconds or less, the application follows its own plan of operation.

LOAD MENU
CREATE WINDOW
CREATE SCROLLBAR

Windows 95, or Win95, opens with a desktop view like the one shown in figure 7.8. The basic system icons, which are arranged down the left side of the screen, are as follows:

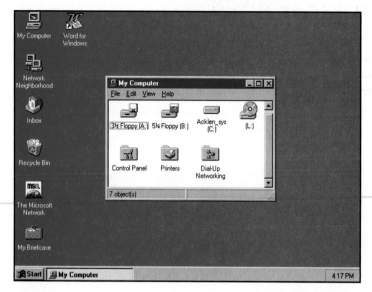

Figure 7.8
The Win95 opening desktop screen is simple and highly graphic.

- *My Computer*, a file management and program management utility that displays the basics—everything you want to know about your computer: information about disk drives, printers, the Control Panel, and networking, if applicable

- *Network Neighborhood*, which displays information about your computer and whatever else is connected in your network(s)

- *The Recycle Bin*, where discarded files are stored until you empty it, at which point the files are permanently deleted

- *The Microsoft Network*, Microsoft's on-line information service

You may see some additional icons for a briefcase, which enables you to exchange data with other computers, and an inbox, which is used for e-mail. The rest of the desktop may be blank, unless you have created icons called shortcuts. A **shortcut** is a small file linked to a program, document, or folder that immediately starts an application or a function. You can create shortcuts not only for applications but also for folders or individual documents.

The **taskbar** appears at the bottom of the screen, beginning with the Start button. Clicking the Start button opens a menu that displays all the folders on your computer that contain applications. To start any of these applications, simply select it from the menu. Shortcut icons and the taskbar highlight the versatility of Win95, and the many ways it enables you to individualize the desktop and the way you work with applications and documents.

At the far end of the taskbar are the system information display and the clock. You hold the mouse pointer on the time to display the date. Between the Start button and the clock are buttons for each open application in the Win95 multitasking environment. Clicking one brings that application on to the screen; others are left active but "parked" until you need to use them. This taskbar is visible at the bottom of the screen, regardless of the application in use, unless you choose to hide the taskbar by placing your pointer on the line that separates the taskbar from the application window and pulling the line down, as if you were pulling down a window shade.

To exit Win95, you click the Start button and then select Shut Down, which presents several options for exiting. Selecting the most common choice closes all applications and opened files and then displays the message, "It's now safe to shut down your computer."

Other Popular Operating Environments

IBM's *OS/2 Warp* is the operating environment that competes with Windows (see figure 7.9). It is more often used in large companies, where IBM has established a presence over the years. OS/2 Warp works well with other IBM computer systems. It uses a Workplace Shell that is similar to the Windows Program Manager and File Manager. OS/2 Warp is designed to run applications specifically written for OS/2, as well as DOS and Windows applications. A network version, called OS/2 Warp Connect, is also available.

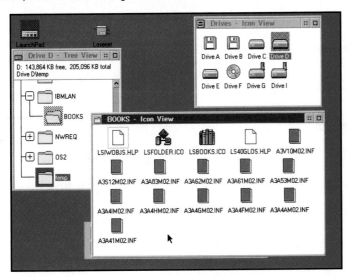

Figure 7.9
OS/2 Warp is widely used in corporate environments.

X Windows is a GUI and operating environment that runs on top of UNIX. X Windows was developed at MIT in the early 1980s and is licensed to developers by the X Consortium, which is comprised of 35 vendors. X Windows enables developers to create applications for a variety of platforms, all presenting the same windows-like GUI to knowledge workers. X Windows runs on workstations, minicomputers, and terminals of all kinds (see figure 7.10).

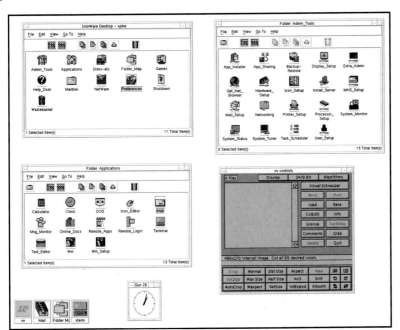

Figure 7.10
An X Windows screen.

Windows NT, Windows 95, and the new release of the MacOS (System 8) demonstrate the advanced state of operating environments. In marketing terms, they are mature products: each represents a tight integration of the operating system and operating environment. In the future, there will be little, if any, need to distinguish between the two.

Indeed, if operating system software technology continues to advance, there should be less and less need for people to use either the operating system or operating environment. Research is underway to develop *intelligent agents*, small software programs that pick up where icons leave off. An agent is a type of program that carries out instructions for you, working in the background while you perform other tasks. For example, you might instruct an agent to find information on X Windows for you on the Internet. Once the agent finds the information, it automatically loads the text into your word processing program on your screen.

Standards like OpenDoc promise to bring knowledge workers closer to working with information in documents, rather than twiddling with various levels of software and a myriad of commands. There are many signs that the industry is researching and exploring the next generation of systems software. As a rock group once put it, "The future's so bright, I gotta wear shades."

Knowledge Check

1. What are the origins of the GUI operating environment?
2. What is the Macintosh operating environment called?
3. Previous to Win95, what was the most successful version of Windows?
4. In what fundamental way is Windows 95 different from its predecessors?
5. Where is OS/2 Warp used most often?
6. What is the advantage of X Windows?

Key Terms

File Manager	Finder	Program Manager
shortcut	taskbar	

ISSUES AND IDEAS

Isn't It Just Computer Software?

Microsoft pulled out all the stops in introducing Windows 95. Press releases reported that more was spent on this event than was spent to make *Waterworld*, the most expensive movie in history. Turning a software introduction into a media event heightens the stakes in a competitive industry. What will Apple do to herald the introduction of MacOS System 8?

Consider these remarks about the introduction of Windows 95 from two key industry people:

There is no question that 18 months from now—pick your date—there aren't going to be people actively using Windows 3.1 on a widespread basis. It's just a question of which way they move up to the new generation. The sooner they do, the better off they are.

Microsoft chairman Bill Gates, quoted in the *Wall Street Journal*, August 24, 1995

Windows 95 will create enough hype to get people into the stores, and we intend to capture them at the door.

Apple chairman Michael Spindler, quoted in *Business Week*, July 31, 1995

Microsoft sold $700 million worth of Windows 95 in the first 24 hours. Yet over the next three months, Apple's computer sales rose to from 8–9 percent to 13 percent of market share. Who was right?

CRITICAL THINKING

1. Research the rivalry between Microsoft and Apple in terms of operating environment software. What was the result of Apple's look and feel lawsuit against Microsoft?

2. Visit a computer store and ask the salesperson to demonstrate both operating environments. Which do you prefer, and why? Make a list of pluses and minuses of each.

3. Do you feel that turning the introduction of a product into a media event is appropriate or necessary? What does this event say about our society?

Module C

Working with the Graphical User Interface and Multitasking

Why It's Important to Know

Because new operating environments use a GUI and also support multitasking, you need to be proficient in using these features. The information in this module will help you be more efficient and enjoy your work at the same time.

Working with the graphical user interface (GUI) and multitasking requires a special kind of concentration and attention. Commands and functions are represented by buttons or listed in pull-down menus; therefore, you must use your pointing device carefully to click buttons. Multitasking permits using more than one application at a time and exchanging data between them. Moving between applications; opening, saving, and closing files; transferring data; and performing the many tasks on the button bars demands your close attention. For these and many other reasons, always remember to take your time, do things carefully, and never begin a task or operation that you don't know how to reverse or end.

Advantages of the GUI

The graphical user interface has distinct advantages over its predecessors—the command line interface and the menu-driven interface. They are

- Ease of use
- Color
- Graphics and icons
- Pull-down menus
- A pointing device to issue commands quickly
- Common functionality among applications

The main advantage a graphical user interface provides is ease of use. *Ease of use* means that anyone, regardless of computer knowledge, skills, or background, can quickly become productive. This ease of use is accomplished through both the commands (such as the menu bar) and the graphical images (icons); the knowledge worker can readily understand the commands and icons, even with little prior training or experience.

The Commands

The use of color, graphics, and icons in the graphical user interface makes learning the screen elements easy and fast. Pull-down menus organize the commands for easy access, and the pointing device helps the knowledge worker quickly accomplish tasks. The GUI design and functionality are established by the operating environment and are usually shared by the applications designed to run under the operating environment.

The Macintosh was the first to extend the ease of use concept throughout all its application software: all applications work nearly identically. Apple established this close similarity as a prerequisite in its closed architecture for independent software developers. The software developers creating applications for Windows have also applied this concept to a great extent.

Applications

The GUI screen below the menu bar displays icons that help you work with applications and files. Each application usually has a unique icon created by the software publisher. Starting applications is much easier with a GUI. Double-clicking a folder launches an application; in many cases, double-clicking the file you want to work with launches the application and opens the file at the same time (see figure 7.11).

The folder icon usually holds any number of individual files, each depicted by a sheet of paper with one corner bent over. These folders and files are generally named using everyday

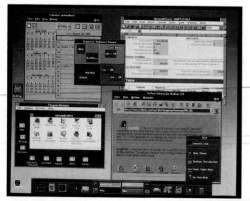

Figure 7.11

The graphical user interface provides the advantage of ease of use.

Courtesy of
TriTeal Corporation

English. For example, a database folder might be named Access Files and a file in it named Last Month's Production Reports. The buttons replace the directory structure common to DOS; instead of having to issue commands to change from one directory to another, you simply move the pointer (commonly using the mouse) from one folder to another and click.

Trade-Offs with the GUI

Although you can use keyboard commands or arrow keys, the GUI and its compatible applications really *require* the use of a mouse or pointing device to be productive. Otherwise, the GUI is just too slow and awkward. This requirement is one of the trade-offs associated with working in a graphical environment. Using the mouse to move to the selected icon and double-clicking it is often slower and requires more hand-eye coordination than simply pressing a few keys to issue a command.

On the other hand, the mouse often makes certain tasks easier to accomplish or enables you to combine a series of key commands under an icon, requiring only a single mouse click. Using buttons, knowledge workers don't have to remember a command's syntax or a file name's format.

Another trade-off has been speed. Both the Macintosh and the PC compatibles have been slow running GUI operating environments. However, the development of hardware always lags behind software; and new fast microprocessors, additional RAM, and faster video processing have increased the speed of GUI environments. Speed is not as great a consideration in using an operating environment as it once was.

The development of the GUI is almost paradoxical. It was created for first-time or novice knowledge workers; but its development took so long (even with the Macintosh, introduced in 1984) that many users had already learned the command line interface or settled comfortably into using menus. However, new knowledge workers can derive great benefit from GUIs. The advantages to having one software design that applies to both the system software and the application software are great—chiefly, learning takes less time, and productivity increases more quickly.

Advantages with Multitasking

Multitasking is the capability to execute and run more than one application at the same time. The knowledge worker can have a number of different applications and desktop tools available to use whenever they are needed (see figure 7.12). For instance, you can have a spreadsheet, a graphics program, and Windows File Manager all loaded and running at the same time. In addition, an application program may have multiple open documents.

How Multitasking Works

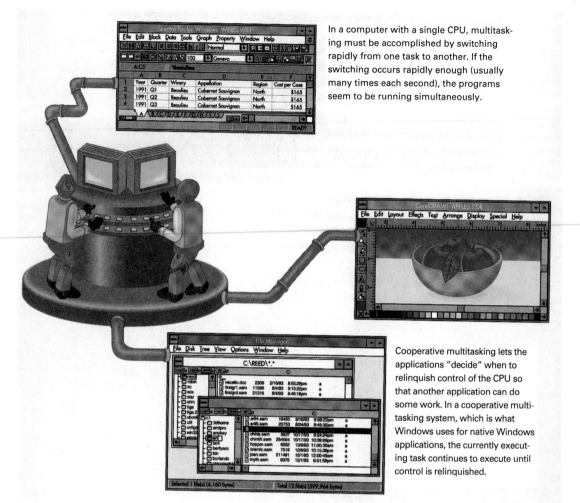

In a computer with a single CPU, multitasking must be accomplished by switching rapidly from one task to another. If the switching occurs rapidly enough (usually many times each second), the programs seem to be running simultaneously.

Cooperative multitasking lets the applications "decide" when to relinquish control of the CPU so that another application can do some work. In a cooperative multitasking system, which is what Windows uses for native Windows applications, the currently executing task continues to execute until control is relinquished.

Figure 7.12
Windows switches between Windows applications using cooperative multitasking.

Running Foreground and Background Programs

Certain tasks can be performed in the *background*, without your having to wait or to monitor them while working at another task in the *foreground*. For example, if your communications program is programmed to dial out and send or pick up your e-mail every few hours, the program will do so without interrupting you at another task. You can also print a long word processing file while working on another.

The 32-bit microprocessor and 32-bit operating systems have made true multitasking available. Before them, the processing and memory constraints of PCs permitted only a limited form of multitasking—swapping programs in and out of available memory, which meant that you had to wait during the exchange. Now, each 32-bit application has its own memory space to run in.

Sharing Data among Applications

Multitasking greatly simplifies sharing data, which is highly desirable when you are working with others. Both the Macintosh and PC compatibles have their own communications software technology to enable sharing data. The Macintosh/IBM technology is called OpenDoc.

The Microsoft technology is called **object linking and embedding**, or **OLE**, and is more widely used. OLE creates compound documents that can contain text, worksheets, database tables, graphics, audio, video, and so forth. To accomplish object linking, you create an **object**, which is a portion of a document or an entire document. Then you move the object to another application's document using the Cut or Copy and Paste or Paste Special functions. You can see how OLE works in figure 7.13.

Windows and Finder both use a Clipboard to hold data while it is being shared by applications. For example, suppose that you cut or copy a portion of a spreadsheet for insertion into a word processing document. Now you can either link or embed the object.

Linking

OLE creates a **dynamic link** with the object between the two documents. If you link a portion of a spreadsheet into a word processing document, any subsequent changes you make in the spreadsheet are updated in the word processing document as well.

Embedding

Sometimes you don't need a dynamic link. In those cases, OLE simply embeds, or places the object in a document, and moves the object from one application to another without the dynamic linking—for example, when you are inserting a graphic image. Objects can also be selected and embedded from the Insert pull-down menu.

How OLE Works

Figure 7.13

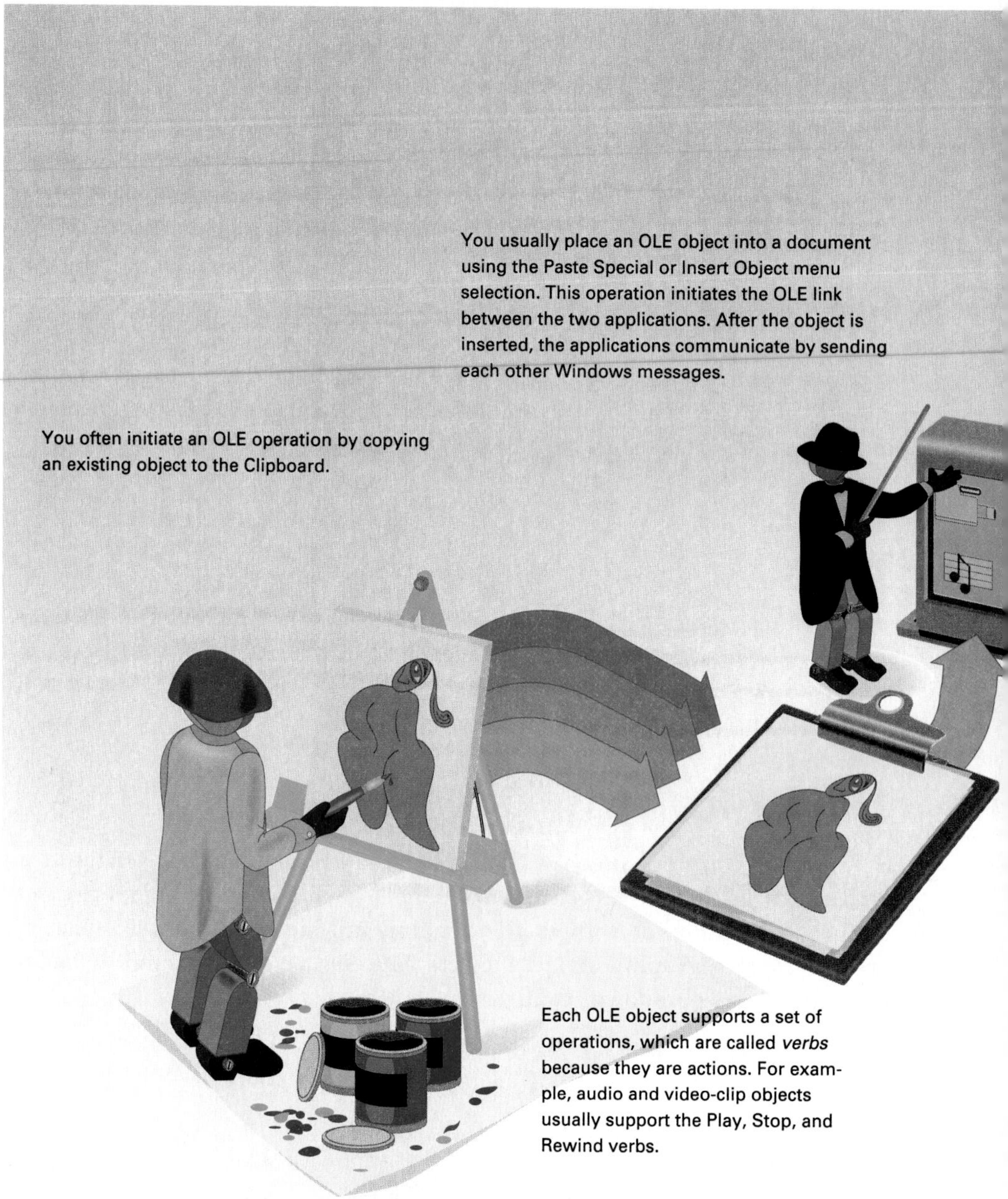

You usually place an OLE object into a document using the Paste Special or Insert Object menu selection. This operation initiates the OLE link between the two applications. After the object is inserted, the applications communicate by sending each other Windows messages.

You often initiate an OLE operation by copying an existing object to the Clipboard.

Each OLE object supports a set of operations, which are called *verbs* because they are actions. For example, audio and video-clip objects usually support the Play, Stop, and Rewind verbs.

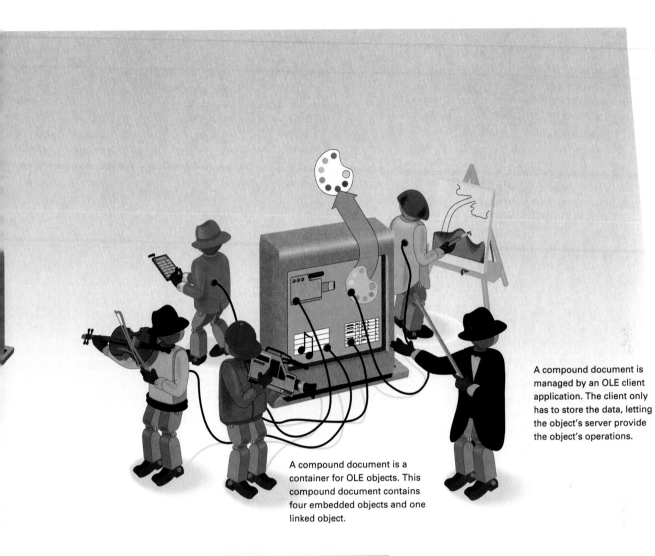

A compound document is managed by an OLE client application. The client only has to store the data, letting the object's server provide the object's operations.

A compound document is a container for OLE objects. This compound document contains four embedded objects and one linked object.

OLE works behind the scenes to display a compound document. The client application calls on servers, as necessary, to display and manage their parts of a document.

Courtesy of Ziff-Davis Press

USING THE GUI AND MULTITASKING

How do knowledge workers take advantage of the GUI? Here's an example. Bonnie works at a travel agency that plans and promotes adventure tours, such as rock climbing in Yosemite National Park and kayaking on the Colorado River. Experienced tour guides propose their own tour itineraries. Bonnie is responsible for preparing the cover letter and descriptive brochure, as well as coordinating airline flight schedules and reservations. She uses a PC compatible running Windows and a number of different applications.

In preparing the brochure, Bonnie uses a map program, from which she clips a graphic with directions to the Yosemite section of California for cover art, pasting the graphic into the document she is creating with her graphical word processing program. She also cuts text from a U.S. Forestry Service publication provided on computer disk describing the physical characteristics of the climbs in the park (being certain to give copyright credit to the publication). She combines this text with a graphic.

Next, Bonnie writes her own marketing copy describing the tour, using various text fonts and clip art to highlight the copy.

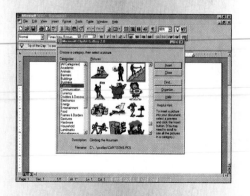

Then she opens the database management system application and selects the itinerary file from the disk provided by the tour guide. She highlights the portion she needs for this trip, selects Copy, switches back to the word processing document, and selects Paste to insert the itinerary. She has several different fee schedules that she's worked up using the spreadsheet application, so next she uses a dynamic link to copy and paste them into the document. That way, fee changes in the spreadsheet will change in the brochure, too.

Finally, she opens the on-line travel guide window, copies the appropriate airline flight information schedules, and pastes them into her brochure. Once she's finished, she prints a copy to see how it all looks. It looks great, so she decides to use it as a one-sheet description to mail to selected clients. But she also decides to make some improvements: using a desktop publishing application, she'll redesign it as a barrel-fold brochure to be professionally printed.

HOME PAGE REVIEW QUESTIONS

1. How many applications did Bonnie use?
2. What operating environment tools did she use to assemble her document?
3. How was OLE helpful to her in her work?

Knowledge Check

1. What are some features common to all GUIs?
2. Name two ways to open files in a GUI.
3. Why does using a pointing device increase the demand for our attention?
4. What is the main advantage with true multitasking?
5. What do *foreground* and *background* mean in multitasking?
6. Why are dynamic linking and embedding useful?

Key Terms

dynamic link   object   object linking and embedding (OLE)

ISSUES AND IDEAS

The Cost of Technical Support

SoftLetter is a newsletter that reports trends and strategies for the personal computer industry. Every few years, editor Jeffrey Tarter and his staff survey the industry to find out how much it costs to provide tech support for software licensees. Following is information from their latest report:

Instead of adding endless numbers of new technicians and phone lines, support managers are now actively exploring cost-control solutions— paid support, outsourcing, automation, usability enhancements, better customer research, workflow management, and the like. It may be too early to predict which of these solutions will deliver the biggest payoffs, but there are certainly more bets on the table than ever before.

Here's a quick summary of what our survey shows:

- The median cost of support for PC software companies currently amounts to 6 percent of total revenues.

- Based on a median call length of eight minutes, the average cost of answering a tech support call is about $3.00 a minute.

- Employee productivity is highest in organizations with four or more employees, which average 200–300 calls monthly per employee (equal to 11–14 calls per day).

- Typically, users place about three-quarters of all tech support calls while products are still under warranty.

- Especially in high-end product categories, paid support programs are already widely accepted.

The productivity question: We feel strongly that the real problem with tech support costs is the industry's failure to grapple with fundamental productivity issues. Expensive manpower is too often used to answer routine and repetitious calls; too much time is spent on training, research, and other tasks that drastically reduce the amount of time technicians actually spend on the phone. Rather than rely on paid support plans (which may be desirable for other reasons) to reduce support costs, we think it makes far more sense for software companies to focus on automation and other productivity-enhancing techniques. When the industry figures out how to handle more customer questions with fewer people, a genuine revolution in support economics will finally get under way.[7]

CRITICAL THINKING

1. Do you think that tech support calls are costly?

2. How could software companies handle routine and repetitious calls more effectively?

3. If you had to pay for tech support calls, would you be more motivated to try to find the solution yourself—for example, in the manual?

---

7. "Benchmark Report: Technical Support Cost Ratios," *SoftLetter*, September 21, 1993.

ETHICS

The "Look and Feel" Legal Issue

In the 1980s, software applications were expensive. A company named Paperback Software brought out versions of popular software programs that worked nearly like the more expensive ones but cost only $99 each. Lotus Development Corporation, maker of the Lotus 1-2-3 spreadsheet, sued Paperback Software for copyright infringement, claiming that its menu command structure, including the choice of command terms, the structure and order of the terms, and the screen presentation, were copyrightable. In Massachusetts District Court in 1990, the judge decided in favor of Lotus, writing:

> The expression of an idea is copyrightable. The idea itself is not. When applying these two settled rules of law, how can a decision maker distinguish between an idea and its expression?

> Answering this riddle is the first step—but only the first—toward a disposition of this case in which the court must decide, among other issues, (1) whether and to what extent plaintiff's computer spreadsheet program, Lotus 1-2-3, is copyrightable, (2) whether defendants' VP-Planner was, on indisputable facts, an infringing work containing elements substantially similar to copyrightable elements of 1-2-3. . . .

> Though their influence in our society is already pervasive, digital computers—along with computer "programs" and "user interfaces"—are relatively new to the market, and newer still to litigation over "works" protected by intellectual property law.[8]

Within a few years of the court's decision, the DOS version of Lotus 1-2-3 that had sparked the litigation was in sharp decline, due to the rise of Windows and the subsequent software redesign it necessitated. Paperback Software went out of business as a result of the judgment.

In another "look and feel" litigation, Apple Computer attempted to sue Microsoft for copying the Macintosh look and feel in Microsoft Windows. To date, no judge has deemed the case to have merit.

---

8. "Lotus Development Corporation v. Paperback Software International and Stephenson Software, Limited," from *Computers, Ethics & Social Values*, Deborah C. Johnson and Helen Nissenbaum, editors (Englewood Cliffs, NJ: Prentice-Hall, 1995), 236.

Critical Thinking

1. What do you think was the real reason for the Lotus suit against Paperback?

2. Research the Apple-Microsoft "look and feel" case. Why has it not been prosecuted?

3. Does the "look and feel" argument have legal merit? Defend your position.

THE LEARNING ENTERPRISE

In previous chapters, you and your fellow knowledge workers have been making decisions that shape your enterprisewide computer systems. In this chapter, you make several of the most important decisions regarding the standards under which your computers, from PCs to mainframes, will use.

First, you need to recognize that you will have more than one standard for the operating systems and operating environments. Your enterprise might have

- Two PC standards: Macintosh and Windows (and possibly two Windows standards)

- Two or more network standards: one for Windows PCs, one for Macintosh PCs, and another for enterprise networking, such as UNIX

- More than one operating system in use for minicomputers and mainframes, which also link to networks and smaller workgroups

The preparation you've done up to this point will help you determine your operating system standards—the *platforms* in your enterprise. You need to determine workgroup standards first, then department or function standards, and then enterprise standards. Remember, the goal is to facilitate the productivity of each knowledge worker, so you must start with the individual and work up to the broadest organizational level rather than work from the top down.

You need to manage the process. Keep in mind that all human activities with a goal, such as your enterprise, need to include planning, organizing, directing, guiding, encouraging, and focusing. You may want to choose one person from your department or function to oversee activities and act as your mentor, guide, and manager. That person would ensure that each knowledge worker will have the personal productivity tools he or she needs and that workgroups will collaborate productively.

In order to help choose this person, discuss the following questions:

1. What are our goals as individuals, workgroups, departments?
2. How will we track and record our progress?
3. Who will help support us, guide us, focus us, and enable us to reach our goals?
4. How will our operating platforms be designed and coordinated to accomplish our goals?

Chapter Review

Fill in the Blank

1. System software includes the _____ software and the _____ software.
2. The most widely used personal computer operating system is _____.
3. The operating environment for the PC compatible is called _____.
4. The operating environment for the Macintosh is called the _____.
5. An operating environment used on many other types of computers is called _____.
6. _____ is an operating environment that runs under UNIX.
7. UNIX, a(n) _____ operating system, can be used on different computers, regardless of manufacturer.
8. The capability to execute and run more than one application at the same time is called _____.
9. Microsoft's technology for sharing data is called _____.

Circle the Correct Answer

1. The first screen you see in Windows 3.1 is (Program Manager, File Manager).
2. In Windows 95, (My Computer, My Documents) takes the place of Program Manager.
3. The (toolbar, taskbar) appears at the bottom of the Windows 95 screen.
4. Files that you delete are stored in the (My Computer, Recycle Bin) until you empty it and permanently delete them.
5. UNIX commands are typed in (uppercase, lowercase) letters.

Review Questions

1. Name five of the fundamental operations that system software performs.
2. What is the difference between stand-alone and network operating systems?
3. What is the main purpose of a network operations system (NOS)?
4. Differentiate between proprietary and open systems.
5. Name three advantages of using a mainframe.

6. Name several advantages the graphical user interface has over a command line interface or a menu-driven interface.

7. Discuss some disadvantages of a graphical user interface.

8. Describe OLE.

9. What is an object?

10. In Windows 95, what is a shortcut?

Discussion Questions

1. Discuss the advantages of multitasking. How would you use it?

2. Discuss the trends in operating environments, and brainstorm what might be next.

3. Compare and contrast these operating systems: Windows 3.1 to Windows 95; Windows 95 to the Macintosh Finder. Prepare a report listing the strengths and weaknesses of each operating system, and conclude by stating which you would prefer to use.

INTERNET DISCOVERY

Avantos Performance Systems, a software company that provides software tools and services for managing people and computers, may be reached at

http://www.avantos.com

8

THE WORD PROCESSOR

The word processor can concentrate your mind on the craft of writing, revising and editing—much more powerfully than this has ever been possible, because your words are right in front of you in all their infinite possibility, waiting to be infinitely reshaped. Technology, the great villain, turns out to be your friend.[1]

William Zinsser

Your ability to work with words is critical to your job success. Communicating through the written word is a primary way that business information is formally shared, whether the communication is a letter to an individual, a memo to a work group, a report prepared for an advisory committee, or an annual report to stockholders.

Word processing is used more than any other application software. IBM coined the term *word processing*—derived from data processing—to mean using computers to manipulate written words. The company created the first word processing system in 1964. Called the MT/ST (for Magnetic Tape/Selectric Typewriter), it used magnetic tapes to store work. In 1969, IBM updated the MT/ST so that it stored information on magnetic cards and, logically, named the new system the MC/ST.

A number of computer systems designed solely to perform word processing tasks followed. Word processing became a buzzword in business; and companies like A.B. Dick, Xerox, and even Exxon introduced *dedicated* word processing systems: word processing was all these stand-alone machines did. In 1976, the Wang WP 55 was introduced and became the most highly successful office word processing system of the time. Digital Equipment Corporation followed suit with a word processing system called the WPS-8.

Once personal computers became widely used, word processing turned from a hardware orientation into a software application. One early word processing program for the personal computer was The Electric Pencil, but the first widely successful program was WordStar, introduced in 1979. Since then, several word processing programs have ascended the bestseller lists—for example, WordPerfect and Microsoft Word for both the Macintosh and PC compatibles.

---

1. William Zinsser. *On Writing Well*, 3rd edition (New York: Harper & Row, 1985), 214.

Module A

The Word Processing Process

Why It's Important to Know

Word processing involves five simple steps: writing, revising, formatting, saving, and printing. Understanding which step you're performing helps you identify the work you're doing and know what to do next.

Written information must be *structured* to convey meaning to its audience. An informal letter to a friend is not written in the same way as a press release announcing a new computer product or a description of your not-for-profit organization's next fund-raiser. The goal is to have the message you send be the message that is received. Such structured information is called a *document*.

A word processing application is software designed to write, revise, format, save, and print documents. Word processing is a tool for working with two primary forms of human communication: words and ideas. Whether you are writing term papers or letters, composing the lyrics to a tune, or creating a business memo, word processing helps you perform various writing tasks more easily. Word processing helps you focus on creating and revising content. It is a much more powerful productivity tool than noncomputerized writing tools and methods. Using word processing consists of five steps: writing, revising, formatting, saving, and printing. Refer to the Word Processing Process Chart in figure 8.1 as you read this module.

Writing

Word processing automates many aspects of **writing**, the process of conveying information with words, and makes writing easier in three ways:

- You can type continuously without pressing the typewriter's carriage return key at the end of each line of text. A word processing feature called **word wrap** automatically pushes the text to the next line.

- You don't have to insert a new piece of paper after each page as you do with a typewriter, because the document is stored in random-access memory (RAM) as you work on it. A feature called *scrolling* enables you to view the successive portions of a document on the screen. You scroll through this *soft copy* in memory by using the scroll bars at the bottom and right side of the screen.

- You don't have to retype the entire document when you reorganize or make changes or corrections. All changes can be made in soft copy before you print hard copy.

An example of a word processing document is illustrated in figure 8.2.

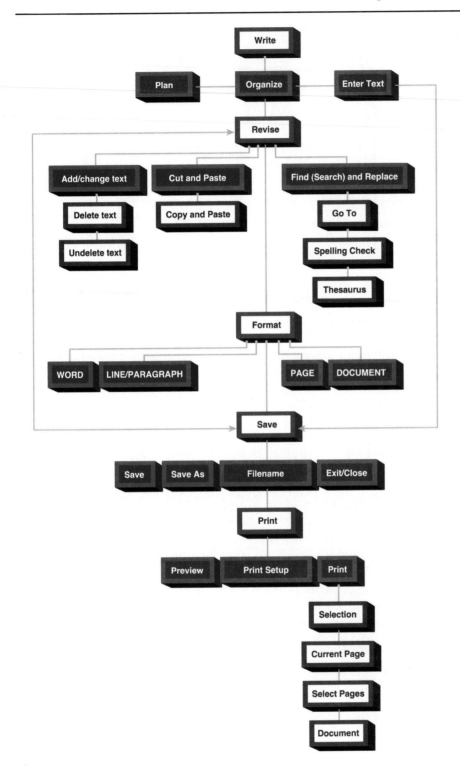

Figure 8.1
*The Word Processing
Process Chart.*

Figure 8.2
Word wrap and scrolling set word processing apart from the typewriter.

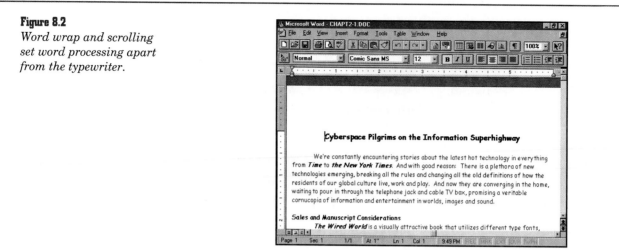

To help you keep your place in a document, most word processing programs have a *status bar* at the bottom of the screen that shows precisely where you are in the document: page number, line, column, and so on. The scroll box on the scroll bar also provides an approximate visual indication. Scrolling and a number of other movements are easily accomplished using the mouse or the cursor-movement keys.

Revising

Revision, or **revising**, is the process of re-reading, changing, deleting, and replacing text you have written. Each time you revise a document, you create a new **draft**, or version of your document. Most knowledge workers edit a document at least once or twice to make changes and corrections. Word processing has made revising as painless as possible because you are working with soft copy on the monitor. The soft copy is a copy of your document that is temporarily stored in RAM and thus easy to revise and modify. Using a typewriter, you may spend many hours typing and retyping on sheet after sheet of paper to produce a good final draft. With word processing, you can make changes until you are satisfied with the document and then print the final draft. Revising includes the following:

- Moving or rearranging portions of the document
- Replacing specific characters, words, or phrases
- Deleting and undeleting portions of the document
- Adding new text

Formatting

Formatting (not to be confused with formatting disks) is the process of emphasizing and arranging text on-screen or on the printed page. Word processing enables you to format and stylize your written documents in the following ways:

- Format *words* by underlining, boldfacing, or italicizing
- Format *lines* by centering text and setting margins and tab spaces

- Format *pages* by setting line spacing, justification, and page breaks
- Format *documents* by choosing a typeface, setting page numbering, and creating headers or footers

Author Alice Kahn tells an interesting story about writing using word processing. When Delacorte Press was working on *My Life as a Gal*, they sent her a mock-up of the cover showing a photograph of her face rolling out of a typewriter. She was embarrassed enough at being on the cover, but seeing the typewriter made her sick because she didn't associate it with her career as a writer. She had them replace it with a picture of her face on a computer screen.

The phrase *What You See Is What You Get* describes a distinct advantage of word processing over the typewriter. With the exception of underlined words, the typewriter produces characters that lack emphasis. But with word processing software that runs in a GUI operating environment, you can **boldface** or *italicize* text, use different type styles, and more. **What You See Is What You Get**, or **WYSIWYG** (pronounced "wizzy-wig"), means that what you see on the screen (in soft copy) is exactly what you'll see on the printed page (on hard copy). Figure 8.3 shows this difference.

```
The phrase What You See Is What You Get describes a distinct
advantage of word processing over the typewriter. With the
exception of underlined words, the typewriter produces characters
that lack emphasis. But with word processing software that runs
in the GUI operating environment, you can boldface or italicize
text, use different type styles and colors, and more. What You See Is What
You Get, or WYSIWYG (pronounced "wizzy-wig"), means that what you
see on the screen (in soft copy) is exactly what you'll see on
the printed page (on hard copy). Figure 8.3 shows this
difference.
```
— Laser

Figure 8.3
The differences of laser printout text, on-screen text, and typewritten text.

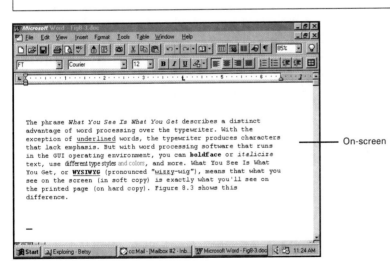
— On-screen

```
The phrase What You See Is What You Get describes a distinct
advantage of word processing over the typewriter.  With the
exception of underlined words, the typewriter produces characters
that lack emphasis.  But with word processing software that runs
in the GUI operating environment, you can boldface or italicize
text, use different type styles and colors, and more.  What You See
Is What You Get, or WYSIWYG (pronounced "wizzy-wig"), means that
what you see on the screen (in soft copy) is exactly what you'll see
on the printed page (on hard copy).
```
— Typewriter

Formatting wasn't much of an option with typewriters, unless you had an IBM Selectric and a desk drawer filled with various "golfballs" with different typefaces. And before the GUI, formatting was often difficult or awkward because you had to use various key combinations or pull-down menus to insert invisible codes into the text. The GUI screen displays many of the formatting choices in the toolbars at the top of the screen, as you can see in figure 8.4.

Figure 8.4

Two different approaches to WYSIWYG: Word 5.1 for the Macintosh and Microsoft Word for Windows for the PC-compatible.

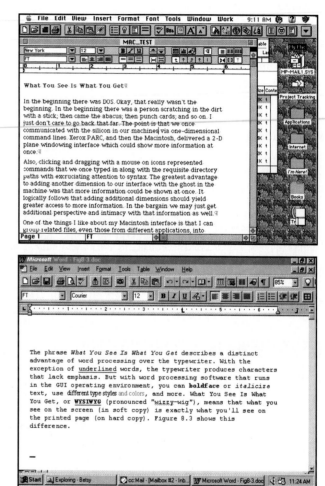

Formatting can be categorized according to text attributes and text positioning. Table 8.1 lists and describes common word processing formatting features.

You can accomplish some of this formatting with a typewriter; however, the word processing advantage is that the software can apply many formatting techniques automatically. For example, you can issue the instruction to begin page numbering on page 2, leaving page 1 unnumbered. The software takes over and consecutively numbers each page.

Another advantage is that you can change a format setting whenever you want. If you want to remove a boldfaced word, change the line spacing, use a different typeface, or insert new headings, you can do so quickly and easily. You make changes on-screen rather than on paper; then when you have your work exactly as you want it, you can print the final document.

Table 8.1
Common Formatting Features

Term	Description
Text Attributes	
Boldface	Accentuates type characters by making them darker and heavier.
Italic	Slants characters for emphasis; also used for book and magazine titles.
Underline	Draws a line under words.
Typeface (font)	The type character design, such as Times Roman or Arial.
Type size	Varies the size of the characters; for example, smaller characters in a footnote or larger characters in a title.
Bullet	Insert a symbol, such as •, in front of items in a list.
Subscript/Superscript	Characters may appear below the line or above the line.
Text Positioning	
Justification	Aligns text against the left, the right, or both margins (sometimes called full justification); centering places text equidistant from each side of the page.
Line spacing	The space between lines of text; as in single-spacing, double-spacing, triple-spacing. Line spacing is also called leading.
Margins	The blank space on either side of the text, usually one inch.
Page break	Determines the last line of text at the bottom of a particular page.
Page numbering	Automatically inserts consecutive page numbers into a document.
Header	Information about the document that appears at the top of the page, in most cases repetitively throughout a document, such as the document title or chapter name.
Footer	Information about the document that appears at the bottom of the page, in most cases repetitively throughout a document, such as the page number or file reference.

Saving

Saving is the process of storing the document in a file and giving it a unique file name. Saving is the means by which you protect your work while writing and preserve the finished document. *The most important thing to remember is to save your work frequently*, regardless of the application software you are using.

When you're beginning a new document, pause after the first paragraph to save the document and give it a file name. After that, a good rule of thumb is to save at the end of every page or every 5 or 10 minutes, whichever comes first. Some word processing programs have a built-in automatic save feature, set on a timer so that you don't have to worry about it. Just make sure you use it!

Most word processing programs now assign a unique DOS file name extension to documents that have been created with that particular program. For example, WordPerfect uses WPD, and Microsoft Word uses DOC. Knowing how various word processing programs assign file name extensions can be helpful when converting a document from one to another. If you're using a PC running Windows 95 or a Macintosh, you don't have to be concerned with this convention; you can give the file any name you choose.

Printing

What you see on the monitor is referred to as *soft copy* because it is visual but intangible. At any point in the writing process, however, you can print what you have written. **Printing** lets you read and review a draft of your document on paper, often called *hard copy*. Hard copy provides a permanent record of a document that can be conveniently shared with other knowledge workers. It is also another form of backup for a disk file, in case of loss or damage. It may not be fun to retype the file, but at least you still have it.

Printing combines software and hardware technology. The word processing software must be capable of taking advantage of the printer's capabilities, but the hard copy is only as good as the printer itself. Yet using the two together, you can create simple documents that look typewritten or complex documents as elegant as the typeset page you are reading. Some word processing programs have a *print preview* feature that enables you to see what the document will look like when printed, including the headers, footers, pagination, type fonts, and so forth. Print preview should display the document in the same way as WYSIWYG.

HOME PAGE

THE NEW NOVEL

Twenty years ago, people were predicting that the computer would mean the death of the printed word. But like many things in the Information Age, the computer has not eliminated anything, but rather added dimensions. Take books: the printed novel, a fictional, imaginary story, continues to thrive but has also found new form in software and on-line versions. These new, computer-based forms involve writing, and you can be sure that the authors used word processing. Some include text and graphics, and others are more graphics than text.

All contribute to an emerging new art form which has many names. It has been called *hypertext* or *hypertext fiction*. **Hypertext** is a method of preparing and publishing text, ideally suited to the computer, in which readers can choose their own paths through the material. Hypertext applications are useful for working with massive amounts of text, such as encyclopedias. An example of *nonfiction* hypertext that knowledge workers encounter regularly is the Help feature built into most applications. Clicking key words that appear in color or with underlining takes you to other related topics. The reader can pursue trails that fork off in alternate directions, which is why this text is often referred to as *tree-based text*. This feature becomes more interesting when you are reading a hypertext novel. Here are a few descriptions:

From *Hyperfiction: Beyond the Garden of the Forking Paths*: "Computer-based fiction ranges from straightforward electronic books with search features to highly interactive texts that invite the user to choose alternative plots, experience a scene from a different character's point of view, or call up information on topics of interest. . . . The principal publisher of the new electronic fiction is Santa Monica, California's The Voyager Co., whose Expanded Book Series repackages classics such as John Steinbeck's *Of Mice and Men* and bestsellers like Michael Crichton's *Jurassic Park*."[2]

From *Tree Fiction on the World Wide Web*: "Hypertext fiction, [is] called 'tree literature,' or 'plot branching,' or 'choose your own fiction.' It consists of short sections of conventional narrative, each ending with a choice for the reader that determines what happens next and thus which section of the narrative should be read next. When presented on paper, such a fiction usually consists of numbered paragraphs connected by directions.

"Tree literature reached the masses with the publication of the 'choose your own adventure' series (beginning in 1981 with *The Circus* by Edward Packard and now numbering more than eighty titles) and the 'fighting fantasy' series (beginning in 1982 with *The Warlock of Firetop Mountain* by Steve Jackson and Ian Livingstone). Both series are adventure stories for children, almost entirely in the science fiction and fantasy genres, and presented as games rather than stories, the aim usually being to complete some task specified at the start of the book by finding the (often unique) sequence of choices that takes you from the start section to the winning section."[3]

This hypertext version of the poet William Blake's illuminated manuscripts is available on the Internet at http://luigi.calpoly.edu/Marx/Blake/blakeproject.html

HOME PAGE REVIEW QUESTIONS

1. What three forms can a hypertext document take?

2. What are the unique features or attractions of hypertext documents?

3. Read a hypertext fiction document, and explore its branches. Report on your experience.

---

2. Domenic Stansberry. "Hyperfiction: Beyond the Garden of the Forking Paths," *NewMedia*, May 1993, 52–55.

3. Gareth Rees. "Tree Fiction on the World Wide Web," posted September, 1994.

Knowledge Check

1. What are the five aspects of the word processing process?
2. Describe several advantages in writing with word processing instead of a typewriter.
3. What do we create each time we revise a document?
4. Describe at least two ways to revise text.
5. What are the two types of text formatting?
6. What is hypertext?
7. What is another name for a printed document?

Key Terms

boldface	draft	formatting
hypertext	printing	revising
saving	What You See Is What You Get (WYSIWYG)	
word wrap	writing	

ISSUES AND IDEAS:

Requiem for the Typewriter

by Matt Friedman

Remember the typewriter? Not many people do. It passed away in obscurity this month, after a long and painful bout with obsolescence. Smith Corona, the last company to devote its entire energy to the design, manufacture and production of typewriters, finally bit the big one and went the way of the dodo, the passenger pigeon and co-rec-tape.

Like most writers, I remember my very first typewriter. It was a chemical blue Smith Corona electric. It was about 1973, and all that I could think of doing with the machine was type out a long, detailed and fastidiously-tabbed catalogue of my father's vinyl record collection. I used a now-obsolete technology to create a database of a now-obsolete technology. True, if I had had a personal computer and a good database program, the job would have been easier . . . but that wasn't an option then.

I used that typewriter to write my first short stories, my first poems, and my first attempts at reportage. I remember sitting up, late at night in my first apartment on Duluth Street, too poor to afford a real PC and too proud to use the ones at the university, hammering-out immense undergraduate essays on Canadian labour history and "Georg Trakl and the Mythology of Fin de Siecle Europe. . . ." And it all would have been easier if I'd had a personal computer and a decent word processor. . . .

There was something satisfying and reassuring in the typewriter—the way each keystroke resulted in a resounding thwack, and the way the letters appeared engraved in an ink-ribbon-patterned bas relief on the page. The noise was the one thing that kept me going when I pulled my university all-nighters. You can't fall asleep at the keyboard when you make that much racket.

The truth is that, while I don't miss liquid-paper, or the fine art of making sure your paper was fed straight on the spindle (something I could never quite do), or the impossible task of keeping margins consistent from page to page, I do miss the sound.

When you walk into a newspaper newsroom today, you become instantly aware that something is missing. Sure, work is getting done, and probably more efficiently than before, but the industrious sound of a few dozen typewriters crashing away in aleatoric rhythm just isn't there.

Like many writers of my post-hippie-pre-generation-x generation, I grew up on a steady diet of Ernest Hemingway stories and movies featuring hard-boiled Hollywood hacks. When I think of a writer, I think of watching William Holden play Joe Gillis on a late-night telecast of *Sunset Boulevard*, his hands flying over the keyboard of a Remington portable, pulling finished pages with a tearing flourish . . . and the sound, the chorus of little hammers striking paper, violently giving flesh to the word.

On the other hand, I can't complain. As much as I'm saddened by the passing of one of the icons of my youth, I know as well as anyone that time marches on, and the reason why few people except inveterate Luddites use typewriters anymore is that, with computers around they just didn't make much sense. Smith Corona and the typewriter died because there was no place for antiquated tools when the new technologies do the job so much better.

I can never imagine myself actually working with one of those relics of the pre-computer age, but I miss the romance of writing that the typewriter seemed to represent. If my laptop supported sound, I'd get one of those neat programs that simulates the noise of a real typewriter. . . . But I'd soon get tired of it. For a writer, the idea of a simulated typewriter is a little like simulated sex or processed-cheese-product. . . . It's not the real thing.[4]

CRITICAL THINKING

1. Do you have memories or experiences of using a typewriter? Are they happy or not?

2. What are the primary ways in which the author recalls his experience with the typewriter?

3. Do the emotional or sentimental aspects of the typewriter keep the author—or you—from taking advantage of word processing?

---

4. This essay originally appeared in slightly different form in the July 21, 1995, edition of *Hour* magazine, published in Montreal, Quebec, Canada.

Module B

Word Processing Basic Tools and Advanced Features

Why It's Important to Know

The word processing document is the most common and frequently used type of document. Mastering basic features speeds and improves routine written communications. Advanced features help people create persuasive and sophisticated documents.

Knowledge workers use word processing to create written communication. The word processing document is one of the most frequently used documents. A word processing document is primarily text characters—the ones that appear on a standard keyboard. The word processing document has value both in form and content.

The *form* may be a memo, a letter, a poem or short story, a report, a proposal, a brochure, a contract or warranty, a newsletter, or a document used for on-line information delivery. *Form* also refers to margins, typeface, use of headers and footers, and other formatting settings.

The *content* has immediate usefulness and often long-range value. The document may express your feelings, explain a new project, or outline the department's personnel policies. The document may include data from a spreadsheet, a summary report from a database management system, or graphics. Content also refers to the words, numbers, and graphic images that convey meaning and information.

Some examples of word processing documents are shown in figure 8.5.

A word processing document may become a published brochure, pamphlet, manual, or even a book. Whatever the finished product, it must conform to the enterprise's requirements for quality and presentation. For example, a letter written by a representative of the enterprise to alumni, potential customers, or business partners must be clearly written, error-free, formatted according to corporate conventions, and printed so that it can be easily read, as seen in figure 8.6.

Join us for a planting a garden party!!

WHEN: Saturday, November 2
               10AM to 6PM

WHERE: 380 South Lincoln

RSVP: Randy Rhodes
               568-4390

Amateur Homebuilders News

Volume 15   Summer 1995

Log Cabin Update

In last month's edition, we surveyed various types of log cabin kits available on the market today. We received numerous letters about the article. Many of the letters pointed out that log cabins may not meet building codes in some areas. Be sure to check with your local planning and zoning commission before you order a kit or start harvesting logs for your cabin. Take a lesson from the experience of Marty Burton, who finished his log cabin in Woodsy, Oregon December of 1994, and was ordered to tear it down in January of 1995 because it violated the local building ordinances.

How Many Blueprints Should You Order?

A single set of blueprints is sufficient to study and review a home in greater detail. However, if you are planning to get cost estimates or are planning to build, you will need a minimum of 4 sets and more likely 8 sets. If you will be modifying your home plan, we recommend ordering a Reproducible Blueprint set.

Stair Design Tips

Those of you who are constructing staircases should be aware of the "rise and run" theory of building steps. For each vertical step (rise), there is a recommended horizontal measurement (run) to the next step. The rise and run work together to create the slope of the staircase. And we all know what happens if the slope of the stairs is too steep!

Here are some basic rules for building staircases:

- The slope of the stairs (rise-run ratio) should be between 30 and 35 degrees.
- The sum of the two risers and one tread should equal 25 inches.
- The product of the riser height multiplied by the tread width should equal approximately 75 inches.

Foundation Options and Exterior Construction

The most common foundation choices are slab, crawlspace or basement foundation; the exterior walls are typically constructed using 2x4s or 2x6s. Most professional contractors or builders can easily adapt a home to meet the foundation and exterior wall requirements that you desire.

If the home that you select does not offer the foundation or exterior wall requirements that you prefer, you may wish to purchase a typical foundation and framing conversion diagram.

Group by Color

FlowerColor	CommonName	Genus	Species	NumberPlanted
BLUE				
	GOLDEN CHAMOMILE	ANTHEMIS	TINCTORIA	10
	PRITCHARD'S BLUE	CAMPANULA	LACTIFLORA	8
	BUXTON'S BLUE	GERANIUM	WALLICHIANUM	12
	FLEABANE AZURE BEAUTY	ERIGERON	SPECIOSUS	20
				50
				55.00%
DARK RED				
	BLACK PRINCE	HEMEROCALLIS	FLAVA	6
				6
				3.87%
GOLD				
	GOLDFINCH	ZALUZIANSKYA	SCABRA	9
				9
				5.81%
PINK				
	GREEK MALLOW	SIDALCEA	MALVIFLORA	6
	SWEET WILLIAM	DIANTHUS	BARBATUS	10
				16
				10.32%
PURPLE				
	BERGAMOT	MONARDA	DIDYMA	3
				3
				1.94%
WHITE				
	STAR OF THE VELDT	OSTEOSPERMUM	PLUVIALIS	10
	BABY'S BREATH	GYPSOPHILA	PANICULATA	10
				20
				12.90%
YELLOW				
	SKUNK CABBAGE	LYSICHITUM	AMERICANUM	3
	DUSTY MILLER	LYCNIS	CORONARIA	12
				15
				9.68%
			Grand Total :	**155**

Figure 8.5
The variety of documents that word processing produces.

Figure 8.6
A document's appearance can be as important as the message it contains.

October 20, 1995

Rachel Simon
The Magic Touch Literary Agency, Inc.
One Rockefeller Center, 44th Floor
New York, New York 10001

Dear Ms. Simon:

Dan Egan is recognized as one of the world's top skiers. I'm part of a team of committed professionals working with Dan to create an innovative multimedia package: *Dan Egan's Chairlift Guide to Skiing.* We are looking for an agent who shares our vision, excitement, and commitment to sell the *Chairlift Guide to Skiing* to an equally committed publisher.

In a series of 24 lessons, the *Chairlift Guide to Skiing* uses three learning tools to explain everything skiers need to know about skiing basics and about improving their skiing. Lessons begin with mental preparation followed by, physical preparation. Next they explain proper use of equipment , and the lessons conclude with ways to understand terrain and snow conditions. The tools we employ are

- A paperback book with complete lessons and instructions, keyed to the other two tools
- A professionally produced instructional videotape, synchronized with the book lessons
- A pocket-sized version of weatherproof lesson cards, with cards and instructions for performing 24 basic and advanced ski drills

We have a complete 22-page book proposal ready to show you. This proposal includes a sample lesson from the book, a video introducing Dan and the instructional techniques, and prototypes to the cards. Our team produces high-quality work on stringent deadlines.

If you're interested in working with us, please call me at 603.555.5000 or reply by fax at 603.555.5353. Thank you for your time. We look forward to hearing from you.

Sincerely

Celeste K. R. Kelly

enclosure

A Word Processing Work Session

The best way to become familiar with word processing is to begin a work session and follow the five steps in the word processing process to create a document. If you need to refresh your memory of these five steps, refer to figure 8.1. Figure 8.7 shows a typical word processing screen from Word for Windows 95.

Figure 8.7
The first screen you see when you start the Microsoft Word for Windows 95 word processing program.

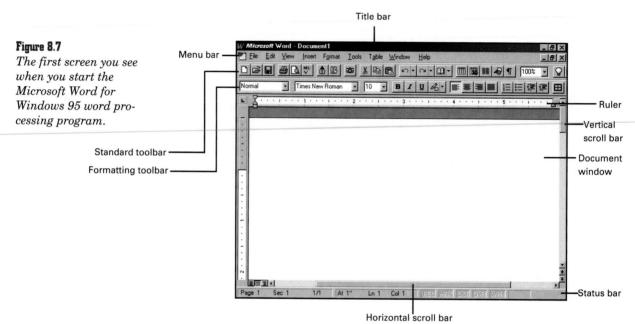

The screen is designed to provide information about the document you're working on. From the top of the screen down, identify the following items in figure 8.7.

- *Title bar.* Displays the program name and current file; *Document1* means that the current file is a new document, that you have not yet saved with your own unique file name.

- *Menu bar.* Lists the available pull-down menus, which contain commands

- *Standard toolbar.* Displays icons that execute commands used most frequently (most also appear in pull-down menus)

- *Formatting toolbar.* Displays information and icons that pertain to text formatting options

- *Ruler.* Displays the margin and tab settings

- *Document window, or work space.* The area in which you create the document

- *Scroll bars.* To the right and across the bottom of the document window; they enable you to move through text in the document

- *Status bar.* Displays information about your current location in the text and other useful information such as the date

Writing

Writing begins with planning and organizing your thoughts. Once you're ready to begin, you use word processing to enter text. It's important to understand the following word processing terms before you start:

- The insertion point and pointer

- Editing modes

- Text appearance

- Saving

The Insertion Point and Pointer

A DOS program has only one cursor; you issue commands by pressing keys or choosing from menus. In a GUI program, the cursor is called the *insertion point* (also called the I-beam). It performs one set of tasks, and the pointer performs others.

The Insertion Point. When you begin a new document, you see a vertical line and a horizontal line at the top left corner of the document window. The vertical line is the insertion point. It marks the position where the next character you type will appear. The horizontal line shows you where the last line in the document is. The insertion point moves along as you type, and the horizontal line moves down when you press the Enter key.

The pointer. The pointer performs two tasks. One, in the document window the pointer is the I-beam, and it moves through the text to reposition the insertion point or perform text highlighting tasks. The I-beam will turn back into the arrow when moved outside the left margin, where it is used to highlight entire lines or paragaphs of text. Two, when you move the I-beam out of the workspace or document window, it becomes an arrow or pointer, ready to issue commands. These two modes of operation can be seen in figure 8.8.

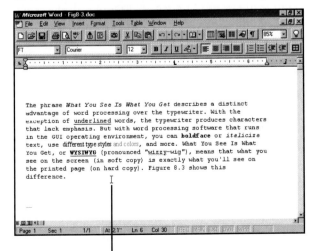

I-beam

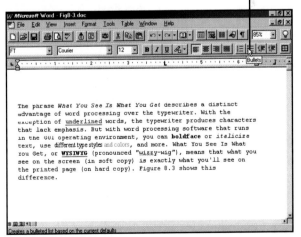

Pointer

Figure 8.8
The pointer is an I-beam in the document window and an arrow outside of the document window.

Editing Modes

Word processing applications have two editing modes: Insert and Overtype. The Insert key is a toggle key that enables you to switch between the two modes. The *default* mode, meaning the mode that the program automatically selects, is normally Insert. In the Insert mode, each text character you type is inserted at the insertion point; any following characters are pushed to the right and, because of word wrap, down. In the Overtype mode, each character you type replaces any existing characters at the insertion point.

Text Appearance

Before you begin writing a new document, you need to consider a few basic aspects of text appearance. Word processing programs have a number of default settings, such as the typeface, type size, line spacing, margins, and tabs. You can see all these settings on the screen in the Formatting toolbar and ruler. If you want to change any of these settings, it is best to do so before you have typed any characters to make sure that the changes apply to the entire document. In most cases, you make these changes by positioning the pointer on an icon or arrow on the Formatting toolbar and clicking or by making selections from pull-down menus.

Saving

Saving your work as a file is essential. In the Word Processing Process Chart, saving is shown as a feedback loop linking Writing and Saving and Revising and Saving (refer to figure 8.1). You should save your work frequently and regularly.

As you write, your work is held in RAM until you use the Save command to save the work as a file on disk. After writing for ten minutes or so, or after you have written the first few paragraphs, save your work. The first time you save, you are asked to assign a file name to your document. After you've typed the name and the file has been properly saved, that file name appears in the title bar. After that, save every ten minutes, or use the program's automatic saving feature—this saves any changes to the file on disk.

Revising

Revising your text is the first step toward producing high-quality documents. There is no written work that cannot be improved through revision. Whenever possible, allow some time between creating the first draft and beginning the revision. This delay gives you a fresh perspective from which to evaluate your work and note ways it can be improved. If you want to keep the original file intact, open the file, and then use the Save As menu option to give the file a new file name for your first revision. You can compare versions later. Some of the basic procedures you use during revision include the following:

- *Add new text* by moving the I-beam to the point where you want to add this text

- *Copy and paste* text to repeat terms, symbols, or text phrases

- *Cut and Paste* (or Move) text to reorganize text for clearer meaning

- *Delete* unwanted text, and *undelete* text that was accidentally deleted

- *Find*, or *Search*, to locate specific words or phrases

- *Search and Replace* to make global changes to a word or phrase—such as replacing a misspelled word that occurs frequently in the document

- *Go To*, to move to specific pages, footnotes, and other specific locations

- Use the *Spelling Checker* to check spelling and other simple vocabulary or syntax errors, such as a repeated word ("the the")

- Use the **Thesaurus**, a word-finding program that suggests synonyms, antonyms, and related and contrasting words

- Use the *revisions* tool to edit a document—usually one created by a fellow knowledge worker—using different colors so that the suggestions or changes are easy to see. A reporter, for example, writes a story and gives it to an editor who works with it as soft copy on the screen—this task is called *on-line editing*.

- The other tool is a *grammar checker*, which enables you to review a document for reading level. Some readability formulas that are commonly used are the Flesch Reading Ease test, which counts the average number of syllables per word and assigns a score of 0 to 100; the average is 60–70. The Coleman-Liau Grade Level test determines readability as a grade level (for example, 6th grade or 10th grade) based on the number of characters per word or the number of words per sentence.

Formatting

Once the text has been written and revised to the point that you are relatively satisfied with it, you can refine and enhance the basic formatting you set up when you started the document. Although it's likely you'll do more revising, you are beginning to finalize the document design. Bear in mind that it's usually most productive to wait until the content and language of the document are in pretty good shape before you begin making extensive formatting changes. Some of the basic formatting tools are listed in table 8.2.

Table 8.2
Basic Formatting Tools for Text Elements

Word	Line/Paragraph	Page	Document
Bold	Left/Right	Margins	Headers
Italic	Center	Layout	Footers
Underline	Full Justification	Portrait/Landscape	Page Numbering
Font Style	Spacing	Tables	Date or Time
Font Size	Bullets/Numbering	Graphics	Insert Worksheet
	Tabs	Borders	
		Columns	

Saving

You simply can't save often enough. That's why you're encouraged to save your work in a file in the early stages of document creation, and to save it frequently while you're revising. You can save by using the disk icon or button, the File pull-down menu, and Autosave.

You can save a file from the File pull-down menu or with the "disk" button on the Standard toolbar. Basically, this button is a way to save quickly; clicking it saves the existing file. If you haven't yet named the file, you are prompted to do so. After that, you see a "saving file" message in the status bar.

The File pull-down menu offers more options. Save is the first and prompts you for a file name. Save As enables you to select a different file name—for example, when you're giving a revision a different name. Save All saves all open files, which are listed in the Window pull-down menu; if you've made changes, you're prompted to save each file. Exit, the last option in the File pull-down menu, similarly prompts you to close each open file before quitting word processing. Close saves each file and then exits word processing.

The **autosave** feature, available with all better word processing applications, is preprogrammed to save open files without your command (see figure 8.9). The usual interval is ten minutes, although you can set it for any length of time. The time autosave takes depends on three factors: the size of the file, the clock speed of the CPU, and the access time of the storage media. With disk storage, saving on a floppy disk usually takes longer than saving on a hard disk. Some word processing programs offer additional choices for autosaving, such as a *fast save,* which only saves the changes you've made, and creating a *backup file,* which makes an extra copy in case the original is lost.

Figure 8.9

The Autosave feature helps you avoid losing your work.

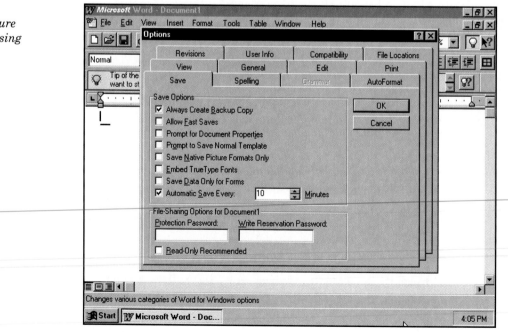

Printing

Printing is another way to make a copy of your work. Although saving a file is storing your work on a disk, paper (hard copy) is a backup copy in case the file is lost or damaged. For that reason, it's a good idea always to print a copy of important work. If you lose the file, you can always type a new copy from paper.

In order to print, you must have a logical interface between the word processing program and the printer. And don't forget the physical interface–the cable connecting the printer to the computer. The software driver that identifies your printer is installed during the initial setup procedures for your word processing program. Any printer you use with Windows or with the Chooser on the Macintosh can be used with word processing. The Print selection on the File pull-down menu offers a variety of printing options. You can

- Print the entire document

- Print a group of selected pages, such as 5 through 9

- Print the current (single) page

- Print a highlighted section if you just want a printed excerpt from a document

- Print more than one copy

- Print the text in *portrait orientation*, where the height of the page is greater than the width, as in a normal letter, report, or term paper, or in *landscape orientation*, where the print appears sideways across the paper, its width being greater than its height. Landscape orientation is good for tables and multiple columns of text.

Another option on the File menu is Print Preview, which enables you to view on-screen the pages of the document exactly as they will appear when printed—in true WYSIWYG. A Print Preview icon appears on the toolbar next to the Printer icon.

Understanding Advanced Word Processing Features

Learning to use word processing is a skill-building process. This statement is true of all the applications you'll learn to use. Most people find that they learn simple skills at first and additional skills as they discover a need for them. This way of learning is nearly always the case with advanced word processing features.

Advanced features are added to word processing for the simple reason that people want them and ask for them. For instance, at one time, word processing didn't have a spelling checker; today, you can check grammar as well as spelling. Here is a list of some of the more popular advanced features:

- *Bookmarks,* as the name implies, identify a specific place in the document. They are used to identify specific text or graphics or to mark a location that you use frequently.

- *Customized toolbars* can be created by the individual knowledge worker to suit work habits. Buttons can be added, reorganized, or removed.

- *Footnotes* cite sources of research and are required whenever you prepare a proper research document. They can be placed at the bottom of each page or at the end of the document (as endnotes).

- *Indexes* and *tables of contents* for long documents can be created. You create an index by marking the words you want to include. You create a table of contents by formatting the headings into categories (1, 2, 3, and so on). Both the index and table of contents for your textbook were created in just this way.

- *Macros*. A **macro** is a program consisting of recorded keystrokes and an application's command language that, when run within the application, executes the keystrokes and commands to accomplish a task. A macro can automate tedious tasks and can also automate a series of procedures, such as taking pages from a document and faxing them. Macros are often written in a simple programming language.

- *Mail merge* enables you to insert individual names and addresses into a form letter and print a copy addressed to each individual.

- *Master documents* combine a number of files, such as the chapters in a book, into a single document that's easier to work with. Each individual chapter file is a subdocument that can be viewed as a normal file or together with the others in a detailed outline form.

- *Revisions* can be recorded and stored so that you can see what you've changed. For example, this sentence was rewritten:

  | Icon buttons can be added, ~~regrouped~~, reorganized, or removed.

- *Sort* enables you to reorder a random collection of text or numbers into alphabetized or numerical ascending or descending order. For example, this list of advanced features was compiled and then sorted alphabetically.

- *Tables* are a simple way to organize data that can be easily grouped. For example, table 8.2 is a table created in word processing. More sophisticated tabular material is often created using a database management system program, and the results are inserted into a word processing document.

- *Templates*. A **template** is a predesigned form to help you quickly create commonly used documents, such as letters, resumes, reports, fax forms, and memos. Templates often contain *styles*, or a particular use of various kinds of text formatting for headers, body text, page layout, and so on. Other applications, such as the spreadsheet, often use templates, too.

Ending a Work Session

The last two things to do when finishing a work session are

1. Save your work.
2. Exit the program.

HOME PAGE

WORD PROCESSING TIPS

1. Use word processing instead of pen and paper to brainstorm and for prewriting. Because you can move, add, delete, and edit so easily, your work will take shape much more quickly. It's tedious—and rather pointless—to write ideas or drafts on paper and then type them into a word processing file. Refer to the document summary information; you'll learn a great deal about your work habits.

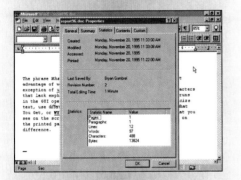

Microsoft Word's Properties menu selection displays document summary information.

2. Edit on the screen whenever possible. The idea behind word processing is that you don't need to retype drafts over and over. If you always edit drafts on paper, you're defeating one of word processing's major advantages and wasting paper, an increasingly expensive natural resource.

3. Don't overuse formatting features. Use underlining, boldface, italic, and different typefaces sparingly; otherwise, the text becomes difficult to read and emphasis is lost.

4. Avoid typing all uppercase words in the body of the text because large blocks of capitals are hard to read—save uppercase for titles or headings. Italicize the titles of magazines and books—underlining the names of publications went out with typewriters. Use boldface for emphasis—it is more effective than underlining. Serif fonts (which have little "feet" and short bars or curves at the top of each letter) are easier to read and better suited for the body of your text than sans serif fonts (letters do not have extra curves or bars). Sans serif is often used for headings.

5. If you're using software that allows you to use only the standard DOS eight-character file names, name your documents carefully. Choose words that convey the content rather than the type of file. For example, it's much easier to remember what's in a file called TOYSTORY than one called FICTION. If you're using a program that allows long file names, you can be as creative as you like.

6. Most people use about 10 commands on a regular basis. Memorize the commands you use most frequently. Customize your toolbar so that you'll have the commands you need at the click of the mouse.

7. Use the document templates for improved productivity. Don't be afraid to modify them or create your own. If you use a particular block of text frequently, save it in a file of its own, and use the Insert File command to place it in other documents. Use macros or Word's AutoText tool for phrases you use repeatedly in a variety of documents; another method is to use Find and Replace from the Edit pull-down menu.

8. Use your word processing program's multiple document feature, which enables you to open and work with more than one file at a time. Multiple documents make it easy to view and edit more than one manuscript, or several portions of the same manuscript, at the same time.

9. Try to learn a new command or technique once a week or at least once a month. Open menus, such as Tools, and explore all the functions; practice creating tables; use the various typefaces; try the graphics utility. Extend your knowledge and your software's capabilities. This habit makes you more productive and makes your work more interesting and fun.

10. Save your work frequently. This statement applies to any application you use. If your word processing software has an autosave feature, set it to save at least every 10 minutes. If it doesn't, get in the habit of performing a quick save at the end of every page. Make backup copies of your work on separate disks.

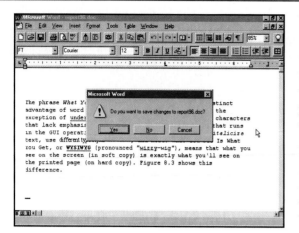

Figure 8.10
*Word prompts you to save
your work before you exit
the program.*

Working in the GUI environment makes these steps easy and nearly foolproof. If you attempt to exit or close the program without having saved the file, a message appears asking you whether you want to save the file or exit without saving (see figure 8.10). Now you have a choice, and you won't lose your work through an oversight.

It's very important to remember to exit or close the application you're working with and then to exit or close Windows. This step ensures that all the important information about your programs is safely stored before power is shut off.

Knowledge Check

1. Describe the form of a word processing document. Describe the content.
2. Explain the difference between the word processing insertion point and the pointer.
3. What are the two editing modes, and how do you switch between them?
4. From a memory and storage standpoint, why is it important to save frequently?
5. What are the four aspects of the document that we format?
6. Describe the purpose of autosave.
7. Why use the pull-down menu to print instead of the print icon?
8. Why use a macro?
9. Why use a template?

Key Terms

autosave   macro   template   thesaurus

ISSUES AND IDEAS

On Writing Well

"Omit needless words! Omit needless words! Omit needless words!" was the clarion call of English professor William Strunk, Jr., co-author of the classic work on writing, *The Elements of Style*.[5] No less passionate is author and writer William Zinsser about word processing. In his book *On Writing Well*, he discusses how he works with words—and word processing:

---

5. 3rd ed. (New York: Macmillan), xiii.

What you must do, in short, is to make an arrangement—one that hangs together from beginning to end and that moves with economy and warmth. Such a structure can only be achieved with a fair amount of trial and error. And doing this on a screen certainly beats doing it over and over on a typewriter. My last book, *Willie and Dwike*, in which I was working mainly with oral material—information that people had given me in their own words—took less than a year to write on a word processor. On a typewriter it would have taken at least two years. The difference was not only in speed and morale; it was also in control. At the end I felt I had made exactly the arrangement that I had in mind when I started.

. . . I learned a lot about myself by learning to write on a word processor. I found that I could trust my powers of logic more than I ever thought I could. When you realize that you're as smart as the machine, you try to figure out how it has been programmed to "think," and you find that you don't have to be Einstein to think in the same sequential way.

. . . Which shouldn't be so surprising. The ability to think logically is one of the fundamental skills of nonfiction writing. Anyone who thinks logically should be able to write well; anyone whose thinking is fuzzy will never write well. I often think we should teach children simple logic before we teach them how to write.[6]

CRITICAL THINKING

1. Why should we omit needless words?

2. Discuss what Zinsser might mean when he refers to "time, energy, enthusiasm, output, and control."

3. Zinsser says thinking logically is the nonfiction writer's skill; does it help to think logically when using a computer and word processing, too?

6. William Zinsser. *On Writing Well*, 3rd ed. (New York: Harper & Row), 218–19.

ETHICS

The Issue Was Plagiarism

Plagiarism is the unauthorized use of another person's original words or ideas. You may have heard discussions at your college about plagiarism, for it has been around a long time. People sometimes plagiarize by copying another's writing from a book or a term paper. Plagiarism is not only unethical behavior; it is also a violation of copyright law—a form of intellectual theft. Unfortunately, the Information Age and word processing have made plagiarism much easier.

For example, a college student loaned a fellow student the disk containing her bibliography for the class term paper. He used it for his term paper and then passed it along to ten other students. The professor saw identical bibliographies in their papers, and all received a reprimand for their actions. This accessibility means that each student must take more stringent measures to avoid plagiarizing, even unintentionally.

All kinds of information are distributed on floppy disks and optical disks these days. This information includes magazine articles, the works of William Shakespeare, book excerpts, work from the Internet—the list goes on and on. In addition, it is not uncommon to obtain information from electronic sources over the telephone lines. When using this information responsibly and ethically, you must cite the source—whether your work is a paraphrase or a direct quotation—in a reference or citation, providing the author's name, the article title, where it was published, the date, and so on.

Most information can easily be plagiarized simply by copying portions of text into a word processor and creating a file. The plagiarist may simply put his or her name on the document. Some try to obscure the plagiarism by changing a few words, modifying some sentences, adding or deleting a paragraph here and there, and calling the result an original work. But the plagiarist knows that he or she has committed an unethical act. And although a short-term goal may have been met— that of getting a term paper in on time—*the long-term goal of acquiring knowledge through the learning process and disseminating it through the effective use of language has not.* Plagiarism, like other unethical acts, really hurts the plagiarist most of all.

A recent college graduate was hired as staff writer of a well-known investment advice newsletter. Key to the newsletter's success were its original insights into the market and unique perspective on how to invest. This young woman worked hard but often ran late on her deadlines. Fearful that she would not have her article done in time, she plagiarized an article from a magazine published by an investment services company, typing it into her word processor and submitting it as her own work. The editor immediately sensed the lack of insight in the work and challenged its originality. The young woman confessed she had plagiarized the work, and although her editor understood the reason, the plagiarism was the grounds for her dismissal. The writer couldn't be trusted to report and write ethically and responsibly again, and thus her career as a writer and journalist came to an abrupt and unfortunate conclusion.

Critical Thinking

1. Why is it unethical to plagiarize?
2. What law was broken?
3. What is the proper and ethical way to use someone else's written work?
4. Discuss the staff writer's plagiarism and its consequences. Was the treatment fair? Why or why not?

THE LEARNING ENTERPRISE

Every department and function in the enterprise uses word processing. In this chapter, your assignment is to

1. Describe the kinds of documents you'll need to write, revise, and share with other knowledge workers
2. Describe any templates that would be help you do your writing work and aid your productivity
3. Explain what advanced features would be helpful, and tell how you would use them
4. Express your opinions about plagiarism, and what you think should be done if one of your fellow knowledge workers plagiarized your work or something from a published work.

Chapter Review

Fill in the Blank

1. A word processing feature called _____ automatically pushes the text to the next line.

2. You can view successive portions of a document on the screen using the feature called _____.

3. Each revision of a document is called a(n) _____.

4. The process of emphasizing and arranging text on the screen is called _____.

5. Name some text attributes you can use in formatting a document.

6. A(n) _____ feature in enables you to see what a document will look like when printed.

7. The _____ feature is preprogrammed to save open files at predetermined intervals without your command.

8. _____ can be used to identify specific text or to mark a location in a document.

9. _____ enables you to reorder a random collection of text or numbers into alphabetized or numerical or ascending or descending order.

10. Unauthorized use of another person's original words or ideas is called _____.

Circle the Correct Answer

1. In (portrait, landscape) orientation, the height of the printed page is greater that the width.

2. In (portrait, landscape) orientation, text is printed across the widest measurement of the paper.

3. (Serif, Sans serif) fonts are easier to read in the body of a text than (serif, sans serif) fonts.

4. The space between lines of text, such as single- or double-spacing, is called (justification, leading).

5. A document that can be read or retrieved nonsequentially is called a (WYSIWYG, hypertext) document.

Review Questions

1. Using computers to create written documents is called what?

2. What are the five steps in word processing?

3. Word processing makes the process of writing and revising easier in three ways. What are they?

4. What is hypertext?

5. What are the three most frequently used text attributes?

6. What is a macro?

7. What is the advantage of the mail merge feature?

8. What is the advantage of using templates?

9. What are some basic formatting tools for text elements?

10. What word processing tips would you give to someone new to word processing?

Discussion Questions

1. Describe the formatting features you would use to create your resume.

2. Express your opinions about plagiarism, and tell what should be done in case someone plagiarizes.

3. For your next written assignment, use the word processing document summary information feature; use revision marks; save subsequent drafts; and then ask your instructor to edit your paper on-line. Evaluate whether the ease with which you can rewrite and reformat sections in word processing improves your paper.

INTERNET DISCOVERY

Learn about some of the different word processing programs that are available. Log on to the following site:

http://search.yahoo.com/bin/search?p=word+processing&y=y& r=Computers_and_Internet%2FSoftware

Learn more about Xerox, an industry leader in document management, at this address:

http://www.xerox.com/

THE SPREADSHEET

Oh, but he was a tightfisted hand at the grindstone. Scrooge! A squeezing, wrenching, grasping, scraping, clutching, covetous old sinner! Hard and sharp as flint, from which no steel had ever struck out generous fire; secret, and self-contained, and solitary as an oyster.

Charles Dickens, *A Christmas Carol*[1]

In the 1700s, businesses began recording financial transactions, such as credits and debits, in a large book called an accountant's **ledger**. Each page in the ledger was called a *columnar page,* or *ledger sheet,* because the page contained a number of vertical *columns* running down the page. In addition, lines drawn across the page created *rows* running from left to right.

As business grew more sophisticated and complex, columnar, or ledger, sheets were used for other purposes than just calculating the company's profits and losses. They were used to keep track of manufacturing, advertising, and research and development costs. Ledgers were used to calculate interest, taxes, salaries, and sales figures. They were used for tracking a company's current financial picture and also for creating projections of what management anticipated in the future.

Over the years, the green-tinted paper ledger sheet grew in size to accommodate these more complex financial situations. As ledger sheets grew, they also became more complicated to work with. People created ledger sheets with pencils and erasers for many years, working with columns and rows of figures they had to total either by hand or with an electronic calculator. If an incorrect number was written in one of the boxes or if projections changed, it meant a great deal of tedious erasing, refiguring, and recalculating—*until* the electronic spreadsheet came along.

1. Charles Dickens *A Christmas Carol*. (Mt. Vernon, NY: Peter Pauper Press), 8.

CHAPTER 9

Module A

The Spreadsheet Process

Why It's Important to Know

Spreadsheet work involves five simple steps: designing the worksheet, creating the worksheet, organizing and revising it, saving it, and printing it. Understanding which step you're performing helps you identify the work you're doing and know what to do next.

The **spreadsheet** makes it possible to create a visual, mathematical model of a specific financial situation on the personal computer's screen. A *model* is a mathematical or graphical representation or a copy of something that exists in the real world. The model can be tested or changed without disturbing the original, in the same way an engineer creates and tests a model of an auto or an airplane. Because the spreadsheet model is financial, it involves the use of numbers and formulas. Here are some of the basic terms you need to know as you begin working with spreadsheets (other important terms are defined later in this chapter as they are introduced):

- A **column** is a vertical set of cells, identified with alphabetic letters: A, B, C, and so on.

- A **row** is a horizontal set of cells, identified with numbers: 1, 2, 3, and so on.

- A **cell** is the intersection of a column and a row, identified A1, B2, C3, and so on. Cells can contain text, numbers, or a formula.

Consider a model used to compute sales figures for a hiking boot company. Although people buy hiking boots all year long, there is a peak sales season. The spreadsheet records the sales figures by month, showing the peaks and valleys in the sales year. At the end of the year, sales are totaled, costs are subtracted, and the resulting figure is profits. Now management can use the spreadsheet to plan next year's sales. If the sales force sells 20 percent more than last month or last year, what will the company earn in profits? The spreadsheet will quickly calculate the new figures. This example is a simple mathematical model; you can represent all this information and more by using a spreadsheet.

The first modern digital computer was used to perform tedious logarithmic calculations. Today's fastest supercomputers also perform complex calculations and sophisticated modeling. Therefore, when you use the spreadsheet, you see the computer doing what it does best: performing calculations very quickly. You must enter the formulas and values carefully so that you get accurate results, and you must follow certain procedures. Those procedures are explained in the five steps of the spreadsheet process: designing the worksheet, creating the worksheet, organizing and revising the worksheet, saving the worksheet, and printing the worksheet. Figure 9.1 diagrams the Spreadsheet Process Chart.

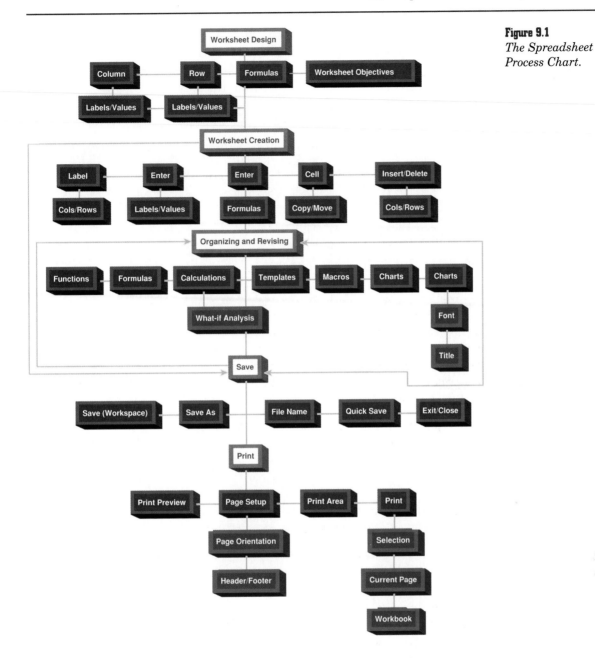

Figure 9.1
*The Spreadsheet
Process Chart.*

Although the program is a spreadsheet, the document created by the spreadsheet is a worksheet. The **worksheet** is like the sheet of ledger paper accountants use to perform and record calculations, except that this worksheet is created by the spreadsheet and you work with it on-screen (see figure 9.2). Be careful to remember the difference between the spreadsheet program and the worksheet document as you study this chapter.

Designing the Worksheet

Designing the worksheet is the first step in using an electronic spreadsheet, and most knowledge workers use paper and pencil for this step. This stage is the planning phase, in which you determine such things as the objectives of the spreadsheet, its size, complexity, and ways to achieve the objectives. Refer again to figure 9.2 and note the design. How many columns will your worksheet have? How many rows? Will the column or row contents be labeled? What formulas will be needed for totaling columns or for other more complex mathematical computations? Finally, what is the objective—what precisely do you want to obtain from the spreadsheet after it has been built? Working out and finalizing these details on paper before setting up the spreadsheet is much easier than doing it on the computer screen.

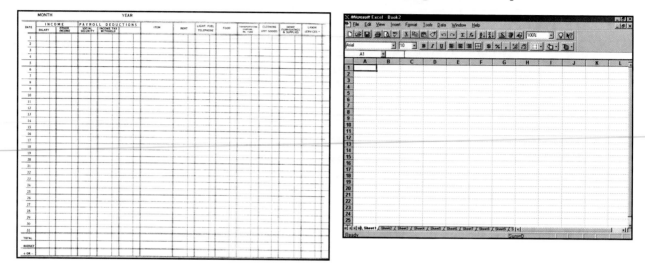

Figure 9.2
The worksheet is an electronic version of a sheet of ledger paper.

Creating the Worksheet

Working with numbers in the spreadsheet is much more efficient than working with them on a paper ledger page. Creating a worksheet means putting all the information you want to work with—both words and numbers—into the proper form. Creating the worksheet is the actual work of building it, as you have described it in the design phase. Typically a worksheet contains labels, values, and formulas.

A **label** is text used to describe the numerical contents of a spreadsheet, such as text listing each sales representative's name or the region name.

A **value** is a number assigned to a cell. Spreadsheets can handle all kinds of numbers, including currency, percentages, and dates. Values are numbers and take two forms. One is the **constant**, the raw number or data you enter for processing: 14,520 toasters or $755,900. The other form is the mathematical formula used for performing calculations on the constants. The simplest formula is A + B, where the letters A and B represent values (*variables*) that can change. For example, say that the constant 12 is in cell A1 and the constant 24 is in cell A2. Using the formula +A1+A2, you can arrive at the answer, 36. Any time the cell contains a constant, that is what you see.

A **formula** is a mathematical statement that sets up a calculation. It is a sequence of steps that takes the values, or numbers, in specified cells and combines them with mathematical operators or functions to produce a new value. A formula is more sophisticated than a simple mathematical *problem* like 1 + 2 because a formula defines a relationship between variables in cells. A simple formula might be to add the values in cells A6, B6, and C6. But if the number (variable) in C6 changes, the stored formula produces new results. A formula is created by the knowledge worker. Formulas reside in cells but are not actually displayed in the cell itself because that's where the value is displayed. Formulas appear in the formula bar.

As you enter words, numbers, and formulas, you begin to see the worksheet take form and shape. Automating the process of entering letters and numbers means no more pencils; the computer's penmanship is always readable. Mistakes are also much easier to correct than on paper, so no more erasers.

For example, you don't have to enter labels alphabetically; you can use the Sort function to alphabetize them after you have entered them all. (Functions are discussed in more detail later in this chapter.) You can make the spreadsheet extremely large, so the size of the paper is no longer a constraint. The following list shows you a few everyday uses for a spreadsheet program:[2]

Address book	Sports scores
Day planner pages	Checkbook
Mortgage amortization	Emergency phone numbers
Exercise log	Calendar
Chores list	Home (or personal) inventory
Car maintenance	Wedding planner
Presentation graphics	Sales contacts
CD/video collection	Student grades
Project management	Household budget
Class schedule	Invoice

Organizing and Revising

Organizing the spreadsheet involves entering the formulas in the appropriate places so that the formulas can perform calculations on the values. Worksheet organization is important for two reasons. One, ensuring that numbers and formulas are in the correct place and order is essential to obtaining the proper results. Two, a well-organized worksheet is easier to read and understand—which is especially important if you're presenting it to someone else.

Revising a spreadsheet is almost as easy as creating and organizing one. As with word processing, *revising* means changing (and improving) something—specifically the organization of words, numbers, or formulas. There are several types of worksheet revisions:

- Reordering data for more efficiency

- Recalculating the worksheet when certain numbers have been changed

- Improving its appearance for presentation

Because you can make worksheet revisions simply by typing them where they appear on the computer screen, you can have new results in moments. This way, you can test the worksheet and ensure that the changes you made worked.

In addition, some spreadsheets have built-in features to assist you in making revisions. Revising a paper ledger sheet is arduous and prone to error. When you use a calculator, you must re-key the numbers and formulas

---

2. Adapted from *The Complete Idiot's Guide to Excel*, Ricardo Birmele (Indianapolis: Alpha Books, 1993), 223–242.

every time you make a new calculation. You're less likely to make errors using the spreadsheet because values that don't change don't have to be rewritten. Here again, the spreadsheet achieves its superior convenience and ease of use by automating this process: formulas have to be entered only once and can be used again and again.

Figure 9.3 shows two popular spreadsheets. Note the similarities and differences in their visual appearance.

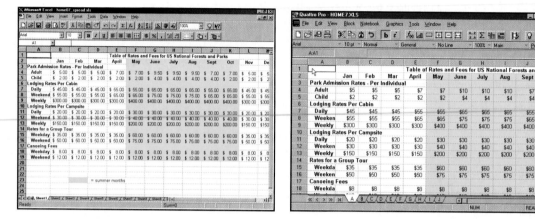

Excel   Quattro Pro

Figure 9.3

Two approaches to the spreadsheet: Quattro Pro for Windows and Microsoft Excel. Quattro Pro began as a DOS application and was redesigned for Windows. Excel was specifically designed to run under Windows.

Saving

The computer's capability to save your work in files gives the spreadsheet another distinct advantage over paper. Instead of having to erase and rewrite or copy information from one ledger sheet to another, you can quickly and easily save each version of the spreadsheet in a separate file. This capability is particularly handy when you have large quantities of data or many formulas. Saving at intervals makes it much easier to save different versions of a what-if analysis or to find a mistake. Again, the need to save your work frequently cannot be overemphasized.

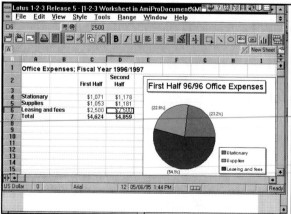

Figure 9.4

You can also print this worksheet to display its data both numerically and graphically.

Printing

Printing lets you see the results of your work in hard copy. It gives you a permanent paper record, in case the computer file is lost or destroyed. Printing also provides another important advantage for spreadsheets. Often, many knowledge workers are involved in the financial planning process, and each needs to study the figures and the results. A clearly understandable worksheet not only helps you explain your work and the way you arrived at your results, but the printed worksheet also gives others the opportunity to suggest improvements in the construction or formulas. In final form, the printed worksheet helps you demonstrate your knowledge and ability and can present data that others can understand easily and quickly.

HOME PAGE

THE BIRTH OF THE SPREADSHEET

The spreadsheet is an interesting example of a software application created to solve a problem. In 1978, Dan Bricklin was a student in the Master's of Business Administration program at Harvard University. Like the other MBA students, Dan had to use a ledger sheet, pencil, and calculator to solve problems posed in the case studies. Any corrections had to be recalculated by hand, and the ledger sheet erased or redone. There had to be a better way, he thought. Couldn't a computer help? "I visualized an electronic blackboard and electronic chalk in a classroom," he said. Dan, who sought a business solution, asked Bob Frankston, a friend with programming skills, if he could help solve the problem.

Courtesy of Dan Bricklin

Cofounders of Software Arts, Inc., and creators of VisiCalc: Bob Frankston (standing) and Dan Bricklin (seated).

Frankston was fascinated with the idea of creating a new kind of program. "Our goal was to provide a high-performance tool that would allow financial planners the same kind of flexibility enjoyed by people using word processors," Frankston said. He worked every night, pounding the keys of his Apple II in his attic apartment, and then slept all day. By January of 1979, Frankston was done. Bricklin chose the name VisiCalc, for Visible Calculator, and the first spreadsheet program soon became a software bestseller.[3]

Even though the personal computer software industry is less than twenty years old, we've already learned that no program dominates the market forever. In the case of spreadsheets, VisiCalc was soon overtaken by Lotus 1-2-3, which was at the top of the software best-seller lists for many years. But even Lotus proved vulnerable in time, in part because it did not keep pace with other technological advances. Microsoft Excel was the first spreadsheet designed specifically for Windows.

The spreadsheet was also the first program originally developed for the personal computer and then adapted for use on larger computers. Before the spreadsheet, most software was created for mainframes and then adapted to run on minicomputers and, finally, on personal computers. Other kinds of specialized financial programs were available for mainframes and minis, but there was nothing quite like the spreadsheet.

HOME PAGE REVIEW QUESTIONS

1. What was the impetus for developing the first spreadsheet?

2. What made Bricklin and Frankston a good team?

3. What was unique about the evolution of the spreadsheet?

---

3. Adapted from "A History of Software Innovation in Massachusetts," Jack B. Rochester, from *The Complete Guide to the Massachusetts Software Industry* (Boston: Executive Office of Economic Affairs, Commonwealth of Massachusetts, 1989), 1.

Knowledge Check

1. What type of model can the spreadsheet create?
2. Explain the difference between a spreadsheet and a worksheet.
3. Why should the spreadsheet design process be done on paper?
4. Name the five steps in the spreadsheet process.
5. How can the spreadsheet present data in another way besides columns and rows of numbers?

Key Terms

cell	column	constant	formula
label	ledger	row	spreadsheet
value	worksheet		

ISSUES AND IDEAS

Outsmarted by a Spreadsheet

Microsoft Excel Version 7 for Windows 95 has many "smart" features, such as AutoFill, which if you type *Jan* in a cell, automatically places *Feb* through *Dec* in subsequent cells. Another smart feature replicates the contents of the last cell as soon as you type one or two characters it recognizes in the current cell. It may be convenient, but it also can cause problems, as this story from the RISKS Forum on the Internet explains.

Date:	Tue, 21 Nov 1995 04:35:32 -1000
From:	"Ray Panko"
	<PANKO@busadm.cba.hawaii.edu>
Subject:	Outsmarted by a Smart Spreadsheet

I was entering exam grades in my class spreadsheet file. I formatted the column as percent. Then I started typing in the grades as usual. I typed *89%* for 89 percent sometimes. Other times, I typed in *.89*.

Fortunately, before I printed the results, I sorted in decreasing order of score on the exam. I noted that one of my usual top students was missing. Checking, I found that he has the lowest score in the class.

The new version of Excel for Windows 95 allows you to type numbers like 89% as 89%, .89, or 89. It figures that if you are typing 89, you mean percent.

Well my student received a 100% score. So I typed a 1 (1.00). It literally gave him 1%.

The new Microsoft algorithm had run into an ambiguous case. Numbers below 1 were recognized properly, while numbers above 1 were recognized properly. Logically, however, the two methods of treating numbers clash as 1. Is the proper thing to do in such cases to throw up a dialog box, explain the situation, and ask the person if he or she wants to make this 1% or 100%? The dialog box could even explain the new (I believe) way of handling percentages.

As we add more and more intelligence to software, it becomes easier to use in most cases but rather dangerous in other cases. Just as programmers need to consider boundary values when they test programs with data, designers of intelligence will need to consider boundary values. They should then "open the box" and bring the user into the decision.

Raymond R. Panko, Decision Sciences Dept., College of BusAdmin, U. of Hawaii 2404 Maile Way, Honolulu, HI 96822
Panko@dscience.cba.hawaii.edu (808)956-5049

CRITICAL THINKING

1. What is the advantage to having "smart" features, such as the one described in a spreadsheet program?

2. What did Professor Panko do incorrectly? What did the program want him to do that he didn't do?

3. Do you agree that the software should be designed to check with the knowledge worker—using a dialog box, as Professor Panko suggests—if there is doubt about how to handle a situation?

4. How would you like having a "smart" feature that prompted you every time you entered the same data into the next cell? Would that be more or less desirable than having it do it automatically?

Module B

Spreadsheet Basic Tools and Advanced Features

Why It's Important to Know

The spreadsheet document, or worksheet, can display and work with several different kinds of data: numbers, words, and graphic images. This versatility makes spreadsheet skills valuable and useful in many knowledge worker activities.

The spreadsheet largely replaces three manual tools for working with numbers: paper, pencil, and the calculator. The paper is the blank worksheet you see on the computer screen. The keyboard and mouse take the place of the pencil. The calculator is actually your personal computer's microprocessor—to be more precise, the arithmetic-logic unit, or ALU. The ALU is activated by the spreadsheet software when you issue to the spreadsheet certain commands called formulas.

Working with Spreadsheet Documents

While sharing some things in common with its paper counterpart, such as columns and rows, the worksheet has a different look and feel. A paper ledger sheet is static; the lines are drawn, and you can't change them. Paper is also a fixed size, such as 8 1/2 by 11 inches, which can't be changed. It's quite another case with the worksheet. You can change columns and rows easily, and the average spreadsheet program contains as many as half a million cells. Figure 9.5 shows how only a portion of the worksheet appears on the screen.

Some spreadsheet programs are designed to resemble a ledger book. The file is a book, which contains a number of individual sheets, appropriately called *worksheets*. This format can make working with financial data easier. Instead of having a single, large spreadsheet, you can create specific worksheets for such things as fiscal year budget, expenses, raw materials, sales and marketing, fixed costs, and so forth, and keep them all together in a workbook. This approach is not simply a neat and tidy way to organize financial information—the worksheets are dynamically linked. If a figure changes in, say, the worksheet for raw materials for manufacturing, the change is automatically reflected in the worksheet with budget bottom-line figures.

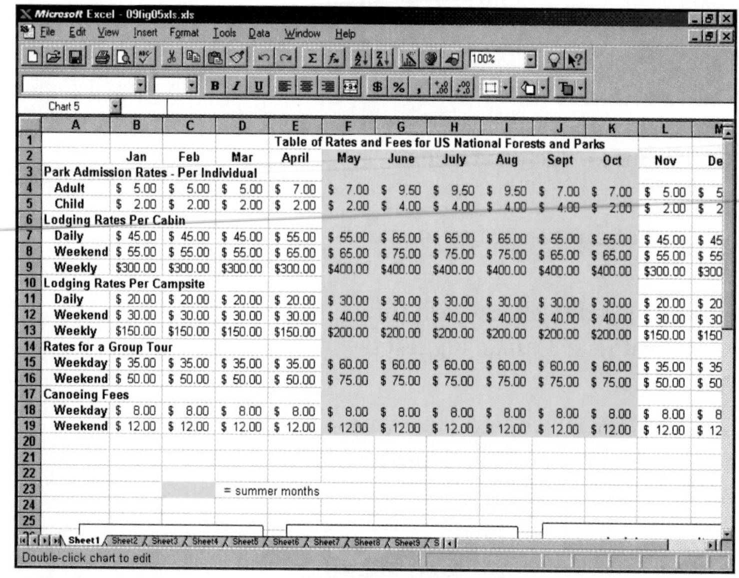

	A	B	C	D	E	F	G	H	I	J	K	L	M
1					Table of Rates and Fees for US National Forests and Parks								
2		Jan	Feb	Mar	April	May	June	July	Aug	Sept	Oct	Nov	De
3	Park Admission Rates - Per Individual												
4	Adult	$ 5.00	$ 5.00	$ 5.00	$ 7.00	$ 7.00	$ 9.50	$ 9.50	$ 9.50	$ 7.00	$ 7.00	$ 5.00	$ 5
5	Child	$ 2.00	$ 2.00	$ 2.00	$ 2.00	$ 2.00	$ 4.00	$ 4.00	$ 4.00	$ 4.00	$ 2.00	$ 2.00	$ 2
6	Lodging Rates Per Cabin												
7	Daily	$ 45.00	$ 45.00	$ 45.00	$ 55.00	$ 55.00	$ 65.00	$ 65.00	$ 65.00	$ 55.00	$ 55.00	$ 45.00	$ 45
8	Weekend	$ 55.00	$ 55.00	$ 55.00	$ 65.00	$ 65.00	$ 75.00	$ 75.00	$ 75.00	$ 65.00	$ 65.00	$ 55.00	$ 55
9	Weekly	$300.00	$300.00	$300.00	$300.00	$400.00	$400.00	$400.00	$400.00	$400.00	$400.00	$300.00	$300
10	Lodging Rates Per Campsite												
11	Daily	$ 20.00	$ 20.00	$ 20.00	$ 20.00	$ 30.00	$ 30.00	$ 30.00	$ 30.00	$ 30.00	$ 30.00	$ 20.00	$ 20
12	Weekend	$ 30.00	$ 30.00	$ 30.00	$ 30.00	$ 40.00	$ 40.00	$ 40.00	$ 40.00	$ 40.00	$ 40.00	$ 30.00	$ 30
13	Weekly	$150.00	$150.00	$150.00	$150.00	$200.00	$200.00	$200.00	$200.00	$200.00	$200.00	$150.00	$150
14	Rates for a Group Tour												
15	Weekday	$ 35.00	$ 35.00	$ 35.00	$ 35.00	$ 60.00	$ 60.00	$ 60.00	$ 60.00	$ 60.00	$ 60.00	$ 35.00	$ 35
16	Weekend	$ 50.00	$ 50.00	$ 50.00	$ 50.00	$ 75.00	$ 75.00	$ 75.00	$ 75.00	$ 75.00	$ 75.00	$ 50.00	$ 50
17	Canoeing Fees												
18	Weekday	$ 8.00	$ 8.00	$ 8.00	$ 8.00	$ 8.00	$ 8.00	$ 8.00	$ 8.00	$ 8.00	$ 8.00	$ 8.00	$ 8
19	Weekend	$ 12.00	$ 12.00	$ 12.00	$ 12.00	$ 12.00	$ 12.00	$ 12.00	$ 12.00	$ 12.00	$ 12.00	$ 12.00	$ 12
20													
21													
22													
23				= summer months									
24													
25													

Figure 9.5
The spreadsheet's scrolling window functions similarly to the word processor's scrolling window; however, the spreadsheet window's dimensions are often much greater.

Columns and Rows

Refer to figure 9.6 as you become familiar with the spreadsheet screen. The spreadsheet has borders that run horizontally across the top of the screen and vertically down the left margin. Within the borders is a grid composed of columns and rows. Columns run vertically, up and down, like the columns used for support in buildings. Rows run horizontally, left and right, like rows of bricks on a building. The horizontal border designates the columns with the letters of the alphabet: A, B, C, and so on. When the columns reach Z, they begin again with AA, AB, AC, and so on. The vertical border numbers the rows: 1, 2, 3, and so on.

Columns are commonly used to create time categories such as months or years. For example, in a spreadsheet for managing a school budget, the first column may be September and the last one may be June. Columns are designed with a uniform width, although you can widen or narrow them. People often widen the first column in order to enter words or phrases to identify the rows.

Rows are commonly used to designate sales regions, companies the firm does business with, or areas of expenditures such as manufacturing, marketing, shipping, and so on. In a personal budget, the rows may list such things as rent, clothing, entertainment, books, supplies, and so on.

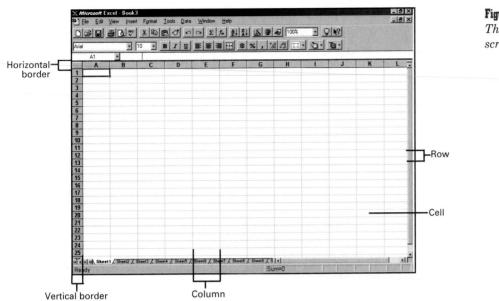

Figure 9.6
The opening spreadsheet screen of Microsoft Excel.

The Cell

On the ledger sheet, the point where a column and a row intersect forms a rectangle on the paper. In the spreadsheet, that rectangle is called a *cell*, indicating a place where you can type data or formulas. That data may be either words or numbers. Cells are where you do your spreadsheet work.

Cells are identified by their column-and-row position, called the **cell address**. For example, when you begin working with a new spreadsheet, the command line shows that the pointer is located in column A, row 1, so the cell address is A1.

The Cell Pointer

The **cell pointer** takes the place of the cursor found in other programs. The cell pointer highlights the cell in which it is located in order to indicate where data can be entered. You use the arrow keys or the mouse to move the pointer from cell to cell. You use other keys to move the pointer to specific locations, such as the home cell, A1, or cell B155.

When the cell pointer is positioned in a cell, its contents appear in the formula bar. If a cell contains a formula, the number is highlighted by the cell pointer, and the formula appears in the formula bar. Therefore, if the answer is incorrect, you can easily check the formula for accuracy.

The pointer and page-movement keys enable you to scroll from left to right and up and down, moving to different areas of the spreadsheet as you enter labels or values into the cells. In most cases, you fill the cells in the portion of the spreadsheet visible on the screen and then scroll to the right or downward to continue filling more cells. Pressing Ctrl+Home or Ctrl+End usually takes you, respectively, to the first or last cell containing data. As your spreadsheet grows larger than a single screen, you can use other commands that shift the spreadsheet an entire screen or jump to a particular cell, such as L22 or BB655.

A Spreadsheet Work Session

The best way to become familiar with the spreadsheet is to begin a work session and follow the five steps in the spreadsheet process to create a document. As you begin, refer to figure 9.7 to familiarize yourself with the spreadsheet screen.

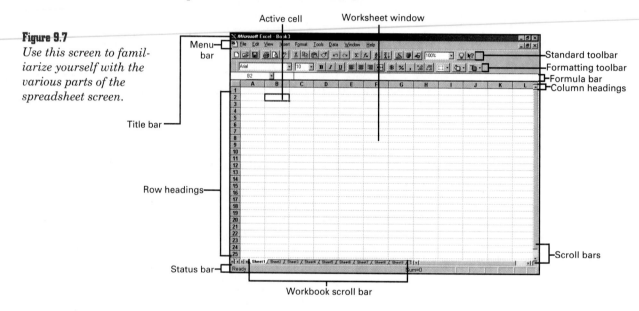

Figure 9.7
Use this screen to familiarize yourself with the various parts of the spreadsheet screen.

Note the following elements in figure 9.7:

- *Title bar*. Displays the program name and current file; *Book1* means that the current file is new and has not been saved with a unique file name

- *Menu bar*. Lists the available pull-down menus, which contain commands

- *Standard toolbar*. Displays buttons that execute commands used most frequently (most also appear in pull-down menus)

- *Formatting toolbar*. Displays information and buttons that pertain to text formatting options

- *Formula bar*. Displays the current location of the cell pointer and cell contents, if any

- *Worksheet (document window)*. The area in which you create the document

- *Column headings*. Column identification across the top of the work sheet

- *Row headings*. Row identification down the left margin of the work sheet

- *Scroll bars.* To the right and across the bottom of the document window, they enable you to move through text in the document

- *Workbook scroll bar.* Displays tabs for various worksheets; arrows at the left enable you to scroll through worksheets

- *Status bar.* Displays information about your current location in the text, such as identifying buttons when the pointer touches them, formula results, the status of the Num Lock key, and so on

Speaking of the Num Lock key, now is the time to toggle it on. Most of your spreadsheet work is entering numbers, and using the calculator-style numeric keypad makes this process quick and easy.

As in other GUI-based programs, the pointer changes its shape according to its assignments. In the work area, the spreadsheet pointer is a cross, or plus sign. When you move the pointer to a cell location and click the mouse button, that cell becomes the **active cell** (or current cell), where data can be entered. Within a cell, the pointer is an I-beam, indicating that you can enter data. When moved to a toolbar, or when moving cells, the pointer changes to an arrow, ready to issue a command. Note the location of the pointer and active cell in figure 9.8.

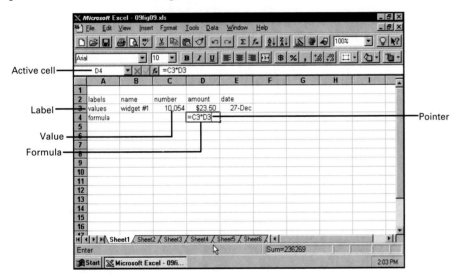

Figure 9.8
The elements you may find in cells.

Designing the Worksheet

What exactly do you put into the cells in a worksheet? You put words that describe various characteristics of the financial or numerical data (labels), the numbers themselves (values), and formulas that perform calculations on those numbers. Take a closer look at figure 9.8, and you can see that cells can contain labels or values and may also hold a formula.

Creating the Worksheet

After you have planned exactly what your worksheet will contain, you are ready to begin the actual on-screen creation process.

Learning the Commands

Commands issue instructions to the spreadsheet program to perform tasks or to alter the design of the spreadsheet itself. Most commands are issued by you, the knowledge worker. Here are some of the most commonly used commands:

- *Copy and Paste*. Copies the contents of a cell or group of cells into another cell or group of cells

- *Cut and Paste*. Moves the contents of a cell or group of cells into another cell or group of cells

- *Delete*. Removes a cell, column, or row; *undelete* reverses the deletion

- *Insert*. Adds a cell, row, or column

- *Find*, or *Search*. Locates words or numbers

- *Search and Replace*. Makes global changes to a word or phrase—such as replacing a budget item that is the same every month but has changed in value

- *Spelling Checker*. Checks spelling and other simple vocabulary or syntax errors

Using Autosum

After you have identified your rows and columns and have entered the data, you can insert formulas. These formulas are usually good old-fashioned algebraic notations that link cells by means of one of the four arithmetic operators. In some spreadsheets, or example, adding three cells is expressed as

=A1+A2+A3

This formula is inserted into another cell, such as A4, and when the Enter key is pressed, the sum is displayed in cell A4.

A spreadsheet is more than a calculator, however, and built-in functions (explained shortly) can take the tedium out of creating formulas. *Autosum*— the sigma Σ button in Excel—does this. Simply indicate the cells you want to total, move to a clear cell, and then click the Autosum button once to see the formula and again to perform the calculation.

Organizing and Revising

Don't mistake the spreadsheet for a calculator. Most of its powerful features are employed after the worksheet is created and you begin working with— *massaging*, as it's called—the data in the spreadsheet. One way you massage the spreadsheet data is with the Calculate feature.

Calculate

Calculate, or recalculation, runs new totals on your worksheet whenever you make a change. Recalculation is one of the spreadsheet's most powerful features, taking the place of an eraser and pencil to make corrections and updates. If you have to change a number for any reason, you don't have to enter the entire column of constants again, one at a time, as you do with a calculator. Instead, you simply enter the change, and Calculate totals the column for you.

In most spreadsheet programs, after the formulas are created, calculation occurs automatically without your having to issue a separate command. Every time you make a change, Calculate runs through all the constants and formulas, updating the results for you. That's fine if you are making only one change. However, if the spreadsheet is very large and you are making a number of changes in different areas, manual recalculation is more convenient. The spreadsheet doesn't have to perform unnecessary and time-consuming recalculations after every change; instead, you recalculate after all the changes are completed. Calculation significantly sets the spreadsheet apart from using paper, pencil, and calculator.

Financial Modeling and What-If Analysis

The spreadsheet makes possible speculation about numerical scenarios and the financial future. In the same way in which you can quickly recalculate a column of numbers when you make a mistake, you can test a variety of financial models. A **financial model** is a mathematical representation of a real-world financial or economic situation, used to test different hypotheses in order to find a solution.

Using the spreadsheet for financial modeling is called performing a what-if analysis. A **what-if analysis** involves substituting one number for another to see what difference the change will make. For example, *what if* a charitable organization has a 20 percent increase in donations next year? *What if* we build a new manufacturing facility with twice our current capacity? *What if* we decide to raise or lower the college tuition by 6 percent? *What if* we want to lengthen an auto loan from 36 months to 48 months to lower the monthly payment?

To do a what-if analysis, you replace certain numerical data and let the spreadsheet perform a recalculation. For example, say that your collegiate spending money comes from what you saved while working last summer. You create a budget in a worksheet and find that you can't cover all your expenses. You need to make more money, but you don't want to cut into your study time too much. Two work-study jobs on campus are hiring—one job pays a dollar more an hour than the other, but it requires a bigger commitment in hours. If you plug in the earnings from these two prospective jobs and create a financial model, you can then run a what-if analysis to help you make your decision.

The capability to perform what-if analyses and test various financial models is one of the most useful features of a spreadsheet. What-if analysis has become a widely used and powerful planning tool that is used every day in government, business, and other enterprises. Figure 9.9 shows an example of the what-if analysis just mentioned.

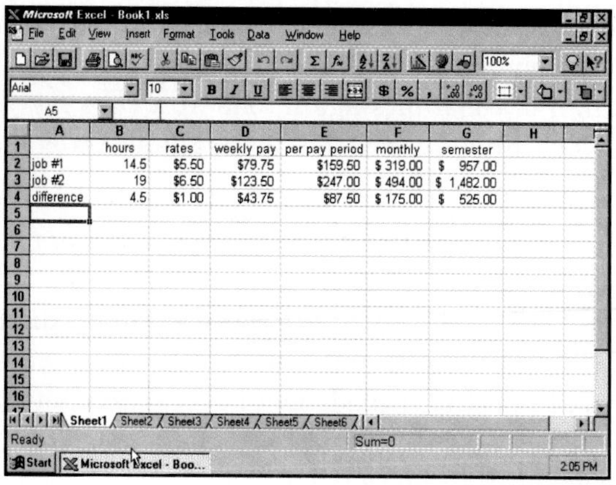

Figure 9.9
What-if analyses clearly show you the data so that you can make informed decisions.

An interesting event involving a computer model occurred in Boston in 1970. The World Dynamics Model was intended to help the mayor solve some of the problems confronting a large city, but the model's conclusions proved somewhat surprising. According to the results of the model, aiding the unemployed would actually draw more unemployed people to the city. This, in turn, would cause the planned social reforms to backfire. Free public transportation, for example, would result in overcrowded subways and would create more traffic from commuting workers. Building city-funded housing would take up space that businesses would have occupied, resulting in fewer jobs. Ultimately, the model was useful because it raised issues that city planners had not considered.

Functions

A **function** is a built-in procedure (or set of procedures) predefined and programmed into the spreadsheet. The function performs mathematical, financial, statistical, and other operations to produce a mathematical result or value. The **PMT** function, for example, tells you the periodic payments on a loan or an investment.

A function combines built-in formulas that perform special mathematical tasks with a minimum of keystrokes. Functions, like formulas, work with the data in the spreadsheet, whereas commands work with the spreadsheet itself. Formulas and functions act on values in a range of cells. A **range** is a defined or highlighted section of the spreadsheet, identified by its column and row designations, that contains the cells on which you want to perform some operation. The cells are identified by their column and row designations.

In some spreadsheet programs, the function is typed at the command line. A special character, such as the = sign or @ sign, is used to signify that what follows is a function. In other spreadsheet programs, a function menu is selected from a pull-down menu or a button, and categories of functions are displayed. You click the category you want, such as financial, date and time, or statistical, and then select the appropriate function from a list. Here are five commonly used functions:

- *=Average (@AVG)* finds the average of a set of constants.

- *=Count (@COUNT)* literally counts the contents of cells; for example, the number of cells with a dollar amount of $5 or more.

- *=Maximum (@MAX)* gets the largest number within a range of cells.
- *=Minimum (@MIN)* gets the smallest number within a range of cells.
- *=Sum (@SUM)* totals the contents of a range of cells.

SUM probably is used most frequently because it is the basic adding machine function. AVERAGE is another useful function because knowledge workers are often interested in averages—the average cost over time of a procured item, the average sales figures for all 12 territories, and so on.

Special Formatting

Worksheet data is often formatted using buttons on the Formatting toolbar. Worksheet titles or column headings may be centered, for example, while dollar amounts may be right-aligned within the cell. Indeed, a variety of number formats—currency, percentages, decimals, and so on—can be selected for entering and formatting.

In addition, note that special formatting is often applied to negative numbers, and shading and various line styles on a grid can make a spreadsheet easier to read. Figure 9.10 shows some of the special formatting possible in a spreadsheet.

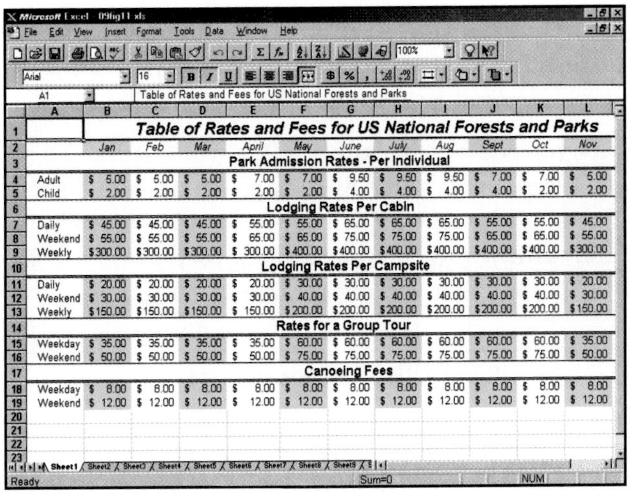

	Jan	Feb	Mar	April	May	June	July	Aug	Sept	Oct	Nov
Park Admission Rates - Per Individual											
Adult	$ 5.00	$ 5.00	$ 5.00	$ 7.00	$ 7.00	$ 9.50	$ 9.50	$ 9.50	$ 7.00	$ 7.00	$ 5.00
Child	$ 2.00	$ 2.00	$ 2.00	$ 2.00	$ 2.00	$ 4.00	$ 4.00	$ 4.00	$ 4.00	$ 2.00	$ 2.00
Lodging Rates Per Cabin											
Daily	$ 45.00	$ 45.00	$ 45.00	$ 55.00	$ 55.00	$ 65.00	$ 65.00	$ 65.00	$ 55.00	$ 55.00	$ 45.00
Weekend	$ 55.00	$ 55.00	$ 55.00	$ 65.00	$ 65.00	$ 75.00	$ 75.00	$ 75.00	$ 65.00	$ 65.00	$ 55.00
Weekly	$300.00	$300.00	$300.00	$ 300.00	$400.00	$400.00	$400.00	$400.00	$400.00	$400.00	$300.00
Lodging Rates Per Campsite											
Daily	$ 20.00	$ 20.00	$ 20.00	$ 20.00	$ 30.00	$ 30.00	$ 30.00	$ 30.00	$ 30.00	$ 30.00	$ 20.00
Weekend	$ 30.00	$ 30.00	$ 30.00	$ 30.00	$ 40.00	$ 40.00	$ 40.00	$ 40.00	$ 40.00	$ 40.00	$ 30.00
Weekly	$150.00	$150.00	$150.00	$ 150.00	$200.00	$200.00	$200.00	$200.00	$200.00	$200.00	$150.00
Rates for a Group Tour											
Weekday	$ 35.00	$ 35.00	$ 35.00	$ 35.00	$ 60.00	$ 60.00	$ 60.00	$ 60.00	$ 60.00	$ 60.00	$ 35.00
Weekend	$ 50.00	$ 50.00	$ 50.00	$ 50.00	$ 75.00	$ 75.00	$ 75.00	$ 75.00	$ 75.00	$ 75.00	$ 50.00
Canoeing Fees											
Weekday	$ 8.00	$ 8.00	$ 8.00	$ 8.00	$ 8.00	$ 8.00	$ 8.00	$ 8.00	$ 8.00	$ 8.00	$ 8.00
Weekend	$ 12.00	$ 12.00	$ 12.00	$ 12.00	$ 12.00	$ 12.00	$ 12.00	$ 12.00	$ 12.00	$ 12.00	$ 12.00

Figure 9.10
This spreadsheet uses boldface, centering, shading, and special rules to enhance its appearance and make it easier to read.

Saving

Saving is a repetitive but essential step in the spreadsheet process. You can never save often enough. Save your work in a file in the early stages of worksheet creation and frequently while you're organizing and revising it. You can save your file using any one of three methods: clicking the Save button, choosing Save from the File pull-down menu, and activating the Autosave feature.

The button on the toolbar is a way to save quickly: simply clicking the button saves the existing file. If you haven't yet named the file, you are prompted to do so. After that, you see a "saving file" message in the status bar.

The File pull-down menu offers several options for saving. The Save command prompts you to provide a file name; Save As enables you to give your file a name different from its current name, such as when you open a blank template file, turn it into a worksheet, and want to give it a new name; and in Microsoft Excel, you can use the Save Workspace command to save a group of related workbooks using a single file name.

If you choose to activate the spreadsheet's Autosave feature, you can choose how often (in minutes) you want your file to be saved automatically.

Printing

Printing a worksheet is a real WYSIWYG experience. The Print command options enable you to select exactly the kind of printout you want. The capability to use various fonts, headers, footers, and page orientations produce professional-looking documents. The Print selections usually offered include the following:

- *Page Setup* enables you to select page orientation, set margins, create headers and footers to label your worksheet, and specify (work)sheet characteristics, such as grid lines.

- *Print Area* enables you to highlight the area of the worksheet you want to print so that no blank cells are included.

- *Print Preview* displays the page just as it will look when it is printed.

- *Print* enables you to choose to print a selected area from a worksheet, specific (not all) worksheets, or an entire workbook. It also enables you to choose the individual pages you want to print.

Printing is a way to create a backup copy of your work for safekeeping. Whereas saving a file is storing on a disk, paper (hard copy) is a backup copy in case the file is lost or damaged. For that reason, it's a good idea always to print a copy of important work. If you lose the file, you'll still have a paper copy of the data, even though it will not display the formulas (see figure 9.11).

Figure 9.11
A handsomely printed worksheet.

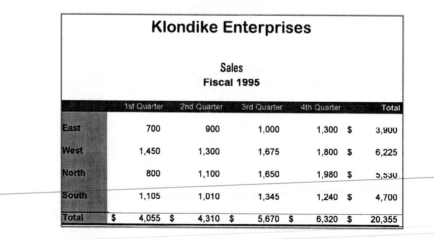

Klondike Enterprises					
Sales					
Fiscal 1995					
	1st Quarter	2nd Quarter	3rd Quarter	4th Quarter	Total
East	700	900	1,000	1,300 $	3,900
West	1,450	1,300	1,675	1,800 $	6,225
North	800	1,100	1,650	1,980 $	5,530
South	1,105	1,010	1,345	1,240 $	4,700
Total	$ 4,055 $	4,310 $	5,670 $	6,320 $	20,355

Advanced Spreadsheet Features

What-if analysis might be considered an advanced feature if it were not used so often, but every time you speculate—"plug in" some numbers, as the power users say—you're doing a what-if analysis. Although it's simple, it's also very sophisticated. Three other advanced spreadsheet features are templates, macros, and charts.

Templates

Often, you can use a spreadsheet design over and over. A **template** is a worksheet with labels, commands, and formulas already created and saved in a file so that you can begin entering data without doing all the other tedious, repetitive work. The template is like a blank form waiting to have data entered into its cells. You can create templates for what-if scenarios, a monthly or annual budget, for loan or credit card calculations, cumulative departmental expenditures on personal computer software, and so forth.

Templates are available for everything from accounting to tax preparation to home budgets. Many people create their own templates, but your spreadsheet program probably comes with some, and you can also buy ready-made templates as disk files. Sometimes the templates are on a disk packaged with a book or printed in a magazine. You simply load the template as you load any other file and then fill in the cells. All the calculations are performed automatically because the formulas have already been entered.

Macros

A **macro** is a series of commands or formulas that you create and store in the spreadsheet so that you can use them again and again. Macros help you program your spreadsheet in many different ways so that you can use it more productively. They are also timesaving devices that save keystrokes on tasks you frequently perform in your spreadsheet work.

For example, you could create a macro that keeps a running total of the interest you have paid, or the point at which you begin paying on the principal, or many other calculations that change over time. Macros are recorded and identified with their own unique name. Every time you want to use the macro, you simply type its unique name and it is played back into a current cell.

Spreadsheet Charts

Spreadsheet charts are graphs: pictorial representations of the numeric data produced by the spreadsheet. Most spreadsheet programs can turn numeric data into business presentation charts, or graphs. These pictorial representations are most commonly in the form of a bar chart, a line chart, or a pie chart. Each has its own unique usefulness:

- *Bar charts* are used for comparing values to each other.

- *Line charts* are used for comparing values over time.

- *Pie charts* are used for differentiating one value relative to that of the entire quantity.

These three types of charts and other variations are shown in figure 9.12.

Figure 9.12

Many types of charts are available to represent spreadsheet data.

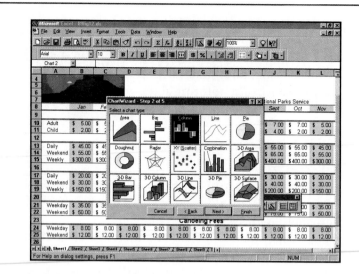

Ending a Work Session

When you finish a work session, here are the last two things you should do:

1. Name your file and save your work.
2. Exit the program.

Working in the GUI environment makes these steps easy and nearly fool-proof. If you attempt to exit or close the program without saving a changed file, you see a message asking you whether you want to save the file or exit without saving (see figure 9.13). Now you have a choice, and you won't lose your work because of oversight.

Figure 9.13

The spreadsheet program prompts you to save your work before exiting.

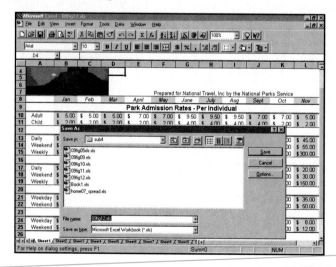

HOME PAGE

SPREADSHEET TIPS

1. Plan your worksheet on paper before you begin working with the program on the computer. Think through the problem you want to solve; draw a rough sketch of the data on a sheet of blank paper or a ledger sheet. Jot down the mathematical equations you'll need to get answers. This planning saves you time, and you'll make fewer mistakes.

2. Learn to use the spreadsheet's powerful Paste feature. You'll find it useful in creating a number of data entry shortcuts, and your data and formulas will be more accurate.

3. If your completed worksheet doesn't work, you'll have to edit and retest it. Copy the worksheet to another sheet, or save it with a different file name; then make corrections to the copy and test it. If the copy works, fine; if not, repeat the process.

4. When you build a spreadsheet model, even a simple one, you have created a template. Save it with the formulas but without any data; then you can use it over and over again.

5. Take advantage of the auditing function, if your spreadsheet has one. It is used to error-check your spreadsheet formulas.

6. Use the spreadsheet's built-in function features instead of typing complicated formulas. Functions are quicker and more accurate.

7. Enter a label in the cell above or to the left of the values you enter, to identify what the value represents.

8. If you see a cell filled with ######## characters, the column probably isn't wide enough to accommodate the data.

9. Learn to use macros, which are a way to record, save, and reuse frequently used commands, equations, labels, and such. A macro lets you fill a cell with data by pressing a key or two rather than performing dozens or hundreds of keystrokes. In addition, macros are a convenient way to customize your keyboard.

10. Save your work often. If you're building a complex spreadsheet, saving each iteration as a separate sheet makes corrections much easier.

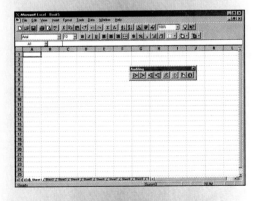

In Microsoft Excel, you open the View pull-down menu and choose Toolbars to select different toolbars, such as Auditing.

Knowledge Check

1. In the spreadsheet grid, what do the vertical lines form?
2. In the spreadsheet grid, what do the horizontal lines form?
3. What is the rectangle formed at the intersection of a column and a row called?
4. What built-in, automatic, feature makes it possible to change figures and perform what-if analyses?
5. What is the term used to refer to text? To numbers?
6. Where do you see commands and instructions for the current cell?
7. What advanced feature creates special files that store commands and keystrokes for reuse?
8. What are pictorial representations of spreadsheet data called?

Key Terms

active cell	calculate	cell address	cell pointer
constant	financial model	function	macro
range	template	what-if analysis	

ISSUES AND IDEAS

Let Your Spreadsheet Do the Talking

One of the most tedious aspects of entering row after row and column upon column of data into a spreadsheet is verifying accuracy. It's not uncommon to see two knowledge workers, heads close together as one stares at the screen and the other reads the data out loud from a sheet of paper in order to make sure that the data is entered correctly.

"Having the latest, most powerful spreadsheet with all manner of sophisticated features is still not going to give you the right answers unless you get the basics right—and that means making sure the right numbers are entered in the first place," says Colin Messit of Oakley Data Services, located in Cheshire, England. "Repeatedly looking up and down between the screen and the input document on your desk is one way of checking, but that's still prone to error and makes your neck ache. Another more accurate alternative is to get a colleague to read the figures for you, but with our SmartChecker software, you have a built-in colleague who won't be out to lunch at the critical time."

SmartChecker is a utility add-in program that audibly reads back rows and columns of figures through the computer speakers. SmartChecker will work with the computer's built-in speaker, although the sound quality is better if there is a sound board with external speakers.

If you'd like to try a copy before you buy, an evaluation copy of SmartChecker is available from the World Wide Web at

http://www.smartcode.com

Once you're convinced, SmartChecker costs a mere $19.95 from Insight Software Solutions of Bountiful, Utah.

CRITICAL THINKING

1. SmartChecker is a utility program that replaces tedious work or the labors of a second person. Does it represent a good use of technology?

2. Discuss the possibilities of finding a niche and a need for a program such as SmartChecker.

3. What does SmartChecker suggest as an emerging voice output technology?

Forensic Accountants

Some accountants now specialize in finding fraudulent bookkeeping in business ledgers. Most businesses employ an accounting firm to audit their books, but it often takes a third party to take a closer look when trouble is suspected or when a business is going bankrupt. Whereas a regular accountant takes samples of inventory, receivables, payables, and so on, a forensic accountant goes back through the books, verifying every piece of paper and number by entering it into a spreadsheet cell.

John Murphy & Associates was hired for the forensic accounting on ZZZZ Best, the carpet cleaning firm started by the now-infamous teenaged Barry Minklow. The Murphy accountants entered reams of ZZZZ Best data into spreadsheets in order to analyze the flow of money into and out of the company. By analyzing the timing of deposits and withdrawals, the accountants were able to determine that there were very few real sales. Instead, the money was going around and around, into and out of different accounts, to make it appear as though there had been a lot of business activity. Murphy says, "I felt what we had was a monstrous check kite. It was a cash race track."

CRITICAL THINKING

1. How would you define forensic accounting?

2. How were the numbers made to lie at ZZZZ Best?

3. See whether you can design the basic worksheet screen Murphy used to find the fatal flaw at ZZZZ Best.

ETHICS

Making Numbers Lie

An old saying in business is "Numbers don't lie." But spreadsheet users must be careful about trusting the numbers they see because the numbers are only as accurate as the person who entered them. It's possible to make errors in formulas or to slip a decimal place or to forget to recalculate when you change something. People have made errors with pencil and paper, adding machines, and electronic calculators for years. Now they make errors with spreadsheet models, too. A faulty model with incorrect formulas will produce errors in the spreadsheet.

It's possible to make a spreadsheet lie, in the same way any numbers can be made to lie. A product manager can simply pluck sales projections out of the air, plug them into the spreadsheet, and project success. Inaccurate data produces inaccurate results: garbage in, garbage out.

Using a spreadsheet program ethically means entering the correct data to arrive at a correct conclusion—and accepting the results. Because you can create what-if scenarios with the spreadsheet, you can just as easily feed in falsified or unrealistic numbers until the desired results are produced as you can insert the correct numbers and accept the results. Deliberately falsifying data is not a good use of the computer, and it doesn't make sense morally, ethically, or practically—from a business perspective.

Humans have difficulty owning up to their mistakes, and we often hear people blaming the computer for errors. In fact, some companies have brought lawsuits against software companies, alleging that a program made a mistake that cost them money. Lacking merit, none has been brought to trial. The problem, as might be expected, is garbage in, garbage out. The spreadsheet has to be used accurately and sensibly. If that's done, using it ethically should follow.

Decision Making and Ethical Values is a course at the Harvard Business School (where the spreadsheet was invented). MBA students take this course to explore the role of conscience and morals in business. To paraphrase one Harvard professor, turning out an excellent manager is one thing, but turning out excellent people is another. John S. R. Shad, who was formerly head of the Securities and Exchange Commission (SEC), has donated $23 million to Harvard for its ethics program. He says, "I think it is a valid question to ask: Is it too late to try to teach ethics to people in their 20s? No school, no matter how good, is going to rehabilitate criminals. But what this ethics course can do is sensitize students to conflicts of interest in business decisions they may never have considered. And I can see the program coming up with research that will demonstrate that the marketplace rewards good conduct. You can do well by being ethical. You don't have to play the edges."

Critical Thinking

1. Is there any difference between altering spreadsheet numbers to induce a favorable outcome and plagiarism in word processing?

2. Discuss why it's hard for "people to own up to their mistakes."

3. Discuss the aspects of ethics that could be taught and those that might be difficult to teach.

THE LEARNING ENTERPRISE

Evaluate the processes and computer system requirements you created in Chapter 5. Determine how much you will need to use the spreadsheet program and for what type of tasks. Your assignment is as follows:

1. Describe the kinds of worksheets you'll need to create and share with other knowledge workers.

2. Will you be turning data into graphics? Which kind?

3. Describe any templates that would be helpful in your spreadsheet work and would aid your productivity.

4. Explain what advanced features would be useful and how you would apply them.

5. Discuss the ethical aspects of working with a spreadsheet, such as falsifying numbers. How can a worksheet be checked for accuracy? Should there be a formal review of all important worksheets? What penalties should be imposed for falsifying data?

Chapter Review

Fill in the Blank

1. Business financial transactions used to be recorded in a book called a(n) _____.

2. A(n) _____ is a specific model of a specific financial situation.

3. The intersection of a column and a row is called a(n) _____.

4. A number entered into a cell is called a(n) _____.

5. A(n) _____ is a defined or highlighted section of cells in a spreadsheet.

6. Cells are identified by their column and row position, called the _____.

7. The _____ takes the place of the cursor found in other programs.

8. The cell where you enter data is called the _____ cell.

9. A series of commands or formulas that you create and store in the spreadsheet is called a(n) _____.

10. In a spreadsheet, a(n) _____ is a worksheet with labels, commands, and formulas already created and saved.

Circle the Correct Answer

1. A (column, row) is a vertical set of cells in a spreadsheet.

2. A (column, row) is a horizontal set of cells in a spreadsheet.

3. A (formula, function) is a sequence of steps that combines the values or numbers in specified cells with mathematical operators or functions to produce a new value.

4. A (formula, function) is a predetermined, stored mathematical procedure that produces a new value.

5. A (template, macro) is a series of commands or formulas that you create and store to use over again.

Review Questions

1. List the five steps involved in working with spreadsheets.

2. How do you know when a value and a formula are both occupying a single cell?

3. Give an example of a what-if analysis.

4. What is a label?

5. What is a value?

6. What is a function? How does it differ from a formula?

7. If a cell is filled with ##### characters, what does it mean?

8. What kind of comparison are bar charts useful for?

9. What are line charts suitable for comparing?

10. For what are pie charts mainly used?

Discussion Questions

1. Create a spreadsheet for your income and expenses for the next four weeks. Create a macro so that you can use your spreadsheet again. After that time, revise your template to make your spreadsheet more useful.

2. Discuss the difference between templates and macros, and tell how you would use each. Come up with a list of five uses for each.

3. Do you think that spreadsheets are useful for you personally? In what ways can they help you stay within a plan for tracking and managing your income and expenditures?

Learn more about how some companies use spreadsheets.

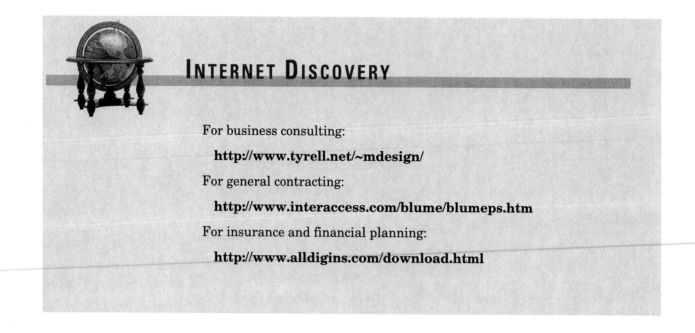

INTERNET DISCOVERY

For business consulting:

http://www.tyrell.net/~mdesign/

For general contracting:

http://www.interaccess.com/blume/blumeps.htm

For insurance and financial planning:

http://www.alldigins.com/download.html

DATABASE MANAGEMENT SYSTEMS

10

CHAPTER

It is extremely important that the development of intelligent machines be pursued. . . We must find a way of organizing ourselves more effectively, of bringing together the energies of larger groups of people toward a common goal. Intelligent systems, built from computer and communications technology, will someday know more than any individual human about what is going on in complex enterprises involving millions of people, such as a multinational corporation or a city."[1]

Avron Barr, computer futurist

Many people collect things. How about you? If you collect anything, you probably are familiar with some of the problems of managing a collection. One way to keep track of a collection is to create a **database**, a group of related records and files.

Libraries use databases to manage their collections. Before and during most of this century, libraries used card catalogs—cards with typed book information, stored in drawers in special file cabinets. Card catalogs hold three kinds of cards for each book in the library. The title index has one card for every book in the library, filed alphabetically by book title. The author index has one card for every book, filed alphabetically by author name. The subject index has a card for each book, arranged in alphabetical order by topic. When a book falls into several subject categories, it has several subject cards.

The card catalog is an excellent manual database, but it has several limitations. Using it is slow; you often have to look through many cards to find the one you want. It is a single-user system; if someone else is using the drawer for the subject you're exploring, you have to wait. And the card catalog is limited in scope. For example, if you want to find all the books that Isaac Asimov has written about Mars, you have to search either all the Mars subject cards or all the Asimov author cards, carefully reading each one. Some searches require looking through several dozen (even several hundred) cards. Turning the libraries' card catalogs into computerized databases for use with a database management system made searches easier and simpler.

---

1. Reingold. *Tools for Thought* (New York: Prentice Hall Press, 1985), 274.

Module A

The Database Management System Process

Why It's Important to Know

A DBMS works with data in a logical and orderly manner. The DBMS is much more efficient than paper and filing cabinets. It enables us to work with large or diverse quantities of data and to more easily turn that data into useful information.

A database is a group of related records and files. A database management system (DBMS) is an application with which you store, organize, and retrieve data from a single database or from several databases. A DBMS helps you manage data better by

- Providing a logical, orderly way to organize data

- Allowing great versatility in selecting the data you want by modifying, searching, sorting, and organizing it in various ways

- Providing many ways to format and print the data in reports

The DBMS can work with both letter characters (usually words) and numbers and can compare and organize the characters and numbers in ways unlike either word processing or spreadsheet software. This process is called data representation.

Data Representation

An **entity** is something about which you collect data. In the library, an entity is a book; in business, it might be the customer. In a not-for-profit organization, such as a public radio station, the entity may be a subscriber. **Data representation** is an organized method for storing data about an entity in a database. For example, a database of customer files may be organized by name, address, phone number, and last order placed. Or the database may be organized by credit card number, phone number, ZIP code, address, and name. All data may be in one file, or it may be in a number of files, depending on the way the database was designed and the data subsequently represented.

Office filing systems use data elements similar to the library card catalog system. Both represent—organize—data in the most logical and easily understood manner possible. For example, in a manual filing system

- Individual sheets of paper, like data items, are stored in folders.

- Folders are collected in file drawers.

- Drawers are components of file cabinets.

These effective manual data management systems were used for many years, but most are now being replaced by the computer DBMS. Figure 10.1 shows some examples of entities and the data representation of each.

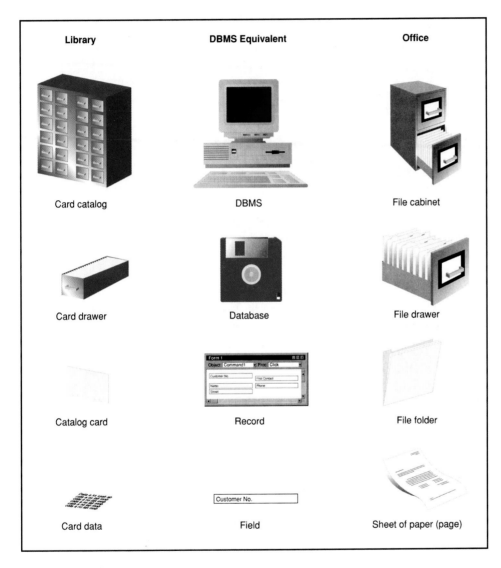

Library	DBMS Equivalent	Office
Card catalog	DBMS	File cabinet
Card drawer	Database	File drawer
Catalog card	Record	File folder
Card data	Field	Sheet of paper (page)

Figure 10.1
Representing data: Computers make it easier.

How does the DBMS represent data? DBMS data is stored in fields, records, files, and databases. As you study each, refer to figure 10.2.

A **field** represents one **attribute**, or characteristic, of the entity. One field is often identified as the **primary key**, or *key field*; this field uniquely identifies the entity. A key field might be a customer's name, account number, or perhaps his or her Social Security number. Other fields might store the customer's address, phone number, and last order. In DBMS terminology, each item is an attribute of the customer—something unique about him or her. In figure 10.2, fields are shown in the vertical columns.

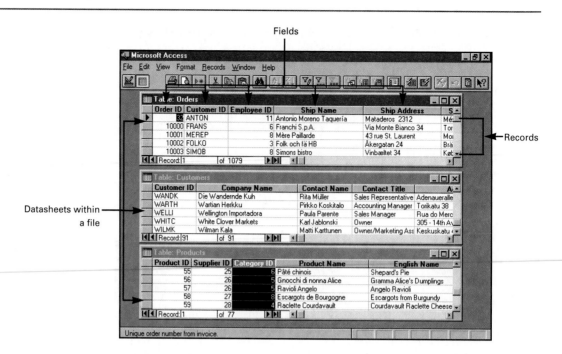

Figure 10.2

A Microsoft Access screen. Identify the various screen components described in the text.

Each field is a data item that is part of a larger whole called a record. A DBMS **record** is a collection of related fields that a DBMS treats as a single entity—in other words, a record contains all the pertinent information about an entity. For example, a record holds all the customer information that is needed to process an order. In figure 10.2, each record is displayed as a horizontal row on the screen. In Microsoft Access, the screen form is called a *datasheet* and is used to collect and organize data into records.

Within the DBMS, a *file* is a collection of related records that serves as a unit of storage—the computer's basic unit of storage. The file may hold all the company's customer records. It may also hold employee records, broken down by divisions. DBMS files are organized however people want. Customers may be grouped into files alphabetically by state, by sales territory, and in many other logical orders. In figure 10.2, the file is called a *table*. The table may contain a number of related datasheets, which, of course, are composed of records.

The simplest database is a single file; however, DBMSs really shine when they work with many files, or tables, linked together as a database. For example, say that an automaker must recall one model of pickup trucks made between 1992 and 1996 to replace a part. The databases holding the customer records for the past five years can be scanned to find only those customers who bought this vehicle so that they can be sent a recall notice. A database is a common pool of data—a single, common storage entity used by the DBMS. A DBMS can work with data from multiple databases, each of which may have dozens, even thousands, of files or tables.

HOME PAGE

MAPPING THE WORLD IN A DATABASE

An important use for database technology has to do with maps. One application is a mapping and guidance system in your car that helps you find your way in unfamiliar cities or towns. The *geographic information system*, or GIS, has been maturing for a decade or more. The GIS combines a database of images with a database of facts. The images are graphics-generated maps, and the data is the names of streets, roads, and highways. Urban planners and government agencies use the GIS, as does the U.S. Bureau of the Census.

Geographic Data Technology of Lebanon, New Hampshire, is the world's leading computer mapping company. As Kathryn Niemela, correspondent for the *Valley News* writes:

> GDT uses . . . computers to create maps—digital maps that are valuable to companies in several ways. For instance, an appliance store manager can use a computer-based map to print out a customized delivery route for truck drivers. Telemarketers at Kmart can tap a caller's address into a computer to instantly find the closest store.

> Those maps can also serve as the base for some interesting research. Geographic references gathered from a corporate data base (customer addresses, for example) can be combined with Census Bureau statistics and other public sources and printed on a GDT base map to yield insights on where to target direct-mail campaigns or open new bank branches.

"There is nothing like it anywhere in the world. The computer map we've got in this building is the most up-to-date in the United States," [GDT founder and president Donald F.] Cooke said.

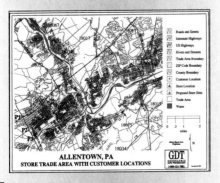

A GDT map.

. . . Cooke says he started the business 15 years ago with a vision of the future—he saw a market for a nationwide street map in digital form. And he was right. Thirteen years prior to starting his business, Cooke had worked for the Census Bureau, researching the bureau's nationwide maps, and he remembers thinking, "Now is the time for a company to come along and sort of take custody of these."

. . . Cooke says initially his idea was a good one but was about 10 years ahead of its time because there really wasn't a market at the time.

. . . Some of the current applications for GDT data surprise him. The Mormon Church in Salt Lake City, Utah, uses GDT technology to locate parishes across the country for families who are moving.

. . . Insurance companies are using GDT maps to figure out how far it is for individual policyholders to drive to work. Roughly 25 percent underreport the drive time to work, and it's the other 75 percent who have been subsidizing them, Cooke said.

. . . Mapping the country is an ongoing process for GDT. As new subdivisions are built, new streets are created and maps need to be adjusted. Inputting the whole United States—interstates, highways, major local roads, railroad systems, rivers, and many more items—is a tremendous task. GDT is working from Census Bureau maps and in some cases the maps are not accurate.

. . . Cooke says Chile is next and . . . Mapping Singapore is also a possible new project—but the challenges are great there as well.[2]

HOME PAGE REVIEW QUESTIONS

1. What is a GIS?

2. What technologies does a GIS combine?

3. Cite some reasons why mapping is a good use for a GIS.

4. What are some of the applications for a map based GIS?

2. Kathryn Niemela. "Mapping a New Direction," *Valley News*, October 1, 1995, E-1, E-5.

The Database Process

The best way to understand the process of creating a database with a DBMS is by studying the DBMS Process Chart in figure 10.3. The process consists of five steps: designing the database (planning it); creating the database (building it); the all-important step of saving your work to disk; querying the database (actually using it); and printing (gathering specific data to analyze in a report). And, as you have already learned, the thinking and planning stage that precedes actual computer work is essential to creating a useful database.

Figure 10.3
The DBMS Process Chart.

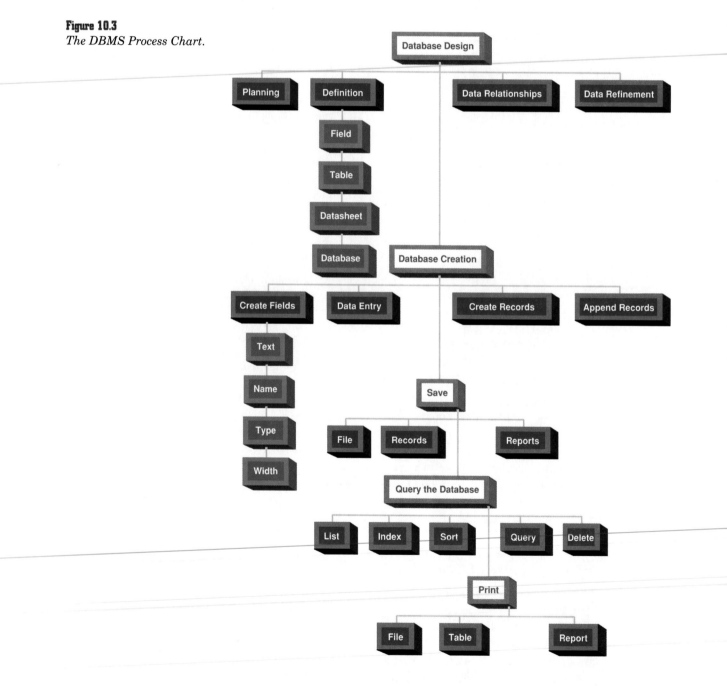

Designing the Database

In *database design*, you use paper and pencil to determine the nature and purpose of a database and to plan its design. An example is shown in figure 10.4. The planner needs to consider the following questions:

- What is the scope of the database? It could be company-wide or intended for a department or product line or perhaps for individual use.

- What kind of data will be collected—from the smallest to the largest?

- What are the relationships among the various types of data? For example, will people be grouped according to geographic area, sex, job description, or salary range?

As you consider each of these questions and transfer the objectives to a diagram on paper, your mental picture of the database design grows clearer.

Figure 10.4
Database design is a pencil-and-paper process.

```
DATABASE: DEPARTMENTAL PCS
FILE: BY WORK GROUP
RECORD: BY PC
FIELD:                  (CHARACTERS)
    BRAND:              (10)
    MODEL:              (5)
    SERIAL #:           (7)
    CPU:                (3)
    RAM:                (1)
    DOS VERSION:        (10)
    APPLICATION #1:     (10)
    APPLICATION #2:     (10)
    APPLICATION #3:     (10)
    KNOWLEDGE WORKER:   (15)
    REMARKS:            (35)
```

The two steps in database design are data definition and data refinement. Once the database is built with the DBMS software, going back and changing it is often difficult; a little planning goes a long way.

Data Definition

Because you're learning about computers, suppose that you are going to create an inventory database to catalog the hardware and software components in a personal computer system. The first thing you need to know is what you're going to inventory. This first step, **data definition**, consists of creating a detailed description of the data. There are many kinds of characteristics you could collect about the system: the computer's brand name and type, name and type of monitor, name and type of printer, and names and types of software applications. You could also collect data such as year purchased, serial number, software version, price paid, and so forth—the list goes on and on. In database terms, each characteristic is an attribute, all of which together make up an entity—the computer system. The entity is stored in the DBMS as a record, which might be the name of the knowledge worker who uses the system.

What do you *need* to know? What are the most important facts you want to store about the office computer systems? If every fact is collected in the database, it might be too large or impractical to use. One way to determine what you need to know is to think about how you'll use the database. Is its purpose to manage ownership and security matters? Is it to ensure compatibility among knowledge workers' computers? Is it for accounting, to amortize expenditures? It's very important to make these determinations during the planning process, for they affect how the data is defined and organized.

Data Refinement

Determining the interaction or relationships among various data elements is called **data refinement**. This part is the condensing and ordering phase in database design. Refinement means that some ideas change while decisions about what stays in or what is left out are made. You don't want your database cluttered with data you'll rarely use, so decide which attributes are least important and take them off the list.

Data refinement also means being economical about the design. DBMSs usually assign all the characters in a field, even when some are just blank spaces. A good example is state names. You don't need to type *Massachusetts* when all the postal service needs is two characters—MA; you can save 11 characters. Although field size can be adjusted, shortening, condensing, or abbreviating a name or title is often a good idea. Some databases will shrink fields to fit later on in the creation process, automatically decreasing wasted space.

Creating the Database

Database creation is transferring the design from ideas and diagrams to the software. Here you load the DBMS software, open a database file, and begin *creating fields* and their characteristics, according to the design.

Remember how you chose attributes for entities in database design? Now each entity, or computer system, will become a record, and each attribute of that entity will become a field.

Fields must be the correct type and size. There are four possible characteristics for each field: name, type, width (in characters), or number of decimal places (for numeric data such as money). Here are some guidelines:

- *Name*. Any characters, including text, numbers, or symbols, may be used.

- *Type*. This choice defines what kind of data will be entered into this field—characters, numbers, currency, or a date.

- *Width* . A field has a definite limit on the number of characters it can hold, usually 255. As mentioned earlier, some DBMSs use a technique that gets rid of unused space.

- *Decimal.* This choice tells the database how many decimal places to assign to numeric data, such as dollars and cents.

With the fields created, the biggest job of all—the task of *entering data*—begins. When all the fields on the screen are filled in, a *record* is created. A database may have any number of records. *Appending records* is the process of creating new records to accompany those already created. For example, adding a new customer means appending a record.

Saving the Database

As with any application, it's very important that you save your work regularly. Working with a DBMS means several different kinds of saving:

- Save and assign a file name to the *file*, or table, as soon as it's designed.

- Save your *records* as you create (append) them; some people—and some programs—save after every new record is finished. (This save is the same as saving the file.)

- Save the database queries you create.

- Save the *report* you have created to organize and display the information from the database. (Reports are explained in the section on printing.)

As in other applications, a good rule of thumb is to save all your work every ten minutes. If your DBMS has an autosave feature, make sure that it is operating and set for ten-minute increments—or less.

Querying the Database

After you have completed the data entry and saved the file, you can actually *use* the database. This action is called a **query**, or *querying the database*, because you retrieve and examine selected data. This is where the DBMS differs from other applications. You can see the results of your work and the computer's processing immediately in word processing or spreadsheet operations; you don't see the result of the DBMS's work until you complete the creation process and begin the query process.

You make your queries by using **logical operators**, which are symbols that specify the different relationships between items in a database. For example, an equal sign (=) logical operator finds everything that is the same as the specified item—such as every customer who purchased a yellow mountain bike. The greater than symbol (>) identifies items greater in value than the specified item, for example, every contribution to the public radio station of more than $35. Other logical operators include the symbols < (less than), and <= (less than or equal to) as well as the words And, Or, Not, Between, and Like.

The data you retrieve with a query can be subsequently narrowed down, or selected—in some cases referred to as *filtering*—in a variety of ways. Here are the most common commands:

- **L̲i̲s̲t̲** (or View) retrieves all the records in the file or database. It's the standard table view when you enter data. List can display your data in other ways, such as selected fields in different groupings. But a list is just a list; other querying tools are more powerful.

- **I̲n̲d̲e̲x̲** retrieves data quickly. Ordinarily, a DBMS indexes on the primary key, or field, that you select. The index helps you search more quickly, whether you are looking for customer records stored by invoice number or records stored by customer name. A list of record numbers is sequential and not normally changed, although you can organize an index any way you want. You can find data much more quickly after it has been indexed and, if two databases have been combined, indexing becomes even more useful.

- **S̲o̲r̲t̲** arranges data in alphabetical or numerical order; this command is useful for ordering information. The fields Sort uses are called **s̲o̲r̲t̲ k̲e̲y̲s̲**; the first is the primary key, and you may specify others. Sort arranges records in either ascending or descending order. You can also sort across fields, whereas you can index only within a single field. Figure 10.5 shows the same data listed, indexed, and sorted.

- *Search*, or Find, is a powerful tool borrowed from word processing and used in the same way. You can search for any unique character string—a word, a number, whatever—in a field or record. You can also search and replace, a feature helpful for updates and misspellings.

- *Delete* is used to remove a record from the database.

Printing

Database management systems provide for printing data in a variety of formats, including the following:

- Printing the raw data as entered into the record or table—just as the data appears on-screen. This printout is handy for keeping a hard copy of the data.

- Printing selected records from the record or table.

- Printing reports that present the data in useful, customized informative formats.

This last feature is often called a **report writer**. Basic features built into most DBMS report writers combine the capability to select data you want to display with the formatting capabilities of word processing, the number processing of spreadsheets, and the capability to display the data graphically. Such a report is shown in figure 10.6.

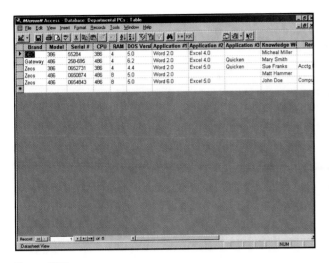

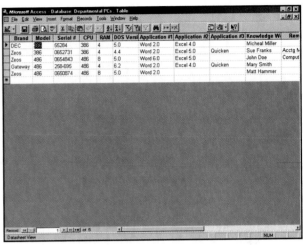

Figure 10.5
Note the difference in the same data as it is listed, indexed, and sorted.

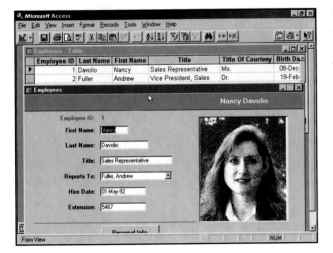

Figure 10.6
Handsomely printed reports can be used for presentations.

Knowledge Check

1. What are the five steps in the DBMS process?
2. Name the two types of data elements in a DBMS.
3. What is the relationship of an entity to an attribute?
4. What is the relationship of a field to a record?
5. What do we call actually working with the database data?
6. Explain the difference between a DBMS file and a DOS file.
7. What can be used to format a printout?

Key Terms

attribute	data definition	data refinement	data representation
database	entity	field	index
list	logical operator	primary key	query
record	report writer	sort	sort key

Issues and Ideas

Databases, Privacy, and You

Privacy is a growing concern in most technologically advanced countries, especially in the United States. A number of laws have been enacted to help ensure the individual's right to privacy; among them are the following:

- *Fair Credit Reporting Act (1970).* Forbids giving credit information to anyone other than "authorized customers"; however, this restriction means that anyone who has a "legitimate business need" can gain access.

- *Privacy Act (1974).* Bars federal agencies from using information for a purpose other than that for which it was obtained—but exceptions in the law let them do it anyway.

- *Right to Financial Privacy Act (1978)*. Restricts the government's access to citizen's bank records but does not apply to state and local governments, the FBI, or U.S. attorneys.

- *Video Privacy Protection Act (1988)*. Retailers cannot disclose (or sell) video-rental records; privacy advocates want the same rules to apply to medical and insurance files.

- *Computer Matching and Privacy Protection Act (1988)*. Regulations restrict searching various federal computer systems to compare data on an individual when verifying eligibility for federal benefits or programs or for verifying delinquent debts, but there are many holes and gaps.

Yet laws are not enough; an informed citizenry is the best deterrent, and unceasing vigilance is the price of freedom. That is why knowledge workers and citizens in the Information Age must accept personal responsibility for being computer literate.

You can keep informed about privacy issues by subscribing to several forums on the Internet once you have obtained an account (either in the class you're now taking or privately). These forums have a moderator who is like an editor or talk-show host, but he or she is highly participative. Like newspapers or magazines, the forums are meant to be read. Submissions from readers are not only welcome but necessary to sustain these forums. Here are two of the most popular forums on the Internet that you can subscribe to without charge:

- *The Privacy Forum Digest* is a selectively moderated digest that spans the full range of both technological and nontechnological privacy-related issues (with an emphasis on the former). For information regarding the Privacy Forum, please send e-mail to privacy-request@vortex.com containing this exact line as the body of a message:

      information privacy

  You will receive an automated response. To submit contributions, send to privacy@vortex.com.

- *The Computer Privacy Digest* is a more casually moderated forum for discussions about technology's impact on privacy. The moderator suggests that, all too often, technology is way ahead of the law and society as it presents new devices and applications and also suggests that technology can both enhance and detract from privacy. To subscribe, send an e-mail request to comp-privacy-request@uwm.edu.

  Send submissions to the e-mail address comp-privacy@uwm.edu.

CRITICAL THINKING

1. Some people are more concerned about privacy than others. For example, one person may not care if others have his or her Social Security number, but another may consider access to that information an invasion of privacy. What does privacy mean to you?

2. Research what rights the U.S. Government has to information about you and what rights you have to not disclose information to the government.

3. Find out what rights the credit reporting agencies and merchants you do business with have to your personal information and what rights you have to obtain the information about yourself that they have.

Module B

DBMS Tools and Advanced Features

Why It's Important to Know

> **A database management system is capable of organizing, sorting, and sifting data according to your needs. Many of its features and capabilities are due to its capability to organize data *relationally*. The data can be combined with information from other documents, represented graphically, or can be printed in customized reports.**

A **relational database management system**, or **RDBMS**, is a DBMS where the data is organized in different tables so that it can be easily stored and retrieved. Data from the different tables can be related to other data, as long as the tables share a common field, called a key field.

Working with DBMS Documents

Most personal computer DBMSs use the relational model. In fact, the RDMBS, or relational database, has become the computer industry standard. It is easy to understand because all data is viewed as essentially alike; you can locate a field with a first name as easily as you can with a last name, an address, or a phone number. By contrast, an older-style DBMS might find only a last name or perhaps just a ZIP code. In RDBMS terminology, this creates *any-to-any relationships*. An example is shown in table 10.1.

Table 10.1
A Relational Database

Territory	Rep Last Name	First Name	Residence City
California	Paterson	Chris	Santa Rosa
Arizona	Sorenson	Janet	Phoenix
Oregon	Robertson	Joshua	Portland
Washington	Antonelli	Michael	Tacoma
Utah	Denton	Patricia	Salt Lake City

The RDBMS resembles nothing so closely as it does the human brain's ability to freely associate people, places, and things. For example, if you want to find the personnel file for Josh in the Oregon sales territory but can't recall his last name, the RDBMS can find all files with those two relations—Josh and Oregon.

You can classify, organize, analyze, cross-reference, and access data because every item is indexed, or *related*. For example, you can find all the sales reps whose first name starts with *J* or who live in a city that starts with a *P*. Note too that the relational database eliminates duplicate data elements and is more flexible in organizing data. Because of this flexibility, you can focus on working with your data, rather than spending time maneuvering through the DBMS.

For a simple example of the relational database in action, consider direct-mail solicitations for bank credit cards. Have you ever received a solicitation for a credit card that you already hold? That occurrence means that the bank either is not using a relational database or is using it inefficiently because the bank sends all direct mailings to everyone in the database. However, the relational database permits narrowing the list by selecting relationships. For example, the relational database could select only customers who have a home mortgage, who earn more than $25,000 a year, and who do not have the bank's Visa card but have reserve checking.

A Database Work Session

The best way to familiarize yourself with the DBMS application is to work with it, following the five steps in the DBMS Process—designing, creating, saving, querying, and printing—to create a database document. This text assumes the use of Access, so refer to figure 10.2 to become familiar with the first Microsoft Access screen. It has the following parts:

- *Title bar.* Displays the program name.

- *Menu bar.* Lists the available pull-down menus, which contain commands.

- *Standard toolbar.* Displays icons that execute commands used most frequently (most also appear in pull-down menus).

- *Datasheet (document window).* The area in which you create the document.

- *Table.* The columns and rows that make up the blank table—more than one table can be displayed at a time. The table title is the same as a file name.

- *Column headings.* Column identification across the top of the table.

- *Row headings.* Row identification down the left margin of the worksheet.

- *Table scroll bars.* To the right and across the bottom of the table window, they enable you to move through text in the table.

- *Status bar.* Displays information about your current datasheet view, the name of the file, and the name of any toggle keys that you have pressed, such as Num Lock or Caps Lock.

- *The insertion point and pointer.* As in other GUI-based programs, the pointer changes its shape according to its assignment. In the work area, the insertion point is a vertical bar. When moved to a toolbar, the insertion point changes to an arrow, or pointer, ready to issue a command.

Designing the Database

Database design has always been a pencil-and-paper operation. Follow these general steps and consider the following points as you create a database design:

1. *Determine the contents of the database.*

   A database contains one or more tables, each of which contains a specific kind of data. For example, you might have a videotape movie database with individual tables for comedy, drama, science fiction, and mystery.

2. *Determine what data you need and the best way to organize it.*

   If you're creating a movie database, each movie field probably should list the title, director, starring actors, release date, running time, and a few other facts. However, be careful not to include too much detail or something you may never need to reference—for example, the date you recorded it or what cable channel it played on.

3. *Determine how you're going to organize and enter data into records and fields.*

   Your goal is to achieve maximum efficiency and ease of use when you're querying your database. You might want to organize the records in the same way that a directory of movies that you refer to often is organized: title, year, length, director, and so forth. You might want to create separate fields for last names and first names, or perhaps one field for both first and last names. If you choose the latter method, be sure to enter the last name first for querying purposes. Otherwise, you may end up with many occurrences of James but none of Spader. Be consistent with numbers as well; don't enter 114 minutes one time and 1:54 hours the next.

Bear in mind that common fields help you get the most from your database. If you establish categories, such as mystery, comedy, drama, and so forth, use the same category names in the same order in every table. That will help you find the common field—Arnold Schwartzenegger—in any table no matter whether the film was a comedy or a drama.

4. *Choose your primary key before you begin.*

   The primary key identifies the field that you decide to use to identify each record in the table. If you want to catalog your videotape collection by numbering the videocassettes, the tape number may be the best choice for your primary key. Otherwise, the DBMS may number your entries in the order that you enter them.

By now you probably realize that good database design is important. Done well, it makes creating the actual database faster and easier, simply because you understand the process and have decided how the data will be organized.

Creating the Database

Some DBMS applications provide software tools to help you get started. One tool is the *Wizard,* which you use to create objects in the database. A *database object* may be a table, form, query, report, or any other element with which you can create or use a database. You usually use Microsoft Access Wizards, for example, when you're starting a new task, such as creating a new table, as shown in figure 10.7. Once selected, a Wizard takes you through the process step by step, using dialog boxes to prompt you.

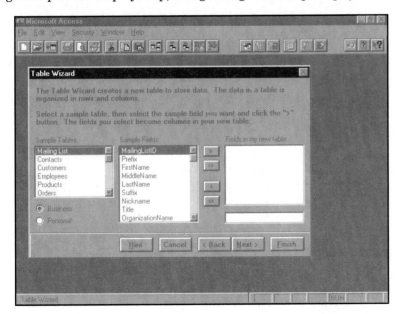

Figure 10.7
Wizards show you procedures one step at a time.

First, you select New Database from the Access File pull-down menu, as shown in figure 10.8. Then the DBMS takes you through a series of screens.

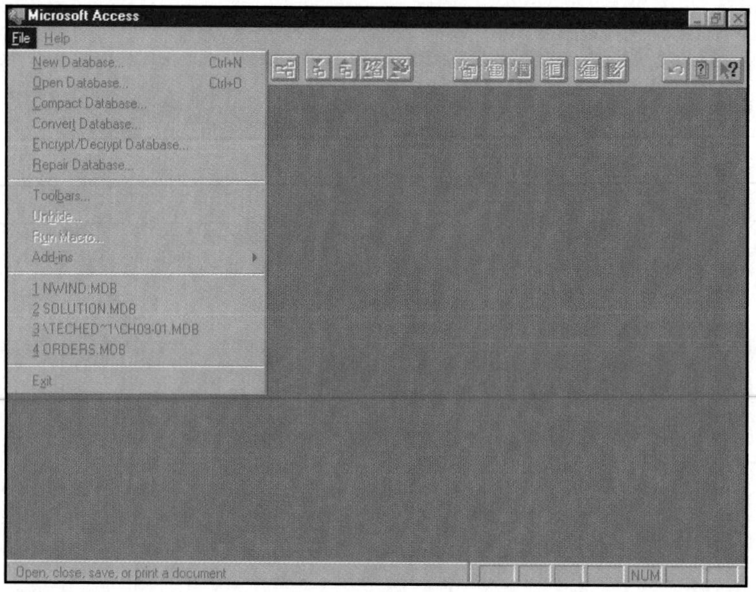

Figure 10.8

Choose New Database from the File pull-down menu to create a new database.

If you don't use a Wizard to create the table, you'll see a screen similar to the one in figure 10.9. In either case, this point is where you transfer your paper design to the on-screen table.

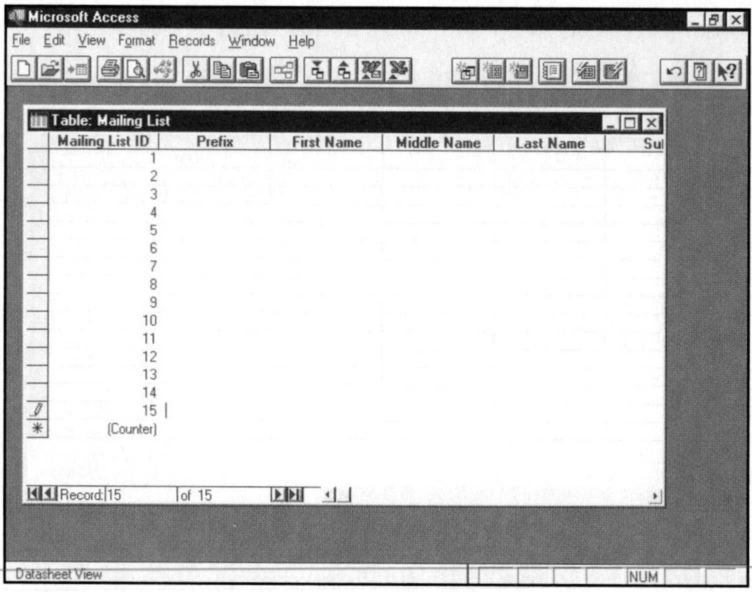

Figure 10.9

Setting up fields in a table.

Tables must be set up with the following elements:

- *Field name.* Names should be short but descriptive of the data the fields will contain, such as Film Title, Director, Release Date, Length, and so on.

- *Field data type.* Fields accept text, numbers, or both; date and time; currency or counting numbers; or yes or no.

- *Field description.* Identifies the table contents and, once entered, appears in the table title bar. The description for each file appears in the status bar.

- *Field properties.* Set down rules for use of fields, such as field size, format for dates or numbers, the kind of value in the field (number, text, date); also specify whether a field is required and whether the field should be indexed. (For example, you probably want to index movie titles or directors but not the running times.)

You can also select various text formatting options such as boldfacing; different font styles and sizes; and alignment (left, right, center). With this initial work completed, save the file and give it a file name. If you decide to make changes later, you can come back to redesign your table.

With the design and creation completed, the least enjoyable part of working with the DBMS begins—entering data. Although this task is time-consuming and often tedious, the graphical user interface often makes the task easier. Data, such as an actor's name, can be copied and pasted from one field to another. Fields can be resized as needed. Some DBMS programs offer the advantage of using a form to enter data, as shown in figure 10.10. This feature at least relieves the tedium of typing data into columns and rows of blank fields.

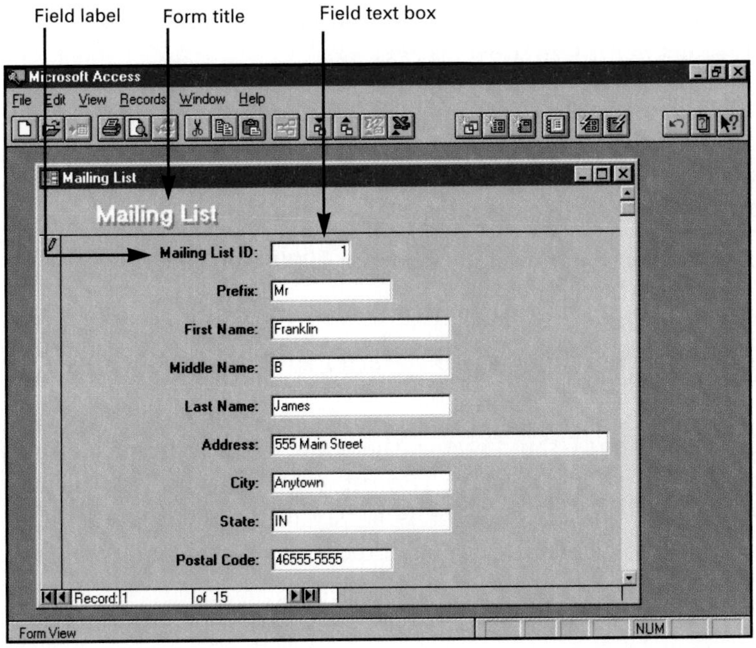

Figure 10.10
Entering data is less tedious when you can just fill in forms.

Saving

Saving is a recurring step in the DBMS process. Save your work as frequently as you can; some knowledge workers save after entering every record. There are three common ways to save: use the File pull-down menu, click the floppy disk icon, and autosave.

If you haven't already done so, you save and name the file from the File pull-down menu or from the disk icon on the toolbar. The icon is a way to save quickly; clicking it saves the existing file. If you're saving a new file you haven't yet named, you are prompted to do so. After that, you see a "saving file" message in the status bar. Autosave is handy because it saves every record automatically for you.

Querying the Database

Once you've built your database, you can begin using it. This process, called querying the database, consists of making a request to retrieve certain data and present it in a specific way. There are many ways to query, ranging from simple to complex.

Find is the simplest command for locating a record quickly and easily. You can also use Find to search for a key word or other unique data, if, for example, you can remember only a word or two from the movie's title.

Find and Replace works the same as it does in word processing: If you've consistently misspelled a word—perhaps you typed *Patterson* when the person's name was spelled *Paterson*—you can correct all occurrences at once.

Sort is the command for placing records in alphabetical order, based on the field you select. You can sort according to film title, director's name, lead actor's name, or whatever you choose. You can sort in ascending (A to Z) or descending (Z to A) order. Sort may also be used for numbers and for dates. You also find the sort feature in word processing.

Filter is the command to retrieve only the records you want to see. You can use Filter to make a quick query that you don't save for re-use. Whereas Sort retrieves all the films by, say, the director John Hughes, Filter enables you to select any of the following (or more):

- Only the films John Hughes made between 1990 and 1995

- Only the John Hughes films that starred Macaulay Culkin

- Only the John Hughes films starring Macaulay Culkin and with a running time longer than 90 minutes

These facts about the films—the director, the actor, the running time—are called *criteria* in the filtering process. The filter will display only records that meet the criteria you select. Filter is a way of viewing records; once you've finished with a selected view, you can return to viewing all records in the database.

Query is the most complex and versatile command for selecting data. As with Filter, you establish a set of criteria to identify the kind of data you want to work with. But instead of simply displaying the data, the query makes a copy of the records and creates a new table for them. Thus, the query enables you to save those records as a permanent file. In this respect, creating and using a query is almost identical to creating and using a table. Queries can be used to

- Summarize data in a table

- Locate duplicate records

- Move or delete records

- Reorganize data in a table into a new format in the query

Once the query is complete, you can use Find, Sort, and Filter just as you use these commands in a table. Here is one way you might use the query in your movie database. Say that you last updated it a year ago. Now you want to find all the films in which Tom Cruise appeared. You find that you are missing Tom's last two movies, so you use the Query Update function to add the new records. (You can also delete selected records.) You can then use the query to update the database while you retain the new updated actor's filmography as a separate, saved query.

Printing

Printing, like querying, can be simple or sophisticated. You can print a datasheet or a portion of one by selecting Print from the File menu. This step produces a printout of the raw data, just as it appears on the screen.

If others are going to see your work, you probably want to create a report to show them the data as information—organized and professionally formatted so that it is easy to use and understand. Three kinds of formatting are available in Microsoft Access:

- AutoReport quickly and automatically provides you with a simple report.

- Report Wizard lets you select from seven report formats, such as single-column, groups or totals, mailing labels, summary reports, and so forth. Figure 10.11 shows a professionally printed report.

- You can create your own report from the New selection on the File menu, which enables you to custom-design your own format.

Reports are like tables and queries: They are saved as permanent files. In some cases, you may want to create a quick AutoReport, print it, and not save it. In most cases, saving a report as a file is a good idea.

Figure 10.11
A custom report printout.

Products by Category

20-Nov-95

Category: Beverages		Category: Condiments		Category: Confections	
Product Name:	**Units In Stock:**	**Product Name:**	**Units In Stock:**	**Product Name:**	**Units In Stock:**
Chai	39	Aniseed Syrup	13	Chocolade	15
Chang	17	Chef Anton's Cajun Seasoning	53	Gumbär Gummibärchen	15
Chartreuse verte	69	Genen Shouyu	39	Maxilaku	10
Côte de Blaye	17	Grandma's Boysenberry Spread	120	NuNuCa Nuß-Nougat-Creme	76
Ipoh Coffee	17	Gula Malacca	27	Pavlova	29
Lakkalikööri	57	Louisiana Fiery Hot Pepper Sauce	76	Schoggi Schokolade	49
Laughing Lumberjack Lager	52	Louisiana Hot Spiced Okra	4	Scottish Longbreads	6
Outback Lager	15	Northwoods Cranberry Sauce	6	Sir Rodney's Marmalade	40
Rhönbräu Klosterbier	125	Original Frankfurter grüne Soße	32	Sir Rodney's Scones	3
Sasquatch Ale	111	Sirop d'érable	113	Tarte au sucre	17
Steeleye Stout	20	Vegie-spread	24	Teatime Chocolate Biscuits	25
				Valkoinen suklaa	65
				Zaanse koeken	36
Number of Products:	11	**Number of Products:**	11	**Number of Products:**	13

Advanced DBMS Features

Some advanced DBMS features make more sophisticated use of standard features. For example, you can use several different query techniques, or query languages, to produce more focused results. You can also create relationships between tables and databases so that you can compare or contrast data from different sources.

One advanced feature that is similar to the spreadsheet is the capability to create graphics from numeric data. The easiest way to create the graph in Microsoft Access is to use the Wizard feature, which guides you through to the finished graph. It can then be saved as a file.

Another advanced feature creates custom applications by using the DBMS's built-in programming language. In this respect, this feature is often referred to as an **application development environment** because, with the right computer hardware, a knowledge worker can develop and use a complete computer system. For example, the owner of a small mail-order business could use the DBMS programming language to create an application with the custom capabilities to

- Present an order entry screen
- Manage inventory
- Prepare replenishment orders
- Prepare customer orders
- Print the invoice and shipping label
- Track payments and print reports

Once created, these applications can be used regularly by the business.

In the past, the knowledge worker or business owner needed to know a formal programming language or else had to hire a programmer to write the application. Today, the DBMS programming language makes this a do-it-yourself project. What's more, the knowledge worker can do most of the programming work either by using English-like commands or by making selections from menus. The software used to accomplish this is called an **application generator**. Figure 10.12 shows an application generator screen.

Menu name

Command name

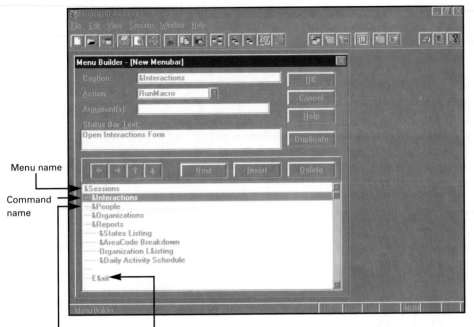

Submenu name   Separator bar

Figure 10.12
In Access, the Menu Builder enables you to create menu names, menu items, and submenus that invoke macros, built-in menu actions, or Basic code.

A Comparison of the Big Three Applications

Most knowledge workers use word processing, the spreadsheet, and the database management system most frequently. The features and advantages of each application overlap to some extent:

- *Word processing.* You can search word processing files for a name and address or a specific phrase, but this application's strength is managing small and large quantities of text.

- *Spreadsheet.* A spreadsheet is capable of producing sales or manufacturing reports, but its strength is performing a wide range of sophisticated mathematical calculations.

- *DBMS.* A database management system can draw on the strengths of word processing by sorting through large quantities of text and on the strengths of a spreadsheet by tabulating numeric data, but the DBMS's real strength is presenting textual and numeric data in many different ways.

Word processing is the application that unites all three. You can bring portions of the spreadsheet and DBMS, and the charts and graphs they generate, into a word processing document. So although each application has its primary purpose, their capability to work compatibly with each other is an important asset in knowledge work.

HOME PAGE

HOME PAGE: DBMS TIPS

1. DBMS programs range from easy to learn and intuitive to extremely difficult. The simplest is the flat-file address book; the most difficult require the use of a programming language, creating the database nearly from scratch. Choose your DBMS carefully; study comparison reviews before you buy.

2. Design your database carefully and thoroughly on paper before you begin using the application. Study the design frequently to determine whether you've left out anything and to ensure that the structure is logical.

3. Define data that you'll want to search for. If you want to be able to search for an area code or ZIP code, be sure that you distinguish them as such. Otherwise, the DBMS will stop at every sequence of numbers. And if you want to sort alphabetically by last name, type the last name first.

4. If you have large quantities of existing information in another data format, you can often convert it into a format the DBMS can read. You can find the specifics for performing this task in the DBMS user manual.

5. Use forms, or templates, to enter repetitive data and automate its collection. It's easier than staring at the columns and rows.

6. Learn the DBMS programming language to create the command files that automate your work and simplify ways to retrieve data.

7. Use the DBMS query language instead of the programming language to learn easier, quicker ways to retrieve data.

8. Explore the features of the report writer—there are many types of reports and ways to use reports. Master the various methods of formatting reports, from the use of type fonts to formats.

9. Learn to use the DBMS's relational characteristics; there are many more ways to define relationships between files than are immediately apparent.

10. Find out whether there are add-on utility programs that will assist in automating tasks you commonly perform with the DBMS.

Knowledge Check

1. What is meant by a relational DBMS?
2. What are the main criteria to consider in database design?
3. What is a primary key?
4. What is the main area where data is entered, organized, and formatted?
5. Why should you save before you query the database?
6. What is the simplest type of query called? The most complex?
7. Why do we save queries and reports?
8. What is the most advanced activity you can do with a DBMS?

Key Terms

application development environment

application generator

relational database management system (RDBMS)

ISSUES AND IDEAS

The Importance of Backing Up Data

The following message was posted on the World Wide Web.

Date: Fri, 24 Nov 95 16:15:26 GMT

Subject: Can you have enough backups?

I was talking to a friend yesterday about the fear of losing our computers and did we have adequate backups for the work we did at home. As a result, she recounted the following cautionary tale. Although it was from a number of years ago (as the technology will show), the lessons remain relevant.

She was responsible for a major health research project, which involved the collection of a large quantity of survey data.

The data was coded onto punched cards.

The punched cards were read into the computer.

Two tape backups were kept, one locally and one at a secure, distant location.

Adequate precautions one would think, the same data existed in five different forms. However:

1. The computer crashed, eliminating the current file.

2. Someone had written over the first part of the local tape—making the tape unusable.

3. When the computer centre was contacted they said that a boiler explosion had destroyed many of the tapes in the storage area and the records of who they belonged to. They were waiting for clients to contact them so that they could identify the scope of the damage. The backup my friend was seeking was one of those destroyed.

4. They went back to the punched cards. This meant losing the analysis of the data, but this could be redone if the original data was available, . . .BUT

Someone had dropped the cards on the floor. There were several thousand of them and they could only be entered in the right order. They were now in random order. There was a faint dot matrix printed number on each card.

5. The project team were faced with three options:

   a. sorting the cards

   b. re-punching all the data

   c. abandoning the project

They chose c.

CRITICAL THINKING

1. List each of the five forms of backup used, and analyze why, under normal circumstances, they would be sufficient precautions.

2. What is the purpose of backup, and why can you (obviously) never take enough precautions?

3. What might have been done to ensure that one or more forms of backup might have survived intact?

4. Develop a backup plan for your data—for your DBMS data and all other files.

Module C

The Personal Information Manager

Why It's Important to Know

Personal Information Manager software is a type of DBMS designed specifically to work with the day-to-day information in your life. It combines personal information tools, such as an appointment calendar, address book, notebook, and sometimes other types of desktop applications into one integrated database program.

The traditional DBMS structures data into fields, records, and files. But the data that people use to manage their everyday lives doesn't always fit neatly into this structure. Philippe Kahn came up with a solution to the problem in the early 1980s with a utility program called Sidekick. First designed for programmers, Sidekick included a calculator, a calendar, a telephone dialer, and an ASCII character table to help the programmer remember the codes for various keyboard characters. Sidekick was a *terminate and stay resident* (TSR) program; that is, it could be called up and used while the person was using another program.

The advent of multitasking operating environments meant that TSR programs were no longer needed, but Philippe Kahn's software company, Borland International, still sells Sidekick (now much improved, of course). Moreover, most of the tools in Sidekick became desktop accessories or applets in the operating environment software. But what was still lacking was integration; you had to use each separately, and they didn't share data.

A new kind of relational DBMS called the personal information manager emerged. Figure 10.13 shows the screen of a typical PIM. The **personal information manager** (**PIM**) is a database program that stores, organizes, and retrieves personal information once kept on paper. The PIM uses a suite of integrated desktop applications, such as an appointment calendar, address book, notebook, and other desktop or pocket organizing tools. Think of the PIM as a software version of a Daytimer. Although no two are alike, all PIMs have one thing in common: They are innovative and flexible in the way they organize data. For example, a PIM might associate information by items or topics, prioritize it by time or urgency, or sort it using a specific category or a **keyword**, a term common to several topics. PIMs are effective for keeping small bits of information—phone messages, reminders, names and addresses, or an Action Item list.

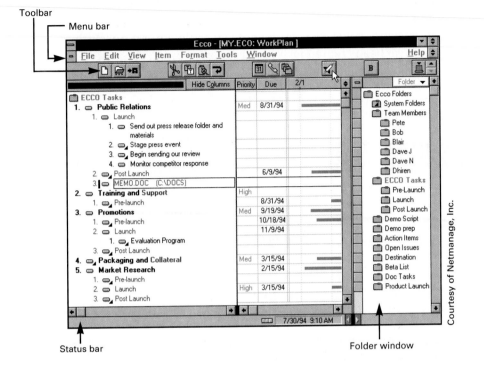

Toolbar

Menu bar

Status bar

Folder window

Courtesy of Netmanage, Inc.

Figure 10.13
A Personal Information Manager.

Some PIMs use the principles of the DBMS so that you can make assumptions and create relationships. For example, suppose that your things-to-do list says to get the leaky faucet fixed, but your address book has no listing for a plumber. However, a handyman named Jim did some repair work for you once. A PIM might use the keyword *repair* to help you find Jim's phone number and address.

In many PIMs, the DBMS file structure is replaced by an information base. An *information base*, which resembles a cross between a text file and a free-form database, combines many kinds of data in a single file. A PIM can hold data in many formats and move it between the desktop applications. The information base structures data by logical relationships; for example, short text (notes); long text (letters, reports, and book chapters); databases; names or addresses or phone numbers; calendar items; business forms; and so on.

With the information base, you can easily link one type of data to another according to your needs, and you can make changes whenever you like. For example, say you reach Jim and he agrees to fix your leaky faucet on Monday at 3 P.M. You can copy his name and phone number into the appointment calendar on your PIM. After the repairs are completed, you can copy the appointment and his address into the notepad with a reminder to send him a check. You can create *dynamic links* between any form of information in the PIM's information base for any kind of searching, organizing, copying, or moving. These links can be more effective for organizing data than a primary key in a DBMS.

The PIM Process and Work Session

The five steps in the PIM process are shown in the PIM Process Chart in figure 10.14. You organize the data, create the information base, save it, use it, and print it. If you were using a DBMS for the first time, you would have to create tables or fields or forms before you could enter data. With the PIM, the forms have been created for you. Organizing the PIM is your first step.

Figure 10.14
The Personal Information Manager Process Chart.

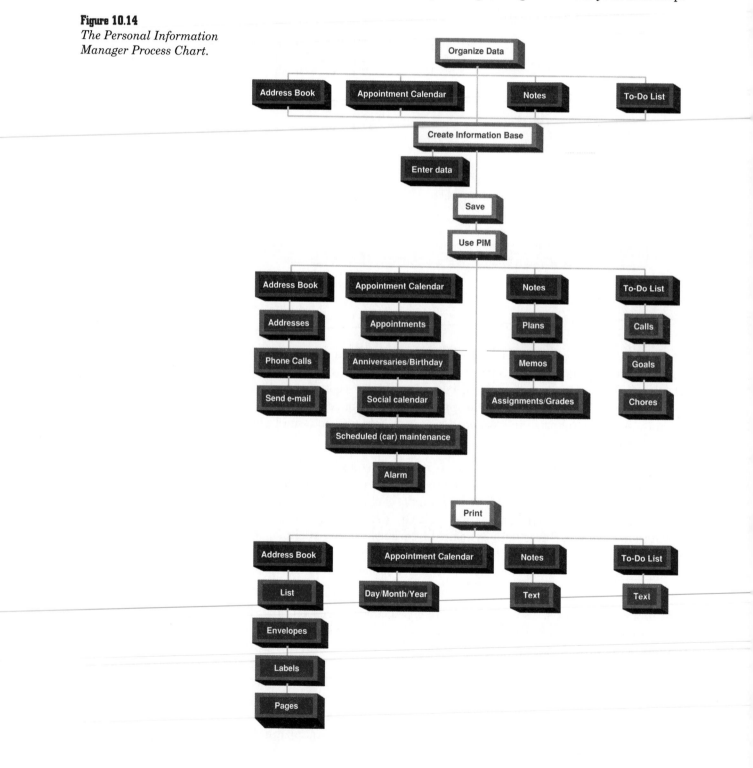

Organize Your Data

You organize your PIM by entering your personal information. As figure 10.15 shows, several desktop applications are combined in the PIM. Each requires you to enter data into it in an organized manner, just as you would if you were using a paper-based desktop tool. By virtue of its storing all data in the information base and making it available to all applications, the PIM adds value to the process.

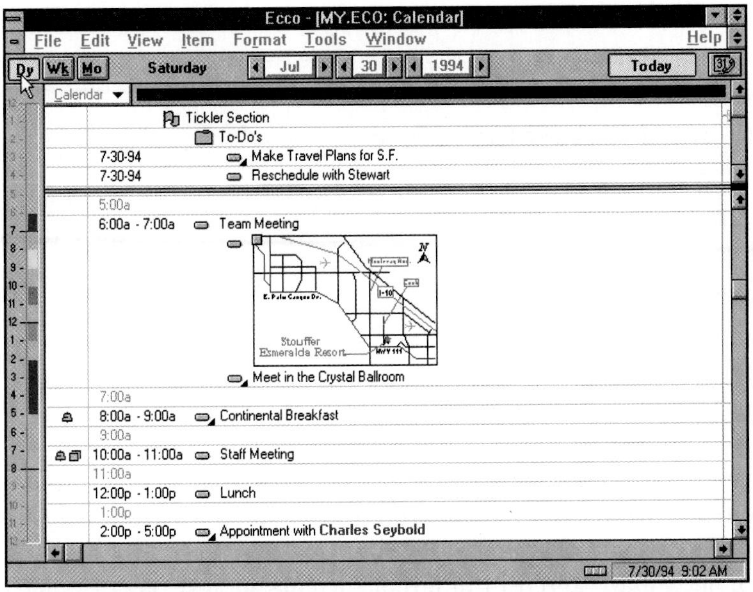

Courtesy of Netmanage, Inc.

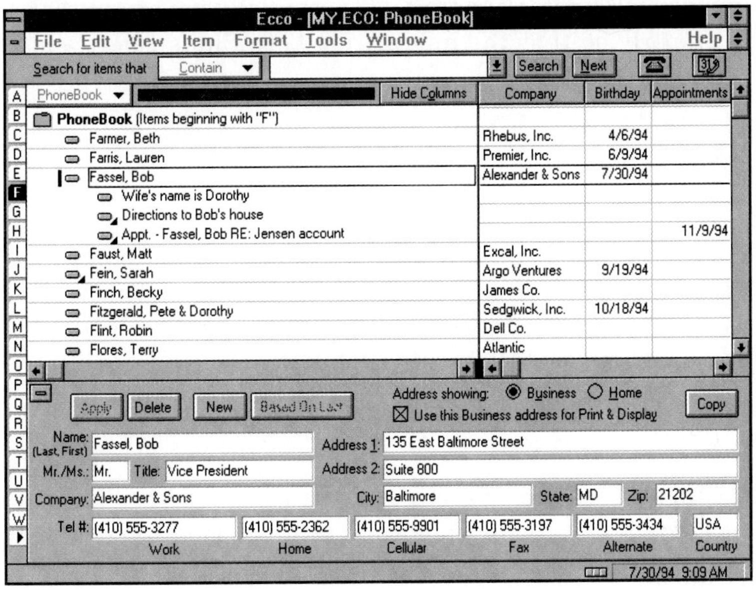

Courtesy of Netmanage, Inc.

Figure 10.15
Two views of desktop applications in a PIM.

Here are some examples of what you can do with your PIM:

- Search the address book using a keyword.
- If you have aerobics every Tuesday, enter the class as a recurring appointment.
- Create lists of activities in the notebook and prioritize them.
- Use the notepad to take notes valuable for memos or reports later on.

The PIM adds value in another way: It's customizable, so you can design the various applications to suit your personal style.

Create the Information Base

All the data you store in the individual desktop applications is kept together in the information base. Having a single repository for all the data is essential to sharing information—not only between desktop applications but also between knowledge workers using a PIM in work groups. The information base is a single file or folder and may be quite large. In most cases, it can be accessed only by the PIM.

Save

Just as when you are using a DBMS, saving your work often is important to ensure that no data is accidentally lost. Because the information base contains complex data stored in different formats for various desktop applications combined with dates and times, it's especially important that you save and exit properly so that the information base file is safely and properly closed.

Use PIM

Now that your data is entered and you have created an information base, you can begin using your PIM. You'll get the most value from the PIM if you use it regularly and use it for everything. Don't keep notes on paper or try to maintain a separate address book or appointment calendar. Here are some additional uses for each desktop application:

- *Address book.* Use it to make phone calls and connect to e-mail services.

- *Appointment calendar.* Record business meetings, travel itineraries, project due dates, product launches, as well as anniversaries, birthdays, auto maintenance; set alarms for appointments and office meetings.

- *Notes.* Create plans or draft outlines; write down assignments; write e-mail messages.

- *To Do list.* Organize class assignments; keep track of your grades; create shopping lists; set personal goals.

- *Share information.* The PIM not only lets you share information between desktop applications, it lets you share it with other applications you use. For example, you can copy and paste a name and address from the address book into a letter you're writing in word processing. You can transfer a list of recently purchased CDs into your DBMS library, or a list of expenditures into your spreadsheet budget. Sharing information moves to a whole new dimension when you're part of a workgroup.

- *DBMS formats.* Some PIMs enable you to organize data the same way a regular DBMS does, by creating forms, sorting, filtering, and so forth.

Print

The PIM has a versatile print function, similar to the report writer in a DBMS. Your address book can be printed as a list on regular paper, on envelopes, on labels, or on special forms for use in, for example, a Daytimer. You can print your daily, weekly, monthly, or annual calendar. You can print notes in various formats as well. Figure 10.16 shows an example of printing.

For many years, we have had to work with data in ways that conform to the computer's method of data processing. A trend now is toward designing software that guides the computer to do our work the way we do it. PIMs are a step in that direction. Some PIMs are designed for use by groups so that people who work together can share the necessary information. They use the calendar to schedule group meetings. They share phone numbers through the address book. They use the notes and action item sections to write and converse informally and arrive at group decisions. With e-mail capability, much of the information stored in the PIM can be shared in electronic messages. In fact, PIMs and e-mail are tailor-made partners for work groups.

Knowledge Check

1. What is a desktop application?
2. Name some desktop applications found in the PIM.
3. On which application is the personal information manager based?
4. What is the main distinguishing characteristic of the PIM (from this application)?
5. What desktop applications are usually found in a PIM?
6. List the five steps in the PIM process.
7. What is a hand-held computer with PIM software called?

Key Terms

keyword   personal data assistant (PDA)   personal information manager (PIM)

Figure 10.16
PIMs can print in many different formats.

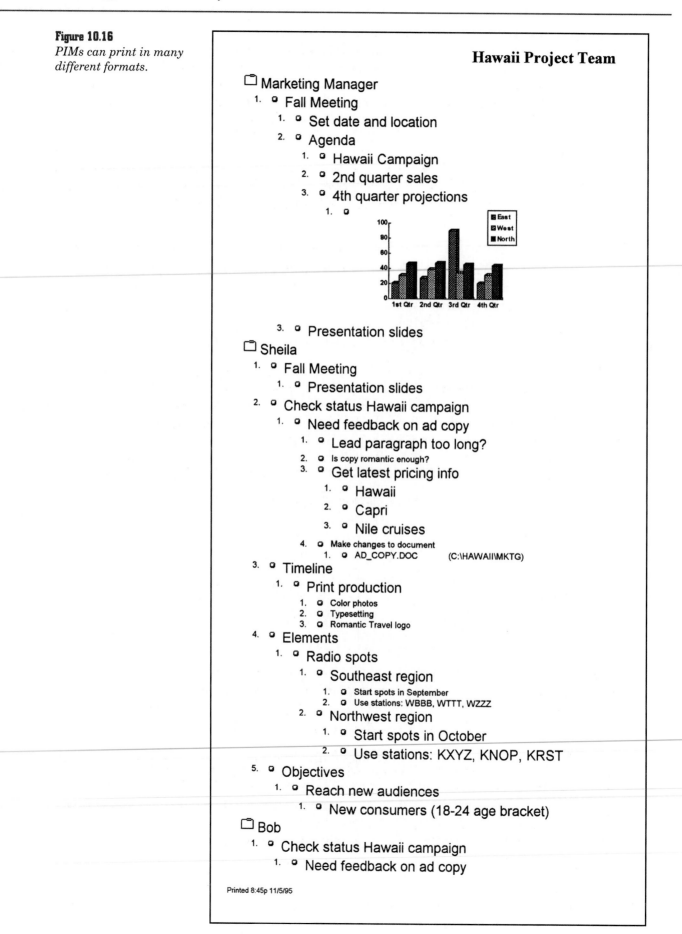

ISSUES AND IDEAS

Is This Going Too Far?

Using a computer and PIM software to manage your life is a fine idea. Being able to take your PIM with you in a pocket-sized computer, or even a wristwatch, is pretty cool. But isn't implanting an integrated circuit memory chip in your brain going just a bit too far?

That's what occurs in the film *Johnny Mnemonic*. Johnny, played by Keanu Reeves, is a messenger who delivers data—a mnemonic courier who can store up to 320 gigabytes of data in his "wetware," or computer-enhanced memory cells—his brain. Of course, something goes wrong—in this case, Johnny gets a dose of "information overload," and unless he gets the code required for downloading in time, he'll die. Meanwhile, a number of other people are looking for Johnny and his data, and they don't care how they get it or what happens to him in the process.

The film was based on a short story by William Gibson, acknowledged as the originator of cyberpunk fiction. Writing in *Wired* magazine about Gibson and *Johnny Mnemonic*, Rogier van Bakel says:

> Gibson created a gritty, credible future that wasn't about glass-domed space cars or intergalactic laser battles. In novel after novel, he populates his universe with computer jockeys on junk food, hookers and hackers, all manner of high-tech hipsters who are probably a lot closer to the soul of the nascent 21st century than George Jetson ever was.

> The movie is about "the politics of information," muses Gibson. "It's phrased as an action-chase piece, but our real agenda is a little more serious than that."

> "We want to see him get the information for himself, escape, turn the tables on the bad guys," says Gibson. "But in the end he does something else, and manages to become a human being in the process. I see it as a fable of the information age."[3]

CRITICAL THINKING

1. If we have a pocket or wristwatch personal information manager today, is it conceivable that we'll have one directly connected to our brains in the future?

2. Why does the desire to meld people with computers seem to be so prevalent? Is it desirable?

3. Examining the history and development of computers over the past fifty years, are we being near-sighted about what might happen in the next fifty years?

4. Create a list of the desirable reasons to use computers in managing our daily affairs. Then create a list of the undesirable side effects of doing so.

---

3. Rogier van Bakel. "Remembering Johnny," *Wired*, June 1995, 157.

HOME PAGE

THE POCKET PIM

PIMs run on most types of PCs, including portable laptop computers. As a knowledge worker on the go, you can install a version of the PIM application on both your desktop and your portable PC and then copy the information base from the desktop to the portable before leaving on a trip. This capability enables you to use PIM data during your absence and update the information base on your desktop PC when you return.

But PIMs can get even more portable. Now you can copy your PIM from the desktop PC to your wristwatch. The transfer couldn't be easier: It's done with infrared technology. Just hold the face of the special watch in front of the monitor screen and touch a button.

Pocket calculators with PIM features are called electronic organizers and have large display screens and standard (although small) QWERTY keyboards. In addition to transferring data to and from a desktop PC, some electronic organizers can send faxes and e-mail and permit using a special stylus to enter data on the display screen.

Just slightly larger than a pocket electronic organizer is a hand-held computer called the **personal data assistant**, or **PDA**. When first introduced, the PDA was lauded for its capability to accept handwritten input on the screen. However, the PDA takes time to "learn" to recognize individual handwriting and is not always completely accurate. Some people felt that handwriting was a step backward from a keyboard input.

Courtesy of Motorola

The Motorola Envoy is a pen-based wireless PDA.

Most PDAs aren't designed to exchange data with a desktop PC. Some have wireless communication capabilities.

PDAs, like the Apple Newton, are useful and convenient. Yet Stewart Alsop, formerly editor-in-chief and now a columnist for *InfoWorld* newsmagazine, believes that their incompatibility with office PCs is a shortcoming. He writes:

> I still believe the key to this whole business is to design a device that is intended to work with a primary computer.

> . . . I would make a device that really does fit in my shirt pocket with my cards and pens or is small and tough enough to coexist in my pants pocket with my loose change and car keys. It would last for months on an AA or AAA battery. And it would be designed to suck just the data I want—the appointments and contacts and notes I need with me all the time—out of my computer, whenever I am close by the main computer.

Fortunately, vendors still think there's an opportunity to make money in mobile devices. So I think we have a serious chance of getting just such a product.[4]

HOME PAGE REVIEW QUESTIONS

1. What is the advantage in using the PIM on more than one computer?

2. What is the most advanced technology for transferring data between desktop and portable devices?

3. What was the main feature of the personal data assistant when it was introduced?

---

4. Stewart Alsop. "HP OmniGo should perk up PDAs, but I may not be able to pocket one just yet," *InfoWorld*, October 23, 1995, 122.

ETHICS

Toward a More Ethical and Responsible Use of Public Information Databases

David Chaum, a professor of computer science, wrote an article entitled "New Paradigm for Individuals in the Information Age" that takes a straightforward, realistic view of the personal information about individuals stored in business and government databases. (A paradigm is a model or pattern for something.) Chaum doesn't argue that database information should be constrained, deleted, or managed better, which would be absurd at this point in database evolution. Instead, he writes:

As the use of computers becomes more pervasive, they are bound to have substantial influence on our relationships with organizations. Currency and paper checks as a way to pay for goods and services will largely be replaced by electronic means. Electronic mail will be the main way we send and receive messages. Our personal credentials will often be presented in electronic form. [Here I discuss] two different paradigms for automation of the informational relationships between individuals and organizations.

The current paradigm is characterized by "identification" of the individual during every transaction. . . . identification is required presumably to allow detection and remedies against abuses and frauds . . . the systems are set up to protect the organizations, not to protect the individuals whose personal information is stored in those systems.

These [systems] allow various records and transaction details relating to a particular individual to be linked and collected together in a "dossier" or comprehensive file on that individual. While limited . . . today, the amount and nature of data which could automatically be captured . . . would radically increase the significance of the dossier.

In the new paradigm, instead of identifying information, individuals provide each organization with a different "pseudonym" or alternate name. Pseudonyms would be created and stored in the credit card-sized computer held by the individual. The critical advantage of systems based on such pseudonyms is that the information they contain is insufficient to allow data on an individual to be linked together, and thus they can prevent the formation of a dossier society, reminiscent of [George] Orwell's [novel] *1984*.

Chaum believes that the new paradigm requires three fundamental kinds of interactions: "Individuals must communicate with organizations; individuals need to pay or be paid by organizations; and organizations need to exchange information about individuals." In his new paradigm, the communication is improved for these reasons:

- The individual is protected from the system provider because messages cannot be traced.
- The organization is protected from the individual because of the authenticating credit card.
- Society is protected from the individual because threats can be traced back if agreed upon by a consensus of parties interested in locating the individual (for example, if the person is perpetrating credit card fraud with many merchants).
- The individual is protected from the organization because the person can send routine messages that are untraceable, subject to the provisos of number 3.[5]

Critical Thinking

1. Does this new paradigm give back control of personal information to individuals?
2. What flaws would individuals find in it? Organizations?
3. What would be required to implement this new paradigm?

5. David Chaum. "A New Paradigm for Individuals in the Information Age," *Computers, Ethics, and Social Values*. (New Jersey: Prentice-Hall, 1995), 366–373.

THE LEARNING ENTERPRISE

Evaluate the processes and computer system requirements you created in Chapter 5. Now you must determine the ways DBMSs will be used in your enterprise. First, use the DBMS Process Chart to determine the following:

1. As an individual knowledge worker, what you will use the DBMS for
2. As a workgroup, what it will be used for
3. As a department or function, what it will be used for
4. What types of databases your enterprise will require (for example, separate ones for accounting, human resources, and so on)

Have each person fill out a Process Chart describing his or her personal use of the DBMS and individual databases the person will use.

Once you have made these determinations, create a chart with the enterprise database in the center and three concentric rings of squares around it. The inside ring represents the department, the next workgroups, and the outer ring the individuals. Write down what everyone's database uses, or requirements, will be. The database work is continued in a subsequent chapter.

Chapter Review

Fill in the Blank

1. A(n) _____ is a group of related records and files.
2. Something that you collect data about is called a(n) _____.
3. An organized method for storing data about an entity is called

    _____ _____.

4. A characteristic of an entity is called a(n) _____.
5. A(n) _____ represents one attribute or characteristic of an entity.
6. A collection of related fields that the database treats as a single entity is called a(n) _____.
7. The symbols that you use to query the database are called

    _____.

8. A(n) _____ combines many kinds of data in a single file.
9. The command to retrieve only the records in a database that you want to see is _____.
10. Data in two separate tables can be related if the tables share a common field called a(n) _____ field.

True/False

1. A record represents one characteristic in a database.
2. A record represents a collection of related fields.
3. A file is a collection of related records.
4. To arrange data in alphabetical or numerical order, choose the Sort command.
5. To retrieve data from a database, you perform a query.

Review Questions

1. In what three ways does a database help you manage data better?
2. What are the five steps in the database process?
3. Explain the difference between data definition and data refinement.
4. To see the results of the database you create, what must you do?
5. What are some logical operators?
6. To retrieve data from your database, what are three commands you might use?
7. What are some reasons to query a database?
8. What is a relational database management system?
9. What is a personal information manager?

Discussion Questions

1. Do you think that pen-based technology will encourage more people to use electronic technology to store and retrieve data? Is the need to use a keyboard a hindrance to the spread of computer use? Which technology do you prefer?
2. Would a PIM be more useful to you than data stored in various paper-based products?
3. Are word processing, spreadsheet, and database applications useful in managing your own data and information? Think of reasons to use the ones that you do not consider useful to you now.

INTERNET DISCOVERY

Learn more about how DBMSs are used. Log on to these Web sites:

http://www.omniscience.com/

http://www.harte-hanks.com/corporate/hh-database.html

http://www.cs.virginia.edu/~vadb/

11

PC COMMUNICATIONS

I've simply reached the point where I can't answer my E-mail, nice or not. If somebody really wants to reach me, I'm listed in the phone book in Oakland. Send me a letter. . . . Come over to my house and we'll go to the coffee shop and talk about it there.

Clifford Stoll, astronomer and author of *The Cuckoo's Egg*[1]

Using technology to communicate has always fascinated people—from the telegraph to the telephone, from ham radio to the CB, from fax to voice mail—these earlier communications technologies have converged in the PC and communications software.

According to *The Economist* magazine, the number of people using their personal computers for data communications is growing half again its size every year: 20 million in 1995, 30 million in 1996. "No communications medium has ever grown as quickly; not the fax machine, not even the PC. At this rate, within two years the citizens of cyberspace will outnumber all but the largest nations."[2]

What's all the excitement about cyberspace? MIT professor Norbert Wiener coined the word **cybernetics**, defined as the comparative study of human and machine processes. In 1948, Wiener wrote *Cybernetics*, an important book that addressed the analogies between the human brain and nervous system and the computer's CPU and other electronic systems. *Cybernetics* quickly became a catchword for things having to do with computers. Today, we use the term *cyberspace* to refer to the "virtual space" created by computers. That space defies the normal boundaries of daily life. A virtual space may be similar to reality, or it may resemble a 3-D movie; the computer's virtual space may be a computer game like Doom or Myst or a 3-D holographic "virtual reality" world like the one in the movie *Disclosure*.

Or cyberspace may simply be the world that beckons from on-line computer communications. **On-line** means, literally, that your computer is in direct communication with another computer. This chapter shows you how this communication is done. So get your computers on-line, connected to the Information Superhighway, and see what's happening in cyberspace!

1. "A Disillusioned Devotee Says The Internet Is Wearing No Clothes," *The New York Times*, April 30, 1995.

2. "The Accidental Superhighway," *The Economist*, July 1, 1995.

Module A

The PC Communications Process

Why It's Important to Know

> **Any computer engaged in on-line communications must be running communications software. Mastering your PC communications software enables you to send and receive electronic mail and to get valuable programs and data from many on-line resources.**

PC communications software is your on-ramp to the Information Superhighway and its myriad routes to news, libraries, entertainment, games, conversations, and more. Communications software makes connections between computers. If you want to communicate with another PC, it too must be running PC communications software for one-to-one communication. To provide on-line services and data to many computers, a computer must be running communications management software. As its name implies, this type of software is designed to *manage* many simultaneous connections and communications work sessions from individual PCs.

PC communications software is an application that turns your PC into a *terminal* capable of sending data to and receiving data from other computers. These other computers are commonly referred to as **host computers** because they invite you to visit, browse, and make copies of programs and data stored at their home sites. Using your terminal computer to connect to the host computer is similar to switching on your television *terminal* to see what's on the cable or satellite *host*. America Online, for example, is considered a host computer. Any computer can be a host computer, even a PC.

The PC Communications Process

As with the other software you've studied, there is a communications software process, as shown in figure 11.1.

The steps in the communications software process are these:

1. *Connect.* Open the phone line circuit and get a dial tone.
2. *Dial up.* Place a call to the host computer.
3. *Handshake and log on.* Make the connections and establish a session.
4. *File transfer.* Send or receive data to or from the host computer.
5. *Disconnect.* Hang up the phone line and reset the communications software to place or receive the next communication.

Now take a closer look at each step in the process.

Figure 11.1
The PC communications process.

Connect

To use on-line communications, your PC must be connected to a modem and the modem connected to the telephone lines. Once the modem connects to the other computer, the two computers' communications protocols must be set to match. **Communications protocols** are the hardware and software standards for communications. Both computers must have the same settings, called **parameters**, and must adhere to the same standard. Table 11.1 lists the most common parameters.

Table 11.1

Communications Protocols

Parameter	Description	Normal Setting
Baud rate	Data transfer speed between modems	Slower modem sets the speed
Data bits	Number of bits required to represent a character	Usually set to 8
Start and stop bits	Begin and end a character	Usually set to 1
Parity	Checks the data bits	Usually set to even to ensure accuracy
Duplex channel	Link between the two computers that permits two-way communication	Usually set to full-duplex

Most computers use *full-duplex*, enabling simultaneous two-way communication. *Half-duplex* enables data to flow in only one direction at a time. Telephones are full-duplex communication devices.

Dial Up

Dialing the phone is the easy part. The modem performs this task, which initiates the handshaking and logon that follow. In the past, you had to enter the phone number each time you dialed; today, the numbers and all the communications parameters are saved in the communications software's address book. When you issue a command to the software to begin a communications work session, the software in turn sends codes for these commands to the modem. Often you can see the codes on your screen (see table 11.2).

Table 11.2
Dialup Codes and What They Do

Code	Action
ATH1	Instructs the modem to open the line to place a call
ATDT	Gives the modem the phone number to dial
ATA	Instructs the modem to answer
ATH0	Instructs the modem to disconnect
ATQ, ATV	Instructs the modem to display result codes, such as RING, CONNECT, connect baud rate, and so on

Handshake and Log On

After your modem establishes contact with the host computer's modem or communications link, the two must "talk" to each other briefly. This step, called **handshaking**, ensures that when one computer transmits, the other is ready to receive. If your software displays the handshaking technique, you may see either ETX/ACK or XON/XOFF.

After the two computers are communicating, you are asked to **log on**, or present your on-line identification granting you permission to use the on-line service. Logging on consists of two steps: (1) typing your user name and (2) typing your password. Your **user name** is often your first initial and part of or all your last name. In most cases, the on-line service determines your user name, and it can't be changed. Your **password** is a unique set of characters known only to you and the on-line service. The combination of the two protects your account from use by unauthorized persons.

Communications software has evolved just like the human-to-computer interface. The earliest programs used a simple command structure, which then evolved to a menu; now most applications are designed to work with the Macintosh or Windows GUI. Today, knowledge workers use one (or more) of these categories of communications software: terminal, full-featured, or proprietary.

Terminal Communications Software

Operating environments like Windows often come with a simple communications program, referred to as **terminal emulation,** which turns your PC into a terminal for communicating. In Windows 95, HyperTerminal, shown in figure 11.2, is such a program. It enables connecting to a bulletin board service (BBS), using simple on-line services like MCI Mail (electronic mail), or emulating (acting like) the French Minitel terminal.

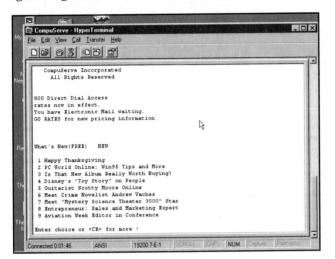

Figure 11.2
HyperTerminal is one of several, and perhaps the simplest, communications software applications that come packaged with Windows 95.

Full-Featured Communications Software

Most knowledge workers use a full-featured communications software. More sophisticated than simple terminal programs, modern full-featured communications programs are able to connect to a wide variety of on-line services. These programs perform terminal emulation and also offer these features:

- An address book for storing the phone numbers, protocols, and other information about the computers (or services) with which you communicate

- A utility to activate, or *initialize*, the modem in preparation for placing a call and to automatically disconnect the modem from the phone lines at the end of the call

- A modem dialer to place the call

- *Handshaking* and *error-checking* utilities to ensure that data is sent and received properly

- The capability to create and save *script files*, which perform certain specific tasks, such as logging you on to the host computer

- File transfer utilities to send (upload) as well as receive (download) programs and data

Figure 11.3 shows a full-featured communications program. Some communications programs also have the capability to send and receive faxes.

Figure 11.3

ProComm Plus is a popular full-featured PC communications program. It works with just about any computer that runs Windows.

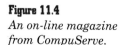

Proprietary Communications Software

Proprietary means privately owned by an individual or company. A proprietary communications software is designed to work exclusively with a specific on-line information service, such as America Online, CompuServe (see figure 11.4), or Prodigy (see figure 11.5). These services charge a monthly or usage fee for *connect time*, and the software helps the service monitor and manage your account. To subscribe to one of these services, you must install their proprietary communications software and use it for all communications with that service. (An exception is CompuServe, which may be accessed with nonproprietary programs as well.) It's not uncommon to get a free copy of the software and some initial free connect time packaged with the monthly issue of a personal computing magazine when you start subscribing.

Figure 11.4

An on-line magazine from CompuServe.

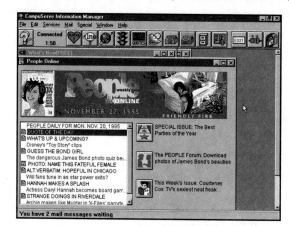

Figure 11.5

The redesigned Prodigy for Windows, an example of how proprietary communications software makes an on-line service easier to use.

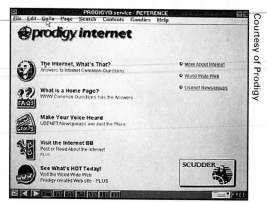

Courtesy of Prodigy

HOME PAGE

NETIQUETTE

Netiquette refers to on-line manners and behavior. We should treat other people in cyberspace as respectfully as we do in everyday situations, and in some cases our manners need to be better. After all, other cyberspace citizens cannot see you or hear your voice inflections—all they know is what you type. So follow these simple rules to avoid offending, angering, or hurting others:[3]

1. Before you write, think about your reader, yourself, and your image. Remember, the person on the other side is human, too. Make sure that your messages use a tone and language your readers will understand and appreciate; the way you write to your teacher is probably not the same way you write to a fellow student. Be sure that your communications present you in the way you want—and be willing to stand behind what you say.

2. Treat e-mail you receive as confidential unless the sender *specifically* gives you permission to share it with others.

3. Respect the copyright and license agreements of material written by others. If you quote someone from a book or magazine, mention your source.

4. Do not participate in chain letters. Doing so could result in a loss of on-line privileges.

5. Typing messages in ALL CAPS is equal to shouting. DON'T SHOUT! A single word in uppercase for emphasis is fine, but not much more.

6. Use abbreviations sparingly; overuse can make your message difficult to understand.

7. Be careful with humor. Use *emoticons*, or Smileys, such as :) or the <g> symbol for "grin," if you think your tone is unclear or if you want to emphasize that you're being friendly or kidding around.

Smileys: when you care enough to let them know your mood.

8. Reply promptly to e-mail received from others. Let them know that their messages got through and that you value their correspondence.

9. When replying to specific topics in another person's message, include only the pertinent phrases or sentences. Don't return the entire message in your reply—it is a waste of resources and usually unnecessary. Preface reply portions with a greater-than arrow (>).

10. If you receive a message that was intended for another person, either return it to its sender or forward it to the recipient—but let both parties know that you received it in error.

11. Don't *flame* or reply to a provocative message when you're upset. Wait a while to cool down before answering. Always assume that every word you send is part of a permanent document. Don't say something you'll be sorry for later.

Flaming is the most serious breach of on-line netiquette.

12. Before participating in chats, forums, or e-mail on services like America Online or Prodigy, make sure that you're familiar with their rules of netiquette.

HOME PAGE REVIEW QUESTIONS

1. What is netiquette, and why is it important?

2. What is the best way to express your emotions in a message?

3. Give some examples of unacceptable on-line behavior.

---

3. Donald Rose. Adapted from *Minding Your Cybermanners on the Internet* (Indianapolis, IN: Que), 20–40.

File Transfer

The most common communications activity is transferring files that contain useful programs or data. Figure 11.6 shows a typical menu of selections from an on-line information service.

Figure 11.6

The Macmillan on-line service offers a variety of software programs you can download for your own use.

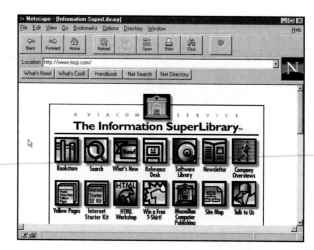

Uploading means *sending* a file from your PC (referred to as the remote computer) to another computer, an electronic mail service, or an information service (referred to as the host computer). The opposite is **downloading**, or receiving files from the host computer. Most knowledge workers download programs but upload data files. Whether uploaded or downloaded, files must be in the correct *format* for transmission.

The ASCII File Format

Applications like word processing and spreadsheets format data to make it appear correctly in the documents you create. For example, word processing sets tabs and boldfaces type; spreadsheets format numbers for currency or other purposes. Communications software has the capability to transmit just about any kind of data, but not always in the format of the originating application.

ASCII (pronounced "as-key") stands for the American Standard Code for Information Interchange, which applies to all aspects of communications and networking. ASCII data interchange requires that all the special codes and formats from the application program be stripped from a file. Even incompatible programs can share a file in ASCII format. You send or receive the basic 96 uppercase and lowercase keyboard characters. If you are in an on-line conversation, or *chat mode,* you're sending and receiving ASCII characters.

Most applications offer the option of storing your work as an ASCII file (sometimes referred to as a *text file*) as well as, say, a WordPerfect or Excel file. But what if you want to send a file with all its original formatting? Then you must send a binary file.

The Binary File Format

A *binary file* has been created by a specific application program, contains special encoding and formatting, and can usually be read only by the same program that created it. If the transmitted file is not ASCII, it's probably binary. The following example shows how the same sentence appears on-screen in text and binary:

Text: The moondog looked over his shoulder at the grinning man.

Binary: &\ Ms è HxX

Remember protocols? Well, the ASCII protocol is used to transfer—you guessed it—ASCII files. Different protocols, such as XMODEM or COMPUSERVE B+, are used to transfer binary files. Sometimes the protocol is determined automatically by the communications application. In any event, a binary file is transmitted intact. A binary file can be transmitted with an ASCII file; in this case, the binary file is known as an attachment. For example, you might write someone an e-mail message (in ASCII) and attach a file containing a spreadsheet template (a binary file).

Graphics Files and File Compression

Two other important aspects of file transfer are graphics file transfer and file compression. Any file designated by the file name extension GIF (Graphics Interchange Format) is instantly recognizable as a graphics file. The GIF file format enables exchanging graphic images, such as photographs and illustrations, between different computer systems. Keep in mind that graphics files are often very large and can take a while to download.

File compression reduces the size of a file so that it can be transferred more quickly and economically. You can use a utility program, such as PKZIP or Compress, to compress files before transmission. For example, in transferring chapters for this book, I compressed an 84,480K file to 27,200K for transmission. To uncompress the file, you can use the same software program you used to compress the file.

Disconnect

An on-line communications session ends when the software issues to the modem the command to disconnect. Although this step sounds simple, it is easy to forget or not complete. Once you issue the command to exit or **log off**, as it is often called, the two computer software programs and hardware devices begin disconnection. This procedure can take a few seconds. Make certain that you are completely disconnected after logging off. If you have a smart modem with LEDs (light emitting diodes), the OH (for *off hook*) LED should be out.

Communications Management Software

The software discussion thus far has centered on the software for a stand-alone remote computer. The host computer also requires software, called **communications management software**, or sometimes called **dialup** or host software. This software controls computers that receive calls requesting access from remote computers. Like an airport traffic controller, this software determines which computers can participate in its network and the proper paths for the data to take.

Communications management software manages the use of the network, ensuring that only properly authorized knowledge workers get connected, keeping records of their on-line time, and charging their accounts when services are used. This software also manages all the services and makes them available to knowledge workers. When a network becomes overloaded, communications management software decides which computers have priority. Figure 11.7 shows how communications management software works with an on-line research service.

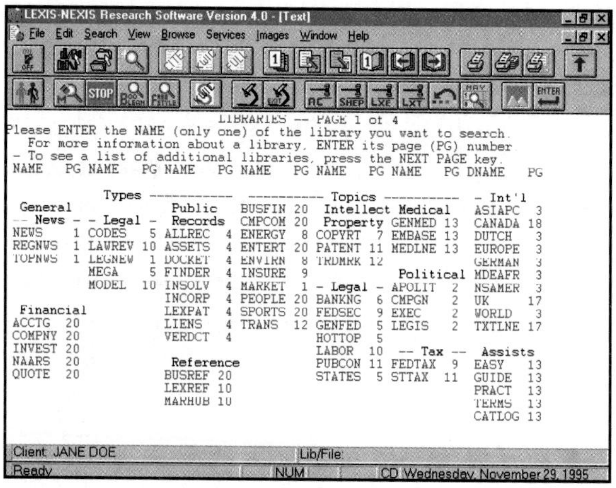

Figure 11.7

When you log on to the LEXIS®-NEXIS® services, the communications management software displays this screen.

Courtesy of Lexis-Nexis

Knowledge Check

1. Define the term *on-line*.
2. What are the two terms used for sending and receiving file transfer?
3. What are the most common formats for file transfer?
4. What are the two types of data communications software?

Key Terms

communications management software	communications protocols	cybernetics
dialup	downloading	handshaking
host computer	log off	log on
on-line	parameters	password
terminal emulation	uploading	user name

ISSUES AND IDEAS

What about Your Password?

When you begin using an on-line service, you're given a password, such as WE204AX1. You are expected to change it to something you can easily memorize and type. Some services may ask you to change your password at regular intervals, perhaps every six months. You may want to change it yourself from time to time. Here are some guidelines for password use:

- Take care not to select a password that will be easy for others to figure out. Don't use the name of your dog or cat. Don't use the same word as your logon name. Don't use *password*, *secret*, or *none*. Use a random word, but one that you'll remember. Include a special keyboard character such as $ or %.

- Never write down your password. Especially don't write it down and stick it to the monitor, or slip it under the keyboard. If you must write down your password, put it in a safe place—such as where you keep other valuables, under lock and key.

- Never give your password to someone else—under any circumstances. That person may write it down, and it could fall into the hands of someone else.

- If you lose or forget your password, don't expect to be able to call the on-line service and get it. If that were possible, anyone could get your password.

CRITICAL THINKING

1. Password protection is for your good but also for the good of the on-line service. Explain both perspectives.

2. Discuss some of the problems an unethical or unprincipled person could cause if he or she gained access to your on-line account.

3. What should you do if you see the password of a roommate or friend taped to the computer?

Module B

PC Communications and the Internet

Why It's Important to Know

The Internet is an assortment of services used for different tasks. Special communications programs and applications accomplish these different tasks. Knowing which programs and tools will give you access to the data or service you need makes navigating the Internet much easier.

If you ever dine at sophisticated restaurants, you probably notice a great deal more silverware on the table than you usually use. There may be special forks for the appetizer, salad, and main course; a spoon for soup; and a knife just for buttering your bread. Each of these eating utensils is specially designed for a single purpose.

Think of the Internet as a restaurant's menu. The **Internet** is a system of linked computer networks that encircle the globe, facilitating a wide assortment of data communications services including e-mail, data and program file transfers, newsgroups, and chat groups, as well as graphic images, sound, and video of all kinds.

The various communications programs, applications, and tools used with the Internet are your silverware. You must have the right tool to accomplish the task. If you understand the tools, you'll know which one to choose to get the service or data you need. Before you learn about these individual tools, the Home Page provides a brief overview of the Internet.

Traveling the Information Superhighway

Using the metaphor of an Information Superhighway, what is it like to tour the Internet? Imagine that you're traveling this superhighway through information cyberspace in a spacecraft equipped with electronic devices for sending and receiving every imaginable kind of communications: text, audio, video, graphics—the works. Now, look at figure 11.8. This illustration represents the Internet cyberspace, and in it are a number of planets, each of which has a unique kind of data, program, or other type of information service in which you're interested. The only hitch is that each planet's communicating language is completely different—that's why you need all the communicating applications and tools mentioned earlier.

Figure 11.8
Navigating Cyberspace:
The Internet.

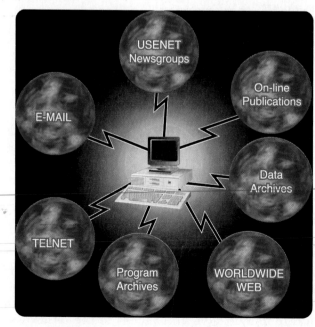

HOME PAGE

WHAT IS THE INTERNET?

The Economist magazine dubbed it "The Accidental Superhighway."[4] Here are some excerpts:

> *The Economist* magazine dubbed it "The Accidental Superhighway," for no one had any idea that, literally overnight, the Internet would become the hottest thing in computing. The Internet was started in 1969 as ARPANET, by the Pentagon's Advanced Research Projects Agency (ARPA). It was suppposed to provide a means of sharing research for computer scientists and engineers working on military projects. These people soon found a way of exchanging "electronic mail." In tiem, many colleges and universities were hooked into the ARPANET. A man who was a graduate student at the University of Pennsylvania in the mid-1970's says that it used to take three or four days for an e-mail message to reach its recipient—not much better than the U.S. Post Office "Snail Mail."

> But over time, everything grew faster, better, and mopre interconnected. In 1983, about 500 computers were connected in the "Internet." As it was now known. Four years later, that number had grown to about 28,000 host computers, connecting more and more academic institutions and research labs around the world. As *The Economist* reports:

> It grew, fast, because it was left to its own devices and filled unmet needs. The Internet's builders laid no cables and dug no trenches; they simply leased existing telephone lines. When the Internet linked up with public and commercial networks in the mid-1980s, its growth accelerated. Yet most of the big telephone companies still wrote it off as nothing more than a playground for bitheads and boffins.

> In mid-1993 something new happened: the Internet sprouted multimedia wings…Thanks to the friendly, multimedia side of the Net, called the World Wide Web, a much broader audience started to catch on to it.

> Last year the Internet doubled in size, as it has done every year since 1988. . . . At the same time the Web grew almost 20-fold; in just 18 months users created more than 3 million pages of information, entertainment, and advertising.

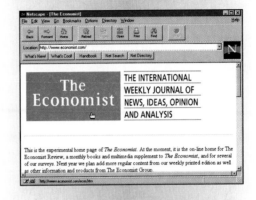

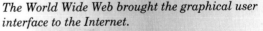

The World Wide Web brought the graphical user interface to the Internet.

> . . . the Internet already offers, albeit in embryonic form, most of the services and technologies that cable and telephone companies are still a decade from delivering. You can make a telephone call on the Internet; watch a video; listen to an audio broadcast, or broadcast yourself; shop; learn; and, of course, communicate. Every day the Internet delivers more of the features of the fabled superhighway. It may be doing these things clumsily, unreliably and slowly, but it is doing them, now.

> The growth of the Net is not a fluke or a fad, but the consequence of unleashing the power of individual creativity. If it were an economy, it would be the triumph of the free market over central planning. In music, jazz over Bach. Democracy over dictatorship.[4]

HOME PAGE REVIEW QUESTIONS

1. Describe the Internet.
2. Who uses it?
3. What was the first use of the Internet?
4. What is the most recent service added?

4. Special Report, "The Accidental Superhighway," *The Economist*, July 1, 1995. Downloaded from *The Economist* Web site, http://www.economist.com.

Another way to think of the situation is this: You have an electric hair dryer you bought in the United States, and you are planning to take it with you on an around-the-world trip. Because each country you visit has different electrical wall outlets, you need a complete set of adapter plugs.

Now, what makes navigating in cyberspace a little easier is that the onboard computer (remember your spacecraft?) manages all these communicating devices automatically. It has the adapter plugs, so to speak. All you have to know is which one to select to communicate with a specific planet. All these hardware connections are selected and managed with software applications and utility programs. It's as if an invisible software hand is reaching out and plugging the right communicating devices into the right outlets.

Internet Software Tools

Exploring the Internet opens a new realm of information. Your responsibility is to select the proper software program or utility to access what you want. Each program performs a specific task, ranging from providing basic connections to accessing resources to preparing e-mail. Internet tools include the following types:

- *Connection and logon software.* Utilities that set up the communications work session and make the initial connections to the Internet.

- *Web browser.* An application used to navigate among the thousands of World Wide Web sites.

- *E-mail manager and editor.* An application for creating, sending, receiving, storing, and organizing e-mail.

- *Newsreader.* An application used for connecting to newsgroups and for writing and sending messages.

In addition, other tools and utilities search for and retrieve files from various sources. Follow along on the PC communications process shown in figure 11.1 in Module A as you take a closer look.

Connect and Dial Up

The custom connect program (whatever its name may be) starts the procedures for logging on to the Internet. **TCP/IP** (for **Transfer Control Protocol/Internet Protocol**) is the set of standards and protocols for sharing data between computers on the Internet.

If you're using Internet on a computer or terminal at your college or university, the school has probably designated a computer as the **Internet Service Provider**, or **ISP** (sometimes referred to as Internet Access Provider, or IAP). A protocol program, such as Custom TCP/IP, connects your ISP to the Internet. In all likelihood, you'll never come in contact with the custom connect program because the people who support and maintain the computers take care of it for you.

Internet Service Providers must remain connected to provide Internet services 24 hours a day, 365 days a year. There are literally thousands of providers, ranging from small private local providers to educational institutions to businesses. Some are commercial and run as for-profit services, and some, like colleges or governmental agencies, are not-for-profit. Commercial ISPs usually require a monthly or connect-time fee.

If you're connecting to the Internet from your own PC and modem, you use a custom connect protocol program. However, PCs must use another type of protocol, either SLIP or PPP. **SLIP (Serial Line Interface Protocol)** is one of the older Internet protocols. **PPP (Point-to-Point Protocol)** is much preferred because of its efficiency and its capability to correct transmission errors. Often your ISP provides the protocol software. In other cases, it may be included with other software; for example, Windows 95 includes PPP. Figure 11.9 shows how protocols work with the Internet.

Handshake and Log On

Once the protocols have connected your PC and the ISP's computer, you must establish your identity and authorization to use the Internet services. The ISP also has its own identity on the Internet—it is known as a domain.

Domains

The provider's computer has a name and is referred to as a **domain**. The service provider chooses the domain name. The domain name, listed to the right of the @ sign in the address, has an extension that identifies it according to its purpose. Domain name extensions resemble DOS file name extensions. Figure 11.10 shows the many domains on the Internet.

The Internet's Protocols

Your computer sends data to receives data from a host computer over the Internet. A program such as Telnet breaks up the data into packets. Protocols, which are standards on which the computing community has agreed, specify how packets should be layered, or packaged, into even smaller packets. Different layers of packets address a variety of software and hardware needs in order to send information over different networks and communication links.

Figure 11.9

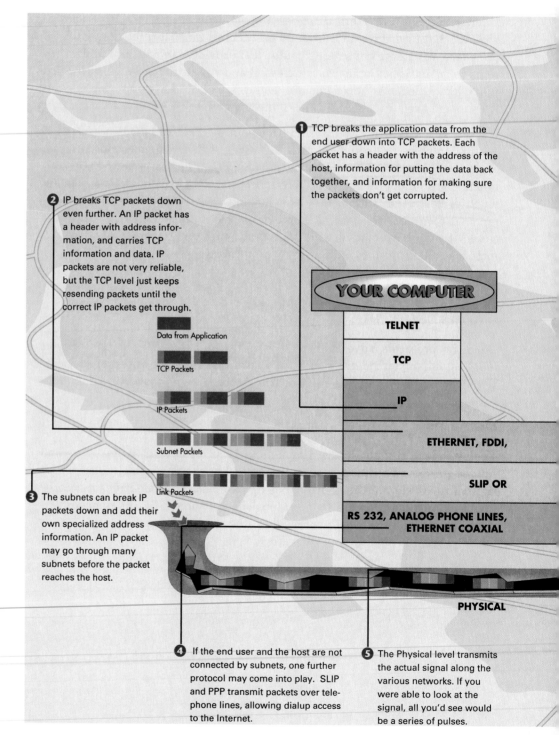

❶ TCP breaks the application data from the end user down into TCP packets. Each packet has a header with the address of the host, information for putting the data back together, and information for making sure the packets don't get corrupted.

❷ IP breaks TCP packets down even further. An IP packet has a header with address information, and carries TCP information and data. IP packets are not very reliable, but the TCP level just keeps resending packets until the correct IP packets get through.

Data from Application

TCP Packets

IP Packets

Subnet Packets

Link Packets

❸ The subnets can break IP packets down and add their own specialized address information. An IP packet may go through many subnets before the packet reaches the host.

YOUR COMPUTER

TELNET

TCP

IP

ETHERNET, FDDI,

SLIP OR

RS 232, ANALOG PHONE LINES, ETHERNET COAXIAL

PHYSICAL

❹ If the end user and the host are not connected by subnets, one further protocol may come into play. SLIP and PPP transmit packets over telephone lines, allowing dialup access to the Internet.

❺ The Physical level transmits the actual signal along the various networks. If you were able to look at the signal, all you'd see would be a series of pulses.

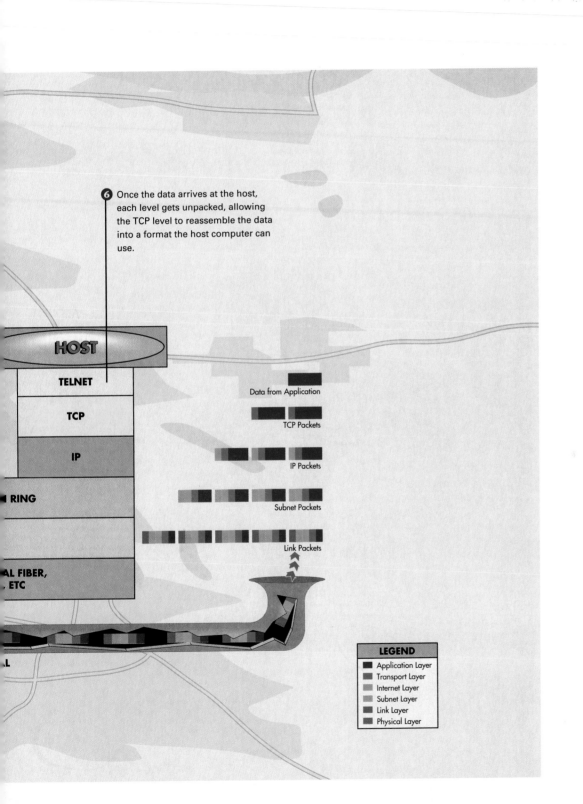

6 Once the data arrives at the host, each level gets unpacked, allowing the TCP level to reassemble the data into a format the host computer can use.

HOST

TELNET

TCP

IP

RING

AL FIBER, , ETC

Data from Application

TCP Packets

IP Packets

Subnet Packets

Link Packets

LEGEND
Application Layer
Transport Layer
Internet Layer
Subnet Layer
Link Layer
Physical Layer

Domain Name System

The Domain Name System is a way of dividing the Internet into understandable groups, or domains. The name of each domain is tacked onto the Internet address, starting from the right with the largest domain. An end user at the end computer is often hooked onto the domain name by an @ sign.

Figure 11.10

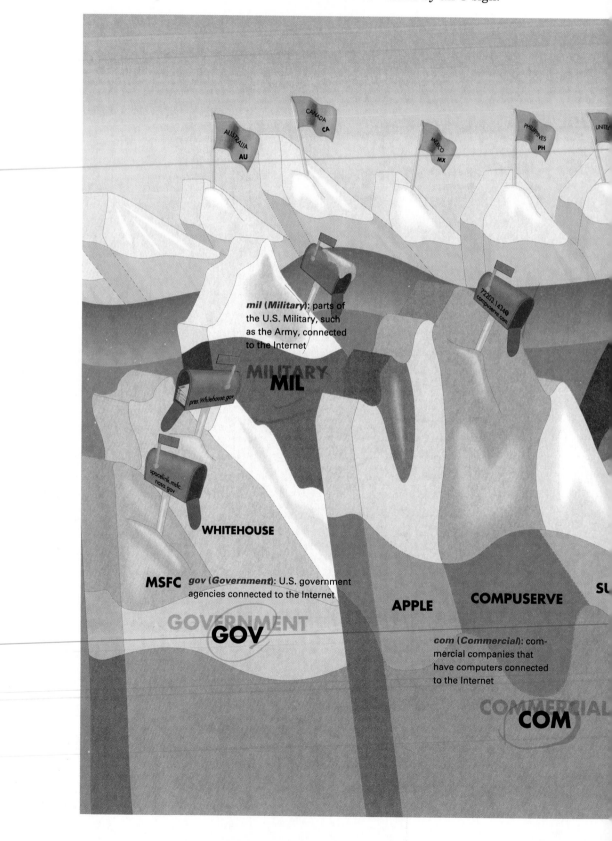

Although the United States uses three-letter domains that are divided by application or theme, such as *edu* for education or *com* for commercial, the rest of the world uses a two-letter country code as the top domain.

FRANCE
FR

GERMANY
DE

ITALY
IT

GREECE
GR

net (*Network*): Companies and groups concerned with the administration of the Internet

NETWORK
NET

library.dartmouth.edu

scilibx.ucsc.edu

liberty.uc.wlu.edu

UC

org (*Organizations*): other organizations on the Internet

ORGANIZATIONS
ORG

UCSC

DARTMOUTH

WLU

EDUCATION
EDU

edu (*Educational*): schools and universities that are connected to the Internet

Logon User Names — CALLen @ cabin.LLCC.cc.IL.u

With the service provider's computer identified on the Internet, you, as an individual subscriber, must register. You are literally logging in, as if you were signing a guest register in a hotel. Each subscriber is a resident in a domain and has a logon, or user, name. Your user name is unique and also identifies your domain (see figure 11.11 for an example). Dana Skiffington is a student at Santa Lucia Community College. The college has dedicated one of its computers, which it calls Sierra, for Internet service. Therefore, Dana's logon identification is

> dskiffington@sierra.slcc.edu

Figure 11.11
The composition of an Internet e-mail address.

If you are logging on to your own Internet service provider's computer, all you need to type your user name, which appears before the @ sign.

Logon Passwords

Because others can know your logon name, a password helps ensure that no one else can read your mail or files, thus maintaining your privacy and security. Although your logon name doesn't change, your password can—and should—frequently. Your password should be unique, something only you know. Again, don't use your pet's name. Never give anyone your password. If you believe someone else has used your account, change your password at once. Many service providers recommend changing your password every three to six months.

Launching the custom connect program to establish the TCP/IP connection and entering your user name, followed by your personal password, completes the link and logon procedures for getting on the Internet.

Navigating Internet Services

After you have properly logged on, you can begin using Internet services. Your activities will include (but not be limited to) the following:

- Sending and receiving e-mail.

- Establishing sessions, such as chat groups.

- Reading news or subscribing to various newsgroups or on-line publications.

- Searching topic-specific databases for information.

- File transfer, or the exchange of files between two computers; the standard for file transfer is called File Transfer Protocol, or FTP.

You need to consider what applications and software utilities are available in order to use these services. The following sections describe these services and provide examples of software.

E-Mail: Eudora

Eudora is an e-mail reader, your on-line post office software. It is a text-editing—simple word processing—program that enables you to create and send messages as well as receive and read messages. While you are on-line, Eudora checks for incoming e-mail every ten minutes and displays a message window that says **You have new mail** when mail arrives. Eudora also manages your incoming, outgoing, and stored mail messages (see figure 11.12).

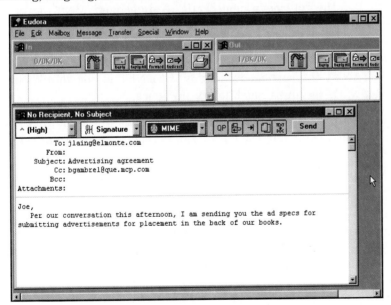

Figure 11.12
An e-mail reader program.

E-mail works much like a post office mailbox. Someone sends a letter to your post office box, and, when you open it, you find the letter waiting. You write a reply, which is sent to your correspondent's mailbox. With e-mail, however, the letter is electronic, and it arrives very quickly.

Internet has its own mail system, as do America Online, Prodigy, CompuServe, MCI Mail, and others. You can send mail to correspondents on other mail systems because *gateways,* special links that translate the messages between the systems, have been created. It's like sending mail to someone who speaks and writes another language: the gateway translates the message so that it will be understood.

Chat Groups: Internet Relay Chat (IRC)

The Internet Relay Chat was created by Jarkko Oikarinen, a Finnish college student who was interested in interactive conversations on the computer. Participating in IRC is like having a conversation with a bunch of your friends at the snack bar or a coffeehouse. The differences are that you're typing instead of talking and the conversation is on-line rather than in person. Many people adopt a nickname when they chat on IRC.

When you join a *chat group,* your computer establishes a connection with a host computer that has a number of chat groups, or *channels,* most of which are devoted to specific topics. You can also set up private chats with another person or group. Everything that each person writes appears on the screen, and because of delays in replies or transmission speeds, the conversations often appear disjointed. Figuring out who's replying to whom and to what is part of the fun.

Newsgroups and USENET: Trumpet

USENET is the Internet's democratic reading room. Here, people from all walks of life converse and share their thoughts on specific topics of interest. There are more than 10,000 newsgroups, and the number grows daily. Although part of the Internet, USENET was originally developed outside the ARPANET-Internet model. Today, USENET is distributed through the Internet while serving a much larger audience.

People post *articles* to USENET newsgroups, ranging from alien abductions to the full-text version of *USA Today* to Zoroastrianism. An article may be a simple question, a personal opinion, a story about personal experiences, or just about anything else. You could say that USENET is an electronic newspaper written by and for its readers.

To be able to read the news in your favorite USENET newsgroup, you need newsreader software. Trumpet for Windows is widely used with PC compatibles, and Newswatcher is used with the Macintosh. A shareware program created in Australia, Trumpet performs the following tasks:

- Connects your computer to the host computer and downloads all the newsgroup names for your selection

- Subscribes you to selected newsgroups and unsubscribes (or "zaps") you, too

- Gathers news on related topics from newsgroups

- Organizes articles in folders, deletes articles, and saves articles in files

- Provides an editor for you to use in writing articles for posting to newsgroups and for writing e-mail

Searching for Information: FTP and Gopher

In the Information Age, what knowledge workers want is—information, of course! And the Internet has it in large quantities stored virtually every-where. The question is, How do you find and retrieve it? The two most popular software tools for this task are FTP and Gopher.

File Transfer Protocol (FTP)

FTP stands for **File Transfer Protocol**, a means of transferring files while ensuring that no errors occur during transmission. FTP is both a standard and a program for uploading and downloading files on the Internet. In the GUI operating environment, FTP is easy to use; you just point and click. The catch with FTP is that in order to download files, you have to know on which host computer the files reside.

Gopher

The solution to not knowing where the programs or data files reside is to use Gopher. Having Gopher is like having the ultimate library index. You simply browse through menus until you find what you want; Gopher does the rest. Gopher has an electronic library card to nearly every source of information on the Internet. Put another way, with Gopher, every source of information on the Internet is in your own library.

Gopher software is similar to other communications software. You must be running Gopher on your remote computer in order to connect to a host computer running Gopher. Your Gopher looks at what's available on the host Gopher and displays the menu (see figure 11.13).

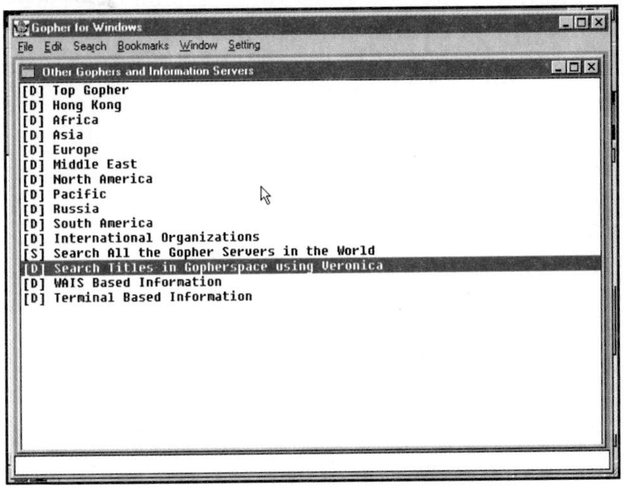

Figure 11.13
Gopher is so widespread that working with it is referred to as "being in Gopherspace."

You can use several additional software utility programs with Gopher to speed or simplify searches. Three of them are Jughead, Veronica, and Archie, named for the comic book characters. The fourth is Wide Area Information Server, or WAIS.

Jughead creates a *search index* of all the menu items you've browsed so that you can easily go back and find the one you want to download. Jughead searches one Gopher host at a time.

Veronica is a master index of some 15 million items; this index is updated regularly. You can search for interesting menu items by using a *keyword search*. Veronica searches for Gopher items worldwide.

Archie is slightly different; it finds and creates databases of files from anonymous FTP computer sites. *Anonymous FTP* refers to a computer host that does not restrict logons to people with logon names and passwords. It's a public access computer, and all you need to do to log on is type *anonymous* at the password prompt. Archie keeps tabs on more than 2 million files on public access computers worldwide.

Wide Area Information Server, or WAIS, is designed to handle searches much larger in size or scope than the other three utilities. WAIS searches databases that are devoted to specific types of content. There are databases for computers, White House documents, aeronautics, movies, music, poetry, and more. Using WAIS, you first identify the database you want; then you search it for the files you want to download. WAIS manages more than 700 indexed databases worldwide.

Telnet

Another Internet resource similar to FTP is **Telnet**, a program that enables you to connect to a remote computer and interact with it. FTP is used to download files. Telnet also uses programs or other resources on the remote computer, just as if you were sitting in front of it.

Disconnect

After you've completed your on-line work session, you must log off the Internet and, depending on the circumstances, disconnect from your ISP. If you're using the college's Internet services, you'll probably log off but not disconnect, as the service is provided to many others at the terminal or computer you used. If you're using a private commercial ISP, you must be sure that you've made a complete disconnection between your computer and theirs, or else you may still be paying fees.

Applications: Suites or Stand-Alone?

You've just covered the basic services available on the Internet, along with examples of the applications or software utilities you'll need so that you can work with them. Even though specific program names are mentioned, be aware that many different versions exist. Some are commercial versions, offered by competing software publishers and bearing different product names. Others are freeware or in the public domain; in some cases, they can be downloaded from the Internet without charge.

You can purchase these applications either as an integrated application *suite* or as individual *stand-alone* applications. Here are some examples from both categories:

- *Internet suites.* An integrated collection of applications and utilities designed to work together smoothly, not unlike integrated office applications such as Microsoft Office. Examples are Internet Chameleon (see figure 11.14), Internet in a Box, Internet Office, Internet Anywhere, and many others.

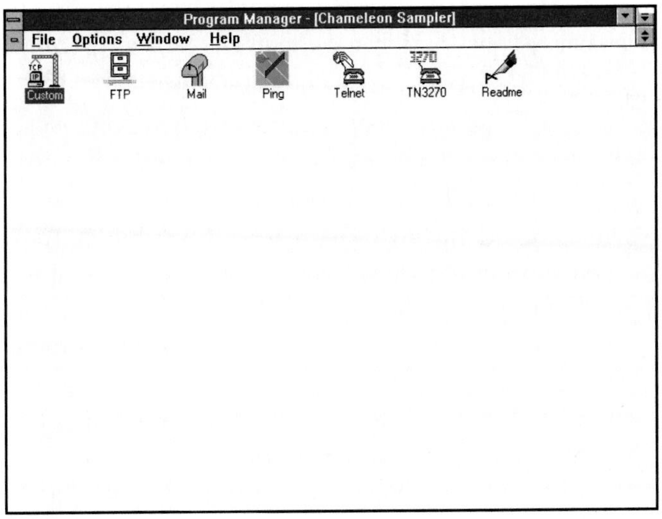

Figure 11.14
Internet Chameleon was PC Magazine's 1995 Editor's Choice.

- *Stand-alone applications and utilities* that you can choose and use as separate programs. These include Netscape Navigator or HotJava for the World Wide Web, Eudora for e-mail, WinGopher for locating files, and SPRY News for use in newsgroups.

The suites are easier to install and handy to use. Purchasing individual stand-alone applications means that you can select the ones you prefer. Reviews in popular personal computing magazines will help you find the ones best suited to your needs.

Knowledge Check

1. Why do you need to have many different software tools in order to use the Internet?
2. For what are the TCP/IP and SLIP protocols used?
3. What is a domain?
4. Identify the different components of this logon user name: jbabiarz@endor.com.
5. Why do you need an e-mail reader?
6. What two purposes does FTP serve?

Key Terms

domain	File Transfer Protocol (FTP)
Internet	Internet Service Provider (ISP)
Point-to-Point Protocol (PPP)	Serial Line Interface Protocol (SLIP)
Telnet	Transfer Control Protocol/Internet Protocol (TCP/IP)

ISSUES AND IDEAS

The Internet as Job Opportunity

Opportunities are where you find them and what you make of them, as Nina Brown of Baltimore, Maryland, will attest. She has started her own business, GenX Internet Training Services, which teaches people how to take people on tours of the Information Superhighway.

Nina Brown is 22 years old. She teaches adults how to use the Internet, at their homes or businesses, on their own computers. "I never get 20- to 30-year-olds," she says. "I would be shocked—we all had it at college, even high school."

E. J. Woznicki, a Baltimore County librarian, had Nina work with him, one on one. "She doesn't come across like 'I know everything about the Internet and you don't know anything,'" he says.

Nina Brown majored in anthropology at Johns Hopkins University but studied a nontraditional culture: cyberspace. She explored Prodigy, America On-line, and the Internet. She first saw Prodigy when she was 16: "My then-boyfriend took me to the basement to show me his new Prodigy system," and she was hooked.

After graduation in 1994, Nina found herself without a job. When people kept asking her questions about how to get on the Internet, she realized that she knew a great deal about it and that she could sell her skills. She has worked with more than 130 customers and offers an array of services from a basic course to advanced skills for the power user. Business is good.[5]

CRITICAL THINKING

1. What skills did Nina Brown use to create her business?
2. Does Brown's enterprise demonstrate how the Information Age is creating new jobs and opportunities?
3. Discuss or write down your skills and interests; then see whether you can find markets and opportunities where you could use them to start your own business.

Module C

The World Wide Web and Browser Software

Why It's Important to Know

> **The World Wide Web is the newest and fastest-growing information service on the Internet. It also offers easy access to many older, text-based Internet resources. Browser software is used to access the Web and may prove useful for other purposes in the future.**

5. Melissa Grace. Adapted from "Savvy Teen Gives Tours on Internet," originally published in *The Baltimore Sun*, reprinted in the *Valley News*, 1995.

The **World Wide Web** (**WWW**) is the newest on-line information service on the Internet. Introduced in 1993, the Web is to the Internet what Windows is to DOS: a graphical environment that offers not only text but also sound, video, and even animation. Many experts say that the advent of the World Wide Web with its color and graphics was responsible for the growth of the Internet. What kind of growth? How about 25 million by 1997?

Other Internet services—e-mail, chat groups, and most file transfers—are strictly text (although you can use FTP to download graphics files and view them in a separate graphics application). But the Web is different: it's graphical as well as textual, it has its own GUI, and it's a world full of compound documents. A software tool called hypertext is what makes Web documents so interesting and versatile.

Hypertext is a way of preparing a computer-created document that allows you to move through it nonsequentially. You don't have to start at the beginning and read each word and sentence in order. The document's author specifies **key words**, which are highlighted, underlined, displayed in a different color, or otherwise distinguished so that they are easily recognizable as hypertext. Clicking a hypertext word or phrase issues the command to create a link to other text or documents. Clicking the hypertext link takes the place of moving back to a command line, toolbar, or menu to issue a command to go somewhere else.

Hypertext was the brain child of a computer visionary named Ted Nelson, who conceived an on-line library implemented with hypertext links in 1969. He called this library Project Xanadu. Unfortunately, because of limitations in computer power and software design, Xanadu was an idea whose time had yet to come. Today most applications use hypertext links in their help files to help you find the information you need.

Hypertext is ideally suited to on-line documents. Files can contain vast amounts of information, and hypertext links enable you to locate quickly what you're looking for. Almost all World Wide Web documents use hypertext links. The primary limitation is that the author defines those links, and they may or may not associate with the information you're looking for. Even so, hypertext is a dramatic leap forward in making documents more useful (see figure 11.15).

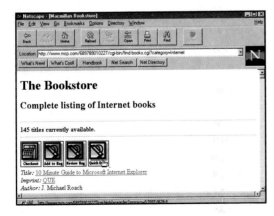

Figure 11.15
Hypertext: Click here to go there.

HOME PAGE

THE BIRTH OF THE WORLD WIDE WEB

The World Wide Web is a global hypertext document-delivery system. A Web document is like a report filled with various kinds of information in different media: text, graphics, sound, and video. The report is found at a Web site, which has an address similar to a drive designation, directory location, and file name. The report cover is called the *home page*; it's where you begin. But instead of turning pages, you click on colored, underlined text—the hyperlinks in the hypertext document. They jump you to another location, where you can find more multimedia information.

About the only thing that can be reliably stated about the World Wide Web is that its growth is phenomenal. According to Matthew Gray, there were 130 Web sites in June, 1993; there were 23,500 in June, 1995.[6] Here is how the Web got started:

> In 1989, some researchers at CERN (the European Laboratory for Particle Physics) wanted to develop a better way to give widely dispersed research groups access to shared information. Because research was conducted between distant sites, performing any simple activity (reading a document or viewing an image) often required finding the location of the desired item, making a remote connection to the machine where it resided, and then retrieving it to a local machine. In addition, each activity required running a number of different applications (such as Telnet, FTP, and an image viewer). What the researchers wanted was a system that would enable them to quickly access all types of information with a common interface, removing the need to execute many steps to achieve the final goal.

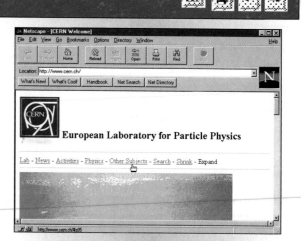

CERN, birthplace of the World Wide Web.

> Over the course of a year, the proposal for this project was refined, and work began on the implementation. By the end of 1990, the researchers at CERN had a text-mode (non-graphical) browser and a graphical browser for the NeXT computer. During 1991, the WWW was released for general usage at CERN. Initially, access was restricted to hypertext and USENET news articles. As the project advanced, interfaces to other Internet services were added (WAIS, FTP, Telnet, and Gopher).

> During 1992, CERN began publicizing the WWW project. People saw what a great idea it was, and began creating their own WWW servers to make their information available to the Internet. A few people also began working on WWW clients, designing easy-to-use interfaces to the WWW. By the end of 1993, browsers had been developed for many different computer systems, including X Windows, Apple Macintosh, and PC/Windows. By the summer of 1994, WWW had become one of the most popular ways to access Internet resources.[7]

---

6. From Matthew Gray, NetGenesis, http:/www.compinfosystems.www.announce.

7. Mary Ann Pike. "How the World Wide Web Works," excerpted from *Special Edition Using the Internet* (Indianapolis:Que, 1994) 677–78.

If you'd like to learn more about the Web, here are some Web sites for information:

Frequently asked questions (FAQs):
   http://sunsite.unc.edu/boutell/faq/
   www_fafaq.html

About CERN: http://cern.ch

About how people use the Web (updated twice a year): http://www.cc.gatech.edu:80/gvu/user_surveys/

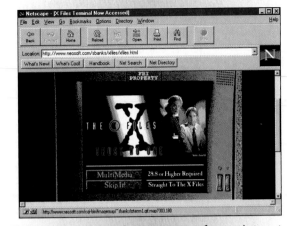

There is a home page for everyone and every interest. This one is for a popular television show.

HOME PAGE REVIEW QUESTIONS

1. How and where did the WWW get its start? Compare your findings to the origins of the Internet.
2. What were some of the primary goals in designing the WWW?
3. Why do you suppose the WWW gained popularity so quickly?

Surfing the Web

Exploring the extraordinary depth and range of information resources on the World Wide Web is known as "surfing the Web." This term aptly describes the way most people move from topic to topic, area to area, studying one thing and then having a quick peek at another before moving on. Writing in *Popular Science*, Chris O'Malley characterizes his on-line adventures on the World Wide Web this way:

> Information superhighway? Alice in Wonderland is more like it. The Internet is a surreal world filled with words and pictures and sounds that manages to be fascinating while remaining largely impractical. You can see pictures of what it's like to stroll down the streets of Paris or London, but you can't stop and make plane or hotel reservations if the experience moves you. Its scope is incredibly broad—yet it's remarkably shallow. There are countless spots devoted to music and movies, for example, but don't expect to get more than a tiny snippet of sound or video through your PC. . . And, oh yes, the Internet is one more thing: It's the trendiest non-place in the universe."[8]

---

8. Chris O'Malley. "Drowning in the Net," *Popular Science*, June 1995, 78–79.

A WWW Work Session

You access the World Wide Web through the Internet, so the first three steps in the PC communications process—connect, dial up, and handshake and log on—have already been completed. To navigate the Web and work with its hypertext documents, you must start a special software program designed specifically for use with the WWW. This kind of program is called browser software.

Web Browser Software

A **browser** is an application designed to help you search for WWW sites and display Web documents. Browser software is a full-featured application that enables you to view hypertext documents. You can scroll through the document's pages or move from one hypertext link to another. If there's sound, you can listen to it. If there's video, you can watch it in a window on the screen. Browser software also enables you to control the work session, upload and download files, and, of course, surf the Web. As you can see in figure 11.16, browser software takes full advantage of the graphical user interface.

Figure 11.16
Mosaic was the first popular GUI browser software application.

Mosaic, the first popular browser, was created at the National Center for Supercomputing Applications (NCSA) at the University of Illinois. It was a freeware program, distributed over the Internet. Its creators, led by a 24-year-old programmer named Marc Andreessen, went on to produce a commercial version called Netscape, which made Andreessen an overnight millionaire.

Browser software is a *killer app*, and new features are constantly being introduced. Netscape itself has undergone a transformation in newly developed versions of its program, such as for Windows 95, and new competitors like Netshark seem intent on outdoing the competition. The latest browser that people are excited about is HotJava. David Cappucio, vice president of network technologies at the Gartner Group market research firm, says, "Any Web browser purchased today should be considered to have a half life of six months at the most."9

9. Quoted in *Information Week*, October 23, 1995, 81.

Using the browser software, you can begin visiting Web sites. But how do you know where you want to go? If you don't have a specific site in mind, you can select some sites using one of the various search engines, or searchers, available on the WWW.

Web Searchers

A *Web searcher* is a software program that searches for, stores, and indexes the names of Web sites; describes them; and provides their names in hypertext hot links so that you can jump right to them. No two navigators are the same, but the most popular (including their Web site addresses) are the following:

- *Yahoo* at http://www.yahoo.com

- *World Wide Web Virtual Library at* http://www.w3.org/hypertext/DataSources/bySubject/

- *Whole Internet Catalog* at http://gnn.com/gnn/wic/index.html

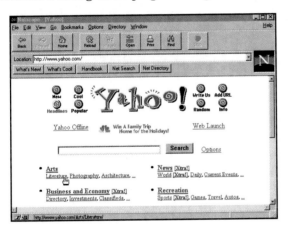

Figure 11.17
Yahoo can take you to many Web sites.

You can also use a *Web searcher* that looks for key words or menu choices. Two of the most popular are these:

- *Lycos* at http://lycos2.cs.cmu.edu/ or http://www.lycos.com/

- *WebCrawler* at http://webcrawler.com/

You can type these addresses into the blank space near the top of the browser screen (see figure 11.18). When you know where you want to go, you can type the Web site's *URL* here. What's a URL?

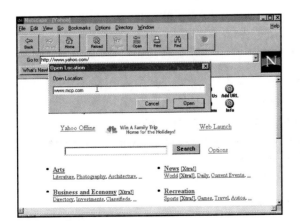

Figure 11.18
You type the address of a searcher near the top of the browser screen.

URL

Like your home, a Web site has an address. It's called a **Universal Resource Locator**, or **URL**. You must know a site's URL address to visit the site. The address is similar to your Internet address. URLS are used for many services including USENET news, Gopher, FTP archives, and, of course, Web HTML documents. You must type URLs exactly as they appear: spaces or no spaces, lowercase, capitals, colons, and diagonals. (Note the URL in figure 11.18.)

All URLs begin with http://, which identifies the protocol used with WWW hypertext documents. **HTTP** stands for **Hypertext transport protocol**, which is designed to support the hypertext links between documents.

Home Pages

The home page is the primary document on the Web. When you surf to a Web site, you land first on the home page. Individuals, colleges, governmental agencies and bodies, businesses, and all sorts of other enterprises create home pages. They range from the ridiculous—one is devoted to showing what a certain individual is currently watching on TV and another belongs to a cat—to the sublime, which might be NASA to one person, or the rock band U2 to another.

A home page combines text, graphics, hypertext, and possibly sound and moving video to give you a good idea where you're visiting and what it's all about. The home page may be entertaining, informative, or both (or neither, depending on your taste). People often put a great deal of effort into creating interesting, artistic, and unique home pages. These are often referred to as *cool sites*. Many magazines and newspapers publish regular reviews and descriptions of cool sites for you to explore.

Some home pages contain a great deal of interesting information providing links to many additional pages. In those cases, you may encounter a hypertext link to something called **FAQ**, which stands for **frequently asked questions**. FAQs are very handy because they do exactly what they say they do: they answer most of the questions you'll have about that site.

You can create your own home page and do just about anything you want with it (although your ISP may charge a fee for maintaining it). You create a home page with an easy-to-use programming language called **HTML**, or **hypertext markup language**. Most people who are fairly proficient with the PC and application software can create a home page using HTML. Some word processing programs now make designing a home page document as easy as creating a word processing document. When you capture Web site data in a file, the data is stored with the HTM file name extension, indicating that the file was created with HTML. The browser program is best suited to displaying the file with all its graphic and hypertext characteristics.

You can keep track of visits to your home page; each visit is called a *hit*. If you get many hits, your home page is probably a hit! As this book goes to press, estimates are that more than 4 million home pages have been created and that about 6,000 a day are being added to the World Wide Web.

Ending a WWW Work Session

In addition to browsing home pages, you can access files using FTP, Gopher, and many other Internet services. During the course of a WWW work session, you may visit a number of Web sites, clicking hypertext links to leap through cyberspace and capturing data in files. When you're finished, all you need to do to leave the World Wide Web is exit the browser software. This step takes you back to the Internet, where you're still on-line. Depending on the ISP you're using, you may or may not disconnect the phone line connection.

Knowledge Check

1. What is the difference between the Internet and the World Wide Web?
2. List some characteristics of hypertext.
3. For what two things is browser software used?
4. What does a Web navigator find?
5. For what is HTML used?
6. What is a URL, and what four letters does one usually begin with?
7. What is a FAQ?

Key Terms

browser

hypertext

hypertext transport protocol (HTTP)

Universal Resource Locator (URL)

frequently asked questions (FAQs)

hypertext markup language (HTML)

key words

World Wide Web (WWW)

ISSUES AND IDEAS

Why the Internet Scares Me

The following excerpt from the book *The Future Does Not Compute*, by Stephen L. Talbott, takes issue with three widely touted advantages of the Internet: information at your fingertips, the on-line community as a new social environment, and the true democratization of politics. Consider his arguments:

The Internet does not promise to redeem education. Rather, it is bringing to perfection the "shoveling facts" model of instruction. The overwhelmingly dominant metaphor for the knowledgeable mind is now found in the computer database stuffed full of informational bytes. The sleepwalking vacancy within us has become a void to be filled with information rather than that place of waking, inner activity wherein information can find its meaning.

The Internet does not promise the renewal of community and the revival of personal relationship. Rather, it is reducing to abstraction whatever human connections remain. The easy warmth and confessional quality of so much electronic correspondence is not altogether unlike what one finds in the shallower reaches of New Ageism, where good feelings thrive in direct proportion to the escape from any genuine sharing of life's gritty responsibilities and blows. Likewise, the supposed "victory over prejudice" (we cannot see each other's skin color or handicaps though e-mail) is in reality an ignoring of the concrete, earthly humanity of the other. And the Net flame is anger gone dry, detached, and self-absorbed, not at all engaging the supposed antagonist.

The Internet's interactivity does not promise a greening of the television wasteland. The important thing about interactivity is not that it redeems old forms of entertainment (it doesn't), but rather how it adapts much more of our lives to the video screen. Making sitcoms interactive will not lead to cultural transformations, but there's every reason to suspect, for example, that moving local, face-to-face politics on-line will tend to change the character of those politics in the direction of what we've already seen happen to televised politics.

Interactivity, in other words, does not salvage the preexisting wasteland, whereas it may well reduce huge tracts of once-thriving adjacent territory to semi-aridity. Yet the pundits have been content to exclaim, "Look how much greener than the desert this new, semi-arid land is!"[10]

CRITICAL THINKING

1. How does the author characterize the Internet method of delivering information? What seems to be the opposite method?

2. How does the author characterize the on-line sense of community?

3. Why does the author think that nothing will change as a result of on-line political discourse?

4. Generally, do you agree or disagree with Talbott? Should we be careful not to expect too much from the Internet? State your reasons.

---

10. Stephen L. Talbott. *The Future Does Not Compute.* (Sebastopol, CA: O'Reilly & Associates, 1995).

ETHICS

What to Do about PornoNet?

A controversy rages about pornography on the Internet, specifically as it affects children. In 1995, *Time* magazine published an extremely controversial cover story entitled "Cyberporn," with accompanying photos that were nearly pornographic themselves. The article proved to be a lot of hype: reports are that pornography, in both text and graphic forms, account for less than three percent of Net usage.

Many feel that "market demand" and self-regulation, both by service providers and consumers, will quell the pornography. Yet many others feel that safeguards should be "built in" to the Internet to ensure that it is porn-free. The two safeguards that have been discussed are blocking software and government regulation.

Blocking software lets parents set up the access routes so that kids won't be able to access certain sites and will not receive e-mail from certain sources. A parent can accomplish this by entering characters or key words that, when recognized, block that service or correspondent.

Both the U.S. Senate and the House of Representatives introduced legislation governing the Internet in 1995. The Senate bill, sponsored by Senators James Exon of Nebraska and Dan Coats of Indiana, would make transmitting "indecent" materials over the Internet a criminal offense.

More than two dozen computer industry companies—including America Online, CompuServe, IBM, Microsoft, Prodigy, and TimeWarner—have formed a consortium called the Platform for Internet Content Selections, or PICS, to address the pornography issue. They have asked Congress to let them self-regulate the Internet, and are in the process of developing a standard for rating on-line content, similar to the rating system of the Motion Pictures Association.

Critical Thinking

1. Should pornography be kept off the Internet? If so, should it also be kept out of movies, books, "adult" stores and everywhere else it appears in society?

2. Is blocking software a good solution to the porn problem? Defend your position.

3. Should the government legislate pornography in the Internet? Research other incidents of government legislation of so-called pornography, such as the novel *Tropic of Cancer* by Henry Miller or the film "I Am Curious-Yellow." What is the precedent for government legislation of morals? Is the Internet case different?

THE LEARNING ENTERPRISE

Many, if not all, of the knowledge workers in your enterprise will find on-line capabilities useful. Most will want to use e-mail, and that should be encouraged. However, the use of on-line information services can become time-consuming and result in lost productivity.

To ensure that everyone has a sound business reason to use on-line services, prepare a survey to determine how your enterprise's knowledge workers plan to use communications. This survey should be kept short—no more than five questions—and should be developed by all knowledge workers who want to participate in its design. Otherwise, if designed by only a few, it will become a tool for keeping people off-line, and that is not your goal. The survey should help people make sound decisions for themselves.

If possible, have each knowledge worker become familiar with on-line communications and spend some time—an hour or more—on the Internet and World Wide Web. Then have them respond to the survey. Here are some ideas for survey questions:

- After spending ____ hours researching on-line information services, I have concluded that I (do) (do not) need them to improve my work.
- I have concluded that the only thing I need is e-mail.
- List the on-line information services you feel would be most beneficial in your work. Be as specific as possible.
- What aspect of your work pertains to on-line applications?
- How would your work be enhanced by using on-line applications?
- What specific types of on-line information would you like to obtain, and how would it be used in your work?
- Describe how the quality of the information you work with and produce would be improved with the value added by on-line information?
- How would you share the information you obtain with other knowledge workers?
- Explain how your personal productivity would be enhanced through the use of on-line information services.
- Explain how the enterprise as a whole would benefit from the information you obtain from on-line information services.

Once all the knowledge workers have had a chance to make a decision, do some research as a work group to choose the software applications and utilities you want to use. Practice using e-mail among yourselves, using the campus system. Keep copies of both sent mail and received mail, and create a log of your work group's activities. If you or others are capturing information, share it with one another—either electronically, through e-mail, or as a circulating memo.

Chapter Review

Fill in the Blank

1. _____ is the comparative study of human and machine processes.

2. A terminal sends data to and receives data from other computers called _____.

3. Communication _____ are hardware and software standards.

4. A step called _____ ensures that when one computer transmits, the other is ready to receive.

5. A communications program, referred to as _____ , turns your PC into a terminal for communicating.

6. To navigate among the thousands of World Wide Web sites, you use an application called a(n) _____.

7. The primary document on the World Wide Web is called a(n) _____.

8. HTTP stands for _____.

9. HTML stands for _____.

10. A FAQ is a(n) _____.

True/False

1. On-line means that your computer is in direct communication with another computer.

2. You can send and receive data from other computers.

3. Sending a file from your PC to another computer is called uploading.

4. The Internet is a system of linked computer networks that encircle the globe.

5. To visit a site on the World Wide Web, you must type its Universal Resource Locator (URL) or address.

Review Questions

1. List the five steps in the communications software process.

2. What is the difference between half-duplex and full-duplex?

3. List four characteristics of a full-featured communications software program.

4. Give several examples of netiquette.

5. What is flaming?

6. Identify the four parts of this Internet e-mail address: matherton@msu.edu.

7. What four letters begin the address or URL of a Web site?

8. What is a chat group?

9. Name two popular software tools for finding and retrieving information on the Internet.

10. What is the name of the programming language that you use to create a home page?

Discussion Questions

1. The Internet enables us to communicate with people we would not otherwise have an opportunity to talk with. Choose a topic that interests you and research it on the Internet.

2. Do you think that your communicating through e-mail is preferable to face-to-face interactions or phone conversations? What is lost or gained in each means of communicating? For example, how important is tone, voice, or facial expression in communicating with others?

3. Is the anonymity factor an encouragement to Internet communication? How do you feel about people presenting a different persona over the Internet?

INTERNET DISCOVERY

You can find a good guide to using the Internet at the following address:

http://www.earn.net/gnrt/notice.html

You can use e-mail in various ways.

To contact government officials in Washington:

http://www.xmission.com/~insearch /washington.html

To find business e-mail addresses:

http://yellowwweb.com/

To list your e-mail address:

http://www.infop.com/phone/index.html

To contact other writers:

http://www.generation.net/~straycat /workshop.html

PRESENTATION GRAPHICS AND DESKTOP PUBLISHING SOFTWARE

One picture is worth more than ten thousand words.
Chinese proverb

Publishing is every company's second business.
Electronic publishing expert David Henry Goodstein[1]

Because human beings are visually oriented, the computer should also be visually oriented. The early constraints of a monitor filled with text characters have given way to graphically oriented operating environments and applications capable of providing detailed colors and images.

Early graphics software enabled programmers only to draw lines to create simple figures. This capability led to the **paint program**, which creates colorful freehand drawings and paintings, and to the *illustration applications* that designers use. The illustration applications then led to applications that enabled creative manipulation of photographs and art. Today, applications are available for every type of artist and for every conceivable aspect of visual communication, including moving video.

Graphics were intended to be displayed with accompanying text. Some of the earliest handmade books were heavily illustrated *illuminated manuscripts*.

The basics of printing didn't change much from the eleventh to the twentieth century. Type—letters and characters—and the art blocks were made first of wood and then of lead. Type was set by hand and then by printing presses. For hundreds of years, printing presses remained in the hands of newspaper owners and book printers.

The computer industry was among the first to see the need for internal publishing operations: the operation and instruction manuals for a typical computer system filled a shelf from six to twenty feet long! The computer companies soon realized that it was far more cost-effective to write, print, and publish their own manuals. The companies therefore developed publishing software, first called *electronic publishing software*, which ran on high-powered workstations or minicomputers.

1. Personal interview with author.

CHAPTER 12

Module A

Presentation Graphics

Why It's Important to Know

Presentation graphics are the graphics created most frequently by knowledge workers. The ability to transform numeric data into meaningful images or to convey information in graphic form greatly increases productivity. The capability of presentation graphics to translate numeric data into a meaningful and memorable report makes this form of communication one of the most important ways to present information.

Graphics are pictorial representations. A graphic can be a photograph, illustration, cartoon, painting—just about any visual image is a graphic. A graphics application enables you to work with computer-generated graphic images. At one time, graphics were used mostly by artists, engineers, and programmers, but the Macintosh has changed that. The Mac demonstrated that computers are capable of producing high-quality graphics at an affordable price. Professional graphic artists quickly began using the Mac, and it also brought flocking to computers many people who previously hadn't been interested. Many of the examples of graphic art and illustration in this book were created by artists and designers working on Macintoshes at Que.

Figure 12.1 shows some examples of the variety of art forms that graphics software is capable of creating. Many graphics applications on the market can be used for this work. A thorough examination of the creative aspect of graphics applications, however, is beyond the scope of this text. The focus of this chapter is to discuss the types of graphics that most frequently accompany documents to present work-related information. These types of graphics are called presentation graphics.

Figure 12.1
These graphics were created on computers.

Adobe Photoshop

CorelDraw

Adobe Illustrator

Presentations can take the following forms:

- Paper—usually as reports

- Transparencies—displayed with an overhead projector

- Color slides—displayed with a slide projector

- Screen displays—projected from the computer on to an overhead projector

Presentation graphics are simple graphs, or charts, that represent business data and usually include titles, legends, and explanatory text. With regard to computers and software, the terms **graph** and *chart* both refer to a graphic or a diagram that displays data—usually numeric—in pictorial form. The terms *graph* and *chart* are synonymous; for convenience and consistency, *graph* is used in this book. Similar to spreadsheet graphics, the most commonly used graphs include pie graphs, bar graphs, and line graphs. Figure 12.2 shows some of the available Microsoft Excel graph types.

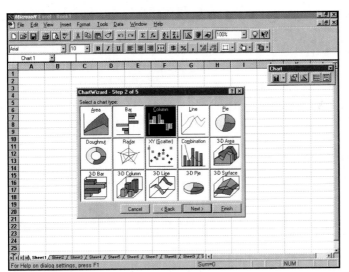

Figure 12.2
Microsoft Excel provides many different graph types for use with the spreadsheet data.

You can create graphs by using a graphics application, such as CorelDraw, or a Windows applet, such as Microsoft Graph. You can also create graphs from within another application—for example, a spreadsheet application. Most popular software applications contain some graph capabilities.

The Computer Graphics Process

The computer graphics process is not complicated. In fact, it's very straightforward because the computer and the software do most of the work for you.

Figure 12.3, "The Computer Graphics Process Chart," shows the steps involved in creating a graphic. These steps include designing the page, creating, displaying, saving, and printing the graphic.

Figure 12.3
*The Computer Graphics
Process Chart.*

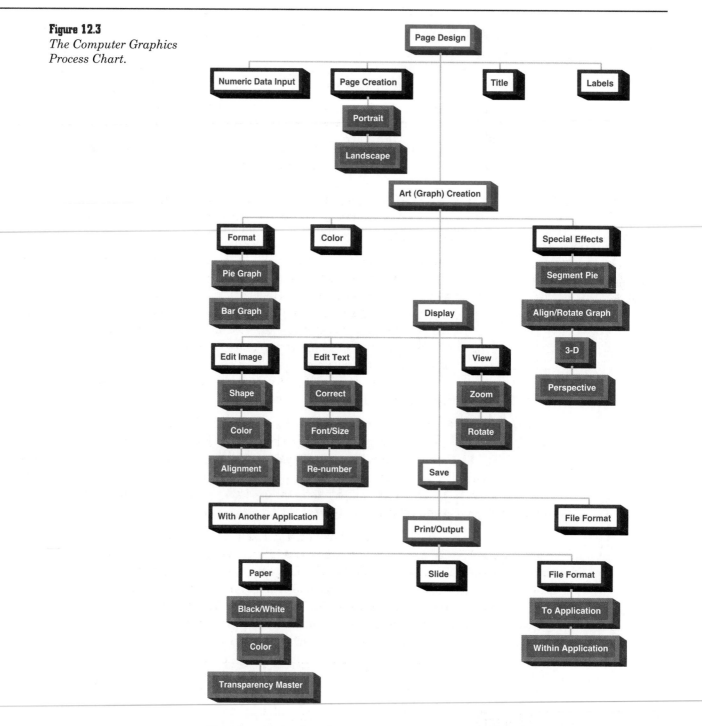

Designing the Page

The first step in creating a graph is to design the page. This step involves
adding a title and labels, or text, to define and describe the numeric data.
The numeric data you use may be something you have on paper, or it may
have been generated by a spreadsheet or database management system
(DBMS) application. Labels, such as months, sales territories, or divisions of
the company, identify the data.

Creating the Art (Graph)

The second step is creating the graph. First, you select the type of graph that will represent your data most effectively. Consider the following points in choosing your graph types:

- Pie graphs are good for representing portions of a whole—for example, how a nonprofit organization distributes varying percentages of each dollar contributed.

- Bar graphs are useful for representing growth, in time or value, of unrelated items—for example, how much a sales territory or product line has grown over two consecutive years.

- Line graphs are effective for showing variations of data over a period of time—for example, the number of influenza cases over a five-year period.

Once you have selected the type of graph that you want to represent your data, you can customize the color and design of the different representations. In a pie graph, for example, portions of the graph can be highlighted, the largest pie slice can be enlarged and separated, or a three-dimensional image can be rotated.

Displaying the Graph

The third step is to display the graph on the screen. WYSIWYG, "what you see is what you get," enables you to see how the data, colors, and labels have been graphically formatted. This step is the one in which you can make changes. For example, if you have created a bar graph, you may find that the numeric increments on the vertical axis are too small or too large. If you have created a pie graph, you may need to change the font size of the pie section labels so that they fit. In screen display, you can revise and view your graph again and again until it looks the way you want it to.

Saving the Graph

The fourth step when creating a graph is to save it. In the graphics application, saving isn't a periodic activity because you don't want to save the graph until it is correct. You save the graph as a file after the image is final. If you have created the graph within another application, check to see whether the graph is saved with the data used to create it. Some graphics applications permit saving the graph in different file formats for use by other applications.

Printing the Graph

The final step in creating a graph is to print it. If you don't have a color printer, the graph will print in different shades of gray. It might be more accurate to say that the final step of creating a graph is output, because you can save the graph as a file that can be used by another application. For example, you can include the graph with the numeric data from a worksheet in a spreadsheet application; or you may have created the graphic from within a presentation graphics application.

Presentation Graphics

Combining graphs with text for a presentation is becoming common practice. Whether you are creating a report for a weekly staff meeting or an annual report, using numerical data graphically with text is highly effective communication. Applications like Microsoft PowerPoint can be used to create these presentations. In addition to working with graphs, most applications enable you to insert **clip art**, which is a collection of simple images of people and objects, such as arrows, animals, buildings, and trains—to name but a few. These clip-art graphics are stored as files on disk and can be used in a wide variety of documents. Figure 12.4 shows a typical presentation screen using clip art.

Figure 12.4

Clip art can enhance textual presentations.

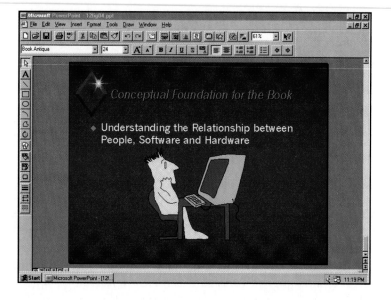

Some applications prompt you through the process of creating a presentation with a help tool like a Wizard or with menu screens that guide you step by step. These tools enable you to focus on content rather than the workings of the program. The steps in creating presentation graphics are the following:

1. Determine the type of presentation—business, informal, or personal— and the manner in which you want to display it, for example, printed on paper or a computer-based slide show.

2. Create the presentation title page (or slide).

3. Create and lay out consecutive pages as text, text and graph, and so on. You may want to use the application's outlining feature to structure your presentation.

4. Write, format, and position text.

5. Select and position the graph.

6. Edit and review your presentation.

7. Preview the presentation.

8. Save the presentation.

9. Print or display the presentation.

An additional feature of a presentation graphics program is the capability to format and use the presentation in different ways, such as

- Summary or outline

- Speaker's or presenter's notes

- Overhead transparencies

- Computer-generated slides

- WYSIWYG handouts

Knowledge Check

1. List the steps in the computer graphics process.

2. What are the most common types of presentation graphs?

3. Describe different ways that graphs can be displayed.

4. What is the most common use of graphics for business purposes called?

5. Name two things that are combined in presentation graphics.

6. What is clip art?

Key Terms

clip art   graph   graphic   presentation graphics

ISSUES AND IDEAS

The Future of the Well Made

Graphics software often encourages the notion of a computer-simulated object or environment being somehow real and approachable. This illusion can lead to an estrangement from the material world and an unnatural immersion in the computer's "virtual" world. Consider, then, these excerpts from the essay "The Future of the Well Made" and see how you feel about the impact of technology after you have read it.

Since that early, twentieth century outburst of optimism and faith in the promise of technology, the idea of the well made seems to have lost its way. . . . Glorifying past crafts has a long and noble tradition in the West, spurred most notoriously by the art critic John Ruskin, who convinced his fellow Victorians that handmade objects had a soul all their own, far superior to anything machines made. . . .

HOME PAGE

GRAPHICS FOR FUN AND PROFIT

What do you do with a love of baseball; a team of award-winning programmers, artists, animators, writers, music and sound editors; and some of the most advanced and sophisticated graphics software? If you're Stormfront Studios, you create a CD-ROM interactive simulation called *Old Time Baseball*. *Interactive* means that as the player, you have an active role in the game or simulation; what you do makes a difference in the outcome.

"We're the industry leaders in baseball software for the PC," says president Don Daglow in a videotaped press release, because of "a deep love of baseball, an attention to historic detail, and a strong understanding of the available technology. With *Old Time Baseball*, we've delivered baseball's past with a faithfulness and accuracy that is unparalleled."

Stormfront uses software products from Autodesk Inc., a company known for its innovative applications. *Old Time Baseball* presents more than 12,000 players and teams from 1871 through 1971. The high-resolution player animation was created using Animator Pro. Video footage was shot using professional baseball players and used to create realistic pitching, hitting, and fielding. Player statistics are displayed on interactive "cards" as shown in the illustration.

Old Time Baseball's player cards are interactive.

Games are played in 16 authentic baseball parks (only five of which still exist today), including Old Comiskey Park in Chicago and the original Yankee Stadium. The stadiums were recreated from original architectural drawings, photographs, videos, and blueprints by using AutoCAD, a computer-aided drafting application. Three-dimensional modeling, rendering, and adding textures was accomplished with an application called 3D Studio.

Vintage play-by-play "broadcasts" are provided by Baseball Hall of Fame radio personalities Curt Gowdy and Mel Allen. Players can play on their original teams or can be drafted to other teams—and seasons. For example, you can see the late Babe Ruth pitch to today's all-time top hitter, Cal Ripkin, using Stormfront's Time Machine.

At the heart of Stormfront's products are high production values and state-of-the-art visual and audio effects that make interactive play and storytelling come alive. Stormfront's latest creations include (John) *Madden NFL Football '96* and *Star Trek: Deep Space Nine—Harbinger*.

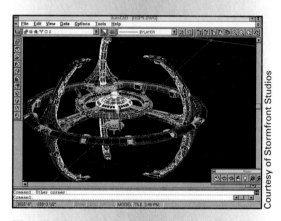

This wireframe of the DS9 space station was created using AutoCAD.

HOME PAGE REVIEW QUESTIONS

1. What does *interactive* mean?

2. What types of software does Stormfront use to create its ballparks?

3. What is involved in the process of animating the ball players?

It is good to consider how we will cultivate the well-made object in the future. . . . I think I have caught a glimpse of it in the studio of Robin Mix, a glass blower in Vermont. He uses centuries-old techniques learned from Venetian craftsmen. However, he does not have to stoke his furnace to keep it at the right temperature; a computer does that for him. Perhaps that kind of collaboration is the ideal marriage of new technologies and old crafts. If we let Robin Mix stand for a new generation of artisans, there is hope yet for the future of the well made. For here, technology, far from robbing the rich tradition of its soul, has helped to keep its spirit very much alive.[2]

CRITICAL THINKING

1. How does the issue of the "well made" relate to computer graphics?

2. Is it in our best interests to live in a re-created world of computer graphics simulations? Can you make a case for playing simulated base-ball games?

3. What would be a good marriage of computer graphics simulations and the "real world" of the well made?

Module B

Desktop Publishing

Why It's Important to Know

> **Mastering desktop publishing skills enhances your word processing skills, turning a writer into a publisher. Desktop publishing offers sophisticated typesetting and layout capabilities that result in attractive and professional-looking published documents.**

<u>**Desktop publishing**</u> (<u>**DTP**</u>) is the use of a personal computer to create typeset-quality text and graphics. Desktop publishing enables you to compose, design, typeset, and incorporate artwork into a professional-looking document or form ready for printing. Typically, *documents* include anything from books and instruction manuals to magazines, brochures, leaflets, flyers, advertisements, newsletters, and pamphlets. Figure 12.5 shows some examples of desktop publishing capabilities.

---

2. Julie V. Iovine. "The Future of the Well Made," *Home Design* magazine, *The New York Times*, October 22, 1995.

Figure 12.5
This desktop publishing program offers many choices for newsletters and other documents.

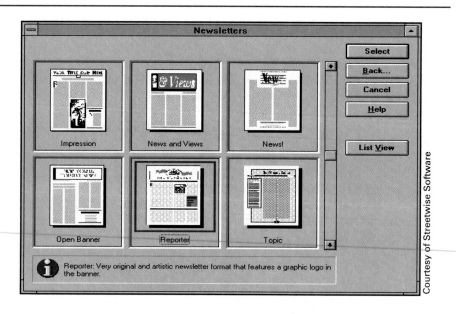

Courtesy of Streetwise Software

Desktop publishing creates *typeset-quality* documents as opposed to *type-written* documents. DTP is often called a *page composition* application, which means that you can design and lay out a document in one or more distinctive page formats. As Sharyn Venit, author of a desktop publishing book says, "When reading a publication, how can you absorb all the information you need to know as quickly as possible? How can an author or publisher catch the reader's attention? The answer, of course, is to design the information to invite the reader's attention, to include headings and subheadings that make it easy to skim the material for key points, and to include illustrations that can convey complex ideas much more quickly than words. Desktop publishing enables you to create the kinds of effective, eye-catching publications that you need in this information age."[3]

In just ten years, the desktop publishing (DTP) process has dramatically changed from the traditional, centuries-old publishing process. Figure 12.6 shows the traditional publishing process. As you can see, a great deal of handwork is involved. But now look at figure 12.7, which shows the desktop publishing process. Most of the work is now accomplished using personal computers, which can reduce the costs of publication by as much as 75 percent.

3. Sharyn Venit. *Using PageMaker 5 for Windows* (Indianapolis, Que, 1993), 14.

The Desktop Publishing Process

Figure 12.8 shows the Desktop Publishing Process Chart. There are six activities in which you, the editor and desktop publisher, are actively engaged: designing the page layout or template, pouring in and copy-fitting text, creating and sizing graphics, formatting, saving, and printing. Because you have already learned about creating graphics, this module discusses only five of these steps.

Designing the Page Layout

Page layout involves determining the placement of text and graphics for the type of publication you want to create. It can be a one-page flyer, newsletter, report, brochure, advertisement, business form, catalog page, stationery, invitation, menu, program, directory, manual, or book. From a single page to a bound and printed 500-page book, everything can be done with DTP.

Knowing the scope of a project helps you plan the work. Some documents have more than one design; for example, some textbooks use a two-column design for text but a one-column design for boxed features. DTP pages use a **frame**, or box, that contains text or graphics. The frame can hold a column of text or a graphic element, a banner (as in a newsletter title), or a footer with newsletter subscription information. A frame is not restricted by the column layout or format. The **ruler** is a tool for measuring the size of frames and columns.

Templates are used by many applications, and desktop publishing is one of them. A DTP template is the page layout grid that serves as the starting point for creating documents with a consistent look. The use of a template helps make the process of creating a document easier. Templates often have a **style sheet**, which is a list of all the specific design characteristics—for example, margins, headers, footers, font styles for the various elements of the document, and so on. If your layout specifies four different page formats, you can create a style sheet for each and then apply styles when necessary.

Pouring Text

Text in a desktop publishing document can be **imported** from a word processing application. Most DTP applications permit importing text in its **native file format**, meaning from the originating application—most commonly word processing. To *pour text* means to take the word processing text and move it into the frame or template that you created in the DTP application. Some DTP programs have a built-in word processing application so that text can be entered directly into a column or template. The only drawback to doing so is that the DTP software often formats the text as you write, making the program work somewhat slowly.

The Traditional Publishing Process

Editor

Once the copy is polished to her specifications, the editor prints a clean copy of the text and gives it, along with the corrected electronic file, to the typesetter.

Typesetter

Working off specifications given to him by the designer, the typesetter encodes the copy with style and size attributes. He then creates *galleys*, strips of styled text set in columns according to predetermined widths.

Writer

After writing text on a word processor, the writer sends the editor an electronic text file (soft copy) along with a text printout (hard copy). The editor marks the printout with corrections and returns it to the writer for review. Hard copy lets the editor track errors in the editing process.

Words

Soft/hard copy

Designer

Working with the editor, the designer creates page layouts. She decides what size the type should be, how wide the columns are, how big the illustrations will be, and so on. For consistency and efficiency, most publications create a *template*, a set of design and format specifications applied to each layout.

Type specs

Type and design specs

Design sp

Artist

The artist works with the editor and designer to create art that reflects the text. He may use a variety of media—water color, pastel chalks , collage—to create an illustration, so it's necessary to shoot the art with a process camera, which produces reduced-sized images on special paper.

Art

Camera operator

The boards are sent to the camera operator. They're photographed with a special camera to create film negatives of the entire page.

Film

Boards

Press operator

In order to proof the film, the press operator first exposes the negatives on to either photosensitive paper (in the case of black and white) or on to a laminated substrate (in the case of color). The proof shows what the final print job will look like.

Next, the proofed film negatives are exposed on to special photosensitive material, which will be used as printing plates on the press. (On critical jobs, a press proof, printed on the actual printing press, is made as a final check before the press run.)

Then, the final pages are printed on the press. Depending on the nature of the press and of the job, pages may be printed one at a time or grouped together on a sheet that can be folded and cut to produce a group of pages (a *signature*). *Perfecting* presses print both sides of the paper in a single pass. The pages are trimmed and bound into books or folded into newspapers.

Paste-up artist

The type galleys and camera-ready art are handed over to the paste-up department for integration into the designer's layout. Here the type and art are cut, trimmed, and pasted (using a special wax) on to stiff boards.

amera-ady art

Final pages

Figure 12.6
Courtesy of Ziff-Davis Press

The Desktop Publishing Process

Writer

The writer enters text into his computer. He sends this file electronically to the editor. After editing, the file is sent electronically to the designer for layout. (If you're writing, editing, and designing your project yourself, the file stays put.)

Words

Edited cop

Designer

Working from an established template, the designer pours text into the electronic layout on her computer. The text flows directly into columns, even jumping to another page where necessary. She applies type styles and sizes with a few keystrokes. Because she gets instant feedback, she can make changes immediately. Graphics are inserted, resized, even rotated and cropped, quickly and easily. Throughout the layout process, the designer prints intermediate copies on a laser printer to check the positioning of the text with the graphics. When the layout is done to her satisfaction, she sends the electronic file to a service bureau.

Art

Artist

The artist creates graphics on his computer. Computer-generated graphics can be resized instantly, so there's no need for a stat camera. He sends his electronic file to the designer for layout.

Service bureau

Modeled on photocopying shops, the service bureau provides high-resolution printing in preparation for final printing at the print shop. The service bureau also prepares film negatives of the file.

Film

Final layout file

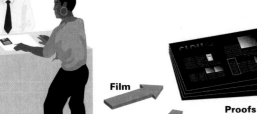

Proofs

The film is used to make proofs as in the traditional process, but the proof may be supplied by the service bureau *or* by the print shop. The proof now serves as an understanding between the service bureau, the client, and the printer as to what the final print job will look like.

Press operator

The press operator either makes plates from the proofed film negatives, or in some state-of-the-art facilities, the plates are made digitally directly from the electronic page data, bypassing film altogether. On direct-to-plate jobs, a press proof, printed on the actual printing press, is vital. The final pages are printed on the press, trimmed, and bound.

Figure 12.7

Courtesy of Ziff-Davis Press

Figure 12.8
*The Desktop Publishing
Process Chart.*

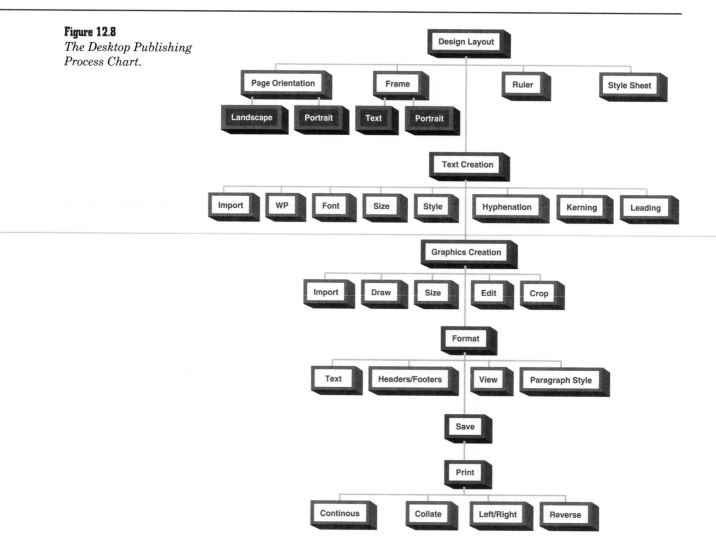

DTP enables you to fit and design text just as a typesetter does. Regardless of the document, length must be monitored and text fitted accordingly. This restriction usually necessitates some editing—usually shortening the text. In the newspaper business, fitting text used to be defined simply as "cutting from the bottom," or from the end backward until the text was the right length.

You can select different fonts, such as boldface, italic, boldface italic, and so on, in a variety of sizes and styles. Like sophisticated word processing software, DTP also enables you to decide whether to hyphenate words at the end of a line; the DTP program knows where to separate a hyphenated word and makes justifying margins easy. **Kerning** proportionally separates individual characters within a word so that text is easier to read. **Leading** refers to the space between lines.

Formatting

When you format a document, you manipulate the text and graphics to make sure that all the elements are in place. When you use the DTP application to design and create a professional document, text must be checked to make sure that it has no widows or orphans. The word **widow** describes a bad line break that results in the last line of a paragraph appearing alone at the top of a page or column. An **orphan** is the first line of a paragraph or a heading that appears alone at the bottom of a page. You don't want a paragraph to end at the top of a new page or column, nor do you want a chapter or topic heading to begin at the bottom of a page or column. Figure 12.9 shows examples of widows, page breaks, and column breaks that should be avoided.

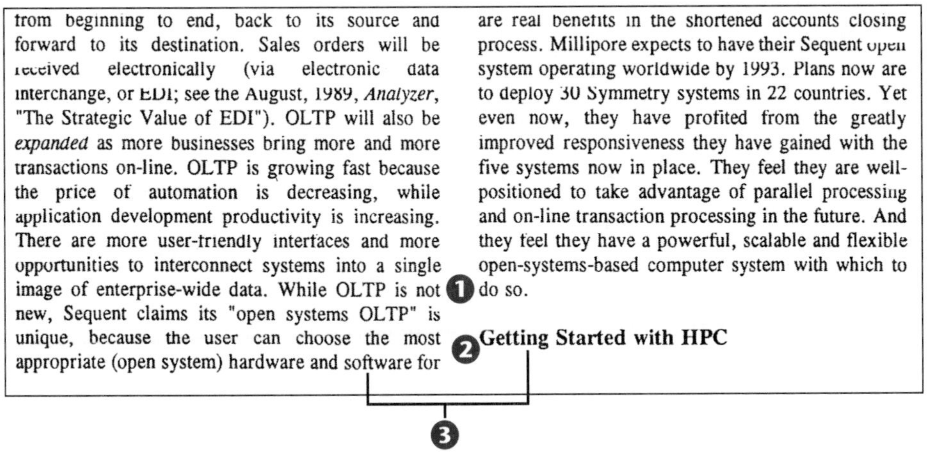

from beginning to end, back to its source and forward to its destination. Sales orders will be received electronically (via electronic data interchange, or EDI; see the August, 1989, *Analyzer*, "The Strategic Value of EDI"). OLTP will also be *expanded* as more businesses bring more and more transactions on-line. OLTP is growing fast because the price of automation is decreasing, while application development productivity is increasing. There are more user-friendly interfaces and more opportunities to interconnect systems into a single image of enterprise-wide data. While OLTP is not **(1)** new, Sequent claims its "open systems OLTP" is unique, because the user can choose the most **(2)** appropriate (open system) hardware and software for

are real benefits in the shortened accounts closing process. Millipore expects to have their Sequent open system operating worldwide by 1993. Plans now are to deploy 30 Symmetry systems in 22 countries. Yet even now, they have profited from the greatly improved responsiveness they have gained with the five systems now in place. They feel they are well-positioned to take advantage of parallel processing and on-line transaction processing in the future. And they feel they have a powerful, scalable and flexible open-systems-based computer system with which to do so.

Getting Started with HPC

(3)

Figure 12.9
Examples of poor DTP management in a newsletter.

1. The two-word widow could have been cleaned up with editing.

2. The heading orphan at the end of the column distracts the reader's attention.

3. The column lines are not even.

Formatting often involves altering paragraph styles, such as indenting, alternating between type fonts or between plain and boldface or italic type styles. Formatting also includes changing entire page styles. The most common page orientation is called **portrait**; in this orientation the height of the page is greater than the width (usually 8 1/2 by 11 inches). **Landscape** orientation is the rotation of a page in which the text and/or graphics are printed sideways on the paper (usually 11 by 8 1/2 inches) You can use style sheets to combine the both portrait and landscape orientation in a single document.

Most DTP applications have a *view* feature that you can use to see how the document will look before you begin printing. Some applications provide multiple views: a single page, side-by-side pages, partial pages, and multiple pages.

Saving

The most important step before printing is, of course, to save your work. Frames, templates, style sheets, drafts, pages, and completed document files need to be saved. Saving in DTP is a continuous process. If you plan to use a template again—for example, if you are going to publish a monthly newsletter using the same format, you should save the empty templates before you pour text into them. After you pour text into the template, you can save the finished publication with a new file name. Many DTP applications automatically save *interim versions* of your document so that only small portions of your publication will be lost in case of an accident. These DTP applications have a *file recovery* capability that automatically recovers the file from the last interim version saved.

Printing

Printing is the final step, but it takes on added dimensions in desktop publishing. The print function enables you to select whether you want to print a single page or the whole document. You can print specific pages, such as only the right or left page, and choose to collate the pages. In some cases, you can print pages in reverse order.

Most people look forward to seeing how the finished product will look. Text, with its various fonts or styles, combined with graphic images, will look like it just rolled off a printer's press. Laser printer quality is acceptable for many publications, such as newsletters. But magazines and books require higher print quality, which is measured in dots per inch. Simply put, **dots per inch**, or **dpi**, is the measure of printer resolution that counts the number of dots that can fit into a linear inch.

Most laser printers today are at least 300 dpi; some of the newer inkjet and laser printers are 400 dpi. Production-grade laser printers have 600 dpi and are now available at reasonable prices. The electronic typesetting equipment used in many print shops and service bureaus produces 1200 to 2400 dpi and often even higher resolution. This equipment is called Linotronic, named for its manufacturer. Linotronic is a laser image setter, which means that extremely high-quality art, photo images, and type can be created. The 1200 dpi laser printer is affordable for the serious desktop publisher.

Knowledge Check

1. What is a major difference between desktop publishing and word processing?
2. Why do you use a template?
3. What is the difference between kerning and leading?
4. What is the difference between portrait and landscape orientations?
5. How do you get high-quality images in DTP printing?

Key Terms

desktop publishing (DTP)	dots per inch (dpi)	frame	imported
kerning	landscape	leading	native file format
orphan	portrait	ruler	style sheet
template	widow		

ISSUES AND IDEAS

Digital Shadows

The following was posted to the Risks Forum and is reproduced in its entirety.

Date: Mon, 15 Aug 1994 19:04:59 -0700

Subject: Desktop check forgery

Saul Hansell, "New breed of check forgers exploits desktop publishing," *The New York Times*, 15 August 1994, pages A1, C3.

This article reports that it's easy to manufacture fake checks with widely available desktop publishing software. You need an original check, which you can get from the trash, from a paid insider (usually a low-level employee), or by standing outside check-cashing shops and paying people to let you photocopy their payroll checks. Then you need a scanner, and software to manipulate the image. Then you need check paper and a check printer (both of which are readily obtained). Finally, you need someone to pass the check—someone who'll take a cut to risk getting arrested.

The forgers and the banks are engaged in a technological arms race. Tellers can run checks through scanners to make sure they've got the right kind of magnetic ink on them, but then magnetic-ink printers are widely available. Image manipulation programs allow for "authenticating" stamps and signatures to be forged as well. When forged checks are discovered, some banks fax the pertinent information to every other bank branch in the same region of the country, figuring that the forgers have made several copies of the check and are driving around cashing them as fast as they can before the alarm is sounded. And so on.

This story illustrates one of the many subterranean interactions between computer technology and social institutions—the tendency of applied computing to change physical objects into hybrid things that have one foot planted in cyberspace. We've always relied on the relative immutability of physical objects to do various kinds of work for us. Computers make it easier to synthesize many kinds of objects, including mutated copies of originals. The obvious solution—at least, the solution that's obvious within the conventions of computer design—is to give every check a digital "shadow." For example, when an employer issues a payroll check, the check number and amount might be registered digitally and made available on a server. When a check is presented for payment, the teller feeds the check into a scanner that recovers the check number and payment amount from the magnetic ink and then, rather like credit cards now, consults that server to see if the check has been presented yet. This is only one of the many social mechanisms through which people, places, and things acquire digital shadows. Each mechanism has a seemingly inexorable logic through which the shadows cast by human artifacts and activities grow more expansive and more detailed. This process might be planned out in advance or it might proceed through a reaction to unanticipated holes in the system. When the trends that precipitate further growth in the shadow system are bad, or at least stigmatized, little attention is paid to alternatives that might minimize the amount of personal information that is being gathered while still providing genuine benefits and helping to prevent genuine ills. What's your shadow like?

Phil Agre, UCSD

CRITICAL THINKING

1. Does the inherent problem with paper-based checks say anything important about the digital Information Age?

2. What is a digital shadow?

3. Discuss Professor Agre's solution. Does it sound plausible? What problems can you foresee?

A Brief History of Publishing

Ancient approaches

The development of the phonetic alphabet by the Phoenicians in the second millennium B.C. shaped the history of the written word in western civilization. Unlike alphabets based on ideograms , which contained 40,000 or more characters, the phonetic alphabet represented language with only 26 or so symbols.

Illuminated manuscript

The books produced by the Celtic church in Ireland in the eighth century represented the peak of the scribe's art. But such books were unique, costly, and difficult to read.

Printing press c. 1450

Gutenberg adapted a wine press to make a printing press. His Bible, published in 1455, is considered to have heralded the birth of modern publishing. About 180 Bibles were printed (30 copies are believed to have been printed on vellum, requiring 170 calves per Bible). Gutenberg's type drawers contained 300 characters, letter combinations, and punctuation marks. Today's printers use about 50.

Rotary-web press c. 1865

By the 1850s, rotary presses made of metal had largely replaced the old wooden flatbed presses. The development of the "endless sheet" of paper, the web, made it possible for steam- or water-powered rotary-web presses to feed the growing demand for mass-circulation newspapers.

Halftone

The halftone process works by exploiting an optical illusion. If different-sized, regularly spaced dots are printed in a sufficiently fine grid pattern, the eye sees them as shades of gray rather than as clusters of dots. The halftone process made it possible to reproduce photographs to print, first in black and white and later in color.

Linotype machine c. 1890

The Linotype machine allowed the typesetter to compose type using a keyboard: It automatically positioned the *matrices* (or molds) for entire lines of type, then cast each line in a *slug* (a single piece of lead).

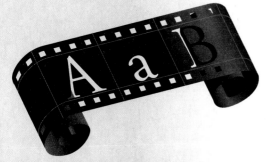

Phototypesetting

In phototypesetting machines, each character is stored as a transparent shape on a piece of opaque film. The characters in a font were arranged on a wheel or a strip. When the typesetter pressed a key on the keyboard, the appropriate character would rotate into position in front of a light source and an arrangement of lenses, which projected the character's shape on to photosensitive paper. Using lenses of different focal lengths, different sizes of type could be produced from the same character outline.

Digital type

In digital type, the character's shapes are recorded as mathematical descriptions. Digital typesetting machines use a grid of tiny dots (typically 1200 to 2500 per inch) that are so finely spaced that they appear continuous to the naked eye. When a character is called for in a particular size, the computer in the digital typesetter calculates which dots to print and which to leave blank to produce the type on the photosensitive paper.

HOME PAGE

THE AUTOMATION OF THE WRITTEN WORD

For thousands of years, people could only scratch words on paper with a sharp-pointed device—often the shaft of a feather, called a quill. The first mechanically printed book was the Bible, produced in Europe in about the year 1455, on a press invented by Johannes Gutenberg. Originally a goldsmith, Gutenberg developed his process of printing by using movable type made from punch-stamped matrices, a press similar to a wine press, and oil-based printing ink. Each page of the Bible held about 2,500 individual pieces of lead type in the German Gothic typestyle of the period. Six presses worked on the Bible simultaneously, printing 20 to 40 pages a day. Fewer than 50 copies are still in existence.

Printing remained in the shops of the printers for another 400 years, until W.A. Burt, an American, built the first desktop printing device, which we call a typewriter. Then in 1857, Christopher Latham Sholes developed the first commercial typewriter, WHICH COULD TYPE ONLY IN UPPERCASE LETTERS. The Remington company bought the rights to Scholes' typewriter, and Mark Twain was the first author to buy and use one.

Thomas Edison invented the electric typewriter in 1872, but it was so crude that it could be used only as a stock market ticker tape printer. A commercial electric typewriter wasn't available until IBM introduced one in 1935. IBM proceeded to lead the field in typing innovation, introducing the "golfball" typewriter in 1961. Replacing the striker arm keys with a rotating golfball greatly improved productivity.

It took the personal computer—specifically the Macintosh—to give birth to desktop publishing. PageMaker has established itself as the best-selling DTP software. But the first desktop publishing program was created by teenager Rob Doyle in 1984. He called it MacPublisher and sold 10,000 copies before selling the rights to Letraset. By the way, his parents are innovative in their own right: they invented Merlin, the first handheld electronic game, and are now working with desktop digital video.

HOME PAGE REVIEW QUESTIONS

1. What was the first book printed on a printing press?

2. What was a limitation of the first type writer?

3. Why was the IBM golfball an advance in typing?

4. For what computer was the first desktop publishing software designed?

ETHICS

A Code of Business Ethics

Working with intellectual property—the ideas and expressions of others—requires finesse, good manners, and moral and ethical behavior. A case in point: a rising young manager was asked by his superior to gather research for a new product launch. The younger man prepared a thorough, professional-looking report using desktop publishing, bound it in a cover, and gave it to his boss. The older man put his name on the report and submitted it to the corporate executives as his own work.

No law was violated here; work done for your employer belongs to your company, not to you. In this example, trust was violated, and hard, honest work was not recognized or rewarded. This behavior is not what most people would call moral or ethical.

Knowledge workers want recognition when they write documents, create graphic art, take photographs, or help produce something for print. If someone writes a document, he wants a byline—his name on it. If a knowledge worker took the photo or created the graph, she wants it to be acknowledged. If they helped publish a newsletter, they want their names and work recognized on the publication's masthead.

What guidelines can you follow in business ethics? Perhaps you'll find guidance in the following "Code of Ethics for Government Service."

1. Put loyalty to the highest moral principles and to country above loyalty to persons, party, or Government department.

2. Uphold the Constitution, laws, and regulations of the United States and of all governments therein and never be a party to their evasion.

3. Give a full day's labor for a full day's pay; giving earnest effort and best thought to the performance of duties.

4. Seek to find and employ more efficient and economical ways of getting tasks accomplished.

5. Never discriminate unfairly by the dispensing of special favors or privileges to anyone, whether for remuneration or not; and never accept, for himself or herself or for family members, favors or benefits under circumstances which might be construed by reasonable persons as influencing the performance of governmental duties.

6. Make no private promises of any kind binding upon the duties of office, since a government employee has no private work which can be binding on public duty.

7. Engage not in business with the Government, either directly or indirectly, which is inconsistent with the conscientious performance of governmental duties.

8. Never use any information gained confidentially in the performance of governmental duties as a means of making private profit.

9. Expose corruption wherever discovered.

10. Uphold these principles, ever conscious that public office is a public trust.[4]

Critical Thinking

1. How do these ethical principles for government apply in a business or any other form of enterprise?

2. Do these principles seem idealistic or unrealistic to you? If so, why? Be specific.

3. What are the consequences when no law is broken but ethical principles are violated?

---

4. Adapted from artwork in *Practical Ethics* by Gordon F. Shea (New York: AMA Management Briefing, American Management Association Publications), 1988.

THE LEARNING ENTERPRISE

If, as David Goodstein says, publishing is everyone's second business, your department or enterprise needs to make publishing part of your business processes. You may find needs for graphic design and desktop publishing for many types of both internal and external printed communication. Following are some suggestions:

Internal	External
Brochures	Advertising materials
Announcements	Marketing brochures
Employee manuals	Press releases
Health plan descriptions	Corporate communication
Newsletters	Product or service documents
	Annual reports

The creative services people are often in charge of the tools and resources for preparing professional documents. But that fact doesn't mean that your department or function can't have a graphics and DTP person. Ask whether anyone is interested in this position as a part-time adjunct to his or her work, and then determine what kinds of documents you'll need to produce. The document may be as simple as a presentation report or slide show for enterprise management or as complex as an advertisement or annual report.

Next, read up on graphics and DTP, perhaps from a book or magazine on the subject in the library. Decide on an initial document that you want to produce. Then determine the following:

- What do we need to communicate?

- What type of document would communicate best?

- What is the message or intent of the document?

- What graphic elements should the document have?

- What does the text convey? How should it be arranged?

Once these basic questions are answered, define and refine your document plans. Then create the document and print a draft. Be sure to share it with others in the document workgroup for comments, suggestions, and revisions. If you don't have graphics and desktop publishing programs, use clip art and word processing. When the document is as good as you can make it, submit it to your instructor.

Chapter Review

Fill in the Blank

1. A collection of graphics stored on disk is called _____.

2. A pictorial representation is called a(n) _____.

3. The terms _____ and _____ both refer to a graphic or diagram that displays data in pictorial form.

4. Using your PC to produce professional-looking documents with typeset-quality text and graphics is called _____.

5. DTP is often called a(n) _____ application.

6. A(n) _____ is a list of all the specific design characteristics for your document.

7. A(n) _____ is a page layout grid helpful in creating documents with a consistent look.

8. _____ proportionally separates individual characters within a word.

9. _____ refers to the space between lines.

10. A formatting flaw that isolates a line of text or a word at the top of the page is a(n) _____; an isolated word or phrase at the bottom is a(n) _____.

True/False

1. You can import text from a word processing application into your desktop publishing document.

2. Leading refers to the space between lines.

3. Kerning adjusts the spacing between words.

4. A frame is a box that contains text or graphics.

5. Text in a DTP document can be imported from a word processing application.

Review Questions

1. Define graphics and give some examples.

2. What are the five steps involved in creating a graphic?

3. Define desktop publishing.

4. List five steps in the desktop publishing process.

5. What is the difference between the terms *widow* and *orphan*?

6. Define presentation graphics.

7. Name several forms of presentation graphics.

8. What is involved in page layout?

9. What is a style sheet?

10. What does *dpi* refer to in desktop publishing?

Discussion Questions

1. Find some examples of business reports, financial statements, annual reports, or magazine articles that include charts or graphs. Evaluate their effectiveness; do the graphs give you a clearer understanding of the data? Defend your position.

2. In your library, find a computer running an application that uses audio input and/or output, or visit a computer store for a demonstration. Decide whether you think audio capability enhances the usefulness of the program.

3. Using a DTP application, create a flyer or advertisement for an activity you are involved in or for an article that you want to sell.

INTERNET DISCOVERY

For information about the leading graphics and desktop publishing software products, visit the Adobe Systems Web site:

http://www.adobe.com

PART IV
HOW KNOWLEDGE WORKERS USE COMPUTER SYSTEMS

Chapter 13 Programming Languages and Concepts

Module A   The Programming Process
Module B   High-Level Programming Languages
Module C   The Future of Programming

Chapter 14 Software Engineering

Module A   System Analysis and Design
Module B   Information Engineering

Chapter 15 Management Information Systems

Module A   What is MIS?
Module B   The Three Components of MIS
Module C   Corporate Database Concepts

Chapter 16 Voice and Data Communications Systems

Module A   Data and Voice Communications Systems
Module B   Types of Networks
Module C   Network Information Services

Chapter 17 Office Automation

Module A   Text and Document Management
Module B   Business Analysis
Module C   Workgroup Computing

ORACLE®

Jolin Marie Salazar-Kish
Sr. Applications Engineer
Applications Division

Oracle Corporation   500 Oracle Parkway   Phone   415.506.3313
                      Box 659305   Fax   415.506.7294
                      Redwood Shores   jsalazar@us.oracle.com
                      California 94065

KNOWLEDGE WORKER INTERVIEW WITH JOLIN MARIE SALAZAR-KISH

Jolin was born on September 1, 1966, in Metheun, Massachusetts, and now lives in Lake Sunappee, New Hampshire. She received an M.S. in Biotechnical Engineering from Dartmouth College in 1988, and an M.S. in Construction Engineering and Management from Stanford University in 1991. She is hoping to complete a Ph.D. in Civil Engineering and Business from Stanford by 1997 and is currently working at Oracle Corporation.

AUTHOR: What are your work responsibilities?

JOLIN: My work at Oracle includes nearly all aspects of the financial applications product development cycle. Oracle sells relational database management software, and it also sells development tools used to create software applications using Oracle DBMSs. As an application developer, I use the DBMS and software tools to create generic financial applications that Oracle sells to customers, such as order entry, general ledger, accounts payable, accounts receivable.

A typical day at work varies greatly depending on the point in the system development life cycle we are at. If it's early in the cycle, much of my day is spent creating designs and documenting them for coordination with other developers and for marketing approval. Later in the cycle, I focus my attention on coding pieces of the design for the testing team.

After the product goes into production, I spend most of my time speaking with customers to solve their setup problems and correct bugs in the software. Sometimes I've even gone to the customer site to teach them how to use the application! Post-production work is considered software maintenance, and it's a considerable portion of my work. Another is upgrading customers when we bring out a new version of the software they're using.

AUTHOR: What computers and software do you use?

JOLIN: Our processing is done on Sequent parallel processing computers, which I access from a Sun UNIX workstation or remotely via an NCD X Windows terminal. I mostly use emacs, a UNIX-based text editor and shell, and Oracle development tools such as query languages and report and form generators.

AUTHOR: What do you like about your employer and your work?

JOLIN: I especially enjoy working with a team of software developers. Each of us has the opportunity to work on all aspects of the product,

How Knowlege Workers
Use Computer Systems

from initial design to customer support and everything in between. This eliminates the pigeonhole effect—when one person gets really good at something and then gets stuck doing it all the time to the exclusion of all else.

I'm a telecommuter. Oracle headquarters is in Redwood Shores, California, but I usually work from my home in New Hampshire. When I'm designing new code, I fly out and work with my team in California. However, when I'm doing support for existing software, I work independently at home.

AUTHOR: How do you view the future of knowledge work?

JOLIN: With the continually improving telecommunications tools, we'll see more people doing some portion of their work at home, for many reasons. One, it's technologically feasible. Two, it often reduces corporate costs. Three, with the growing number of working mothers, there are many more day care options when you work at home and have a flexible work schedule. Four, without constant interruptions for meetings, a programmer can really focus work efforts and big productivity gains can be achieved. Five, telecommuting offers more flexibility for professional couples. But I don't think offices will go away either, because people always need to be around other people.

AUTHOR: Where do you think future opportunities lie?

JOLIN: There will always be jobs for programmers who know how to manage and manipulate large amounts of data. Currently, there are many opportunities to make advances on the home computing front. Software companies want to bring the World Wide Web services and a wealth of data into people's homes. They need programmers to help create the software solutions, such as how to monitor use and charge for it.

AUTHOR: What advice would you give today's college student?

JOLIN: Understand the basics of computing first: these will always help you, especially structured programming techniques. Learn how to program in one language and operate a system really well. The industry is very diverse, so find an area that interests you—operating systems, compilers, programming languages, databases, development tools—and follow it closely. Keep track of the current technology in your area of interest, and the companies that provide or use that technology. This will really help you in your job searches.

AUTHOR: What are your favorite nonwork uses for the computer?

JOLIN: I generally use my computer for two nonwork related tasks: e-mail and personal record keeping, such as recipes and finances. I spend a lot of time working at the keyboard, so when I have free time I usually get away from computers and books.

AUTHOR: What do you do for fun?

JOLIN: Step aerobics, Nautilus, dancing, singing, downhill skiing, water-skiing, hiking, biking, canoeing, rowing crew, and cooking.

PROGRAMMING LANGUAGES AND CONCEPTS

CHAPTER 13

*Programming is, among other things, a kind of writing. . . .
Unlike novels, the best way to read [programs] is not always
from beginning to end. . . . Instead, we might base our reading
on a conceptual framework consisting of the origin of each
part. In other words, as we look at each piece of code, we ask
ourselves the question, "Why is this piece here?"*

Gerald M. Weinberg[1]

Programming is an activity for all kinds of knowledge workers—from the programmer to the information systems professional, from an administrative assistant to a marketing manager. Preparing instructions for the computer is an everyday activity; the type of instructions and the way they are prepared may differ.

Programming can be traced to the textile industry in 1801. A Frenchman, Joseph-Marie Charles Jacquard, was probably the first to program a machine. He was a weaver who dreamed of a machine to help him do his weaving more quickly, inexpensively, and accurately.

Jacquard studied the weaving process and the loom. In his studies, he displayed the analytic qualities of a good programmer. The result was a loom that used a punched card and could be programmed to create patterns and designs. Jacquard's punched card, a wooden slat with holes punched in it, would be used for more than 180 years.

Jacquard's loom demonstrated two important ideas: complex designs can be translated into codes, or programs, that machines readily understand, and machines can be instructed to perform repetitive tasks.

Traditionally, programming was the domain of people specifically trained in programming skills. More and more, the meaning of *programmer* is blurring. As more knowledge workers begin creating computer instructions that can be saved and used, over and over, the traditional definition of a programmer must be broadened.

---

1. Gerald M. Weinberg. *The Psychology of Computer Programming* (New York: Van Nostrand Reinhold, 1971), 5–7.

Module A

The Programming Process

Why It's Important to Know

As knowledge workers who have not been formally trained as programmers assume many of the traditional duties of programmers, the knowledge workers must also learn some of the traditional programming skills.

Programs are created by programmers who use special programming languages to create instructions that the computer can understand. Over the years, many programming languages have been devised—some for special purposes. Some have become more sophisticated programming tools, but by and large, programming languages have become more English-like and easier to use.

Programming is the process of creating instructions, in the form of programs, for computers. Programming has been called an art and a science. Interestingly, programming attracts people from almost every kind of educational background: anthropology, music, physics, and everything in between.

Computer programming has been with us for more than fifty years. Many types of machines, computers included, are programmed with ordered, organized instructions. These instructions are written in a **programming language**—a formally designed set of commands used to create sequential instructions that can be processed and executed by the computer. The instructions programmers create with a programming language often are referred to as **code**. Figure 13.2 shows how a program is created.

Learning a programming language is like learning a foreign language. Mastery of the language, however, is only one part of a programmer's job. The programmer must know how knowledge workers will use the program and know how to design a good human-computer interface. In addition, the programmer must have expertise in the algorithms that make up the program and know the characteristics of the hardware components the program will use.

Programming languages have evolved greatly over the years. Each evolutionary stage is commonly referred to as a *generation*. Table 13.1 shows the five generations of computer languages.

Table 13.1
The Five Generations of Programming Languages

1st	2nd	3rd	4th	5th
1951–58	1958–64	1964–71	1977–88	1988–present
Low-level	Low/ high-level	High-level	Very high-level	Object-oriented
Machine, assembly	Assembly, COBOL, FORTRAN	BASIC, Pascal	C++, Turbo Pascal 4GLs	OOP, CASE, Visual Basic

The Jacquard loom's programming language took the form of a series of cards punched with holes. ENIAC (the first electronic computer) was initially programmed by flipping toggle switches and changing cables. Needless to say, this process was slow and awkward. Information systems professionals quickly began searching for a better, faster way to issue instructions to the computer. Better and faster was especially desired when repetitive instructions had to be issued—exactly the same every time, without errors. In a payroll program, for example, no one wants a program that cannot produce consistent, reliable results. One solution was the punched card.

Punched cards evolved into other methods, such as punched metal, paper tape, and then magnetic tape. The most effective solution, however, was what is now called *programming languages*. The first language closely resembled the toggle-switch method, issuing 0s and 1s to the computer with software instructions instead of manually flipping switches. As programming languages evolved and improved, they became more English-like. The following sections explore the development of programming languages.

JACQUARD LOOM CARDS

Courtesy of International Business Machines Corporation

Figure 13.1
The Jacquard loom. The punched cards are fed through a primitive processing device to program the loom.

Machine Language

Electronic digital computers understand only **machine language**—the language of the 0s and 1s that make up bits and bytes. Machine language requires no translation in order to be understood by the CPU. From ENIAC to today's most sophisticated digital computers, machine language is essentially the same. Machine language is directly understood, or executed, by hardware. Electronic circuitry turns these 0s and 1s into the operations the computer performs. It is extremely tedious, however, for a programmer to sit at a keyboard and type the instructions in endless sequences of 0s and 1s.

Assembly Language

Assembly language was the first method used to address the problem of programmers' having to sit and type a steady stream of 0s and 1s. **Assembly language** uses letters, numbers, and symbols to represent instructions that the computer can understand. For example, to give the command to multiply in machine language, you would have to type *001011*; in an assembly language, you can simply type *MUL*. *MUL* is then translated by a special program, called an *assembler,* into the 001011 of machine language. Assembly languages greatly simplified programming, made the programmer's job much less tedious, and made the programmer more productive.

Designing a Program

1 You can design a program in many ways, but usually the first step is to figure out the requirements of the program—determine exactly what you want the program to do. In this example, the requirement is to add a sequence of numbers from 1 to a number specified by the user.

2 One of the traditional ways to design a program is to use a flow chart. The top of the flow chart indicates input from the user. Rectangles contain statements, and diamonds indicate decisions.

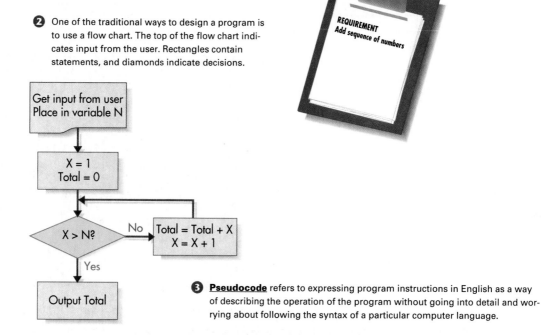

3 **Pseudocode** refers to expressing program instructions in English as a way of describing the operation of the program without going into detail and worrying about following the syntax of a particular computer language.

```
Function AddSequence
 Integer N, X, Total      ' Three integer variables
 N = Get a number from the user
 For X = 1 to N     ' Loop through the values 1 through N
       Total = Total + X
 Next X
 Return Total
End Function AddSequence
```

4 There are many techniques for designing complex programs. In fact, there are programs that can help you design software and keep track of the flow of data through the components of your application. These software-engineering tools are most frequently used for large projects that involve many programmers.

Courtesy of Ziff-Davis Press

5 One common approach to developing applications is called *top-down design.* This technique involves creating a hierarchy of functions for your program. The top functions closely reflect the requirements of the program. Then you define the functions that will be called by these top-level functions, moving down the hierarchy to the lowest-level functions. When it is time to write the actual code, you start by coding the lowest-level functions and work your way up.

This example illustrates the hierarchy of functions that might be used by a washing machine.

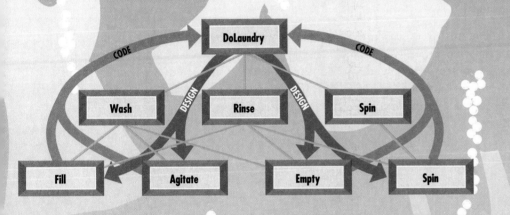

6 A **prototype** is a demonstration version of a proposed program. *Prototyping* is one of the best design techniques for testing a program's user interface. Unlike earlier prototyping tools that could only design screens, modern programming environments let you build on the user interface to create your final program. Many high-level languages, including C++, SmallTalk, and Visual Basic, provide powerful user-interface design tools that enable you to position objects such as buttons and text fields on the screen to see how the application will look and behave when it is complete. This user interface for a washing-machine program took less than five minutes to create using Visual

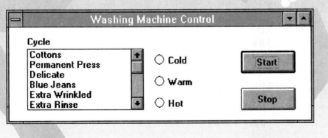

Figure 13.2

Assembly languages are powerful programming tools because they give programmers a great deal of direct control over the hardware. They provide greater ease in writing instructions but preserve the programmer's ability to declare exactly what operations the hardware performs.

Assembly languages are *machine-specific*, or *machine-dependent*. *Machine-dependent* means that the instructions are specific to one type of computer hardware. The assembly language used for a Prime mini won't work on an IBM PC because the two computers use different processors. Because assembly languages are so closely tied to the hardware used in the computer, they often can't be transferred even between different models of computers built by the same manufacturer. However, all assembly languages use the same letters, numbers, and symbols.

For the most part, assembly languages are used by systems programmers to develop operating systems and their components. Thus, one early programming problem was solved, but another remained: how to make programming languages portable, or transferable from one computer to another. The answer was, in theory at least, the creation of high-level programming languages.

Knowledge Check

1. How were the first computers programmed?
2. What fundamental language do digital electronic computers understand?
3. What is an example of assembly language?
4. What does the term *machine-dependent* mean?
5. For what is an assembly language primarily used?

Key Terms

assembly language	code	machine language	programming
programming language	prototype	pseudocode	

ISSUES AND IDEAS

Tech Support: The Final Frontier

Answering questions and solving problems for customers has always been the "Oh, no!" aspect of software development. In the early days of the IBM PC, when such programs as WordStar, VisiCalc, and dBASE were popular, tech support was often regarded as a nuisance—why couldn't people just read the documentation? The problem became so acute that one company started a third-party service called Mayday! to provide—for $199 a year—both software and hardware support. The service began building a database of common problems and took unlimited calls from customers. Mayday, undercapitalized, soon went out of business; but many other similar services followed in its footsteps.

HOME PAGE

"DON'T FLIP THE BOZO BIT"

Jim McCarthy is director of the Microsoft Visual C++ Program Management Team at Microsoft Corporation in Redmond, Washington. His book, *Dynamics of Software Development*, discusses his experiences working with and managing programming teams. In the book, he explains 54 rules for delivering software on time. One of them, "Don't Flip the Bozo Bit," has relevance for any knowledge worker. Here's an excerpt:

A screen for working with Visual C++.

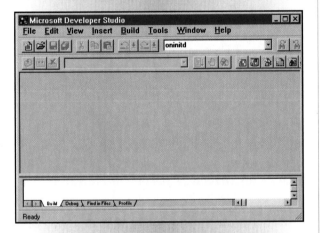

. . . Shipping ordinary software on time is . . . hard. Shipping great software in any time frame is extraordinary. Shipping great software on time is the rarest of earthly delights.

. . . Software is intellectual property, and creating software is primarily an intellectual endeavor. The bits on the disk or the CD embody the cumulative intellectual output of the software product development team. The more intellect embodied on the disk, the more intellectual property created and the higher the value of the product.

. . . You have to have intellects at work in order to get software. And the more intellects you have working at a higher rate of speed, the more value in intellectual property you're going to end up with. The obvious point is that people have to be thinking. Someone once asked me, "What's the hardest thing about software development?"

I didn't hesitate. "Getting people to think."

Believe it or not, most people don't want to think. They think they want to think, but they don't. It's easier not to and to instead flip the bozo bit—that's what we call it at Microsoft. "That dude's a bozo!" Then nobody pays any attention to anything the putative bozo says or does forevermore.

. . . If you focus your attention on the movement of intelligence from people to bits as the central activity of the software development team, you'll have a valid point of view from which to monitor or lead the development of software.[2]

HOME PAGE REVIEW QUESTIONS

1. According to McCarthy, what are the requirements for great software?

2. What is the single most important aspect of software development?

3. Even though developing software is an intellectual process, why do you suppose it's hard to get people to think?

2. Jim McCarthy. *Dynamics of Software Development* (Redmond, WA: Microsoft Press, 1995), 2–3, 30.

Today, it's not uncommon for users to pay for customer support, or at least to pay for the long-distance phone call. And many software companies are becoming more savvy about tech support. When Microsoft launched Windows 95 on August 24, 1995, the company anticipated the flood of calls from early buyers. They had learned a great deal from their launch of Windows 3.0, and this time they were ready with 1,600 support engineers on the phones. At first, callers spent about 10 minutes on hold waiting for help; but within two weeks, that wait had dropped to under 5 minutes, and finally to 30 seconds. For several months, Microsoft also offered free weekend tech support.

InformationWeek magazine reported, " 'Microsoft's support has gotten better with each successive operating system rollout,' says Jesse Berst, editorial director for *Windows Watcher*, a Redmond, Washington, newsletter that tracks Microsoft. 'The Win95 support team executed superbly.' "[3]

Technical support was not as great with CompuServe, an on-line information service. Author and columnist Stephen Manes writes that a service he used, Executive News Service, one of CompuServe's on-line services, suddenly stopped working properly. "Sometimes it was inaccessible; other times it delivered heaps of stale information. I couldn't get past the customer-service busy signal, and never did CompuServe post a single public message informing its customers of any problems."

After sending an e-mail message and receiving a vague response, Manes says, "A couple of days later, everything returned to normal. All I'd lost was a week's worth of news and a lot of my time. Hey, it's only my business!"

According to a CompuServe spokesman, a "significant hardware crash" caused the trouble. . . . Yet the only public notice that the system wasn't working was the on-screen error message when it was inaccessible.

. . . The lesson: If you run a system that's not working properly, 'fess up. Announce the problem at logon or via broadcast e-mail. Explain it clearly. State how soon a solution can be expected. If you're late, 'fess up again. Slight embarrassment and a few refunds are better than users who think the problem may be their fault.[4]

CRITICAL THINKING

1. Why do you suppose that providing technical support is poorly regarded?

2. Is having to pay for tech support fair?

3. Joseph C. Panettieri. "Windows 95 Support Gets High Marks," *InformationWeek*, November 6, 1995, 122.

4. Stephen Manes. "System Problems? 'Fess Up," *InformationWeek*, October 9, 1995, 120.

3. Why aren't companies more honest about problems with their products?

4. What can you as a knowledge worker who uses a program do to reduce the burden of tech support?

Module B

High-Level Programming Languages

Why It's Important to Know

High-level languages are the programmer's tools-in-trade for creating programs. Some are designed for general-purpose programming; others for specific purposes. The goal is to make languages easier to use and maintain while creating highly reliable programs.

Assembly languages were the first bridge between the language we speak and the computer's binary language. Soon, however, programmers realized that they could take programming one step closer to a spoken language. The creation of high-level programming languages followed. **High-level languages** use English-like words as program instructions. Figure 13.3 shows the evolution of high-level languages.

High-level programming languages combine several machine-language instructions into one high-level instruction. So, as you move up the ladder from machine language to high-level languages, *less is more:* fewer program instructions actually do more work. To issue a command in machine language, a programmer has to write correctly a string of 0s and 1s. In assembly language, that same command requires only a single letter or a short **mnemonic**—a term or word that is easy to identify, such as *ADD* for addition. Programming an operation in a high-level language, however, enables you to replace several assembly-language instructions with a single statement.

Statements and Syntax

A **statement** is an expression that can generate instructions in a programming language. A statement usually translates into one or more instructions at the machine-language level. For example, the following statement tells the program to display on-screen the words shown in quotation marks:

```
PRINT "Welcome to MetaSoftware version 6.0"
```

Each programming language includes a set of statements and a syntax. **Syntax** is the set of rules governing the way you put the language's statements together to make valid commands. To write a program in any programming language, the programmer must use the statements required by that language and adhere strictly to its syntax rules. These syntax rules may include the way statements are written, the order in which statements occur, and the way sections of programs are organized.

The Evolution of Computer Languages

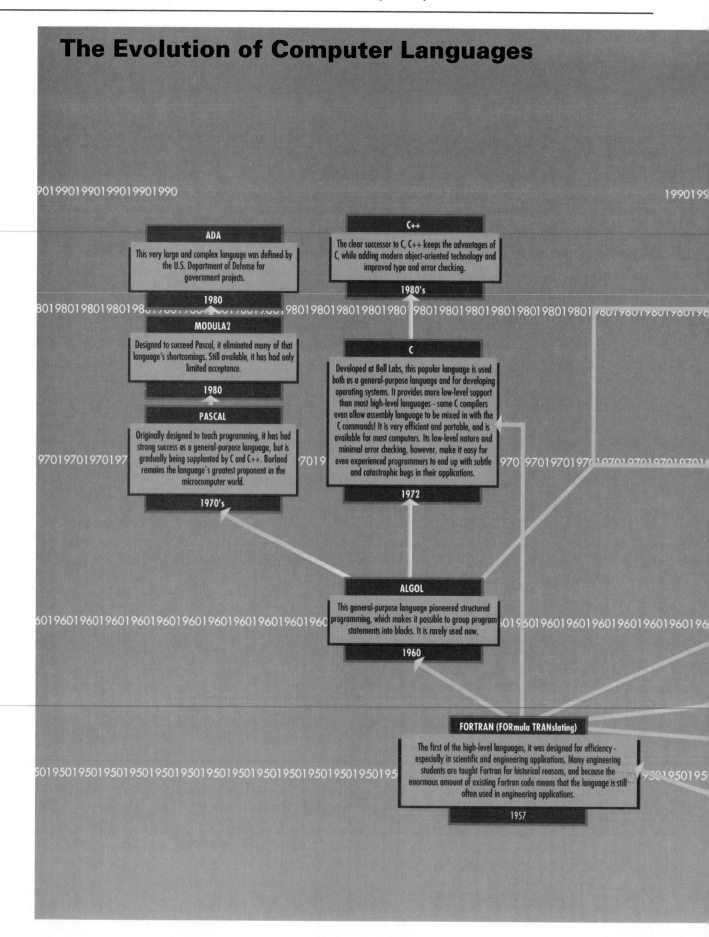

ADA

This very large and complex language was defined by the U.S. Department of Defense for government projects.

1980

C++

The clear successor to C, C++ keeps the advantages of C, while adding modern object-oriented technology and improved type and error checking.

1980's

MODULA2

Designed to succeed Pascal, it eliminated many of that language's shortcomings. Still available, it has had only limited acceptance.

1980

PASCAL

Originally designed to teach programming, it has had strong success as a general-purpose language, but is gradually being supplanted by C and C++. Borland remains the language's greatest proponent in the microcomputer world.

1970's

C

Developed at Bell Labs, this popular language is used both as a general-purpose language and for developing operating systems. It provides more low-level support than most high-level languages - some C compilers even allow assembly language to be mixed in with the C commands! It is very efficient and portable, and is available for most computers. Its low-level nature and minimal error checking, however, make it easy for even experienced programmers to end up with subtle and catastrophic bugs in their applications.

1972

ALGOL

This general-purpose language pioneered structured programming, which makes it possible to group program statements into blocks. It is rarely used now.

1960

FORTRAN (FORmula TRANslating)

The first of the high-level languages, it was designed for efficiency - especially in scientific and engineering applications. Many engineering students are taught Fortran for historical reasons, and because the enormous amount of existing Fortran code means that the language is still often used in engineering applications.

1957

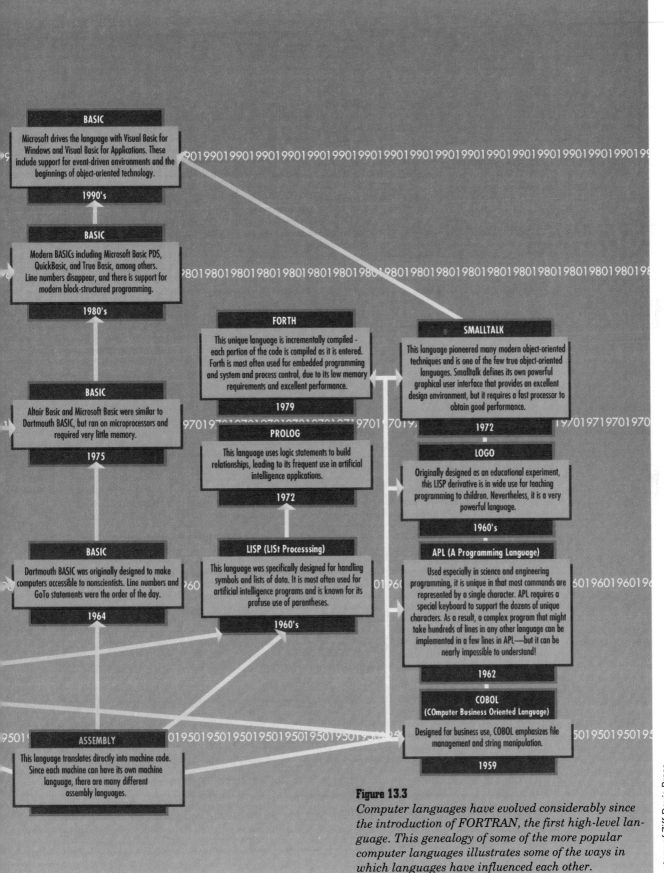

BASIC

Microsoft drives the language with Visual Basic for Windows and Visual Basic for Applications. These include support for event-driven environments and the beginnings of object-oriented technology.

1990's

BASIC

Modern BASICs including Microsoft Basic PDS, QuickBasic, and True Basic, among others. Line numbers disappear, and there is support for modern block-structured programming.

1980's

BASIC

Altair Basic and Microsoft Basic were similar to Dartmouth BASIC, but ran on microprocessors and required very little memory.

1975

BASIC

Dartmouth BASIC was originally designed to make computers accessible to nonscientists. Line numbers and GoTo statements were the order of the day.

1964

ASSEMBLY

This language translates directly into machine code. Since each machine can have its own machine language, there are many different assembly languages.

FORTH

This unique language is incrementally compiled - each portion of the code is compiled as it is entered. Forth is most often used for embedded programming and system and process control, due to its low memory requirements and excellent performance.

1979

PROLOG

This language uses logic statements to build relationships, leading to its frequent use in artificial intelligence applications.

1972

LISP (LISt Processsing)

This language was specifically designed for handling symbols and lists of data. It is most often used for artificial intelligence programs and is known for its profuse use of parentheses.

1960's

SMALLTALK

This language pioneered many modern object-oriented techniques and is one of the few true object-oriented languages. Smalltalk defines its own powerful graphical user interface that provides an excellent design environment, but it requires a fast processor to obtain good performance.

1972

LOGO

Originally designed as an educational experiment, this LISP derivative is in wide use for teaching programming to children. Nevertheless, it is a very powerful language.

1960's

APL (A Programming Language)

Used especially in science and engineering programming, it is unique in that most commands are represented by a single character. APL requires a special keyboard to support the dozens of unique characters. As a result, a complex program that might take hundreds of lines in any other language can be implemented in a few lines in APL—but it can be nearly impossible to understand!

1962

COBOL
(COmputer Business Oriented Language)

Designed for business use, COBOL emphasizes file management and string manipulation.

1959

Figure 13.3
Computer languages have evolved considerably since the introduction of FORTRAN, the first high-level language. This genealogy of some of the more popular computer languages illustrates some of the ways in which languages have influenced each other.

Courtesy of Ziff-Davis Press

Human and computer languages have two similarities:

- They consist of a set of words.
- They are governed by a set of language usage rules.

In human language, sentences are constructed in a specific way—subject, predicate, and so on. Programmers, when using a computer language, write instructions using statements and syntax.

For example, in the following statement written in a popular programming language, you must include the quotation marks around the letter *Y*:

```
answer = "Y"
```

A programming language also may support the use of *control structures*, which are blocks of programming code that define how the statements within the block should be executed. The syntax of most programming languages requires that control structures have a beginning and an end. When you use an IF statement, for example, at some point you must have an END IF statement. If you don't include a termination statement, the program will produce an error message when run.

Some high-level languages also require that you organize programs in sections. A typical first section identifies the program and the programmer. This section may be followed by a declarations section and then by a program section. Whatever the language requires, you must abide by its rules. As with most other aspects of computing, close is not good enough!

Structured and Unstructured Languages

High-level programming languages can be divided into two categories: structured and unstructured. Once again, you encounter yet another use for the word *structured*, which is distinct from either structured design or structured programming. A **structured** high-level programming language requires the programmer to write programs in well-defined sections that are then compiled in sequence. An **unstructured** language allows the programmer to create programs randomly.

Translating High-Level Languages into Programs

A high-level program must be translated before it becomes an executable program that can be read by the CPU. Each language must be converted from its English-like expressions into machine language.

A **compiler** is a special type of program that translates entire files of source code into machine-readable **object code,** but that object code still cannot be executed by the computer. The final step in turning object code into an executable file requires a linker. A **linker** is a special program that combines various object code files, resolves the differences between them, and creates a finished executable file. The **executable** file can be read and run by the

CPU. Files used to start a word processing or graphics application program are executable files.

Some compilers and linkers also produce other kinds of files, such as analysis and program-error files. Programmers find these files very useful because they contain important information about how clearly the computer understands the source code as it was written.

An **interpreter** translates source code one line at a time for immediate execution by the CPU. Like a compiler, an interpreter translates from the language the program was written in to instructions the computer understands. Whereas a compiler and linker create an executable file, an interpreter creates only executable statements, one at a time. Interpreters are very useful: they stop the program when an error is found so that the programmer can quickly and easily solve the problem. Once the error is corrected, the interpreter runs the program again. Interpreters were widely used on early personal computers and are still used in some programming languages to develop prototypes of programs.

Advantages and Disadvantages of High-Level Languages

The advantage of a high-level programming language is the programming power offered by its concise statements. The downside, however, is that programmers forfeit some of the direct control over hardware that they have when they use assembly language. When high-level languages are compiled, statements are translated into specific machine instructions determined by the compiler, not necessarily by the programmer. Programmers can't alter these translations without rewriting the compiler—a huge task.

An additional problem that high-level languages were meant to address is that of portability. Programmers initially hoped that programs could be written in one version of a programming language—no matter what kind of hardware they were using. This goal has never really been reached. In attempting to ensure customer loyalty, most computer manufacturers customize one of the major high-level languages specifically to fit their hardware.

The reality of this situation is that program code written for an IBM PC, for example, often must be modified before it will run on a system from Sun Microsystems. Nevertheless, code written in a high-level language is much more portable than assembly code. Usually modifying high-level source code to work on different hardware is much easier than modifying programs written in assembly language.

Application Creation

High-level languages are used for all kinds of programming, but are especially valuable to applications programmers. Figure 13.4 shows how an application is created.

Coding and Documentation

1 Coding starts with a programmer working at a computer. The most important tool for a programmer is an *editor,* a program that creates text files called *source code modules.* An editor is similar to a word processor, except that the editor is optimized for programming. For example, it might display language commands in one color and comments in another to make it easier to see the structure of the program. Additional tools can be used to create other program components, such as bit maps or icons.

2 A *compiler* translates each text file into machine code and places it in an object file. A computer can execute only machine code. However, an object file is not entirely ready for execution. Some of the locations for variables and functions have not yet been assigned because they may be in a different object file.

3 A program called a *linker* combines all the object files into an executable program that can run directly on the target computer.

SOURCE TEXT FILE

SOURCE TEXT FILE

Interpreter

4 The *interpreter* program is executed by the computer. This program reads text from the source file and performs the operations specified by the commands in that file.

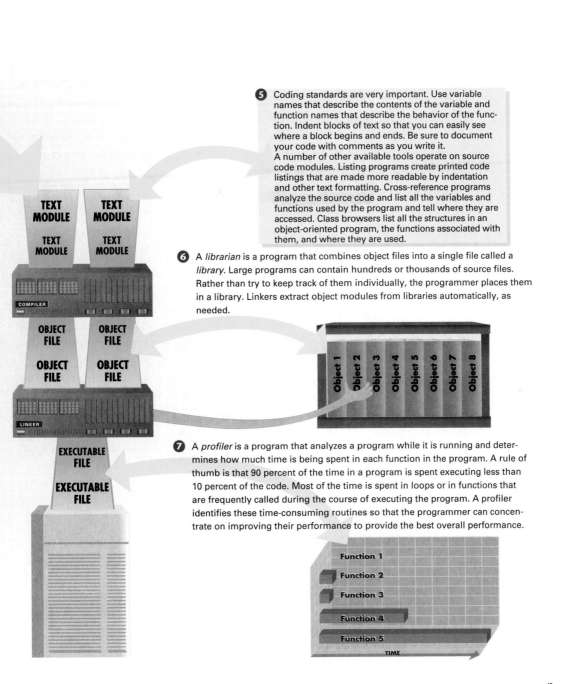

5 Coding standards are very important. Use variable names that describe the contents of the variable and function names that describe the behavior of the function. Indent blocks of text so that you can easily see where a block begins and ends. Be sure to document your code with comments as you write it.
A number of other available tools operate on source code modules. Listing programs create printed code listings that are made more readable by indentation and other text formatting. Cross-reference programs analyze the source code and list all the variables and functions used by the program and tell where they are accessed. Class browsers list all the structures in an object-oriented program, the functions associated with them, and where they are used.

6 A *librarian* is a program that combines object files into a single file called a *library*. Large programs can contain hundreds or thousands of source files. Rather than try to keep track of them individually, the programmer places them in a library. Linkers extract object modules from libraries automatically, as needed.

7 A *profiler* is a program that analyzes a program while it is running and determines how much time is being spent in each function in the program. A rule of thumb is that 90 percent of the time in a program is spent executing less than 10 percent of the code. Most of the time is spent in loops or in functions that are frequently called during the course of executing the program. A profiler identifies these time-consuming routines so that the programmer can concentrate on improving their performance to provide the best overall performance.

TEXT MODULE
TEXT MODULE
TEXT MODULE
TEXT MODULE
COMPILER
OBJECT FILE
OBJECT FILE
OBJECT FILE
OBJECT FILE
LINKER
EXECUTABLE FILE
EXECUTABLE FILE

Object 1 Object 2 Object 3 Object 4 Object 5 Object 6 Object 7 Object 8

Function 1
Function 2
Function 3
Function 4
Function 5
TIME

Courtesy of Ziff-Davis Press

Figure 13.4

Popular High-Level Languages

More than two hundred general- and special-purpose high-level languages are in use today. The following sections examine four widely used high-level programming languages and the features that make them powerful and effective tools for programming computers.

FORTRAN: A Scientific Language

One of the first high-level languages was **FORTRAN**, which stands for FORmula TRANslator. FORTRAN was created in 1954 by IBM's John Backus for developing scientific and engineering applications. FORTRAN enables programmers to calculate complex formulas with a few source code instructions. Like a wise mathematician, FORTRAN readily understands and executes the language of numbers.

FORTRAN is an unstructured language and was patterned after the CPU: it reads and executes instructions, one after the other, without much regard to categories and classes. If you want to define a data item, you can do so at any point in the program.

As with most high-level programming languages, FORTRAN has been revised and refined over the years. Even John Backus continues to improve FORTRAN. Standardized versions, approved by the American National Standards Institute (ANSI), were released in 1957, 1958, 1962, and 1978. Computer manufacturers who adopt these standards make it possible to use the same version of FORTRAN on nearly any computer hardware. Figure 13.5 shows a sample FORTRAN program. For the sake of comparison, each of the programming language examples in this module performs the same task—averaging 10 numbers—so notice how differently each approaches the problem.

Figure 13.5

A FORTRAN program that produces the average of 10 numbers.

```
C COMPUTE THE SUM AND AVERAGE OF 10 NUMBERS
C
      REAL NUM, SUM, AVG
      INTEGER TOTNUM, COUNTR
C
      SUM=0.0
C INITIALIZE LOOP CONTROL VARIABLE
      COUNTR=0
      TOTNUM=10
C
C LOOP TO READ DATA AND ACCUMULATE SUM
  20 IF (COUNTR .GE. TOTNUM) GO TO 30
      READ, NUM
      SUM = SUM + NUM
C     UPDATE LOOP CONTROL VARIABLE
      COUNTR = COUNTR + 1
      GO TO 20
C END OF LOOP - COMPUTE AVERAGE
  30 AVG = SUM / TOTNUM
C PRINT RESULTS
      PRINT, SUM
      PRINT, AVG
      STOP
      END
```

COBOL: A Business Language

About the same time FORTRAN was invented, COBOL was developed by the COnference on DAta SYstems Languages (CODASYL). The language was issued by the U.S. Government Printing Office in 1960. **COBOL** stands for COmmon Business-Oriented Language. Its developers represented a cross-section of computer users in business, industry, government, and education.

COBOL is a structured programming language. This statement means that COBOL "has a place for everything" and requires programmers to "put everything in its place." COBOL programs are separated into the following four sections, called divisions:

1. The Identification Division documents the program name, the programmer's name, dates, and any other important identification information.
2. The Environment Division names the computer hardware, including the CPU and I/O devices.
3. The Data Division identifies all associated files and working storage sections of the program.
4. The Procedure Division contains all the instructions in the COBOL program.

COBOL divisions are further divided into paragraphs and sections. This structure helps programmers write code efficiently with a minimum of repetition and confusion. COBOL is the nearest thing to a standard in business programming in the United States. Over the years, one programming language after another has threatened to displace COBOL, but so many COBOL programs have been written for large computer systems that changing them would be very costly. The American National Standards Institute (ANSI) standardized COBOL in 1968 and in 1974 issued a revised form called ANSI-COBOL. After long years of industry debate, COBOL 85 was approved. Today, COBOL is among the most standardized high-level programming languages. Versions of COBOL have been released for every major computing platform, including personal computers. Figure 13.6 shows a sample COBOL program.

Figure 13.6
A COBOL program that produces the average of 10 numbers.

```
        IDENTIFICATION DIVISION
        PROGRAM-ID.     AVERAGES.
        AUTHOR.         DEB KNUDSEN.
        DATE-COMPILED
        ENVIRONMENT DIVISION.
        CONFIGURATION SECTION.
            SOURCE-COMPUTER. HP-3000.
            OBJECT-COMPUTER. HP-3000.
        INPUT-OUTPUT SECTION.
        FILE-CONTROL.
            SELECT NUMBER-FILE ASSIGN TO "NUMFILE".
            SELECT REPORT-FILE ASSIGN TO "PRINT,UR,A,LP(CCTL)".
        DATA DIVISION.
        FILE SECTION.
        FD  NUMBER-FILE
            LABEL RECORDS ARE STANDARD
            DATA RECORD IS NUMBER-REC.
        01  NUMBER-REC              PIC S9(7)V99.
        FD  REPORT-FILE
            LABEL RECORDS ARE STANDARD
            DATA RECORD IS REPORT-REC.
        01  REPORT-REC             PIC X(100).

        WORKING-STORAGE SECTION.
        01  END-OF-NUMBER-FILE-FLAG    PIC X(3) VALUE SPACES.
            88  END-OF-NUMBER-FILE              VALUE "YES".
        01  SUM-OF-NUMBERS         PIC S9(7)V99.
        01  AVERAGE-OF-NUMBERS     PIC S9(7)V99.
        01  NUMBER-OF-NUMBERS      PIC 9(5).

        01  WS-REPORT-REC.
            05 FILLER              PIC X(2)    VALUE SPACES.
            05 FILLER              PIC X(17)   VALUE
                                   "SUM OF NUMBERS = ".
            05 WS-SUM-OF=NUMBERS   PIC Z,ZZZ,ZZZ.99-.
            05 FILLER              PIC X(3)    VALUE SPACES.
            05 FILLER              PIC X(15)   VALUE
                                   "# OF NUMBERS = ".
            05 WS-NUMBER-OF-NUMBERS   PIC ZZZZ9.
            05 FILLER              PIC X(3)    VALUE SPACES.
            05 FILLER              PIC X(21)   VALUE
                                   "AVERAGE OF NUMBERS = ".
            05 WS-AVERAGE-OF-NUMBERS  PIC Z, ZZZ, ZZZ.99-.
        05 FILLER                  PIC X(8)    VALUE SPACES.
        PROCEDURE DIVISION.

        100-MAIN-PROGRAM.
            OPEN INPUT NUMBER-FILE
                 OUTPUT REPORT-FILE.
            MOVE SPACES TO REPORT-REC.
            MOVE ZEROS TO SUM-OF-NUMBERS.
            MOVE ZEROS TO AVERAGE-OF-NUMBERS.
            MOVE ZEROS TO NUMBER-OF-NUMBERS.

            READ NUMBER-FILE
              AT END MOVE "YES" TO END-OF-NUMBER-FILE-FLAG.

            IF END-OF-NUMBER-FILE
              NEXT SENTENCE
            ELSE
              PERFORM 200-PROCESS-NUMBER-FILE.
                 UNTIL END-OF-NUMBER-FILE.

            PERFORM 300-COMPUTE-AVERAGE.
```

```
            AT END MOVE "YES" TO END-OF-NUMBER-FILE-FLAG.

    300-COMPUTE-AVERAGE.
        DIVIDE SUM-OF-NUMBERS BY NUMBER-OF-NUMBERS
          GIVING AVERAGE-OF-NUMBERS.

    400-PRINT-RESULTS.
        MOVE SUM-OF-NUMBERS TO WS-SUM-OF-NUMBERS.
        MOVE NUMBER-OF-NUMBERS TO WS-NUMBER-OF-NUMBERS.
        MOVE AVERAGE-OF-NUMBERS TO WS-AVERAGE-OF-NUMBERS.

    WRITE REPORT-REC FROM WS-REPORT-REC.
```

BASIC: A Personal Computer Language

BASIC, or the Beginners All-purpose Symbolic Instruction Code, was developed over a period of years by professors John Kemeny and Thomas Kurtz and students in the computer science program at Dartmouth College. BASIC was first released in 1965. Although originally developed on mainframe computers, BASIC is the most popular programming language used by personal computer owners. In most versions, BASIC is an unstructured language. Its creators intended for it to teach programming concepts as students wrote programs. BASIC is sometimes called *conversational* because it uses such terms as START, READ, INPUT, and STOP.

The original BASIC was easy to learn and enabled novice computer users to write simple programs within a few minutes. Today, many manufacturers have developed varieties of BASIC that are as complex as other high-level programming languages.

BASIC uses these five major categories of statements:

- Arithmetic statements enable users to use BASIC like a calculator. Typing *PRINT 2 + 2* programs your computer to display the result: *4.*

- Input/Output statements, including READ, DATA, INPUT, and PRINT, provide fundamental data-flow functions.

- Control statements, including GOTO, IF-THEN, FOR, NEXT, and END, control the sequence of instructions executed by the computer.

- Other statements, including REM and DIM, help document BASIC programs and set up data dimensions, respectively.

- System commands tell the operating system how to work with BASIC programs. For example, RUN means execute a program; LIST directs the computer to display a BASIC program.

There are many popular implementations of BASIC. Perhaps the most popular versions are offered by Microsoft. This popularity is due to the fact that for years Microsoft BASIC shipped automatically with virtually every PC sold. Today, even though Microsoft BASIC is no longer shipped with PCs, it remains as popular as ever. The most recent version of the language, Visual Basic, takes full advantage of the popular Windows environment.

Another popular version of BASIC is True BASIC, a structured version developed by Kemeny and Kurtz. It was developed in response to criticism of unstructured BASIC and is available for many computers. In addition, ANSI issued a standard for structured BASIC in 1987. Figure 13.7 shows a sample BASIC program.

Figure 13.7

A BASIC program that produces the average of 10 numbers.

```
Rem Compute sum and average of 10 numbers
DIM N(10)

Sum = 0
FOR I = 1 to 10
    INPUT N(I)
    Sum = Sum + N(I)
NEXT I

Avg = Sum / 10
PRINT "Sum ="; Sum
PRINT "Average ="; Avg
END
```

C: A High-Level Language

C is a popular programming language originally developed by Bell Laboratories. Like assembly language, C gives programmers a larger measure of control over the hardware, but it also incorporates many of the statement features of high-level languages. Although it was originally designed to work with the UNIX operating system, C has been adapted to virtually all operating systems running on nearly every hardware platform you can think of. C is a structured language that can be used effectively for just about any kind of programming. C owes its versatility to the fact that it was standardized by the American National Standards Institute (ANSI), making it almost universal for personal computer and workstation programming tasks.

C is a compiled language that uses a number of *libraries* of functions. To use a specific function, such as printf (which is similar to the PRINT statement in other languages), the programmer looks it up in the appropriate library and inserts it into the program. The newest variation of C is called C++. C++ builds on the C language, providing the programmer with *object-oriented programming* features. Figure 13.8 is an example of a C program.

Figure 13.8

A C program that produces the average of 10 numbers.

```
#include <stdio.h>

main ()
   {
        int i, num;
        float sum;

        printf("Enter numbers \n");
        sum = 0;
        for (i = 0; i < 10 i++)
         {
              scanf("%d",&num);
              sum = sum + num;
         }
        printf("Sum = %3.1f\n",sum);
        printf("Average = %3.1f\n",sum / 10.0);
   }
```

Other High-Level Languages

The discussion thus far has been limited to only a few of the high-level programming languages. The following list provides some facts about some of the other specialized programming languages, and table 13.2 shows the characteristics of some of these languages:

- *Ada*. Named for Augusta Ada Lovelace Byron, the first female programmer (1816–1852), Ada was developed by the Department of Defense for military programming.

- *APL*. The abbreviation stands for A Programming Language. APL is best suited for writing mathematical programs.

- *PL/1*. Developed by a committee especially for the IBM System/360, PL/1 was originally to be called NPL for New Programming Language. However, the acronym was already being used by the National Physics Laboratory in England.

- *Pascal*. Designed by one of the world's foremost programmers, Niklaus Wirth of the Netherlands, Pascal is a teaching language that can help students learn structured programming and good programming habits. It was popularized by Borland International with the introduction of Turbo Pascal in 1984.

- *RPG*. The Report Program Generator language is an easy-to-learn programming language used mostly with mainframe computers and their DBMS applications. It is especially useful for creating reports.

Table 13.2

Selected High-Level Programming Languages and Their Characteristics

Feature	Ada	APL	BASIC	C	COBOL	FORTRAN	Pascal	PL/1	RPG
Scientific		✓	✓	✓		✓	✓	✓	
Business			✓	✓	✓		✓	✓	✓
Problem oriented									✓
Procedure oriented	✓	✓	✓	✓	✓	✓	✓	✓	
Standardized	✓		✓	✓	✓	✓	✓	✓	
English-like			✓	✓	✓		✓	✓	
Widely used			✓	✓	✓	✓			✓
Interactive		✓	✓				✓		

Programming languages have increased in number and have become much more diverse over the years. Some were designed for specific purposes, whereas others were intended to set broad standards or to encompass a number of computer platforms. Each language has served a useful purpose. Some languages, such as Jovial (1960), have faded into obscurity, while others, such as COBOL, seem destined to be around forever.

HOME PAGE

JAVA: A HOT CUP OF PROGRAMMING LANGUAGE

A software designer named James Gosling, working at workstation manufacturer Sun Microsystems, led a research group in developing Java, a new programming language being used extensively for developing content on the World Wide Web. "People are going to see a Web that's much livelier," says Mr. Gosling.[5]

Here's what John December, author of *Presenting Java: An Introduction to Java and HotJava*, says:

> What do the Rolling Stones and Sun Microsystems have in common? First, both organizations have sites on the World Wide Web to promote their work. Second, both have chosen Java as a new way to enliven their World Wide Web pages.

The Rolling Stones' Home Page has been animated using Java.

Java is a programming language developed by Sun Microsystems that brings animation and interaction to the World Wide Web. HotJava is the name of the software developed by Sun that you can use to observe and interact with Java programs. Java unleashes a level of interactivity that has never been possible on the Web.

. . . Java enables developers to create content that can be delivered to and run by users on their computers. This software can support anything that programmers can dream up: spreadsheets, tutorials, animations, and interactive games. With the Web page as the delivery platform, this software can support a variety of information tasks with true interactivity. Users can get continuous, instanta-

neous feedback for applications in visualization, animation, and computation.

. . . One metaphor for hypertext is that it offers a visually static page of information (which can include text, graphics, sound, and video). The hypertext page can also have "depth" where it contains hyperlinks connecting to other documents or resources.

Java transforms this static page metaphor into a more dynamic one. The information on a Java page on the Web does not have to be visually static or limited to a pre-defined set of ways to interact with users. Users encountering Java programs can take part in a wider variety of interactive behavior, limited only by the imagination and skill of the Java programmer. Java thus transforms a hypertext page into a stage, complete with the chance for actors and players to appear and for things to happen. And, instead of the user being in the audience, you, as a user of a Java-enabled Web browser, are actively a part of the activity on this stage.

The Java programming language marks a significant advance for interactivity on the Web, and the HotJava browser that showcases Java marks the start of a new generation of smart browsers for the Web. . . . The HotJava browser opens new possibilities for new protocols and new formats never before seen on the Web.[6]

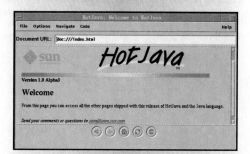

HOME PAGE REVIEW QUESTIONS

1. What is Java, and what is HotJava?

2. Where is Java being used, and for what?

3. What are Java's major assets and advantages?

5. N'Gai Croal and Adam Rogers. "Now for Some HotJava," *Newsweek*, November 13, 1995, 88–9.

6. John December. *Presenting Java: An Introduction to Java and HotJava* (Indianapolis: Sams.Net, 1995).

Knowledge Check

1. What is a statement?
2. What is syntax?
3. Explain what is meant by an unstructured language, and identify one.
4. Explain what is meant by a structured language, and identify one.
5. Describe three of the most popular programming languages, and tell the specific purposes for which each is used.
6. For what is an assembly language primarily used?

Key Terms

BASIC	C	COBOL	compiler
executable	FORTRAN	high-level languages	interpreter
linker	mnemonic	object code	statement
structure	syntax	unstructured	

ISSUES AND IDEAS

No Bugs in Microsoft Software?

Bill Gates, chairman and CEO of Microsoft Corporation, was interviewed by Dr. Juergen Scriba in Focus, a German magazine (Issue 43, October 23, 1995). Dr. Scriba made the following excerpts available to Klaus Brunnstein, who posted them to the Risks Forum (17.42, November 4, 1995) on the Internet. These excerpts were from the original interview, prior to editing and before publication in the magazine. The interviewer is asking Mr. Gates about software bugs.

FOCUS: Every new release of a software that has fewer bugs than the older one is also more complex and has more features . . . .

Gates: No, only if that is what'll sell!

FOCUS: But . . . .

Gates: Only if that is what'll sell! We've never done a piece of software unless we thought it would sell. That's why everything we do in software . . . it's really amazing. We do it because we think that's what customers want. That's why we do what we do.

FOCUS: But on the other hand, you would say: "Okay, folks, if you don't like these new features, stay with the old version, and keep the bugs."?

Gates: No! We have lots and lots of competitors. The new version—it's not there to fix bugs. That's not the reason we come up with a new version.

FOCUS: But there are bugs in any version, which people would really like to have fixed.

Gates: No! There are no significant bugs in our released software that any significant number of users want fixed.

FOCUS: Oh, . . . I always get mad at my computer if MS Word swallows the page numbers of a document that I printed a couple of times with page numbers. If I complain to anybody they say "Well, upgrade from Version 5.11 to 6.0."

Gates: No! If you really think there's a bug, you should report a bug. Maybe it's that you're not using it properly. Have you ever considered that?

FOCUS: Yeah, I did . . . .

Gates: It turns out Luddites don't know how to use software properly, so you should look into that. The reason we come up with new versions is not to fix bugs. It's absolutely not. It's the stupidest reason to buy a new version I ever heard. When we do a new version we put in lots of new things that people are asking for. And so, in no sense, is stability a reason to move to a new version. It's never a reason. Guess how much we spend on phone calls every year.

FOCUS: Hmmm, a couple million dollars?

Gates: $500 million a year. We take every one of those phone calls and classify them. That's the input we use to do the next version. So it's like the world's biggest feedback loop. People call in—we decide what to do on it. Do you want to know what percentage of those phone calls relate to bugs in the software? Less than one percent.

FOCUS: So people call in to say, "Hey listen, I would love to have this and that feature."?

Gates: Actually, that's about five percent. Most of them call to get advice on how to do a certain thing with the software. That's the primary thing.

FOCUS: So where does this common feeling of frustration come from that unites all PC users? Everybody experiences it every day—that these things simply don't work like they should.

Gates: Because it's cool. It's like, "Yeah, been there done that—oh, yeah, I know that bug." I can understand that phenomenon sociologically, not technically.

CRITICAL THINKING

1. It is an accepted fact that no software is bug free. What, then, is Mr. Gates trying to say?

2. Is it fair to ask the knowledge worker, as Mr. Gates does, if what is perceived as a bug might, in fact, be an error or misunderstanding of the software?

3. What ulterior motive might an employee at a retail software store have for blaming a problem on the software vendor and then recommending that the customer wait for the next version to correct it?

Module C

The Future of Programming

Why It's Important to Know

For the foreseeable future, programming by programmers will be with us. As programming languages become easier to use, more nonprogrammer knowledge workers will be able to create their own programs. New tools and techniques are constantly being introduced to make programming more efficient and accurate.

Programming has changed dramatically over the past five decades, as figure 13.9 shows. What does the future hold? Will computers eventually be able to program themselves? This module explores some recent advances in programming and what the future holds in store.

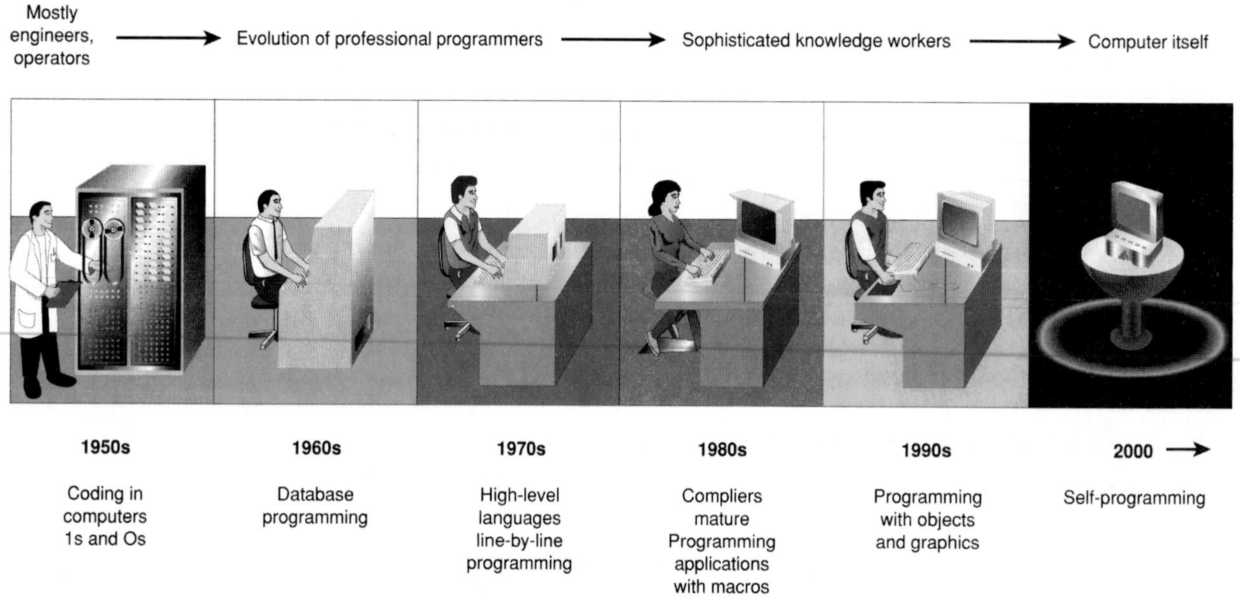

Mostly engineers, operators ⟶ Evolution of professional programmers ⟶ Sophisticated knowledge workers ⟶ Computer itself

1950s	1960s	1970s	1980s	1990s	2000 ⟶
Coding in computers 1s and Os	Database programming	High-level languages line-by-line programming	Compliers mature Programming applications with macros	Programming with objects and graphics	Self-programming

Figure 13.9
Advances in programming.

Object-oriented programming, or OOP, is a tool for both skilled programmers and knowledge workers who have never programmed. Bits of code and the data required by the code are put together to form an **object**. An object, for example, could be developed to place an icon on the screen. The data necessary to create the icon is contained within the object, as well as the programming code necessary to display the icon. Figure 13.10 shows the object browser screen in Delphi, an object-oriented programming language.

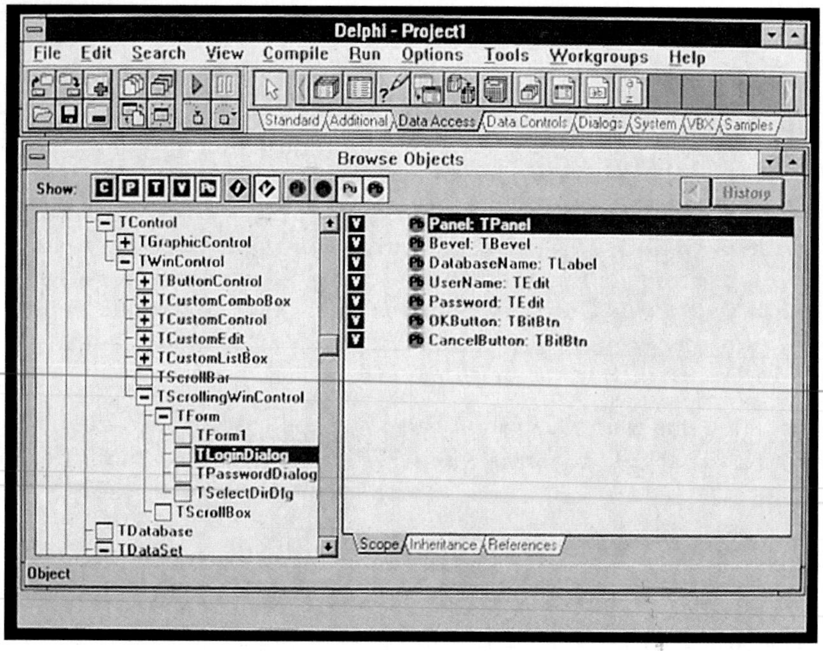

Figure 13.10
In Delphi, objects are stored as files in the Visual Component Library, a collection of more than 75 objects — such as dialogs, buttons, and list boxes — and reusable objects — such as database controls, notebook tabs, grids, and multimedia controls.

Courtesy of Borland International, Inc.

The Nature of Objects

Objects have both *attributes* and *behaviors*. For example, if the icons are buttons, clicking one with the pointing device launches an action. That action is the object's attribute. Its behavior is seen in the way in which it launches the action. It may zoom the action on to the screen, for example, or change the colors.

To make objects easier to create, they are derived from an organized hierarchy of *classes*. The class defines the kind of instructions and data found in an object. Some objects, for example, perform specific actions (such as calculating a column of spreadsheet numbers), whereas others ensure that instructions (such as closing a file) are properly carried out.

Objects are put together to form a program. Using OOP is similar to building a modular house in which parts are prefabricated and put together according to the buyer's desires. In that respect, OOP differs greatly from the way programming is traditionally accomplished in high-level languages.

A COBOL programmer, for example, may write portions of a program in no particular order. Then the programmer may outline other sections and go back later to "flesh out" the outlined portions. The programmer may find it necessary to write small bridge programs to link larger portions after the fact. The result is often called **spaghetti code** because the code is convoluted and tangled. Deciphering the spaghetti code may take longer—even for the original programmer—than rewriting the program. Spaghetti code has been a common programming occurrence for the past 40 years and often makes program maintenance extremely difficult.

Basic Principles of Object-Oriented Programming

OOP avoids the frustration of spaghetti code by using practical engineering techniques, much the way an architect or engineer designs a building or an aircraft. OOP utilizes three basic principles: encapsulation, inheritance, and polymorphism.

Encapsulation

Encapsulation means that a high degree of functionality is integrated, or bundled, into each object. Encapsulation makes an object *reusable* because it is totally self-sufficient. Therefore, you can easily link different objects when you are creating new programs or modifying old ones.

Inheritance

Inheritance means that objects derived from a specific class can derive attributes from the original class. Because the important traits are already built in (using encapsulation), the programmer can easily create a new program that is similar to an existing one.

Suppose that a programmer develops an object for editing text in a highly sophisticated desktop publishing program. If the programmer later writes a word processing program, he or she can create a new object, based on the original object, that inherits the capabilities and behaviors of the original object. The new object can then be modified to include new features, but the original features inherited from the original object remain intact. In essence, encapsulation ensures functionality, and inheritance permits defining—or redefining—objects to suit them to the new application.

Polymorphism

Polymorphism enables a programmer to describe a set of actions, or routines, that will perform exactly as they are described *regardless of the class of objects they are applied to*. In a conventionally written application program, the programmer has to be concerned with the type of data being printed by a routine and must assign a distinct name to each routine. The programmer also has to know when to use the proper routine to print the desired data. Polymorphism means that the program can still create, say, two routines, but the routines will have the same name. This way, the programmer has only one name to remember, and the compiler takes care of detecting the nature of the data being operated on and selecting the proper version of the print routine to match the data.

OOP Languages

SmallTalk, developed by Alan Kay at the Xerox Palo Alto Research Center in 1972, was the first widely available object-oriented language. SmallTalk pioneered the concept of programming with icons, rather than with statements and syntax. Instead of typing character strings, the programmer constructs object-oriented programs by linking icons that take over the task of creating character strings—in other words, writing the code.

Today, C++ is the most widely used object-oriented language. It is anticipated that C++ will be standardized by the ANSI committee in the near future. Many different C++ compilers have been released, and many commercial software programs originally written in C or in assembly language have been translated into C++. It seems likely that C++ will be a dominant force in the future.

Besides SmallTalk and C++, many other object-oriented languages are now available. Many older languages are starting to be released with object-oriented extensions that enable them to work in program environments based on objects. Future programs most likely will be developed in some sort of OOP dialect.

OOP Advantages

OOP acknowledges that changes in programs will occur and enables the programmer to plan for those changes. Like a well-planned city, OOP is capable of withstanding change. OOP speeds application development and requires less actual programming than a conventional high-level language.

Object-oriented programming simplifies programming for information systems professionals, but it also opens the door for knowledge workers to create software they need without having to learn a formal language or get a programmer involved. Another advantage with OOP is that modules can be reused in other programs. In addition, software created with OOP can be modified and revised by adding or subtracting modules. You can create an application simply by selecting objects or icons from a menu.

CASE: Computer-Aided Software Engineering

An interesting new kind of software tool emerged in the 1980s: **computer-aided software engineering**, or **CASE**. It is a methodology designed especially for programmers in large information systems organizations who need to create new applications quickly or re-engineer older applications containing spaghetti code.

CASE automates the design and implementation of applications and the procedures linking various applications so that they can be created more rapidly and efficiently. In this respect, CASE is similar to object-oriented programming. It differs primarily in that CASE is designed for applications that were created using high-level programming languages. CASE tools are used in three ways: for program design, for re-engineering, and as an integrated set of application development tools.

Program Design

Program design is the process of creating a new application; the process includes analysis, design, and documentation. CASE dramatically lowers these so-called front-end development costs by automating many manual operations and tasks. Paper, pencil, and the flow chart template are replaced by the computer.

Excelerator is a CASE tool developed for the personal computer; Excelerator designs, validates, and prepares specifications for applications and information systems. The systems analyst can create a system design, show it to end users, work with them to tailor the design to their needs, and then create the program specifications. Figure 13.11 shows Asymetrix InfoModeler, another CASE program.

Re-Engineering

The second way in which CASE tools are used is to correct programming errors and to maintain software applications—the back end of development. These tools streamline and automate many programming tasks and include text editors with built-in language templates, source-code management libraries, and program-performance and efficiency analyzers. Many companies have at least one enormous database that has become increasingly expensive or difficult to maintain and update. Using CASE for *re-engineering* modifies and updates older applications to meet current business requirements.

Figure 13.11

Asymetrix InfoModeler, CASE software available for Oracle, FoxPro, Access, Paradox, and Sybase / Microsoft SQL Server.

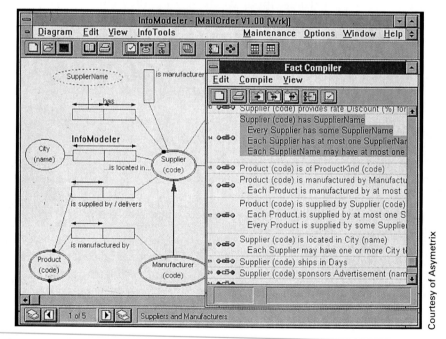

Courtesy of Asymetrix

Suppose, for example, that a company began using a database 30 years ago. Many of the departments in existence when the database was created may no longer be in operation. Accidentally accessing a portion of the database designed for these departments can cause a malfunction or even a failure. A CASE re-engineering tool cleans up existing files and redesigns the database to bring it more in line with the company's current and future needs. The CASE tool also paves the way for migrating from the old database to a new one. CASE re-engineering tools have extended the life and usefulness of existing software applications that otherwise would cost millions to replace

6. Will Tracz. *Confessions of a Used Program Salesman* (Reading, MA: Addison-Wesley Publishing Co., 1995), 7–8, 25–26.

Knowledge Check

1. What is an *object* in object-oriented programming?
2. What is the term used to describe disorganized programs?
3. What does the word *reusable* mean in OOP?
4. How does OOP offer an advantage in addressing changes in programs?
5. What is the main difference between OOP and CASE programming tools?
6. What does *re-engineering* mean, and when and how should it be used?
7. Who uses OOP tools, and who uses CASE tools?

Key Terms

code generator	computer-aided software engineering (CASE)	encapsulation
inheritance	object	object-oriented programming
polymorphism	spaghetti code	

ISSUES AND IDEAS

Game Programming

If you've ever played a computer game, such as Doom, you might consider all the programming skills that went into creating that game. Clayton Walnum has written a book on the topic of creating computer games called *Dungeons of Discovery*. Here are a few of his thoughts:

A programmer who can write commercial-quality computer games can write just about any other type of software as well, especially considering today's focus on graphics and sound in applications. Good computer games push your computer to its limits. In fact, a good computer game must excel in many areas. To write computer games that people will want to play, then, you must gain some expertise in the elements of game programming:

Game design. Whatever type of computer world you envision for your game, it's imperative that the world have consistent rules that the player can master. For a game to be fun, the player must be able to figure out how to surmount the various obstacles that you place in his path.

Graphic design. How a games looks is often as important as how well it performs. You want your gaming screens to be neat and uncluttered, logically laid out, and, above all, exciting to look at. Your screens should scream "Play me!" to anyone who comes into viewing distance.

Sound generation. . . . There is not a computer game on the planet (or, I'd venture to say, in the universe) that could not be improved by better sound effects. . . . Music . . . can also add much to a computer game.

Controls and interfaces. . . . To enable the player to control the game, the programmer must provide some sort of interface that the player can use to manipulate the data that exists inside the computer. . . . Menus and on-screen buttons enable the user to select options and commands . . . (and) the keyboard or mouse acts as the player's hands.

Image handling. Every computer game must deal with various types of images. These images may be full-screen background graphics, icons that represent game commands or game pieces, or tiles that you use to create a map or other complex game screen. You want your game to use enough quality graphics to look as professional as possible . . . but you must consider the amount of memory the graphics will consume . . . .

Animation. Animation is the process of making objects appear to come to life and to move around the computer screen. . . . Because animation consumes so much of your computer's power and requires that you design two or more images of each object you want to animate, you don't want to go overboard with the programming technique.

Game testing. The best way to test a game is to give it to a few trusted friends and watch as they play, taking notes about things that don't work quite the way you expect. Remember to watch not only for program bugs . . . but also interface bugs, which may make your program confusing to use.

So, why program Windows computer games? Mostly because it's fun! But remember that your game-programming experience will help you with every other program that you ever write. Gee, learning and fun. What a great combination![7]

CRITICAL THINKING

1. What kind of programming does the author believe requires the most skill?

2. What are the concerns with graphics and animation?

3. What two types of bugs do you need to watch for?

---

7. Clayton Walnum. *Dungeons of Discovery: Writing Dazzling Windows Games with WinG* (Indianapolis: Que, 1995), 5–13.

ETHICS

Ethics in Programming

As you have learned, programming involves a degree of creativity. As a means of solving problems, programs are creations or inventions. To underscore this fact, consider that in recent years, many companies and individuals have sought U.S. Government patents on programs. Of course, any time individual origination is concerned, ownership often becomes an ethical issue.

Many computer corporations feel that they own the programming ideas and finished work of their employees. They insist that any and all programming output while an employee is on the payroll is actually the property of the corporation. This output includes both the programs themselves and even "intellectual property"—ideas. If you examine this perspective, you can see why corporations take this stance.

Employees work together, attend meetings and seminars, and generally discuss programs under development. The problem-solving they do is valuable and has the potential to create profitable products. If an employee turns this information into a product he or she sells for personal gain outside the corporation, the act may be considered a form of theft. In this instance, the ideas of the individual are subordinated for the group's advantage.

The line between ethical and unethical behavior in this type of situation is often drawn on the basis of monetary gain or loss. Has the programmer used company resources, such as computer time or corporate data? Does the company authorize using the computer to work on individual projects on personal time? Did the employee agree that all work he or she does belongs to the company? Was the project originally intended for company use?

Many companies now have a set of ethical guidelines for employees to follow; failure to follow these guidelines often results in immediate dismissal. When systems professionals are found breaking the rules, it is not uncommon to see them escorted out of the building by the security guards. This humiliating scenario is prompted by fear that employees will take programs or software with them or possibly cripple the system with bugs.

Clearly, ethical behavior means not breaking company rules. However, the rules must be clear: if the programmer is hired on a freelance basis, he or she may be entitled to retain ownership. If the company wants to keep its system development private, management must inform employees of this fact. When it comes to programming, discretion plays a big part in determining what is right and what is wrong. Most important, ethical behavior means developing and adhering to a strict set of personal ethical guidelines.

Critical Thinking

1. From your understanding, would you say that programming is a creative activity?

2. Should programs be treated the same as any other company property, or should they be considered intellectual property, owned by the individual who created them?

3. Where does one draw the line between an idea and property? Does this line separate the ethical from the unethical?

THE LEARNING ENTERPRISE

The Management Information Systems department is where most of the enterprise's programmers work. However, it is not uncommon to see a programmer or two in other departments or functions. A programmer assigned to, say, marketing can quickly and efficiently create a custom application because he or she understands the business needs of that department.

Your assignment is to determine your department's or function's programming needs, both in terms of people and programming languages. To begin with, ask who in the class might be interested in learning more about programming. Perhaps there is someone with programming experience. Next, see whether that person or someone else will do some preliminary research to learn more about programming and programming languages. With the exception of the MIS department, use the following check list to determine your needs:

1. Will you need a full-time or part-time programmer?

2. Will the programmer be creating new applications?

3. What language(s) should the programmer know?

4. Will you need someone for application programming (setting up, teaching, or facilitating the use of programming in applications, such as word processing mail merge or spreadsheet formulas)?

5. Will you need someone for database programming or to teach others how to do it?

For the MIS department, consider the following questions:

1. What programming services will you offer to the rest of the enterprise?

2. Will you help train departmental programmers?

3. What advanced techniques, such as CASE, will you use?

4. Will you re-use software?

5. Will you teach others how to set up programming development teams?

6. Will you look for ways to market corporate information and sell the programs or applications that result?

Chapter Review

Fill in the Blank

1. _____ is the process of creating instructions for computers

2. A(n) _____ language is a set of commands used to create sequential instructions for computers.

3. In a programming language, a(n) _____ is an expression of instruction.

4. _____ is the set of rules governing how to put statements in a programming language together to make valid commands.

5. In OOP, bits of code and the data required by the code are put together to form a(n) _____.

6. The Jacquard loom was the first machine to be programmed with _____.

7. _____ is a way of expressing a program's instructions in English before actually writing it.

8. The language used to write programs in 1s and 0s is called _____.

9. A(n) _____ language most popular because it is closest to English.

10. Using computers to create programs is called _____.

Circle the Correct Answer

1. (Machine, Assembly) language is the only language the computer understands.

2. The (punched card, compiler) is the earliest means of programming machines.

3. (CASE, C++) is often used in re-engineering.

4. (SmallTalk, COBOL) was the first object-oriented programming language.

5. (Basic, CASE) is one of the most popular high-level programming languages.

6. Another name for program instructions is (code, assembler).

7. A (mnemonic, statement) is a short, English-like term or word in assembly language.

Review Questions

1. What is the difference between CASE and I-CASE?
2. What are the three characteristics of object-oriented programming?
3. Why do programmers need an editor program?
4. For what do programmers use a compiler?
5. What is the difference between a compiler and an interpreter?
6. What is an executable file, and why is it important?
7. What is syntax, and why is it important?
8. Explain the purpose of a statement.

Discussion Questions

1. Discuss the different uses for particular high-level programming languages.
2. How do tools like CASE and OOP improve programming productivity? Be specific; discuss the uses for CASE tools, program design, and code generators, and the three characteristics of OOP and tell why they're important.
3. Describe a program you or your group would like to create; then discuss program design in the context of how you would create it.
4. In the Home Page "Don't Flip the Bozo Bit," what does the author mean by "bozo bit?"
5. Define what you consider ethical or unethical behavior of programmers.

INTERNET DISCOVERY

To learn more about a variety of MIS resources, log on to one of the following sites:

http://www.smeal.psu.edu/misweb/

http://www.smeal.psu.edu/misweb/plibrary.html

SOFTWARE ENGINEERING

One of the most urgent concerns in enterprises today is the need for information systems organizations to create and modify applications much faster than with the traditional development life cycle.

Dr. James Martin, *Rapid Application Development*[1]

A computer system consists of people using software and hardware. In using software and hardware, people tend to create new computer systems—a process often called *system development*. Most system development work centers around the creation of software—either system software or application software. The applications used on the system often determine how effectively knowledge workers use that system. A well-designed application should increase productivity for the enterprise.

Software engineering refers to the design, development, and implementation of production software systems. A *production* software system is one designed and used within an enterprise to accomplish its mission. For example, an accounting or human resources management software system is a suite of various applications, all developed exclusively for those particular departments and their knowledge workers. The other primary kind of software development is *product software*, such as the applications you purchase from a software publisher.

Software engineering can be accomplished on PCs, workstations, mini, and mainframe computers. As defined by the Study Group on Computer Science of the NATO Science Committee in 1967, software engineering embraces all the human aspects, from programming to management, and all project details, from concept to execution to documentation.

1. (New York: Macmillan), 1991, vii.

Programmers, systems analysts, application programmers, and other software and information systems professionals should all take part in software engineering, as should managers and the knowledge workers who will use the system. The degree of complexity and the number of steps in software engineering vary depending on the size of the company, the number of information systems professionals on the development staff, the size and complexity of the problem that must be solved, and the number of knowledge workers who will use the system. But regardless of these factors, the most important thing is to use the best software engineering methods and tools available to create high-quality, error-free systems in the shortest time possible.

Module A

System Analysis and Design

Why It's Important to Know

The system development life cycle is the basis for creating computer systems. When you understand the steps involved, you can see that it's a human process that involves both computer professionals and the knowledge workers who will use the system.

In the past, all the computer systems for an enterprise were developed by the information systems staff. This development technique is called the **system development life cycle** and is a way of describing each of the steps involved in the development of a computer system or an application. In this context, a computer system may include a number of programs, utilities, and applications, all of which are designed to work together in the business process. An example is an accounting system with accounts payable, accounts receivable, general ledger, management reports, invoices, transaction reports, and so forth. A system may also be a single application, such as a report generator for a DBMS. But regardless of the end use of the system or application, the system development life cycle includes the following:

- *Analysis*. Identifying and defining the problem

- *Design*. Planning the solution to the problem

- *Coding*. Writing the program

- *Debugging*. Correcting program errors

- *Testing and Acceptance*. Ensuring that the system works properly and turning it over to users, with accompanying training as necessary

- *Implementation*. Releasing the system for regular use

- *Maintenance*. Keeping the system working properly and improving it as necessary

- *Documentation*. Writing software, user, and reference documentation

The following sections take a closer look at each of these steps.

Analysis and Design

The first two steps in the system development process are systems analysis and design. **Systems analysis** is the study of an activity, a procedure, or an entire business to determine what kind of computer system can make it more efficient. **Systems design** is the act of planning the technical aspects of the new system. In the past, these two steps were accomplished with paper and pencil; today, these tasks are often performed with software tools.

System development is usually triggered by a knowledge worker requesting a new system, as when members of a company's telemarketing department ask for an application to keep track of customer ordering information. Large software development companies have found that effective systems analysis and design can cut the overall program development time and costs by as much as 60 percent.

The **systems analyst** gathers and analyzes the data necessary to develop the new system. Depending on the organization and its size, the systems analyst may also be called a systems consultant, a systems engineer, an information analyst, or a business analyst. Whatever the title, the job includes the following tasks:

- Analyzing the problem to be solved, including the data to be input, the expected output, and other system considerations

- Interviewing the knowledge workers who will use the system to determine their needs, problems, and expectations

- Determining which people and what kinds of software, hardware, and monetary resources are necessary or available to solve the problem

- Writing the specifications and designing the computer system and the methods that enable the information system to solve the problem

- Guiding or managing the project to a successful conclusion

Coding

The next two steps of the system development life cycle—coding and debugging—are the nitty-gritty work of developing the system or application. **Coding** means programming in a specific programming language—in other words, writing the *source code* for the program. The code is then *compiled* into instructions the CPU can execute.

Source code is the program, written in a specific high-level programming language, that is sent to the computer for processing. *Coding* is often used interchangeably with *programming*, but refers specifically to the process of writing source code. By the time a programmer begins writing code, the program planning stage should be finished. If the programmer has defined the problem adequately and has created a good design, coding can often take less time than the other steps in the system development process.

An essential tool for the coding step in the system development process is the **text editor**. A programmer uses a text editor program to write, erase, and manipulate words on the screen. A text editor is similar to a word processor but without many of its formatting features; in fact, text editors are the predecessors of word processors.

Programming languages have certain rules or *conventions* that programmers must follow. Advanced text editors help programmers adhere to those conventions. For example, if a programming language requires each line of source code to be indented a certain number of spaces and end with a period, the text editor can be set to automatically begin each line with a tab and end each line with a period. Other text editor features, such as search, cut and paste, automatic word wrap, and automatic line spacing, also make the job of coding a little easier.

Structured coding resulted from the need for a more organized way to write programs. The concept of structured coding maintains that all programs can be written using three basic constructs: sequence, selection, and looping, as shown in figure 14.1. Programs written using structured coding techniques are easier to read, understand, and maintain. Structured coding is different from other structured techniques. You can use structured *coding* whether or not you use structured *design* techniques.

Figure 14.1
The three primary control structures used in structured coding.

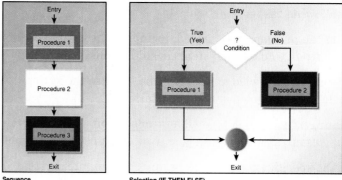

Sequence

Selection (IF-THEN-ELSE)

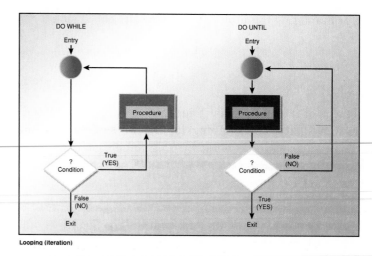

Looping (iteration)

Debugging

In the early 1940s, a programming team discovered a moth in a computer; that moth had caused a program to fail. Ever since that incident, the term *bug* has been used to describe a program or hardware problem.

Detail and precision are required, almost to the point of perfection, to make a program run successfully. Program bugs, therefore, are quite common. A **debugger** is a system software program that helps programmers identify program errors. For example, a debugger may be used when a program runs but fails to produce the correct output. A debugger reports problems as *error messages*.

The compiler also identifies program errors so that the programmer can debug, or correct, the program. Programmers use error message listings, as shown in figure 14.2, to track down bugs. Debugging can be a costly process and can consume as much as 50 percent of program development time. Modern debugging tools help programmers find trouble spots more quickly.

Figure 14.2
Error messages produced when a BASIC program is compiled.

```
Diagnostic on source line 16, listing line 16
source file: CHECKBOOK.BAS;1

                IF answer = "Y"

%BASIC-E-INSERTB,          assuming THEN before end of statement

Diagnostic on source line 17, listing line 17
source file: CHECKBOOK.BAS;1

                WHILE

%BASIC-E-FOUND,     found end of statement when expecting an expression

Diagnostic on source line 21, listing line 21
source file: CHECKBOOK.BAS;1

                THEN
.............1

%BASIC-E-FOUND, 1:        found keyword THEN when expecting one of:
                                an operator
                                end of statement
                                "("

Diagnostic on source line 30, listing line 30
source file: CHECKBOOK.BAS;1

                THEN
.............1

%BASIC-E-FOUND, 1:        found keyword THEN when expecting one of:
                                an operator
                                end of statement

Diagnostic on source line 35, listing line 35
source file: CHECKBOOK.BAS;1

                END IF

%BASIC-E-MISMATFOR,        missing NEXT for UNTIL at listing line 25

%BASIC-E-ENDNOOB J, CHECKBOOK.BAS;1 completed with 5
diagnostics - object deleted
```

Testing and Acceptance

No system is truly worthwhile unless it meets the needs of the knowledge workers it was designed for. Therefore, once a system is debugged, it goes into testing so that people can see how it works. There are two types of testing:

- **Alpha testing** involves entering various kinds of data to see how the system or application reacts under different conditions. These tests are normally conducted "in-house," meaning by the people who created the system, whether they work for a company that is developing its own system or for a software publisher that is developing a commercial application.

- **Beta testing** means letting knowledge workers test the system under actual working conditions but before it goes into production and is released. They not only look for system malfunctions but also for such things as ease of use, speed, and a number of design characteristics.

In beta testing, knowledge workers often are asked to try to cause the system to fail by performing unanticipated functions, such as opening the same file repeatedly without closing the previous one. Remember, a system should not only work as it is designed to work, but it should not fail even when used improperly. When used improperly, the system should give the knowledge worker an error or help message suggesting a course of corrective action.

Implementation

Implementation means the release of a system for use by its intended knowledge workers. Another term is going into **production**, which means putting it to work in daily use. In organizational terms, implementation means that the system development people have to stop tweaking the system and give it to the department or workgroup for which it was designed. The transition from testing to implementation is always difficult; the systems people usually want to continue making improvements. On the other hand, the knowledge workers are anxious to begin using the new system in earnest and obtaining its benefits. The system is not necessarily perfect at this stage. Even after release and implementation, the relationship between the people who created the system and the people who are using it doesn't end.

Maintenance

Even after going into production, most systems are constantly being corrected, updated, and improved. This ongoing phase of the system life cycle is called **maintenance**. Knowledge workers may request that the system be modified to run faster or perform more tasks, or changes in business procedures or conditions may necessitate updating the system. And because the system is not perfect, subtle bugs may reveal themselves after the system is in use, especially during periods of high-volume use or when the system is being used in unanticipated ways.

Regardless of the reasons, far more time and attention are put into systems maintenance than into systems design (see figure 14.3). Whether the software being developed is a corporate-wide inventory control system or a commercial product such as a new spreadsheet, ongoing maintenance and support are essential. Knowledge workers expect assistance during a system's entire life cycle.

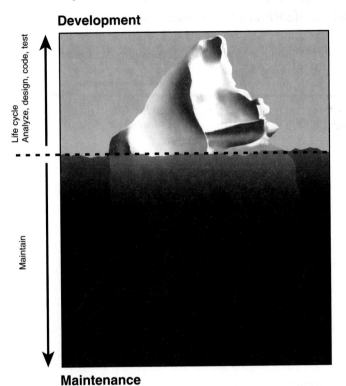

Development

Life cycle
Analyze, design, code, test

Maintain

Maintenance

Figure 14.3
The relationship between the amount of work involved in systems design and in systems maintenance is compared here to the portions of an iceberg above and below the surface of the water.

Documentation

Documentation is the set of instructions that accompanies a system or an application. The three types of documentation are software, user, and reference, and the type is determined by how it is being used. **Software documentation** is chiefly for programmers who maintain the program. **User documentation** and **reference documentation** are for the knowledge workers who use the program. Software documentation explains *how* a program works. User and reference documentation explains *what* a program does and *how* to use it.

Preparing documentation is the final step in the system development life cycle, but ideally it is a *process* that continues throughout development and even after implementation. Although the final details cannot be written until the programming is finished, waiting until the end of the project to begin writing often results in poor documentation.

Good documentation is no accident; it is the result of careful planning, thoughtful development, and a thorough explanation of all important system characteristics. Well-prepared documentation enables knowledge workers to be more productive in their day-to-day work. Documentation can take many forms:

- Conventional paper manuals or memos

- Readme files provided on program disks

- Context-sensitive help screens or messages, such as Microsoft's Wizards

- On-line, hypertext guidance using the Help key or Help pull-down menu

In addition, knowledge workers can get help and learn more about a system or application from on-line forums where others using the software to answer each other's questions. Sometimes, these forums are moderated by the software publisher or an expert user. Books published by third-party publishers (as opposed to the software publisher) are also an excellent source of helpful documentation. The experts who write third-party books often explain the subject more thoroughly than it is explained in the documentation that comes with the software.

Knowledge workers often contribute to producing a system's documentation, both during and after development. They tell the systems people what doesn't work—or doesn't work properly—and suggest ways to make the system better.

Structured Techniques

By the mid-1960s, government institutions and corporations were floundering in a sea of programming problems. Programs written using the personal styles of many individuals led to chaos in software development and maintenance. In response, people like Edsger Dijkstra, Corrado Bohm, and Guiseppe Jacopini developed and advocated a variety of **structured techniques**. Programming using structured techniques facilitates the creation of more reliable and easily maintained programs that are also orderly, readable, and easily understood by others.

There are a number of structured techniques, including structured analysis, structured design, and structured programming or coding. Structured techniques often result in reduced program development time, increased programmer productivity, less testing and debugging, and programs that are simpler and easier to maintain. The next section more closely examines structured coding techniques, but first you explore some of the more common structured analysis and design techniques.

Structured Analysis

Structured analysis uses a *data flow diagram*, like the one shown in figure 14.4, to chart a system's progress. By showing how data moves from one point to another, the resulting concept is that of a *logical system*. Structured analysis requires the analyst to think logically through what the system should do before determining how it should be done. The emphasis is on the end result—what knowledge workers need from the system to do their jobs. Interestingly, the logical base of structured analysis often enables the analyst to come up with more creative solutions to problems.

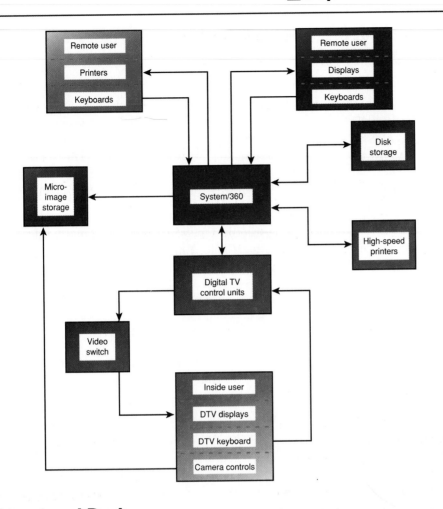

Figure 14.4
*Data flow diagrams
chart the course of data
in an information system.*

Structured Design

Structured design commonly uses a method called the *top-down approach,* which breaks the problem into parts and arranges these parts according to their size and level of detail. The result is a *hierarchy,* or series of steps, that begins with the overall problem to be solved and continues down in increasingly more detailed parts of the problem.

Computers perform tasks in a step-by-step fashion. For this reason, they are good at working with algorithms. An **algorithm** is a set of instructions or procedures that solves a problem. After the steps are well defined, programmers can easily go on to write code in **modules**—distinct, logical parts of a program.

Structured Programming Techniques

Structured programming techniques help programmers understand what they're doing before they begin writing code. These techniques provide several kinds of road maps, in various levels of detail, to serve as guides in coding. After the systems analyst has defined the problem and designed the most appropriate algorithm for solving it, the next step is coding the program. Using structured techniques makes for a smoother coding process and results in a neater, more organized program that other programmers can read and understand.

Structured Programming Techniques Case Study: *The New York Times*

The first software engineering project to use structured techniques began in 1969 at *The New York Times*. IBM was brought in to develop an information system that would replace the manual clipping file, or *morgue,* as it was known. The system would make it possible to research articles by date of publication, section of the paper, key words, and so on. The system was developed using what was called a *chief programmer team,* which was comprised of specialists, each of whom was responsible for specific tasks or modules of the programming code.

The project began with structured design, which involved creating data flow diagrams that explained how data would move between various hardware components, as shown in figure 14.4. The team identified descriptors—bibliographic data that would be needed—such as a date or a date range; whether the writer was a staff reporter or freelancer; the type of article (news, editorial, feature); accompanying illustrations or artwork; the section and page numbers; and the relative importance of the article.

The project used the top-down approach for its structured analysis. The team completed the *control code* (primary programming) first, followed by the functional code that would work with the already-functioning computer system. This approach made it easier to integrate the new system and resulted in fewer program errors, which meant less debugging. Because debugging occurred in modules, or stages, overall system reliability was improved.

The experienced team members were highly motivated to finish the project on time; remarkably, the project was finished in just 6 months. Using traditional development techniques, it would have taken an estimated 132 months. Its small size was considered a benefit to its manageability and responsiveness to change. And because only 20 errors were discovered, debugging, testing, and acceptance proceeded quickly and smoothly. The project's success was attributed in large part to structured programming techniques and to the organization and tools used in the process.

HOME PAGE

BETA ADDICTS

Beta testing can help companies understand where technology is heading, which products appear promising, and—equally important—which software isn't worthy of deployment. On the other hand, the beta process has been diluted in recent years, say critics. Beta testing used to be a final spot-check of software that was about to ship. Now, in many cases, it's become a massive bug hunt on products that aren't even close to completion.

Yet beta testing is burgeoning. Just ask Microsoft, which (in the spring of 1995) distributed test versions of Windows 95 to more than 400,000 users, charging each $30 to participate in what the vendor called the *Windows 95 Preview Program*. All told, Microsoft estimates more than one million users worked with Windows 95 prior to the operating system's final release on August 24, 1995.

. . . Beta testers get a thrill from seeing software prior to its release and enjoy hacking products to find their weaknesses. A select few even become technology-industry celebrities. Beta tester Matt Merrick . . . is regularly quoted in the computer trade press—and even in Microsoft press releases.

. . . Getting started as a beta tester can be difficult. Software suppliers usually verify an applicant's expertise and the intended use of the software. Also, in a Catch-22 situation, vendors want applicants who have already tested other packages. But, says tester Merrick, "Once you're approved and you do a good job, it snowballs into beta testing more and more software."

. . . Many (beta testers) strive to find a "show stopper"—a bug so major it can permanently damage data or delay the product's release. "The best beta testers thrive on finding show stoppers," says Richard Buchanan, a consultant in Peterborough, NH.

. . . Are beta-testing employees doing work that should be done by software vendors? "Years ago, a beta product was something with no known bugs," says Rich Finkelstein, president of Performance Computing, a consulting firm in Chicago. "The vendor viewed a beta product as something that was ready to ship as soon as selected customers gave it a go. Now, betas aren't even complete products."

. . . Indeed, vendors such as Microsoft and IBM generally ship several beta releases of software over a period of months, incrementally adding functionality and bug fixes before shipping a final product.

. . . Proponents of beta testing say . . . snags are to be expected, given software's complexity. Besides, they add, beta-testing helps the industry. "Software vendors need a slew of PCs to test their software, and the beta process provides that," says *BugNet* editor (Bruce) Brown.[2]

HOME PAGE REVIEW QUESTIONS

1. Why is beta testing important?

2. What has beta testing become?

3. Prepare a brief letter stating why you would like to be a beta tester.

---

2. Joseph C. Panettieri. "Beta Addicts," *Information Week*, October 9, 1995, 34–42.

Knowledge Check

1. What is software engineering?
2. Which two program development steps work hand in hand to define the software project?
3. Who is in charge of system development during the early development stages?
4. What makes coding different from programming?
5. What tasks does a text editor perform?
6. What term is used to refer to the problems the debugger reports?
7. Name the two types of testing.
8. Why is more effort expended on maintenance than system design?
9. Name the three categories of documentation.

Key Terms

algorithm	alpha testing	beta testing
coding	debugger	documentation
implementation	maintenance	module
production	reference documentation	software documentation
software engineering	source code	structured analysis
structured coding	structured design	structured programming techniques
system development life cycle	systems analysis	systems analyst
systems design	text editor	user documentation

ISSUES AND IDEAS

Will the Computer Save Humanity?

In the novel *Microserfs*, three bright, twenty-something people who work at Microsoft Corporation are having a discussion. Todd and Daniel are testers, or program debuggers. Karla is a programmer.

Todd said, "What we do at Microsoft is just as repetitive and dreary as any other job, and the pay's the same as any other job if you're not in the stock loop, so what's the deal . . . why do we get so *into* it? What's the engine that pulls us through the repetition? Don't you ever feel like a cog, Dan? . . . wait—the term *cog* is outdated—a *cross-platform highly transportable binary object?*"

I said, "Well, Todd, work isn't, and was never *meant* to be, a person's whole life."

"Yeah, I know that, but aside from the geek-badge-of-honor stuff about doing cool products first and shipping them on time and money, what else is there?"

I thought about this. "So what is it you're really asking me?"

"Where does *morality* enter our lives, Dan? How do we justify what we do to the rest of humanity? Microsoft is no Bosnia."

Religious upbringing.

Karla came into the room at this point. She turned off the TV set and looked at Todd square in the eyes and said, "Todd, you exist not only as a member of a family or a company or a country, but as a member of a *species*—you are human. You are part of *humanity*. Our species currently has major problems and we're trying to dream our way out of these problems, and we're using computers to do it. The construction of hardware and software is where the species is investing its very *survival*, and this construction requires zones of peace, children born of peace, and the absence of code-interfering distractions. We may not achieve transcendence through computation, but we *will* keep ourselves out of the gutter with them. What you perceive as a vacuum is an earthly paradise—the freedom to, quite literally, line-by-line, prevent humanity from going non-linear." [3]

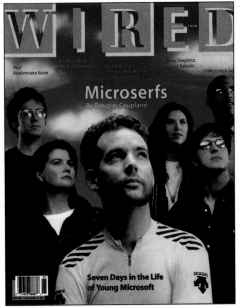

Courtesy of Information Week

CRITICAL THINKING

1. What is Todd questioning about his work?
2. Do you think Karla is right about how humanity is using computer systems?
3. Will, as Todd fears, technology ultimately overcome morality, or will it ultimately free humanity as Karla predicts?

Module B

Information Engineering

Why It's Important to Know

> **Information engineering is a more modern and efficient form of system development. It is a more people-oriented approach than the system development life cycle, and supports the use of the latest tools and techniques.**

Information engineering is a software development methodology developed by Clive Finkelstein, an Australian information systems professional. In 1982, Finkelstein wrote: "Software engineering is intended primarily for use by analysts and programmers. It was not designed to be applied directly by users (knowledge workers). Communication with knowledge workers comes primarily through the data flow diagram. Information engineering, on the other hand, brings user department personnel, management, and data processing (the information systems organization) together in a partnership. Its techniques draw on the experience of all three groups."[4]

---

3. Douglas Coupland. *Microserfs* (New York: HarperCollins, 1995), 60–61.

4. Clive Finkelstein. "Information Engineering," InDepth section, *Computerworld,* June 15, 1981.

Finkelstein, working with James Martin, has refined and perfected this methodology over many years. Information engineering goes beyond the boundaries of a specific methodology. It creates a framework for developing enterprise-wide computer systems to automate an entire business and all its processes. In fact, its concentration is on creating systems that serve the business needs and the company's goals.

Knowledge workers play an integral role in information engineering; indeed, systems cannot be designed or created without their participation. Information engineering uses the latest software tools and techniques to design and create systems. The idea is to do quality work, but to do it quickly so that the system can be put to use.

In almost all respects, information engineering is superior to traditional development techniques. By way of comparison, refer to table 14.1.

Table 14.1
Traditional Development versus Information Engineering

Traditional Development	Information Engineering
Emphasis on coding and testing	Emphasis on analysis and design
Paper-based specifications	Computer-based specifications
Manual coding	Automatic code generation
Manual documentation	Automatic document generation
Often fails to meet user specs	Joint application development
Requires debugging	Automated design verification generates bug-free code
Constant code maintenance	Code regenerated according to updated design specifications

Information Engineering Development

Everyone participates in an information engineering project: senior management, knowledge workers, and information systems professionals. An information engineering project consists of the following four simple components:

- *Information strategy planning.* Top management reviews the goals of the enterprise and establishes the information needed to support these goals.

- *Business area analysis.* This analysis models the enterprise's activities and data, with respect to prior planning.

- *System design.* The actual specifications and attributes of the system are presented in a manner that is understandable to both senior management and knowledge workers. This design is periodically reviewed and updated.

- *Implementation.* Data and activities are integrated with the enterprise-wide plan to accomplish business goals. The business now can react more quickly and effectively to changing conditions. Management has a better understanding of the enterprise and the strategic uses of technology. Knowledge workers work more productively, resolve problems faster, and produce both short-term and long-term returns.

Information Engineering Approaches

There is no single use for information engineering. Rather, it is a new way of thinking about system development. Some of the techniques or methodologies and development tools may be "home grown"—developed within a business as part of its own approach or to use for a single project. Other information engineering techniques may be developed by a consultant, a software company, or a software developer. Here are a few ways information engineering may be used:

- *Application development without programmers.* Nonprogrammer knowledge workers create applications for their departments or areas using languages or development tools that do not require extensive training.

- *Rapid application development (RAD).* A team of information systems professionals and knowledge workers is assembled on a one-time basis to work intensively on a single project using RAD techniques or software.

- *Prototyping.* A partially working model of the system is quickly put together to show the knowledge worker how it will perform. If it seems appropriate, the working system is built with the knowledge worker's participation.

- *CASE projects.* A team of information systems professionals who have demonstrated an interest in using CASE tools work together to complete a system project.

In the following sections you take a closer at two information engineering techniques: RAD and prototyping.

Rapid Application Development

Rapid application development, or **RAD**, is an information engineering technique promoted by James Martin, who defines RAD as a development life cycle designed to take maximum advantage of the integrated CASE (I-CASE) tools. The goal is to produce systems of high quality, at high speed, and with low cost. Although better, faster, cheaper has certainly always been the ultimate goal of computing, Martin appends this goal by saying, "A top criteria for IS must be that it never interferes with business's ability to seize a competitive opportunity. Speed is essential." Table 14.2 shows how some companies have improved development times using the RAD approach to systems development.[5]

---

5. Adapted from *Enterprise Engineering* by James Martin (Lancashire, England: Savant Institute, 1994), Volume I, 98–99.

Table 14.2

How Some Businesses Have Used RAD to Stay Competitive

Company	Systems Improvement	Results
IBM Credit Corporation	Reduced financing approval time from seven days to four hours	Staff size remained the same, but productivity rose 100 fold
Wal-Mart	Reduced shelf restocking time from six weeks to 36 hours	Customers rarely find stores out of product they desire
Harley-Davidson	Reduced time to manufacture a cycle frame from 72 days to two days, while raising product quality from 50% to 99%	Renewed company image for a quality product and demand soared
Motorola	Cut customer request time for a pager from three weeks to two hours	Massive increase in the volume of pager business

In the traditional development approach, the knowledge worker is commonly involved in the process at the outset, *prior to design*, and then not again until the application reaches the testing stage. In the RAD life cycle, the knowledge worker is involved during the entire process; only during actual construction does that involvement diminish.

The RAD life cycle is based on four foundations: the Information Engineering methodology, high-quality software engineering tools, use of highly skilled people, and strong management support and involvement. RAD also presumes a departure from what James Martin calls the "classical development life cycle," in which applications are built "by hand" using line-by-line coding and plastic templates.

RAD Case Study: Imperial Oil

Imperial Oil, Ltd., of Canada is a $5 billion petroleum refiner and marketer with headquarters in Toronto. In 1986, at a time when the oil business was recovering from its worldwide slump, Imperial's information systems organization decided that it must deliver to the various business functions better services in a shorter period of time. The company had tentatively settled on a methodology, but on closer examination realized that it could never manually implement a rigid methodology in a company the size of Imperial and be sure that knowledge workers would conform to its design criteria. In addition, Imperial had begun developing an architecture that used PC-based tools but soon realized that it needed a mainframe-based, shared-data environment.

Imperial's Esso Petroleum Canada division employed the services of James Martin Associates (JMA) to develop a mission-critical system for retail sales reporting and cash management for its retail outlets. The system was to include a management reporting system for these two functions. The developer used the Information Engineering methodology with rapid application development (RAD) techniques, employing the Texas Instruments Integrated Engineering Facility (IEF) I-CASE development environment.

The system was designed to accomplish four goals. The first was to develop an application that processed transactions at the retail outlet and then gathered that data from the outlet's point-of-sale (POS) terminal and stored it. The second goal was a management and control system that balanced the books, provided a quality assurance component, and returned data results to the outlets for review. The third goal was a management and control system that put this data into a shared database. And the fourth goal was a series of applications to extract and report on the data in the database. Because Imperial was building a new system within a suite of systems, they used JMA's Information Engineering techniques to design the bridges between old and new.

A great deal of planning, communicating, and decision-making took place before the project began. Moreover, Imperial felt it was essential that everyone on the development team—both the information systems professionals and the knowledge workers who would be using and managing the system—thoroughly understand the business aspects of the system they were building. All had to understand what they were working on and why they were working on it; delivering the system would mean giving the company a strong competitive advantage.

Certain areas identified for automation in the business area analysis were considered a business priority, so they were discussed with analysts who understood the current systems, as well as with employees in the retail operations who used the data. In this way, Imperial was able to gauge how the new system would work with existing systems and what obstacles might stand in the way.

Development team issues were very important at Imperial. The project team consisted of three subteams, each with a group leader reporting to the project manager. Team members were information systems professionals and knowledge workers from the comptroller's and retail departments. No one had any prior IEF experience; some, in fact, had never worked on a project before. One team worked on changes to the POS units, another on constructing the on-line transaction processing system and databases, and the third on connections to and from those databases to the corporate database. Imperial learned that not all people come to a project like this with the appropriate skills. Some team members needed training in tools other than CASE, so training was delivered during the project.

This project taught the people at Imperial several important things. First, they found that they didn't have to analyze the business excessively in order for the system to produce results. Second, Imperial found that CASE tools are a means to an end, not an end themselves, and they must be used under proper project management to produce results. Third, a project's success is based, in large part, on having "responsive, enthusiastic, and hungry knowledge workers who want the system."[6]

---

6. Jack B. Rochester. "Improving Application Development Productivity," *I/S Analyzer*, March, 1990.

Prototyping

Prototyping is creating a working model of a new application or system. The subject warrants some additional attention here because it can be used in just about any application development environment, regardless of the methodology used—structured design or information engineering—because prototyping is performed early in the process. Prototyping involves both knowledge workers who will use the system and the application programmers or developers. The primary purposes of prototyping are to determine whether the system can meet the following criteria:

- Simulate the important interfaces between the system and knowledge worker

- Perform all the major functions

- Be built quickly

A prototype does have limitations. It may not perform on par with the actual system—for example, the prototype may not be able to access all the databases. It may not respond correctly to all the situations that will be encountered when the actual application is in use. A prototype is similar to a designer's model of an auto: it has form and some function, but it can't be driven. Early prototyping tools created a prototype and nothing more. When the knowledge workers were satisfied with it, the developers had to begin again from scratch using development tools. However, that is no longer the case. The prototype is the model on which the real system is built, and it almost always evolves into the final system. In this way, prototyping speeds the development process.

Prototyping is usually accomplished with a prototyping software development tool. This tool may be a stand-alone software product or part of an integrated CASE product. Figure 14.5 shows a working screen of a prototyping tool.

Figure 14.5

A prototyping tool at work.

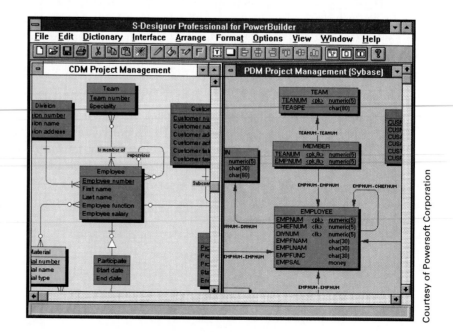

Courtesy of Powersoft Corporation

HOME PAGE

WORKING IN DEVELOPMENT TEAMS

Working in a development team or group is complex social behavior, because there are many people with often differing goals, priorities, needs, and agendas. That is why a team often has a senior management *sponsor* who does not actually work regularly with the group, but who is available to make team decisions and resolve issues and disputes. The sponsor is more of a mentor and an equal than a supervisor and superior.

J. Daniel Couger of the University of Colorado at Colorado Springs has long been considered an authority on programmer motivation and training. He has identified the following mix of factors that enhance programmer motivation and productivity:

- *Skill variety.* The different activities necessary

- *Task identity.* Completion from beginning to end

- *Task significance.* The job's final outcome or effect

- *Autonomy.* Freedom, independence, and discretion

- *Feedback.* Clear communication about performance

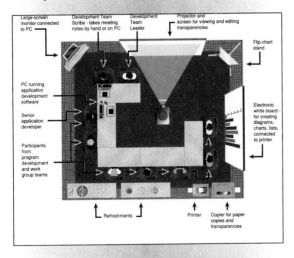

Modern development teams work in specially designed rooms, using the latest tools, where team members can discuss, design, prototype, and test system designs.

All five, in the correct amounts, can produce meaningfulness, responsibility, and knowledge of results, according to Dr. Couger.[7] The result is more satisfied programmers, lower turnover, and higher quality programming.

These same factors can apply to development teams in which programmers work with knowledge workers. And when working in a mixed group such as this, conflicts occur less frequently when the atmosphere is open and free of the usual corporate bureaucracy. According to Gerald M. Weinberg, an internationally recognized software consultant, many development projects get into trouble not because of technological issues but due to people problems such as "status walls" and "boundary problems."[8]

In all development projects, individuals must be called on to set aside their individual agendas and focus on the good of the company. As a member of a development team, that focus is on creating software. As Weinberg says, "When I didn't think right about a program, the program bombed. The computer, I learned, was a *mirror* of my intelligence. . . . Later . . . I learned that the computer was not just a mirror, but a *magnifying* mirror. Any time I didn't think straight about a software project, we made a colossal monster. I began to learn that if we were ever to make good use of thinking machines, we would have to start by improving our own thinking."[9]

HOME PAGE REVIEW QUESTIONS

1. Why is it better for teams to have a sponsor rather than a manager?

2. Why are the people aspects of computer systems so important?

---

7. Based on interviews with the author.

8. Gerald M. Weinberg. *Quality Software Management* (New York: Dorset House, 1992), 226.

9. Ibid., xiv.

Knowledge Check

1. What is the most significant difference between traditional system development and information engineering?
2. What is the central concept behind prototyping?
3. What is the central concept behind rapid application development?
4. Why is it important to develop applications more rapidly?

Key Terms

Information engineering   prototyping   rapid application development (RAD)   version

ISSUES AND IDEAS

Upgrading Software: No Pain, No Gain?

Few programs—whether system software, utility software, or applications—cannot be improved. When a program is released, it normally is identified with a **version** number. The first release is Version 1.0. When some modifications or improvements are made, it may have an interim version number, such as 2.4. If you're using Windows, you can usually find a program's version number by clicking Help from the menu bar and choosing About. On the Macintosh, you can click the apple in the menu bar and choose About.

When a single knowledge worker changes from one version of a program to another, it normally is referred to as *upgrading.* Sometimes, software publishers sell new versions either as a complete package for new users or as an upgrade for those already using the program. When companies and large organizations change software, it usually is called a *migration* because many computers must be upgraded.

For example, many enterprises are migrating from a previous version of Windows. "Keeping up with user demand for Windows 95 won't be easy, but the process doesn't have to be completely chaotic," writes Leo Spiegel in *InfoWorld.* A well-planned, systematic migration methodology can facilitate smooth transitions from Windows 3.1 or Windows for Workgroups 3.11 to Windows 95.[10] Adhering to a well-defined process that covers the basics can keep the migration project on-track, on time, and within budget.

"When budget plans fail, it's typically because those implementing plans lack sufficient discipline."

---

10. Leo Spiegel. "Well-Developed Plans, Teamwork, and Discipline Ease Transitions," *InfoWorld*, August 24, 1995.

"Migrations are like dieting," says Jesse Berst, editorial director of *Windows Watcher* newsletter in Redmond, Washington, quoted in an article in *InfoWorld* newsmagazine. "We know how to lose weight: Eat less, exercise more. We know how to plan a successful migration: Stress training, roll it out in stages. What's missing from both diets and migrations is discipline."[11]

The *InfoWorld* article lists the following 12 stages to a successful migration:

1. Develop team and tools, including migration and communication plans
2. Train the migration team
3. Document the existing environment
4. Do the comprehensive "Does it work?" testing
5. Plan end-user training
6. Design preferred configurations
7. Develop a rollout methodology
8. Arrive at a support plan
9. Do a pilot rollout
10. Get feedback from a pilot program
11. Finalize the rollout process
12. Initiate company-wide rollout plans

CRITICAL THINKING

1. What software do you use and what versions?
2. Discuss any experiences you have had, good or bad, in installing or upgrading software.
3. What does Berst mean when he mentions the need for discipline? Cite some specific examples.

---

11. Ibid.

ETHICS

Liability for Defective Electronic Information

Those who develop computer programs know programs often contain defects or bugs, some of which can cause economic or physical harm. Many people in the computing field are rightly concerned about what liability they or their firms might incur if a defect in software they developed injures a user.

The general public seems largely unaware of the risks of defective software. Even the popular press generally subscribes to the myth that if something is computerized, it must be better. Only certain freak software accidents ("Robot Kills Assembly Line Worker") seem to capture the mass media's attention. Within the computing field, Peter Neumann deserves much credit for heightening the field's awareness of the risks of computing through the RISKS Forum Digest. But even this focuses more on technical risks than legal risks.

It is fair to say that there have been far more injuries from defective software than litigation about defective software. Some lawsuits have been brought, of course, but they have largely been settled out of court, often on condition that the injured person keep silent about the accident, the lawsuit, and the settlement. No software developer seems to want to be the first to set the precedent by which liability rules will definitively be established for the industry.

. . . I can summarize in a sentence what the law's likely response would be to a lawsuit involving defective software embedded in machines such as airplanes, X-ray equipment, and the like: The developer is likely to be held liable if defects in the software have caused injury to a consumer's person or property; under some circumstances, the developer may also be held liable for economic losses (such as lost profits). That is, when an electronic information product behaves like a machine, the law will treat it with the same strict rules it has adopted for dealing with defective machines.[12]

12. Pamela Samuelson. "Liability for Defective Electronic Information," from *Computers, Ethics and Social Values*. Deborah G. Johnson and Helen Nissenbaum, editors (Englewood Cliffs: Prentice Hall, 1995), 539.

Critical Thinking

1. Do you think that software publishers should be held liable for errors incurred due to bugs in their products?

2. Where do you draw the line between what should reasonably be expected from the person using the software and what should reasonably be expected from the software publisher? Is this determined by the person's formal training? By the publisher's warranty?

3. Research a story from the press concerning an actual legal case of software causing either physical or economic harm, and discuss its pros and cons.

THE LEARNING ENTERPRISE

Systems development is an essential aspect of any enterprise. Existing systems must be maintained and new systems must be created for the changing needs and goals of the enterprise. In this section, you have the opportunity to develop a new system.

First, the MIS department must make some key assignments: a systems analyst and designer, a technical support specialist, and a project leader and mentor.

Next, two departments must be selected for systems work. One department has an existing system that is having problems. Have various knowledge workers ask for help with problems you are familiar with, such as word processing or spreadsheet applications. Help the technical support specialist learn how to provide customer-oriented service.

Then decide on a new system, preferably one that will be used by more than one department or function. Create a rapid application development team and assemble them in a RAD room where they will work together. Furnish this room with as many RAD tools—PC, marker board, and so on—as your classroom provides. Try both systems analysis and design and information engineering to see whether one development methodology works better than the other. Use this first-hand experience to see what it's like to develop a system as a team.

Chapter Review

Fill in the Blank

1. The process of creating new computer systems is called
_____.

2. Systems _____ is the study of a procedure to determine what kind of computer system can make it more efficient.

3. Systems _____ is the act of planning the technical aspects of the new system.

4. Programming in a specific programming language is also known as
_____.

5. Programmers use _____ to write messages and take notes as they code.

6. A(n) _____ is a system software program that helps programmers identify program errors.

7. The first trial of a new system is called _____.

8. The testing knowledge workers often participate in is called
_____.

9. The set of instructions and explanations that accompanies a system or application is called _____.

10. Using the computer to create software is called _____.

Circle the Correct Answer

1. The process of creating new systems and applications quickly and effectively in teams is called (RAD, CASE).

2. The phase of testing where knowledge workers help find bugs and problems is called (alpha, beta) testing.

3. The documentation that is available on-screen is (Help, Readme).

4. A stand-alone software tool for developing systems is called (CASE, I-CASE).

5. Information engineering places more emphasis on (people, debugging).

6. A system ready for use is called a (production, presentation) system.

Review Questions

1. What is software engineering?
2. List the steps involved in the system development life cycle.
3. Define coding.
4. What is a debugger?
5. What is the difference between alpha testing and beta testing?
6. Name the three types of documentation for a system or an application.
7. What is information engineering?

8. Define prototyping.
9. Why is RAD a more effective means of developing a system?
10. What does the version number mean on a software program?

Discussion Questions

1. What are the limitations of the traditional system development life cycle?
2. Why is it important to use as many computer-automated software tools as possible to create new systems?
3. Discuss maintenance and why it consumes so much time and attention. Describe as many aspects of maintenance as possible.
4. Why are the various approaches to information engineering so important to system development?
5. Research I-CASE and determine what it's currently being used for.

INTERNET DISCOVERY

To learn more about how a consulting firm helps an enterprise develop systems, visit Copley Systems and CIC Systems Education Services at the following address:

http://www.copley.mv.com/copley/edserv

To learn about how Visual Basic is used to develop systems, visit Microsoft at the following address:

http://www.microsoft.com

To learn about Delphi, a rapid application development software tool, visit Borland International at the following address:

http://www.borland.com

MANAGEMENT INFORMATION SYSTEMS

Never before has the job of managing an IS department been so difficult.

Charles P. Lecht[1]

The term Management Information System (MIS) refers to the computer resources, people, and procedures used throughout the modern enterprise. The term gained acceptance in 1968, when the Society for Management Information Systems (now the Society for Information Management) was founded. MIS also refers to the organization that develops and maintains most of or all the computer systems in the enterprise. The goal of the MIS organization is to deliver information systems to corporate knowledge workers. So MIS refers not only to the computer system but also to a specific function in the enterprise.

MIS serves many types of knowledge workers in business; these workers use computers to perform a variety of tasks that help the company achieve its business objectives. These tasks include management, administration, order processing, accounting, purchasing, manufacturing support, sales, and marketing.

MIS professionals create and support the computer systems throughout the company. Trained and educated to work with corporate computer systems, these professionals are responsible in some way for nearly all the computers, from the largest mainframe to the desktop and portable PCs.

Business processes, automated by MIS, ensure that work gets accomplished and that the company achieves its goals, such as producing a service or product, satisfying customer needs, creating a profit, and distributing dividends to shareholders. The MIS organization's mandate is to ensure that knowledge workers have all the information needed to do their work, that each business process achieves the highest level of performance, and that the business remains competitive in its market.

1. "Now More Than Ever, A Plan," *Computerworld*, April 27, 1992, 88.

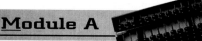

Module A

What Is MIS?

Why It's Important to Know

> **MIS refers to complex computer systems as well as to the department or organization that creates and maintains these computer systems. MIS is integral to the modern enterprise; without MIS and its services, it would be difficult, if not impossible, for a business to function.**

MIS: A Definition

The term **management information system** refers to a complex computer system, its people, and certain procedures that work with the enterprise to achieve business goals. Figure 15.1 illustrates a business process supported by a management information system. Like the various hardware components in a computer system (such as the CPU, main memory, and peripherals), various business processes including order processing, accounting, manufacturing, and shipping form a system for business.

Figure 15.1
A custom manufacturing business process, where specialty products are created on demand for customers.

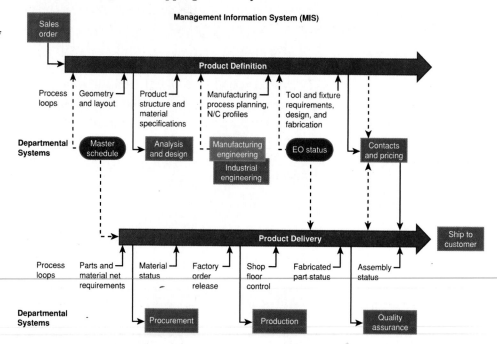

In this example, the process is triggered by a sales order, which stimulates the *product definition* cycle. Each phase is supported by computer systems and software applications in the *departmental systems* linked to the cycle. The master schedule triggers the *product delivery* cycle, which is supported by additional departmental systems of the enterprise-wide management information system until the product is shipped to the customer.

The management information system monitors, directs, and controls various processes to ensure that the work gets accomplished satisfactorily and that the business achieves its goals and objectives. These objectives may include the following:

- Ensure that knowledge workers have all the information needed to do their work in a timely manner

- Produce a useful service

- Manufacture a quality product

- Satisfy customer needs

- Help the company remain strong and competitive in its market

- Support each business process to achieve the highest level of performance

- Create a profit

- Distribute dividends to shareholders

The **MIS** computer systems are integral in providing the data that various knowledge workers in the business use—in the form of information—to solve problems, plan strategies, and make decisions affecting the health and livelihood of the business or enterprise.

For example, L.L. Bean is a small ($1.1 billion in 1994) but well-known outdoor clothing and equipment mail order company, famous for its duck boots. The company's focus is entirely on the customer, as is its MIS operation, which is designed for individualized service. In 1980, L.L. Bean installed its first on-line order entry system. It provides immediate answers to 92 percent of the questions customers ask the customer representatives.

In the past, customers might have to wait a month for a mail order. L.L. Bean's system has drastically reduced the turnaround time to fulfill an order; now an order can be delivered in two days. The on-line system captures and retains customer information so that the order-taker does not have to ask the repeat customer for an address. L.L. Bean continues to develop the customer representative's knowledge and helping skills. The company has also established a World Wide Web site with information on outdoor activities for Bean products.[2]

Why Use a Management Information System?

Why would an enterprise use a management information system? Perhaps better to ask how an enterprise could get along without one! For an answer to this question, consider the abbreviation for management information system: *MIS*.

- *M (Management).* Regardless of its mission, a business or enterprise must have some form of management to plan, organize, direct, control, and staff it. Management accomplishes objectives through the efforts of many people. Lack of good management is responsible for more failures than any other single aspect of the enterprise.

---

2. Adapted from "IT Accent on the Real Customer," *Babson College Center for Information Management Studies Newsletter*, November 1995, 3–4.

- *I (Information).* An enterprise needs information for making management decisions, planning strategic directions for the future, improving performance, and developing or sustaining a competitive advantage in the marketplace.

- *S (System).* An enterprise must develop and maintain one or more computer systems and software applications that help make knowledge workers more productive and contribute to supporting its mission.

Who Uses MIS?

Who uses MIS? This question has two answers. First, MIS is used primarily in enterprises of all kinds: business, government, and nonprofit organizations, as well as the computer and information industry itself. MIS is important in organizations large and small, but the larger the organization, the more important MIS. *InformationWeek*, a magazine for information systems professionals, ranks the top 100 MIS organizations in business each year. The smallest of these organizations has an annual budget of $100 million; the largest is greater than a quarter of a billion dollars!

Second, management information systems are used by managers and knowledge workers at all levels of the enterprise. The most important objective is for MIS to provide information to the right people, at the right time, so that they can make the right decisions. Because organizations are changing, the way MIS delivers information has changed, too. Peter G. W. Keen says, "Today's [management information] systems focus on alerting managers to problems and trends, answering their ad hoc questions, and providing information in the form they want, when they want it."[3]

Figure 15.2 shows a typical organizational structure, often referred to as hierarchical. In this organization, information can flow only vertically, up and down channels. For sales information to reach another department, the information must flow upward to management for approval, then downward to the appropriate person for action. Information—and access to it—is much more controlled in this organizational environment.

The old hierarchical organization is top-heavy with managers and is giving way to the flattened, or clustered, organizational style shown in figure 15.3. Here, knowledge workers work in peer groups, where information can be readily exchanged between workers, between one group and another, and between groups and management. In the flat organization, information is regarded as an essential asset for every employee and is shared, not controlled. For that reason, MIS may be referred to as simply IS, for information systems, or IT, for information technology.

---

3. Peter G. W. Keen. *Every Manager's Guide to Information Technology* (Boston: Harvard Business School Press, 1995), 185.

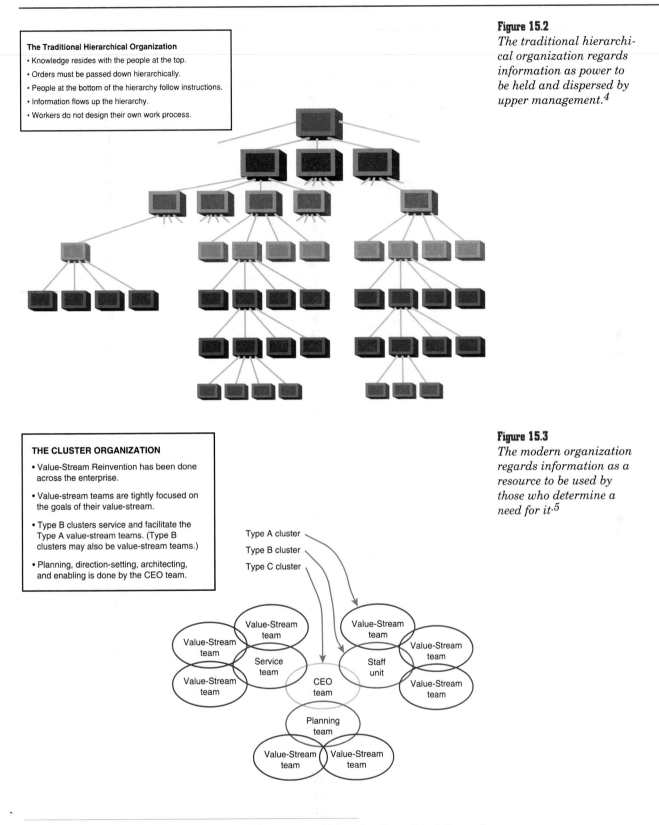

The Traditional Hierarchical Organization
- Knowledge resides with the people at the top.
- Orders must be passed down hierarchically.
- People at the bottom of the hierarchy follow instructions.
- Information flows up the hierarchy.
- Workers do not design their own work process.

Figure 15.2
The traditional hierarchical organization regards information as power to be held and dispersed by upper management.[4]

THE CLUSTER ORGANIZATION
- Value-Stream Reinvention has been done across the enterprise.
- Value-stream teams are tightly focused on the goals of their value-stream.
- Type B clusters service and facilitate the Type A value-stream teams. (Type B clusters may also be value-stream teams.)
- Planning, direction-setting, architecting, and enabling is done by the CEO team.

Figure 15.3
The modern organization regards information as a resource to be used by those who determine a need for it.[5]

Type A cluster
Type B cluster
Type C cluster

Value-Stream team
Value-Stream team
Value-Stream team
Service team
CEO team
Value-Stream team
Staff unit
Value-Stream team
Value-Stream team
Planning team
Value-Stream team
Value-Stream team

4. Adapted from James Martin. *The Great Transitions: Using the Seven Disciplines of Enterprise Engineering to Align People, Technology, and Stragegy* (New York: AMACOM), 398.

5. Ibid., p. 399.

How MIS Is Used

Management information systems are most widely used in business, where they are often considered a "strategic weapon" in "corporate combat." Management collects business data, and with the help of MIS, a system or an application is created to work with that data. A *system* usually involves both hardware and software. An *application* is software to support an enterprise activity.

Either a system or an application may be referred to by the MIS organization as a **project**, or an assignment. The project might be a way for a fast-food chain to gather the daily receipts from its many restaurants, or to set up a new customer database for a division introducing a new product.

Once the new system or application is up and running, it collects the necessary data. Then the data is stored, processed, and retrieved as strategic information. The data collected in various computer systems in the MIS comes from three sources:

- *Outside sources*, such as feedback from customers, sales rep surveys, magazines or trade publications, on-line database information, and the informal human networks or "grapevines."

- *Inside sources* about the company, provided by operational management concerning its productivity and resources, or provided by middle management regarding opinions or analyses of short-term goals, opportunities, and accomplishments.

- *The information system itself*, by feeding specific data into the computer to produce analyses or scenarios for senior management to set future goals, plan strategic directions, or create new competitive advantages. These customized information systems are often called *decision support systems* or *executive information systems*, designed especially for top-level managers who lack extensive computer skills.

A typical large company has many types of information systems. Although some are designed to assist customers, such as a network of ATMs at a bank, most are for internal use. In most organizations, each department usually has one or more of its own information systems. Some of the computers used are unique to that organization, and some are centralized and shared by other departments. For example, central MIS provides sales figures that are used by the following departments:

- *Manufacturing*, to set production goals and monitor inventory

- *Finance*, to determine the firm's profitability

- *Marketing*, to set quotas

- *Human resources*, for employee evaluations

- *Accounting*, or payroll, to pay salaries and sales commissions

From a management perspective, the sales information helps the operational manager know how much product to manufacture and how many workers to hire. This information also helps the middle manager set goals for new products or for an increased market share, and helps senior management decide on plans for expansion or growth. So, in a sense, anyone who is involved in decision making uses management information systems.

The MIS Concept

The underlying concept of MIS is that it is a system which works in connection with the business system—like an overlay that helps conceptually chart, support, and verify the business plans, directions, and strategies. MIS usually provides three levels of information management:

- *Record keeping,* the simplest (and earliest) use for information systems

- *Operations control,* improving such operations as order entry and processing (or inventory control)

- *Strategic planning,* for such goals as increasing market share, outperforming the competition, and generally gaining a competitive advantage

Consider this case study of the airline industry. Airlines are noted for their advanced application of information technology. Yet in many cases, they have lost or overlooked competitive advantages because of concentrating too much on record keeping and operations, with a resulting lack of focus on the strategic aspects of their business.

The main problem for airlines is that a seat is just a seat, and an airport is just an airport. Passengers want only to get from point A to point B in relative comfort and the shortest period of time. They couldn't care less about parsley on their dinner plates or how good the movie was. Most airlines are relatively efficient, and most flights arrive on time; thus, differentiating the products has become increasingly difficult.

American Airlines set the pace in defining and exploiting certain advantages. It recognized that its computer-based reservation system was not operational overhead, but rather the key to distribution—the industry term for marketing and sales, mainly through travel agents. Its AAdvantage frequent-flier program transformed the airline industry's entire marketing processes. American also led in hubbing during the 1980s, a practice adopted by all major airlines. Yet all these competitive advantages have run their course and—because of overcapacity, price competition, falling margins, and foreign competition—have become liabilities rather than assets.

Southwest Airlines has been successful and profitable for more than two decades. Between 1971 and 1992, it provided the highest returns to shareholders of any publicly quoted company: 22,000 percent. Southwest does not hub. It has labor agreements, entirely unlike its competitors, that allow it much more flexibility in handling operations, aircraft, and staffing. Following the workgroup model in white collar offices, Southwest is made up of small, individual airlines and discrete teams. It has cut its amenities and simplified many outdated, cumbersome, paper-based processes, from reservations through boarding passes. Southwest listens to the voice of the customer, delivering high-volume service at the lowest fares.

If all the airline industry profits were totaled since the day the Wright Brothers took off, they would amount to zero. New competitive advantages for the airline industry must be built around cost. Customers have made it clear that price dominates all other factors to the extent that a $2 difference on a $200 fare can sway customers. The use of strategic information systems to develop innovations and new ways of doing business will be critical in the survival of the airlines industry.

HOME PAGE

A MISSION STATEMENT FOR MIS

Charles P. Lecht (1933–1992), computer guru, consultant, and once an MIS columnist for *Computerworld* newspaper, wrote the following about the mission of the MIS organization:

Courtesy of IDG Books World Wide

The primary mission of the information systems department is to create the proper procedural environment for the orderly regeneration of the corporation's operational environment as it pertains to

1. the acquisition, purification, storage, processing, retrieval, presentation and dissemination of information for management at all levels and

2. the creation of organic harmony in the integration of man/machine information technology systems into the day-to-day affairs of the corporation.

The IS department's primary mission is supportive of, subservient to, and embedded in the overall corporate plans, procedures, and objectives as established by the corporate planning committee.

Its role in the corporate environment is unique in that it cannot create a product to be delivered to the corporation without the dynamic and day-to-day participation of the various corporate organizations that the product is to serve.

Its measure of success is in its ability to proliferate its capabilities throughout the corporation and to ultimately lose its identity as a corporate organization.

In concert with the broad objectives outlined above are those involving the IS department's role in providing guidance in the allocation of funds to be invested in data processing resources. In doing this, the IS department is required to achieve a proper, timely and in-context capability to ascertain the technical, political, psychological and financial impact of the use of information technology in support of the corporation.

Courtesy of International Business Machines Corporation

The IS department will prepare and maintain a plan to include long-range objectives, each defined as the outgrowth of a set of short-range accomplishments. The IS department must prepare and maintain its own operational procedures and standards to serve as an in-flight guidance system to ease the corporation's transition from systems of the past to those of the future in an atmosphere of realism dedicated to fulfilling the urgent needs of the present.[6]

HOME PAGE REVIEW QUESTIONS

1. What makes the IS department's responsibilities so important?

2. In what ways are the IS department's tasks and responsibilities unique?

3. How, and by what criteria, does Lecht measure the IS department's success?

---

6. Charles P. Lecht. "Now More Than Ever, A Plan," *Computerworld*, April 27, 1992, 88.

Knowledge Check

1. What is the name given to computer systems used in enterprises to achieve business goals?
2. Explain what the three letters in the abbreviation MIS stand for.
3. Who in an organization uses MIS?
4. What is a project?
5. What are the three sources of data used for strategic or competitive information?
6. Explain the various aspects of the MIS concept.

Key Terms

Management Information System (MIS)   project

ISSUES AND IDEAS

The IT-Enabled Network Organization

In the book *Creative Destruction*, authors Richard Nolan and David Croson write: "Information technology has enabled business transformation both directly and indirectly. . . . Now it is obvious that IT is responsible for the emergence of a powerful and flexible new form of organization: the IT-enabled network, which marries network organization structures with network technologies. . . . Mainframe and microcomputers in organizations were important technologies, of course, and resulted in important, organizational learning that was the prerequisite for the marriage of network technologies and network organization structures."

The authors cite some principles that have emerged in the new IT-enabled network organization:

1. *Leadership principle*. Senior management formulates and coordinates the firm's vision and plays a central role in defining projects.
2. *Information principle*. All organization members have open access to all information, instead of restricting the flow based on need rather than position.
3. *Worker-class principle*. All employees are treated as a uniclass of knowledge workers, versus the two-class system of white/blue collar workers.
4. *Task principle*. Work is organized into projects and carried out by team members assigned to these projects based on the expertise necessary to accomplish the project goals.
5. *Reward principle*. Rewards are performance-based, not position-based.[7]

---

7. Richard L. Nolan and David C. Croson. *Creative Destruction* (Boston: Harvard Business School Press, 1995), 187–197.

CRITICAL THINKING

1. Analyze and discuss each of the five principles. Make a list of each principle's pluses and minuses.
2. Determine why this new organization has emerged as a result of MIS.
3. Describe your position in this new network organization, and explain why you would like or not like to work in it.

Module B

The Three Components of MIS

Why It's Important to Know

> **MIS is both an organization and a computer system. As such, MIS is made up of people, software, and hardware. Each element is unique in MIS and integral to the success of the enterprise.**

In the early days, a business had a computer that kept track of accounting data and records. It was considered an office machine or just a large calculator that helped speed processing. Today, computer-based management information systems are essential in every aspect of a well-run business. A company literally grinds to a halt without MIS. Even when the computer function is lost, or "goes down," for just a short period of time, the losses quickly add up. MIS represents a multi-million-dollar investment in large companies. In some of the Fortune 100 firms, that investment is in the billions of dollars. MIS is the lifeblood and nerve system for most enterprises today; without computers, there is no life.

This book stresses that the computer is a system—made up of people, software, and hardware. The same is true of MIS, but perhaps more so, because MIS has become a mission-critical aspect of the enterprise. There are many people to consider in MIS: managers, staff, and end users. MIS software takes many forms; MIS hardware is often complex and dispersed throughout the enterprise. In this module, you take a closer look at all three components of MIS.

The People Component

MIS is unique in that it touches just about everyone in the company. MIS is a department or organization itself, with its own internal computing needs. Yet it is also an organization providing services to other departments. Within those departments are many specialized knowledge workers who support computers and the people who use them to do their work.

The MIS Organization

In years past, data processing functions were loosely managed; the atmosphere was casual. Projects often ran over budget and past the scheduled completion date, because programmers tended to write and rewrite code, or "tweak" it, to make it better. Often, the improvements were barely noticeable to the user and were a waste of time and money. In other cases, the application was a programming marvel but was difficult to use or did not provide the information managers needed.

Without firm management controls, MIS often ran afoul of other business departments and gained a reputation for being difficult to work or communicate with. However, more and more departments and functions wanted information systems, creating a work overload in MIS. As a result, an application backlog grew; in large companies, a lag time of five to six years might be estimated for the completion of a project. A closer alignment between MIS and the functional aspects of the enterprise has helped get MIS better organized and better able to accomplish its tasks.

MIS Management

At the head of the MIS organization is the senior executive, sometimes known as the vice president, general manager, or chief information officer. In most cases, this individual has worked up through the ranks over a period of 10 to 20 years. Many senior executives have an undergraduate degree in computer science or MIS and often an MBA to go with it. They are highly paid individuals with a great deal of authority and responsibility. They often report to the executive vice president or even the president of the company. These executives spend a great deal of time in planning meetings—helping chart directions for the company and determining the role of MIS in corporate strategies. Consider the following profiles of MIS managers.

Dawn Lepore is executive vice president and chief information officer at Charles Schwab & Company in San Francisco. Her biggest project is moving the company off its older mainframes and on to 6,100 IBM and Compaq Pentium workstations. "Our overall goal is to provide better service to customers by putting the right tools in the hands of our people," she says. In 1995, Ms. Lepore reorganized her MIS department into "Enterprise Technology Solution areas," each of which is tightly integrated with individual business units at Schwab. This reorganization gives each business group its own IT staff.

Dennis Jones is senior vice president and chief information officer at Federal Express in Memphis, Tennessee. "We don't watch what our competitors are doing—we listen to what our customers want," he says. Mr. Jones created the PowerShip system, which gave large customers a PC that enables them to create their own shipping waybills, print them, and track their FedEx expenditures. This program was expanded to provide the application to smaller customers with their own PCs, and the program was renamed FedEx Ship. Over a quarter-million customers use PowerShip and FedEx Ship daily. In addition, FedEx has a World Wide Web site that customers can use to obtain real-time information about where their packages are. Both programs reduce paperwork, for FedEx and its customers, and provide a level of customer service unequaled in the package-shipping business.[8]

---

8. Adapted from "The Innovators: Changing the Face of Business Technology," *InformationWeek*, November 20, 1995, 34–64. "Leveraged: Charles Schwab & Co.'s Dawn Lepore sees desktop systems as key to the future," by Doug Bartholomew. "Powering Up: FedEx CIO Dennis Jones takes overnight delivery to the next level," by Marianne Kolbasuk McGee.

Reporting to the head of MIS are the operational managers. They oversee such things as software maintenance, new application development, user training, and a number of other MIS functions. These managers are often appointed to head a team of programmers working on a specific application or project. They are given specific instructions and schedules for completing portions of the projects, some of which take years to complete.

MIS Staff

The MIS staff is made up of people with many different skills, aligned with many of the same organizational tasks of the business itself. Most staff members have completed college programs in computer science. Systems analysts are responsible for analyzing and designing new applications and complete systems. For example, the head of manufacturing might ask a systems analyst to create a system, from hardware to software, to control the entire manufacturing process of a new product.

Courtesy of Chen Systems

Figure 15.4

Programmers write software using programming languages. The programmers can be found working at terminals or personal computers in conventional office environments, just like any other knowledge worker. In a Fortune 500 firm, several hundred programmers might be working on various projects. Some are system programmers, whose work involves expanding, improving, or maintaining the systems software or the existing software applications, such as the accounting system or the manufacturing resource planning (MRP) system.

Others are application programmers. They are assigned to work with different departments in the company, such as customer service, or they help users develop new applications. For example, a company planning to implement electronic data interchange, or EDI, might have several systems programmers working in the MIS department and have application programmers working with order processing, inventory, and shipping to set up and install the EDI applications.

Courtesy of International Business Machines Corporation

Figure 15.5

Still other staff members are operations technicians, responsible for maintaining the hardware. Some are responsible for installing terminals and setting up personal computers; others troubleshoot malfunctioning equipment. Some technicians are in charge of backup systems, such as changing disk packs, tapes, and tape cartridges. Last (but far from least), some MIS knowledge workers are help-desk personnel, answering phones and making in-house calls to knowledge workers who are having difficulties with their computers.

End-User Computing

The IBM PC, introduced to corporate America in 1981, truly changed the way the world computes. Its proliferation was spurred by the users' growing frustration with MIS and its inability to provide them with computing services. The result became known as **end-user computing**, or giving knowledge workers their own computers so that they could be more productive in their work. Because MIS could not (or would not) provide workers with computing power, the end-user departments funded the purchase of PCs from their own budgets. In time, large companies actually opened their own computer stores, where knowledge workers could select their own PCs.

But PCs do not remedy all the shortcomings of MIS. Naomi Karten, editor of *Managing End-User Computing*, has identified a number of erroneous assumptions about what PCs can or cannot do. Note some examples:

- *PCs do not reduce work load.* They often increase the work load because they can do so many tasks that simply weren't possible before.

- *Training results in immediate expertise.* Training is the beginning of the expertise-building process, not the end.

- *All we need to know is how to make the software work.* Clients who ask only for features or functions and don't want to be bothered with understanding how to analyze a business problem from a computer perspective, or how to evaluate alternative systems solutions, need more training.[9]

At first, knowledge workers with personal computers were content with spreadsheets and word processing and so were not interested in using central MIS services. But workers soon realized that to be truly productive, they must have access to mainframe data. This need resulted in a number of significant changes in the way MIS functions and in the way companies use information, as you learn in the following discussions of software and hardware components.

The Software Component

MIS is responsible for keeping many applications running every day and for making them available to knowledge workers. These applications may be for order processing, accounting, inventory control, computer-aided drawing, manufacturing, database management, and so on. Remember that large computer systems are multiuser, multitasking machines; a hundred or more applications could be running at once. The manner in which these systems and applications are organized and monitored has been given various names over the years, in much the same way physicists test theories about how the universe and its particulate matter evolved and organized itself. The distinctions often blend into one another, but what follows describes the evolution of the MIS software component.

---

9. Naomi Karten. *Managing End-User Computing*, April 1992 (New York: Auerbach Publishers), vol. 5, no. 9, p. 11.

Distributed Computing

For many years, all MIS functions were **centralized**, or kept in the central MIS facility. Eventually, MIS had more to do than it could handle. For this reason as well as others, many computers and applications are **distributed**, or placed where they would be most effective.

Cooperative Processing

For most of the half-century in which computers have been in use, computer systems have been intentionally incompatible with each other. The effort to correct this incompatibility is called **cooperative processing**, which means that different computer systems can exchange data among their diverse operating platforms. The **operating platform** includes the computer itself, its operating system, its networking system, its applications (such as databases) and services (such as transaction processing), and its development languages and tools. The ultimate goal is to enable any application to share data with any other.

The term **interoperable** is a way of saying that you can perform any work task, regardless of its original resident operating platform, from whatever computer you are using. Interoperability is illustrated in figure 15.6. The reality today is that knowledge workers who have to use applications that reside on different platforms either must know complex login and logout procedures to be able to change from one platform to another, or may have two or three different terminals on their desk. You can easily see why interoperability is highly desirable. It enables workers to have mainframe, minicomputer, workstation, and PC application work sessions available or even running simultaneously

John R. Rymer, editor of *Network Monitor: Guide to Distributed Computing*, writes: "Interoperability is the defining user requirement for the 1990s. All large corporations and public institutions are trying to use distributed computing technology to get more value from their older stand-alone applications . . . [and are] seeking to integrate existing applications with new applications [with] a set of distributed computing structures known as *cooperative processing*. In cooperative processing, two or more systems collaborate to perform a task. . . . We are moving slowly but inexorably toward distributed, object-oriented computing as the most important applications platform for the '90s and beyond."[10]

---

10. John G. Rymer. *Network Monitor*, April 1992, vol. 7, no. 4, 2–3. Patricia Seybold's Office Computing Group.

Figure 15.6
Interoperability is the basis for all new systems software and applications.

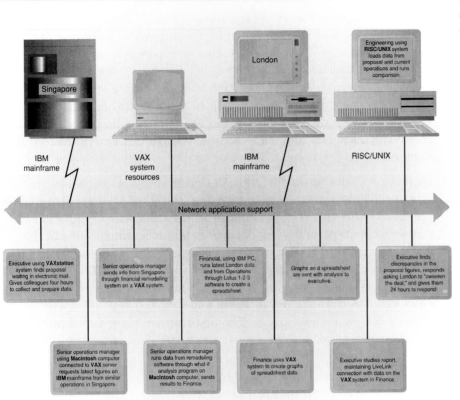

The Hardware Component

In the early days of business computing, the computer was kept in a separate room. By the late 1950s, most businesses had IBM computers, so they called the computer site "the IBM Room." Over the years, the names *data processing* (DP) and *electronic data processing* (EDP) became fashionable. By the mid-1970s, the term MIS was commonplace. In the 1980s, MIS was shortened to information systems, or IS. In the 1990s, the commonly used term is information technology, or IT.

These changes reflect the desire of the information systems professional to provide the kinds of computer services the enterprise seeks. There is still a computer room today, but more often it is an area, perhaps an entire floor in the building, designed to house the computer equipment. Usually, a shift supervisor and several operations people are on duty, monitoring the system, backing up hard disk drives on tape, and performing other maintenance tasks.

But MIS extends throughout the business. Minicomputers are in manufacturing, workstations are in engineering, and personal computers are in offices everywhere. This proliferations has created a demand for high-level, managerial organization of the software and hardware components. These complex, interconnected systems need modern techniques of software engineering or information engineering at the development level, and cooperative processing at the application level. And as you will see, there is also managerial organization at the hardware level.

New Computer Architectures

As with nature and its systems, the evolution of computers and management information systems hasn't always been logical or carefully planned. A **computer architecture** is the design and implementation of computer systems in an organization. With the wide variety of peripherals and separate systems that must connect to the centralized computer, new computer architectures have emerged. A computer architecture is quite similar to a building architecture; both determine how best to use physical facilities to help people get their work done efficiently. Many businesses have devised their own architecture designs, and some businesses use designs promoted by computer vendors.

Figure 15.7 shows an architecture design used by an aerospace division of TRW, Inc. This design maximizes the distributed computing concept. Centralized MIS services are retained as they are, with smaller mainframes and minicomputers connected; departmental processing is done in the appropriate departments. Personal computers and workstation computers are connected to departmental computers. The strategy behind TRW's architecture is to disperse computer power to reach as many users as possible. The company's belief is that the newest uses and innovations with the information system come from those users. The architecture shown in figure 15.7 is a basic design for modern information systems. The most significant trend today is client/server computing.

Figure 15.7

Computer architectures are created to take maximum advantage of all types of computer systems.

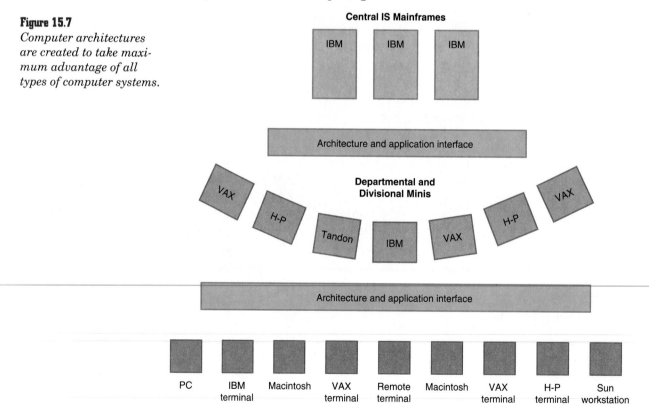

Client/Server Computing

Client/server computing is a hardware architecture that takes advantage of the processing power of two computers working together to perform a task. One is called the **client**, usually a PC used by a knowledge worker, which is the "front end" of the system. The other computer is called the **server**, which is the "back end" that holds data the client needs to process.

The server might be a mainframe, a minicomputer, a workstation, or even another PC. Often, servers are the most powerful PCs available, and they serve many PCs. Although this architecture resembles the traditional distributed model with its mainframe and terminals, the design differs significantly in that *both computers are involved in the data processing.* Each computer processes its data in the best way it knows how; for example, if the knowledge worker is working with a large DBMS stored on the server, the PC works only with the data it needs; the rest stays at the server. If the server database is updated, that processing is done at the server. In addition, servers often serve more than one client PC, thus requiring more processing power. Figure 15.8 shows a client/server architecture.

Authors Patrick Smith and Steve Guengerich write:

> The client/server model makes the enterprise available at the desk. It provides access to data that the previous architectures did not. Standards have been defined for client/server computing. If these standards are understood and used, organizations can reasonably expect to buy solutions today that can grow with their business needs without the constant need to revise the solutions. Architectures based on open systems standards can be implemented throughout the world, as global systems become the norm for large organizations. . . . From the desktop, enterprise-wide applications are indistinguishable from workgroups and personal applications.[11]

Courtesy of Compaq Computer Corporation

Figure 15.8
Rack-mounted like high-end stereo gear, these powerful personal computers act as servers.

Consider as a case study The Solaris Group of San Ramon, California. As a company that makes lawn- and garden-care products, this business is highly seasonal and also erratic because of the weather. All this inconsistency makes most forecasting and planning difficult. In 1991, Solaris management was using a pencil, a calculator, and a PC for its forecasting. "The best you could say was that it was better than nothing," says Dwight Maloney, manager of planning and logistics.

---

11. Patrick Smith and Steve Guengerich. *Client/Server Computing*, Second Edition, (Indianapolis: Sams, 1994), 2.

In 1992, after much consultation, Solaris began to implement a client/server system. The hardware consisted of an IBM midrange computer and several PCs in a network. One PC was set up as the server, running server software and a database management system. The DBMS allows capturing sales information and applying it to a demand model to forecast for future market conditions.

Thus began a period of great change, but by 1994, the system was stabilizing. In the past, the company often found itself without enough inventory to fill customer orders. Today, Solaris fills more orders while keeping less inventory on hand. Plans are to implement a customer-by-customer forecast to sharpen its customer service even more.[12]

Facilities Management

In the 1960s, many companies wanted to install data processing equipment but lacked the staff or the expertise to do it themselves. So they brought in **facilities management** companies, which contract for and run the entire information systems operation. One such company, Electronic Data Systems (EDS), was formed by H. Ross Perot, a Texan with firm convictions about himself, his employees, and his company. Facilities management takes many forms today. It is used to get a new MIS operation up and running quickly, and to breathe new life into one that is performing below par. Facilities management is used also by companies that simply no longer want to operate their own MIS; this strategy is often termed **outsourcing**.

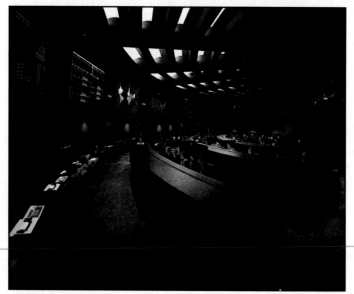

Courtesy of Electronic Data Systems

Today, industry leader EDS is a $5 billion company, with employees in 26 foreign countries. Figure 15.9 shows the EDS Data Center in Dallas, Texas. EDS buys more computers than any other corporation on earth, installing and operating them at customer sites. EDS has created management information systems for insurance companies, banks, the Federal government, and agencies of the armed forces. In the 1980s, it has had contracts with the U.S. Army, First City Bancorp of Houston, and Blue Cross/Blue Shield—each contract representing well over half a billion dollars.

In 1984, Perot sold EDS to General Motors, to help GM enhance its computer operations and develop sophisticated factory automation systems. Perot became a significant investor in Steve Jobs' NeXT computer company and went on to form Perot Systems, a more specialized counterpart to EDS, in 1988.

Figure 15.9
The EDS Data Center in Dallas.

HOME PAGE

GETTING THE LATEST SCOOP ON MIS

In 1995, *InfoWorld* newsmagazine launched a new World Wide Web site called InfoWorld Electric, a resource for people in MIS. The Web site is http://www.infoworld.com

It has some interactive features not found on most Web sites. According to Stewart Alsop, executive vice president, "InfoWorld Electric is made up of four basic components with a few other features and experiments."

Real-time news. InfoWorld Electric will cover and update news stories continuously. "We only report stuff that makes a difference while it's happening. We report it in smaller chunks. And we report really important events by updating the story until every event is concluded," says Alsop.

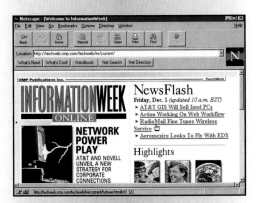

Interactive forums. Nearly 70 percent of *InfoWorld* subscribers have on-line accounts. Qualified readers will be admitted to forums for serious discussions about technology and problems.

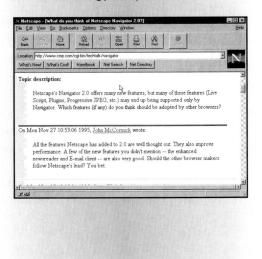

Searchable archives. "You can search our back issues using the coolest search technology on the planet today from Architext Software Inc.'s Architext," says Alsop. Searching may be done through back issues of *InfoWorld*, or by key word.

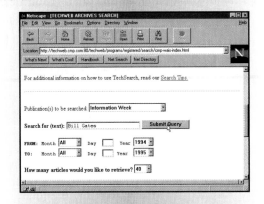

Interactive advertising. "We are working on ways . . . to make the advertising buttons you see on Electric lead you directly to the relevant content from the advertiser. . . . Apple, Hewlett-Packard, IBM, Microsoft, Novell and Oracle . . . will be working with us . . . to develop our interactive advertising approach."[13]

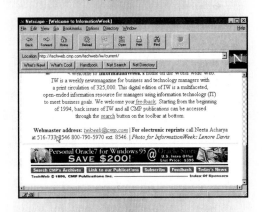

HOME PAGE REVIEW QUESTIONS

1. What is the main feature that makes InfoWorld Electric different from other Web sites?
2. Who would be attracted to InfoWorld Electric? Why?
3. Log on to InfoWorld Electric. In what other ways does InfoWorld Electric differ from Web sites you've browsed?

---

13. Steward Alsop, "Distributed Thinking," *Infoworld,* November 13, 1995, 166.

Knowledge Check

1. What is the senior MIS manager called, and to whom does he or she report?
2. Name several MIS staff positions.
3. What kinds of applications is MIS responsible for running?
4. Why is cooperative processing desirable?
5. Why do we say there is a computer "room," yet MIS extends throughout the business?
6. Describe the purpose of a computer architecture.
7. What is the advantage with client/server computing?
8. Name some of the reasons for facilities management.

Key Terms

centralized	client	computer architecture
cooperative processing	distributed	end-user computing
facilities management	interoperable	operating platform
outsourcing	server	

ISSUES AND IDEAS

MIS as a Corporate Resource

As information systems have evolved, the manner of collecting data and transforming it into information has itself become a strategic tool, with true value. Just as a manager becomes more valuable as he or she gains experience, so have information systems. Companies are often reluctant to discuss certain aspects of their information systems, for fear that competitors may gain a competitive advantage by employing the same strategies.

For this reason, many corporate information systems use a security system that restricts access to certain types of information. For example, access to the data center is restricted to key personnel by use of passwords and special locks. Security systems create passwords and security levels, so a clerk cannot read memos between senior executives discussing a new product introduction. Programmers are often asked to sign employment agreements stating that they will not divulge details about the projects they are working on or the contents of programs they write. For example, a manufacturing system might contain proprietary details about a product's ingredients or proprietary manufacturing techniques that would cause great loss if it fell into a competitor's hands.

Often, computer-generated information and, in some cases, proprietary programs have demonstrated a usefulness that does not conflict with the company's strategic goals. Smart companies realize that this material can be sold to others, providing a return on the investment made in developing it and perhaps even a profit. Mailing lists are a profitable information resource. Banks and insurance companies often sell specialized programs they have developed in-house. Clearly, MIS is a valuable corporate resource in many different ways.

VOICE AND DATA COMMUNICATIONS SYSTEMS

Computers did it. Computer melted other machines, fusing them together. Television-telephone-telex. Tape recorder-VCR-laser disk. Broadcast tower linked to microwave dish linked to satellite. Phone line, cable TV, fiber-optic cords hissing out words and pictures in torrents of pure light. All netted together in a web over the world, a global nervous system, an octopus of data.[1]

Bruce Sterling

1. Bruce Sterling. *Islands in the Net* (New York: Ace Books, 1989), 17.

CHAPTER 16

Module A

Data and Voice Communications Systems

Why It's Important to Know

Computer networks are systems comprised of hardware and software. Increasingly, networks carry both voice communications and a wide variety of data communications. The need for more versatile and powerful networks continues to grow, as does the need to manage them and ensure that they are secure.

Not too many years ago, voice communications and data communications were completely separate technologies in a company. Rarely did the two interact. But in the late 1980s, that situation changed dramatically. Today, voice and data communications technologies are often merged, working together to meet the rapidly expanding needs of businesses.

Voice Communications Hardware

Knowledge workers use the telephone every day, but the phone used in the office is often very different from the one used at home. Office phones usually have many calling and messaging features that are attributable to the computer circuitry that lies within its case. In voice communications, your desk phone is a terminal attached to a powerful computer-powered device called a PBX.

PBX

Aside from the telephone, probably the most common voice communications hardware device is the **private branch exchange**, or **PBX**—also known as the switchboard. The PBX was modeled after the public branch exchange switchboard used at the telephone company to route calls. In the past, the switchboard was controlled by an operator who connected outside callers with the destination phone by plugging cables into a panel. In time, it became possible to dial the extension number; today, many PBXs enable direct dialing. Most modern PBXs have computer power built in so that many of the functions are automatically performed by the operator. The "intelligent PBX," sometimes called either a computerized branch exchange (CBX) or private automated branch exchange (PABX), has many other features, some of which are discussed in the section on software.

A number of voice communications peripheral devices are also used in voice communications and integrated voice/data communications. The following sections describe a few of the peripheral devices required for voice and/or data communications.

T-1 switch

The **T-1 switch** makes it possible to turn one incoming phone line into a number of lines. T-1 switches are electronic devices that split the incoming calls using binary logic—2, 4, 8, 16, 32, 64, and so on—and then route them to another computer or controller that disperses them to their destination. For example, a company may have one incoming line that splits to 24 lines, routing them to the PBX; or, it might route them to the order processing or customer service department, where the calls are answered by the first available representative.

Automatic Call Dialing

Automatic call dialing, or ACD, is a computer-managed electronic dialing function for outgoing calls often used by telephone marketing companies. It selects an exchange, such as 745, and then begins dialing all the suffix numbers in that exchange. Each time a call is answered, it is routed to the salesperson or customer service representative.

Automatic Number Identification

—caller ID

Automatic number identification, or ANI, is used to determine the number of the caller. ANI uses its computer circuitry to identify the number from the telephone network, displaying it on a computer screen or an LCD readout. ANI, too, is used in telephone marketing as a tool for determining customer demographics. For example, a customer calling an 800 toll-free number to order a product or magazine subscription can be identified regionally (city, state, Midwest, and so on) by the area code and phone number prefix. In this way, companies can perform targeted test marketing to learn about their customers.

Bridge

Bridge is the term used for computer circuitry that links phones and computers. Some bridges are simple; all they do is enable the computer to perform dialing tasks, such as speed dialing or predictive dialing, which combines the features of automatic call dialing with a screening function, where unanswered calls or those picked up by an answering machine are rejected so that the knowledge worker's time is not wasted.

Besides the bridge, the two other devices in the bridge family include the *router* and the *gateway*. Both perform similar functions—making connections between communications systems, whether voice or data. The goal of all bridge devices is to create enterprise-wide open systems.

More sophisticated bridges answer an incoming call and use ANI to identify the caller as a new or existing customer. If the customer is an existing one, the computer finds the customer's file and automatically routes *both* the call *and* the on-screen file to the customer service representative. This technique is called **voice/data integration**, and it not only saves time but also helps customers feel that they are being treated courteously, efficiently, and professionally.

Data Communications Hardware

In order to connect a computer to any kind of communications network, such as the public phone system or an internal phone system, there must be a device that links the two. The most common communications device is a modem, which is used to convert digital information to a form that can be transmitted over phone lines. Other common communications devices are discussed in the following sections.

Controller

Communications controllers perform the same functions as regular computer controllers. A controller routes data between the CPU and the terminal, making it possible for many knowledge workers to work more efficiently. The controller acts as a middleman, handing work off to the terminal and then, when the CPU is ready, passing the work on to the CPU for processing.

Communications controllers are used primarily with minicomputers and mainframes, and act as an intermediate computer between the terminal and the CPU. A controller is useful when sales representatives are submitting their daily sales reports. A file arrives and is routed by the controller to an operator at a terminal, where the file is checked and prepared for processing. Then it is sent to the CPU for processing and storage.

Multiplexer

The T-1 switch is a voice multiplexer; the term **multiplexer** is used to describe the peripheral device that splits one incoming *data line* into many so that more than one terminal or PC can be used to service incoming data transmissions. Multiplexers also speed up the data transmission, often raising it from 9600 baud to 56,000 baud (often shown as 56Kbps, for kilobits per second). A multiplexer might, for example, be used when multiple credit card authorizations are being handled at a processing center. Another use is to connect multiple users on a local network to multiple users on another network.

Concentrator

A **concentrator** is a controller and multiplexer combined into one peripheral to manage, amplify, and ensure the integrity of data signals. The concentrator is usually a computer or microprocessor-controlled device, and like its two counterparts, it is connected between the primary computer and the terminals and other peripherals (such as a printer or modem). A concentrator is useful when terminals or peripherals perform operations slowly, but the tasks need to be processed promptly. A customer at a bank ATM, for example, may take all the time he wants to check account balances and decide how much to withdraw from his account, but the debiting is quickly accomplished. The concentrator is also used when the data must be passed through wires or cables over long distances and needs to be boosted, or amplified. This use ensures that the processing tasks are performed promptly and accurately.

Voice Communications Software

Computers have made it much easier to work with PBXs. For example, if a marketing department was launching a new promotion that asked customers to place orders over the phone, the department might need additional incoming lines. In the past, this change meant physical rewiring, but today, it simply means a little reprogramming. The same is true of the messages and manner in which incoming calls are placed on hold until answered.

Voice Mail

Perhaps the most familiar voice communications software is **voice mail**, which uses the computer to capture, digitize, store, and forward voice messages. Voice mail usually permits each employee to record a personal outgoing message. Voice mail is the corporate answering machine at every extension so that no one ever misses a call.

Call Center Management

The most sophisticated voice—and often voice/data integration—communications application is in customer service. The call center is the department that works with customers and often handles the largest volume of calls. Customer service is one of the most important services that any company delivers because satisfying the customer is a top priority; therefore, the way calls are handled is extremely critical. Customer service is much more than simply handling incoming orders or complaint calls, as figure 16.1 shows. Using computer systems that integrate voice and data is often referred to as *computer-telephone integration,* or CTI. CTI systems make it possible for businesses not only to help customers but also to add value to services and to increase business as well.

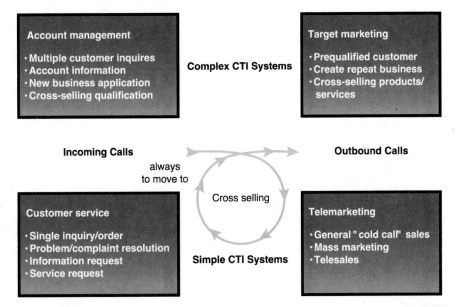

Figure 16.1
Computer-telephone integration uses voice and data communications to create new business opportunities from simple customer service calls.

Data Communications Software

The two types of data communications software *include communications software* and *communications management software*. Communications software is used to make connections from the individual computer making the inquiry to the **host** computer (the computer in charge of the work session and where the data that the knowledge worker seeks is stored). Communications management software is used to establish connections from host computers to individual computers to provide services and data.

Communications Software

Communications software programs work just like any other application, such as word processing or spreadsheets. Some communications software applications use a simple command structure; some use a menu; others are graphical and designed to work with Windows. Communications software can usually be programmed with telephone numbers that dial the modem and connect to another computer. Once connected, or on-line, you can send or receive communications. On-line means, literally, in direct communication with another computer. In a few cases, there are proprietary communications software programs that are designed to provide access to a single vendor's computer. This approach is used to restrict and control access to these information sources and thus ensure security and fiscal accountability.

Communications Management Software

Up to this point, the discussion on software has centered on a stand-alone computer calling a host computer. Communications management software, sometimes called *host* software, controls computers that receive calls from a number of individual knowledge workers. Like an airport traffic controller, this software controls which computers can participate in a network and determines the proper paths for communications to take place.

Communications management software manages the use of the network, ensuring that only authorized knowledge workers get connected, keeping records of their on-line time, and charging their accounts when services are used. It also manages all the various services and makes them available to knowledge workers. When a network becomes overloaded, communications management software decides which computers have priority and which have to wait.

Commonly, all communications management software performs error checking and security procedures. **Error checking** is the process by which networked computers ensure the accuracy and integrity of data transmissions. Many factors, such as typing errors, electrical power surges, and telephone line noise, introduce errors. Often when errors are found, the software tells the transmitting computer to resend the data. **Security procedures** are used to prevent someone from intruding in a network without proper authorization. The software requests that potential knowledge workers identify themselves and prove that they are authorized to use the computer before they actually get into the network's computers.

Communications management software runs on mainframes, minis, and personal computers; its characteristics and capabilities are determined by the number of people using it and the extent of the services it offers. Figure 16.2 shows the main menu for a popular on-line information service. This menu is generated and controlled by the communications management software used by the on-line service. You learn more about on-line information services later in this chapter.

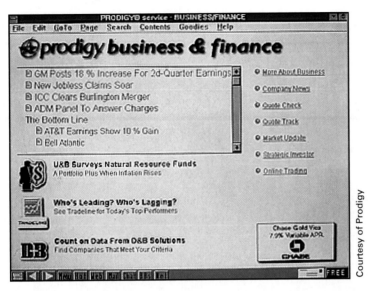

Figure 16.2
Communications management software provides access to the on-line service.

Courtesy of Prodigy

Knowledge Check

1. Name the voice and data devices that turn a single incoming line into multiple lines.
2. What is the difference between a controller and a concentrator?
3. What is the most common voice communications application?
4. What does the term *on-line* mean?
5. What are the two types of data communications software?
6. Why is error checking important?

Key Terms

automatic call dialing	automatic number identification	bridge
communications software	concentrator	error checking
host	multiplexer	private branch exchange (PBX)
security procedures	T-1 switch	voice mail
voice/data integration		

HOME PAGE

THE NATIONAL INFORMATION INFRASTRUCTURE

The U.S. Government's National Institute of Standards and Technology (NIST) is in charge of setting policy for the country's National Information Infrastructure (NII). Standards help ensure that technology is compatible and that people are able to use various information resources, whether radio, television, or the Internet. The following description was obtained from the World Wide Web (http:/www.nist.gov/).

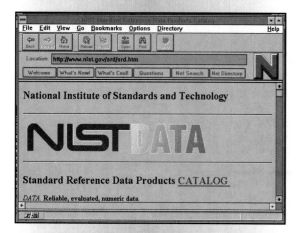

America has always had an information infrastructure, going back to smoke signals. But today, the nation is developing an information infrastructure with unprecedented sophistication and benefits for all Americans. The modern National Information Infrastructure (NII), sometimes called the "information superhighway," is an interconnection of computers and tele-communication networks, services, and appli-cations.

The phrase "information infrastructure" has an expansive meaning. The National Information Infrastructure (NII) includes more than just the physical facilities used to transmit, store, process, and display voice, data, and images. It encompasses a wide range and ever-expanding range of equipment including cameras, scanners, keyboards, telephones, fax machines, computers, switches, compact disks, video and audio tape, cable, wire, satellites, optical fiber transmission lines, microwave, nets, switches, televisions, monitors, printers, and much more.

The NII is not a cliff that suddenly confronts us, but rather a slope—one that society has been climbing since postal services and semaphore networks were established. An infor-

mation infrastructure has existed for a long time, continuously evolving with each new advance in communications technology. What is different is that today we are imagining a future when all the independent infrastructures are combined. An advanced information infrastructure will integrate and interconnect these physical components in a technologically neutral manner so that no one industry will be favored over any other. Most importantly, the NII requires building foundations for living in the Information Age and for making these technological advances useful to the public, business, libraries, and other nongovernmental entities. That is why, beyond the physical components of the infrastructure, the value of the National Information Infrastructure to users and the nation will depend in large part on the quality of its other elements:

- The information itself, which may be in the form of video programming, scientific or business databases, images, sound recordings, library archives, and other media. Vast quantities of that information exist today in government agencies and even more valuable information is produced every day in our laboratories, studios, publishing houses, and elsewhere.

- Applications and software that enable users to access, manipulate, organize, and digest the proliferating mass of information that the NII's facilities provide.

- The network standards and transmission codes that facilitate interconnection and interoperation between networks, and ensure the privacy of persons and the security of the information carried, as well as the security and reliability of the networks.

- The people—largely in the private sector—who create the information, develop applications and services, construct the facilities, and train others to tap its potential. Many of these people will be vendors, operators, and service providers working for private industry.

Every component of the information infrastructure must be developed and integrated if America is to capture the promise of the Information Age.

HOME PAGE REVIEW QUESTIONS

1. What technologies and infrastructures does the NII encompass?

2. How does the NII foresee these various technologies in the future?

3. What four elements are essential to help the NII grow and remain viable?

4. Why do you think we need an NII?

ISSUES AND IDEAS

Free Phone Calls on the Internet?

Cnet Central, the computer television show, broadcast a segment on using the Internet to make telephone—yes, telephone—calls. Using the Internet could reduce the cost of phone calls to practically nothing once you have the proper software and hardware. *Digital Dispatch, Cnet Central*'s on-line newsletter, reported:

To send voice communication over the Internet, all you need is a Mac or a Windows PC equipped with a microphone and a sound card, a standard modem (for most programs 14.4 kbps is sufficient), a SLIP or PPP Internet connection, and special voice communications software. To make a call, you type in the host IP address or the name of the person you want to reach, and you communicate by speaking directly into your computer's microphone. Your computer digitizes your voice, and whichever voice application you're using compresses the digitized sound and sends it across the Internet. At the other end, the same program decompresses the file and plays your voice through the other computer's speakers. (Most voice communications applications require that the other party use the same software.)

But before you cancel your long distance service, keep in mind that Internet voice communications have a long way to go to match the quality you'll get from the cordless phone on your desk. While audio sent over the Internet is for the most part understandable, it does sound distorted—how distorted depends on the application and the type of compression you're using, the speed of your computer, and the quality of your speakers and microphone. A good external microphone improves sound quality, and using external speakers or headphones can minimize the effects of distortion.

One major drawback is that both parties must use the same software in order to communicate. Another is that some software permits only one person to speak at a time—half-duplex, to use the data communications term. No doubt, these limitations will be overcome shortly, and knowledge workers will see both data *and* voice communications flooding the Internet airwaves.

CRITICAL THINKING

1. Does using the Internet for making phone calls sound like a good idea or a gimmick?

2. Although the call itself might be free, the article goes on to say "all you need..."—and it's a lot. How much must you spend on computer hardware and software before you can make a call?

3. What other drawbacks does the article mention? Would they be serious drawbacks to you?

Module B

Types of Networks

Why It's Important to Know

Networks connect two or more computers so that information can be quickly and accurately transmitted from one location to another. Increased productivity is one advantage of the use of networks because of the capability to share data.

A **network** is any system that connects two or more computers for the transfer of information. Practically speaking, a network is made up of three components: computers and peripheral devices, one or more communications media, and a set of standards, or protocols, that ensure proper understanding and communication. In the following sections, you learn about the many kinds of networks—how they differ and how they often interconnect with one another. Communications media is discussed first.

Communications Media

Communications media are the methods in which information is transferred over a network. The medium can be as simple as a string between two tin cans. In computer communications, each point in a network is a **node**. These nodes are physically connected to each other using the communications medium. Thus, the tin cans are nodes in a network, and telephones are nodes of a voice communications network. For telephones, the oldest communication medium is two copper wires, termed **twisted-pair** wiring. These two wires and a little electricity are all that phones need to function. Yet those same twisted pairs are quite adaptable to data communications as well. Many networks are built with twisted-pair wiring. Refer to figure 16.3 as you study these other common communication media, all of which are used to send communications signals:

- **Coaxial cable**. Used by cable television companies and many computer networks

- **Fiber optic cable**. Thin wires of glass fiber that replace standard copper wire

- **Infrared transmission**. A beam of infrared light

- **Microwave transmission**. High-frequency radio signals beamed between earth stations

- **Satellite transmission**. High-frequency radio signals beamed between satellites and earth stations

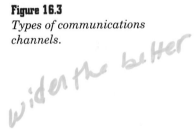

Figure 16.3
Types of communications channels.

Two additional factors that affect the use of communications media are bandwidth and speed; covered in the following text.

Bandwidth

Why are there so many different types of communications media? Because of the need for increased **bandwidth**, or the capacity of a particular medium to carry information. Voice bandwidth is not much of a concern; the frequency range of the human voice is quite narrow. But what happens when a friend plays music for you over the phone? Chances are that it doesn't sound nearly as good as your stereo. The reason is that twisted-pair wiring has a limited bandwidth and cannot accurately carry the full spectrum of sound that you might otherwise hear.

Limited bandwidth becomes problematic in two ways. The first is the *number of messages* the medium can carry, in both voice and data. The more, the better. The second is the nature and quality of the signal. Data must have a very, very clear channel; what you hear as noise on the phone line can completely corrupt a data transmission. Coaxial cable is affected by inclement weather, and falling autumn leaves can downgrade microwave transmissions. Imagine the significance of this to a bank that is electronically transferring several billion dollars. In addition, full-motion video used in multimedia applications requires very high bandwidth channel capabilities. The channel must be as wide as possible to accommodate a large number of complex signals.

Speed

Speed is the rate at which information is conveyed over a communications channel and is expressed in bits per second, or bps. This is a measure of the number of individual data bits that can be transmitted every second. When bandwidth and speed are considered, communications channels are classified into three categories:

- *Narrow band transmission*. The slowest at 45–150 baud; used by telegraph and teletype machines; commonly twisted-pair wires

- *Voice-grade transmission*. The middle speed at 300–28,800 baud; the human voice is in this range and so are telephones and inexpensive or home-use modems; commonly twisted-pair wires

- *Wideband transmission*. For highest speed at 19,200 baud to 500Kbps or more; this is for commercial grade channels used in business, finance, the government, and so on; commonly coaxial, fiber optic, or microwave transmission

Network Standards

Communications network standards are the rules and guidelines for achieving satisfactory performance and communication between different networks and computer systems. Each new communications technology or application seems to require its own standards. Here is a sampling:

- FDDI for high-speed fiber optic transmissions

- T-1 (and T-3) for wideband circuits

- CCITT X.400 for electronic mail message handling

- SNA for IBM mainframe communications

- DECNET for Digital minicomputer communications

These are just a few of the literally scores of different communications protocols in use today. There is no practical reason for you to know them all; however, for the purpose of understanding the importance and usefulness of standards, OSI is discussed because it is a good model of uniformity in data communications.

OSI, or **Open Systems Interconnect**, is a standard that separates computer-to-computer communications into seven layers or levels, each building one on top of the next. The OSI model was created by the European International Systems Organization in the 1970s. In the 1980s, it became regarded as a solution, not just for communications, but for the enterprise-wide open systems issue. As its name implies, its stated goal is to make differing systems "open" from the hardware through the application, as shown in figure 16.4. Dr. Peter G.W. Keen, author, professor, and consultant on communications, says of OSI: "The OSI model has generated several of the most important and useful standards in the telecommunications field. The architecture, not OSI, is the strategy, although OSI may be a key element of the architecture."

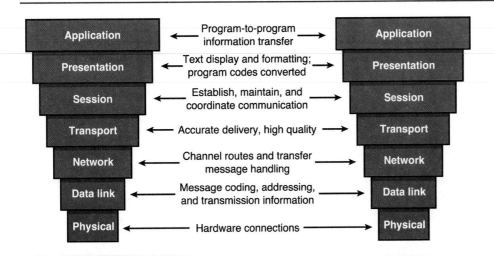

Figure 16.4
The seven layers of OSI. When properly implemented, the only layer the knowledge worker interacts with is the application.

Types of Networks

Many different types and sizes of networks exist, each designed for a different purpose. Basically, they fall into two groups: public networks, which individuals and businesses can use for a fee, and private networks, whose use is limited by its owners.

Public Networks

A **public network** is an *open* communications network available for use by anyone, usually on a fee basis. The AT&T, Sprint, and MCI telephone networks are examples of public networks. They span the United States and the world. Even though telephone networks were initially designed for voice messages, today they carry a large volume of computer communications.

In France, the telephone network was intentionally turned into a computer network by a project called Teletel. It was launched in 1981, when the French telephone and post office department put a terminal called "Le Minitel" in every home in France. Over 4 million have been installed. Initially, Teletel was to replace printed phone books by giving people on-line directory assistance. However, enterprising companies soon realized that they could provide other on-line services to the public. The program was a success: the number of on-line services in France has jumped from 200 to well over 10,000.

Data Communications Networks

In the United States, some networks are used exclusively for computer communications. These are called **packet-switching networks**. A **packet** is a block of data prepared for data transmission. Packets are routed to their destination in just a few milliseconds. On a packet-switching network, for example, you could send the entire text of the novel *Moby Dick*—220,000 words—in less than 30 seconds. There are two advantages to packet-switching. First, it is more economical to send data in packets. Second, packets are less prone to errors and corruption. The most prominent packet-switching networks are Tymnet and Telnet in the U.S., and Datapac in Canada. The first packet-switching network was **ARPANET**, created in 1968 by the U.S. Department of Defense Advanced Research Projects Agency. It links various government agencies, research labs, and universities. Today it is called Internet, and it links millions of computers around the world.

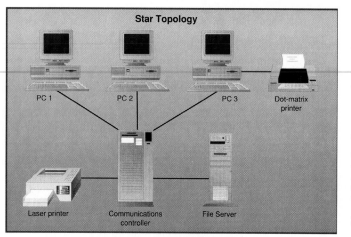

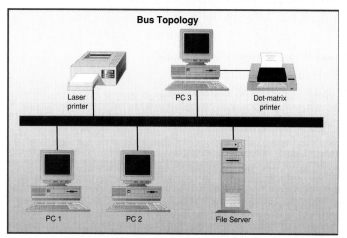

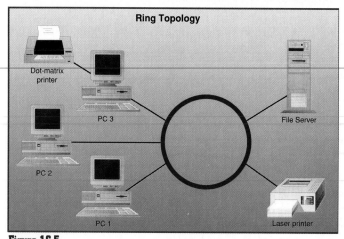

Figure 16.5
The three most common network topologies.

Private Networks

In addition to public networks, many private networks exist in the United States. A **private network** is a *closed* communication system, usually confined to a particular company, governmental entity, or other group. An example of a private network is American Airlines' SABRE reservation service. SABRE stands for Semi-Automated Business Research Environment. Developed by IBM in the mid-1960s, SABRE now has more than 68,000 terminals that connect 8,000 reservation operators and 14,000 travel agents around the world. Over 470,000 reservations are made on SABRE every day.

Several types of private networks exist in business today, serving a variety of needs for knowledge workers. The networks are categorized by topology, or the physical layout of network devices and nodes, and by the proximity of the devices and nodes to each other. Now look at these types of networks and examples of how they are used.

Network Topology

Topology defines the layout of computers and other devices and how they are connected. Figure 16.5 illustrates the three most common topologies: star, bus, and ring networks.

- A **star network** gives many knowledge workers access to central files and system resources through a host CPU.

- A **bus network** has no central computer but shares other network resources, such as printers, in the same way as the star network.

- In a **ring network**, individual computers are connected serially to one another. This arrangement is somewhat more expensive, but has the advantage of providing many routing possibilities.

Local Area Networks

A widely used type of private network is the **local area network**, or **LAN**. As the name suggests, LANs are set up to enable a small group of knowledge workers in the same geographic location, such as an office or a small company, to share data, programs, and hardware resources. A LAN may use any of the three types of networks—star, bus, or ring. The two general classifications of LANs that you can use are client/server LANs and peer-to-peer LANs.

Client/Server LANs

Local area networks that have quite a few nodes utilize the **client/server** hierarchy. In this arrangement, dedicated computers (called servers) on the network are used for specialized purposes. These servers are accessed by general-purpose computers on the network (called clients) in order to complete a necessary function. At a minimum, the network includes a file server, which is used to centralize files or security functions for the network. Other types of common servers include print, communications, fax, or database servers. In a client/server environment, all resources for which the server is designed are shared from that server. In a sense, a client node is subservient to the server, because it must rely on the server for the successful completion of a task.

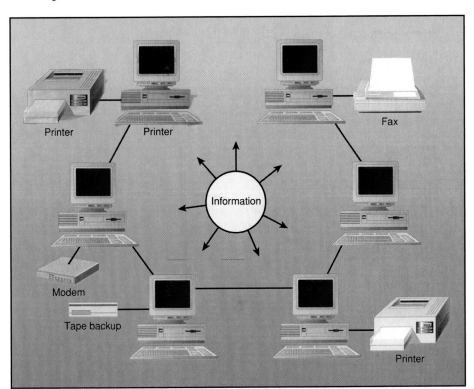

Figure 16.6
Peer-to-peer networking is ideally suited to workgroups.

Peer-to-Peer LANs

Peer-to-peer means that every computer on the network is an equal so that it can act as a server, a workstation, or both. Programs, data, and peripherals on the network can be made available to all knowledge workers. Exchanging files and programs between workstations becomes very easy to do with peer-to-peer networking. Figure 16.6 shows a typical peer-to-peer networking architecture.

The PCs and server(s) in most LANs are usually hard-wired, meaning that they are physically connected with cables. An exception is infrared LANs. Each PC has a network adapter card installed in an expansion slot that is connected to the cable. Hard-wired LANs don't require modems. The cable may be twisted-pair, but coaxial cable is often used and fiber-optic use is growing, because it can handle more data and transmit it much faster.

LAN Software

All networks require software, and the LAN is no exception. Refer to figure 16.4, showing the OSI layers. The LAN utilizes four of these layers:

- *Application.* Network applications

- *Transport.* Network operating system

- *Network.* Network BIOS

- *Physical.* Network adapter card

The network BIOS functions in the same way as the DOS operating system BIOS. The network operating system, or NOS, performs functions similarly to a computer operating system such as DOS. NOS tasks include the following:

- *File service.* Sending files from the server to the workstations

- *Print service.* Routing print jobs from workstations to printers

- *Security.* Ensuring that file integrity is maintained; for example, two knowledge workers cannot be allowed to edit and change the same file at once

- *Utilities.* Managing and directing certain tasks and helping to configure the network

By far the most popular NOS for PCs is Novell Netware, which is compatible with most topologies and is capable of supporting several hundred knowledge workers, depending on the specific Netware version in use.

Today, more and more operating systems for personal computers include built-in networking. This fact means that there is no difference between the regular OS and the NOS. For instance, Windows 95 includes all the operating system features you need to implement a peer-to-peer network.

Knowledge workers use many of the same software applications in a networked environment that they would use on a stand-alone PC. Most major applications, such as WordPro, Lotus 1-2-3, and Oracle, have LAN versions.

In addition, special applications have been designed for knowledge workers who work in teams or groups. One of the best-known is Lotus Notes. A very common application on networks of all kinds is e-mail.

Wide Area Networks

The **wide area network**, or WAN, is another type of private network. WANs use phone lines, microwave relaying stations, and satellites to connect computers located miles apart. Even over great distances, WANs enable users to send electronic mail, share data and programs, and use the printers and memory devices linked to the network. Figure 16.7 is an example of a WAN.

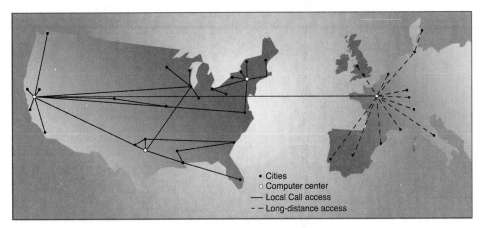

Legend:
- Cities
- ○ Computer center
- — Local Call access
- – – Long-distance access

Figure 16.7
The enterprise-wide WAN enables sending voice and data transmissions anywhere in the world at greatly reduced cost.

Knowledge Check

1. What is the term used to refer to points on a network?
2. Name several methods for creating communications channels.
3. Why is bandwidth important in networks?
4. What is the purpose behind a standard such as OSI?
5. Name a type of public network.
6. What is the most widely used type of private network?
7. What is the difference between a LAN and a WAN?

Key Terms

bandwidth	bus network	client/server
coaxial cable	fiber optic cable	infrared transmission
local area network (LAN)	microwave transmission	network
node	Open Systems Interconnect (OSI)	packet
packet-switching networks	peer-to-peer	private network
public network	ring network	satellite transmission
speed	star network	topology
twisted pair	wide area network (WAN)	

HOME PAGE

ISDN COMES OF AGE

When American Telephone and Telegraph introduced Integrated Services Digital Network (ISDN) in the early 1980s, it was widely regarded as nonsense. Who would need a digital network? Why would we want our processing and storage to take place on the network? Who would care if phone, data, television, radio, movies-on-demand, and a dozen other on-line or interactive services all came out of the phone jack in the wall?

Sometimes it takes a while for a new technology to gain acceptance, and ISDN was no exception. Here's how it looks from Pacific Bell's perspective.

ISDN, An Introduction

Integrated Services Digital Network (ISDN) is here, today, in California. In a Bay Area publisher's office and a Los Angeles bank, in a giant research lab, and a small artist's studio, it functions as intended and has begun to bring increased capabilities, reduced costs, and improved productivity to organizations both large and small.

ISDN offers dramatic increases in the speeds of data and document transfer. But that's just the beginning. It empowers a whole new breed of applications made possible by high-speed transmission:

- telecommuting
- inexpensive video conferencing
- teleradiology and remote health care
- teleteaching
- remote broadcasting and sound transfer
- collaborative CAD/CAM engineering connectivity
- interactive publishing

and many, many more.

And improvements are being made every day to the ISDN services offered by Pacific Bell, to the equipment produced by the world's leading manufacturers, to the statewide and worldwide telecommunications network that dynamically responds to the way the world does business.

Why Is ISDN So Important?

More than just a means for fast, accurate data transmission, ISDN truly represents the next generation of the world's telephone service for all forms of telecommunications, including voice.

ISDN brings the digital network to the individual user. Thus, the same twisted-pair copper telephone line that could traditionally carry only one voice, one computer, or one fax "conversation," can now carry as many as three separate "conversations" at the same time, through the same line. ISDN is the "magic" that makes this happen.

How is this possible? The basic ISDN-to-user connection, called a Basic Rate Interface, contains three separate channels, or "pipes." Two of these channels (the B channels) carry user "conversations" from a telephone, computer, fax, or almost any other device. The third channel (the D channel) carries call set-up information for the network, but can also carry user data transmissions.

This means that two separate "conversations," such as a voice call and a computer transmission, can take place at the same time through the same ISDN line. Simultaneously, a third "conversation," a CompuServe session or a credit-card authorization, for example, can also take place through the same connection. The power of ISDN enables all three of these transmissions to happen at the same time, through the same copper twisted-pair telephone line that once could handle only one transmission at a time.

Furthermore, as many as eight separate devices (telephones, computers, fax machines, and more) can be connected to the same ISDN line and each given as many separate telephone numbers as needed. [ISDN does not require a modem for data transmission between computers.] All of which means it is no longer necessary to have multiple telephone lines to handle multiple telephone devices, telephone numbers, or telephone calls. One ISDN line does it all.

Basic Rate ISDN

ISDN telephones can, of course, call and receive calls from ordinary telephones everywhere, because the digital and analog systems are fully interconnected. Digital ISDN connections also produce voice conversations that are absolutely quiet and crystal-clear.

Most of the telephone wiring in place today (the copper twisted pairs that have carried telephone conversations since the days of "number, please?") can successfully transmit ISDN digital signals. Although some older buildings and homes may need to upgrade wiring, most are "ISDN ready" today.

Access to a suitably equipped digital switching system is also required. The availability of these switches is growing rapidly. By the end of 1994, Pacific Bell schedules indicate that a vast majority of businesses and residences in most of California will be able to access the power, speed, and amazing flexibility of ISDN.

A Statewide Fiber Optic Network

Pacific Bell has also announced a $16-billion plan to expand the power and capacity of its digital network. Called *California First*, the program calls for new high-speed fiber optic information highways throughout the state, as well as the replacement of copper phone lines serving California's 10.4 million businesses and residences. By the year 2000, more than 6.5 million customers will be equipped with either fiber optic or coaxial cables. The purpose of this emerging digital network is twofold. In its own interest, Pacific Bell expects to return significant yearly savings in maintenance, parts inventories, training, and other operating expenses. More important in the long term, however, is the impact that digital communications will have on the economy and quality of life in California.

Advantages of a Digital Network

Why is a digital network important? There are two basic reasons: clarity and speed.

First, digital signals ignore the static and noise that often affect analog transmissions, especially over long distances and older telephone lines, producing connections of the highest possible quality. They offer quiet, static-free voice conversations, and virtually error-free data connections, worldwide.

Second, they carry data at significantly higher speeds, and promise even greater speeds as digital compression and other techniques become more sophisticated and available.

HiFi on the Digital Highway

In both the Los Angeles and San Francisco areas, radio stations now use ISDN for clear, quiet sound transmissions from baseball, basketball, and other games, concerts, news conferences, political conventions and similar events. At most locations, temporary ISDN lines are installed, although at more and more venues, permanent ISDN lines have been put in place by both broadcasters and entrepreneurs who lease them to others for major functions. Sophisticated sound studios are also beginning to use ISDN for remote recording of an announcer's voice, live music, or other components of a film, video, advertising, or audio-visual presentation. Many studios also download stereo tracks recorded elsewhere for mixing and enhancement on their more sophisticated equipment, or for incorporation into a film or television presentation.

Hollywood's Byron Wagner, of Genius, Inc., is convinced that ISDN transmission of CD-quality sound is in its infancy. Wagner is not only an equipment innovator and technology consultant to the entertainment industry, but has been the recording engineer of choice for some of the world's leading popular and country performers.

At a digital media demonstration at Texpo '93, he used ISDN lines and state-of-the-art compression to link singers in San Francisco, Hollywood, and Hawaii into a single real-time concert. He believes that the emerging technology opens many possibilities, from remote concerts, talent auditions, and collaborative "jam sessions," to tele-jukeboxes in which customers link their stereo systems to a compact disc library to hear and perhaps even buy new releases or hard-to-find classics.[2]

HOME PAGE REVIEW QUESTIONS

1. What is the difference between the phone networks used today and ISDN?

2. How does ISDN improve voice, data, and computer communications?

3. What are the advantages in using ISDN?

---

2. From the PacBell WWW site: htpt://www.pacbell.com /isdn/isdn.bhpm/

The Battle for Your Internet Connection

Fortune magazine reported that the cable TV industry is getting wired—maybe. Cable companies, eager to compete with the telephone companies and pay off some of their multibillion dollars of debt, plan to lure Baby Bell customers with fast Internet access.

Explore and the Personal Cable TV modem, the first commercially available complete solution for cable modeming was demonstrated in September, 1995, at NetWorld + Interop. The cable modem delivers Internet access at speeds up to 1,000 times faster than is currently possible using phone lines at 9600 baud. The combination of Explore and the Personal Cable TV modem makes World Wide Web access practical and affordable for many data-intensive applications that until now have required expensive ISDN connections reaching speeds of only 56Kbps or T-1 telephone lines at 1.5 Mbps. Internet access via cable TV promises to reduce greatly user frustration with file download times and server availability, as well as lower the cost of high-speed data transmission. This easy-to-install-and-use turnkey solution immediately opens new business opportunities for cable operators to provide high-speed World Wide Web and Internet access services to more than 60 million cable TV subscribers nationwide, plus a host of households and businesses currently not using cable.

In one interesting experiment in the Netherlands, the SURF foundation commissioned SURFnet, in cooperation with Wageningen Agricultural University (WAU) and the Dutch Cable System Association (DCSA), to carry out an innovative project. A practical experiment was made in Wageningen using Zenith "HomeWorks" 0.5M technology through the cable TV network.

The aim of this project was to gather knowledge of and experience with data communications through a cable TV network using a standard Zenith modem. With the help of this technology, thirty students were able to access the computer network of the WAU, as well as the Internet, from their own rooms. The experiment was carried out in a students' flat complex in Wageningen from August 1994 to March 1995.

Through TCP/IP, the students were able to use graphic World Wide Web browsers (Mosaic and Netscape) and many different Internet applications. The current state of affairs shows that the use of Zenith "HomeWorks" 0.5M offers good possibilities for individual connections with LAN functionality through the cable TV network. The suitability of the Internet can be classified as excellent, one participant reported.

But don't buy that cable modem just yet, says *Fortune* magazine (September 18, 1995): If the cable companies don't invest millions to upgrade their networks, they'll have to stick to offering HBO and the Home Shopping Network. A paper prepared for CableLabs by Rogers CableSystems, Canada's largest cable operator, said the current cable infrastructure is rife with signal interference that makes two-way communications nearly impossible.

CRITICAL THINKING

1. Often the best technology is not the predominant technology. Does it make sense to change from conventional modems to cable modems?

2. It's likely that cable modems will be more expensive—$500 compared to around $100—until sufficient demand is created. But won't cost be a barrier to acceptance?

3. Given that cable is connected to a different system—the television, not the computer—what benefits would having a cable modem provide?

4. Will ISDN make the modem obsolete?

Module C

Network Information Services

Why It's Important to Know

> **Network information services are invaluable because of the amount of information they provide. News, database services, and interactive services can all be easily accessed by way of the computer. Privacy is an issue that needs to be considered when on the net.**

Networks provide a wide range of personal, business, and governmental services. In general, these network services fall into two categories: information services, which enable us to read local and remote databases, and interactive services, which enable us to exchange information via networks. The following are some examples of these two kinds of network services.

Information Services

Information services maintain and provide access to data repositories, which offer a wide variety of information. Subscribing to an information service is similar to subscribing to a magazine. Once you are registered, you're given a telephone number that enables your computer to connect to the service. Many information services require an initial fee and then bill you for usage on a monthly basis.

Information services are one-way services; you can read their data but you can't add to their databases. The two general categories into which information services fall are news and database services. You can begin by looking at news services.

News Services

As the name implies, **news services** provide the latest news, including general interest, business, and financial news. You can read *The New York Times*, *Forbes*, *USA Today*, and many newsletters on news services.

Figure 16.8

ZDNet news service.

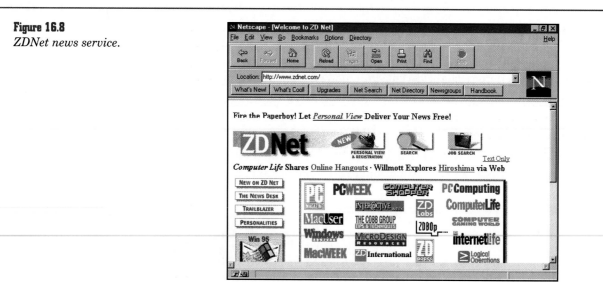

The Dow Jones News/Retrieval (DJN/R) service is an example of a news service. DJN/R provides financial information, stock quotations for thousands of companies, and other investment information. Because it's owned by Dow Jones, it also offers the full text of articles from *Barron's* and *The Wall Street Journal*. But DJN/R doesn't confine itself to financial information, it also provides film reviews, a college selection service, an encyclopedia, and a medical and drug reference.

Database Services

A **database service** is an information service whose primary purpose is to provide comprehensive information. These services store very large amounts of data on large-capacity hard disk drives. Database services enable you to connect your personal computer to a host computer, read the data, and download it to your computer. Writers, students, lawyers, medical practitioners, and other knowledge workers use database services to research topics of interest. Figure 16.9 shows a topic researched on a database service.

The U.S. Government has hundreds of specialized databases for such topics as agriculture, population, jobs, health, and science. In some ways, subscribing to a database service is like having the Library of Congress on your desktop.

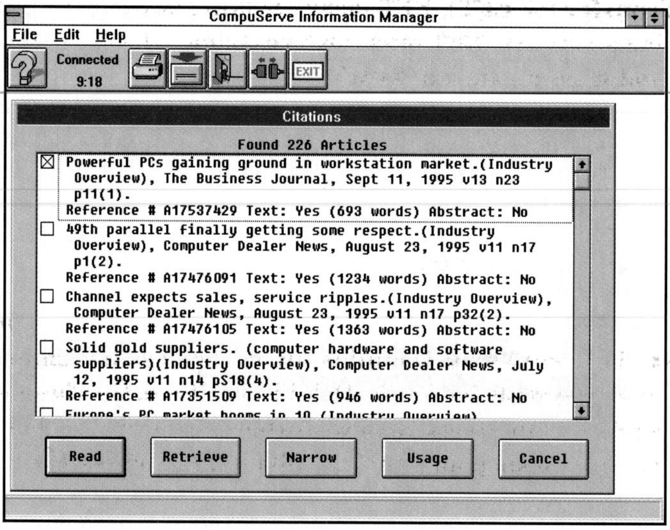

Figure 16.9

A screen of downloaded data. Downloading enables you to pull what you need from the network and save it as a file.

Many commercial databases are available to businesses and individuals as well. One of the largest and most widely used is Dialog, which contains hundreds of industry-specific databases (chemistry, petroleum, and so on), as well as news, magazines, and special-interest topics. Dialog is used by businesses but offers a limited number of its databases to individuals as Knowledge Index. Other commercial databases include Nexis for news and articles; Lexis for legal research; Bibliographic Retrieval Services (BRS) for news and articles, and Investext for financial information.

Interactive Services

Interactive services enable you to connect your personal computer to a community of computer users both to obtain and to exchange information. You can interact with other users in the same way you would over the telephone, but with added dimensions. In effect, you get all the benefits of a database service, as well as being able to add your own information to whatever extent you choose.

Electronic Bulletin Boards

One of the most popular interactive services for personal computer users is the electronic bulletin board, often called a BBS, or bulletin board system. An **electronic bulletin board** enables people to read and post messages on an information service. Bulletin board messages are topic-specific or personal, depending on the type of bulletin board. A bulletin board, for example, may specialize in bringing buyers and sellers of personal computers together, much like classified ads. However, you may also read and post personal messages on any of thousands of topics, from business topics to politics to personal hobbies or outdoor activities. For example, during the Tour de France bicycle race, fans watching the race posted daily race results. Bulletin boards are available for just about any and every interest.

EFT and Consumer Services

Probably the most common example of an interactive service is **Electronic Funds Transfer** (or **EFT**). EFT means making any type of financial transaction using a network. EFT often involves using a bank card to make withdrawals and deposits via an ATM. Consumer shopping networks are also growing in popularity. These services enable shopping worldwide for virtually every kind of product or service, from dry cleaners that pick up and deliver to large volume auto sales dealers.

Information Utilities

A third type of interactive service is sometimes referred to as **information utilities**. This category includes such services as America Online, CompuServe, Microsoft Network, Delphi, and Prodigy. These services provide subscribers with access to news, extensive databases, bulletin boards, electronic mail, and shopping services, all for a reasonable fee.

Business and Governmental Networks

Business and government regard communications and networking as serious tools, even as they experiment with this technology to create new services. Now look at a few ways business and government use networks.

Electronic Data Interchange

Electronic Data Interchange (or EDI) is using networks to transfer forms, such as invoices, purchase orders, shipping notices, and even payments with computers. The data is loaded into EDI software with the appropriate forms, similar to on-screen templates. The completed forms are most commonly transmitted from computer-to-computer using compatible hardware and software, or via a private network. Figure 16.10 shows a diagram of an EDI transaction.

Figure 16.10
Electronic Data Interchange has made order fulfillment and inventory much more efficient.

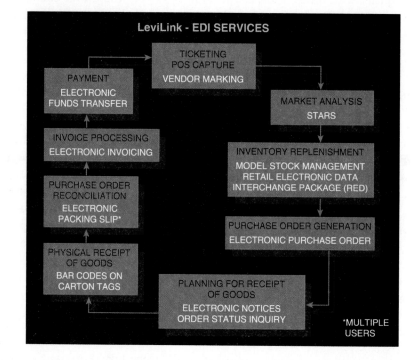

Many accountants and individuals are now using EDI technology to submit federal income tax returns. The Internal Revenue Service makes it possible for many people to use their personal computers to file tax returns. To do so, you use an income tax preparation software application and electronically transmit the files to IRS computers.

CALS

Some years ago, the U.S. Department of Defense instituted *Computer Aided Acquisition and Logistics Support* (CALS), a program conceived for image processing and paperless document management associated with the design, manufacture, acquisition and maintenance of weapons systems. Under the CALS requirement, defense contractors involved in large weapons systems for the Air Force, Army, and Navy must now submit engineering drawings and text information in digital form—usually computer tapes or CD-ROM—instead of paper.

A new aspect of the CALS network, made operational in 1992, links NATO offices and contractors in France, Germany, Italy, and the United Kingdom for the access and exchange of weapons systems data stored on mainframes at the Huntsville, Alabama, Missile Command (MICOM) in CALS format. The new network will use fiber optic channels to link over 10,000 workstations and Macintoshes to the MICOM mainframe.

The Internet — security

One of the fastest growing networks in the world is the Internet. In reality, the Internet is a "network of networks," meaning that it is a collection of networks that you can access individually once you are connected to the Internet. The Internet began in 1969 under the name of ARPANET, which was a packet-switched network for the U.S. Department of Defense. The Internet has grown to the point where there are now more than 6 million hosts connected, and experts are predicting that if current growth rates persist, there will be more than 200 million connected by the turn of the century.

Unlike other commercial services, there is no central location or company that you need to contact in order to get access to the Internet. Chances are good that you may already have access because most post-secondary schools in the United States are already connected to the Internet. If you want personal access, separate from your school, you need to establish an account with an Internet service provider, or ISP. The names and addresses of ISPs can be found in the phone books of most large cities, under the heading Internet Services. Any of these groups (your school or an ISP) can get you started with the proper software and information you need to tap into the power of the Net.

Network Security

Computer security and the need to physically protect data is critical in networking. Whenever a computer is connected to a phone line, it is extremely vulnerable to people gaining unauthorized access to the stored data stored. The following section explores some of the problems and their remedies and discusses the ethics of networking.

Protecting Networks

Because networks can make computer systems vulnerable to intrusion, security systems exist to protect computers and networks. One such system employs user names or account numbers, accompanied by a password, to differentiate between authorized users and intruders. To make this system work, knowledge workers must keep their passwords both unique and confidential.

Another method of ensuring network security is *callback*. In this type of system, you begin by connecting to the computer with a telephone and modem. Next, the computer prompts you for your user name and password, which you enter. At this point, the computer terminates the connection. The computer verifies your user name and password and then calls you back to establish your work session.

Despite the various security systems, unauthorized parties still find ways to intrude on computer systems. One term used for these computer abusers is intruders. Who are these people and what are the crimes they commit?

Intruders

People who intrude, or break in to computer systems, are sometimes inappropriately called hackers. A **hacker** is someone who demonstrates great skill in programming and working with computers. A computer abuser is an **intruder**, sometimes called a cracker, who is either behaving unethically or illegally in the use of computer systems. Intruders interfere with computer systems owned or operated by others. They usually gain access by circumventing user name or password security. They use an automatic telephone dialer to find the numbers of computer systems. When they locate a number, their computer attempts to guess user names and passwords by trying every possible combination of letters and numbers.

Intruders have been known to attack voice communications systems as well. A few years ago, two teenage intruders were able to gain unauthorized access to the phone mail system of a publishing house. Angered that they had not received a free poster for subscribing to the publisher's magazine, they left lewd voice mail messages and erased valuable incoming advertising queries. The voice mail system had to undergo extensive reprogramming, rendering it out of service for almost three weeks.

To thwart intruders, some systems use **lockouts**—software that allows you to have only three tries at entering a user name or password. After several incorrect attempts, the phone connection is broken. This protection can certainly impede the efforts of an intruder. Another security measure requires that authorized users change passwords at assigned intervals.

The latest technology uses keycards, fingerprints, voiceprints, and retinal eye scans to secure multiple-user systems. Although these require additional sophisticated hardware and software, many military, government, corporate, and private institutions often feel that their information security is worth the extra cost and effort.

There are many other ways to break into computers and networks. Some computer owners try breaking into their own systems to try to figure out the loopholes before intruders do. The U.S. Air Force, for example, employs experts from Mitre Corporation to look for weaknesses in their computer security. Following are two other methods to thwart unauthorized access to computer systems.

Encryption

Encryption involves putting coding devices at each end of the communication line. Before transmitting a message, one computer encodes the information to be transmitted by substituting gibberish characters for real letters.

At the other end, the process is reversed by the receiving computer. This method makes it very hard for transmissions to be intercepted and read by unauthorized individuals.

File Protection

File protection is now common on personal computers, whether they are used by one person or connected in a network. Programs have been created so that individual workers can protect their personal files from others. In addition, programs "lock" a floppy disk or hard disk drive against prying eyes. Figure 16.11 shows how a program of this type works. The program prompts the user for a password, and reveals if unauthorized attempts to log on have been attempted.

The Computer Virus

In recent years, computer systems have been plagued with an insidious program called a **computer virus**, which corrupts or "infects" computer files by inserting a copy of the virus itself. Most computer viruses are very small, short programs that enter computer systems via other programs or through communications networks. A virus can go unnoticed for long periods as it insidiously infects the computer and then, at a predetermined time and date, or often when the computer is powered up, causes it to crash.

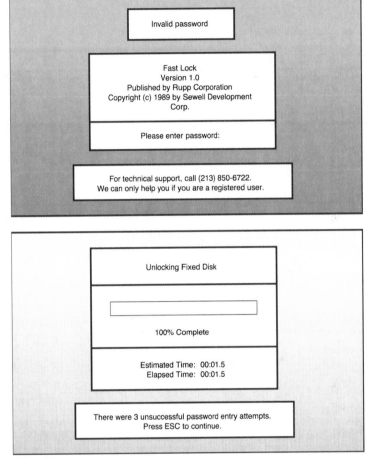

Figure 16.11
A password protection program for an individual's PC.

Viruses are often created by an employee who has been fired and wants to strike back at the company in anger; by talented young intruders who want to demonstrate their computer skill; or by programmers with antisocial tendencies or a perverted sense of humor. Many virus attacks have occurred over the past few years, and although they can be stopped there does not seem to be a way to prevent them.

The Computer Worm

A relative of the computer virus is the **computer worm**, which duplicates itself from one computer's memory to the next. Once in memory, it continues to propagate itself, over and over, consuming ever more space until the computer crashes. The most widely publicized worm attack in history occurred in 1988. Robert Tappan Morris, a graduate computer science student at Cornell University, placed a computer worm on ARPANET. It brought 6,000 computers to a halt. Morris was brought to trial, convicted, fined, and sentenced to a year of public service.

HOME PAGE

POWER PROTECTION: NOT A TRIVIAL CONCERN

A few years ago, an AT&T facility near Chicago caught fire, destroying equipment and disrupting telephone service across the nation. Millions of calls went uncompleted; no backup or disaster recovery system was in place. Most corporate and government computer systems do have plans and provisions for a disaster or a power outage. Power outages are quite frequent in most parts of the country and are mostly weather-related, due to storms or lightning or sometimes electrostatic discharge (ESD).

A backup power system for a personal computer is just as important. High-quality PCs have a rugged power supply that is capable of withstanding minor power disruptions, called *surges*. But not only can a sudden power outage cause loss of data, but a voltage spike or electrical brownout can destroy sensitive electronic circuits and damage software configurations. PCs in networks are especially vulnerable; corrupted data on a client machine affected by a power outage can corrupt data on a server.

In these more severe cases, what is required is an uninterruptible power supply, or UPS, which contains sophisticated electronic circuitry that switches from the line to a battery in case of disruption or outage. Although the battery cannot power your computer indefinitely, it allows you the time to close all applications safely and power down normally. In addition, good UPSs have built-in network card or modem surge protection for times when lightning or electrical discharge travels down the phone lines.

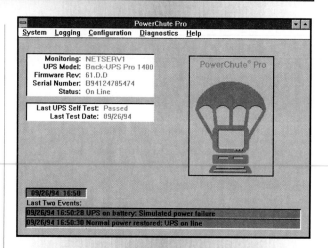

American Power Conversion is a leader in power protection and uninterruptible power supplies and offers a product line called Smart-UPS. These UPSs have features that can be configured using software that runs on the computer. One of the most recent offerings is for Windows 95. The software takes advantage of Win 95's "plug and play" feature, which detects the presence of certain hardware devices. The software provides automatic shutdown in case of a power outage. The software also provides continuous monitoring of the UPS, recording power events and displaying the status of the unit.

HOME PAGE REVIEW QUESTIONS

1. What is the most common electrical irregularity that affects computers and communications systems?

2. What is the ultimate form of protection against power problems?

3. What advantage does a UPS with software provide?

Knowledge Check

1. What is the difference between an information service and an interactive service?
2. Identify two types of information services.
3. Identify two types of interactive services.
4. What is an information utility?
5. What does EDI stand for?
6. Describe how encryption provides computer security.

Key Terms

computer virus	computer worm	database service
electronic bulletin board	Electronic Data Interchange	Electronic Funds Transfer (EFT)
encryption	file protection	hacker
Information Services	information utilities	intruder
lockouts	news services	

ISSUES AND IDEAS

E-Mail Abuse

Privacy and identity on the Internet are subjects of great concern and great abuse. The two common types of abuse are individuals abusing their privileges and employers or other parties abusing the rights of others.

In the first instance, consider that most people want to believe the person that they are corresponding with is exactly who says she is, in name, gender, and all other aspects. Yet two common abuses, according to Larry J. Hughes, Jr., author of *Actually Useful Internet Security Techniques*, are

- *To pose as somebody else.* This act is usually considered highly unethical under any circumstance—even as a joke between friends. In the worst case, the recipient of a forged message is led to believe that someone has said something that he or she did not, and perhaps would not, say. (Imagine this coming from your "boss": "Don't bother coming into work tomorrow. . . you're ugly and you're fired.")

- *To communicate anonymously.* There are countless justifications for sending e-mail anonymously, just as there are for sending anonymous paper mail and making anonymous telephone calls. Consider a tip to the authorities about a child pornography ring that is selling crack to buy automatic weapons for disgruntled postal employees—probably a good thing to report with a low profile. Yet there are better ways to achieve this than through e-mail forgery. . . Unfortunately, forged e-mail can also be used for harassment, libel, and similar malevolent behaviors.[3]

---

3. Larry J. Hughes, Jr. *Actually Useful Internet Security Techniques,* (Indianapolis: New Riders Publishing, 1995), 131.

In the second instance, consider that most individuals and employees would prefer to feel that their e-mail accounts are not "subject to postal inspection" as the case may be. Yet many employers, colleges, and government agencies consider any work or correspondence, whether it is between employees or going outside the enterprise, as the property of the enterprise. Remember the widely publicized case a few years ago of Epson, the computer and printer maker, whose supervisors were reading employee e-mail?

L. Detweiler, author of "Privacy & Anonymity on the Internet FAQ (Frequently Asked Questions)," says:

> Generally, you should expect little privacy on your account for various reasons:
>
> - Potentially, every keystroke you type could be intercepted by someone else.
>
> - System administrators make extensive backups that are completely invisible to users which may record the states of an account over many weeks.
>
> - Erased files can, under many operating systems, be undeleted.
>
> - Most automated services keep logs of use for troubleshooting or otherwise; for example FTP sites usually log the commands and record the domain originations of users, including anonymous ones.
>
> - Some software exacerbates these problems.
>
> Independent of malevolent administrators are fellow users, a much more commonly harmful threat. Following are some ways to help ensure that your account will not be accessed by others, and compromises can often be traced to failures in these guidelines:
>
> 1. Choose a secure password. Change it periodically.
> 2. Make sure to log off, always.
> 3. Do not leave a machine unattended for long.
> 4. Make sure that no one watches you type your password.
> 5. Avoid password references in e-mail.
> 6. Be conservative in the use of the .rhost file.
> 7. Use utilities like "xlock" to protect a station, but be considerate.[4]

CRITICAL THINKING

1. In the first instance explained here, describe some instances where the Golden Rule applies to e-mail.

2. List some reasons why you should always assume that someone is reading your e-mail. Which of these instances actually threaten your privacy?

3. What steps can you take immediately to have more e-mail security?

4. L. Detweiler. Privacy & Anonymity on the Internet FAQ: http://www.cis.ohio-state.edu/hypertext/faq/usenet/net-privacy/top.html

ETHICS

Protection for Hackers, Prosecution for Crackers

The following excerpt is from "Civil Liberties in Cyberspace: When Does Hacking Turn from an Exercise of Civil Liberties into Crime?" by Mitchell Kapor.

During the past several years, dozens of individuals (using computers) have been the subject of . . . [Secret Service] searches and seizures. In any other context, the warrant might never have been issued. By many interpretations, it disregarded the First and Fourth Amendments to the U.S. Constitution, as well as several existing privacy laws. But the government proceeded as if civil liberties did not apply. . . [because it] was investigating computer crime.

Our society has made a commitment to openness and to free communication. But if our legal and social institutions fail to adapt to new technology, basic access to the global electronic media could be seen as a privilege, granted to those who play by the strictest rules, rather than as a right held by anyone who needs to communicate. To assure [*sic*] that these freedoms are not compromised, a group of computer experts, including myself, founded the Electronic Frontier Foundation (EFF) in 1990.

. . . There are, of course, real threats to network and system security. The qualities that make the ideal network valuable—its popularity, its uniform commands, its ability to handle financial transactions and its international access—also make it vulnerable to a variety of abuses and accidents. It is certainly proper to hold hackers accountable for their offenses, but that accountability should never entail denying defendants the safeguards of the Bill of Rights, including the rights to free expression and association and to freedom from unreasonable searches and seizures.

We need statutory schemes that address the acts of true computer criminals. . . while distinguishing between those criminals and hackers whose acts are most analogous to noncriminal trespass. And we need educated law enforcement officials who will be able to recognize and focus their efforts on the real threats.

The question that arises: How do we help our institutions, and perceptions, adapt? The first step is to articulate the kinds of values we want to see protected in the electronic society we are now shaping and to make an agenda for preserving the civil liberties that are central to that society. Then we can draw on the appropriate legal traditions that guide other media.

. . . The EFF's agenda extends far beyond litigation. Our larger agenda includes sponsoring a range of educational initiatives aimed at the public's general lack of familiarity with the technology and its potential. That is why there is an urgent need for technologically knowledgeable people to take part in the public debate over communications policy and to help spread their understanding of these issues. Fortunately, the very technology is at stake—electronic conferencing—makes it easier than ever before to get involved in the debate.[5]

Critical Thinking

1. Describe the ethical issue involved here, regarding the relationship between the government and its citizens.

2. Research the First and Fourth Amendments. Make a list of ways they can be violated in electronic communications.

3. Research some cases of computer crimes and determine their disposition. Develop a position about what constitutes computer crime and noncriminal hacking.

THE LEARNING ENTERPRISE

Your department, and subsequently your enterprise, has decided that it needs the latest voice and data networking technologies in order to fulfill its mission and improve overall productivity. Here are the steps to create a fully networked enterprise, where each knowledge worker is connected and everyone is a citizen of cyberspace.

1. Begin with your workgroup. What kind of computer network (LANs) do you need? What hardware and software must be acquired? Refer to the chapter, and be specific.

2. Next, determine how your workgroup will be networked into your department or function.

3. Have a representative from all departments and functions meet and decide how they will be interconnected. Make decisions about enterprise-wide e-mail and how the enterprise will network with the external world (wide area networks). Also, decide on the voice communications and voice mail at this time.

4. What information services will the enterprise need? Will you need Internet access? An up-to-the-second news service? EDI?

5. What kinds of network security will departments and the enterprise as a whole need? How will you safeguard e-mail, and how can you prevent viruses and worms?

6. Report these decisions in a memo to your department.

7. What information services will individual knowledge workers and workgroups need?

8. Have each department's scribe report all these decisions and choices in a memo and collect them from each department. This collection becomes the departmental and enterpise-wide networking policy. Submit the report to your teacher.

---

5. Mitchell Kapor. "Civil Liberties in Cyberspace: When Does Hacking Turn from an Exercise of Civil Worberties into Crime," *Computer Ethics* (Prentice Hall: 1995), 644–650.

Chapter Review

Fill in the Blank

1. The voice communications hardware device used to distribute phone calls is the _____, or _____

2. The most common data communications hardware device is the _____.

3. Using the computer to store phone messages is called _____.

4. There are two kinds of data communications software: _____ software and _____ software.

5. The capacity of a particular medium to carry information is called _____.

6. The standard that separates computer-to-computer communications into seven layers is called _____, _____, or _____.

7. The three most common network topologies are _____, _____, and _____.

8. A private network called a _____ _____, or _____, enables knowledge workers in the same geographic location, such as an office, to share date, programs, and hardware resources.

9. The _____, or _____, is a private network that enables knowledge workers to share data, programs, and hardware resources over great distances.

10. One of the fastest growing public networks in the world is the _____.

Circle the Correct Answer

1. In computer communications, each point in a network is (router, node).

2. The oldest telephone communicating medium is (twisted pair, fiber optic).

3. An (interactive, information) service enables you to obtain and exchange information through your personal computer.

4. Using your bank card to carry out financial transactions is an example of (EDI, EFT).

5. A computer (hacker, intruder) is someone who behaves unethically or illegally in the use of computer systems.

Review Questions

1. List five common communications media.
2. Describe several purposes of communications management software.
3. Describe packet-switching networks and give an example of one.
4. What functions do bridges, routers, and gateways perform?
5. Name the three components that make up a network.
6. Differentiate between information services and interactive services and give an example of each.
7. Describe some methods for network security.
8. What is a computer virus?
9. Differentiate between hackers and intruders.
10. Name two methods that prevent unauthorized access to computer systems.

Discussion Questions

1. Research a topic on an on-line information service that interests you.
2. Discuss the advantages and disadvantages of electronic news services.
3. Discuss some guidelines for the selection and care of passwords.
4. Why is it necessary to have security measures on networks? Research and discuss situations in which security is breached, who does it, and how it can be prevented.

Use Yahoo to explore some networking topics. Log on to these sites:

INTERNET DISCOVERY

http://www.yahoo.com/Computers_and_Internet/

Networking_and_Communications/General_Information/

For example, to find information on Windows 95, use these addresses:

http://www.yahoo.com/Computers_and_Internet/
Operating_Systems/

Microsoft_Windows/Windows_95_Win95/Networking/

For client/server information, use this address:

http://dgoats.onr.com/clients.html

For loads of network management information, use this address:

http://smurfland.cit.buffalo.edu/NetMan/index.html

OFFICE AUTOMATION

A consensus . . . emerged in the late 1980s that the danger of sharing information with employees was minimal compared to the advantage of having an informed work force. . . . When employees had access to the same information as their managers, they were much more likely to understand decisions about needed workplace changes and to work cooperatively to implement those changes.[1]

<u>Office automation (OA)</u> is using computer and communications technology to help people better use and manage information. Office automation technology includes all types of computers, telephones, electronic mail, and office machines that use microprocessors or other high-technology components.

Knowledge workers using office automation include senior executives, managers, supervisors, analysts, engineers, and other white-collar office workers. In most offices, information is the end product, often in paper form. Office automation is essential for managing, organizing, analyzing, and conducting the company's business. OA systems keep track of the information originating in various processing operations throughout the company, such as order processing, accounting, inventory, manufacturing, and so on. Office automation provides knowledge workers with information-producing systems to collect, analyze, plan, and control information about the many facets of the business, using text, voice, graphics, and video display technologies.

The term office automation was first used in 1955 to describe computer-automated bookkeeping, an adjunct of data processing. The term—and to some extent the entire notion of automating the office—fell into disuse as the emphasis turned to management information systems. Toward the end of the 1970s, renewed interest came about when futurists such as Alvin Toffler envisioned the "office of the future." By the mid-1980s, office automation was a popular concept once again. The road to OA has been a bumpy one, from being a poor cousin to data processing to finding its own identity in text and information processing.

---

1. Joseph H. Boyett and Henry P. Conn. *Workplace 2000: The Revolution Reshaping American Business* (New York, Dutton, 1991), 49.

CHAPTER 17

Module A

Text and Document Management

Why It's Important to Know

Text and document management is an activity in which all knowledge workers participate. The nature of the document and the way knowledge workers use it is changing dramatically. Learning to work with documents of various types, in various forms, is a key productivity skill.

In the past, a single knowledge worker may have been responsible for collecting, organizing, analyzing, and formatting a printed monthly report of his or her department's activities. Today, several people contribute information based on their individual areas of expertise—supervisor, analyst, sales manager, and so on. Data is collected from several applications, either on disk or transmitted across the local area network. Significant tables or charts are electronically turned into overhead transparencies or color slides. The monthly report may be distributed electronically rather than on paper, and the subsequent meeting to discuss its contents may occur on-line, using electronic mail, without all parties being present in a conference room. In fact, the sales manager, who is traveling, may participate from a remote site using a notebook computer.

Today's office automation technologies are used to managing the following types of information:

- *Text*. Written text form

- *Data*. As in numbers or other nontext forms

- *Electronic data*. Such as e-mail

- *Graphics*. Including drawings, charts, and photographs

- *Video*. Such as captured images, videotapes, or teleconferencing

- *Audio*. Such as phone conversations or dictation

Figure 17.1 shows a state-of-the-art office.

In some cases, two or more of these types of information are combined in a compound document. Figure 17.2 shows a system designed to handle these various types of information.

As this text has stressed, people are the most important component in any computer system. Knowledge workers are found in many different occupations in modern business, turning data into useful information. A hundred years ago, office workers were treated in much the same way as factory workers, performing rote tasks under strict supervision. As you will see, today's knowledge workers, and the work they perform, have redefined office work.

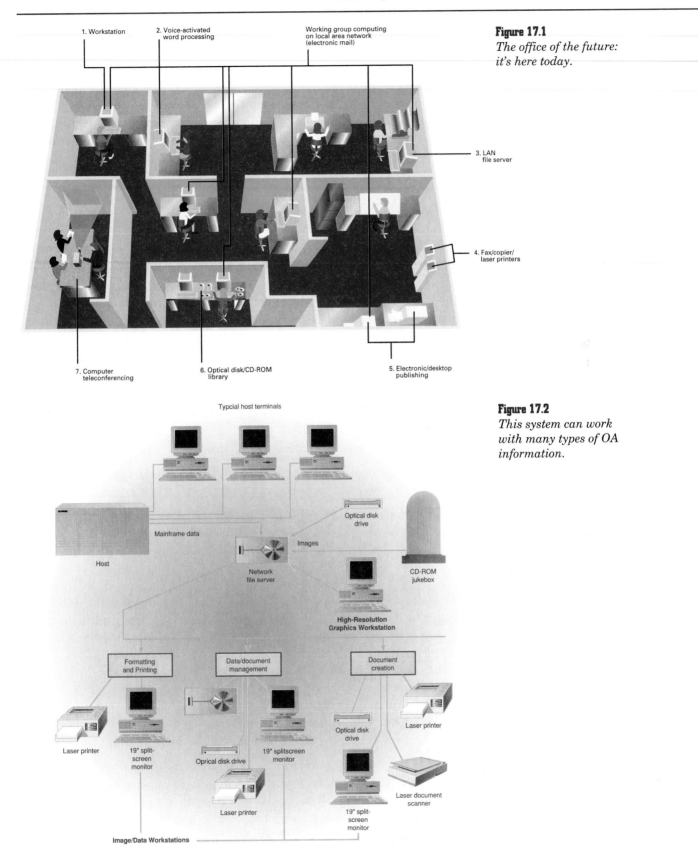

1. Workstation
2. Voice-activated word processing
Working group computing on local area network (electronic mail)
3. LAN file server
4. Fax/copier/laser printers
5. Electronic/desktop publishing
6. Optical disk/CD-ROM library
7. Computer teleconferencing

Figure 17.1
The office of the future: it's here today.

Typcial host terminals
Mainframe data
Host
Network file server
Images
Optical disk drive
CD-ROM jukebox
High-Resolution Graphics Workstation
Formatting and Printing
Data/document management
Document creation
Laser printer
19" split-screen monitor
Oprical disk drive
19" splitscreen monitor
Laser printer
Optical disk drive
19" split-screen monitor
Laser printer
Laser document scanner
Image/Data Workstations

Figure 17.2
This system can work with many types of OA information.

Office tasks involve a great deal of thinking and decision making. People need to be comfortable but alert for knowledge work. As a result, hardware and software engineers turned to the study of ergonomics in order to ensure that office systems be easy and healthy to use. Office equipment must be designed so that it can easily be used by any knowledge worker, regardless of background. With the advent of computers, ergonomics engineers became particularly interested in OA systems, furniture, and environments for the knowledge worker.

Text Management Systems

A **text management system** is a database management system (DBMS) that is capable of locating, sorting, retrieving, indexing, and storing large quantities of text-based documents. The scope of a text management system includes documents created by typewriters, word processing systems, PCs with word processing, desktop publishing, text editing systems, and even computerized typesetting equipment. Text management systems are used for

- Writing memos, notes, letters, and other short documents requiring little if any revision

- Printing envelopes and labels

- Preparing preprinted forms, such as invoices or purchase orders

- Composing longer documents, such as proposals and reports, that involve several reviews and revisions

- Retrieving and editing documents that are often reused, such as form letters and contracts with standard replaceable (boilerplate) text

- Creating display documents, from advertising brochures to in-house or client newsletters or other documentation

AT&T Federal Systems Advanced Technologies has a Proposal Development Engineering facility in Greensboro, North Carolina. Their work involves preparing high-quality documents, or proposals, for U.S. Government bids. Technical writers from all over the country write and edit the text and send it on disk or electronically to Greensboro. The documents are then published, incorporating different fonts, drawings, graphic images, and formatting. Because these proposals must be published without delay, and they often must meet strict federal guidelines for size, length, and other details, timeliness and accuracy are extremely critical to the publishing operation.

In addition to its ongoing proposal preparation, the Proposal Development Engineering facility is developing a proposal database. Most proposals contain approximately 50 percent new information, but a great deal of repetitive information can be reused, such as facility and business plans, personnel resumes, product descriptions, and so on. Knowledge workers are currently creating a text library of this boilerplate information. The key is to index the library so that items can be easily found. Using a text management system has eliminated a great deal of paper, as well as an awkward and outdated system for organizing and storing old paper proposals.

Document Management Systems

OA demands that data be immediately accessible and instantaneously retrievable. For that reason, businesses are slowly moving away from paper toward document forms that can be stored on the computer. In order for computer systems to be truly useful, they must be information managers. Managing raw data is not enough; it is far more important to manage and retrieve the information stored in documents.

A **document management system** aids in filing, tracking, and managing documents, whether they are paper- or computer-based. The document may be a word processing file, a spreadsheet, a database, or a file from another application, such as an image file. Document management systems exist for many different uses, such as an on-line information retrieval company or insurance agency client files. These systems can organize documents for entire divisions of a company on a mini or a mainframe, or on a personal computer for smaller applications.

InfoWorld magazine reports, "To hear certain analysts and vendors talk about it, compound document management will be the next killer application for the enterprise. These emerging systems, which provide access, storage, and tracking of discrete document elements, will enable large organizations to make better use of the information stored in memos, letters, and reports. Once used only by isolated departments, document management systems are being enhanced to appeal to entire organizations through support for a broad range of data type—including images, video, and sound."[2]

Office Automation Technologies at Work

Three technological trends have created today's office automation environment. One trend is the rise of the personal computer because of its suitability to perform many routine office tasks. Knowledge workers who previously didn't have access to the corporate computer are now able to do their own computing. Another trend is the local area network, which has greatly facilitated sharing information. The third trend is client/server technology, helping people work together while ensuring that all have the computing power they need. This is the ideal OA environment.

The Integrated Desktop

Software makes it possible for today's knowledge worker, using a PC or workstation, to have an integrated electronic desktop. In the new highly integrated office applications environment, all the various office management functions are available on the PC, at the touch of a key. An example is Microsoft Office 7.0 for Windows 95, which creates an integrated work environment for all productivity applications: word processing, spreadsheet, database management system, presentation software, and personal scheduler. E-mail can be created and sent using the word processing application.

2. Doug Van Kirk. "Getting a Grip on Unstructured Data," *InfoWorld*, May 22, 1995, 51–54.

According to Microsoft, desktop productivity software is 59 percent of all software sold; sales of Microsoft Office have increased fourfold between 1993 and 1995.

The key to this integration is a compound document architecture called OLE, which stands for object linking and embedding. OLE was developed by Microsoft as a way to transfer portions of documents between applications without losing any of the characteristics of the originating application. OLE works like this:

- An *object* is a document, or a portion of a document. If the object is a word processing object, it retains all its text formatting. If the object is a worksheet, it retains its spreadsheet formulas.

- A *link* is a connection between two documents, where the document in the receiving application contains a reference to the document from the originating application. Changes made in the original document are made in the receiving application when the original document is updated.

- *Embedding* means that a copy of the document from the originating application is made in the receiving application. Changes made in the original document are not transferred to the linked document.

OLE is a copy and paste operation. Linked or embedded objects are inserted using the Paste Link or Paste Special commands. Microsoft has created a new version of OLE for Office 7.0 called DocObjects, that makes it possible for documents created by several different applications to be treated as if they were a single object. Once this compound document, or document object, is created, it is saved in a file format called an Office Binder. Figure 17.3 shows an example of an Office binder document.

Figure 17.3

An Office binder holds various documents as a single compound document.

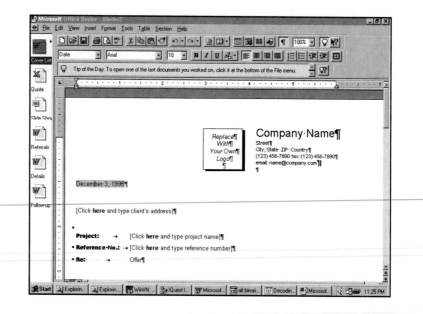
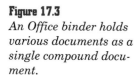

Large System Integration

Office automation in large systems expands on the multitasking, multiuser concept. In large systems, it isn't always necessary that every knowledge worker use the same brand of application, such as WordPerfect; sophisticated software interfaces and file conversion utilities make it possible to exchange data between PC, mini, and mainframe applications. This additional functionality makes it possible to create standards for applications that apply across the company so that the emphasis is on the business benefits, not on trying to make the technology work properly. The ideal situation is to make the entire computer system transparent to knowledge workers so that their concentration is on obtaining and properly utilizing information in order to make decisions.

Digital Equipment Corporation's All-in-1 integrated OA software includes word processing and text management, electronic mail, facsimile, database management, a calendar and appointment scheduler, computer teleconferencing, and many other features. With All-in-1, if a knowledge worker receives an e-mail message, her terminal or PC beeps to signal an incoming message. If a meeting time or date is changed, each attendee automatically receives an electronic message.

What the knowledge worker cares most about is the type of work—writing, calculating, referencing, and so on—and quality of the work being accomplished in this kind of OA environment. Because All-in-1 operates on an all-digital network of high bandwidth, it is capable of voice, data, and image processing. For example, an editor can make voice edits to a written document; an insurance underwriter can view a videotape of a ship that he is to insure; and digitized color photographs of employees and work-in-progress can be filed.

Perhaps the best thing about All-in-1 is the diversity of the applications that run seamlessly with one another in a full multitasking environment. It's hard to tell when you leave one application and begin another because all applications perform similarly. Clicking a file name opens the application that created it. Whenever the knowledge worker is presented with a new task or challenge, Help brings answers.

Integrated OA technology is confirmation that knowledge workers want applications that perform consistently, from word processing to spreadsheets to database management systems. Unfortunately, the element of selectivity is removed; if you don't like the way one application works, you're stuck. The alternative is to cobble together separate applications that often won't share data easily or effectively.

As object-oriented computing takes firm hold over the next few years, great improvements in individual and office-wide systems will be seen. With each improvement in technology, we move closer to working with information and documents, without being constrained by a particular vendor's software. More and more, software is being designed with the knowledge worker involved in the process.

HOME PAGE

WORKFLOW AUTOMATION: ANOTHER FORM OF DOCUMENT MANAGEMENT

One of the pervasive problems of the Information Age is productivity. Computers were intended to improve knowledge worker productivity. Even though the American knowledge worker's productivity leads the world, it still isn't repaying the investment made in technology. Put another way, the computer still requires too much manipulation, and the knowledge worker still has to do too many nonessential tasks, such as backups, moving files, converting data, and so on. The computer is not yet the brain lever it was envisioned to be.

Workflow automation software is designed to address this problem. It is a set of tools for developing applications to manage work processes, measure the results, and revise the processes to make them more efficient. Workflow automation software works with the DBMS. It performs many of the simple, repetitive tasks that computers ought to do for knowledge workers but don't.

Workflow automation software addresses the work *process*, looking not at tasks but at the cumulative results. Its main feature is its capability to shorten the time that work sits around waiting for someone to do it. Any time a number of tasks are involved in a work process, the software can find ways to take up the slack, reduce wasted time, and speed up the process.

Workflow automation software was born due to a need to manage the complex tasks computers are capable of while still being able to manage the work people do. For example, a mail order company might install hardware and software that speeds up the input phase of customer orders, but unless the orders can be directed to appropriate processing, they back up and slow down the input phase.

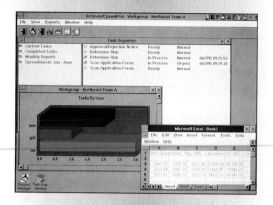

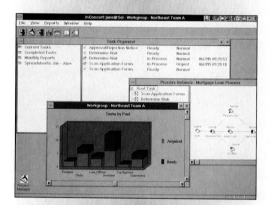

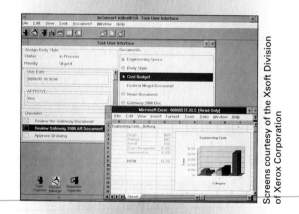

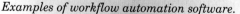

Examples of workflow automation software.

Screens courtesy of the Xsoft Division of Xerox Corporation

An example of a simple use for workflow automation software is managing expense reports for a group of sales reps, in which various categories of expenditures must be separated and categorized. A more complex use is exemplified by *TV Guide* magazine, which uses workflow automation software for the overwhelming task of producing more than 100 distinct editions of TV listings for 21 million viewers each week. The new system, called Workflow Management System or WMS, coordinates all the documents that comprise the magazine and coordinates them for various editions. For example, local baseball or basketball games are compiled for inclusion in one region, while general-interest articles are included in all editions. The *TV Guide* staff previously had to accomplish 10,000 separate tasks each week to publish the magazine—most of them by hand. Now, WMS does many of these tasks automatically, without errors or forgetfulness.[3]

HOME PAGE REVIEW QUESTIONS

1. What kind of tasks are a lingering knowledge work problem?

2. How does workflow automation software solve this problem?

3. What aspect of the process does the software address?

---

3. Lee Thé. "Workflow Tackles the Productivity Paradox," *Datamation*, August 13, 1995, 65–73, and Deborah Asbrand, "TV Guide stays on schedule with workflow app," *InfoWorld*, September 11, 1995, 56.

Knowledge Check

1. What is office automation?
2. What is the purpose behind ergonomics?
3. What are the different types of information used in OA?
4. For what is text management used?
5. For what is document management used?
6. What technology is used in creating compound documents?
7. What is an object?
8. What is the goal of all office automation?

Key Terms

document management system   office automation (OA)   text management system

Is There Privacy in On-line Groups?

The following excerpt was posted to the RISKS Forum on the Internet:

Date: Tue, 24 Oct 1995 19:09:53 -0400

Subject: DejaNews [Deja vu all over again]

Internet Services Accused of Privacy Violations

[This appeared in *The Boston Globe*, 23 Oct 1995.]

(C) 1995, Simson L. Garfinkel

Simson L. Garfinkel, Globe Correspondent

An Internet service that catalogs and indexes messages from electronic bulletin boards is drawing criticism for possibly violating the privacy of the network's users. DejaNews Partners taps into the Usenet global electronic bulletin board network, makes a copy of every message, and stores and indexes them for easy public retrieval. The service has quickly become the fastest and most powerful way for savvy Internet users to find answers to questions, locate lost friends, or even take the pulse of the wired public.

Executives at San Antonio-based DejaNews seem perplexed at the near daily messages they receive from computer users who complain that what the company is doing amounts to an invasion of privacy. "When you post to Usenet, it automatically gets propagated to tens of thousands of computers," said Steve Madre, president of DejaNews Partners. "So anybody who posted something to Usenet and then later on has any kind of privacy concerns about it must have seriously misunderstood what they were doing."

But it's not just DejaNews' archival retrieval system that has some cyber-surfers worried. It is the fact people are unaware their messages are being archived and, perhaps even more insidious, the program's capability to form user profiles of people who post messages—grouping them by the specific subject matter on which they most frequently correspond.

"No one ever mentioned to me that it was possible to take a different program and run a search on what you've written," says Peter Crone, a local graphics designer who reads Usenet through his account with The Internet Access Company, of Bedford. "Maybe this is as obvious as the sky being blue to techies, but this is the first I've heard of it." According to Dejanews, Crone posted three articles to the Usenet between July 27, 1995, and September 2, 1995, to the user groups "rec.arts.startrek.current," "rec.arts.sf.tv," and "rec.arts.sf.starwars." Thus, simply by looking up Crone's name on DejaNews, it is possible for anybody on the Internet to conclude that Crone is a science fiction buff and that he likes *Star Trek* and *Star Wars*. "It feels a little like a phone tap or something," says Crone. The Usenet system is divided into more than 10,000 such special interest "groups," each with its own self-descriptive name, such as "rec.autos.makers.saturn," for Saturn car lovers, and "alt.politics.usa.republican," for devotees of the Republican National Party.

CRITICAL THINKING

1. Is capturing names from a public source, as described in this article, an invasion of privacy?

2. At what point does the data—a person's name—become information?

3. If the person's name and interests are made public information, should the person be permitted to decide whether that information should be made public?

4. How might this information be used? List any harmful or harmless ways you can think of.

Module B

Business Analysis

Why It's Important to Know

> **Business analysis systems track business performance and help analyze various productivity factors. Office automation tools for business analysis are essential for strategic planning.**

A manager or executive needs solid data from which to extract the information necessary to make good decisions for the business. In the past, these knowledge workers had to rely on their experience and other personal factors to make decisions. A **business analysis system** provides data that when used with the proper software, aids in business analysis and decision making.

Spreadsheets are routinely created by corporate power users for such things as cost-benefit analyses and creating budgets. Yet there are other computer-based software tools for performing business analyses, as well. Two that are commonly used are decision support systems and executive support systems.

Decision Support Systems

Since its origins in the late 1970s, the **decision support system**, or **DSS**, has evolved in its usefulness and the tasks it performs. A decision support system, as its name implies, helps a manager extract information from various MIS databases and reporting systems, analyze it, and then formulate a decision or a strategy for business planning. The DSS does this by collecting data and then analyzing it with special modeling software.

A manager, for example, can create a scenario to see what would happen if a product's sales skyrocketed or if a division were closed down. The software creates charts and graphs from the data, showing how expenses, profits, and other financial factors would be affected. Some DSSs have an artificial intelligence component to help formulate decisions and analyze outcomes.

Executive Support Systems

The **executive support system**, or **ESS**, is designed for top management who often want nothing to do with a computer. Typically, the ESS is a PC with brilliant color graphics and easy-to-use software that can present data with just a keystroke or two, as shown in figure 17.4.

Figure 17.4

An executive support system.

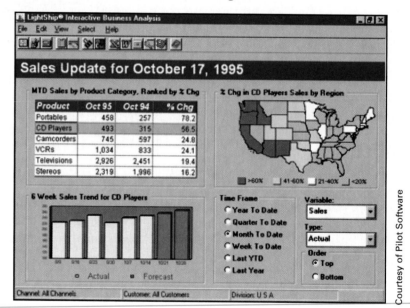

Courtesy of Pilot Software

The idea is to create an executive tool that isn't intimidating. The ESS replaces conventional reports, such as a thick stack of computer printouts, that contain only a few items of interest to the executive. The ESS has access to the corporate mainframe and is capable of projecting most of the information in graphical form. Using the ESS, the executive can evaluate the company's performance and track product lines, create scenarios for future product introductions, plot emerging trends in the industry, or plan new directions in which to take the company.

A Case Study

TransCanada PipeLines (TCPL), with headquarters in Calgary, Alberta, Canada, transports natural gas over 11,000 km of pipeline in Canada as well as the United States. Several years ago, a number of changes in business dynamics, such as deregulation, pipeline expansion, the need to expand markets, and the demand for new services, led to TCPL's reevaluation of its information systems directions. This, in turn, led to the installation of a network of Macintosh personal computers. Once the new information infrastructure was in place, the MIS organization was able to create an important application that has helped transform the way senior management uses information systems at TCPL.

Up until a few years ago, the chief executive officer, chief operating officer, senior vice presidents, and vice presidents received mostly paper-based reports. They felt that the Macs on their desktops were being underutilized and wondered if they could be used to better access the information they needed. The project became known as GIS, or Graphical Information for Senior Executives. A team of three or four people worked on two aspects of the project. One aspect was interpreting and translating the paper-based reports to the user interface. The second was working with other information systems staff and knowledge workers to understand what information was needed.

The team conducted short interviews with the knowledge workers—senior managers—and then quickly created modules for them to work with for a few weeks. The modules contained specific information, presented graphically as a pie graph, line graph, bar graph, or as custom layouts, such as maps or diagrams. After soliciting feedback, the team adjusted the module and returned it to the knowledge worker. This cycle was usually done for two to three iterations, until the module was complete. Each module was created by a member of the project team and took between two and four weeks to complete, depending on each member's experience.

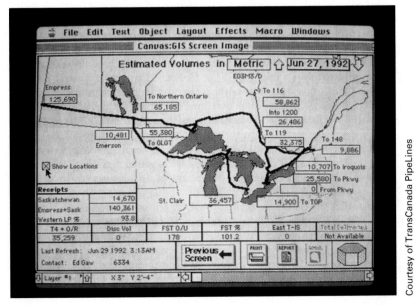

Figure 17.5
The TransCanada PipeLines GIS.

Courtesy of TransCanada PipeLines

The various report categories helped determine the visual metaphor on the opening screen—a rotating hexagonal nut that reflects the engineering nature of the company with each side representing a control panel. Each control panel corresponds to a report category, with a title and accompanying icon for identification. Reports provide information in the categories of Pipeline, Construction, Planning, External Information, Human Resources, and Financials. Clicking and holding the mouse button on an icon produces a pop-up menu list of the modules available in the category.

Pipeline is the largest category, containing extensive information about the pipeline, its operation, and the gas flows. The screen presents a map of the TCPL pipeline with gas flow information displayed at key points. Volume can be displayed in either metric or Imperial units. The date in the upper right corner is the current date; the arrows permit moving ahead or back in time. Clicking any value on the map results in the display of a line chart showing the trends at that location over the current month, as well as the preceding month. When the screen is loaded, all the past, present, and forecast data is retrieved at once, so that it is instantaneously accessible.

At the bottom left corner of the screen is a status box, displaying the date and time the data was last refreshed and the name and telephone extension of the *information custodian* responsible for the information presented in the modules. Generally, these custodians were previously responsible for providing senior management with paper reports; now they do the same work electronically. The information is either automatically updated from the source system and transferred to GIS from a Microsoft Excel spreadsheet, or GIS reads the source files directly.

Senior management enjoys using GIS; they are receiving more information than was previously available, in a more useful and understandable format and more quickly than on paper. What's more, GIS has triggered a constant stream of ideas and requests for ways to make the system even more worthwhile.

"No amount of technical expertise alone can create a system such as this," says Dr. Doron Cohen, vice president of MIS. "It is important to understand that first you must have a technical infrastructure. By that I mean you must understand the hardware, software, and communications architecture that is the basis for information systems. Second, you must have a cultural infrastructure; that is to say, there must be a sound relationship within MIS as well as between MIS and the business people we serve. We strongly believe in teamwork, and we have a clearly defined set of values that guide the way we work and interact with people. We believe in forming partnerships with the users and that providing continuing support for them is extremely important. Yes, the GUI is a beautiful screen, and we are very proud of our GIS. But it was only possible because we looked at the changing business world of TransCanada PipeLines, and changed our MIS infrastructure along with it."[4]

4. Jack B. Rochester. "Presenting Information," *I/S Analyzer*, July, 1991.

Artificial Intelligence

The software technology called **artificial intelligence**, or **AI**, attempts to replicate many human thought processes, such as reasoning, learning, self-improvement, and associative learning in a computer. The goal that many AI researchers are striving for is a machine that can think. On the immediate horizon is simply to have smarter programs. Raymond Kurzweil, a leading proponent of artificial intelligence, says, "I believe that by the end of this century, AI will be as ubiquitous as personal computers are today. The majority of software will be intelligent, at least by today's standards."

Expert Systems

Computer systems are capable of storing and randomly retrieving information in close approximation to how a human would do it, and it is here that AI has achieved the most success. These computer systems are called expert systems. An **expert system** offers solutions for problems in a specialized area of work or study, based on the stored knowledge of human experts. Expert systems have been developed for medicine, oil exploration, civil engineering, food preparation, monitoring plant operations, and hundreds of other applications. For example, MYCIN is an expert system that can diagnose blood and bacterial infections, based on information from doctors stored in its knowledge base, and then recommend antibiotics for treatment. In another example, when the chief cook at Campbell's soup decided to retire, they stored his recipe preparation knowledge in an expert system.

Neural Networks

Another AI technology is **neural networks**, which use various connections between input, processing, and output. A neural network may be either a software or hardware technology; recently, the first neural network integrated circuit chip was developed. Neural networks in software have been in use in business for several years, where their great strength is in recognizing patterns in data. For example, Chase Manhattan Bank, the second largest credit card issuer, uses neural network software to detect credit card abuse patterns in transactions. If a card is used repeatedly in a short time, or just after a card has been reissued, it could mean that the card has been stolen. The neural network was exposed to the patterns of legitimate and illegitimate credit card use until it "learned" how to detect fraud. The neural network also learned to detect new and emerging types of fraud. In this way, Chase Manhattan Bank was able to reduce the time between detecting possible misuse or fraud from three days to just one, saving the bank untold millions of dollars.[5]

---

5. Jack B. Rochester. "New Business Uses for Neurocomputing," *I/S Analyze,* February, 1990.

HOME PAGE

THE WISDOM OF TEAMS

In *The Wisdom of Teams*, Jon R. Katzenbach and Douglas K. Smith define a team this way: "A team is a small number of people with complementary skills who are committed to a common purpose, performance goals, and approach for which they hold themselves mutually accountable."[6]

James Martin cites Katzenbach and Smith in his book, *The Great Transition*, and goes on to say, "It is important to distinguish between a team and a working group. A team and a working group may be the same size and may have the same work to accomplish, but they operate altogether differently. In a workgroup, one individual is in charge, and each member behaves as an individual. There is *individual accountability*. In a team no one individual gives orders to the members; the members work out collectively what to do. The team has *collective accountability*."[7]

Katzenbach and Smith cite six characteristics of real teams: small size, mutual accountability, the right mix of skills, common meaningful purpose, specific performance goals, and a common approach. They also demonstrate the ascendancy of team work over group work, as shown in the following chart:

6. Jon R. Katzenback and Douglas K. Smith. *The Wisdom of Teams* (Boston: Harvard Business School Press, 1993), 45.

7. James Martin. *The Great Transition: Using the Seven Disciplines of Enterprise Engineering to Align People, Technology, and Strategy* (New York: AMACOM, 1995), 85–93.

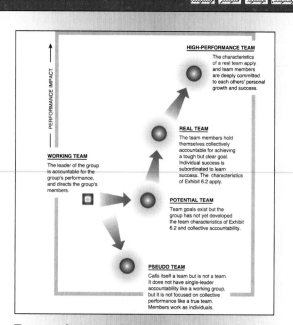

Team performance (based on Katzenbach and Smith).

HOME PAGE REVIEW QUESTIONS

1. What is the difference between a workgroup and a team?

2. Describe some situations where a workgroup is preferable; where a team is preferable.

3. From your experience, characterize a high-performance team.

4. All things being equal, would you rather work in a group or a team?

Knowledge Check

1. What is the simplest form of a business analysis system?
2. Who uses a decision support system?
3. What is the purpose for executive support systems?
4. When would you need an expert system?
5. What advantages are gained with a neural network?

Key Terms

artificial intelligence (AI)   business analysis system   decision support system (DSS)

executive support system (ESS)   expert system   neural networks

ISSUES AND IDEAS:

Monitoring Employees by Computer

According to the U.S. Government Office of Technology Assessment, more than 26 million employees have their work tracked electronically, and more than 10 million employees are paid according to computer-monitored performance evaluations. The personal habits of knowledge workers can be monitored either by viewing their computer screens to see what they are doing or by reading their electronic mail messages. Some say that we live in a surveillance society and that we make daily choices about what we are willing to give up about ourselves.

Apparently, the purpose behind tracking employees is to ensure high productivity, but people being people, it often turns into something more. Some recent studies have shown that tracking employees is counterproductive because, among other reasons, it increases stress. A focus on quality of work, not quantity of output, makes workers happy and productive.

CRITICAL THINKING

1. What do you think about tracking employees?
2. Is there ever a time when it would be a good idea to track employees?
3. If some tracking of employees is done now, is it fair to assume that more will be done in the future?

Module C

Workgroup Computing

Why It's Important to Know

Workgroup computing is the most important trend in office automation and knowledge work. It is a means of bringing people together to use collaborative work methods with client/server computing and networking in order to be more productive.

Knowledge workers used to be defined by department or function. Today, people are selected to work together for their knowledge and skills to accomplish a task or project and then regrouped to work on the next project. This is called **collaboration**, and it simply means working together.

Collaboration becomes more effective with the aid of computer systems. Collaboration is sometimes referred to as computer-supported collaborative work, and the knowledge workers working together are often referred to as a workgroup. Collaborative workgroups make use of PCs and workstations in local area networks, often connected to the corporate computers for downloading data, using everyday applications, electronic mail, and sometimes special workgroup software.

Workgroup Computing

Many knowledge workers are more productive and enjoy their work more when they work together in small, collaborative groups. A workgroup is comprised of knowledge workers, each with different job duties or tasks, but all are working toward a common goal. Workgroup computing is spreading throughout business organizations and encompasses all four of the different systems discussed previously.

Groupware is a software product designed for sharing information—both text and graphical—from both corporate and on-line sources among networked PCs and workstations. Lotus Notes is groupware that helps people track ideas, analyze data, create continuing dialogs with one another, and present results. Groupware such as Lotus Notes, shown in figure 17.6, helps knowledge workers present ideas, organize information, create brainstorming sessions, obtain feedback, and solve problems within workgroups.

Lotus Notes reduces the time that a workgroup spends in live meetings by providing a 24-hour forum. People can log on or off the system from their office, from a PC at home, or from a notebook on the road. Recipients can read the meeting dialog and add their comments; the group then works on the project until everyone agrees on a decision or course of action. Some people say that in an on-line forum, they feel more comfortable saying what's really on their minds.

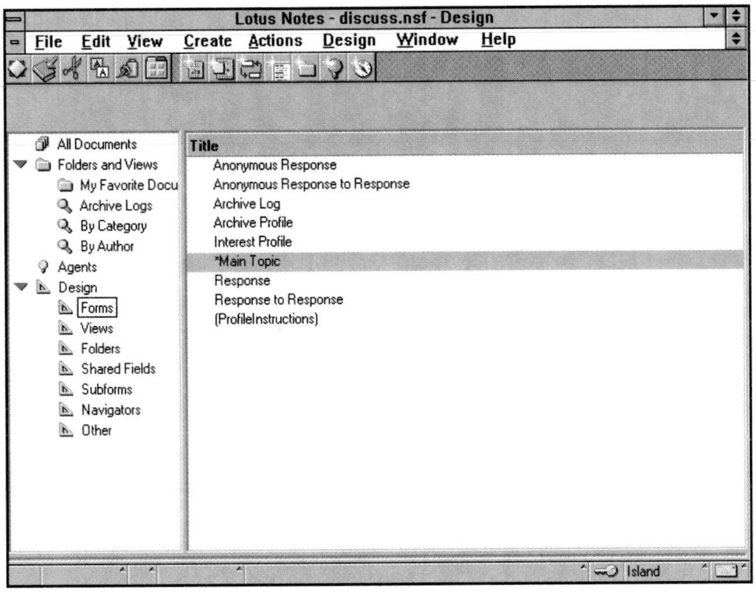

Figure 17.6
*Lotus Notes uses folders
to organize workspaces.*

Lotus Notes is a client/server application that requires three computers. One computer is the server, which maintains the primary databases and acts as an administrator for work and communication between the client computers (there must be at least two clients). Each client has a set of folders for his or her personal use as well as for workgroup and enterprise-wide purposes. Enterprise-wide folders, for example, can be for products, sales, research, administration, finance, customer service, and so on.

All clients share in the use of databases, which they can access from the server. Clients can work with a dynamic copy of a database at their PC for better access and convenience. Clients can communicate with each other via e-mail and through discussion groups. The discussion groups are an especially good way to share information and help each other solve problems. Other services include a real-time news service and an on-line electronic library.

Lotus Notes is used by executives for planning and strategy, by groups, such as traders in a mutual funds financial brokerage, and by information systems developers creating software requirements for new applications. Once again, we see how the Information Age has changed the way we communicate.

A Case Study

The Coast Guard's National Pollution Fund Center (NPFC) plays a major role in the nationwide pollution response system. Among NPFC's daunting responsibilities are all liability and compensation issues related to oil spills, including certifying financial responsibility for vessels operating in U.S. waters, providing funding for assessing damages due to spills, funding efficient clean-up efforts, compensating for damages, and recovering clean-up costs from polluters. All these duties fall to a staff of fewer than 100, so high productivity is key to NPFC.

NPFC must move quickly to respond to all requests and situations because time is always crucial when dealing with oil spills. As anyone who watches the evening news knows, oil spills are a serious problem, and the NPFC has a steady and substantial caseload, with more than 1,000 active cases at any given time. Cases generate a great deal of information, claims, and documentation from many different sources including state and local governments, natural resources trustees, fishermen affected by coastal spills, insurance agencies, clean-up contractors seeking payment, and Native American tribes. In short, NPFC deals with anyone affected by an oil spill.

All this case information must be integrated into one comprehensive case file accessible to each member of an NPFC case team. NPFC's responsibilities also require a great deal of correspondence, including responding to Freedom of Information Act (FOIA) requests.

Finally, because NPFC is a relatively new agency (created by the Oil Pollution Act of 1990), it is still developing internal policies, which must be thoroughly discussed before they are approved. The agency's charter also specifies that the group must be managed using the principles of Total Quality Management (TQM).

Given NPFC's geographically distributed staff and strategic charter, workgroup computing and Lotus Notes emerged as a possible solution to the challenges faced by NPFC. The agency decided to perform a pilot test with one case team. "Most of our business is information," says Lt. Commander Ernest Del Bueno of the NPFC. "Our whole case team concept depends on the ability to share information efficiently." These teams include case officers and other individuals who provide the various expertise necessary to handle a case.

The NPFC pilot test identified the following major benefits of workgroup computing and Lotus Notes:

- *Better access to case information.* The paper-based case files used by the NPFC were bulky, inefficient, and vulnerable to loss. The shared databases of Lotus Notes enable all authorized NPFC staff members to enter and access case information. Using Lotus Notes Document Imaging, the NPFC scans all case-related faxes and mail, ensuring that comprehensive records are available to all team members at all times. Now when an oil spill is assigned a Federal Project Number, all related information is automatically routed to the case file.

- *Better case management.* At any given time, the NPFC faces approximately 2,200 half-active or "open" cases on-line. Lotus Notes helps ensure that no case information falls through the cracks. Each case officer may handle more than 100 cases at a time; therefore, efficient case management is a priority. Case officers appreciate the "tickler" system, which reminds them of actions required on their cases.

- *More efficient correspondence.* Generating forms and correspondence can be a chore for any business, and even more so given NPFC's high volume of paperwork. Now that Lotus Notes enables NPFC to develop a library of standard correspondence, staff can enter and customize the letters, add information, and route the correspondence electronically for on-line review and approval.

- *Faster response to customers.* An important part of NPFC's vision is rapid response to the public it serves, and Lotus Notes helps speed up this response. The NPFC's hotline staff has complete, on-line case files for reference during customer calls. Lotus Notes also enables the NPFC to quickly respond to Freedom of Information Act (FOIA) requests with the click of a mouse, automatically generating FOIA versions of case files for approval and immediate release.

As the NPFC works with Lotus Notes, they continue to find new ways to use Lotus Notes' advanced technology to improve the quality of their work. The quick development capabilities of Lotus Notes enable the NPFC to create new applications and adjust current applications to better match their needs. The NPFC finds the flexibility of Lotus Notes a welcome change from previous applications developed in other platforms, which were not as fast or flexible.

Officials at the NPFC praise the unique benefits that Lotus Notes brought to their organization in a relatively short period of time:

"Lotus Notes' development capabilities let us get up and running quickly. We were able to develop and prototype the system on the fly and create applications that users feel comfortable with. It's a very good package, and is easy to use from all perspectives—users and developers." - George Cognet, Chief of the Information System Branch

"We're a fairly new group, so we don't have established processes. Two years ago, as we began to get established, we lost a lot of information and thinking. Now, with Lotus Notes, our people are beginning to create databases for policy discussions. Lotus Notes gives us a record of these discussions so we can see someone's reasoning and track responses. Now good ideas don't go out the window. Lotus Notes captures good thinking. I've been very impressed with Lotus Notes. As someone who has been in software development for years, I know it really is a super set of software. I've been trying to break it, and so far I haven't been able to." - Linda Burdette, Claims Manager

"With our pilot Lotus Notes system, we can tap our case files to create collective information that wasn't available before. That's a major step forward for case management. In our case team pilot, Lotus Notes has really improved our work processes and saved time. I'm totally sold on workgroup computing for increasing productivity." - Robert Hildebrand, Senior Case Officer

HOME PAGE

RAY OZZIE, THE MAN WHO CREATED LOTUS NOTES

"One of the top five programmers in the universe," is what Bill Gates said of him in "The Office That Ozzie Built," an article in The New York Times Magazine. "A Chicago native, [Ray] Ozzie graduated from the University of Illinois at Urbana in 1978 and entered the world of offices, bouncing from Data General to Software Arts to Lotus before coming up with the Iris business plan, which had been turned down by several venture capitalists by the time [Lotus's then-CEO Mitch] Kapor signed on." In 1984, Kapor provided Ray Ozzie with $1.2 million in seed money to start Iris Associates, and to create one of the most innovative software applications in the world.

. . .Naturally, Iris's programmers spend most of their time alone with their computers. They don't like being interrupted by phone calls and knocks on the door. Meetings are infrequent. When they do happen—a brief encounter in the hallway or periodic gatherings around computers to resolve disagreements—they're not for exchanging information. Ozzie believes that's a waste of time because computers do that far more efficiently. People, on the other hand, are necessary for one thing Ozzie admits computers aren't very good at: expressing emotions.

. . . By funneling most of the daily office work through Lotus Notes, Iris tried to prove that a company can scatter its departments all over the world. And it can draw important people from the outside—suppliers, subcontractors, consultants—into its cyberspace office. All the information is encrypted with sophisticated technology available within Notes. Time and distance become meaningless as entire companies can "live in Notes," as users phrase it.

In 1995, IBM paid $3.5 billion for Lotus Development Corporation, the parent company of Iris Associates, twice its market value. "Soon it became clear who IBM was after. Within days, the press was referring to Ozzie as "the franchise," the Shaquille O'Neal of the software world. His colleagues teased him as "the three-billion-dollar man."

. . . The new industry in office networking programs, called groupware, is booming. Sales of Lotus Notes have at least doubled every year since its release in 1989; 10,000 companies are using it, including Chase Manhattan, General Motors and Delta airlines. Some believe that IBM now owns the most promising challenge to Gates and Microsoft's hegemony this side of a court order. Ozzie's ambition is for Lotus Notes to be on every last one of the world's estimated 70 million networked business PCs.

The most frequent claim about Lotus Notes is that it will fundamentally and forever change the way people work. More than our physical space, Lotus claims, the computer screen will *be* the office. To compete in a fiercely competitive global economy, companies will need to forsake the old, slow way of doing business—with meetings, by telephone, on paper, through the mail—and communicate almost entirely with networked computers. In other words, the way Ozzie works.[8]

HOME PAGE REVIEW QUESTIONS

1. Why do you think IBM bought Lotus?

2. How will Lotus Notes "fundamentally change the way people work"?

3. Explain how Lotus Notes is a product of "the way Ozzie works" and a particular style of working in his profession. Compare that with the comment about how businesses need to change their old ways in order to compete. What does this say about the direction of communication in the business world?

---

8. Paul Keegan. "The Office that Ozzie Built," *The New York Times Magazine*, October 22, 1995, 49-51.

Knowledge Check

1. What does collaboration mean?
2. What is workgroup computing?
3. What kind of software is required for workgroup computing?
4. What are some of the characteristics of this software?
5. What are some of the benefits of workgroup computing?

Key Terms

collaboration   groupware

ISSUES AND IDEAS

The "Dumbing Down" of the Workforce

A recent concern has been the issue of what is termed the "dumbing down" of the workforce. Rebekah Wolman, writing in *Information Center* magazine, says, "Sometimes the introduction of computer technology 'deskills' jobs—allowing grocery store clerks to slide items over bar-code readers or fast food cashiers to press illustrated buttons on their cash registers." The result is that people will not learn or will forget how to use a simple calculator or make change without the help of the machine.

Wolman continues, "But often, technology introduces reading into jobs that never required it before. And the overall effect of the information revolution has unquestionably been to make jobs more demanding. By making it easier to produce goods inexpensively, quickly, and flexibly, technology has changed the terms on which our economy competes, and with them, the jobs of our workers."[9]

CRITICAL THINKING

1. What does "dumbing down" mean to you personally?
2. Are the skills people have lost important skills? Should we make efforts to preserve them?
3. How can we help people to work with common sense as well as with computers?

---

9. Rebekah Wolman. "Technology and the Basic Skills Crisis," *Information Center*, January 1990, 16.

ETHICS

Working in a Group

Human beings are, by nature, competitive. It's part of the survival instinct to want to get ahead in life. For many years, people have used war terminology and metaphors to describe business practices. It's no secret that certain people will do unethical—even illegal—things to make money or boost their careers. But can we say, "All's fair in love and war?" This is an issue of particular concern in the office, where so many people can easily gain access to your computer and the data stored on it.

Workgroup computing is founded on the premise that people work *together* to achieve common goals. There should be respect for others' rights, privacy, and data in such an environment. However, it is likely that in the real world unethical people will read other knowledge workers' private files; in fact, some might even sabotage a colleague's work to make him or her look bad. To some extent, security systems should take care of this, but as the old saying goes, locks only keep honest people honest.

What can you do? You can help keep honest people honest by not creating temptations. Keep your computer secure; conceal your password, and follow the company's security precautions. Keep your personal data on a floppy disk; lock it in your desk, or take it home with you at night. Be sure that all your important work is backed up and stored in more than one location—on more than one computer system or on a disk you keep with you.

Finally—and this is the hardest part—realize that you are part of the problem as well as part of the solution. Encourage your fellow employees, through polite conversation and example, to behave ethically. Find shared values and beliefs and discuss them; people who are moral and honest find it difficult to wrong those they know personally. And when you see illegal or unethical things occurring, discuss them with your supervisor. To do otherwise makes you an accomplice to wrongdoing, and it also makes it easier to look the other way the next time it happens.

Kenneth R. Andrews, a former professor of management and editor of the *Harvard Business Review* for many years, writes in his book, *Ethics in Practice: Managing the Moral Corporation*, that "Commitment to quality objectives—among them compliance with law and high ethical standards—is an organizational achievement. It is inspired by pride more than by the profit that rightful pride produces."[10] Everyone must work together for an ethical workplace.

---

10. Kenneth R. Andrews. *Ethics in Practice: Managing the Moral Corporation* (Boston: Harvard Business School Press, 1989).

Critical Thinking

1. How must competitiveness be balanced with respect for others?

2. What is the single most important way that you would want other workers to behave ethically toward you?

3. What actions can you take to ensure that the rights and values of others are respected?

THE LEARNING ENTERPRISE

Conduct a performance analysis of your workgroup, comparing it to the benefits that can be derived from using workgroup software such as Lotus Notes. You'll probably find that workgroup software brings everything you've been doing together with a high degree of integration.

Prepare a proposal for your instructor in support of having workgroup software installed. Explain your document management systems, your business analysis systems, and how you're presently using stand-alone or integrated application software. Make it a collaborative document; have each knowledge worker in your department or function offer his or her opinion of why you need workgroup software.

Finally, prepare a collaborative report assessing how your workgroup, your department, and your enterprise are using information technology to achieve your organizational goals and accomplish your mission.

Chapter Review

Fill in the Blank

1. The technology used to create compound documents is called
   _____ or _____.

2. The _____ helps managers extract and analyze business information in order to formulate business strategy.

3. Hardware and software engineers study _____ in order to ensure that office systems are easy and healthful to use.

4. The software technology that attempts to replicate human thought processes is called _____.

5. In the field of AI, a(n) _____ offers solutions for problems in a specialized area of work or study based on the stored knowledge of human experts.

6. An AI technique that mimics the way nerve cells are connected in the human brain is called _____.

7. Working together on a project to accomplish a task is known as

   _____.

8. A software product designed for sharing information among networked computers is called _____.

9. Knowledge workers in offices spend most of their time working with

   _____.

Circle the Correct Answer

1. In OLE, the (object, link) is a document or part of a document.

2. The (executive support system, decision support system) is an easy-to-use software application that enables management to analyze and evaluate information.

3. The study of human safety factors in working with machines is called (ergonomics, neural networks).

4. (Expert, Decision support systems) require the stored knowledge of experts to perform their tasks.

5. (Groupware, Embedding) means a copy of the document from the originating application is made in the receiving application.

6. (Document management systems, Business analysis systems) help keep track of important information in a type of database management system.

7. Business analysis systems may use the (spreadsheet, DBMS) for analysis.

Review Questions

1. What is meant by office automation?
2. What are three technology trends that have created the office automation of today?
3. Give several examples of the kinds of information that office automation manages.
4. Define text management and give several examples of how it is used.
5. Define document management and describe how it is used.
6. Name the technology that enables you to create compound documents.
7. Differentiate between linking and embedding.
8. Name two commonly used computer-based software tools for performing business analyses.
9. What are the short-term and long-term goals of artificial intelligence?
10. Describe four major benefits of workgroup computing.

Discussion Questions

1. Lotus Notes, which helps knowledge workers share information and track discussions, is an example of which type of application?
2. Discuss the different aspects of working in groups, and compile a list of advantages and disadvantages.
3. Why is business analysis so important? Be specific.
4. Explain how OLE works and why you would personally find it useful.

ON LINE DISCOVERY

To learn more about Lotus Notes, obtain the Groupware White Paper from

http://www.lotus.com

To learn more about collaboration and document management, visit

http://www.collabra.com/

accumulator. A register that temporarily stores the results of continuing arithmetic and logical operations.

acoustic coupler. A modem with two cups into which the telephone receiver fits.

active cell. The current cell, highlighted in a spreadsheet.

algorithm. A limited set of step-by-step instructions that solves a problem.

alpha testing. Entering various kinds of data to see how the program reacts under different conditions. These tests are normally conducted in-house by the people who created the system.

applets. Small programs that act like desktop accessories. Some of these simple programs are small applications that work only within the operating environment.

application. A specific purpose for which the computer is used.

application development environment. In DBMS, a set of programming tools used to create custom applications.

application generator. A DBMS programming tool that permits programming either by using English-like commands or by making selections from menus.

application software. Computer programs designed to perform tasks with the computer.

arithmetic-logic unit (ALU). One of three components of the central processing unit; performs arithmetic and logical operations. See also *central processing unit (CPU), storage*.

arithmetic operations. ALU functions that perform addition, subtraction, multiplication, and division.

artificial intelligence. A software technology that attempts to replicate in a computer many human thought processes, such as reasoning, learning, self-improvement, and associative learning.

ASCII. Acronym for American Standard Code for Information Interchange. A standard for telecommunications file transfer requiring that all the special codes and formats from the application program be stripped from a file. An ASCII file is also called a text file.

attribute. A characteristic of an entity.

automatic call dialing (ACD). A computer-managed electronic dialing function for outgoing calls.

automatic number identification (ANI). A computer-assisted operation used to identify the number of the caller dialing in. ANI uses its computer circuitry to identify the number from the telephone network, displaying it on a computer screen or an LCD readout.

autosave. A feature that is preprogrammed to save open files without your command.

back up. To make extra, or duplicate, copies of your programs and files for safekeeping.

bandwidth. A measurement of the amount of data that can flow through a communications channel.

BASIC. The most popular programming language used by personal computer owners; most commonly an unstructured language. BASIC stands for Beginner's All-purpose Symbolic Instruction Code.

batch processing. Taking data that is collected in a batch over a period of time, and then usually input, processed, and output in one session. See also *transaction processing*.

baud (bps). The unit for measuring signal speed, roughly equivalent to one *bit per second* (bps).

baud rate. The data transmission speed at which modems are classified.

beta testing. Letting knowledge workers test a new system under actual working conditions but before the program goes into production.

binary number system. A mathematical system based on just two numbers or digits, 1 and 0.

BIOS. Acronym for basic input/output system. Programs permanently stored in the computer. The BIOS programs load the operating system and also check and coordinate the peripherals, such as the keyboard, monitor, and disk drives. BIOS is often called system software.

bit. The basic unit of data recognized by a computer.

bit map. A high-resolution display in which each dot, or pixel, on the screen is represented by one bit by the computer.

bit-mapped graphic. The graphic image created by a pattern of pixels; usually color.

boldface. To accentuate type characters by making them darker.

boot. To load the operating system in computer memory.

bridge. Computer circuitry that links phones and computers together.

browser. An application designed to help you search for WWW sites and display Web documents.

bug. A program or hardware problem.

bus. On a main circuit board, an electronic pathway between computer components.

business analysis system. A system that provides data which, when used with the proper software, aids in business analysis and decision making.

bus network. A network with no central computer that shares other network resources in common. See also *local area network (LAN)*.

byte. A group of bits on which the computer can operate as a unit.

C. A programming language similar to assembly language but incorporating many of the statement features of high-level languages.

cache memory. A special set of fast random-access memory chips used to store data that the CPU most frequently accesses from RAM.

Calculate. An automatic calculation command built into a spreadsheet's operation.

carrier or **carrier signal.** A tone indicating that the computer is available.

cell. The intersection of a column and a row. Cells can contain text, numbers, or a formula.

cell address. The column-and-row position used to identify cells.

cell pointer. The highlight that illuminates the particular cell in which it is located, taking the place of the cursor to indicate where data may be entered.

centralized computing. The concept of keeping all MIS functions in one location or facility.

central processing unit (CPU). The computer's processing, control, and internal storage circuitry. The CPU is an integrated circuit chip containing the electronic circuitry that controls the interpretation and execution of instructions that are issued by an input device. See also *arithmetic-logic unit (ALU), storage.*

click. To make a selection using the mouse.

client. A PC used by a knowledge worker; the "front end" of a client/server system.

client/server. A database system used by a group of knowledge workers in a specific workgroup, division, or department.

clip art. Universally recognized images available in books or stored on computer disks.

clock speed. The measure of CPU speed, or the pace at which processing takes place.

coaxial cable. A type of wiring used by cable television companies and many computer networks.

COBOL. A structured programming language most widely used in business; COBOL stands for COmmon Business-Oriented Language.

code generator. A software program used to create a large portion of the source code.

coding. Programming in a specific programming language or languages; creating source code for a program.

collaboration. Working together. In today's office, collaboration is sometimes called computer-supported collaborative work. See also *groupware*.

column. The cells running vertically down a spreadsheet screen, identified with alphabetic letters (A, B, C, and so on).

command. An instruction given to the computer.

command language. A collection of terms, often called keywords, and special expressions that the operating system understands and executes.

command line. The portion of the screen where DOS commands or instructions are issued.

command line interface. A human-computer interface that requires typing a command in the proper syntax. See also *graphical user interface, menu-driven interface*.

communications management software. An application that controls computers that receive calls requesting access from remote computers. Also called dialup or host software.

communications protocol. The hardware and software standards for communications between computers.

communications software. An application that turns a PC into a terminal capable of sending data to and receiving data from other computers.

compact disc read-only memory (CD-ROM). An optical disk that holds approximately 650M, the equivalent of 452 1.44M floppy disks.

compiler. A special type of program that translates entire files of source code into object code, which in turn becomes an executable file.

complex instruction set computing (CISC). A microprocessor or CPU architecture and operating system design that can recognize 100 or more instructions. See also *reduced instruction set computing (RISC)*.

compound document. A single file that has been created using two or more applications.

computer-aided software engineering (CASE). A methodology especially designed for programmers in large information systems organizations who need to quickly create new applications or reengineer older applications.

computer architecture. The design and implementation of computer systems in an organization.

computer literacy. (1) Being knowledgeable or educated in how to use a computer. (2) Having an understanding of the computer's impact on your daily life. In addition, computer literacy means using computers properly and ethically.

computer-output microfilm (COM). Miniature photography used to condense, store, and retrieve data on film.

computer system. People using data and procedures to work with software and hardware components.

computer-to-machine output. The I/O process that controls machine operations, maintains heating and cooling, and turns lights on and off at prescribed times.

computer virus. A program that corrupts or "infects" computer files by inserting a copy of the virus itself.

computer worm. A program that damages computers by duplicating itself from one computer's memory to the next; a relative of the computer virus.

concentrator. A controller and multiplexer combined into one peripheral to manage, amplify, and ensure the integrity of data signals.

constant. The raw number or data entered for processing.

controller. A peripheral device that routes data between the CPU and the terminal.

control unit (CU). One of three components of the central processing unit; directs the step-by-step operation of the computer. See also *arithmetic-logic unit (ALU), central processing unit (CPU), storage.*

conversion. A change from one DBMS program (or other application) to another.

cooperative processing. The capability of different computer systems to exchange data among their diverse operating platforms.

coprocessor. A microprocessor support chip that takes over when additional or special processing is needed.

copyright. Information ownership, including the areas of personal, business, and external sources. Copyright applies to unique and individual expression in writing.

cursor. Usually a blinking rectangle or a blinking underline that indicates where the next keyboard character typed will appear on the screen.

cut and paste. To move portions of files, often created by different applications, from one file to another. See also *object linking and embedding (OLE).*

cybernetics. The comparative study of human and machine processes.

cycle. The length of time it takes the CPU to process one machine instruction.

cylinder. A vertical stack of tracks on a disk.

data. Facts, numbers, and other symbolic representations, suitable for communication or interpretation. A single unit of data is termed a *datum*; *data* is the plural term. See also *information, knowledge.*

database. A group of related records and files.

database administrator (DBA). The information systems professional responsible for maintaining the DBMS and ensuring the accuracy and the integrity of its data.

database management system (DBMS). An application that organizes data into records in one or more databases and allows organizing, accessing, and storing of the data in a variety of formats.

database services. Information services whose primary purpose is to provide comprehensive information.

data collection device. A hand-held, computer-like source-data input device used for such tasks as scanning UPC codes for inventory purposes.

data definition. In DBMS, the process of creating a detailed description of the data.

data dictionary. In DBMS, a list of all the fields, files, and commands used in manipulating the database.

data entry. The process of entering data into computer memory and issuing commands that tell the processor how to work with the data.

data processing. Preparing, manipulating, and storing data.

data refinement. In DBMS, the interaction or relationships among various data elements.

data representation. In DBMS, the characters used to present data to the computer for processing in a language it understands; or an organized method for storing data about an entity in a database.

debugger. A system software program that helps programmers identify program errors.

decision support system (DSS). A system that helps a manager extract information from various MIS databases and reporting systems, analyze it, and then formulate a decision or a strategy for business planning.

demodulate. To reconvert the analog telephone signals into digital signals the computer understands.

desktop publishing (DTP). Combined word processing and graphics applications with advanced formatting capabilities.

digital camera. A video input device that takes still photographs and transfers them directly into the computer through the serial port.

digital computer. A computer that uses the binary arithmetic system as the basis for its operation.

digitizer. An electronic drawing tablet used as an input device.

direct access. A method to quickly retrieve data stored in a particular memory location with a specific address. Also called random access. See also *sequential access*.

direct access storage device (DASD). Magnetic disk drives used for secondary storage. They may be either floppy disks or hard disks.

directory. A list of the files stored on a disk or a portion of a disk.

directory designation. An indication of which directory you are using presently.

disaster recovery. A plan or program that goes into effect in case of fire, flood, or loss of electrical or telecommunications services.

disk drive designation. A letter telling you which drive is "logged," or in use.

disk operating system (DOS). The collection of programs that manage the computer's internal functions and control the computer's operations.

distributed computing. Placing MIS functions where they are most effective.

document. A self-contained work, created by a knowledge worker using a computer and an application program, that can be saved and later retrieved as a file.

documentation. The instructions that accompany a system or an application. See also *reference documentation, user documentation*.

document management system. A system that aids in filing, tracking, and managing documents, whether they are paper or computer-based.

domain. The description of a particular computer on the Internet, identified by name and type of organization. An example is endor.com.

dot-matrix. Output produced by printers that use wires in the print head.

dot-matrix printer. A printer that produces output by moving wires in the print head.

dots per inch (dpi). The measure of printer resolution that counts the number of dots that can fit into a linear inch.

double-density disk. A disk that doubles the capacity of a double-sided disk. See also *high-density disk*.

double-sided disk. A disk that can be written to on both sides.

downloading. Receiving files from a host computer.

drafts. Successive versions of a document.

drag. To hold down the pointing-device button while you move the pointer through data.

driver. A software program used to provide a common logical interface between two hardware devices. Sometimes referred to as a *device driver*.

dumb terminal. A video monitor and keyboard connected to a large system that performs the simplest input and output operations, but no processing.

dynamic link. A connection created with the object between two documents. See also *object linking and embedding (OLE)*.

electronic. A machine that uses components such as vacuum tubes, transistors, or silicon chips.

electronic bulletin board. An interactive service that permits posting and receiving electronic mail messages; sometimes called a BBS or CBBS.

Electronic Data Interchange (EDI). The use of communications networks to transfer forms, such as invoices, purchase orders, shipping notices, and even payments.

Electronic Funds Transfer (EFT). The use of communications networks to perform financial and banking transactions.

embed. In object linking and embedding (OLE), placing an object from one application into another without having the ability to change or update it.

encapsulation. In OOP, the addition of a high degree of functionality to each object, making it reusable. See also *inheritance*, *polymorphism*.

encryption. The use of coding devices at each end of the communication line to prevent transmissions from being intercepted and read by unauthorized people.

end-user computing. Giving knowledge workers their own computers so that they can be more productive in their work.

entity. Data that has a particular meaning; something about which data is to be collected in a database.

ergonomics. A study exploring the human factors surrounding the design of computers, office environments, furniture, and other aspects of the work area to make them more healthy and easy for people to use.

error checking. The process by which networked computers ensure the accuracy and integrity of data transmissions.

executable. A file that can be read and run by the CPU; with PCs, a file with the .EXE extension.

execution cycle. The portion of the machine cycle in which the data is located and the instruction is executed.

executive support system (ESS). A system for top management that utilizes a PC with brilliant color graphics and easy-to-use software that can present data easily.

expansion card. A printed circuit card with circuitry that gives the computer additional capabilities.

expansion slots. Long plug-in strips at the left rear of the main circuit board. Expansion cards are inserted into these strips, or receptacles.

expert system. A system that offers solutions for problems in a specialized area of work or study, based on the stored knowledge of human experts.

Explorer. The program in Windows 95 that permits working with folders and files. See also *File Manager*.

external modem. A modem enclosed in a case and connected to the computer with a cable.

facilities management companies. Vendor companies that contract for and run a corporation's entire information systems operation.

facsimile (fax). The transmission and reception of digitized images over telephone lines. Facsimile turns text, characters, graphics, or whatever type of image into patterns of tiny dots.

FAQ. An abbreviation for Frequently Asked Questions, a document that contains questions and answers designed to help new users of on-line services.

fax modem. A device that can send and receive faxes as well as data.

fiber optic cable. A type of wiring made of glass fibers; used as a communications medium.

field. A group of characters that represents an attribute.

file. A group of related records or a collection of related data, identified and stored with a unique name. The file is the primary unit of data storage.

file conversion utility. A utility that translates files from other formats so that the program you're using can read and edit the files.

file format. A series of patterns, standards, and codes that identify the unique data stored in the file by the application that created it.

File Manager. In Windows 3.*x* and earlier, the feature that enables knowledge workers to work with drives, directories, and files, either graphically as icons or in a conventional tree directory structure. See also *Explorer*.

file name. A unique designation for a file created with an application; in DOS, a file name contains up to eight characters, followed by an optional period and a three-character file name extension.

file name extension. An optional three characters added to a file name.

financial model. A mathematical representation of a real-world financial or economic situation, used to test different hypotheses in order to find a solution.

Finder. The Macintosh operating environment.

floating operations per second (FLOPS). The measurement of supercomputer performance.

floppy disk. An inexpensive, removable storage medium for storing instructions and data.

format. The process of preparing a floppy disk or hard drive for use by the computer system.

formatting. Emphasizing and arranging text on the screen or the printed page, most commonly in word processing.

formula. In spreadsheet applications, a mathematical operation performed on the values, or numbers, in specified cells to produce a new value or relationship. See also *function*.

FORTRAN. A high-level programming language; it stands for FORmula TRANslator.

fourth-generation language (4GL). A database front-end tool that uses English-like phrases and sentences to issue instructions.

frame. In desktop publishing, a box that contains text or graphics.

front end. A software tool that enables knowledge workers to work flexibly with databases, ranging from access to data analysis to creating custom databases and database applications.

FTP. An abbreviation for file transfer protocol; a means of transferring files while ensuring that no errors occur during transmission. FTP is both a standard and a program for uploading and downloading files on the Internet.

function. In spreadsheet applications, a preprogrammed, named and stored procedure or set of routines that performs a specific operation on the values or numbers in specified cells to produce a new value. See also *formula*.

game port. A port used specifically for the joystick.

gas plasma display. A deep orange, flat-panel display composed of three sheets of glass with plasma, an illuminant gas, between them.

general-purpose computers. Computers used for a variety of tasks without the need to modify or change them as the tasks change.

gigabyte (G). Approximately one billion bytes, or 1G.

graph. A graphic or a diagram that displays data.

graphical user interface (GUI). A software design that enables knowledge workers to use color and graphics, icons, pull-down menus, and a pointing device to issue commands and instructions. See also *human-computer interface*.

graphics. Pictorial representations; a photograph, illustration, cartoon, painting—just about any visual image.

groupware. A software product designed for sharing information, both text and graphics, from both corporate and on-line sources, among networked PCs and workstations. See also *collaboration*.

hacker. A person who demonstrates great skill in programming and working with computers.

handshaking. Synchronizing two communicating computers for data exchange.

hard copy. A draft of a document in a paper form.

hard disk drive. A secondary storage medium that uses from two to eight disks, or *platters*, permanently sealed in a case. Each has its own read/write head, but all move together to read and write to the disk.

hardware. The components or physical devices that make up a computer system.

Hertz (Hz). A unit of measurement of electrical vibrations. One hertz equals one cycle per second.

high-density disk. A disk that has the number of tracks doubled or quadrupled. See also *double-density disk*.

high-level languages. Programs written using English-like words as instructions.

highlighting. Either reversing the characters or changing the display color of a selection.

high resolution. The monitor's capability to display sharp, crisp video with curving lines, shading, detail, color, and so on.

host. The computer in charge of a data communications work session.

HTML. An abbreviation for Hypertext Markup Language; an easy-to-use programming language you use to create a home page on the Internet.

HTTP. An abbreviation for Hypertext Transport Protocol; a protocol designed to support the hypertext links between documents.

human-computer interface. The way the computer and its software are presented to the human being who is using them. See also *command line interface, graphical user interface, menu-driven interface*.

hypertext. A way of preparing a computer-created text document that allows you to access and move through it nonsequentially. World Wide Web home pages are hypertext documents.

I-beam pointer. The shape the pointer takes on when you move it into the work area.

icon. A type of graphics; an on-screen symbol that represents a program, a data file, or some other entity or function.

impact printer. A printer that prints by striking characters on paper. See also *laser printer*.

import. To bring a file created by another type or brand of application into the one currently in use.

Index. A DBMS command that retrieves data quickly.

indexing. The process by which the read/write head moves to the outer edge of the disk to find data in its various locations.

information. An organized collection of facts or data. See also *data, knowledge*.

Information Age. A society in which information has become a commodity, has value, and is bought and sold.

information engineering. A software development methodology that brings knowledge workers, management, and information systems personnel together into a working partnership.

information services. On-line services that maintain and provide access to data repositories.

information utilities. On-line services that combine information and interactive services to provide access to news, extensive databases, bulletin boards, shopping services, and so on.

infrared transmission. A communications medium that sends signals via a beam of infrared light.

inheritance. In object-oriented programming (OOP), giving objects within a specific class the capability to share attributes with each other. See also *polymorphism*.

inkjet printer. A printer that transfers characters and images to paper by spraying a fine jet of ink.

input. The instructions or data given to the computer.

insertion point. The place on-screen that identifies where the next character you type will appear.

instruction. A group of characters organized in an action statement, which the computer understands and can execute.

instruction cycle. The portion of the machine cycle in which the CPU fetches, or retrieves, an instruction from RAM and gets ready to perform processing.

instruction register. A register that holds an instruction—for example, to add, to multiply, or to perform a logical comparison operation.

integrated circuit. An electronic component with hundreds or thousands of electronic circuits on a single piece of silicon.

Integrated Drive Electronics (IDE). An interface used with hard disk drives in PC compatibles.

integrated software. The combination of several stand-alone applications, capable of freely exchanging data with each other, into a single program. Also called suite software. See also *stand-alone applications*.

interactive processing. Working on a computer that can display the output so that changes may be made or errors corrected before the processing operation is completed.

interface. The point where either a peripheral device or a human meets the computer. See also *logical interface, physical interface*.

internal modem. A modem mounted on an adapter card that slips into an expansion slot inside your computer.

Internet. A system of linked computer networks that encircles the globe, facilitating a wide assortment of data communications services including e-mail, data and program file transfers, newsgroups, and chat groups, as well as graphic images, sound, and video of all kinds.

Internet Service Provider (ISP). A computer or terminal designated for use with the Internet. It is sometimes called the Internet Access Provider, or IAP.

interoperability. The capability to perform any work task, regardless of its original resident operating platform, from any computer.

interpreter. Software that translates source code one line at a time for immediate execution by the CPU.

intruder. A person who is behaving either unethically or illegally in the use of computer systems; sometimes called a cracker.

italicize. To tilt text for emphasis.

joystick. A pointing device most commonly used for playing computer games.

kerning. Proportionally separating individual characters within a word to make text easier to read.

keyboard. An input device used to enter data or instructions.

keyword. A searchable term common to several topics.

kilobyte (K). One thousand twenty-four bytes, or 1K.

knowledge. A body of information or understanding acquired through experience and/or study. See also *data, information*.

knowledge worker. A person who routinely uses a computer in his or her work to enhance work productivity.

label. Text data in a spreadsheet.

landscape. A page orientation in which the width of the page is greater than the height; text and/or graphics are printed sideways on the paper (usually 11 by 8 1/2 inches). See also *portrait*.

laser printer. A printer that creates output by directing a laser beam onto a drum, creating an electrical charge that forms a pattern of letters or images and transferring them to paper. See also *impact printer*.

leading. Proportionally altering the space between lines of text.

ledger. A large book in which businesses record financial transactions, such as credits and debits. See also *spreadsheet*.

letter-quality printer. A printer that is similar to a typewriter and creates high-quality impact printing.

light pen. An input device used to draw, write, or issue commands when it touches the specially designed video monitor screen.

linker. A special program that combines various object code files, resolves the differences between them, and creates a finished executable file.

liquid crystal display (LCD). A type of flat-screen display commonly used with laptops.

List. A DBMS command to display information, such as fields or records.

local area network (LAN). A network that enables a small group of knowledge workers in the same geographic location to share data, programs, and hardware resources. See also *bus network, peer-to-peer network, ring network, star network*.

lockout. A security procedure in network software that enables you to have a specific number of attempts (usually three) at entering a correct user name or password. If all attempts are unsuccessful, the phone connection is broken. See also *password*.

logical interface. Software that sets up a form of communication between hardware

devices so that they "talk" to one another. See also *physical interface*.

logical operations. Functions of the ALU that compare two pieces of data to determine whether one is greater than, less than, or equal to the other.

logical operators. Symbols that specify the different relationships between items in a database.

log off. To issue a command to exit an on-line service.

log on. To present your on-line identification granting you permission to use the on-line service. Logging on consists of entering your user name and password.

low resolution. A screen image in which you can see lines, jagged edges, and graininess. See also *high resolution*.

machine cycle. The steps involved in processing a single instruction.

macro. A small program within an application or program (such as word processing) that saves a sequence of keystrokes to accomplish a specific task and replays them on command.

magnetic ink character recognition (MICR). A type of source-data input that allows the computer to recognize characters printed using magnetic ink.

magnetic strip. A place where data is encoded using magnetic ink, most commonly on the back of bank or credit cards.

main circuit board. The place where the computer's primary electronic circuitry resides. The main circuit board, which used to be called the motherboard, contains a number of electronic components that are essential in the processing and storage in some of the routing and control operations.

mainframe. A large, general-purpose computer capable of performing many tasks simultaneously for hundreds or thousands of people.

maintenance. The ongoing corrections, updatings, and improvements made to applications; part of the system development life cycle.

management information systems (MIS). A complex computer system, its people, and certain procedures that work with the enterprise to achieve business goals.

massively parallel processing (MPP). A parallel processing computer that uses hundreds to thousands of processors.

media. The physical material used to store data and instructions. An example is a floppy disk.

megabyte (M). Approximately one million bytes, or 1M.

memory. The computer's primary storage for instructions and data. See also *random-access memory (RAM), storage.*

menu bar. An area on the screen that displays related or associated commands grouped under appropriate selections.

menu-driven interface. A human-computer interface that presents a list of the commands, tasks, or projects most often worked with. See also *command-line interface, graphical user interface.*

microprocessor. The personal computer's CPU on a single integrated circuit. An integrated circuit chip combines the processing functions that required multiple—sometimes hundreds of—components or circuits in older, larger computers.

microwave transmission. A communications medium that beams high-frequency radio signals between earth stations.

millions of instructions per second (MIPS). The measure of CPU speed in mainframes and minicomputers.

minicomputer. A versatile, medium-sized computer that can be used by more than one person at the same time.

mnemonic. A term or word that is easy to identify, such as *ADD* for addition.

modem. Short for modulator-demodulator. A hardware device that allows computers to communicate via telephone lines.

modulate. To convert the computer's digital signals so that they can be transmitted over the analog phone line.

modules. Distinct, logical parts of a program.

monitor. A video display screen that presents computer work.

mouse. A hand-held device moved across the desktop surface to electronically move the pointer correspondingly across the screen.

multiplexer. A data communications peripheral device that splits one incoming data line into many so that more than one terminal can be used to service incoming data transmissions.

multitasking. Starting and using more than one program at a time on a single computer system.

native file format. The format in which a file was stored in its originating application.

network. Any system that connects two or more computers for the transfer of information.

network operating system (NOS). An operating system that coordinates activities among various computers and peripherals—ranging from disk drives to printers—connected in a network.

neural network. Either a hardware or software technology that uses many input, processing, and output connections to recognize patterns in data.

news services. On-line services that provide the latest news, including general interest, business, and financial news.

node. A point in a communications channel.

nonimpact printer. A printer that forms a character by means other than striking the paper, most commonly by using laser technology or spraying ink.

nonvolatile memory. A type of memory in which instructions and data are retained regardless of whether the computer is turned on or off.

object. (1) A set of prewritten instructions and data that form a program module. (2) A portion of a document or an entire document that is moved to another application's document using the cut or copy function, and the paste or paste special function.

object code. Programming code turned from source code into an executable file by a compiler.

object linking and embedding (OLE). The Microsoft technology that creates compound documents that can contain text, worksheets, database tables, graphics, audio, video, and so forth. See also *cut and paste*.

object-oriented database management system (OODBMS). A DBMS that uses objects to combine procedures, or instructions, with data and incorporate them together into a software entity.

object-oriented programming (OOP). A programming technique that puts prewritten modules of programming code and data together to form an unique programming entity that perfectly executes a specific routine. See also *inheritance, polymorphism*.

office automation (OA). The process of using computer and communications technology to help people better use and manage information.

on-line. Two computers in direct communication with each other.

open system. A computer environment in which all types and sizes of computers, regardless of their operating systems, can work together.

Open Systems Interconnect (OSI). A standard that separates computer-to-computer communications into seven layers or levels.

operating environment. A type of software that works between the operating system and the application software to make the computer system easier for knowledge workers to use.

operating platform. The computer, operating system, networking system, applications and services, and development languages and tools.

optical character recognition (OCR). Recognition of a specific typeface developed specially to be read by early scanners.

optical disk. Storage media read or written to with the use of a laser beam.

orphan. A bad break that occurs when the first line of a paragraph or a heading appears alone at the bottom of a page.

output. The product or result of computer processing.

outsourcing. A strategy used by companies that no longer want to operate their own MIS; another term for facilities management.

packet. A block of data prepared for data transmission.

packet-switching network. A data communications network that transmits data in blocks, or packets; used exclusively for computer communications.

paint program. An application that enables you to create colorful freehand drawings and paintings; an illustration application that designers use.

parallel interface. An interface designed so that data passes through it simultaneously, or all at once. See also *serial interface*.

parallel processing. Many processors working together so that many programs, operations, or transactions can be processed simultaneously.

parameters. The value or option settings you set to perform the actions you want.

password. A special character string unique to the individual using a computer, a type of software, or an on-line service; used to differentiate between authorized users and intruders. See also *lockout*.

peer-to-peer network. A network architecture in which every computer on the network is an equal and can act as a server, a workstation, or both. See also *local area network (LAN)*.

peripheral hardware. A hardware component that is physically separate from but connected to the processing hardware.

personal computer (PC). A self-sufficient computing machine equipped with everything necessary for a person to perform data processing tasks. It is a *stand-alone* computing machine, is designed for use by a single individual, and is usually small enough to fit on a desktop or to stand beside a desk.

personal digital assistant (PDA). A handheld computer that acts as an electronic organizer.

personal information manager (PIM). A database program that stores, organizes, and retrieves personal information once kept on paper.

physical interface. A connection between two hardware devices. The most common physical interfaces connect the system unit and peripheral devices. See also *logical interface*.

pixel. The dots of light that create the monitor screen display and determine its resolution.

plotter. A type of printer that uses inkjet technology to create scientific and engineering drawings, as well as other graphics, often in color.

point. To move the pointing device to an object on-screen.

pointer. The arrow or character you move across the screen using the mouse.

pointing devices. Peripherals that are used to move the cursor, usually working in conjunction with a keyboard.

point-of-sale terminal (POS). A source-data input device that scans the bar codes of the UPC to register the price, which is programmed into the host computer, as well as to deduct the item from inventory.

polymorphism. In object-oriented programming (OOP), the capability of a set of actions or routines to perform exactly as they are described, regardless of the class of objects they are applied to.

port. A connection from the main circuit board to a peripheral device.

portable. An operating system that can be used on several different computers, regardless of their manufacturers.

portrait. A page orientation in which the height of the page is greater than the width (usually 8 1/2 by 11 inches). See also *landscape*.

power user. A knowledge worker who can learn to use new applications quickly, has mastered most of an application's advanced features, and may know some application programming techniques.

PPP. An abbreviation for Point-to-Point Protocol; the preferred custom connect protocol program used to connect to the Internet. See also *SLIP*.

presentation graphics. Computer graphics or visuals for business that present numerical, statistical, financial, or other quantitative data in a pie chart, bar chart, line graph, or scatter graph.

primary key. A field that uniquely identifies the entity.

primary storage. The memory that holds instructions and data for immediate use by the CPU. See also *cache memory, secondary storage*.

printer. A device that provides a finished paper printout of the results of your work.

printing. Creating a hard copy of your document as the final step in word processing.

private branch exchange (PBX). The voice communications device used for routing telephone calls; also called a switchboard, computerized branch exchange (CBX), or private automated branch exchange (PABX).

private network. A closed communication system, usually confined to a particular company, governmental entity, or other group. See also *public network*.

processing. Executing program instructions by the computer.

processing hardware. All the components and physical devices necessary for the actual computing or processing of data.

production. The act of putting an application into daily use.

productivity. The measurement of an enterprise's efficiency, often defined by labor, or worker productivity.

program. A complete sequence or set of instructions directed to a specific purpose, written in a language the computer understands and executes.

Program Manager. In Windows 3.*x* and earlier, the utility that displays windows with the icons used to start programs and applications.

programmer. A person who understands the problem or task the computer is supposed to work on and can translate it into the language the computer understands.

programming. Creating instructions, in the form of programs, for computers.

programming language. A formally designed set of commands used to create sequential instructions that can be processed and executed by the computer.

project. An assignment for MIS to create an application for users in a business function.

prompt. A character or message that indicates the computer system is ready to accept a command or input.

proprietary. A computer system whose exact workings are private, protected information.

prototyping. In programming, creating a working model of a new application or system.

public network. An open communications network available for use by anyone, usually on a fee basis. See also *private network*.

pull-down menu. A menu of commands or selections that appears when the mouse button is clicked.

quarter-inch cartridges (QIC). Specially designed tape cassettes for backup.

query. In DBMS, a software tool or a function that extracts data from the database and presents it in a usable format.

range. In spreadsheets, a defined or highlighted section of a spreadsheet worksheet specifying the cells on which you want to perform an operation.

random-access memory (RAM). One of the three components of the central processing unit; a form of temporary storage where instructions and data are kept while being used. Also called main memory.

rapid application development (RAD). An information engineering technique designed to take maximum advantage of the integrated CASE (I-CASE) tools.

read. To get data and instructions from a source, such as the keyboard. See also *write*.

read-only memory (ROM). Memory chips that store permanent instructions that perform many routine tasks for the CPU; these instructions cannot be changed.

read/write head. The element in the data storage device that scans the magnetic surface of the disk. Reading the disk is searching for data or instructions; writing to disk is storing data or instructions. See also *read, write*.

real-time processing. Processing data immediately, as soon as it is input, and producing output just as immediately.

record. A collection of related data items or fields that a DBMS treats as a unit.

reduced instruction set computing (RISC). A microprocessor or CPU architecture that uses a condensed set of instructions for its operating system. See also *complex instruction set computing (CISC)*.

reference documentation. For the knowledge workers who will use the program, instructions that organize information in a nonprocedural way, such as listing commands alphabetically. See also *documentation, user documentation*.

register. A high-speed temporary storage area designed to hold instructions and data during processing.

relational database management system (RDBMS). A DBMS where the data is organized in different tables so that it can be easily stored and retrieved.

report writer. A DBMS tool that organizes and formats data into an attractive format for printing.

revising. In word processing, the process of rereading, changing, deleting, and replacing text you have written.

ring network. A network in which individual computers are connected serially to one another. See also *local area network (LAN)*.

root directory. The primary directory; subdirectories are stored under the root directory.

row. The cells running horizontally across a spreadsheet screen.

ruler. A tool for measuring the size of frames and columns in desktop publishing.

satellite transmission. A communications medium that beams high-frequency radio signals between satellites and earth stations.

saving. Storing a document or file on disk and giving it a unique file name.

scanner. An input device that uses a light-sensitive device to enter text (and, depending on the software, graphics) into the computer.

scrolling. Moving the contents of a file through the window you view, either vertically (up and down) or horizontally (left and right).

secondary storage. The hardware components that enable you to store programs and data permanently, or indefinitely, so that they may be used again. See also *primary storage*.

sector. A portion of a floppy or hard disk; pie-shaped wedges that compartmentalize the data into the addresses for the head to locate.

security procedures. Procedures that prevent someone from intruding in a network without proper authorization.

sequential access. The method of storing data in a particular order, such as alphabetically or by date and time. See also *direct access*.

serial interface. An interface in which the data passes through the interface sequentially. See also *parallel interface*.

server. The "back end" computer in a client/server system that holds data the client needs to process. Also called the file server.

shortcut. A small file linked to a program, document, or folder that immediately starts an application or a function.

single in-line memory module (SIMM). A plug-in memory unit used to add RAM to a computer.

SLIP. An abbreviation for Serial Line Interface Protocol; a custom connect protocol program used to connect to the Internet. See also *PPP*.

Small Computer System Interface (SCSI). An interface into which you can connect hard disk drives, CD-ROM drives, printers, modems, scanners, and so on.

smart modem. A modem that can automatically dial a number or answer a call, redial a busy number, and adjust to the characteristics of the modem to which it is connecting.

smart terminal. A terminal that has its own CPU or processing capabilities, as well as a built-in disk drive for storage.

soft copy. The output produced by the video monitor.

software. The programs and instructions that tell the computer what to do.

software ambiguity. The capability of a program to offer more than one way to perform a given task or execute a command, or not to behave in an identical manner each time the program performs a task.

software engineering. The aspect of computer system development that involves the design, development, and implementation of production software systems on large-scale business computers. See also *system development life cycle*.

Sort. A DBMS command to arrange data in alphabetical or numerical order.

sort keys. In DBMS, the fields used by the Sort command to separate records.

source code. The program, written in a specific programming language, that is sent to the computer for processing.

source data automation. The process of feeding data directly into the computer without human intervention.

spaghetti code. Programs, or code, not written sequentially, or with little regard to rules or good organization.

special-purpose computers. Computers designed and used solely for one application.

speed. The rate at which information is conveyed over a communications channel, expressed in bits per second, or bps.

spreadsheet. An application that performs *number processing* and electronically simulates an accountant's worksheet, enabling you to add and revise numerical data and formulas for a wide variety of financial work.

stand-alone applications. Individual applications that work alone. See also *integrated software*.

star network. A network that provides access to central files and system resources through a host CPU. See also *local area network (LAN)*.

statement. An expression of instruction in a programming language.

storage. Holding programs or data in hardware components so that it may be processed. See also *memory*.

storage devices. Hardware components that hold data for long-term puposes; usually housed in the system unit.

storage register. A register that temporarily holds data retrieved from RAM, prior to processing.

streaming tape drives. Specially designed tape cassettes for backup.

structured analysis. The use of data flow diagrams to chart a system's progress.

structured coding. The first structured technique; a result of the need for a more organized way to write programs. All programs can be written using three basic constructs: sequence, selection, and looping.

structured design. In programming, a method that uses the top-down approach to break a problem into parts and arrange them into a hierarchy, according to their size and level of detail.

structured programming. A way of programming that requires the programmer to write programs in well-defined sections, which are compiled in sequence.

structured query language (SQL). The standard query language for relational database management systems.

structured techniques. Structured analysis, structured design, and structured programming used to create more reliable and easily maintained programs that are also orderly, readable, and easily understood by others.

style sheet. A template used by an application and containing a list of all the specific design characteristics—for example, margins, headers, footers, font styles for the various elements of the document, and so on—that makes document design progress more quickly and smoothly.

subdirectory. Additional directories stored under the root directory. Subdirectories help keep your programs and data well organized and easy to find.

supercomputer. A special type of computer commonly used to perform a single, very complex task that requires massive processing power.

syntax. In programming, the set of rules governing a computer language's structure and statements.

system development life cycle. The traditional method of creating a system or an application. Consists of analysis, design, coding, debugging, and testing and acceptance. See also *software engineering*.

systems analysis. The study of an activity, a procedure, or an entire business to determine what kind of computer system would make it more efficient.

systems analyst. The information systems professional who gathers and analyzes the data necessary to develop the new application.

systems design. The activity of planning the technical aspects for a new system.

system software. All the programs used to operate and maintain a computer system.

system unit. The cabinet in which the computer's electronic and mechanical components are stored.

T-1 switch. A peripheral device that takes calls from a single incoming line and routes them to another computer or controller that disperses them to their destination.

taskbar. An application launcher and task switcher, in the form of a bar at the bottom of the Windows 95 screen.

TCP/IP. An abbreviation for Transfer Control Protocol/Internet Protocol; the set of standards and protocols for sharing data between computers on the Internet.

telecommunications. The process of sending data, including voice, from one computer-like device to another. Also called communications or data communications.

Telnet. A program that enables you to connect to a remote computer and interact with it.

template. A predesigned form to help you quickly create commonly used documents, such as letters, resumes, reports, fax forms, and memos

terabyte (T). Approximately one trillion bytes, or 1T.

terminal. A keyboard and monitor connected to a mainframe or minicomputer.

terminal emulation. The use of a simple communications program to turn your PC into a terminal for communicating.

text editor. In programming, a utility used to write, erase, and manipulate words on the screen; similar to a word processor, but without many of the formatting features.

text management system. A database management system (DBMS) that is capable of locating, sorting, retrieving, indexing, and storing large quantities of text-based documents.

thermal printer. A printer that uses heat to form a nonimpact image on chemically treated paper. See also *laser printer*, *nonimpact printer*.

Thesaurus. A word-finding program that suggests synonyms, antonyms, and related and contrasting words in word processing.

time-sharing. A technique in which many people can use a computer system simultaneously for different purposes or applications.

topology. The layout of computers and other devices and how they are connected.

touch-sensitive screen. An input device that permits using the finger as the input device.

trackball. A pointing device that performs like a stationary, upside-down mouse to move the cursor on the screen.

tracks. The concentric storage rings on a floppy or hard disk.

transaction processing. Processing data as soon as it is input. See also *batch processing*.

twisted pair. A communications medium made of two copper wires. It creates a communications channel; commonly used as phone lines.

unstructured programming. Creating programs in a more random fashion.

uploading. Sending files from a remote computer to a large central computer.

URL. An abbreviation for Universal Resource Locator; an address for a Web site.

user documentation. Instructions for the knowledge workers who will use the program, explaining procedures step by step. See also *documentation, reference documentation.*

user name. The identification you use when logging on to an on-line service.

utility programs. Software that provides additional capabilities and sometimes ease of use. Some programs are included with the operating system, and others (often called *add-ons*) are purchased separately.

value. A number entered into a cell in a spreadsheet. Also the number in a cell that is produced as a result of using a formula.

version. A number that identifies the release number of a program.

voice/data integration. The computer-assisted capability to route a data call and a voice call to a knowledge worker so that both transmissions occur simultaneously.

voice mail. The use of the computer to capture (input), digitize (process), store (on disk), and forward (output) voice messages.

voice output. The computer's capability to produce spoken output. Also called speech synthesis.

voice recognition. The act of entering data into a computer by speaking into a microphone. Also referred to as voice input.

volatile memory. Short-term memory; everything stored is lost when the computer's power is shut off.

what-if analysis. In spreadsheets, the process of substituting one number for another to see what difference it will make.

wide area network (WAN). A type of private network that uses phone lines, microwave relaying stations, and satellites to connect computers located miles apart.

widow. In word processing, a bad line break that results in the last line of a paragraph appearing alone at the top of a page or column, making the text hard to follow or read.

wisdom. Organized, distilled, and integrated knowledge. See also *data, knowledge.*

word. A logical unit of information composed of bits and bytes and treated as one entity that can be stored in a memory location. *Word length* is the term used to describe word size.

word processing. An application that enables you to create, write, edit, proofread, and format documents for printing.

word wrap. A word processing feature that automatically moves a word from the end of one line to the beginning of the next.

work group. A number of knowledge workers, each of whom has different job duties or tasks, but all of whom are working toward a common goal.

worksheet. The data document created by the spreadsheet program, containing the words, values, formulas, and so on.

workstation. A powerful desktop computer most commonly used by a single individual but that may be shared by others.

World Wide Web (WWW). The newest on-line information service on the Internet. It is a graphical environment that offers text, sound, video, and even animation.

write. To transfer data to other devices such as auxiliary storage. See also *read.*

writing. Conveying information with words; the first step in using word processing.

WYSIWYG. The capability to display text exactly as it will appear on the printed page; the acronym stands for "what you see is what you get."

INDEX

Symbols

> (greater than) logical operator, 2-22, 3-105

< (less than) condition, logic operations, 2-22

= (equal sign)

DBMS logical operator, 3-105

spreadsheet functions, 3-84

@ (at sign), spreadsheet functions, 3-84

3-D Studio, 2-99, 3-180

3.5-inch floppy disks, 2-112 to 2-113

4GL (fourth-generation language) tool, DBMS front end, 4-93 to 4-94

32-bit operating systems, multitasking, 3-28

101-key enhanced keyboards, 2-68

2001: A Space Odyssey, 2-96 to 2-97

A

Access databases, 3-111

creating databases, 3-113 to 3-114

access time (hard disks), 2-115

accounting, forensic, 3-91

accumulators (CPU registers), 2-25 to 2-26

ACD (automatic call dialing), 4-107

Acer (PC compatibles), 1-94

ACM (Association of Computer Machinery) Code of Ethics, 2-49

ACOG (Atlanta Committee for the Olympic Games), DBMS case study, 4-99

acoustic coupler modems, 2-131

active cells (spreadsheets), 3-81

Actually Useful Internet Security Techniques, 4-133

ADA (programming language), 4-25

Adams, Edie, 2-84

adjustable chairs, 2-77 to 2-78

adjustable keyboard drawers, 2-77

adjustable keyboards, 2-77

advanced features

DBMS (database management systems), 3-118

spreadsheets, 3-86 to 3-87

word processing, 3-59 to 3-60

advertising

InfoWorld Electric Web site, 4-87

Windows 95, 3-24 to 3-25

AI (artificial intelligence), 4-153

airline industry case study, MIS (Management Information System), 4-75

algorithms, 4-51

all-in-1 integrated OA software, 4-145

Allen, Mel, 3-180

alpha testing, 4-48

Alps GlidePoint Keyboard and TouchPad, 2-71

Alsop, Stewart, 3-130, 4-87

Alt key, 2-69

Altair 8800, 1-97

ALU (arithmetic logic unit), 2-17, 2-22, 3-77

registers, 2-25 to 2-26

America Online, 4-127

American Airlines

MIS case study, 4-75

SABRE reservation service, 4-118

American Power Conversion, 4-132

amplitude, 2-129

analog communications, 2-129 to 2-130

amplitude, 2-129

binary codes, 2-129

frequency, 2-129

analysis tool (DBMS front end), 4-93

Andrews, Kenneth R., 4-162

ANI (automatic number identification), 4-107

Animator, 2-99

Animator Pro, 3-180

anonymous FTP, 3-158

antitrust issues (Microsoft), 3-13 to 3-14

APL (programming language), 4-25

appending records (databases), 3-105

Apple Computer, Inc., 1-94

Apple I, 1-97

Apple II, 1-97

Apple key, 2-68

AppleShare, 3-8

applets, 1-71

application development environment (DBMS), 3-118

application generators (DBMS), 3-119, 4-94

applications

ambiguous software, 1-81 to 1-82

applets, 1-71

communications (suites/stand-alone), 3-158

communications software, 1-75

compound documents, 1-85

creating via high-level programming languages, 4-17 to 4-19

DBMS (database management systems), 1-75

DTP (desktop publishing), 1-75

EMACS (Richard M. Stallman), 1-86

freeware, 1-86

GUI icons, 3-26 to 3-27

integrated, 1-83

interoperability, 4-82

introduction, 1-75

"killer", 1-84 to 1-85

license policy, 1-86

presentation graphics, 1-75

public domain, 1-86

shareware, 1-86

spreadsheets, 1-75

stand-alone, 1-82

tips on purchasing, 1-77

word processing, 1-75

see also programs; system development life cycle